Alice Murgier is a Franco-American lawyer. She is a criminal and environmental lawyer specialized in intersectional legal issues, such as business and human rights and corporate due diligence. As an experienced legal professional in international organizations, nongovernmental organizations, and white-collar crime firms both in Europe and the United States, her practice is currently focused on criminal law, freedom of speech, and freedom of the press. In addition to her litigation work at her firm in Paris, Alice advises clients and teaches at the University of Nanterre and Northwestern University.

Thomas Andrew O'Keefe is the President of Mercosur Consulting Group, Ltd. [https://www.mercosurconsulting.net] and currently teaches at Stanford University. A dual US–Chilean national, he has degrees from Columbia University, Villanova University's School of Law, and the University of Oxford. In 1986, he worked for the legal departments of the Chilean Human Rights Commission and the Vicaría de la Solidaridad (the human rights office of the Archdiocese of Santiago). He chaired the Western Hemisphere Area Studies program at the US State Department's Foreign Service Institute between 2011 and 2016 and taught a seminar on International Human Rights Law at Villanova University's School of Law in 2015. He is the author of *Latin American Trade Agreements* (Ardsley, NY: Transnational Publishers, Inc. 1997–), *Latin American and Caribbean Trade Agreements: Keys to a Prosperous Community of the Americas* (Leiden NL: Martinus Nijhoff (Brill), 2009), and *Bush II, Obama, and the Decline of U.S. Hegemony in the Western Hemisphere* (New York: Routledge, 2018).

Austin Pierce helps public and private companies, funds, and their boards to navigate all manner of environmental, social, and governance (ESG) matters. An associate at Latham & Watkins LLP, he has advised clients on their ESG strategy, policy development and implementation, and disclosures (both required and voluntary), in addition to providing targeted environmental and ESG support for specific business goals. Austin's approach to ESG includes an understanding of topics individually—including climate change, biodiversity and natural capital, human rights, Indigenous rights, and corporate culture—as well as how they interact. Austin regularly presents and publishes thought leadership on ESG, as well as the field's intersection with other subjects—from the law of the sea to capital markets. Austin received his JD and LLM in International & Comparative Law from Duke University.

Steven M. Richman holds a law degree from New York University School of Law and is a member of Clark Hill PLC, based in Princeton and New York, with a national and international litigation and arbitration practice. His book publications include the *Photography Law Handbook*. He has written and spoken extensively in the areas of international law, business and human rights, contracts, litigation and arbitration, and professional responsibility. He is a past chair of the ABA's International Law Section and serves as Deputy ABA delegate to the United Nations. His publications in the area of business and human rights include *Ethical Issues for Business Lawyers under the United Nations Guiding Principles*, 51

chapter provides contextual information about HRDD through a discussion of the concept of due diligence and the components of HRDD, and then elaborates the extensive uptake of HRDD, including by bar associations. Section III provides an overview of the growing legislative and regulatory requirements that either explicitly or implicitly require HRDD. Section IV then highlights practical approaches relevant to businesses' HRDD processes, while Section V notes a number of challenging evolving topics related to HRDD. The chapter concludes with some brief observations in Section VI.

II. Context

The term "due diligence" will be familiar to many lawyers, particularly those working with financial entities, on mergers and acquisitions, and in risk management in the areas of anti-corruption and anti-bribery.[11] However, due diligence by businesses related to human rights is a distinct type of due diligence because it focuses on the impact to stakeholders, rather than the business (although in the medium to long term, severe impacts on people and companies will tend to converge). This section is intended to assist the lawyer in understanding the general meaning and broad implications of HRDD. Therefore, it initially situates HRDD in relation to corporate and human rights law concepts of due diligence (Subsection A), identifies its components (Subsection B), highlights the uptake of HRDD by international organizations, governments, the financial sector and investors, business associations, and civil society that is rendering it an essential and integral part of business practices and processes (Subsection C), and demonstrates the support and guidance provided to lawyers by bar associations to assist them as they provide advice to businesses relative to HRDD (Subsection D).

A. The Concept of Human Rights Due Diligence

HRDD is a unique and specialized form of due diligence. As a starting point, Black's Law Dictionary defines due diligence as: "a measure of prudence, activity, or assiduity, as is properly to be expected from, and ordinarily exercised by, a reasonable and prudent man under the particular circumstances; not measured by any absolute standard, but depending on the relative facts of the special case."[12] HRDD is a process that does, indeed, require prudence, activity and assiduity, and close and constant attention by a business. As noted in a paper by John Ruggie, who authored the UNGPs during his tenure as special representative of the UN Secretary-General on business and human rights, and two collaborators: "[t]he construct of human rights due diligence was deliberately adapted from other (legal, financial, technical) due diligence processes traditionally familiar to businesses."[13]

---

[11] According to the survey of Fortune Global 500 Firms, "due diligence is a standard business practice." Human Rights Council, Report of the Special Representative of the Secretary-General on the Issue of Human Rights and Transnational Corporations and Other Business Enterprises, Addendum Human Rights Policies and Management Practices: Results from Questionnaire Surveys of Governments and Fortune Global 500 Firms, A/HRC/4/35/Add.3, para. 98 (2007).

[12] *Due Diligence*, Black's Law Dictionary (11th ed. 2019).

[13] John G. Ruggie, Caroline Rees, & Rachel Davis et al., Making "Stakeholder Capitalism" Work: Contributions from Business & Human Rights 11 (Harvard Kennedy Sch. Faculty Research Working Paper

D. Human Rights Due Diligence and the Legal Profession

Bar associations have provided guidance to lawyers, both those serving as in-house counsel and those in law firms, on businesses' formulation and conduct of HRDD that not only encourages lawyers' advice and counsel to businesses on HRDD, but also recognizes the important role lawyers can play in assisting businesses with respecting human rights.

The Japan Federation of Bar Associations has issued specific guidance on HRDD to lawyers, titled *Guidance on Human Rights Due Diligence*.[52] Numerous other bar associations have provided guidance on HRDD in connection with the formulation of general advice on business and human rights for the legal profession. For example, the American Bar Association (ABA), which in 2012 was the first bar association to endorse the UNGPs, has a web page with key documents.[53] The Law Council of Australia issued *Business and Human Rights and the Australian Legal Profession*;[54] the Norwegian Bar Association prepared a guide, *Business and Human Rights for Lawyers*;[55] the European Federation of Bar Associations published *Guidelines on Business and Human Rights for European Law Societies*;[56] LawAsia formulated *Business and Human Rights: A Guide for Lawyers in the Asia Pacific*;[57] the Law Society of England and Wales issued *Business and Human Rights: A Practical Guide*;[58] the Canadian Bar Association published *Business and Human Rights*;[59] and the International Bar Association issued a *Practical Guide on Business and Human Rights for Business Lawyers*.[60]

Bar associations will continue to have a key role to play in providing information about hard and soft-law developments related to HRDD. A number of bar associations, including the ABA, the Law Society of England and Wales, the Malaysian Bar Council, and the Spanish

---

[52] *Guidance on Human Rights Due Diligence*, JAPAN FED'N OF B. ASS'N (Jan. 2, 2015), https://www.nichibenren.or.jp/en/document/opinionpapers/20150107.html.

[53] *A Lawyer's Guide to Key Business and Human Rights Documents*, AM. B. ASS'N https://www.americanbar.org/groups/human_rights/business-human-rights-initiative/key-business-and-human-rights-documents/ (last visited Feb. 2, 2022).

[54] LAW COUNCIL OF AUSTRALIA., BUSINESS AND HUMAN RIGHTS AND THE AUSTRALIAN LEGAL PROFESSION (2016), https://www.lawcouncil.asn.au/docs/2b2f5f40-6a43-e811-93fb-005056be13b5/1601-Position-Paper-Business-and-Human-Rights-and-the-Australian-Legal-Profession.pdf.

[55] NORWEGIAN BAR ASSOCIATION, BUSINESS AND HUMAN RIGHTS FOR LAWYERS, https://www.advokatforeningen.no/globalassets/17798/businessandhumanrights.pdf (last visited Feb. 2, 2022).

[56] VIDAL MARTÍN HERNANDO, CARLOS CORDERO SANZ, & MAR CAMEIRO FREIRE ET AL., GUIDANCE IN BUSINESS AND HUMAN RIGHTS FOR EUROPEAN LAW SOCIETIES 14 (2017), https://www.sustentia.com/wp-content/uploads/2018/02/GUIDE-ON-BUSINESS-HUMAN-RIGHTS-ICAM-FBE-January-2018-Sustentia-English.pdf (stating that "[t]hrough these Guidelines, the FBE offers its memberLaw [sic] Societies an open door into due diligence in Human Rights").

[57] LAWASIA, BUSINESS AND HUMAN RIGHTS: A GUIDE FOR LAWYERS IN THE ASIA PACIFIC (2019), https://lawasia.asn.au/sites/default/files/2019-11/LAWASIA%20Business%20and%20Human%20Rights%20Toolkit%2029-10-2019.pdf.

[58] Law Soc'y of Eng. & Wales, *Business and Human Rights: A Practical Guide*, BUS. & HUM. RIGHTS RESOURCE CTR. (Aug. 19, 2019), https://www.business-humanrights.org/en/latest-news/pdf-business-and-human-rights-a-practical-guide/.

[59] *Business and Human Rights*, CANADIAN B. ASS'N, https://www.cba.org/Publications-Resources/Practice-Tools/Business-and-Human-Rights?lang=en-ca (last visited Feb. 2, 2022).

[60] INT'L BAR ASS'N, IBA PRACTICAL GUIDE ON BUSINESS AND HUMAN RIGHTS FOR BUSINESS LAWYERS 7 (2016), https://shiftproject.org/wp-content/uploads/2020/01/Default.pdf.

Chapter 12, "The United Nations Guiding Principles on Business and Human Rights and Global Supply Chains," by Andrea Shemberg and Bettina Braun, considers the UNGPs' expanded scope of company responsibility for human rights harms and explores its implications in the context of supply chains. The chapter then demonstrates how recent legislative, case law, and soft-law developments reflect this expanded scope of responsibility and highlights several open questions related to the management of human rights risks in supply chains.

B. Financial Sector

The financial sector, as noted above in Section II.C, has made and will continue to make a significant contribution to businesses' implementation of HRDD as businesses are required by financial institutions, investors, and others to be aware of their adverse human rights impacts and demonstrate that they are taking steps to address those impacts. As the UNWG has noted:

> Increasingly, investors are asking questions about human rights policies and human rights due diligence in line with the Guiding Principles. This practice has moved beyond the niche realm of socially responsible investors to become part of a wider trend of greater focus on managing the social impact of business and integrating environmental, social and governance considerations into mainstream investment decision-making. It is increasingly being recognized that proper human rights due diligence and the integration of human rights risks improve risk management overall—and are good for both people and investments.[89]

Chapter 13, "Leveraging the Financial Sector for Human Rights," by Margaret G. Wachenfeld, considers the application of the UNGPs by financial institutions, which generally includes, as she notes, integrating human rights into their policy commitments and risk management systems and carrying out HRDD to identify and address the human rights risks of their financing. The chapter reviews the role of financial institutions leading up to the adoption of the UNGPs, considers the relevant legal, regulatory, and voluntary initiatives and their applicability to the financial sector, and highlights good practices.

C. Environmental Law and Climate Change

The degradation in the environmental condition of the earth's land, seas, and air is manifesting itself in a multitude of devastating forms, including pollution, health impacts, and climate change, all of which have significant repercussions on individuals' and communities' human rights. The intersection between environmental risks and human rights, and, in particular, the way in which the environmental impacts of businesses affect peoples' human rights is receiving greater research and policy attention, which will only heighten as States adopt

[89] *Id.* at para. 86.

of the adverse human rights impacts.[16] Supporting and promoting human rights through community development, philanthropic initiatives and other social and environmental activities, in the traditional sense of corporate social responsibility, does not offset any failure to respect human rights.[17]

States and companies have complementary roles in effectively preventing and addressing adverse impact linked to business activities.[18] However, the responsibility to respect human rights is undiminished by, and independent from, the inability or unwillingness of governments to fulfil their duty to protect.[19] Furthermore, it exists over and above businesses' compliance with national laws and regulations protecting human rights.[20]

The first element of this responsibility, the *human rights policy statement*, is to be embedded and approved at the most senior business level.[21] Usually developed with relevant internal and external expertise, it sets forth human rights expectations for internal and external stakeholders and should be widely communicated internally and made publicly available externally.[22] The second element, *human rights due diligence*, is a four-step process outlined in Principle 17 of the UNGPs and more fully fleshed out in Principles 18 to 21: (a) an assessment of human rights impacts; (b) an integration of findings and action plan; (c) a system of tracking of adverse human rights impacts; and (d) the communication of human rights impacts, which will be addressed in greater detail in the remainder of this chapter. The third and final element is the *remediation of adverse human rights impacts*.[23]

B. OECD Due Diligence Guidance

The Organisation for Economic Development and Co-operation's *Guidelines for Multinational Enterprises* (OECD Guidelines)[24] were first adopted in 1976 as an annex to the OECD Declaration on International Investment and Multinational Enterprises[25] and further amended in 2011 to include a human rights chapter that incorporates specific recommendations to businesses on risk-based human rights due diligence in alignment with the UNGPs.[26] The OECD Guidelines establish governmental expectations for multinational enterprises on responsible business conduct in the form of nonbinding recommendations.

[16] *Id.* at 15 (Principle 14 Commentary).

[17] *Id.* at 13 (Principle 11 Commentary). *See also* Interpretive Guide, *infra* note 18, at 10.

[18] UN Office of the High Commissioner for Human Rights, *The Corporate Responsibility to Respect Human Rights, An Interpretive Guide*, UN Doc. HR/PUB/12/02 (2012), p. 10 [hereinafter Interpretive Guide].

[19] *Guiding Principles, supra* note 4, at 13 (Principle 11 Commentary).

[20] *Id.* at 30.

[21] *Id.* at 16 (Principle 16).

[22] *Id.*

[23] *Id.* at 24 (Principle 22).

[24] OECD, *Guidelines for Multinational Enterprises*, OECD Publishing (2011), http://mneguidelines.oecd.org/guidelines/ [hereinafter OECD Guidelines].

[25] OECD, Declaration on International Investment and Multinational Enterprises, OECD/LEGAL/0144, last updated in 2011.

[26] OECD *Guidelines, supra* note 24, at 21 (see General Policies para. 10-12 and Chapter IV, Human Rights).

	Prevention	Mitigation		Remediation
Applicability	Potential human rights impacts		Actual human rights impacts	
Actions/Processes	Ensure an adverse impact *does not occur*	Reduce the *likelihood* of an adverse impact occurring	Reduce the *extent* of an adverse impact Any residual impact requires remediation	Provide *remedy* for an adverse impact

Figure 2.7 Terminology Cheat Sheet: Prevention, Mitigation, and Remediation

and reporting to, the C-suite and/or board of directors; and (iii) some cross-functional and operational/site level representation. Departments responsible for activities that may contribute to a human rights impact, in addition to those who determine the terms of the enterprise's relationships with business partners, should be part of this integration process.[65] This usually means the legal and compliance, human resources, purchasing/procurement, sales and marketing, and environment, health, and safety (EHS) functions, at a minimum.

2. *Appropriate Action*

Businesses are required to: (a) avoid *causing or contributing* to adverse human rights impacts through their own activities and address such impacts when they occur; and (b) seek to *prevent* or to *mitigate* adverse human rights impacts directly linked to their operations, products, or services by their business relationships, no matter whether or not they have contributed to such impacts.[66] Potential impacts should be addressed through prevention or mitigation via the integration of findings, and actual impacts through remediation.[67] Figure 2.7 defines and distinguishes prevention from mitigation and remediation.[68]

Following the identification of actual and potential adverse human rights impacts, businesses should first seek to prevent or mitigate those impacts that are the most severe, or for which delayed response would make them irremediable.[69] Preventing and mitigating adverse impacts can be done in a variety of other ways, including: adapting or modifying aspects of an enterprise's operations, products, or services; developing and implementing company policies; training employees and suppliers; adopting red-flag systems and screening mechanisms; and addressing systemic issues.[70] Contracts can also have a positive role in creating incentives to respect human rights—if there is reasonable evidence of the party's willingness or ability to meet contractual requirements.[71]

Appropriate action will depend on whether the business caused or contributed to an adverse impact, or whether it is only directly linked to its operations, products, or services by

[65] Interpretive Guide, *supra* note 18, pp. 47–48.

[66] *Guiding Principles, supra* note 4, at 14 (Principle 13 and Principle 13 Commentary).

[67] *Id.* at 18 (Principle 17 Commentary).

[68] Interpretive Guide, *supra* note 18, at 7.

[69] *Guiding Principles, supra* note 4, at 26 (Principle 24).

[70] OECD Due Diligence Guidance, *supra* note 27, at 75.

[71] *Id.* at 48.

Alex Newton, *Human Rights Due Diligence*, in The Business of Human Rights, Best Practices and the UN Guiding Principles, pp. 104–113 (Routledge ed., 2019).
Marc B. Taylor, *Corporate Human Rights Due Diligence*, in Research Handbook on Business and Human Rights, pp. 88–107 (Deva & Birchall eds., 2020).

C. Reports and Guides

BSR, Conducting an Effective Human Rights Impact Assessment, 2013, https://www.bsr.org/reports/BSR_Human_Rights_Impact_Assessments.pdf.
The Danish Institute for Human Rights, Human Rights Impact Assessment Guidance and Toolbox, 2016, https://respect.international/human-rights-impact-assessment-guidance-and-toolbox/.
International Bar Association, Handbook for Lawyers on Business and Human Rights, 2016, https://www.ibanet.org/LPRU/Business-and-Human-Rights-for-the-Legal-Profession.
International Business Leaders Forum & UN Global Compact, Guide to Human Rights Impact Assessment and Management, 2010, https://www.unglobalcompact.org/library/25.
Shift, Oxfam & Global Compact Network Netherlands, Doing business with respect for human rights, A guidance tool for companies, 2016, https://www.businessrespecthumanrights.org/image/2016/10/24/business_respect_human_rights_full.pdf.

D. Electronic Portals

Business and Human Rights Resource Centre
https://www.business-humanrights.org/en/big-issues/un-guiding-principles-on-business-human-rights/.
BSR
https://www.bsr.org/en/topics/all-channels/Human-Rights.
Danish Institute for Human Rights Learning Hub
https://www.humanrights.dk/learning-hub.
Shift
https://shiftproject.org.
United Nations Forum on Business and Human Rights
https://www.ohchr.org/EN/Issues/Business/Forum/Pages/ForumonBusinessandHumanRights.aspx.
United Nations Global Compact Human Rights Due Diligence Portal
https://www.unglobalcompact.org/library/5.

heightened risk of [corporations] becoming complicit in human rights violations in certain environments, such as conflict-affected areas." In rejecting the motion to dismiss and allowing the case to continue, the Court balanced policy considerations and found policy in support of a duty to care for purposes of a negligence claim in the plaintiffs' argument that "recognizing a duty would support efforts taken by the federal government by encouraging Canadian companies to meet the 'high standards of corporate social responsibility' that are currently expected by the Canadian government."[23]

The UNGPs' fundamental premise is a policy statement as to corporate responsibility in the area of human rights. Ethics codes are not drawn so narrowly as to exclude consideration of such soft law by lawyers in advising clients, and as notably demonstrated in *Choc v. Hudbay Minerals*, such policy consideration assumes legal import.

C. The ABA Model Rules of Professional Conduct

Many American lawyers may not fully know or understand the background of lawyers' ethical obligations under the ABA Model Rules, and how they impact their own local ethical rules. Presumably, they are familiar with those rules of professional conduct governing them in the jurisdictions in which they are licensed to practice. In most instances, those rules are adaptations, in whole or in part, of the ABA Model Rules. ABA Model Rules are not binding rules, but the ABA opinions interpreting them are often relied upon by courts or disciplinary bodies in interpreting their applicable versions under state professional responsibility codes. Consequently, unless otherwise specified in discussing a particular case, reference herein is to the ABA Model Rules.

Notably, Paragraph 16 of the Preamble addressing a lawyer's responsibilities, in the section on scope, makes clear that the rules are not exhaustive, and that a lawyer's responsibilities must be read broadly:

> Compliance with the Rules, as with all law in an open society, depends primarily upon understanding and voluntary compliance, secondarily upon reinforcement by peer and public opinion and finally, when necessary, upon enforcement through disciplinary proceedings. The Rules do not, however, exhaust the moral and ethical considerations that should inform a lawyer, for no worthwhile human activity can be completely defined by legal rules. The Rules simply provide a framework for the ethical practice of law.[24]

There are various places within the ABA Model Rules that consideration of soft-law issues and the UNGPs could be relevant. The primary focus will be on Rules 1.16 (declining or terminating representation), 1.6 (confidentiality), and 2.1 (lawyer as advisor). It is worth

---

[23] *Id.*

[24] https://www.americanbar.org/groups/professional_responsibility/publications/model_rules_of_professional_conduct/model_rules_of_professional_conduct_preamble_scope/.

a soft-law set of principles such as the UNGPs need not be followed when advising clients on the possibility of criminal or civil liabilities. However, ignoring such soft law would not fulfill the requirement of providing competent legal advice. As expressed by one court over half a century ago:

> The modern lawyer almost invariably advises his client upon not only what is permissible but also what is desirable. And it is in the time [sic] public interest that the lawyer should regard himself as more than predicter of legal consequences. His duty to society as well as to his client involves many relevant social, economic, political and philosophical considerations. And the privilege of nondisclosure is not lost merely because relevant nonlegal considerations are expressly stated in a communication which also includes legal advice.[46]

In other words, there is a recognition by courts for purposes of the attorney-client privilege that "mixed" considerations, part legal, part business, part social, do not destroy the fundamental nature of the advice as legal. Legal advice must have context, and its ramifications must be understood.[47]

The comments above regarding the distinctions between client confidentiality and attorney-client privilege should be borne in mind when rendering advice pursuant to Rule 2.1. Though under Rule 1.6 information conveyed in the context of the representation would protect the factors that Rule 2.1 identifies, the same information and context may not on its face meet the more limiting factors under an evidentiary privilege analysis. If intertwined with the factors and policy underlying the plain language of Rule 2.1, arguably the evidentiary privilege should encompass the protection there as well. The finite body of cases interpreting and applying Rule 2.1 suggests support for this approach.

One application could involve advising a client that while a motion may be feasible as a legal matter, the costs of the motion versus the benefit likely to be achieved should be considered, even if the latter factor of cost is a non-legal factor. Another could be where the lawyer advises a client as to the legal feasibility of naming an additional party without addressing whether such a course of action might have a negative public relations impact. The choice of how to act based on the advice remains ultimately with the client, and while the lawyer need not raise every potential issue, the point is that legal advice cannot be given in a vacuum. Lawyers need to be comfortable in speaking candidly with a client about such matters and should not have to worry if they are giving otherwise non-privileged "business advice" in the context of the evidentiary privilege. Ultimately, the test is not a black-and-white one as to whether the advice is "legal" or "business," but rather, whether the primary purpose of the

---

46 United States v. United Shoe Mach. Corp., 89 F. Supp. 357, 359 (D. Mass. 1950)

47 *In re* Cty. of Erie, 473 F.3d 413, 420 (2d Cir. 2007) ("The complete lawyer may well promote and reinforce the legal advice given, weigh it, and lay out its ramifications by explaining: how the advice is feasible and can be implemented; the legal downsides, risks and costs of taking the advice or doing otherwise; what alternatives exist to present measures or the measures advised; what other persons are doing or thinking about the matter; or the collateral benefits, risks or costs in terms of expense, politics, insurance, commerce, morals, and appearances. So long as the predominant purpose of the communication is legal advice, these considerations and caveats are not other than legal advice or severable from it.")

when applying the ethical rules noted above, including ABA Model Rule 2.1. In the disputes area, for example, lawyers can help their clients develop appropriate dispute resolution mechanisms that address issues within the company. In the contracts area, the lawyer's role is to help structure these contracts to "prevent and mitigate human rights harm." Lawyers are warned to avoid boilerplate which is not tailored to the specific situation. In other words, if the client has a desire to effectuate the UNGPs, one of the most readily available means of addressing that in the supply chain is having appropriate provisions in the client's contracts. Such provisions become enforceable as a matter of contract law and therefore transform aspirational into objective hard law. Lawyers, in order to fulfill their ethical obligations to implement the client's objectives, therefore need to understand the UNGPs.

In other words, lawyers have significant opportunities not only to help implement the UNGPs, but also to expand the parameters of their thinking as to what constitutes appropriate legal advice. In-house counsel have the opportunity, in their roles as business advisors as well as lawyers within the company, to help shape not just the philosophy of the company but the practical implementation of its human rights agenda. Outside counsel, through their role of independent lawyer and advisor, can help identify risks.

The IBA Guide identifies several expectations of the UNGPs, and indicates certain "things to think about" for lawyers.[78] For example, one of the UNGPs' expectations involves assessing human rights impacts, and suggests that the lawyer think about those impacts that include the firm's own employment practices, supply chain, and legal advice that is given with regard to supply chain contracts.

The IBA Guide concludes by noting that:

> [c]ompliance with the law is a bedrock requirement of the corporate responsibility to respect human rights under the UNGPs, but it applies even where the law is absent, unenforced, or in tension with internationally recognised human rights. Even though the UNGPs themselves do not and cannot impose legal responsibilities on business, the UNGPs are relevant to many legal practice areas. The UNGPs stress that business should respect internationally recognised human rights even when national laws do not adequately protect them.[79]

Another guide for lawyers has been published by the Advocates for International Development, titled the *UN Guiding Principles on Business and Human Rights: A Guide for the Legal Profession*.[80] Among other things, this guide specifically addresses the relationship between the UNGPs and codes of professional conduct for lawyers. Among its recommendations is for bar associations to consider to what extent it is appropriate to include references to human rights or even the UNGPs in their codes of professional conduct.

---

[78] IBA Guide at 33, found at https://www.ibanet.org/MediaHandler?id=d6306c84-e2f8-4c82-a86f-93940d6736c4.

[79] IBA Guide at 39, found at https://media.business-humanrights.org/media/documents/files/documents/IBA_Practical_Guide.pdf

[80] http://www.a4id.org/wp-content/uploads/2016/04/A4ID-Business-and-Human-Rights-Guide-2013-web.pdf

same time, in a rather paradoxical way, the Law has also been criticized by supporters of corporate accountability; nongovernmental organizations (NGOs) claim that the scope of the Law is too limited. Specifically, some NGOs assert that accountability for social and environmental matters should not be limited to business entities formed as corporations under French law that meet the threshold number of employees, but rather should apply to all companies carrying out business in France whatever their number of employees including all foreign companies operating in France.

What is certain is that the Law impacts international groups with a French subsidiary employing more than 5,000 employees in France or 10,000 employees in France and abroad. The French subsidiary of the foreign group will be required to publish a vigilance plan. As a result, suppliers and subcontractors of French companies, located anywhere in the world, are likely to be required to report any risks and serious breaches of human rights occurring in their supply chain to their French business partners. If a French company has not been alerted by its foreign partner of such risks or breaches, could the French company seek recourse against the foreign partner if the latter is deemed responsible for a lack of vigilance? This question will likely arise.

Thus, the law creates new considerations for foreign lawyers advising clients trading with French entities, even indirectly without having an establishment in France. Certainly, legal proceedings against foreign companies on the basis of the Duty of Vigilance Law will raise complex questions of international law in terms of conflict of laws and determination of the competent jurisdiction. Yet it is not inconceivable that the US parent company of a French group could be sued for the failure of its French subsidiary to comply with the Duty of Vigilance Law. In practice, the issue has been raised against the US group XPO Logistics, whose French subsidiary has been served with a notice of violation of labor rights, including within the group's American companies with which the French subsidiary has an established business relationship.[4] Similarly, in a summons issued against the French retailer Casino, the Brazilian groups JBS, the world's leading meat producer, and Marfrig, the second largest Brazilian food processing company, they are directly targeted for the laundering of livestock responsible for deforestation in the Amazon.[5]

In addition, the Law serves as an important model for other countries that are developing HRDD laws. Since the entry into force of the Duty of Vigilance Law, other European countries have introduced initiatives to adopt legal provisions inspired by the Law, including among others the Netherlands, Denmark, Switzerland, Germany, and Luxembourg.[6] The Duty of Vigilance Law has also served as an inspiration and provided a foundation for provisions in the draft treaty on multinationals and human rights which is being worked on

Sandra Cossart, Tiphaine Beau de Loménie, Antoine Lubrani, « Extension du domaine de la vigilance, la Loi sur le devoir de vigilance, au-delà de la compliance », Revue des juristes de Science Po n° 16, January 2019, accessible here: https://www.asso-sherpa.org/wp-content/uploads/2019/02/Sherpa-Extension-du-domaine-de-la-vigilance.pdf.

[4] Business and Human Rights Resource Centre, « Transport giant served notice under duty of vigilance law in landmark legal move », 1 October 2019, https://www.business-humanrights.org/en/latest-news/transport-giant-served-notice-under-duty-of-vigilance-law-in-landmark-legal-move/.

[5] Envol Vert, « Casino sue in court », 3 March 2021, https://envol-vert.org/en/news/2021/03/casino-in-court/.

[6] European Coalition for Corporate Justice, « Map: Corporate accountability legislative progress in Europe », 25 January 2022, https://corporatejustice.org/publications/map-corporate-accountability-legislative-progress-in-europe/.

way for France to promote social progress, human rights, and environmental rights globally.[36] The bill also received support from France's left-wing majority, viewing this legislation as its human rights counterpart to the so-called Sapin 2 law on prevention of corruption. The final bill submitted to Parliament outlined the duty of vigilance as follows: "[The duty of vigilance] includes reasonable vigilance measures to identify risks and prevent serious violations of human rights and fundamental freedoms, human health and safety and the environment, resulting from the activities of the company and those of companies that it controls (. . .) as well as the activities of subcontractors or suppliers with whom an established commercial relationship is maintained, when these activities are attached to this relationship."[37] On March 17, 2017, the Duty of Vigilance Law was adopted, and was the very last draft bill passed under François Hollande's presidency. It was codified in France's Commercial Code as articles L.225-102-4 and L.225-102-5.

After the Duty of Vigilance Law was adopted, the constitutionality of its provisions was strenuously challenged by a group of right-wing opposition Members of Parliament, including through a constitutional challenge. The Constitutional Court decided the law was constitutional, rejecting all objections raised by the Members of Parliament, except for one. The Constitutional Court stated that the provision regarding the payment of a fine of up to EUR€10 million by a company which has committed a breach is "defined in such insufficiently clear and precise terms" that it is unconstitutional. The decision further stated that the provision was unconstitutional "given the generality of the terms [the legislator] used, the broad and indeterminate nature of the mention of 'human rights' and 'fundamental freedoms' and the extent of companies, businesses and activities falling within the scope of the vigilance plan that [the legislator] instituted."[38] Despite the rejection of the provision on fines as unconstitutional, the Constitutional Court upheld the Law based on the principle that it introduced "a new civil obligation," referring to the arsenal of sanctions, remedies, and damages comprised in the general civil system.[39] This decision was important in defining the scope of the law and affirming its civil nature.

III. Obligations Resulting from the Duty of Vigilance Law

The purpose of this section is to present the new obligations imposed on companies covered within the scope of the law. In particular, this information is presented based on an analysis of the first Vigilance Plans published by companies and how the law is being applied. It will also assess whether this application is consistent with both the intent of the law and the requirements needed to make it fully effective.

---

[36] *Id.*, Reports n° 4184 (March 11, 2015), n° 2628 (November 2, 2016), n° 4242 (November 23, 2016) by member of Parliament Mr. Potier.

[37] Article L.225-102-4-I of the French Commercial Code.

[38] Conseil constitutionnel, Décision n° 2017-750 DC du 23 mars 2017, Loi relative au devoir de vigilance des sociétés m.res et des entreprises donneuses d'ordre.

[39] *Id.* § 7.

The Law provides for two types of judicial enforcement mechanisms. One is the judicial injunction to publish a complying Vigilance Plan enshrined in the Law. Any interested party can send a letter of formal notice to any company subject to the Law requesting compliance with the Law's obligations.[72] If the company still fails to comply within three months of receipt of the formal notice, the interested party may bring an action before the competent court to obtain a judicial order requiring the company to comply with its legal obligations. The second judicial enforcement mechanism is a remediation mechanism, under the general regime of civil liability for tort in the French Civil Code that requires the demonstration of a wrongdoing, a damage and the existence of a causal link between them, and hence the link between the damage and the alleged breach resulting from the company's default of vigilance.[73]

While the judicial injunction mechanism is quite straightforward in the Law, the remediation mechanism deserves to be clarified since it does not create an autonomous liability regime but is based on the application of the principles of civil liability provided by article 1240 of the French Civil Code.

1. Legal Standing

Initially, the claimants must demonstrate legal standing under the Duty of Vigilance Law which is interpreted, according to the general rule of French civil procedure,[74] as requiring that the claimants have: (i) the quality to act, that is, they are the victims of a damage (legal standing), or are NGOs or labor unions that are considered stakeholders of the company, although the issue may also be raised by other parties, such as competitors, that have an interest in the action, and (ii) an interest to act which is actual, present, direct, and personal.[75] In the first decisions, the judges adopted an interpretation of the interest to act, related to the company's duty of vigilance, that extends beyond its management and concerns the company as a whole.[76]

---

[72] Art. L. 225-102-4-II of French Commercial Code: "Where a company that has been given formal notice to comply with the obligations provided for in I does not do so within a period of three months from the date of the formal notice, the competent court may, at the request of any person who can prove an interest in acting, enjoin it, if necessary under penalty payment, to comply with them."

The president of the court, ruling in summary proceedings, may be seized for the same purpose.

[73] According to Article L. 225-102-5 of French Commercial Code: "Under the conditions provided for in Articles 1240 and 1241 of the French Civil Code, failure to comply with the obligations defined in Article L. 225-102-4 of this Code renders the perpetrator liable and obliges him to compensate for the damage that the performance of these obligations would have made it possible to avoid." Article 1240 of the French Civil Code states that: "Any act of man, which causes damage to another, obliges the one by whose fault it occurred to repair it." And Article 1241: "Everyone is liable for the damage he or she has caused not only by his or her own actions, but also by his or her negligence or recklessness."

[74] According to provisions of Article 31 of the French Proceeding Code: "The action is open to all those who have a legitimate interest in the success or rejection of a claim, subject to cases in which the law attributes the right to act only to those persons it qualifies to raise or fight a claim, or to defend a particular interest."

[75] As defined by articles 31 and 32 of the French Civil code and the related case law.

[76] "The letter of Article L. 225-102-4 of the Commercial Code reveals that the preservation of human rights and of nature in general cannot be satisfied with 'insurance-based management' [. . .] mentioned in the work of parliament and the standardisation by the market that is induced by the presentation of the Vigilance Plan at a shareholders'

evidence-gathering procedures, analogous to the discovery procedure that exists in US legal system. Unfortunately, French law lacks an effective evidence-gathering procedure that could be enforced against a nondisclosing company. That is to say that a due diligence process would be more easily applied in a common law legal system, especially those of the United States and the United Kingdom, where the discovery procedure requires the parties to produce all documents related to the dispute, whether favorable or unfavorable, and represents an effective phase of preliminary investigation.

B. Difference between the Duty of Vigilance Law and Existing French Non-financial Disclosure Requirements

The Duty of Vigilance Law can be viewed as an additional corporate compliance requirement in the field of non-financial disclosure of information. Even though the Duty of Vigilance Law and existing French requirements concerning non-financial disclosure, which transposed the October 22, 2014 European Directive relating to the publication of non-financial information (NFRD) into French law,[112] have similarities, in practice, the requirements are very different. Compliance officers and legal counsel who deal with compliance statements should be aware that there are substantial differences.

The French non-financial disclosure requirements in effect require large companies to publish regular reports on the social and environmental impacts of their activities. Although a company's Vigilance Plan must be included in the company's annual report, the duty of vigilance encompasses much more than a mere reporting obligation. It is conceived as a genuine behavioral standard for the company and its executives to act diligently in the conduct of business activities throughout the company's entire sphere of control, including its subsidiaries, suppliers, and subcontractors. The disclosure of information in the Vigilance Plan functions as a means to ensure that the company acts diligently and takes all appropriate measures to limit and prevent harms arising from its activities. In addition, the company may be held liable under the tort law regime for any damage caused by its lack of vigilance.

Two potential solutions could help clarify the true nature of the duty of vigilance and avoid any confusion of mHRDD with the non-financial reporting requirements under the NFRD. First, it can be expected that the EU Commission's proposal for a mHRDD European directive based on the Duty of Vigilance Law and the EU Commission's ongoing revision of the NFRD will establish clear-cut provisions to prevent overlap and provide for consistency between the two EU regimes by eliminating the drafting discrepancies that have led to confusion. Second, the Autorité des Marchés Financiers (AMF), the French financial market

---

[112] Décret n° 2017-1265 du 9 août 2017 pris pour l'application de l'ordonnance n° 2017-1180 du 19 juillet 2017 relative à la publication d'informations non financières par certaines grandes entreprises et certains groupes d'entreprises, accessible here: https://www.legifrance.gouv.fr/jorf/id/JORFTEXT000035401863 For more information on the EU requirements, *see* the EU web page on non-financial reporting: https://ec.europa.eu/info/business-economy-euro/company-reporting-and-auditing/company-reporting/non-financial-reporting_en#overview.

French Commercial Code, articles L.225-102-4 and L.225-102-5. Law on transparency, the fight against corruption and the modernization of economic life, 2016 (Loi n° 2016-1691 du 9 décembre 2016 relative à la transparence, à la lutte contre la corruption et à la modernisation de la vie économique), https://www.legifrance.gouv.fr/jorf/id/JORFTEXT000033558528.

New Economic Regulations (NRE) Law, Loi n° 2001-420 relative aux nouvelles régulations économiques, 15 mai 2001, accessible here: https://www.legifrance.gouv.fr/jorf/id/JORFTEXT000000223114.

Parliamentary debates of the Duty of Vigilance Law, Reports n° [illegible] (March 11, 2015), n° [illegible] (November [illegible], 2016), n° [illegible] (November [illegible], 2016) by member of Parliament Mr Potier.

Report n° [illegible]: https://www.assemblee-nationale.fr/14/rapports/r[illegible].asp

Report n° [illegible]: https://www.assemblee-nationale.fr/14/rapports/r[illegible].asp

Report n° [illegible]: https://www.assemblee-nationale.fr/14/rapports/r[illegible].asp

See p. [illegible] [illegible] (Sherpa [illegible], 2019) available here: https://www.asso-sherpa.org/wp-content/uploads/2019/[illegible]/Sherpa_[illegible]_WEB[illegible].pdf.

false and misleading documentation in purported compliance of an NSW law which may attract a two-year gaol sentence or a fine of 200 penalty units.

4. *Proposed Canadian Modern Slavery Act*

Bill S-211, an Act to enact the Fighting Against Forced Labour and Child Labour in Supply Chains Act and to amend the Customs Tariff (CMSA), was introduced in the Senate on November 24, 2021.[28] According to Section 3, its purpose is to implement Canada's international commitment to contribute to the fight against modern slavery through the imposition of reporting obligations on government institutions and entities involved in the production of goods in Canada or elsewhere or in the importation of goods produced outside Canada.

If passed, it will cover "entities" including a corporation or a trust, partnership, or other unincorporated organization that meets any of the following requirements: (1) that it is listed on a stock exchange in Canada; and (2) that it has a place of business in Canada, does business in Canada, or has assets in Canada and that, based on its consolidated financial statements, meets at least two of the following conditions for at least one of its two most recent financial years: (a) has at least C$20 million in assets, (b) has generated at least C$40 million in revenue, or (c) employs an average of at least 250 employees; or that it is prescribed by regulations (Section 9). Of these entities, the Bill will impose reporting requirements only on those that: produce or sell goods in Canada or elsewhere; import goods produced outside Canada into Canada; or control an entity engaged in the same activities.

Reports would have to be filed with the Minister of Public Safety and Emergency Preparedness (Minister) and should set out the steps taken during the preceding year to prevent and reduce the risk that forced labor or child labor is used at any step in the production of goods in Canada or elsewhere by the entity or of goods imported into Canada by the entity (Section 11(1)). Under Section 11(2), the report should also cover its structure and the goods that it produces in Canada or elsewhere or that it imports into Canada; its policies in relation to forced labor and child labor; its activities that carry a risk of forced labor or child labor being used and the steps it has taken to assess and manage that risk; any measures taken to remediate any forced labor or child labor; as well as the training provided to employees on forced labor and child labor.

The Minister would be empowered to specify the form and way a report is to be provided under Section 11(6). The report would be required to be submitted to the Minister within 180 days after the end of the reporting entity's fiscal year.

The proposed CMSA is stronger than the UKMSA in several respects. Canada will have an electronic registry containing the reports provided to it (Section 22(1)). The registry would be made available to the public on the Department of Public Safety and Emergency Preparedness website.

The proposed CMSA would contain stronger penalties than the UKMSA or the AMSA. As under the NSWMSA, under the proposed CMSA, persons or entities that fail to submit or publish a report that complies with the proposed CMSA could be fined up to C$250,000

[28] An Act to Enact the Fighting Against Forced Labour and Child Labour in Supply Chains Act and to amend the Customs Tariff, 2021, Sen. Bill [S-211] (Can.): https://www.parl.ca/legisinfo/en/bill/44-1/s-211.

According to paragraph 10 of Article 2, the implementation of the due diligence obligations must be documented. The report shall be published no later than four months after the closure of the financial year and shall remain publicly accessible on the entity's website for seven years. At a minimum, the annual compliance report should cover whether risks and violations have been identified, and if so, which ones; what the entity has done to fulfil its obligations, including measures as a result of complaints; how the entity assesses the impact and effectiveness of those measures; and what conclusions it draws for future measures.

The Federal Office of Economics and Export Control *(Bundesamt für Wirtschaft und Ausfuhrkontrolle) (BAFA)* is tasked with enforcing the German Act and monitoring compliance with the obligations. BAFA will impose administrative fines in the case of violations. BAFA also is given investigative powers (for example, search or seizure) for this purpose.[67]

The consequences of violations will be high. Under the German Act, the company will be deemed to contribute to violations if (1) third parties, in particular companies in the value chain and government agencies, or (2) products or services of the company contribute unlawfully to a violation as a result of the company's business activities. Fines of up to EUR€5 million, imprisonment, and exclusion from public procurement contracts can be awarded against an entity.

The German Act has been criticised for establishing a duty of effort, rather than a "duty to succeed" or a "guarantee liability." It creates a positive duty to conduct HRDD, but not HRDD of a standard to ensure that human rights breaches are avoided. Further, it does not create liability for companies that have been implicated in serious human rights abuses, in the way that the French Due Vigilance Law does, according to Human Rights Watch.[68] Human Rights Watch has urged the next German government to address this shortcoming.

4. *China HRDD in Conflict Minerals Guidelines*

China's Chamber of Commerce of Metals, Minerals, and Chemicals (CCCMC), a State-controlled industry association, issued two sets of guidelines, in 2014 and 2015 respectively, setting specific directives for overseas operations of Chinese mining-sector firms. These cover Chinese companies engaged in outbound mining investment and do not appear to capture non-Chinese companies. CCCMC's 2014 *Guidelines for Social Responsibility in Outbound Mining Investment* (2014 Guidelines)[69] were succeeded in December 2015 by the *Chinese Due Diligence Guidelines for Responsible Mineral Supply Chains*,[70] which elaborate the

---

[67] Steinmeyer, Späth & Werner, *supra* note 59.

[68] Human Rights Watch, Germany: *New Supply Chain Law a Step in the Right Direction. Law's Gaps Should be Fixed by Next Government*, June 11, 2021, https://www.hrw.org/news/2021/06/11/germany-new-supply-chain-law-step-right-direction.

[69] China Chamber of Commerce of Metals, Minerals & Chemicals, *Guidelines for Social Responsibility in Outbound Mining Investment*, (2014), http://images.mofcom.gov.cn/csr2/201812/20181224151850626.pdf.

[70] China Chamber of Commerce of Metals, Minerals & Chemicals, *Importers & Exporters, Chinese Due Diligence Guidelines for Responsible Mineral Supply Chains*, (2015): https://mneguidelines.oecd.org/chinese-due-diligence-guidelines-for-responsible-mineral-supply-chains.htm (January 24).

transnational corporations and other business enterprises with respect to human rights, whose mandate shall be to elaborate an international legally binding instrument to regulate, in international human rights law, the activities of transnational corporations and other business enterprises."[89] The elements, scope, and substance of such a UN treaty have been subject to a lengthy debate in the Intergovernmental Working Group, with new iterations of the draft resulting. A third draft was released in August 2021.[90]

The third draft covers all business enterprises but gives States leeway to differentiate businesses enterprises based on "their size, sector, operational context and the severity of impacts on human rights" as to how they discharge their prevention obligations Article 3(1). It extends obligations to business to respect "all internationally recognized human rights and fundamental freedoms." In addition to the Universal Declaration of Human Rights and customary international law, the given definition covers human rights emanating from "any core international human rights treaty and fundamental ILO convention to which a state is a party" (Article 3(3)). Article 6(2) requires States to regulate effectively by taking "all appropriate legal and policy measures" to ensure that business enterprises respect human rights and prevent and mitigate human rights abuses throughout their business activities and relationships. Articles 7 through 11 of the 2021 draft require States to remove barriers to effective remedy faced by victims of business-related human rights abuses, and to provide a comprehensive and adequate system of legal liability of legal and natural persons conducting business activities (Article 8(1)).

It may take many years for such a treaty to be adopted by the UN, and many more for ratification, as there are many roadblocks to its adoption. One such roadblock is lack of business support. The International Organisation of Employers, which represents business in international fora, has taken a deliberate stance against mandated HRDD on the grounds that establishing international human rights obligations directly on business when these duties often do not exist at the national level suggests that States are seeking to place responsibilities on private entities due to their own failure or unwillingness to protect their people's rights. It summarizes its concerns as follows:

> Despite its importance, HRDD – especially in relation to global supply chains – is neither a simple exercise, nor a silver bullet to the world's business-related human rights problems. The push for policy-makers to create hard laws concerning this process raises many questions and concerns. However well-intentioned these laws may be, taking a top-down, prescriptive and punitive approach risks unintended consequences for rights-holders; it risks driving unhelpful action (or inaction) by some States and businesses; and

[89] United Nations Human Rights Council, *Open-ended Intergovernmental Working Group on Transnational Corporations and Other Business Enterprises with Respect to Human Rights*, https://www.ohchr.org/EN/HRBodies/HRC/WGTransCorp/Pages/IGWGOnTNC.aspx#:~:text=At%20its%2026th%20session%2C%20on,to%20elaborate%20an%20international%20legally, (last visited May 25, 2021).

[90] OEIGWG Chairmanship, *Third Revised Draft of a Legally Binding Instrument to Regulate, in International Human Rights Law, The Activities of Transnational Corporations and Other Business Enterprises* (Aug. 17, 2021), https://www.ohchr.org/Documents/HRBodies/HRCouncil/WGTransCorp/Session6/LBI3rdDRAFT.pdf.

was his ability to listen carefully to multiple views from different sides and forge them into principled and pragmatic solutions to the problem of business and human rights.[3]

Therefore, HRDD shares features in common with existing business and legal management systems, corporate governance, and due diligence processes. But HRDD is different because its "very purpose 'is to understand the specific response on specific people, given a specific context' (UNGPs Principle 18, Commentary), and not merely manage commercial risks to the company itself."[4] In order to achieve this purpose, HRDD must be integrated into corporate governance, supported by effective leadership, and embedded in corporate culture.[5]

A. The UN Guiding Principles on Business and Human Rights

Since this chapter is about *corporate* governance, it is critical to understand that the UNGPs were designed to address a gap in *global* governance with respect to business involvement in human rights abuse. The UNGPs combine into a mutually supporting framework three independent sources of governance: (1) voluntary business practices and policies and self-regulation (often known as corporate social responsibility, or CSR); (2) State enforcement of laws to protect people from business-related human rights abuse; and (3) the robust advocacy by civil society. Each is necessary to prevent and address the problem of global business-related human rights abuse. Yet none is sufficient by itself to solve the problem.[6]

Professor Ruggie concluded that to move past the logjam resulting from the bitter debate over voluntary and mandatory measures, an authoritative normative framework had to combine these three distinct governance systems in a manner that draws on their strengths.

The result was the interdependent, mutually supporting, three-pillar Protect, Respect, and Remedy framework. Pillar One is the State duty to protect human rights, which reflects the State's legal duty under international treaties and covenants to protect persons from human rights abuse by third parties, including businesses. Pillar Two is the non-legally binding business responsibility to respect internationally recognized human rights, which expects

[3] For a pre-UNGPs discussion of the relationship between human rights due diligence and corporate governance, see. John F. Sherman III, *Exploring Human Rights Due Diligence*, Discussion Paper, Expert Meeting of North American Corporate and External Counsel (Apr. 30, 2010), https://media.business-humanrights.org/media/documents/29c0373597a09aa834f2bdf87e93070fb6db345e.pdf.

[4] John G. Ruggie & John F. Sherman III, *The Concept of 'Due Diligence' in the UN Guiding Principles on Business and Human Rights: A Reply to Jonathan Bonnitcha and Robert McCorquodale*, 28(3) The Eur. J. of Int'l L., (2017). https://academic.oup.com/ejil/article-abstract/28/3/921/4616676.

[5] John G. Ruggie, Caroline Rees, & Rachel Davis, *Making 'Stakeholder Capitalism' Work: Contribution from Business & Human Rights*, Harvard Kennedy School Working Paper No. 76, (2020), p. 11, https://www.hks.harvard.edu/sites/default/files/centers/mrcbg/files/CRI_WP76.pdf.

[6] *See* John G. Ruggie, Just Business (Norton, 2013); John G. Ruggie, *Life in the Global Public Domain: Response to Commentaries on the UN Guiding Principles and the Proposed Treaty on Business and Human Rights* (2015) https://papers.ssrn.com/sol3/papers.cfm?abstract_id=2554726, and John G. Ruggie, *The Social Construction of the UN Guiding Principles on Business and Human Rights*, 12 Jun. 2017, Harvard Kennedy School Faculty Research Working Paper Series, HKS Working Paper No. RWP17-030, https://www.hks.harvard.edu/publications/social-construction-un-guiding-principles-business-human-rights.

society."[45] This affirmative duty requires corporate fiduciaries to pay close attention to relevant soft-law norms.

Comparing Human Rights Due Diligence and the US Sentencing Guidelines as internal control systems Although they have different purposes, both HRDD and the Sentencing Guidelines are internal control systems that are essential to corporate governance. Both are soft-law systems that are designed to enable corporations to manage critical corporate risks. Both must be integrated into corporate governance, and both require high-level attention within the corporation. Both are grounded in the expectation of a lawful and ethical corporate culture. Both are ongoing rather than single-shot due diligence processes. And both are "knowing and showing" systems that provide prompt information to the board and management regarding the corporation's major risks: by assessing and identifying them; by monitoring the company's performance; by taking appropriate preventative actions; and by reporting on violations.

The focus of the Sentencing Guidelines is to prevent corporate involvement in crime. To accomplish this goal, the affirmative duty of loyalty to act in good faith to further the best interests of the corporation expects that the corporation should do more than insist solely on bare legal compliance with criminal laws. Rather, this duty also requires the corporation to protect the corporation from financial, management, reputational, and other adverse consequences that can harm the corporation, by going beyond the minimum needed to avoid legal liability.[46]

Like the Sentencing Guidelines, HRDD is also predicated on compliance with the law. However, since HRDD's focus is on identifying and addressing corporate involvement in human rights abuse, HRDD is not limited by what the law requires to prevent and address such harm, even where applicable law is absent or insufficient to protect human rights.[47] Nevertheless, HRDD does not operate in a law-free zone. Prior to the promulgation of the UNGPs in 2011, numerous laws protected people from business-related human rights abuse in such fields as workplace and public safety, antidiscrimination, privacy, and environmental protection, to name a few.

Because the Sentencing Guidelines and HRDD have different objectives and origins, they are not identical. However, they share common attributes. Both are internal control systems with heavy normative weight that enable companies to manage their operations in ways that reflect the expectations of society as to responsible business conduct. They therefore inform the responsibility of corporate fiduciaries to act affirmatively in good faith to further the best interests of the corporation.

b. Enterprise Risk Management *(ERM)*

The second relevant COSO framework is ERM. ERM complements internal control systems. ERM is focused on the identification and assessment of strategic risks to the organization, which if not properly identified and managed, will prevent the organization from achieving

[45] Brummer & Strine, *supra* note 40.

[46] Brummer & Strine, *supra* note 40, at 8–9.

[47] *Guiding Principles, supra* note 2, at 17 & 23 (Principles 17 & 23).

A Guide to Human Rights Due Diligence for Lawyers

Corinne E. Lewis and Constance Z. Wagner
EDITORS

AMERICAN BAR ASSOCIATION
International Law Section

Cover design by Jill Tedhams/ABA Design

Printed in the United States of America.

27 26 25 24 23   5 4 3 2 1

Library of Congress Cataloging-in-Publication Data

Names: Lewis, Corinne, editor. | Wagner, Constance Z., 1954– editor. | American Bar Association. Section of International Law, sponsoring body.
Title: A guide to human rights due diligence for lawyers / Corinne E. Lewis and Constance Z. Wagner, editors.
Description: Chicago, Illinois : American Bar Association, [2022] | Includes bibliographical references and index. | Summary: "This book is intended to assist lawyers in navigating the developing area of human rights due diligence (HRDD). It explores the key components and requirements of the HRDD process, considers practical implementation of HRDD into corporate practices and policies, and treats key topics and cross-cutting issues related to HRDD. The 15 chapters in this book should therefore further lawyers' understanding of HRDD and allow them to advise their business clients in a manner that aids those clients with adoption and implementation of good practices to enhance their effectiveness in addressing their potential and actual human rights impacts"-- Provided by publisher.
Identifiers: LCCN 2022042104 (print) | LCCN 2022042105 (ebook) | ISBN 9781639052028 (paperback) | ISBN 9781639052035 (epub)
Subjects: LCSH: International business enterprises--Law and legislation. | Social responsibility of business--Law and legislation. | Liability for human rights violations. | United Nations Human Rights Council. Guiding Principles on Business and Human Rights.
Classification: LCC K1329.5 .H86 2022 (print) | LCC K1329.5 (ebook) | DDC 346/.0664--dc23/eng/20221201
LC record available at https://lccn.loc.gov/2022042104
LC ebook record available at https://lccn.loc.gov/2022042105

Contents

About the Authors

Morvarid Bagheri works as general counsel at an energy efficiency company and has served as a co-chair of the ABA International Law Section's International Human Rights Committee. Morvarid received her LLM in International Law and Justice from Fordham University School of Law and her JD from Suffolk University Law School. She is a member of the Massachusetts State Bar.

Bettina Braun is a policy advisor at the German Institute for Human Rights, where she works in the business and human rights team, focusing on legislative developments in the European Union and worldwide. She previously worked on business and human rights developments and corporate accountability issues with civil society organizations in the United States. Prior to focusing on this area, she worked in a law firm on international arbitration and investment cases and has experience in European Union market regulation and competition law through her work at the Center for European Integration Studies, Bonn, Germany. She holds an LLM from Columbia University School of Law and received her first law degree from the University of Bonn, Germany.

Jared Cole has worked as a design strategist and researcher for over 20 years. His experience includes everything from prototyping reproductive healthcare services in Northern Nigeria, to designing mission control software for nanosatellites, to advising startups and innovation labs, to teaching design research methods to graduate students. Jared has worked with communities across six continents, and with clients as diverse as Mozilla, Wikimedia Foundation, and the US Agency for International Development.

Shauna Curphey is a human rights lawyer and researcher at Just Ground, focused on advancing the visions of communities working to address corporate activity that threatens or violates their human rights. She currently serves on the Steering Committee of the ABA International Law Section's International Human Rights Committee. Her past experience includes serving as associate general counsel for the Coalition of Immokalee Workers and as research director for the Institute for Multi-Stakeholder Initiative Integrity.

Olivia Dean is a PhD candidate with RMIT University in Melbourne, Australia, and an emerging researcher in business and human rights. Her PhD scholarship explores the impact of the Modern Slavery Act on the Australian Finance Sector, focusing on reporting obligations and human rights due diligence. Olivia teaches Company Law (Melbourne and Jakarta), International Commercial Law, Law of Investments and Financial Markets, Corporate Governance and Regulation, and Business and Corporations Law.

François de Cambiaire is a lawyer admitted at the Paris Bar for more than 10 years. He specializes in civil and commercial litigation, white-collar crimes, particularly in the areas of corruption and economic criminality, human rights, and corporate accountability. With his partner Sébastien Mabile at Seattle Avocats, he developed an expertise in corporate social responsibility litigation based on the Duty of Vigilance Law adopted in France in 2017. They have brought cases against French oil major TotalEnergies on climate change and against Casino for its contribution to deforestation in the Amazon. François is a lecturer and an Expert at the European Centre for Economic Law at ESSEC Business School. In 2021, he was distinguished as Laureate of the 1st Palmarès Giverny–Le Point gathering for 50 committed leaders under 40 in ecological and social transformation in France.

Carlos de Miguel Perales is a lawyer and a professor at the Faculty of Law of the Comillas University-ICADE (Madrid, Spain). After more than 30 years as a lawyer in the law firm Uría Menéndez, Carlos continues his activity as an independent legal advisor. His experience includes providing legal advice on environmental and natural resource matters to national and international corporations in various industry sectors and in all types of transactions. When dealing with environmental matters, Carlos also advises on related issues, including human rights. Carlos has authored several books and numerous articles in his areas of expertise. He is a frequent participant in seminars, conferences, and webinars, in Spain and abroad. Carlos is a Doctor of Law and a graduate in Business Administration of the Comillas University-ICADE.

Esmira Hackenberg is an Associate Lecturer in Law at RMIT University in Vietnam. She is a PhD in Law candidate with RMIT University in Melbourne, Australia. Her research areas and interests include corporate law, corporate accountability, and business and human rights. Esmira completed a Master of Laws at the University of Edinburgh with the Distinction Award. She is an active member of the RMIT Melbourne Centre for Business and Human Rights.

Lisa J. Laplante is a professor of law at New England Law in Boston where she also directs the Center for International Law and Policy (CILP). Through CILP, she oversees the Operational-Level Grievance Mechanism Research Project, among other projects on the theme of business and human rights. She first started working on the theme of business and human rights while a Furman Fellow with the Lawyers Committee for Human Rights after earning her JD from New York University School of Law where she was a Root-Tilden-Kern Public

Interest Scholar. In 2012–2013, she became the interim director of the University of Connecticut's Thomas J. Dodd Research Center, where she helped spearhead programming on business and human rights. She teaches and writes on the topic of remedies for human rights, and her prize-winning scholarship appears in leading journals. Recognition of her expertise in the field led to the invitation to become a member of the Institute for Advanced Studies at Princeton in 2008.

Dr. Corinne E. Lewis, a partner in the Brussels-based law firm Lex Justi, is an international human rights lawyer with a specialization in business and human rights. She provides legal advice to a range of clients based on her corporate law background as in-house counsel with a major multinational company and her 30 years of international human rights law experience, including work at the United Nations. She also has taught human rights law and public international law courses at US and UK universities. Having lived and worked in the United States and multiple countries in Asia and Europe, she brings an international perspective to her diverse projects. In addition to a PhD in law from the London School of Economics and Political Science, Dr. Lewis has an LLM (with honors) from Georgetown University and a JD from Indiana University. She is Immediate past co-chair of the ABA International Law Section's International Human Rights Committee.

Shelley Marshall is an Associate Professor and Director of the RMIT University Business and Human Rights Centre and an Australian Research Council DECRA Fellow. She has advised and published on corporate accountability and business and human rights for 25 years, with a focus on the labour conditions of vulnerable workers and modern slavery. Shelley left legal practice in 2001 to join the team setting up Ethical Clothing Australia. Her research has informed labour law reform in several countries and the policies of the International Labour Organization. For example, over 2018–2019 she made frequent trips to Thailand to advise the Thai Ministry of Labor on how to enforce labour laws for home-based workers. Shelley was a cofounder of the Australian Corporate Accountability Network, which has over 100 civil society and academic members from across Australia, and is on its Steering Committee. She has undertaken research consultancies for business and intergovernmental agencies. Her most recent book is *Living Wage*, published by Oxford University Press in 2019.

Hind Merabet has been an in-house counsel within the healthcare sector for more than 15 years. Prior to that, she worked as a litigator in a large Canadian law firm and as a Canadian Junior Professional Consultant in the Office of the Special Representative for Children and Armed Conflict. Hind earned a Bachelor's degree in Law and a Bachelor's degree in Biology from the University of Montreal. She also holds an LLM from New York University School of Law. During her legal studies, Hind was a recipient of the North American Mobility in Higher Education Scholarship and a Graduate Editor for the *NYU Journal of International Law and Politics*. Additionally, Hind is a Certified Information Privacy Professional in the United States (CIPP/US) and Europe (CIPP/E). Her areas of interest include data privacy, business and human rights, and corporate social responsibility.

Int'l Law. 423 (2018). He is a member of the New York City Bar Working Group on Business and Human Rights, the ABA Representative to the Uniform Law Commission Supply Chain Transparency Study Committee, and past member of the ABA Center for Human Rights Advisory Council and the ABA Rule of Law Initiative board.

Andrea Shemberg is Chair of the Global Business Initiative on Human Rights, a business-led organization working to help multinational companies implement the United Nations Guiding Principles on Business and Human Rights (UNGPs). She has worked as a business and human rights practitioner for nearly 20 years. Andrea served as legal advisor at Amnesty International UK and legal officer at the International Commission of Jurists before becoming Legal Advisor to John Ruggie, the then UN Special Representative of the Secretary General for Business and Human Rights. Andrea went on to establish and co-lead the Investment & Human Rights Project at the London School of Economics, where she was also a visiting fellow until 2019. Andrea is a US-trained lawyer and began her legal career as an employment and labor lawyer for a management-side law firm. She has an MSc with Distinction in Human Rights from the London School of Economics.

John F. Sherman III is a well-known expert on the implications of the 2011 United Nations Guiding Principles on Business and Human Rights (UNGPs) for the practice of law. He was senior legal advisor to the late Harvard Kennedy School Professor John Ruggie, the author of the UNGPs. John is general counsel and senior adviser to Shift, an independent nonprofit, which is the leading center of expertise on the UNGPs. He is also a Senior Program Fellow at the Corporate Responsibility Initiative of the Harvard Kennedy School and an Executive Fellow of the Hoffman Center for Business Ethics at Bentley University. John has advised multinational companies, international law firms, and bar associations on aligning themselves with the UNGPs. John is a graduate of Harvard Law School and Dartmouth College and was formerly deputy general counsel of National Grid. His chapter reflects his own personal views and not those of any other person or entity.

Nancy Kaymar Stafford is an attorney licensed to practice in the State of New York. She spent several years practicing as a corporate attorney before turning to rights-based work. She has served as chair of the International Law Section of the ABA and as a board member of its Rule of Law Initiative. Ms. Stafford works pro bono with Georgetown University Law Center's International Women's Human Rights Clinic as a supervising attorney, conducting field work in Uganda, Ghana, Tanzania, Kenya, Eswatini, Lesotho, and Botswana. She has taught International Women's Human Rights Law at Georgetown University Law Center and Emory University School of Law. Ms. Stafford has worked extensively on issues of women's rights, particularly as they relate to the African continent, having published several articles and book chapters on that topic. She has an LLM from Georgetown University Law Center in International and Comparative Law and is working on a PhD in International Relations from Salve Regina University.

Anahita Thoms heads Baker McKenzie's International Trade Practice in Germany. She is a member of its Europe, Middle East, and Africa Steering Committee for Compliance & Investigations and Global Lead Sustainability Partner for the Industrials, Manufacturing, and Transportation Industry Group. She serves on the ABA International Human Rights Steering Committee and served as co-chair of the ABA Export Controls and Economic Sanctions Committee. Anahita has won awards for her work, including 100 Most Influential Women in German Business (*Manager Magazin*), International Trade Lawyer of the Year (Germany) (2020 ILO Client Choice Awards), Young Global Leader of the World Economic Forum, Capital 40 under 40, International Trade Lawyer (New York) (2016 ILO Client Choice Awards). Anahita focuses her practice on global investigations and white-collar crime proceedings before German authorities and courts. She has significant experience advising on internal compliance programs, accompanying internal and external investigations, and self-disclosures involving breaches of sanctions, export control, human rights, data protection, and foreign investment review.

Margaret G. Wachenfeld is an international lawyer and policy adviser with more than 25 years of experience in applying international standards related to human rights, responsible business conduct, human development, and the environment to the work of international organizations and the private sector. She currently holds several concurrent positions: Managing Director, Themis Research; Senior Research Fellow for the Institute for Human Rights and Business; Senior Adviser at the Myanmar Centre for Responsible Business; and Senior Adviser at the Center for Responsible Business Colombia. In addition, she serves on a number of advisory boards including the European Parliament Responsible Business Conduct Working Group, the United Nations Environment Programme FI-PRI Reference Group for the Legal Framework for Impact Project, and the Organisation for Economic Co-Operation and Development Advisory Group on Responsible Business Conduct in the Financial Sector. Margaret previously worked at UNICEF, the International Finance Corporation, White & Case, and the Danish Institute for Human Rights. She has a BA, JD, LLM and PhD.

Constance Z. Wagner is Professor of Law and affiliated faculty with the Center for International and Comparative Law at Saint Louis University School of Law. She focuses her teaching and scholarship on business law and international law, including corporate governance, corporate social responsibility, financial regulation, international trade law, and international business transactions. She holds a secondary appointment as Professor of Women's and Gender Studies. She has taught seminars on women's human rights and has lectured at conferences and published articles on the gender dimensions of international trade treaties, gender mainstreaming, and gender equity. She serves as vice-chair (publications) of the International Human Rights Committee of the ABA Section of International Law. She practiced corporate law in New York City prior to entering the legal academy and is a member in good standing of the New York and Missouri bars. Professor Wagner holds degrees from Columbia University School of Law (JD), University of Konstanz School of Law (LLM), Saint Louis University School of Business (MBA), and Northwestern University College of Arts & Sciences (BA).

PART I

An Introduction to Human Rights Due Diligence

1

The Evolving Concept of Human Rights Due Diligence

Corinne E. Lewis

I. Introduction

When the United Nations (UN) Human Rights Council unanimously endorsed the *UN Guiding Principles on Business and Human Rights* (UNGPs) in 2011, they ushered in a profound shift in the expectations and approach to businesses' adverse impacts on people, including not just their employees, but also workers in their supply chains, local communities, and customers.[1] The UNGPs expressed, in what has become the authoritative global standard, that States have a duty to protect human rights from business-related abuse, businesses have a responsibility to respect human rights, and States and businesses should provide greater access of remedy to those harmed. They also articulated the essential process by which companies can identify, prevent, address, and account for their actual and potential human rights impacts in their own operations and in their value chains: human rights due diligence (HRDD).[2] HRDD is the primary process and tool for businesses to "know and show" their responsibility to respect human rights. As technical legal experts, wise counselors, and

[1] Human Rights Council Res. 17/4, UN Doc. A/HRC/RES/17/4, at para. 4 (Jul. 6, 2011).

[2] UN Office of the High Commissioner for Human Rights, *Guiding Principles on Business and Human Rights: Implementing the United Nations "Protect, Respect and Remedy" Framework*, at 17–21, UN Doc. HR/PUB/11/4 (2011), https://www.ohchr.org/documents/publications/guidingprinciplesbusinesshr_en.pdf [hereinafter *Guiding Principles*].

leaders,[3] lawyers have a key role to play in assisting and supporting businesses with respecting human rights and with HRDD.

Lawyers' representation and advice to businesses occurs against the backdrop of an increasingly international context at both a micro and a macro level. At the micro level, focused on a company's end product, raw materials for a product may be sourced from a mine or mill in one country, additional components may be manufactured in multiple other countries, and the final product may be assembled in a factory in a different country. The end product may then be transported in massive container ships to locations across the globe and driven by trucks or carried by rail to large regional warehouses for pickup and transportation to local distribution centers. Thus, production processes for a single consumer product can be highly fragmented and dispersed throughout the world. The transactions to effectuate this process require lawyers' extensive involvement.

At a macro global level, there is an increasing emphasis on product sustainability, which emphasizes that the needs of the present generation should be met in a manner that does not jeopardize the needs of future generations.[4] Social, economic, and environmental issues, which are inextricably linked and interdependent, are considerations that determine the sustainability of a product.[5] The UN Working Group on Business and Human Rights (UNWG), a body of five independent experts mandated by the UN Human Rights Council to "promote, disseminate and implement" the UNGPs,[6] has highlighted that HRDD not only enables, but also contributes to sustainable development.[7] As the UNWG has stated:

> For businesses, the most powerful contribution to sustainable development is to embed respect for human rights in their activities and across their value chains, addressing harm done to people and focusing on the potential and actual impacts. . . . Businesses need to realize and accept that not having negative impacts is a minimum expectation and a positive contribution to the Goals.[8]

Governmental upheavals, coups resulting in an increasing number of autocratic leaders of countries, and natural disasters can no longer be viewed by businesses, and the lawyers who work with them, as far-off events; nor can the devastating effects of ravaging fires, increased drought, and unusual weather patterns due to climate change. Additionally, the global COVID-19 pandemic continues to upend business practices and has resulted in nearly 6.43 million deaths worldwide, at the time of writing. Political and natural events and health

[3] John Sherman III, *The Corporate General Counsel Who Respects Human Rights*, SSRN, *at* 10, https://papers.ssrn.com/sol3/papers.cfm?abstract_id=3624331 (last revised Mar. 6, 2021) (accepted for publication in Legal Ethics Journal).

[4] *See Goal 12: Ensure Sustainable Consumption and Production Patterns*, Sustainable Dev. Goals (last visited Jan. 31, 2022), https://www.un.org/sustainabledevelopment/sustainable-consumption-production/.

[5] EU Science Hub, https://ec.europa.eu/jrc/en/research-topic/sustainable-production-and-consumption (last updated Jun. 23, 2021).

[6] Human Rights Council Res. 17/4, *supra* note 1, at para. 6.

[7] Working Group Report on the Issue of Human Rights and Transnational Corporations and Other Business Enterprises, at para. 59, UN Doc. A/73/163 (Jul. 16, 2018), https://digitallibrary.un.org/record/1639520?ln=en.

[8] *Id.*

crises, even when occurring in far-off regions of the world, have significant ramifications for a business's operations. Thus, companies require legal counsel and advocacy that incorporate not only an understanding of the practical aspects of a business's operations and relationships but also the larger context in which business is conducted.

A key component of a business's operations and its success is its relationships with stakeholders—the employees of the company, the workers in its supply chain, its customers, and the local community, as well as the rapidly increasing number of investors who pay close attention to a company's environmental, social, and governance (ESG) factors, where the "S" or "Social Impact Factor" primarily concerns human rights. In implementing their responsibility to respect human rights, businesses need to understand their adverse human rights impacts on these persons and reassess their potential and actual impacts in light of changes in the context, especially the impact on the persons who are most marginalized and disadvantaged in countries. Businesses have long had to manage and report on their financial results and, more recently, ensure their business practices were free of corruption and bribery;[9] they are now increasingly accountable for their damages to the environment.[10] The missing component in businesses' responsibilities and accountability has been that of ensuring respect for the human rights of people.

The responsibility of businesses to respect human rights covers a wide range of business activities. The responsibility extends from the business's own hiring and employment practices to use of its products or services by its customers. It also includes responsibility for adverse impacts in the communities in which the businesses operate and throughout their business relationships. The latter, therefore, includes respect for the rights of workers in entities within businesses' value chains, regardless of the country in which those workers are located. The globalization of trade and the outsourcing of production means that businesses must, now more than ever, be aware of and address their adverse human rights impacts at the operational level while taking into consideration the wider macro context. Lawyers, as legal experts, wise counselors, and leaders, are key in assisting them to do so.

Therefore, this book is intended to assist lawyers in navigating the developing area of HRDD. It explores the key components and requirements of the HRDD process, considers practical implementation of HRDD into corporate practices and policies, and treats key topics and cross-cutting issues related to HRDD. The 15 chapters in this book should therefore further lawyers' understanding of HRDD and allow them to advise their business clients in a manner that aids those clients with adoption and implementation of good practices to enhance their effectiveness in addressing their potential and actual human rights impacts.

This first chapter serves as an introduction to HRDD and lays the groundwork for the successive chapters that provide a more in-depth analysis of specific topics. Section II of this

[9] *See e.g.*, U.S. Foreign Corrupt Practices Act, 15 U.S.C. §§ 78dd-1 (1977). *See also*, UN General Assembly, United Nations Convention Against Corruption, UN Doc. A/48/422 (Oct. 31, 2003), https://www.refworld.org/docid/4374b9524.html.

[10] *See e.g.*, *50 Landmark Legal Cases*, EARTHJUSTICE (Sept. 15, 2021), https://earthjustice.org/features/landmark-cases. *See also*, ALEJANDRO GARCÍA ESTEBAN & CHRISTOPHER PATZ, SUING GOLIATH (Cass Hebron & Iva Petkovic eds., Sept. 2021), https://corporatejustice.org/wp-content/uploads/2021/09/Suing-Goliath-FINAL.pdf.

For lawyers advising businesses, due diligence is "a process to manage business risks or to meet a mandated duty of care."[14] In the corporate law area, the Securities Act of 1933 in the United States was adopted during the Great Depression and after the stock market crash of 1929 to ensure that prospective investors in securities such as stocks and bonds receive financial and other significant information about the securities in which they invest and are not defrauded.[15] Liability is precluded for the preparer of the information where a "reasonable investigation" was conducted to ensure that there were no material misrepresentations or omissions.[16] The term "due diligence" is not expressly mentioned in the Act, but became a term of art derived from the Act's provisions and was therefore both a management process and a standard.[17]

Due diligence is also carried out by businesses prior to the acquisition of or merger with another business, to assess and confirm the financial situation of the latter company, its contractual relationships, and other facts about the conduct of its business. In the financial sector context, in 1990, the Financial Action Task Force (FATF), the global money laundering and terrorist financing watchdog, issued *Forty Recommendations* that endorse due diligence by financial institutions to prevent money laundering by customers; these recommendations have been periodically updated and now also cover terrorist financing.[18] Thus, due diligence is a widespread practice in the corporate context that allows the entity to avoid relationships and activities that would cause harm to the company.

The concept of due diligence is also one familiar to human rights lawyers. In the human rights field, due diligence also has the dual characteristics of a standard and a process. General recognition of the concept in this area is most often attributed to the decision by the Inter-American Court of Human Rights in the *Velásquez Rodriguez* case. Velásquez Rodriguez disappeared at the hands of the Honduran secret police with the assistance of civilians who acted pursuant to police orders. The Court held that: "[a]n illegal act which violates human rights and which is initially not directly imputable to a State (for example, because it is the act of a private person or because the person responsible has not been identified) can lead to international responsibility of the State, not because of the act itself, but because of the lack

Series, Working Paper No. RWP20-034, 2020) https://www.hks.harvard.edu/publications/making-stakeholder-capitalism-work-contributions-business-and-human-rights.

[14] John Sherman III, Beyond CSR: The Story of the UN Guiding Principles on Business and Human Rights 1–40 (Corp. Responsibility Initiative, Harvard Kennedy Sch., Working Paper No. 71, 2020), https://www.hks.harvard.edu/sites/default/files/centers/mrcbg/files/CRI_AWP_71.pdf.

[15] Registration Under the Securities Act of 1933, U.S. Sec. & Exch. Comm'n, https://www.investor.gov/introduction-investing/investing-basics/glossary/registration-under-securities-act-1933 (last visited Feb. 1, 2022).

[16] 15 U.S.C. § 77k (1933). *See* Linda S. Spedding, Due Diligence and Corporate Governance 3 (Butterworth-Heinemann 2005); William K. Sjostrom Jr., *The Due Diligence Defense Under Section 11 of the Securities Act of 1933*, 44 Brandeis L.J. 549, 554 (2006).

[17] Dennis J. Block, Jonathan M. Hoff, & Joshua Bloomstein, *Underwriter Due Diligence in Securities Offerings*, FindLaw, https://corporate.findlaw.com/finance/underwriter-due-diligence-in-securities-offerings.html (last updated Mar. 26, 2008). *See* Herman & MacLean v. Huddleston, 459 U.S. 375, 382 (1983).

[18] FATF, International Standards on Combating Money Laundering and the Financing of Terrorism & Proliferation: the FATF Recommendations, (updated Oct. 2021), https://www.fatf-gafi.org/publications/fatfrecommendations/documents/fatf-recommendations.html.

of due diligence to prevent the violation or to respond to it as required by the Convention."[19] The obligation of a State to act with "due diligence" in fulfilling its duty to protect has also been reiterated by the Human Rights Committee (HRC), which is responsible for monitoring the implementation of the International Covenant on Civil and Political Rights by States (ICCPR), in its General Comment 31.[20] The Comment provides that States can breach their obligations under the ICCPR where they permit or fail "to take appropriate measures or to exercise due diligence to prevent, punish, investigate or redress the harm caused by such acts by private persons or entities."[21]

Thus, HRDD conducted by a business may contain aspects that resemble due diligence in the corporate governance and international human rights areas but is a distinctive concept because it considers impacts from the perspective of the person harmed. The process of HRDD is to be conducted by a business entity with the purpose of ensuring, not the protection of the company's interests, but instead, the rights, the human rights, of persons. John Ruggie used the term in a broad sense to mean "a comprehensive, proactive attempt to uncover human rights risks, actual and potential, over the entire life cycle of a project or business activity, with the aim of avoiding and mitigating risks."[22] In doing so, HRDD is an active, transformative process that transcends legal norms, both national and international; it should be viewed as a "transnational social norm," that "meets the company's social license to operate" and "exists 'over and above' all applicable legal requirements."[23]

B. Key Components of Human Rights Due Diligence

HRDD is, as noted above, an essential process to a business's ability to meet its responsibility to respect human rights.[24] The UNWG has emphasized the integral role that HRDD should play within the business by referring to it as the "backbone of the day-to-day activities of a business enterprise in translating into practice its responsibility to respect human rights."[25] UNGPs Principles 17–21 enumerate and provide guidance on implementing the four components to the HRDD process. These four components include:

---

[19] Caso Velásquez Rodríguez v. Honduras, Merits, Reparations, and Costs, Judgment, Inter-Am. Ct. H.R. (Ser. C) No. 4, ¶ 174 (July 29, 1988), https://www.refworld.org/cases,IACRTHR,40279a9e4.html.

[20] UN Human Rights Committee, General Comment No. 31 [80]: the Nature of the General Legal Obligation Imposed on States Parties to the Covenant, UN Doc. CCPR/C/21/Rev.1/Add/13 (May 26, 2004), https://www.refworld.org/docid/478b26ae2.html#:~:text=Refworld%20%7C%20General%20comment%20no.,States%20Parties%20to%20the%20Covenant&text=Adopted%20on%2029%20March%202004%20(2187th%20meeting.

[21] *Id.* at para. 8.

[22] Special Representative of the Secretary-General, *Business and Human Rights: Towards Operationalizing the "Protect, Respect and Remedy" Framework*, para. 46, Human Rights Council, UN Doc. A/HRC/11/13 (Apr. 22, 2009), https://www2.ohchr.org/english/bodies/hrcouncil/docs/11session/a.hrc.11.13.pdf.

[23] John Gerard Ruggie & John F. Sherman, III, *The Concept of "Due Diligence" in the UN Guiding Principles on Business and Human Rights: A Reply to Jonathan Bonnitcha and Robert McCorquodale*, 28 EUR. J. INT'L L. 921, 923-924 (2017).

[24] *Guiding Principles*, *supra* note 2, at 15–16.

[25] Working Group Rep. on the Issue of Human Rights and Transnational Corporations and Other Business Enterprises, *supra* note 7, at para. 10.

a. Identifying and assessing actual or potential adverse human rights impacts that the business enterprise may cause or contribute to through its own activities, or which may be directly linked to its operations, products or services by its business relationships;

b. Integrating findings from impact assessments across relevant functions and company processes and taking appropriate action according to its involvement in the impact [. . . .];

c. Tracking the effectiveness of measures and processes to address adverse human rights impacts in order to know if they are working; and

d. Communicating on how impacts are being addressed and showing stakeholders—in particular affected stakeholders—that there are adequate policies and processes in place to implement respect for human rights in practice.[26]

Briefly stated, HRDD is the process that "all business enterprises should undertake to identify, prevent, mitigate and account for how they address potential and actual impacts on human rights caused by or contributed to through their own activities, or directly linked to their operations, products, or services by their business relationships."[27] In carrying out HRDD, businesses are to focus on the risks to persons potentially or actually impacted by the entity's operations, from the perspective of these persons, in contrast to other forms of corporate due diligence, which, as mentioned above, include those in connection with mergers and acquisitions, anti-corruption, and anti-bribery, and are concerned about the risk to the business entity itself. However, respect for human rights of individuals and groups by businesses is not offset by businesses' positive contributions through job creation, infrastructure development, creation of schools and hospitals, or other activities. These are not, as stated in UNGPs Principle 11, "a substitute for undertaking human rights due diligence." There is no setoff for adverse human rights impacts on people and communities.

Therefore, within businesses and among lawyers who advise businesses on incorporating HRDD into their corporate policies and processes, two key shifts in thinking are required to ensure that HRDD is performed in a manner that allows the business to identify its potential and actual negative human rights impacts and to address them appropriately. First, unlike corporate due diligence in which due diligence is undertaken as a one-time assessment, HRDD should be performed over the life cycle of a project or business activity. Second, individuals and communities that are potentially or actually impacted by the business should be meaningfully engaged in the HRDD process. They need to receive adequate information and be engaged throughout the HRDD process, from the identification of adverse impacts through determination of appropriate remedies.

Chapter 2 of this book, "The Due Diligence Process", by Hind Merabet, furnishes an overview of the HRDD process that will assist legal practitioners to navigate the practical challenges of this process. She analyzes each of the four components of HRDD and explores the distinctions related to the business's responsibility to address its adverse human rights

[26] *Id.*

[27] *Id.* at para. 2.

impacts, based on whether the business caused or contributed to the impacts through its own activities or whether the impacts are directly linked to its operations, products, or services by its business relationships.

C. Uptake of Human Rights Due Diligence

HRDD has become a norm of expected conduct by business entities due to its extensive uptake by international organizations, governments, the financial sector and investors, business associations, civil society organizations, and businesses themselves.[28]

International organizations have incorporated HRDD into their standards. The Organisation for Economic Co-operation and Development (OECD), an intergovernmental economic organization comprised of 38 member countries, updated its *OECD Guidelines for Multinational Enterprises* (OECD Guidelines) to include a human rights chapter and align them with the UNGPs, including providing that business enterprises should "[c]arry out human rights due diligence."[29] The OECD issued more specific guidance on HRDD in 2018 with its *Due Diligence Guidance for Responsible Business Conduct*, which provides an overview of HRDD, explains the process, and provides practical guidance on its implementation.[30] The International Labour Organization, a UN agency that promotes social justice and human rights, particularly labor rights, has issued a revised *2017 Tripartite Declaration of Principles concerning Multinational Enterprises and Social Policy* that contains principles that provide guidance to multinational enterprises, governments, and employers' and workers' organizations, based on international labor Conventions and Recommendations, and specifically provides that: "[e]nterprises, including multinational enterprises, should carry out due diligence."[31] Also, the UN Development Programme, the UN agency mandated to "end poverty, build democratic governance, rule of law and inclusive institutions,"[32] has developed a *Human Rights Due Diligence Training Facilitation Guide*.[33]

International bodies have also encouraged States to adopt legislative and policy measures requiring businesses to adopt HRDD and clarify what the HRDD obligation of businesses entails. For example, the Inter-American Commission on Human Rights recommended in 2019 that mandatory HRDD be adopted by its member States.[34] Also, the Committee on

---

[28] *Id.* at para. 20.

[29] Corinne Lewis, *The ABA's Commitment to Develop and Promote Business and Human Rights within the Legal Profession: What this Means for Lawyers*, 38 Hous. J. Int'l L. 2, 20-21 (2016). *See* Organisation for Economic Co-operation and Development, OECD Guidelines for Multinational Enterprises 31 (2011).

[30] Organisation for Economic Co-operation and Development, OECD Due Diligence Guidance for Responsible Business Conduct 9 (2018).

[31] ILO, Tripartite Declaration of Principles Concerning Multinational Enterprises and Social Policy (5th ed. 2017) (for language on HRDD, see p. 5, Principle 10(d)).

[32] *About Us*, United Nations Dev. Program, https://www.undp.org/about-us#:~:text=UNDP's%20mandate%20is%20to%20end,people%20build%20a%20better%20life (last visited Feb. 2, 2022).

[33] *Human Rights Due Diligence Training Facilitation Guide*, United Nations Dev. Program (Sept. 13, 2021), https://www.undp.org/publications/human-rights-due-diligence-training-facilitation-guide.

[34] *See* Soledad García Muñoz (Relatora Especial sobre Derechos Económicos, Sociales, Culturales y Ambientales), *Informe Empresas y Derechos Humanos: Estándares Interamericanos*, OEA.Ser.L/V/II (Nov. 1, 2019) www.oas.org

Economic, Social and Cultural Rights, the body responsible for monitoring implementation of the International Covenant on Economic, Social and Cultural Rights (ICESCR), has stated in its *General Comment No. 24 on State Obligations under ICESCR in the Context of Business Activities* that:

> The obligation to protect entails a [State's] positive duty to adopt a legal framework requiring business entities to exercise **human rights due diligence** in order to identify, prevent and mitigate the risks of violations of Covenant rights, to avoid such rights being abused, as well as to account for the negative impacts caused or contributed to by their decisions and operations and those of entities they control on the enjoyment of Covenant rights.[35]

Governments have expressed support for HRDD through multinational fora. The G7, in 2015, urged the private sector to implement HRDD.[36] In 2017, at the G20 summit in Hamburg, Germany, G20 States committed to promote sustainable and inclusive supply chains through fostering the implementation of human rights consistent with the UNGPs and "work towards establishing adequate policy frameworks in our countries such as national action plans on business and human rights," and they "underline[d] the responsibility of businesses to exercise due diligence."[37] Governments also have expressed their expectation that businesses will conduct HRDD in their National Action Plans (NAPs) on business and human rights, which have been formulated by some 30 States with nearly the same number in the process of developing NAPs.[38] Many of the adopted NAPs express governmental priorities and actions to support implementation of HRDD.[39] Governments also have issued general

---

/es/cidh/informes/pdfs/EmpresasDDHH.pdf.

[35] [emphasis added] UN, Econ. & Soc. Council, Comm. on Econ., Soc. and Cultural Rights, General Comment No. 24 on State Obligations Under the International Covenant on Economic, Social and Cultural Rights in the Context of Business Activities, para. 16, UN Doc. E/C.12/GC/24 (Aug. 10, 2017), https://tbinternet.ohchr.org/_layouts/15/treatybodyexternal/Download.aspx?symbolno=E%2fC.12%2fGC%2f24&Lang=en.

[36] *G-7 Leaders' Declaration*, The White House (Jun. 8, 2015), https://obamawhitehouse.archives.gov/the-press-office/2015/06/08/g-7-leaders-declaration.

[37] *G20 Leaders' Declaration: Shaping an Interconnected World*, Council of the EU & The European Council (July 8, 2017), https://www.consilium.europa.eu/en/press/press-releases/2017/07/08/g20-hamburg-communique/.

[38] National Action Plans (NAPs) are "policy documents in which a government articulates priorities and actions that it will adopt to support the implementation of international, regional, or national obligations and commitments with regard to a given policy area or topic." *See*, https://globalnaps.org/about/.

For a list of countries that have adopted NAPs or are in the process of doing so *see National Action Plans on Business and Human Rights*, UN Office of the High Commissioner for Human Rights, https://www.ohchr.org/en/issues/business/pages/nationalactionplans.aspx (last visited Feb. 2, 2022).

[39] For an analysis of references to HRDD in government's National Action Plans, *see* Danish Inst. for Human Rights, *Human Rights Due Diligence*, Nat'l Action Plans on Bus. & Hum. Rights, https://globalnaps.org/issue/human-rights-due-diligence (last visited Feb. 2, 2022). The UN Working Group on Business and Human Rights, in its 2016 *Guidance on National Action Plans on Business and Human Rights*, specifically notes that governments should state the "expectation that business enterprises respect human rights in line with the UNGPs, including by implementing human rights due diligence." UN Working Grp. on Bus. & Human Rights, Guidance on National Action Plans on Business and Human Rights, p. ii (2016), https://www.ohchr.org/Documents/Issues/Business/UNWG_NAPGuidance.pdf.

guidance on HRDD,[40] as well as guidance for specific industry sectors.[41] Moreover, a number of countries have adopted HRDD legislation, as discussed in detail in Section III.

Financial institutions, including private sector commercial banks, institutional investors, and development finance institutions, exert a great deal of influence on both public and private business entities. These institutions are in the early stages of requiring businesses to conduct HRDD, but this trend will likely continue to grow with the increased emphasis on ESG factors in investment decisions, in which respect for human rights is the primary component of the "S" in "ESG." According to Reuters, a record amount of US$649 billion was invested in ESG-focused funds throughout the world in 2021 up to the end of November, which is a significant increase from US$542 billion in 2020 and US$285 billion in 2019; ESG funds are estimated to be 10 percent of worldwide fund assets, based on Refinitiv Lipper information.[42] Signs of this trend include the adoption by 126 financial institutions in 37 countries of the Equator Principles, which provide that financial institutions will fulfill their responsibility to respect human rights consistent with the UNGPs "by carrying out human rights due diligence."[43] Additionally, the Sustainable Finance Disclosure Regulation of the European Union (EU) requires investors to disclose information about the adverse impacts of their investment decisions on people and the planet and their due diligence to address those impacts."[44]

Large businesses and business associations have publicly endorsed mandatory HRDD regulation.[45] Business associations are also emphasizing HRDD in guidance to their member

---

[40] Denmark updated its online tool for Danish companies to use "when requiring customers and suppliers to respect human rights and perform due diligence." *See* Danish Inst. for Human Rights, *supra* note 39. The European Union issued *Guidance on Due Diligence for EU Businesses to Address the Risk of Forced Labour in their Operations and Supply Chains* (Jul. 12, 2021), https://trade.ec.europa.eu/doclib/docs/2021/july/tradoc_159709.pdf.

[41] For example, the United States issued *Guidance on Implementing the UN Guiding Principles for Transactions Linked to Foreign Government End-Users for Products or Services with Surveillance Capabilities*, which recommends that businesses incorporate HRDD into their compliance programs. U.S. Dep't. of State, Guidance on Implementing the UN Guiding Principles for Transactions Linked to Foreign Government End-Users for Products or Services with Surveillance Capabilities 1, https://www.state.gov/wp-content/uploads/2020/09/DRL-Industry-Guidance-Project-FINAL-508.pdf (last accessed Feb. 2, 2022). The French Development Agency issued a *Guide to due diligence of agribusiness projects that affect land and property rights: Operational guide*. Tech. Comm. on Land Tenure and Dev., Guide to Due Diligence of Agribusiness Projects that Affect Land and Property Rights: Operational Guide (2014) http://www.foncier-developpement.fr/wp-content/uploads/Guide-to-due-diligence.pdf.

[42] Ross Kerber & Simon Jessop, *Analysis: How 2021 Became the Year of ESG Investing*, Reuters (Dec. 23, 2021), https://www.reuters.com/markets/us/how-2021-became-year-esg-investing-2021-12-23/.

[43] Equator Principles (Jul. 2020), https://equator-principles.com/app/uploads/The-Equator-Principles_EP4_July2020.pdf.

[44] *Sustainability-Related Disclosure in the Financial Services Sector*, Eur. Commission, https://ec.europa.eu/info/business-economy-euro/banking-and-finance/sustainable-finance/sustainability-related-disclosure-financial-services-sector_en (last visited Feb. 2, 2022).

[45] *Companies & Investors in Support of mHRDD*, Bus. & Hum. Rights Resource Ctr., https://www.business-humanrights.org/en/big-issues/mandatory-due-diligence/companies-investors-in-support-of-mhrdd/ (last visited Feb. 2, 2022).

businesses,[46] and have even, alongside civil society, advocated for mandatory HRDD.[47] Civil society organizations have also played an active role in assisting and incentivizing businesses to pursue effective HRDD. They have produced guides on how to conduct HRDD, formulated benchmarks to assess businesses' implementation of HRDD,[48] and called attention to the inadequacies in businesses' conduct of HRDD.[49]

In sum, HRDD is becoming a mainstay of corporate responsibility. However, there is still a great deal of effort that needs to be undertaken by businesses to implement HRDD in a manner that provides them with an understanding of their adverse human rights impacts and includes actions to effectively address those impacts. KnowTheChain, whose aim is to assist companies to prevent forced labor in their supply chains and protect workers' rights, reported in a 2022 report, following five years of benchmarking, that companies in high-risk sectors, such as information and communications technology, food and beverage, and apparel and footwear scored only 29 percent for their HRDD efforts.[50] And the UNWG, in their report taking stock of the first 10 years of the UNGPs, stated that "benchmarking initiatives and stakeholder assessments highlight disconnect between improvements at the policy level and human rights due diligence in business practice."[51] Consequently, businesses require assistance and guidance from their legal counsel on various aspects of the HRDD process in order to meet their responsibility to respect human rights.

[46] For example, *see* Int'l Council on Mining and Minerals, Human rights in the mining and metals industry: Integrating human rights due diligence into corporate risk management processes (Mar. 2012), https://www.icmm.com/website/publications/pdfs/social-performance/2012/guidance_human-rights-due-diligence.pdf, *and* China Chamber of Commerce of Metals, Minerals & Chemicals Importers & Exporters, Chinese Due Diligence Guidelines for Responsible Mineral Supply Chains (Dec. 2, 2015), https://mneguidelines.oecd.org/chinese-due-diligence-guidelines-for-responsible-mineral-supply-chains.htm, for due diligence guidelines. *Also see* the joint publication, *No Way Around Due Diligence: Overview of Human Rights*, by Econsense, an association of leading globally active companies and organizations of German business specializing in the area of sustainable development and corporate social responsibility, and Twentyfifty, a management consultancy. econsense & twentyfifty, Overview of Human Rights Due Diligence Frameworks and Legislation (Jana Heinze et al., eds., 2017), https://econsense.de/wp-content/uploads/2019/07/190322_Due_Diligence.pdf.

[47] ABN-AMRO et al., Support for EU Framework on Mandatory Human Rights and Environmental Due Diligence (Sept. 2, 2020), https://media.business-humanrights.org/media/documents/EU_Business_Statement_Mandatory_Due_Diligence_02092020.pdf.

[48] *See* for example, *Human Rights Due Diligence Framework*, Ethical Trading Initiative (May 19, 2016), https://www.ethicaltrade.org/resources/human-rights-due-diligence-framework. For an example of civil society–formulated benchmarks that explicitly assess human rights due diligence by companies see, *The Methodology for the 2022-2023 Corporate Human Rights Benchmark*, World Benchmarking Alliance (Sept. 30, 2021), https://www.worldbenchmarkingalliance.org/research/the-methodology-for-the-2022-corporate-human-rights-benchmark/ and Ranking Digital Rights (2019), *see* Section 3, subsection 3.3 "*Due Diligence*," https://rankingdigitalrights.org/index2019/report/governance/#section-33.

[49] *See* Business and Human Rights Resource Centre, https://www.business-humanrights.org/en/ (last visited Feb. 2, 2022).

[50] KnowTheChain & Bus. & Human Rights Res. Ctr, Closing the Gap: Evidence for Effective Human Rights Due Diligence From Five Years Measuring Company Efforts To Address Forced Labour, 4 (2022), https://knowthechain.org/wp-content/uploads/2022-KTC-mHREDD-brief.pdf. Also see World Benchmarking Alliance, Social Transformation Baseline Assessment 2022: Are Companies Contributing to Systems Transformations that Leave No One Behind? 9 (Jan. 2022), https://www.worldbenchmarkingalliance.org/research/2022-social-transformation-baseline-assessment/.

[51] Rep. of Working Group on Business and Human Rights, *Guiding Principles on Business and Human Rights at 10: Taking Stock of the First Decade*, at III, UN Doc. A/HRC/43/39 (2021).

National Bar, have expressly committed to "promoting the realization of human rights in the business context," in signing the *Joint Declaration of Commitment on the Development and Promotion of the Field of Business and Human Rights Within the Legal Profession.*[61] As bar associations carry out this promotional, educational, and informative work, they will also be confronted with questions concerning lawyers' professional responsibilities and obligations and how these relate to their provision of advice on HRDD to their business clients.

Chapter 3 of this book, "Lawyers' Ethical Obligations and Human Rights Due Diligence," by Steven M. Richman, examines the obligations governing lawyers' professional conduct that have a disciplinary overlay, related to lawyers' advice to businesses. Mr. Richman, who notes that all lawyers are human rights lawyers now, considers the lawyer's professional principles of independence and the scope of ethics rules from a sampling of jurisdictions around the world. He specifically considers how the ABA's Model Rules apply to the lawyer as an advisor, to address the relevance of the UNGPs with clients, and then provides concrete examples of how lawyers can offer advice to their business clients that advances the UNGPs.

III. Standards: Hard and Soft Law/Express and Implied Obligations

Despite the increasing recognition by businesses of their responsibility to respect human rights since the adoption of the UNGPs over 10 years ago, companies' actual implementation of their obligation, and in particular their performance of HRDD, still lags behind their policy commitments, as the UNWG and nongovernmental organizations (NGOs) have noted (see Section II.C.). Assessments by Germany, the Netherlands, and the Commission of the EU also have demonstrated low rates of implementation of HRDD.[62] This has resulted in increasing calls for mandatory HRDD legislation from the NGO sector and others.[63] For example, in 2021, 94 investors, who represent over US$6 trillion in assets under management and advisement, expressed support for mandatory human rights and environmental due diligence legislation.[64]

---

[61] Am. Bar Ass'n et al., Joint Declaration of Commitment on the Development and Promotion of the Field of Business and Human Rights Within the Legal Profession (Jun. 9, 2015), http://www.americanbar.org/content/dam/aba/administrative/human_rights/joint_declaration.authcheckdam.pdf. The Joint Declaration was presented and signed by the American Bar Association at a meeting held at the United Nations' Palais des Nations in Geneva, Switzerland from June 8–9, 2015 and was attended by the Author.

[62] *Monitoring the National Action Plan for Business and Human Rights*, German Fed. Foreign Off. (Oct. 13, 2020), https://www.auswaertiges-amt.de/en/aussenpolitik/themen/monitoring-nap/2131054; *Evaluation and Revision of Policy on Responsible Business Conduct*, Dutch Ministry of Foreign Aff., https://www.government.nl/topics/responsible-business-conduct-rbc/evaluation-and-renewal-of-rbc-policy (last visited Nov. 2, 2020); Lise Smit et al., Study on Due Diligence Requirements Through the Supply Chain: Final Report (2020).

[63] *See, e.g.*, *Over 100 NGOS Demand Human Rights and Environmental Due Diligence Legislation*, European Coal. for Corp. Justice (Dec. 2, 2019), https://corporatejustice.org/news/over-100-ngos-demand-human-rights-and-environmental-due-diligence-legislation/.

[64] Investor Alliance for Human Rights, *94 Investors with Over US$6T in Assets Voice Support for EU Mandatory Due Diligence Including Liability*, Bus. & Hum. Rights Resource Ctr. (Oct. 8, 2021), https://www.business-humanrights.org/en/latest-news/94-investors-with-over-us6t-in-assets-voice-support-for-mandatory-due-diligence-incl-liability/.

A range of legislative and regulatory measures already necessitate that businesses integrally incorporate HRDD into their business practices in the United States and in other countries. In the United States, at the time of writing, there are two key measures that explicitly require HRDD. At the federal level, pursuant to Section 1502 of the Dodd-Frank Wall Street Reform and Consumer Protection Act (Conflict Minerals Rule), adopted by the US Congress in 2010, the Securities and Exchange Commission (SEC) requires, pursuant to rules issued in 2012, that US listed companies disclose their use of "conflict minerals" (tin, tantalum, tungsten, and gold) if these minerals are "necessary to the functionality or production of a product manufactured."[65] Companies using "conflict minerals" must evaluate whether the minerals originated in the Democratic Republic of the Congo or an adjoining country. Following a positive determination, they must undertake due diligence measures on the source and chain of custody of the minerals and report on these in an annual disclosure.[66] At the state level, the California Transparency in Supply Chains Act requires any company doing business in California that has annual worldwide gross receipts of over US$100 million and that identifies itself as a retail seller or manufacturer on its California tax return, to disclose its due diligence efforts "to eradicate slavery and human trafficking from its direct supply chain for tangible goods offered for sale."[67]

While the Conflict Minerals Rule and the California Transparency in Supply Chains Act address specific human rights issues, conflict minerals in the former and human slavery and trafficking in the latter, there is no current US legislation that mandates HRDD for all human rights by US companies. The draft bill, entitled the Corporate Human Rights Risk Assessment, Prevention and Mitigation Act of 2019, which would have required public companies that file an SEC annual report to identify human rights risks and actual impacts in their operations and value chain and then provide information about the process in their annual reports, was debated in the US House of Representatives Committee on Financial Services.[68] However, this draft bill has not progressed further at the time of writing.

In Europe, many countries have adopted or are in the process of adopting laws that make conducting HRDD a mandatory requirement. France enacted the first general law on HRDD, the French Duty of Vigilance Law, which is considered in chapter 4, "French Due Diligence Law," by François de Cambiaire and Alice Murgier. In the chapter, they provide background to the development of this ground-breaking law. They also thoroughly elaborate its scope

[65] Dodd-Frank Wall Street Reform and Consumer Protection Act, 12 U.S.C. § 1502 (2010). For information regarding the interpretation and application of the provisions, *see Fact Sheet: Disclosing the Use of Conflict Minerals*, U.S. SEC. & EXCH. COMM'N, https://www.sec.gov/opa/Article/2012-2012-163htm---related-materials.html (last updated Mar. 14, 2017); *Specialized Corporate Disclosure*, U.S. SEC. & EXCH. COMM'N, https://www.sec.gov/spotlight/dodd-frank/speccorpdisclosure.shtml (last updated May 30, 2013).

[66] 15 U.S.C. § 78m(p)(1)(A)(i) and (ii).

[67] Cal. Civ. Code § 1714.43 (West).

[68] INT'L CORP. ACCOUNTABILITY ROUNDTABLE, CORPORATE HUMAN RIGHTS RISK ASSESSMENT, PREVENTION, AND MITIGATION ACT OF 2019, (Jun. 10, 2019), https://static1.squarespace.com/static/583f3fca725e25fcd45aa446/t/5d2738f58d73de0001c531a7/1562851574384/Corporate+Human+Rights+Risk+Assessment+Bill+One+Pager.pdf. This took the form of an amendment to the U.S. Securities Exchange of 1934.

and highlight outstanding issues relating to its applicability and businesses' compliance with the law.

A range of other countries have adopted or are considering legislative measures requiring HRDD that covers all human rights or HRDD that addresses a specific human rights issue, such as human trafficking, conflict minerals, or child labor. Chapter 5, "Human Rights Due Diligence Requirements Outside the United States," by Esmira Hackenberg, Olivia Dean, and Shelley Marshall, considers legal requirements for HRDD and disclosure-based mechanisms for the United Kingdom, Australia, Canada, and a range of countries in continental Europe, as well as guidelines in China. The proposed directive by the EU Commission on HRDD and environmental due diligence and the UN Draft Treaty on Business and Human Rights are also discussed. Additionally, the chapter explains how the various laws and mechanisms are applied in practice by using case examples and citing good practices.

Governmental procurement practices are also evolving and increasingly requiring suppliers to respect human rights, in line with Sustainable Development Goal target 12.7, which calls upon States to "[p]romote public procurement practices that are sustainable, in accordance with national policies and priorities."[69] Norway's public procurement law requires public organizations to promote human rights when procuring products with a high risk of human rights violations in the supply chain.[70] In the United States, federal contractors are required to conduct HRDD on specific topics. Executive Order 13627, *Strengthening Protections against Trafficking in Persons in Federal Contracts*, issued in September 2012, prohibits all federal contractors, their subcontractors, and their employees from engaging in certain human trafficking–related practices.[71] Companies that contract or subcontract with the federal government in contracts over US$500,000, under this Executive Order, are required to implement compliance plans and certify that no evidence of trafficking was found or that steps were taken to address the abuses.[72] To address abuses by private security contractors, US federal agencies, such as the Department of Defense and the Department of State, require private security contractors to demonstrate compliance with standards consistent with the International Code of Conduct for Private Security Providers, which explicitly requires HRDD.[73]

Even when legislative and regulatory requirements do not expressly state that "human rights due diligence" is required on a company's value chain, HRDD is essential to ensuring that the company complies with laws and regulations whose aim is to safeguard human rights. For example, Section 307 of the Tariff Act of 1930 bans importation of goods produced with

---

[69] *SDG Indicators*, UN Sustainable Dev. Goals, https://unstats.un.org/sdgs/metadata/?Text=&Goal=12&Target=12.7 (last visited Feb. 2, 2022).

[70] *Public Procurement and Human Rights*, Norwegian Div. for Pub. Procurement, https://anskaffelser.no/en/public-procurement/socially-responsible-public-procurement (last updated Oct. 21, 2021).

[71] Exec. Order No. 13627, 77 Fed. Reg. 60,029 (Oct. 2, 2012).

[72] *Id.* at Section 2(2).

[73] Schweizerische Eidgenossenschaft, International Code of Conduct for Private Security Providers 7 (2010), https://icoca.ch/wp-content/uploads/2020/07/icoc_english3.pdf.

forced labor and thus stops goods at US ports of entry before they enter the United States.[74] The US Customs and Border Patrol has recently increased the number of orders preventing the entry of goods into the US market where there is evidence that the items were produced with forced labor, including child labor.[75] To have the order lifted, the importer must demonstrate that "every reasonable effort" has been made to determine the source and type of labor used to produce the product and its components.[76] Essentially, the importer must show through HRDD that the goods were not produced with forced labor.

In addition, at the time of writing, President Biden had just signed the Uyghur Forced Labor Prevention Act, passed by both chambers of Congress. Under the Act, which is expected to take effect in mid-2022, US Customs and Border Control would presume that any goods produced in Xinjiang, China involved forced labor and, therefore, would not be admitted into the United States unless the importer could demonstrate "by clear and convincing evidence" that the goods were not made with forced labor.[77] As a result, adequate HRDD will be a key way to demonstrate that goods were not made with forced labor in Xinjiang.

Thus, increasing legislation, regulations, and other measures, both those that cover all human rights and those addressing specific issues, such as conflict minerals and modern slavery, are imposing HRDD requirements on businesses. Although the United States has not adopted broad-based HRDD legislation and currently has few measures that directly impose due diligence requirements on companies, a company's awareness of potential risks and actual violations of human rights within its own operations and its value chain can assist it in ensuring that it: is in compliance with laws that protect human rights; qualifies for federal contracts; avoids having components or products seized at the border; and does not receive negative media attention for its own violations of human rights or those in its value chain.

The difference in approach toward HRDD between many European countries and the United States arguably arises from a significant difference in laws. Namely, there are no comprehensive human rights instruments that cover civil and political or economic and social rights in the United States in a manner comparable to the European Convention on Human Rights and the European Social Charter for Europe.[78] In the United States, human rights protections are generally developed through litigation and interpretation of the US Constitution and the Bill

[74] 19 U.S.C. § 1307 (2011).

[75] U.S. Customs & Border Protection, *CBP Combats Forced Labor* (Jan. 2021), https://www.cbp.gov/sites/default/files/assets/documents/2021-Jan/CBP%20Combats%20Forced%20Labor%20Part%201%20for%20.gov_.pdf. In FYI 2021, CBP "detained 1,469 shipments that contained approximately $486 million of goods suspected to be made by forced labor" and issued 7 Withhold Release Orders, which targeted "cotton products and tomato products from China's Xinjiang Uyghur Autonomous Region; silica-based products made by a company that operates in Xinjiang; palm oil from a Malaysian company; and tuna and other seafood harvested by a Chinese fishing fleet, a Taiwan-flagged fishing vessel, and a Fijian-flagged fishing vessel." *See CBP Releases Operational Fiscal Year 2021 Statistics*, U.S. Customs & Border Protection (Jan. 3, 2022), https://www.cbp.gov/newsroom/national-media-release/cbp-releases-operational-fiscal-year-2021-statistics. *See* Cong. Research Serv., Section 307 and Imports Produced by Forced Labor, https://crsreports.congress.gov/product/pdf/IF/IF11360#:~:text=Section%20307%20of%20the%20Tariff,(CBP)%20enforces%20the%20prohibition (updated Dec. 27, 2021).

[76] Cong. Research Serv., *supra* note 75, at 2.

[77] Uyghur Forced Labor Prevention Act, Pub. L. No. 117-78, § 3, 135 Stat. 1525, 1529 (2021).

[78] European Social Charter (revised), Oct. 18, 1961, E.T.S. No. 163; Convention for the Protection of Human Rights and Fundamental Freedoms (European Convention on Human Rights, as amended), Nov. 4, 1950, E.T.S. No. 005.

of Rights, particularly US Supreme Court cases, rather than through a regulatory framework. Consequently, there is no overarching policy on human rights by the US government, and human rights issues are frequently addressed separately and independently by different US agencies, rather than through the more cohesive policy and regulatory approach used in Europe.

Despite this difference, even where businesses are not legally obliged to perform HRDD by law, an effective HRDD approach and practice can ensure that businesses are both aware of and in compliance with laws or other measures that aim to protect human rights. Additionally, laws, regulations, and other measures requiring general HRDD, or HRDD that addresses a particular human rights issue, will not only be binding on the business entities directly covered, but also will impact the foreign subsidiaries and operations of those businesses and the entities in their value chains. Business entities that must comply with the laws will need to ensure that the entities in their value chain are compliant, and the ripple effects of compliance will likely extend to other business entities, including those in the same industry, thereby creating a more generalized expectation of the need of all businesses to implement and account for their HRDD processes.

IV. Identification of Good Practices

Existing processes within companies can serve as a basis for incorporating HRDD. Yet, due to the unique aspects of HRDD, including that it is an ongoing process that should meaningfully and effectively involve stakeholders, "there is not one, single model for HRDD regimes" but many variants of workable approaches.[79] This section provides an overview of some key aspects related to businesses' HRDD practices that assist the business to ensure respect for human rights.

A. Business Practices

Within a company, HRDD is not a stand-alone aspect of doing business, but an integral part of how entities manage their business and address adverse impacts on individuals and communities. HRDD should be integrated throughout the business, including into its corporate governance. In chapter 6, "Human Rights Due Diligence and Corporate Governance," John F. Sherman demonstrates how alignment with HRDD and compliance with laws that reflect or incorporate it are key to good corporate governance. He also examines why corporate legal officers should, in the interests of good corporate governance, help to foster a corporate culture that respects human rights and suggests how they can do so. He then identifies key future issues relating to corporate governance and HRDD.

The incorporation of HRDD processes into businesses' policies and practices does not necessarily mean that businesses must create entirely new processes. Many businesses already have in place compliance approaches into which HRDD can be incorporated. In chapter 7, "Integrating Human Rights Due Diligence into Compliance Approaches," Anahita Thoms

[79] UN Office of the High Commissioner for Human Rights, UN Human Rights "Issues Paper" on Legislative Proposals for Mandatory Human Rights Due Diligence by Companies 1 (Jun. 2020), https://www.ohchr.org/Documents/Issues/Business/MandatoryHR_Due_Diligence_Issues_Paper.pdf.

considers the ways in which HRDD and compliance approaches overlap and differ, and provides concrete suggestions on methods for using HRDD and anti-corruption approaches together.

Company-based grievance mechanisms, which are referred to as operational-level grievance mechanisms in the UNGPs, are an important tool for providing support to HRDD. In chapter 8, "Making the Connection: Operational-Level Grievance Mechanisms and Human Rights Due Diligence," Lisa J. Laplante explores the connection between operational-level grievance mechanisms and HRDD by examining company approaches, and she shares recent developments in State regulation, policy, and voluntary standards that provide insights into ways that this connection can be further developed.

B. Businesses and Impacted Persons and Communities

As emphasized in Section II.B., one of the key differences between corporate due diligence processes and HRDD is that HRDD requires engagement with persons whom the business may potentially or actually adversely impact rather than evaluating the risks to the company. Chapter 9, "Stakeholder Engagement," by Shauna Curphey and Jared Cole, notes that meaningful engagement is the basis for understanding the perspective of persons potentially or actually affected by the business and is essential to the design of accessible and effective grievance mechanisms. The chapter outlines the basic principles that underpin meaningful stakeholder engagement and how the principles work in practice, demonstrates the role of engagement in each step of HRDD, and outlines emerging challenges and opportunities.

In their approach to stakeholder engagement, businesses will also need to be sensitive and consider the human rights of specific groups of stakeholders, such as those of women, Indigenous peoples, children, people belonging to ethnic or religious minorities, and people with disabilities, and how to engage with these persons. Since, as noted in the UNGPs, "business enterprises can have an impact on virtually the entire spectrum of internationally recognized human rights, their respect applies to all such rights."[80] Businesses should understand that "human rights" refers, at a minimum, to international human rights law standards in the International Bill of Human Rights, which includes the Universal Declaration of Human Rights,[81] the International Covenant on Civil and Political Rights,[82] and the International Covenant on Economic, Social and Cultural Rights,[83] as supplemented by the principles on fundamental rights in the International Labour Organization's Declaration on Fundamental Principles and Rights at Work.[84] However, businesses will also need to consider additional standards from other international human rights instruments that protect the rights of specific groups of stakeholders.

---

[80] *Guiding Principles*, *supra* note 2, at 13–14.

[81] Universal Declaration of Human Rights, G.A. Res. 217 (III) A, UN Doc. A/RES/217(III) (Dec. 10, 1948).

[82] International Covenant on Civil and Political Rights, Dec. 16, 1966, 999 U.N.T.S. 171.

[83] International Covenant on Economic, Social and Cultural Rights, Dec. 16, 1966, 993 U.N.T.S. 3.

[84] *Guiding Principles*, *supra* note 2, at 13.

In chapter 10, "Gender-Responsive Human Rights Due Diligence," Constance Z. Wagner and Nancy Kaymar Stafford explore the need for greater attention to be paid to women's human rights in the HRDD process. They provide context to the issue by providing an overview of women's human rights under international law, and then review voluntary standards on conducting gender-responsive HRDD that have been developed by intergovernmental organizations and NGOs. Their chapter also identifies emerging good practices. Chapter 11, "Human Rights Due Diligence Practices for Adequate and Effective Consultation with Indigenous Peoples," by Thomas Andrew O'Keefe, considers key aspects to the engagement and legal rights of Indigenous peoples in HRDD. The chapter examines the legal obligation of prior consultation and the principle of free, prior, and informed consent. Using relevant guidelines and standards related to businesses' adverse impacts on the rights of Indigenous peoples, the chapter provides guidance on how these can be used to fashion a business enterprise's international HRDD policies and practices to ensure that the business supports, respects, and promotes the human rights of Indigenous peoples.

V. Specific Challenges

As HRDD continues to transition from soft-law principles in the UNGPs to hard law in national legislation, regulations, and other measures, lawyers will need to follow developments in a number of key areas that will have significant effects on how their business clients operate. This Section addresses four of those key areas: suppliers in value chains (Subsection A), the financial sector (Subsection B), the intersection of environmental law and climate change issues with HRDD (Subsection C), and high-risk security situations, such as situations of armed conflict (Subsection D).

A. Suppliers in the Business's Complex Value Chains

The UNGPs provide that the business enterprise's responsibility to respect human rights includes not only adverse human rights impacts resulting from its own activities but also those adverse impacts resulting from their business relationships with other parties. These business relationships, linked to its operations, products, and services, include its value chain.[85] The value chain "encompasses the activities that convert input into output by adding value."[86] Thus, the "value chain" includes entities that supply products or services that contribute to the business's own products and services and entities that receive products or services from the business.[87] Businesses' supply chains can be extremely complex with hundreds or even thousands of suppliers in multiple tiers.[88]

[85] *Id.* at 15.

[86] UN Office of the High Commissioner for Human Rights, The Corporate Responsibility to Respect Human Rights: Interpretive Guide, 8, UN Doc. HR/PUB/02 (2012), https://www.ohchr.org/Documents/Issues/Business/RtRInterpretativeGuide.pdf.

[87] *Id.*

[88] Working Group Rep. on the Issue of Human Rights and Transnational Corporations and Other Business Enterprises, *supra* note 7, at para. 48.

laws that require businesses to address their human rights impacts and environmental risks, as Germany has recently done.[90] Though environmental law and human rights law were traditionally two distinct areas, this is no longer the case and their intersection is increasingly acknowledged and relevant to HRDD.

Chapter 14, "Environmental Law and Climate Change," by Carlos de Miguel Perales and Austin Pierce, provides an overview of the evolution of environmental law and its interaction with human rights and identifies environmental standards of particular importance for human rights, including those related to project assessments, air and climate, water, waste, hazardous substances and remediation, and natural and cultural resources. The chapter also considers good practices for identifying risks in environmental due diligence as well as outstanding and evolving issues in the environment–human rights nexus.

D. High-Risk Security Situations

As noted in a report of the UNWG in 2020, since 2011 when the UNGPs were endorsed by the UN Human Rights Council, "the number of civil wars has nearly tripled . . . peaking in 2016 with 53 countries experiencing conflict."[91] Moreover, as the report concedes, "[m]any of these situations are 'protracted crises with multiple adversaries, stalled peace processes, organized crime and attacks from violent extremists or terrorists.'"[92] Since HRDD under the UNGPs is based on the "concept of proportionality, the higher the risk, the more complex the processes."[93] Thus, when businesses operate in conflict-affected or high-risk areas, HRDD should be of a heightened nature, referred to as enhanced HRDD.

Chapter 15, "Due Diligence in Conflict-Affected and High-Risk Areas," by Morvarid Bagheri, provides information about how conflict sensitivity methodology can be integrated into the HRDD process to obtain enhanced HRDD on operations linked to conflict-affected and high-risk areas (CAHRA). The chapter explains conflict sensitivity methodology and identifies standards on complicity in international crimes and key industry-specific regulatory and voluntary frameworks relative to HRDD in CAHRA. The chapter also provides a seven-step framework linked to the four stages of HRDD that incorporates conflict sensitivity methodology results in enhanced HRDD and identifies outstanding issues.

VI. Conclusion

The chapters in this book highlight the importance of HRDD as a method for businesses to understand and address their adverse human rights impacts on individuals and communities.

---

[90] *See* Gesetz über die unternehmerischen Sorgfaltspflichten in Lieferketten [LkSG][Supply Chain Due Diligence Act] July 16, 2021, BGBl 1 at 2959 (Ger).

[91] Rep. of the Working Group on the Issue of Human Rights and Transnational Corporations and Other Business Enterprises, at 3, UN Doc. A/75/212 (Jul. 21, 2020), https://undocs.org/en/A/75/212.

[92] *Id.* (citing 2019 report of the Secretary-General on the Work of the Organization (A/74/1)).

[93] Oral Statement by Ms. Anita Ramasastry (Chairperson, Working Group on the Issue of Human Rights and Transnational Corporations and Other Business Enterprises), Business, Human Rights and Conflict-Affected Regions: Towards Heightened Action, 2 (Oct. 27, 2020), https://www.ohchr.org/Documents/Issues/Business/20201027GA75OralStatement.pdf.

HRDD facilitates businesses' respect for not only the rights of their employees, but also their customers, employees of their suppliers, and local communities, among other persons. HRDD is a process that allows the business to identify the potential and actual adverse human rights impacts that it causes, those to which it contributes, and the human rights impacts that are directly linked to its operations, products, or services by its business relationships, even where the business does not contribute to such impacts. This identification then allows the business to address the impacts in order to ensure that the human rights of persons are respected and restored.

Support for HRDD continues to grow and is accelerating with legislative and regulatory measures rendering HRDD mandatory for businesses and thereby creating a cascading effect of concern by entities throughout the value chain about their effects on human rights. These measures should assist in providing greater clarity about the expectations on businesses and a more level playing field. At the same time, the emphasis on sustainability and ESG is reinforcing the requirement of HRDD that extends well beyond human trafficking, conflict minerals, and forced labor, to encompass all human rights. Fundamentally, HRDD is a key process that facilitates businesses' contribution to sustainable development and the social factor of ESG.

Lawyers will be increasingly called upon by their business clients to assist them with navigating both compliance with legal requirements and the soft-law standards that define governments', investors', and society's expectation that businesses respect human rights and thereby contribute to sustainability. New opportunities are therefore arising for lawyers to provide services and advice that assists, facilitates, and furthers businesses' respect for human rights.

Thus, this book examines the essentials of HRDD, practical approaches to its implementation, and specific challenges that arise, with the intention of contributing to lawyers' understanding and role in assisting businesses to respect human rights, and more generally, to promoting advancement in harmonization, consistency, understanding, and implementation of HRDD. However, challenges remain. There is a need for greater uniformity, cohesiveness, and clarity in the scope and content of HRDD. In addition, the roles of governments, intergovernmental bodies, investors, business associations, and others in evaluating businesses' HRDD processes and outcomes necessitate further development. These issues will certainly receive greater consideration in the coming years. In the meantime, lawyers would be well advised to take steps to integrate human rights considerations into their advice to businesses and to stay abreast of continuing developments related to HRDD.

VII. Resources

Organisation for Economic Co-operation and Development (OECD), *Due Diligence Guidance for Responsible Business Conduct* (2018).

Organisation for Economic Co-operation and Development (OECD), *Guidelines for Multinational Enterprises* (2011).

United Nations Office of the High Commissioner for Human Rights, *The Corporate Responsibility to Respect Human Rights, An Interpretive Guide*, UN Doc. HR/PUB/12/02 (2012).

United Nations Office of the High Commissioner for Human Rights, *Frequently Asked Questions About the Guiding Principles on Business and Human Rights*, UN Doc. HR/PUB/14/3 (2014).

United Nations Office of the High Commissioner for Human Rights, *Guiding Principles on Business and Human Rights: Implementing the United Nations "Protect, Respect and Remedy" Framework*, UN Doc. HR/PUB/11/04 (2011).

United Nations Working Group on Business and Human Rights, *Guiding Principles on Business and Human Rights at 10: Taking stock of the First Decade*, UN Doc. A/HRC/47/39 (2021).

United Nations Working Group on Business and Human Rights, *Improving Accountability and Access to Remedy for Victims of Business-related Human Rights Abuse: The Relevance of Human Rights Due Diligence to Determinations of Corporate Liability*, UN Doc. A/HRC/38/20/Add.2 (2018).

2

The Due Diligence Process

Hind Merabet

I. Introduction

In early 2021, Blackrock called on companies to "implement processes to identify, manage, and prevent adverse human rights impacts that are material to their business, and provide robust disclosures on these practices."[1] This followed a budding recognition that the purpose of the company extends beyond making a profit. Specifically, in his 2019 annual letter to chief executive officers, Larry Fink, chairman and chief executive officer of Blackrock, the world's largest asset manager, highlighted the "inextricable link" between purpose and profit and the increased relevance of environmental, social, and governance issues.[2] That same year, the Business Roundtable, an association of chief executive officers of leading US companies representing every economic sector, redefined the "Purpose of a Corporation" with an emphasis on: diversity and inclusion; dignity and respect; fair and ethical dealings with suppliers; community support; and commitment to transparency and effective engagement with shareholders.[3]

[1] Blackrock, *Our approach to engagement with companies on their human rights impact* (2021), https://www.blackrock.com/corporate/literature/publication/blk-commentary-engagement-on-human-rights.pdf.

[2] Larry Fink's 2019 Letter to CEOs, https://www.blackrock.com/americas-offshore/en/2019-larry-fink-ceo-letter (last visited Nov. 30, 2021).

[3] *See* Business Roundtable Statement, https://opportunity.businessroundtable.org/ourcommitment/ (last visited Nov. 30, 2021). The Business Roundtable has periodically issued Principles of Corporate Governance since 1978, with every version, starting in 1997, reaffirming the Milton Friedman doctrine that proclaims that companies exist primarily to maximize shareholder value.

The *United Nations Guiding Principles on Business and Human Rights* (UNGPs)[4] have been the catalyst for the formulation, recognition, and widespread acceptance of a "corporate responsibility to respect human rights" as a global standard. Under the UNGPs, business enterprises should: i) institute a *policy commitment* to meet their responsibility to respect human rights; ii) undertake ongoing *human rights due diligence* to identify, to prevent, to mitigate, and to account for their negative human rights impacts; and iii) have processes in place to enable *remediation* for any adverse human rights impact they caused or to which they contributed, all appropriate to their size and circumstances.[5]

This chapter provides a general overview of the human rights due diligence process to assist legal practitioners in navigating the practical challenges associated with the conduct of this process. The chapter initially provides, in Section II, some brief background on the key documents to consider when conducting human rights due diligence. Section III then examines the core concepts and practical aspects associated with the various phases of the human rights due diligence process, before Section IV concludes the chapter.

II. Background

Lawyers can find essential human rights due diligence guidance, including definitions of core concepts illustrated by examples, in the two main documents introduced below.

A. UN Guiding Principles

The idea of developing standards to regulate the activities and responsibilities of transnational corporations and other business enterprises with regard to human rights has been debated over more than three decades.[6] In 2005, the United Nations (UN) Commission on Human Rights (the precursor to the UN Human Rights Council) adopted a resolution requesting then-acting UN Secretary-General Kofi Annan to nominate a special representative to identify and clarify standards of corporate responsibility and accountability for transnational

[4] John Ruggie, *Report of the Special Representative of the Secretary-General on the Issue of Human Rights and Transnational Corporations and Other Business Enterprises, Guiding Principles on Business and Human Rights: Implementing the United Nations "Protect, Respect and Remedy" Framework*, Hum. Rts. Council, UN Doc. A/HRC/17/31 (2011). The Guiding Principles on Business and Human Rights are annexed to the Special Representative Report and available now as a stand-alone publication. *See* UN Office of the High Commissioner for Human Rights, *Guiding Principles on Business and Human Rights, Implementing the United Nations "Protect, Respect and Remedy" Framework*, UN Doc. HR/PUB/11/04 (2011) [hereinafter Guiding Principles] https://www.ohchr.org/documents/publications/guidingprinciplesbusinesshr_en.pdf. The term "Principle" is used herein when referencing one of the Guiding Principles individually.

[5] *Guiding Principles*, *supra* note 4, at 15 (Principle 15).

[6] *See generally* Tripartite Declaration of Principles Concerning Multinational Enterprises and Social Policy (1977); UN Sub-Commission on the Promotion and Protection of Human Rights, *Economic, Social and Cultural Rights: Norms on the Responsibilities of Transnational Corporations and Other Business Enterprises with Regard to Human Rights*, UN Doc. E/CN.4/Sub.2/2003/12/Rev.2 (2003); UN Sub-Commission on the Promotion and Protection of Human Rights, *Commentary on the Norms on the Responsibilities of Transnational Corporations and Other Business Enterprises with Regard to Human Rights*, UN Doc. E/CN.4/Sub.2/2003/38/Rev.2 (2003); UN Office of the High Commissioner for Human Rights, *Report of the United Nations High Commissioner for Human Rights on the responsibilities of transnational corporations and related business enterprises with regard to human rights*, UN Doc. E/CN.4/2005/91 (2005).

corporations and other business enterprises with regard to human rights, including the development of materials and methodologies for undertaking human rights impact assessments of business enterprises.[7] Harvard University Professor John Ruggie was so appointed.

For the first three years of his mandate, Ruggie spearheaded an unprecedented, comprehensive research programme that included multistakeholder consultations with government, business, civil society, and community representatives in all regions of the world, which culminated in the development of the "Protect, Respect and Remedy" policy framework.[8] Subsequently, the UN Human Rights Council unanimously welcomed the framework and renewed his mandate for another three years to operationalize the framework and, among various other requests, "elaborate further on the scope and content of the corporate responsibility to respect all human rights and to provide concrete guidance to business and other stakeholders."[9] In June 2011, the UN Human Rights Council unanimously endorsed the UNGPs,[10] which were the first global standard for preventing and addressing the risk of adverse human rights impacts associated with business activity. The UNGPs constitute a "model of widely distributed efforts and cumulative change"[11] for States and businesses, and an authoritative voluntary framework that has since informed numerous domestic and global standards on business and human rights.[12]

The UNGPs are comprised of 31 principles articulated under three main pillars: I, the States' duty to protect individuals from human rights abuses committed by companies; II, the corporate responsibility to respect human rights; and III, access to remedy for individuals and communities whose rights have been adversely impacted by business activities. Pillar II of the UNGPs establishes the corporate responsibility to respect human rights as the global minimum standard of expected conduct for all companies.[13] Specifically, businesses should respect human rights, which means *avoid infringing* on the human rights of others, and *address adverse human rights impacts* with which they are involved.[14] Businesses must take steps to "know and show" that they respect human rights in all their operations, regardless of the particular factors of size, sector, operational context, ownership, and structure.[15] The responsibility applies fully and equally to all businesses, but the scale and complexity of the means used by the business may vary according to these factors and with the severity

---

[7] Hum. Rts. Comm., Res. 2005/69, 61th Sess., UN Doc. E/CN.4/RES/2005/69 (2005).

[8] John Ruggie, *Promotion and Protection of all Human Rights, Civil, Political, Economic, Social and Cultural Rights, including the Right to Development: Protect, Respect and Remedy: a Framework for Business and Human Rights: Report of the Special Representative of the Secretary-General on the issue of human rights and transnational corporations and other business enterprises*, UN Doc. A/HRC/8/5 (2008) [hereinafter UN Framework].

[9] Hum. Rts. Council., Res. 8/7, 8th Sess., UN Doc. A/HRC/RES/8/7 (2008).

[10] Hum. Rts. Council., Res. 17/4, 17th Sess., UN Doc. A/HRC/RES/17/4 (2011).

[11] John Gerard Ruggie, Just Business, Multinational Corporations And Human Rights x/iii (W.W. Norton & Company 2013).

[12] UN Office of the High Commissioner for Human Rights, *Frequently Asked Questions About the Principles on Business and Human Rights*, UN Doc. HR/PUB/14/3 (2014), pp. 15–16 [hereinafter FAQ].

[13] *Id.* at 9.

[14] *Guiding Principles*, *supra* note 4, at 14 (Principle 11).

[15] *Id.* at 15 (Principle 14).

The 2018 OECD *Due Diligence Guidance for Responsible Business Conduct* (OECD Due Diligence Guidance)[27] supplements the OECD Guidelines with explanations, examples, and recommendations for practices on conducting due diligence. In addition, the OECD has developed due diligence guidance for specific sectors, including minerals, agricultural, garment and footwear, extractives, and finance.[28]

III. Due Diligence Phases

This next section focuses on the principles and practical steps described in both the UNGPs and the OECD Due Diligence Guidance for conducting the four phases of human rights due diligence.

A. Identification and Assessment of Human Rights Risks and Impacts

The first stage involves identifying and then assessing potential human rights risks and actual impacts on human rights in which the business is involved directly or through its business relationships.[29] This can be done using existing risk management systems and processes, but only to the extent that these include the identification and management of human rights risks to rights-holders.[30] This has to do with the fact that human rights due diligence is first and foremost about people.[31] The risks to be assessed are those that business operations represent to the human rights of individuals and groups, the so-called *human rights risks* that have the potential to cause human rights impacts.[32]

Additional key characteristics of human rights due diligence are contrasted, in figure 2.1, with those of the due diligence traditionally conducted in a corporate setting in connection with mergers and acquisitions and anti-bribery and anti-corruption screening. One key distinction is that human rights due diligence is a continuous and dynamic process, as human

---

[27] OECD, *OECD Due Diligence Guidance for Responsible Business Conduct* (2018), https://www.oecd.org/investment/due-diligence-guidance-for-responsible-business-conduct.htm [hereinafter OECD Due Diligence Guidance], at 10.

[28] OECD, Practical Actions for Companies to Identify and Address the Worst Forms of Child Labour in Mineral Supply Chains, https://mneguidelines.oecd.org/Practical-actions-for-worst-forms-of-child-labour-mining-sector.pdf (2017); OECD, *OECD Due Diligence Guidance for Responsible Supply Chains of Minerals from Conflict-Affected Areas and High-Risk Areas*, https://www.oecd.org/daf/inv/mne/OECD-Due-Diligence-Guidance-Minerals-Edition3.pdf (2016); OECD, *OECD-FAO Guidance for Responsible Agricultural Supply Chains*, https://www.oecd-ilibrary.org/agriculture-and-food/oecd-fao-guidance-for-responsible-agricultural-supply-chains_9789264251052-en. OECD, *OECD Due Diligence Guidance for Responsible Supply Chains in the Garment and Footwear Sector*, https://www.oecd-ilibrary.org/governance/oecd-due-diligence-guidance-for-responsible-supply-chains-in-the-garment-and-footwear-sector_9789264290587-en. (2018); *OECD Due Diligence Guidance for Meaningful Stakeholder Engagement in the Extractive Sector*, https://www.oecd.org/development/oecd-due-diligence-guidance-for-meaningful-stakeholder-engagement-in-the-extractive-sector-9789264252462-en.htm (2017); OECD, Responsible Business Conduct for Institutional Investors, https://mneguidelines.oecd.org/RBC-for-Institutional-Investors.pdf (2017).

[29] *Guiding Principles*, *supra* note 4, at 19 (Principle 18).

[30] *Id.* at 18 (Principle 17 Commentary).

[31] FAQ, *supra* note 12, at 3.

[32] Interpretive Guide, *supra* note 18, pp. 6–7.

	Corporate Due Diligence	Human Rights Due Diligence
Timing	Prior to new transaction	As a baseline assessment Prior to new activity or relationship, or in relation to external changes
Recurrence	Ad hoc	Ongoing, at regular intervals, throughout the life of an activity or relationship
Risk Perspective	Business	Individuals or groups potentially and actually affected
Risk factors	Legal, compliance, financial, environmental, operational, regulatory, etc.	Human rights
Scope	Dependent on the nature of, and level of risk, associated with the transaction	Risk-based, commensurate to likelihood and severity of adverse impact, proportionate to resources and industry sector
	Focused on target entities, products and operations in relation to the transaction	Across operations and products and throughout value chain and business networks

Figure 2.1 Practical Considerations: Corporate vs. Human Rights Due Diligence

rights risks may change over time as business operations and operating context evolve.[33] An initial human rights impact assessment can serve as a baseline assessment, but additional assessments should also be initiated: (a) prior to a new activity or relationship, major decisions, or operational changes to the business (such as market entry, product launch, policy change, or mergers and acquisitions) or in response to or in anticipation of changes in the operating environment (e.g., rising social tensions); (b) at regular intervals; and (c) periodically throughout the life of an activity or relationship.[34] The extent of the efforts to be devoted is left to be determined on a case-by-case basis by the enterprise using an objective standard, that is, the standard that would be expected from a reasonable and prudent organization under similar circumstances, including sector, operating context, and size, to meet its responsibility to respect human rights.[35] Human rights due diligence should not, however, be conducted as a perfunctory "tick-the-box" exercise.

Businesses that wish to conduct a stand-alone human rights impact assessment (HRIA) (also referred to as a human rights assessment or HRA) often retain outside consultants or lawyers with human rights expertise to coordinate this effort.[36] It is still advisable, under those circumstances, to designate internal contact points who can work in tandem with the outside experts to facilitate the conduct of the process internally, including by: helping

[33] *Guiding Principles*, *supra* note 4, at 18 (Principle 17(c)).

[34] *Id.* at 20 (Principle 18 Commentary).

[35] OECD Due Diligence Guidance, *supra* note 27, at 47.

[36] Resources developed by some of these organizations are presented in Section V of this chapter.

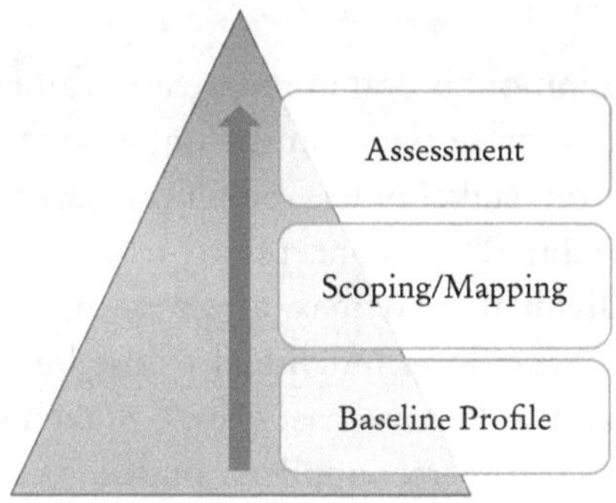

Figure 2.2 Practical Considerations: Identification and Assessment

identify internal and external stakeholders; sourcing company information; and filling any knowledge gaps in terms of the company's operations, strategies, organizational structure, and overall profile. An HRIA can take anywhere between four and eight months to complete, but sometimes longer, depending on the nature of the risks involved and the size of the company. Though the UNGPs do not prescribe a specific methodology for conducting the assessment, there are overarching principles and practical steps that are common to this process, which are summarized in figure 2.2 and more extensively discussed below.

1. Baseline Profile

Human rights due diligence is concerned with identifying and addressing adverse human rights impacts that can be linked to the business's activities or operations, products, or services through its business relationships.[37] Accordingly, there needs to be a baseline understanding of the organization's business relationships, business model, operations at the country and site level, products and/or services, and stakeholders. *Business relationships* include direct or indirect relationships with business partners, entities within the value chain including beyond tier one, and any other entity directly linked to the business operations, products, or services.[38] The *value chain* includes not only regular supply chain activities that convert input into output, but also those activities that add customer value to the products or services of the enterprise.[39]

This information can usually be obtained through desk research, publicly available corporate statements, and external reports and filings (if applicable). Additionally, it is best practice to review business codes of conduct and ethics, policies and processes with a human rights nexus (including those issued in the area of human resources and labor practices, privacy, environment, and health and safety), and other relevant internal company documentation that can provide insights for identifying human rights the business has the potential to impact, or is currently impacting, as well as the stakeholders it may potentially or is actually impacting.

[37] *Guiding Principles, supra* note 4, at 17 (Principle 17).

[38] FAQ, *supra* note 12, at 41.

[39] *Id.* at 45.

2. *Scoping/Mapping*

Scoping or mapping is, by definition, broad in nature and can be done through in-person or telephone interviews, interview or self-assessment questionnaires, inspections, and audits. The goal here is to identify key stakeholders, significant areas of human rights risks and impacts, and salient human rights. These concepts are clarified below.

A *stakeholder* is an individual who may affect or be affected by an organization's activities.[40] An *affected stakeholder* is an individual whose human rights have been affected by an enterprise's operations, products, or services.[41] Stakeholders may be internal (e.g., employees) or external (e.g., customers, suppliers, outside communities, nongovernmental organizations and civil society, human rights defenders, shareholders, and investors).[42] Moreover, the UNGPs should be implemented in a nondiscriminatory manner and consistent with a human rights–based approach[43] with particular attention paid to the rights and needs of, as well as the challenges faced by, *marginalized groups*, those that may be at heightened risk of being exposed to discrimination or other adverse human rights impacts,[44] for example: women; children; Indigenous peoples; lesbian, gay, bisexual, transsexual, transgender, queer, intersex, asexual (LGBTQIA+); persons with disabilities; national, ethnic, religious, and linguistic minorities; undocumented and domestic workers; and persons subjected to modern slavery, such as sex trafficking and domestic servitude.

Similarly, human rights standards and issues also need to be catalogued, with the entire spectrum of *internationally recognized human rights* as a reference point.[45] Those include, at a minimum, such rights guaranteed under the aegis of the International Bill of Human Rights[46] and the fundamental principles expressed in the International Labour Organization (ILO) Declaration on Fundamental Principles and Rights at Work, which include: freedom from discrimination in respect of employment and occupation; freedom from forced labor and child labor; and freedom of association and the right to collective bargaining, to name

---

[40] Interpretive Guide, *supra* note 18, at 8.

[41] *Id.*

[42] Stakeholder engagement is at the heart of every phase of human rights due diligence.

[43] The human rights–based approach is a conceptual framework directed at increasing the ability and accountability of "duty-bearers" to fulfil and protect those rights and empowering the "rights-holders" who have legitimate claims to their rights. All forms of discrimination in the realization of rights must be prohibited, prevented, and eliminated. *See* United Nations Sustainable Development Group, *Human Rights Based Approach to Development Cooperation Towards a Common Understanding Among UN Agencies*, https://unsdg.un.org/resources/human-rights-based-approach-development-cooperation-towards-common-understanding-among-un (2003).

[44] *Guiding Principles, supra* note 4, at 1.

[45] *Id.* at 13 (Principle 12 Commentary).

[46] *Id.* at 13 (Principle 12). The International Bill of Human Rights refers to the Universal Declaration of Human Rights, the International Covenant on Civil and Political Rights and International Covenant on Economic, Social and Cultural Rights. *See* United Nations Office of the High Commissioner for Human Rights, the International Bill of Human Rights, https://www.ohchr.org/sites/default/files/Documents/Publications/FactSheet2Rev.1en.pdf. Specific circumstances may dictate a need to consider additional standards tailored to groups of individuals that require particular attention (e.g., women, children, minorities, persons with disabilities, migrant workers, or groups in conflict areas). *Id.* at 14 (Commentary to Principle 12).

Human Rights	Human Rights Impact
Right to health	Employees working under conditions that create health hazards
Prohibition of slavery, child labor, and forced labor	Supplier using trafficked persons in the production of raw materials
Right to privacy	Unauthorized access to employee personal records
Right to free assembly and collective bargaining	Company shutting down efforts to unionize

Figure 2.3 Practical Considerations: Examples of Human Rights Impacts

Scale	Scope	Irremediable Character
Extent of infringement of access to basic life necessities or freedoms (e.g., education, livelihood)	• Number of individuals impacted • Percentage of identifiable groups of people impacted	• Extent to which the impact can be rectified (e.g., through compensation or restitution) • Whether the exercise of the right of the people affected can be restored

Figure 2.4 Practical Considerations – Examples of Scale, Scope and Irremediability

a few. Once stakeholders and salient human rights have been determined, human risks and impacts across the enterprise's operations and business relationships can be mapped out.

Human rights risks are the risks that business operations may lead to one or more adverse human rights impacts; in other words, the potential to cause human rights impacts.[47] The primary and initial focus should be on the most *salient human rights*, the rights that stand out as being most at risk of negative human rights impacts; those usually vary depending on the sector and operating context in which the business operates.[48] However, other human risks should not be ignored[49] and are to be addressed once the most significant impacts have been handled.[50] An *adverse human rights impac*t occurs when an action removes or reduces the ability of an individual to enjoy his, her, or their human rights. Adverse human rights impacts caused by business are sometimes alternatively referred to as *negative human rights impacts* or *human rights abuses* in the UNGPs. Figure 2.3 displays a few examples of human rights impacts.

The severity of a human rights impact is defined in terms of its *scale* (gravity), *scope*, and *irremediable character*,[51] as further detailed in figure 2.4.[52]

[47] Interpretive Guide, *supra* note 18, pp. 6–7.

[48] FAQ, *supra* note 12, at 44.

[49] Interpretive Guide, *supra* note 18, at 8.

[50] OECD Due Diligence Guidance, *supra* note 27, at 28.

[51] *Guiding Principles, supra* note 4, at 15 (Commentary to Principle 14).

[52] OECD Due Diligence Guidance, *supra* note 27, at 44.

3. *Assessment*

Next, a narrower in-depth assessment of risks for a determined activity or relationship is done in order to identify and assess specific actual and potential adverse impacts.[53] *Potential human rights impacts* are those for which the adverse impact may, but has yet to occur, as opposed to *actual human rights impacts* for which the adverse impact has already occurred or is occurring.[54] Traditional risk assessments often rely on risk heat maps or matrixes that feature the likelihood of the risk on one axis, and the severity of the risk on the other, with each potential intersection of the two yielding a risk level that can be ranked (low, medium, or high), color-coded (green, yellow, red), or scored. Human rights risks are also calculated on the basis of their severity and likelihood, but severity is the predominant driver for determining the risk profile.[55] Assessing all adverse human rights impacts may be reasonably impractical, depending on the particular operating context, suppliers, operations, products, or services involved; it is therefore recommended, in such cases, to prioritize areas where the risk of adverse human rights impacts is most significant.[56] The assessment process should also draw on internal and/or independent external human rights expertise[57]—such as human rights defenders and other experts from civil society—in the latter case, where direct consultation with potentially affected stakeholders to understand their concerns may not be possible.[58]

B. Integration and Action Plan

To prevent and mitigate adverse human rights impacts, it is incumbent upon companies to: (i) effectively *integrate* assessment findings across all relevant internal functions and processes; and (ii) to take appropriate *action*,[59] which actions comprise the second stage of human rights due diligence. The relevant UNGPs principles and concepts are more amply developed in Subsections 1 and 2, with figure 2.5 serving as a checklist of practical considerations for this phase.

1. *Integrating Findings*

Effective *integration* across relevant functions and processes calls for a bottom-up approach with assignment to the appropriate business level and function as well as budget allocations and oversight processes to enable effective responses to such impact to ensure that findings are properly understood and acted upon.[60,61] *Embedding*, in contrast, is a top-down mechanism through which the human rights policy statement, signed at the highest level of the

[53] *Id.* at 27, 61.

[54] FAQ, *supra* note 12, pp. 41–45.

[55] *Id.* at 43.

[56] *Guiding Principles, supra* note 4, at 18 (Commentary to Principle 17).

[57] *Id.* at 19 (Principle 18(b)).

[58] *Id.* at 20 (Principle 18 Commentary).

[59] *Id.* at 20 (Principle 19).

[60] *Id.* at 20–21 (Principle 19(a)).

[61] *Id.* at 21 (Principle 19 Commentary).

- What lines of responsibility and accountability exist for addressing our findings of potential human rights impact? What systematized approaches might help us integrate findings from our assessments across the relevant business units or functions, so that we can take effective action?
- Should we have one or more cross-functional groups to liaise on ongoing human rights challenges or cross-functional communication requirements before certain decisions or actions?
- Can we build scenarios or decision trees for action across the company so that we are prepared to respond to the most likely or severe potential impact? Do staff need training and guidance on these issues?
- How can we best integrate measures to address potential impact at the contract stage of new projects, partnerships or activities?
- If we find that human rights impact is linked to our operations, products or services, are we equipped to address the risk of its continuation or recurrence appropriately and swiftly? How will decisions be made? What credible sources can we turn to for advice?
- How do we assess our leverage in business relationships, especially those in areas of heightened risk to human rights? How can we maximize that leverage from the start of relationships? What opportunities for exercising or increasing our leverage can we see? Do we have any "crucial" business relationships? How should we respond if these relationships lead to adverse human rights impact being linked to our operations, products or services? Are we equipped in terms of internal and external advice for this situation?

Figure 2.5 Practical Considerations: Integration

Source: The Corporate Responsibility to Respect Human Rights: An Interpretive Guide, by United Nations Office of High Commissioner, © 2012 United Nations. Reprinted with the permission of the United Nations.

Embedding	**Integrating**
Macro process	Micro process
Ensuring all are aware of the enterprise's human rights policy commitment; understand its implications for how they conduct their work; are trained, empowered, and incentivized to act in ways that support the commitment; and regard it as intrinsic to core values of the workplace	Taking the findings about impacts, identifying who in the enterprise needs to be involved in addressing it, and securing effective action
Top Down	Bottom up

Figure 2.6 Terminology Cheat Sheet: Embedding vs. Integrating

company, is embedded, that is, reflected in internal operational policies and procedures.[62] These distinctions are further explained in figure 2.6.[63]

To implement such integration, certain businesses opt for the establishment of a stand-alone committee, working group, or task force, while others leverage the resources of a pre-existing committee (such as a corporate social responsibility or sustainability committee). Regardless of how human rights issues are handled within the company,[64] to the extent there is a formal governance structure, it should ideally have: (i) its own charter or terms of reference to delineate roles, responsibilities, and objectives; (ii) some executive oversight from,

[62] *Id.* at 16 (Principle 16).

[63] *See* Interpretive Guide, *supra* note 18, pp. 46–47.

[64] *See generally* United Nations Global Compact, *Organizing the Human Rights Function within a Company*, Good Practice Note (2014).

a business relationship,[72] sometimes referred to conceptually as involvement or attribution. Additionally, the extent of the business leverage in addressing the adverse impact, as more broadly discussed below, will also be a relevant factor.[73] *Leverage* is the power of a business to influence and to drive change in the wrongful practices of another party that is causing or contributing to an adverse human rights impact.[74] Leverage over one entity may reflect a variety of factors, including: whether there is a degree of direct control by the enterprise over the entity; the terms of the contract between the enterprise and the entity; the ability to incentivize the entity or other enterprises to improve human rights; the benefits and disadvantages of working with the enterprise for the entity's reputation; and the ability of the enterprise to engage governments in requiring improved human rights performance.[75]

If a company *causes or may cause* an adverse human rights impact, it should take the necessary steps to cease or to prevent the impact.[76] If it *contributes* to, *or may contribute* to an adverse human rights impact, it should take the necessary steps to cease or to prevent its contribution and use its leverage to mitigate any remaining impact to the greatest extent possible.[77] If the human rights impact is *caused by* an entity with which it has *a business relationship and is directly linked to its own operations, products, or services*, the appropriate action will be determined by a variety of factors, including leverage, how crucial the relationship is to the business, the severity of the abuse, and whether terminating the relationship would have adverse human rights consequences.[78]

A relationship can be *crucial* to the extent it provides a product or service that is essential to the enterprise's business, and for which no reasonable alternative source exists.[79] For crucial business relationships, the risk that the abuse continues or recurs should be mitigated, to the extent the business has leverage.[80] If this effort is not successful or if the business has no leverage, the business should seek to increase leverage and, if it fails, consider terminating the relationship, taking into account the severity of the impact, or demonstrate efforts made to mitigate the abuse, while recognizing possible consequences of any remaining abuse.[81] For *non-crucial* relationships, the business should, with leverage, try to mitigate the risk of the abuse continuing or recurring.[82] If that is not successful, it should take steps to end the relationship, taking into account credible assessments of potential resulting adverse human rights impact: the more severe the abuse, the quicker the change needs to happen before ending the relationship.[83] When it lacks leverage, the company should assess reasonable options

[72] *Guiding Principles*, *supra* note 4, at 21 (Principle 19(b)).

[73] *Id.* at 22 (Principle 19 Commentary).

[74] Interpretive Guide, *supra* note 18, at 7.

[75] *Id.* at 49.

[76] *Guiding Principles*, *supra* note 4, at 21 (Principle 19 Commentary).

[77] *Id.*

[78] *Id.* at 21–22 (Principle 19 Commentary).

[79] *Id.* at 22 (Principle 19 Commentary).

[80] Interpretive Guide, *supra* note 18, at 50.

[81] *Id.*

[82] *Id.*

[83] *Id.*

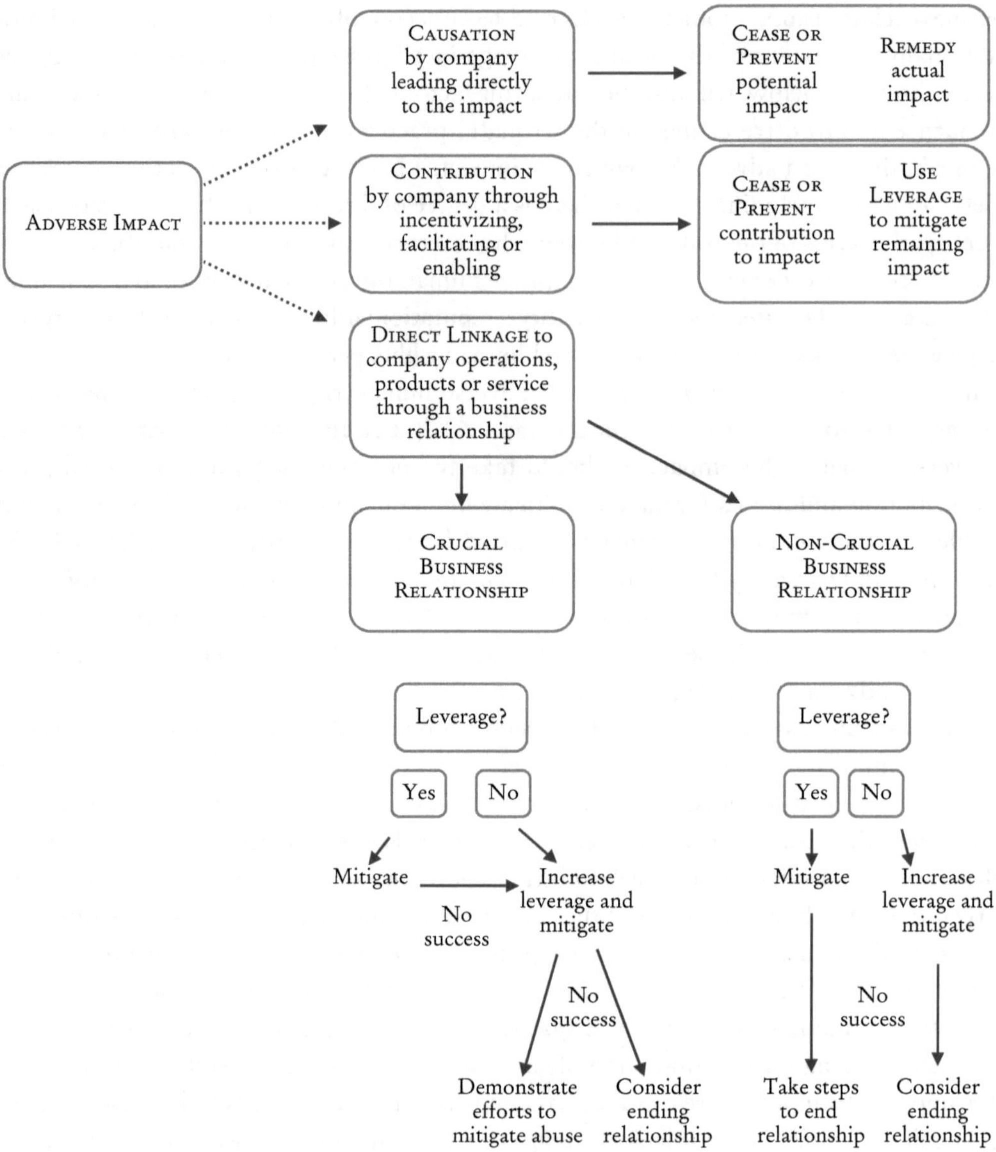

Figure 2.8 Practical Considerations: Appropriate Actions

for increasing leverage to mitigate the risk of the abuse continuing or recurring (through capacity building or other incentives, or collaboration[84]), and otherwise consider ending the relationship.[85] Recommended actionable steps for the various scenarios discussed above are summarized in figure 2.8.[86] The business should ensure that it formulates a plan of action

[84] *Guiding Principles, supra* note 4, at 22 (Principle Commentary 19).

[85] Interpretive Guide, *supra* note 18, at 50.

[86] *Guiding Principles, supra* note 4, pp. 21–22 (Principle 19 Commentary). *See also* International Bar Association, Handbook for Lawyers on Business and Human Rights (2016), https://www.ibanet.org/LPRU/Business-and-Human-Rights-for-the-Legal-Profession [hereinafter IBA Handbook], at 21.

- Do we already have tracking systems into which we could effectively integrate some or all aspects of tracking our human rights impact and responses? If so, are they fit for this additional purpose?
- What measures should we use?
- Are there established and widely accepted indicators we can draw on?
- Are there quantitative metrics that can be applied?
- What qualitative measures do we need to ensure we are interpreting quantitative data correctly and to give us a full picture?
- What indicators can we reasonably include to help us see how our responses to impact relate to women and men separately, and to vulnerable groups?
- What means do we have for gaining feedback from directly affected stakeholder groups or their legitimate representatives? Can our wider stakeholder engagement processes or our grievance mechanism(s) contribute to this process?
- In what kinds of situations should we conduct deeper root cause analyses of impact and our response to it as part of tracking? How can we ensure that lessons are learned across the enterprise?

Figure 2.9 Practical Consideration: Tracking

Source: The Corporate Responsibility to Respect Human Rights—An Interpretive Guide, by United Nations Office of High Commissioner, © 2012 United Nations. Reprinted with the permission of the United Nations.

that includes recommendations for prevention, mitigation, and remediation measures with timelines and priorities, all to be reviewed, approved, and implemented.

C. Tracking

The purpose of this third stage of due diligence is to verify whether adverse human rights impacts are being addressed per the integration and action plan implemented in the previous phase.[87] Tracking helps the business assess the effectiveness of the actions it has taken to address its impacts and to drive improvement,[88] and identify trends and patterns, including repeated problems and best practices.[89] Practical considerations for this phase are listed in figure 2.9.

Effective tracking of adverse human rights impacts is based on appropriate qualitative and quantitative *indicators* and draws on feedback from both internal and external sources.[90] Relevant indicators may include: the percentage of impacted stakeholders engaged who feel adverse impacts have been adequately addressed; the percentage/number of agreed action points implemented according to planned timelines; the percentage of impacted stakeholders who feel channels for raising grievances are accessible, equitable, and effective; and the rate of recurring issues related to the identified adverse impacts.[91] Quantitative indicators offer precision and are easily integrated with or linked to indicators used in different areas of the business, but qualitative indicators that include stakeholders' perspectives will provide a

---

87 *Id.* at 22 (Principle 20).

88 *Id.* at 23 (Principle 20 Commentary).

89 Interpretive Guide, *supra* note 18, at 53.

90 *Guiding Principles, supra* note 4, at 22 (Principle 20).

91 OECD Due Diligence Guidance, *supra* note 27, at 82. *See also* IBA Handbook, note 87, at 24.

more accurate interpretation of quantitative indicators.[92] This may consist in a simple review of the company's response and the extent to which it prevented the impact or, for significant human rights impacts, a root cause analysis to help determine how and why the impact occurred.[93]

Tracking should be integrated into relevant internal reporting processes and may include tools already in use, such as performance contracts and reviews, surveys and audits, and operational-level grievance mechanisms (e.g., anonymous reporting hotlines).[94] Obtaining feedback from stakeholders is paramount, whether it is from individuals within the company or from external expert observers—such as local authorities or civil society—or directly affected stakeholders,[95] with particular attention to individuals and groups that may be at heightened risk of marginalization.[96]

D. Reporting

Companies should be prepared to publicly communicate information about their human rights risks and impacts in a form and frequency that is accessible to its intended audience and with sufficient information to evaluate the adequacy of the company's response.[97] The communication should help establish the business's credibility and transparency in the eyes of the affected stakeholders.[98]

This "showing" phase is primarily about the ability of the enterprise to communicate its *general approaches* to address its human rights risks and impacts, but it may sometimes include communication on *specific responses* to a particular human rights impact with all the facts necessary for those affected to make an informed decision regarding their own interests.[99] With this in mind, there is no expectation for a business to disclose all of the issues identified in its ongoing assessments of human rights impacts or the steps it takes to mitigate every risk identified.[100] Figure 2.10 illustrates how the purpose for which a communication is made will assist in determining the format to be used.[101]

The business should consider a number of additional factors in determining what, how, and when to communicate adverse impacts, such as the intended audience, the accessibility of the information and any barriers to such accessibility (e.g., language, literacy, culture, gender, and other factors specific to certain marginalized groups), as well as issues of importance for

---

[92] *Id.* at 54–55.

[93] Interpretive Guide, *supra* note 18, at 54.

[94] *Guiding Principles, supra* note 4, at 23 (Principle 20 Commentary).

[95] Interpretive Guide, *supra* note 18, at 55.

[96] *Guiding Principles, supra* note 4, at 23 (Principle 20 Commentary).

[97] *Id.* at 23 (Principle 21).

[98] *Id.* at 24. Independent verification of the reporting can strengthen the content of the reporting and its credibility.

[99] Interpretive Guide, *supra* note 18, at 61.

[100] *Id.* at 58.

[101] *Id.* at 59–61. *See also* OECD Due Diligence Guidance, *supra* note 16, pp. 33, 85–87.

Format	Purpose(s)
In-person meetings with the affected stakeholders or their representatives, or online dialogues	Communicate to affected stakeholders how the enterprise is addressing a specific risk
Documents and presentations at an annual general meeting, *web updates, messages to electronic mailing lists* of those who self-identify as interested parties, or similar means of communication	Report to shareholders and other stakeholders on how the enterprise is addressing general or specific risks
Formal public reports (self-standing report on human rights performance alone, or integrated as part of annual reports, CSR/ corporate responsibility/ sustainability reports)	• Report on human rights issues of wider public interest/severe or significant risks to human rights impacts (e.g., risk is extensive or remediable) • Embed within the enterprise an understanding of human rights issues and importance of corporate responsibility to respect human rights • Protect reputation of the enterprise and build wider trust in its efforts to respect human rights

Figure 2.10 Practical Consideration: Purpose, Format, and Content of Communication

affected stakeholders.[102] Furthermore, the communication should be made in a manner that does not pose a risk to affected stakeholders, to personnel or to legitimate requirements of commercial confidentiality.[103] Such confidentiality requirements normally extend to information crucial to negotiations regarding a significant business transaction—for the length of such negotiations—and information legally protected against disclosure to third parties.[104] Actual or potential impact on the safety and welfare of affected stakeholders should be communicated *proactively* to such stakeholders as directly and quickly as possible.[105] Additional practical considerations are highlighted in figure 2.11.

When a company determines that formal reporting is an appropriate format for disclosing its human rights impacts, it should consider which reporting standards or frameworks are more suitable and would best guide the content of the reporting. Figure 2.12 provides a brief overview of some voluntary frameworks and standards for reporting human rights issues.

The *Global Reporting Initiative* is the most widely used standard for sustainability reporting and is composed of (a) universal standards that define report content and quality (regardless of sector) and management approach for each material topic; and (b) topic-specific standards organized into economic, environmental, and social impacts.[106] The *Sustainability Accounting Standards Board (SASB) Standards* contain (a) industry-specific disclosure standards compiled on the basis of an investor interest in an issue and material financial impact on companies in an industry; and (b) industry-specific topics organized into environment,

[102] *Id.* at 85–86.

[103] *Guiding Principles, supra* note 4, at 23 (Principle 21(c)).

[104] Interpretive Guide, *supra* note 18, at 60.

[105] *Id.*

[106] GRI Standards, https://www.globalreporting.org/standards/ (last visited Nov. 30, 2021).

- Do we have the necessary internal communications and reporting systems to gather all relevant information on how we address our adverse human rights impact? If not, what additional systems do we need?
- What different groups can we envisage we may need to communicate to and about what types of issues?
- What means of communication do we need for those different groups, taking account of how they can access information, and what will be the most effective?
- Should those communications be driven by a set timetable, be in response to particular events or both?
- What processes do we have in place to make reasoned and defensible judgments on when we should communicate publicly?
- If our operations or operational contexts pose significant risk to human rights, how do we provide formal public reporting on how we address that risk?
- If we are not in a context of heightened human rights risk and are not required to report publicly on our human rights performance, would there nevertheless be other benefits to formal public reporting? How will we ensure that our communications do not pose a risk to individuals inside or outside the enterprise?
- How might we solicit feedback on our public communication to test how it is viewed and see whether there are ways to improve it?

Figure 2.11 Practical Considerations—Reporting

Source: The Corporate Responsibility to Respect Human Rights—An Interpretive Guide, by United Nations Office of High Commissioner, © 2012 United Nations. Reprinted with the permission of the United Nations.

Frameworks/Standards	Issued By	Primary Target Audience	Purpose
Global Reporting Initiative Standards	Global Reporting Initiative	All stakeholders	Identify and report on material topics
SASB Standards	Sustainability Accounting Standards Board	Investors	Identify ESG factors reasonably likely to have a significant effect on the financial condition, operating performance, or market valuation of companies with an industry.
Integrated Reporting Framework	International Integrating Reporting Council	Investors	Explain to providers of financial capital how an organization creates value over time.
UN Guiding Principles Reporting Framework	Mazars & Shift	All stakeholders	Identify and manage salient human rights issues.

Figure 2.12 Terminology Cheat Sheet: Relevant Voluntary Reporting Frameworks and Standards

Note: ESG = environmental, social, and governance

human, social, business model, and governance dimensions.[107] The *UNGP Reporting Framework* is a series of questions designed to determine if the company is doing business in a manner respectful of human rights and show the progress it is making in that regard.[108] The

[107] SASB Standards, https://www.sasb.org/standards/ (last visited Nov. 30, 2021).

[108] United Nations Guiding Principles Reporting Framework, https://www.ungpreporting.org (last visited Nov. 30, 2021).

Integrated Reporting Framework is an outward-looking framework with principles-based guidance focused on value creation over time.[109]

IV. Conclusion

To summarize, human rights due diligence is a risk management process that aims: to bolster a business's internal policies and processes to avoid causing or contributing to human rights impacts; to help prevent a business's operations, services or products being linked to adverse human rights impacts; and to mitigate and remedy any human rights impacts if they occur.

The corporate responsibility to respect human rights has ushered in a new era of dealing with negative business human rights impacts. Civil society activism and social justice movements, the COVID-19 pandemic—which upended business operations in every industry sector and exposed systemic supply chain vulnerabilities—and the global climate change crisis and its human impacts, to name a few, are providing additional impetus for greater transparency and accountability in managing the business impacts on individual rights and freedoms. Lawyers, no matter their background and experience, are uniquely poised to play an integral role in supporting businesses' efforts to implement the UNGPs and conduct human rights due diligence to help maintain and build the trust and credibility that underlie their clients' social license to operate.

V. Resources

A. UN Guidance

UN Office of the High Commissioner for Human Rights, *The Corporate Responsibility to Respect Human Rights, An Interpretive Guide*, UN Doc. HR/PUB/12/02 (2012).

UN Office of the High Commissioner for Human Rights, *Frequently Asked Questions About the Guiding Principles on Business and Human Rights*, UN Doc. HR/PUB/14/3 (2014).

B. Books, Book Chapters, and Articles

Stéphanie Bijlmakers, *Human Rights Due Diligence as a Legal Concept*, in Corporate Social Responsibility, Human Rights and the Law, 102–134 (Routledge ed., 2018).

Jonathan Drimmer & Michael Torrance, *CSR Risk Management and Due Diligence*, in Corporate Social Responsibility—Sustainable Business, Environmental, Social and Governance Frameworks for the 21st Century, pp. 611–627 (Lindsay & Martella eds., 2020).

Alan S. Gutterman, Business and Human Rights, Advising Clients on Respecting and Fulfilling Human Rights (American Bar Association, 2020).

Robert McCorquodale, Lise Smit, Stuart Neely & Robin Brooks, 2(2) *Human Rights Due Diligence in Law and Practice: Good Practices and Challenges for Business Enterprises*, Bus. Hum. Rts. J., 195–224 (2017).

---

[109] IR Framework, https://www.integratedreporting.org/resource/international-ir-framework/ (last visited Nov. 30, 2021).

3

Lawyers' Ethical Obligations and Human Rights Due Diligence

Steven M. Richman

I. Introduction

A. General Considerations

The lawyer's ethical obligations primarily involve professional conduct[1] rules and regulatory structure governing the lawyer's behavior, violation of which leads to disciplinary action. They are generally not concerned with issues of morality or personal political preference. Indeed, one of the more difficult issues is representing a client where the lawyer is not sympathetic to the client's position. Whether or not to undertake such representation in the initial instance is a matter of personal preference but not an ethical issue unless and until it impacts the ability of the lawyer to exercise competent and independent judgment. This will be discussed in more detail later.

The United Nations (UN) Office of the High Commissioner for Human Rights (OHCHR) defines human rights due diligence (HRDD) as "a way for enterprises to proactively manage potential and actual adverse human rights impacts with which they are involved," and involves four elements: (1) "identifying and assessing actual or potential adverse human rights impacts . . ., (2) integrating findings from impact assessments across relevant company

[1] While the American Bar Association (ABA) Model Rules are termed Model Rules of Professional Conduct, and many states use "conduct" in their adoptions of such Model Rules, some writers use the phrase "professional responsibility." They are used interchangeably here in certain circumstances. The main point is to understand these are rules based on policy considerations that govern behavior for disciplinary purposes. The word "ethics" in connection with professional conduct or responsibility is also used in the same context.

processes . . ., (3) tracking the effectiveness of measures . . ., and (4) communicating on how impacts are being addressed . . ."[2] The *United Nations Guiding Principles on Business and Human Rights* (UNGPs)[3], as explained in more detail below, provide a series of principles and commentary relating to the obligations of public and private entities to implement the UNGPs' three core pillars of protect, respect, and remedy. To the extent legislation is enacted in a jurisdiction, due diligence becomes mandatory in advising clients as to how that legislation affects them and their obligations under such legislation. Consequently, the UNGPs are tied to HRDD and therefore lawyers, in providing competent legal advice, must be aware of this interrelationship.

This chapter addresses the obligations governing lawyers' professional conduct that have a disciplinary overlay, variously referred to as ethical obligations or obligations of professional conduct. It is the thesis of this discussion that the rules of professional conduct support providing advice on HRDD.

B. Hard Law and Soft Law

In addition, this chapter only addresses the responsibility of lawyers in connection with their advice to their clients as business entities, but not in connection with their role in their own law firms or companies as corporate counsel. Under the terms of the UNGPs, law firms, nongovernmental organizations (NGOs) and corporate entities are considered to have their own direct responsibility for complying with the UNGPs. Lawyers therefore draw a distinction between the rules of professional conduct governing a lawyer in terms of practicing law on the one hand, and their own soft-law obligations as they seek to comport themselves with the UNGPs.

Business and human rights is not the province of a select group of lawyers that specialize in human rights and public international law. Legislation—hard law—provides obligations in certain jurisdictions for certain qualifying entities, with criminal and civil penalties for noncompliance. Contract provisions are another example of hard law obligations that can bind a company. In addition, statements appearing in corporate publications may bind the corporation or, to the extent they are aspirational and implicating soft-law principles, may have impact on the corporate client. Such impact may include political, social, or economic issues. Lawyers may not realize the broader implications of professional responsibility obligations to counsel their clients more broadly when it comes to HRDD. In short, all lawyers are all human rights lawyers now. This chapter explores those obligations and offers good practices advice.

Before identifying the ethical obligations of a lawyer with regard to certain principles of international law and the UNGPs, it is important to understand what these soft-law regimes entail. If the UNGPs are considered only aspirational and in the realm of soft law, then

---

[2] https://www.ohchr.org/EN/Issues/Business/Pages/CorporateHRDueDiligence.aspx

[3] UN Office of the High Commissioner for Human Rights, *UN Guiding Principles on Business and Human Rights: Implementing the United Nations "Protect, Respect and Remedy" Framework*, 13–26, UN Doc. HR/PUB/11/04 (2011).

practitioners need to understand what actually is meant by soft law, in order to gauge the lawyer's ethical obligations relating to same. Soft law is not generally defined in case law. It has been defined by commentators as not formally binding, but nonetheless has certain weight and influence.[4]

The line between hard law and soft law is not always discernible. More specifically, soft law falls somewhere between the purely aspirational and the legally significant.[5] This chapter will look at the extent to which a lawyer is ethically obligated to advise with respect to soft-law obligations (advice as to hard law is a given) and the lawyers' obligations where there isn't such clearly defined hard law. In other words, how relevant is soft law to the lawyer's defined obligations of professional responsibility to render independent and competent legal advice, and also to provide that legal advice in an appropriate context as an advisor to the client? In the course of this discussion the primary focus is on the UNGPs' HRDD aspects more closely, because they serve as the framework for this area.

The Universal Declaration of Human Rights and the related (1) International Covenant on Economic,[6] Social, and Cultural Rights,[7] and (2) International Covenant on Civil and Political Rights (ICCPR) and its two Optional Protocols, form the "International Bill of Human Rights."[8] While inchoately soft law, the Universal Declaration of Human Rights "has over time been widely accepted as the fundamental norms of human rights that everyone should respect and protect."[9] To the extent its principles are adopted into national or subnational (state) constitutions or statutory law, or otherwise cited as part of holdings in judicial decisions, those principles "harden" and become legally binding.[10]

[4] "[S]oft law is defined as a residual category [of hard law]: '[t]he realm of "soft law" begins once legal arrangements are weakened along one or more of the dimensions of obligation, precision, and delegation." [citing Kenneth W. Abbott & Duncan Snidal, *Hard and Soft Law in International Governance*, 54 Int'l Org. 421, 422 (2000)]. Thus, if an agreement is not formally binding, it is soft along one dimension. Similarly, if an agreement is formally binding but its content is vague so that the agreement leaves almost complete discretion to the parties as to its implementation, then the agreement is soft along a second dimension. Finally, if an agreement does not delegate any authority to a third party to monitor its implementation or to interpret and enforce it, then the agreement again can be soft (along a third dimension) because there is no third party providing a 'focal point' around which parties can reassess their positions, and thus the parties can discursively justify their acts more easily in legalistic terms with less consequence, whether in terms of reputational costs or other sanctions." Gregory C. Shaffer & Mark A. Pollack, *Hard vs. Soft Law: Alternatives, Complements, and Antagonists in International Governance*, 94 Minn. L. Rev. 706, 715 (2010).

[5] Lantz v. Coleman, No. HHDCV084034912, 2010 WL 1494985, at *16 (Conn. Super. Ct. Mar. 9, 2010) ("Often, declarations of an international organization are regarded as a kind of aspirational 'soft law': rules which are neither strictly binding nor completely void of any legal significance. These may in time 'harden' into customary international law. Thus, for a declaration promulgating a rule of medical ethics to become binding international law, an individual claiming the law's protection would have to demonstrate overwhelming global agreement on the issue.") (internal quotations and citation omitted).

[6] GA Res. 217(III), UN GAOR, 3d Sess., Supp. No. 13, UN Doc. A/810 (1948) 71

[7] G.A. Res. 2200A (XXI), UN GAOR Supp. (No. 16) at 49, UN Doc. A/6316 (1966).

[8] Dec. 16, 1966, 999 U.N.T.S. 171; *see also* https://www.ohchr.org/Documents/Publications/FactSheet2Rev.1en.pdf

[9] https://www.ohchr.org/EN/ProfessionalInterest/Pages/InternationalLaw.aspx

[10] For example, in Switzerland, the Swiss Federal Supreme Court (AFT 140 I 125, § 3.2; ATF 141 I 141, § 6.3.3, stated: "The European Prison Rules—and a fortiori their commentary—are mere guidelines for the member states of the Council of Europe. However, as a reflection of the legal traditions common to the these States, the Federal Supreme Court has long considered them in the realization of personal freedom and other fundamental rights guaranteed by the Cst. and by the ECHR. They are referred to as 'penitentiary detention code' or 'soft law', nevertheless relatively

In this regard, it is notable that the Universal Declaration of Human Rights was a basis for the ICCPR,[11] a treaty which the United States ratified in 1992, although that ratification specifically rendered the treaty non-self-executing and without providing for a private cause of action.[12] The ICCPR provides in Article 6 that "(1) [e]very human being has the inherent right to life. This right shall be protected by law," in Article 7 that "[n] one shall be subjected to torture or to cruel, inhuman or degrading treatment or punishment," in Article 9 that "[e]veryone has the right to liberty and security of person," and in Article 10 that "[a]ll persons deprived of their liberty shall be treated with humanity and with respect for the inherent dignity of the human person." It is notable that whether or not the UNGPs are soft law, its principles find embodiment in the hard law provisions of this treaty to which the United States is a party.

At least one court has suggested that the International Bill of Human Rights constitutes "peremptory norms of international law and the application of federal law in derogation of [such a norm] would violate such peremptory norms."[13] To understand what this means, lawyers need an understanding of what those norms are, that is, what exactly is international law.

C. The Road Map

With the above in mind, this chapter will proceed in Section II to first discuss the legal and regulatory context governing lawyers, focusing on certain globally accepted core values, with an abbreviated comparative discussion of how those core values translate into governing ethics codes, and then focus on the American Bar Association (ABA) Model Rules of Professional Conduct (ABA Model Rules). In Section III, the discussion addresses the different legal, regulatory, and voluntary standards of practice, identifying the principal ABA Model Rules and how they compel the lawyer as an advisor to address the relevance of the UNGPs with clients. Section IV takes all of this into consideration and suggests good practices for lawyers. Finally, Section V looks ahead to the challenges and developments on the horizon regarding ethical obligations and the UNGPs.

binding for the authorities. Unlike the relevant federal or cantonal law, this corpus of legal norms has the merit of specifying the desirable organisation, equipment, cell size, or surface area that every prisoner is entitled inside the latter." Among the more well-known statutory embodiments of certain of the UNGPs principles are the United Kingdom Modern Slavery Act 2015, GBR-2015-L-101872, France's Law on the Corporate Duty of Vigilance, and Germany's Act on Corporate Due Diligence in Supply Chains, 2021. In the United States, California's Transparency in Supply Chains Act of 2010, Cal. Civ. Code § 1714.43.

[11] https://www.ohchr.org/EN/ProfessionalInterest/Pages/CCPR.aspx.

[12] https://www.law.umich.edu/facultyhome/drwcasebook/Documents/Documents/Senate%20Committee%20on%20Foreign%20Relations%20Report%20on%20the%20ICCPR.pdf; https://www.congress.gov/treaty-document/95th-congress/20/resolution-text.

[13] Sablan v. Iginoef, No. APPEAL 89-008, 1990 WL 291893, at *7 (N. Mar. I. Nov. 13, 1990).

II. Legal/Regulatory Context Governing Lawyers

A. Global Principles and Core Values

A lawyer's legal advice is rooted in the law and advising a client entails setting out the parameters of what may be done without penalty. This generally entails a spectrum of risk; not everything is black and white, and as the line is approached, the risk analysis becomes more extended. Still, in the case of hard law, there is a line, and the question is at what point it is crossed. On the other hand, soft law by definition does not contain hard lines, and if soft law is not legally binding, the intuitive response is that it may be safely ignored. The question becomes, then, to what extent does a lawyer's ethical obligation require familiarity with soft law and what role does it play in ethical obligations relating to the attorney-client relationship and the rendering of appropriate advice? Does it matter? There is sufficient scope within the professional rules governing American lawyers to answer the question in the affirmative.

Globally, there are also shared principles that are reflected in varying degrees in different national ethical codes, often referred to as core values. The International Bar Association (IBA) has issued the IBA International Principles on Conduct for the Legal Profession (IBA Principles), which set forth 10 principles, rather than ethical rules, to guide regulatory bodies in fashioning more specific rules of professional conduct. The IBA Principles state that "these principles aim at establishing a generally accepted framework to serve as a basis on which codes of conduct may be established by the appropriate authorities for lawyers in any part of the world."[14] Those principles are: independence; honesty, integrity, and fairness; conflicts of interest; confidentiality/professional secrecy; clients' interest; lawyers' undertaking; clients' freedom; property of clients and third parties; competence; and fees.

A main source of contention between lawyers and business clients surfaces when the client says "yes" and the lawyer says "no." The "no" should be based on two major considerations: first, what the law says and how it may be complied with (if possible) to accomplish the client's objective and second, what other non-legal factors bear on the validity of the legal advice. In other words, where there is room for interpretation of specified hard law that affects the client's goal and conduct, the lawyer's advice is often on a sliding scale that balances risks and benefits. There are, however, occasions where the only legal answer is a "no." A lawyer should try to find ways to get beyond the "no," but if that cannot be accomplished, then "no" is "no." The lawyer needs to always render competent advice and not offer advice that is simply what the client wants to hear because of fear of losing the client or otherwise being punished. This is where the fundamental principle of the independence of the lawyer applies.

Independence of the lawyer is the first identified principle of the IBA Principles, which requires "unbiased advice and representation."[15] Another component of the IBA Principle of

[14] Accessible at https://www.icj.org/wp-content/uploads/2014/10/IBA_International_Principles_on_Conduct_for_the_legal_prof.pdf at 5.

[15] *Id.*

independence is the responsibility of the lawyer to balance the best interest of the client with the lawyer's duty to the court "and the "interests of justice." Though "interests of justice" is not defined, the commentary to the IBA Principles notes that "[t]he requirement of independence calls upon the individual practicing lawyer, government and civil society to give priority to the independence of the legal profession over personal aspirations and to respect the need for an independent legal profession."[16] A client's interests may be read reasonably to implicate more than just legal liability, and as broadly defined, suggests a sensitivity by the lawyer to such concerns.

What all this means is that the lawyer's duty to the client may often involve an element of "tough love," telling the client what they may not want to hear, but also exploring lawful means to accomplish the goal. Conversely, and equally important, is that the public needs to understand that the lawyer's independence is critical to the process, and representation of unpopular clients doing unpopular but lawful things is to be respected.

The global principle of lawyer's independence to render objective advice is also found in the Havana Convention, more formally known as the Basic Principles on the Role of Lawyers, adopted by the UN Congress on the Prevention of Crime and the Treatment of Offenders in 1990.[17] Among the duties and responsibilities identified for lawyers are those that compel the lawyer to advise a client "as to their legal rights and obligations, to the working of the legal system insofar as it is relevant to the legal rights and obligations of the clients." Moreover, lawyers are obligated to assist clients "in every appropriate way." Perhaps most importantly, Principle 14 admonishes lawyers to "seek to uphold human rights and fundamental freedoms recognized by national and international law and shall at all times act freely and diligently in accordance with the law and recognized standards and ethics of the legal profession." As a declaration, this UN instrument is not legally binding in the manner of hard law, but as soft law may be cited for its persuasive value, to the extent that it compels lawyers to consider upholding human rights and fundamental freedoms as recognized in international law.

Other core values of the profession are shared globally, such as client confidentiality, discussed below. However, with regard to the subject of human rights and the UNGPs, the paramount obligation of lawyer independence is a fundamental step in educating international corporate actors in their responsibilities under the UNGPs and in particular, the second pillar addressing private actors, that of respect.

---

[16] *Id.* at 12. ABA Model Rule 5.4, titled "Professional Independence of a Lawyer," essentially addresses independence in terms of prohibiting the sharing of legal fees with a nonlawyer except in certain specified instances, and precluding formation of partnerships with nonlawyers for the practice of law. Model Rule 5.4 also precludes lawyers from practicing law in a professional corporation or association where nonlawyers hold interests, with certain exceptions. Notably, Washington, DC's version of Rule 5.4 permits nonlawyer ownership, *see* https://www.dcbar.org/For-Lawyers/Legal-Ethics/Rules-of-Professional-Conduct/Law-Firms-and-Associations/Professional-Independence-of-a-Lawyer. The issue is in a state of flux as certain jurisdictions are reevaluating this, such as Arizona, which has eliminated its Rule 5.4. *See* https://www.azcourts.gov/Portals/201/Press%20Releases/2020Releases/082720RulesAgenda.pdf.

[17] Adopted by the Eighth United Nations Congress on the Prevention of Crime and the Treatment of Offenders, Havana, Cuba, August 27th to September 7th, 1990. Available at https://www.ohchr.org/en/professionalinterest/pages/roleoflawyers.aspx.

B. Examples of Human Rights Elements in Ethics Codes

Certain jurisdictions emphasize a broader scope to the lawyer's role than a reciter of statutes and case holdings.

For example, in Europe, the Charter of Core Principles of the European Legal Profession and Code of Conduct for European Lawyers (Code of Conduct for European Lawyers) expressly "takes into account" the Universal Declaration of Human Rights, the European Convention on Human Rights, and the European Union (EU) Charter of Fundamental Rights.[18] The Code of Conduct for European Lawyers, per the document, "is a binding text on all Member States: all lawyers who are members of the bars of these countries (whether their bars are full, associate or observer members of the CCBE) have to comply with the Code in their cross-border activities within the European Union, the European Economic Area and the Swiss Confederation as well as within associate and observer countries."[19] In its preamble, titled "the function of the lawyer in society," the lawyer's function "lays on him or her a variety of legal and moral obligations (sometimes appearing to be in conflict with each other) towards . . . the public for whom the existence of a free and independent profession, bound together by respect for rules made by the profession itself, is an essential means of safeguarding human rights in face of the power of the state and other interests in society."[20] This is important, because the Code of Conduct for European Lawyers is binding on lawyers in the EU Member States. It ties together the concept of independence with both legal and moral obligations, while recognizing the potential for conflict in the latter.

In Canada, by way of another example, the Law Society of Ontario's Complete Rules of Professional Conduct provide in its Rule 2.1, titled Integrity, that "a lawyer has a duty to carry on the practice of law and discharge all responsibilities to clients, tribunals, the public and other members of the profession honourably and with integrity."[21] Comment 4.1 to the Rule states that "[a] lawyer has special responsibilities by virtue of the privileges afforded the legal profession and the important role it plays in a free and democratic society and in the administration of justice, including a special responsibility to recognize the diversity of the Ontario community, to protect the dignity of individuals, and to respect human rights laws in force in Ontario." The phrase "human rights" also appears in the Code's rules relating to (1) the marketing of legal services and (2) discrimination.

To the extent that the UNGPs reflect a soft-law policy it nonetheless has relevance in Canadian jurisprudence. This is demonstrated in *Choc v. Hudbay Minerals Inc.*,[22] involving a claim by Indigenous Guatemalan plaintiffs against a Canadian mining company and its subsidiaries. The corporations moved to dismiss. Amnesty International as an intervening party raised the UNGPs among other sources to emphasize, as the Court summarized, "the

---

[18] Accessible at https://www.ccbe.eu/fileadmin/speciality_distribution/public/documents/DEONTOLOGY/DEON_CoC/EN_DEON_CoC.pdf

[19] *Id.*

[20] *Id.*

[21] Rule2.1-1,https://lso.ca/about-lso/legislation-rules/rules-of-professional-conduct/complete-rules-of-professional-conduct.

[22] Choc v. Hudbay Minerals Inc., 2013 ONSC 1414, 2013 CarswellOnt 10514.

noting, though, the others that may arise. As with any other legal representation, a multitude of rules are applicable, some in more self-evident ways than others.[25]

III. Legal/Regulatory/Voluntary Standards

A. The Relevance of the UN Guiding Principles

A detailed explanation of the UNGPs is beyond the scope of this chapter. However, a brief summary of its core points is pertinent to understanding how the lawyer's duty to deliver legal advice on HRDD arises and what ethical challenges exist in delivering such advice. As noted above, HRDD may be said to involve identification, integration, tracking and communication.

The UNGPs have 31 principles, plus commentary, to implement the three pillars of protect, respect, remedy. The "respect" pillar is the one that most concerns the lawyer in private practice, whether in-house or outside counsel, in advising clients. The foundational principles under this pillar mandate that businesses respect human rights (Principle 11); understand what human rights are fundamental (Principle 12); avoid causing or contributing to human rights impacts and seek to prevent or mitigate same (Principle 13); recognize the application of these principles regardless of company size, operational context, ownership and structure (Principle 14); and establish procedures relevant to those factors to enable implementation (Principle 15). As an operational principle, businesses should issue a statement of policy (Principle 16).

For HRDD, businesses should carry out due diligence assessments as to the business's current activities (Principle 17); identify actual and potential risks and engage in meaningful consultation (Principle 18); prevent and mitigate abuses by integrating measures across the components of the business enterprise (Principle 19); verify and track effectiveness (Principle 20); and prepare external communiques (Principle 21).

By way of remediation of human rights violations, business should identify adverse impacts by them (Principle 22), and by way of context, businesses should comply with applicable law and respect international human rights and seek ways to honor them (Principle 23); and, where necessary, seek prevention and mitigation to prevent irremediable situations (Principle 24).

The lawyer's duty regarding HRDD therefore arises in several contexts. Beyond obvious obligations of competence, the lawyer needs to put legal advice into proper context as advisor. A second context involves the initial advice and drafting of documents ranging from contracts to corporate mission statements. In this regard, Principles 11 and 12, therefore, become part of the lawyer's obligation to educate the client, not just as to the differences between soft law and hard law, but to ensure that the client understands that HRDD is no longer solely the province of public interest law. Principles 13 through 16 follow from that

[25] *See, e.g.*, Rule 1.1 (competence), Rule 1.3 (diligence), Rule 1.4 (communications), Rule 3.1 (meritorious claims and defenses), Rule 3.3 (candor toward the tribunal), Rule 3.4 (fairness to opposing party and counsel); Rule 4.1 (truthfulness in statements to others), Rule 4.4 (respect for rights of third persons), Rule 5.1 (responsibilities of a partner or supervisory lawyer), Rule 5.2 (responsibilities of a subordinate lawyer), Rule 5.3 (responsibilities regarding nonlawyer assistance), Rule 5.7 (responsibilities regarding law-related services), Rule 6.1 (voluntary pro bono service), Rule 6.4 (law reform activities affecting client interests) and Rule 8.4 (misconduct).

and involve the lawyer in a more concrete way, in helping shape actual policies and protocols, and means for implementation.

A third context relates to implementation. Principles 17–24 implicate the lawyer's ethical obligations of diligence. It is not enough to draft the documents competently; the lawyer's responsibility is a continuing one to advise as to the risks of a company's failing to comply with its own written protocols. For example, "while widely published, vague corporate mission statements are not sufficient to support a breach of contract action; policy statements that include specific and definite promises may be sufficient to support such an action."[26]

The lawyer's role is to maintain the distinction between the political and the legal. A corporate entity that asserts a position that may become legally binding as a contract or actionable as a representation needs proper legal advice as to the ramifications of such assertions and the need for compliance. The UNGPs therefore provide a starting point for understanding the framework for HRDD.

B. ABA Model Rule 1.16

ABA Model Rule 1.16(b)(4) permits a lawyer to decline or terminate representation of a client if "the client insists upon taking action that the lawyer considers repugnant or with which the lawyer has a fundamental disagreement." Model Rule 1.16 poses a particular set of issues. A client may be acting within the law, but the attorney may feel that from a moral perspective something more is required. The attorney may feel uncomfortable in defending a legal position because the attorney may believe the law is wrong or does not go far enough. All of this must be balanced with the long-held tradition that clients are entitled to legal representation, not just in criminal cases but in civil cases as well. Will a lawyer be able to be relieved as counsel, or refuse to work on a matter within a larger law firm where it cuts against the attorney's personal morality? If the attorney cannot separate out those feelings and it jeopardizes the ability to perform competent and diligent representation, then in the civil law context, the attorney should be able to rely upon Rule 1.16 to withdraw from the representation. In the criminal law context, such a fundamental disagreement may lead to ineffective assistance of counsel, if the attorney's personal moral feelings interfere with competent and diligent representation.

Nevertheless, the ability of an attorney to withdraw under this rule is not absolute and is balanced against competing considerations. In *State v. Hausner*,[27] the Arizona Supreme Court denied defense counsels' motion to withdraw from representing a defendant who waived presentation of mitigation evidence, thereby preventing the lawyers from arguing for leniency in a death penalty case in which the defendant "urged the jury to sentence him to death." The Court held that, under the Arizona equivalent of ABA Model Rule 1.2, the lawyers were required to abide by the client's decision, even though the defendant's decision "put them in a difficult position and one they may have found morally repugnant," and the trial court did

---

[26] Perloff v. Transamerica Life Ins. Co., 393 F. Supp. 3d 404, 409 (E.D. Pa. 2019).

[27] 230 Ariz. 60, 85 (2012).

not err in denying the motion to withdraw.[28] Even in the civil context, assertions of repugnance are not foolproof.[29]

C. ABA Model Rule 1.6

ABA Model Rule 1.6 is a rule of professional conduct that addresses client confidentiality; paragraph (a) precludes the lawyer from revealing any information relating to representation unless the client gives informed consent, the disclosure is impliedly authorized to carry out the representation or the disclosure is permitted under one of the exceptions in paragraph (b). Exceptions in paragraph (b) included disclosures that the lawyer reasonably believes are necessary to prevent "certain death or substantial bodily harm," or to prevent a client from "committing a crime or fraud" reasonably certain to cause another substantial financial injury when the client has used the lawyer's services to perpetuate, or if disclosure is impliedly authorized to carry out the representation or it is necessary to establish a defense or detect conflict, or per court order. The need to be transparent with the client and inform the client as to material considerations in achieving their objectives, is covered by the communications rule (Rule 1.4), and similarly, the ability to speak candidly about possible negative consequences in dealing with UNGPs-covered issues would be protected under the confidentiality provision (Rule 1.6).

The professional conduct obligation embodied in Rule 1.6 is distinct from the evidentiary rules surrounding "attorney-client privilege, which is more limited: it protects from compelled disclosure the substance of a lawyer-client communication made for the purpose of obtaining or imparting legal advice or assistance and applies only in the context of a legal proceeding governed by the rules of evidence."[30] Rule 1.6 "applies in situations other than those where evidence is sought from a lawyer through the compulsion of law."[31] It is "given effect by related bodies of law" such as attorney-client privilege and work product, as well as "the rule of confidentiality established in professional ethics."[32]

There is an important distinction between Rule 1.6's confidentiality obligations and those related to issues of attorney-client privilege. In the course of lawyer-client communications, Rule 1.6 applies to "disclosure by a lawyer of information *relating to the representation* of a client *during the lawyer's representation* of the client" [emphasis added].[33] This would

---

[28] *Id.* at 87.

[29] *See, e.g.*, Cuadra v. Univision Commc'ns, Inc., No. CIV.A. 09-4946 JLL, 2012 WL 1150833, at *7 (D.N.J. Apr. 4, 2012) (rejecting both permissive and mandatory withdrawal).

[30] *See* Rule 1.6, cmt. [3]. *See also, e.g.*, Fed. R. Evid. 502 (Attorney-Client Privilege and Work Product; Limitations on Waiver).

[31] Town of W. Hartford v. Taubman Centers, Inc., No. X02UWYCV075007876S, 2009 WL 1578485, at *2 (Conn. Super. Ct. May 21, 2009) (quoting the comment in Connecticut's version of ABA Model Rule 1.6). That rule further clarifies that "[t]he confidentiality Rule, for example, applies not only to matters communicated in confidence by the client but also to all information relating to the representation, whatever its source." CT R RPC Rule 1.6.

[32] *See* Rule 1.6, cmt. [3].

[33] Comment [4] to the Rule makes clear this applies even to information not intrinsically protected: "Paragraph 9a) prohibits a lawyer from revealing information relating to the representation of a client. This prohibition also applies to disclosures by a lawyer that do not in themselves reveal protected information but could reasonably lead to the

suggest that in discussing with a client potential actions that relate to a human rights situation implicating the UNGPs, information beyond pure legal advice that is related to the information would fall under the black-letter language of the rule. The comments further emphasize the "reasonable precautions" the lawyer must take to ensure a "reasonable expectation of privacy" in conveying the information.[34]

It is important to recognize the strong policy considerations underlying Rule 1.6. While Rule 1.6(b)(1) does provide an exception that allows a lawyer to reveal information relating to the representation where the lawyer "reasonably believes" it is necessary to "prevent reasonably certain death or substantial bodily harm," that may implicate societal rather than simply individual concerns.[35] Similarly, Rule 1.6(b)(3) permits disclosure "to prevent, mitigate or rectify substantial injury to the financial interests or property of another that is reasonably certain to result or has resulted from the client's commission of a crime or fraud in furtherance of which the client has used the lawyer's services." The issue of death or substantial bodily harm is not tied to fraudulent or criminal activity. As noted in Comment [6], a concern about an accidental discharge of toxic waste, for example, would be something that should be disclosed to eliminate the threat or reduce the number of victims.[36]

Rule 1.6 is a rule of professional conduct. It is distinct from evidentiary issues implicating attorney-client communications. The problem arises when information is sought to be disclosed to a third party and the attorney-client privilege is asserted.[37] That privilege may be a function of federal common law or state privilege law, depending upon context of the proceeding. The "scope of protection afforded by Rule 1.6 is far broader than attorney-client privileged information."[38] However, in the narrower context of attorney-client privilege, where forced disclosure is sought in an investigative or dispute resolution context, the

---

discovery of such information by a third person. A lawyer's use of a hypothetical to discuss issues relating to the representation is permissible so long as there is no reasonable likelihood that the listener will be able to ascertain the identity of the client or the situation involved."

[34] *See* Rule 1.6, cmt. [9].

[35] Comment [6] to Model Rule 1.6 recognizes, for example, that "a lawyer who knows that a client has accidentally discharged toxic waste into a town's water supply may reveal this information to the authorities if there is a present and substantial risk that a person who drinks the water will contract a life-threatening or debilitating disease and the lawyer's disclosure is necessary to eliminate the threat or reduce the number of victims."

[36] Paragraph (b)(1) recognizes the overriding value of life and physical integrity and permits disclosure reasonably necessary to prevent reasonably certain death or substantial bodily harm. Such harm is reasonably certain to occur if it will be suffered imminently or if there is a present and substantial threat that a person will suffer such harm at a later date if the lawyer fails to take action necessary to eliminate the threat. Thus, a lawyer who knows that a client has accidentally discharged toxic waste into a town's water supply may reveal this information to the authorities if there is a present and substantial risk that a person who drinks the water will contract a life-threatening or debilitating disease and the lawyer's disclosure is necessary to eliminate the threat or reduce the number of victims. https://www.americanbar.org/groups/professional_responsibility/publications/model_rules_of_professional_conduct/rule_1_6_confidentiality_of_information/comment_on_rule_1_6/.

[37] This privilege may be found at common law or codified by rule or statute. *See, e.g.*, Grace v. Mastruserio, 2007-Ohio-3942, ¶ 18, 182 Ohio App. 3d 243, 249, 912 N.E.2d 608, 612, Fed. R. Evid. 502.

[38] *See* ABA Formal Opinion 480, found at https://www.americanbar.org/content/dam/aba/administrative/professional_responsibility/aba_formal_opinion_480.authcheckdam.pdf. The opinion addresses specifically issues of lawyer blogging, and addresses the strict parameters of what a lawyer must not disclose. It is a different context from issues relating to demands for disclosure in other contexts.

privilege does not generally apply to business advice, but only to legal advice.[39] This becomes important to bear in mind as the lawyer seeks to preserve client confidentiality, protect disclosure of attorney-client privilege issues in discovery, and yet fulfill the role of advisor. As a practical matter, to attempt to receive the maximum benefit of the privilege, the business advice should be intertwined in a discussion of the legal issues, with it being delivered in support of legal advice; the business advice should not predominate.[40]

The fundamental principle underlying client confidentiality is based on trust and is intended to encourage a full and frank discussion, including discussion of embarrassing or legally damaging subjects, and to enable the lawyer to effectively represent the client and advise against further wrongful conduct. The role of the lawyer as advisor under Rule 2.1 is discussed later in this chapter. This is important to the UNGPs and human rights issues, particularly those of soft law, because it provides protection for the lawyer in advising a client to speak more freely, lest there be concern about a communication that would not be fully protected.

Having said that, it is worth emphasizing that adherence to Rule 1.6 may protect the lawyer from a claim of violating this rule of professional conduct, but that does not mean that it avoids a request for information exchanged between the lawyer and the client where the evidentiary privilege is invoked.

The decision in *Honolulu Civil Beat Inc. v. Department of Attorney General*,[41] shows that both Rule 1.6 and the privilege may come into play regarding a request for a report, even though they have different scope and analytical frameworks. In *Honolulu Civil Beat*, plaintiff made a request for information from a government agency regarding the results of an investigation, and the defendant refused, asserting both attorney-client privilege and Hawaii's version of Model Rule 1.6, which is materially the same as the ABA rule. The Hawaii Supreme Court held that to determine the issue of privilege, the predicate inquiry is what was communicated in the context of the attorney-client relation. The Court found that the communication at issue "was not necessarily rendering a legal service," that the contents of the tendered report at issue were factual, but that the government simply had not

---

[39] *See, e.g.*, North Pacifica, LLC v. City of Pacifica, 274 F. Supp. 2d 1118, 1127 (N.D. Cal. 2003) ("In general, legal advice is implicated 'if the nonlegal aspects of the consultation are integral to the legal assistance given and the legal assistance is the primary purpose of the consultation."). *See*, Restatement (Third) of the Law Governing Lawyers § 68 (Am. Law Inst. 2000) ("Except as provided in this Restatement, the attorney-client privilege may be invoked as provided in § 86 with respect to: (1) a communication (2) made between privileged persons (3) in confidence (4) for the purpose of obtaining or providing legal assistance for the client."); *See also*, *In re* Lindsey, 158 F. 3d 1263 (D.C. Cir. 1998), cert. den. sub nom Office of the President v. Office of the Independent Counsel, 119 S. Ct. 466 (1998); *see also* Ullmann v. State, 230 Conn. 698, 713 (1994) ("A communication from attorney to client solely regarding a matter of fact would not ordinarily be privileged, unless it were shown to be inextricably linked to the giving of legal advice.")

[40] *See, e.g.*, Neuder v. Battelle Pac. Nw. Nat. Lab'y, 194 F.R.D. 289, 292 (D.D.C. 2000) ("Where business and legal advice are intertwined, the legal advice must predominate for the communication to be protected. See Memo. Order at 5 (citing Coleman v. ABC, 106 F.R.D. 201, 206 (D.D.C.1985)); *see also* ABB Kent–Taylor v. Stallings and Co., Inc., 172 F.R.D. 53, 55 (W.D.N.Y.1996) ("[o]ften intertwined with legal advice as to substantive issues is counsel's strategic assessment of alternative choices of action available to the client."). Relatedly, "communications by a corporation with its attorney, who at the time is acting solely in his capacity as a business advisor, would not be privileged.")

[41] Honolulu Civil Beat Inc. v. Dep't of Attorney Gen., 146 Haw. 285, 298, 463 P.3d 942, 955 (2020).

proved in this case that legal services were provided. It then noted that the policies underlying both the evidentiary privilege rule and Rule 1.6 supported its holding, and that ultimately "[t]he Department failed to meet its burden to prove that it was acting within a lawyer-client relationship when it prepared the report. Accordingly, it failed to prove that the report itself is covered by either the lawyer-client evidentiary privilege, HRE Rule 503, or the professional conduct rule of confidentiality, HRPC Rule 1.6."[42] While *Honolulu Civil Beat* was decided in the context of a statutory provision governing disclosure, the Court nonetheless analyzed the issue under both the disciplinary rule's policy as well as the evidentiary rule.

The practical differences between Rule 1.6 and the evidentiary privilege rule were also addressed in *Downie v. Superior Ct.*,[43] in which the Court noted that "while both the law of evidence and the law of professional conduct protect the confidences of clients, these two bodies of law are distinct and they apply in separate, discrete situations," with the evidentiary privilege applying "in judicial and other proceedings in which a lawyer may be called as a witness or otherwise required to produce evidence concerning a client" and the latter "in situations other than those where evidence is sought from the lawyer through compulsion of law," where it is broader.

Consequently, understanding Rule 1.6 and its implications functions on two levels. First, by accommodating soft-law concepts as part of the information conveyed relating to the representation, it allows for the communications to remain confidential, under certain circumstances. Second, the lawyer can explain to the client that there are provisions which allow a lawyer to reveal confidential information, which can influence the client's reaction to a particular set of circumstances. However, the fact that the information is protected for purposes of the disciplinary rule does not mean that certain information, otherwise protected in that context, may not be immune from compelled disclosure under the evidentiary privilege analysis. To the extent the attorney is providing advice to a client that may implicate issues relating to human rights that could come up in a litigation or other proceeding where the privilege is relevant, care should be taken to protect such communications within the context of the privilege or work product.

D. ABA Model Rule 2.1

ABA Model Rule 2.1 addresses the role of the lawyer as advisor, and indicates that "[i]n representing a client, a lawyer shall exercise independent professional judgment and render candid advice. In rendering advice, a lawyer may refer not only to law but to other considerations such as moral, economic, social and political factors, that may be relevant to the client's situation."

The rule's two sentences use different words, and suggest that while the obligation to render "candid advice" is mandatory ("a lawyer shall"), the second sentence says that in rendering that advice, the lawyer "may" refer to other non-legal factors that "may" apply to the client's situation. The question arises as to whether there is a duty under the rule to tell a

[42] *Id.* at 298, 463 P.3d at 955.

[43] 888 P.2d 1306, 1309 (Alaska Ct. App. 1995).

client things they may not want to hear by the lawyer as "advisor." If the legal advice permits a client to take a particular course of action but the lawyer believes that such would have negative political, social, and economic repercussions, is communicating that belief part of the mandatory "candid advice" or part of the discretionary "other considerations?"

Views may differ on how far this rule goes. I suggest that the better practice is that the UNGPs should be considered—particularly with regard to ABA Model Rule 2.1, which defines the lawyer as advisor, and its equivalents in other jurisdictions.

Comment [2] to Rule 2.1 amplifies this and emphasizes that legal advice given in isolation from other factors is insufficient, stating, "[a]dvice couched in narrow legal terms may be of little value to a client, especially where practical considerations, such as cost or effects on other people, are predominant. Purely technical legal advice, therefore, can sometimes be inadequate. It is proper for a lawyer to refer to relevant moral and ethical considerations in giving advice. Although a lawyer is not a moral advisor as such, moral and ethical considerations impinge upon most legal questions and may decisively influence how the law will be applied."

Because Rule 2.1 and the role of the lawyer as an advisor extend beyond purely legal advice, a broader and more practical viewpoint and context are required. First, it is not always easy to separate legal from business advice, particularly when the word "reasonable" is part of any law. What is reasonable as a matter of law will depend upon the factual context, which cannot be divorced from legal advice. For example, in considering whether or not an agency's decision to deny consent to a sublease was arbitrary and capricious, the court reviewed the facts and circumstances of the proposed sublessee. The issue involved aquatic lands, and the regulatory agency sought information as to "whether [the proposed sublessee] has any history of causing environmental damage."[44] The appellate court found that the agency had not acted arbitrarily and capriciously in denying consent to a sublease of the aquatic lands, noting that "careful consideration of [the proposed sublessee's] financial condition and business reputation was especially reasonable given the circumstances surrounding the potential sublease."[45] The lawyer would have to evaluate certain "non-legal" factors relating to business reputation that of necessity would involve other than "legal" factors in giving advice in such an instance. While not addressing HRDD, these cases emphasize the need to put legal advice in context based on non-legal but economically relevant considerations, which certainly would include reputational damage in the market.

Second, an awareness of soft law is important in providing context for legal advice. As noted, the rule compels the lawyer to exercise independent professional judgment and render candid advice, but has discretion ("may") in referring to non-legal considerations. While a strict view of what constitutes competent legal advice may lean towards advising a client of what it can or cannot do, the broader, if discretionary, aspects of Rule 2.1 make clear that in appropriate circumstances, advice on soft law may have relevance, and failure to advise on it may be an abuse of discretion on the lawyer's part. A lawyer may correctly determine that

[44] Nw. Alloys, Inc. v. Dep't of Nat. Res., 10 Wash. App. 2d 169, 175–76, 447 P.3d 620, 625, review denied, 194 Wash. 2d 1019, 455 P.3d 138 (2020).

[45] Nw. Alloys, Inc. v. Dep't of Nat. Res., 10 Wash. App. 2d 169, 187, 447 P.3d 620, 630, review denied, 194 Wash. 2d 1019, 455 P.3d 138 (2020).

advice is "legal" and the "business advice" is incidentally involved.[48] There needs to be a legal context; for example, a position paper drafted by lawyers purely for public relations purposes but not for legal purposes may not be afforded attorney-client privilege protection.[49] To the extent that the lawyer advises on such issues in the context of the UNGPs, for example, then arguably the "business advice" or public relations issues are incidental to the broader framing of the advice, and therefore should achieve the appropriate protection.

There is not always an explicit discussion of this issue in the context of privilege, but cases have implicitly indicated the need for adopting a broader viewpoint in rendering legal advice. In *Wise v. Washington Cty.*,[50] an attorney was sanctioned for, among other reasons, failing to properly advise a client as to the risks of litigation separate and apart from legal considerations. In this case, the Court cited Rule 2.1 in the context of a civil rights action. Significantly, Wise himself had a long-standing seizure disorder. Because he had failed to take his necessary medicine, he was in a car accident that resulted in the death of his passenger, and he was convicted of a criminal manslaughter charge. Upon his release, Wise hired a lawyer and initiated a civil action for violation of his rights, including cruel and unusual punishment, and for assaults against him by his treating doctors and nurses. In the context of a motion for sanctions against Wise's attorney, after reciting a litany of applicable rules and statutes, the Court noted, "[s]imilarly, it does not appear that [attorney] Fisher properly counseled his client as to the attendant risks of this litigation, especially in light of his memory and likely credibility issues. Pa. RPC 2.1 (Advisor)."

When it is referenced, Rule 2.1 is commonly cited in the context of other rule violations, including the need for independence of a lawyer. The particular information that was attributable to a violation of Rule 2.1 as opposed to other ethics rules is often not explained.

Wise, above, is an example in which there was clarity of the Rule 2.1 violation. Another example is *Henry v. Henry*,[51] where the Court stated, "Counsel often obtain insights into a client's conduct and behavior which could be relevant and useful in further proceedings. It also must be remembered that counsel in a matrimonial dissolution action must play several roles. These include not only that of advocate, but that of counselor and advisor. See Rules of Professional Conduct, Rules 2.1 and 3.1." *Henry* was decided in the context of a disqualification motion by plaintiff based on conflict of interest, but the Court observed that in a matrimonial case, information as to the client's lifestyle is exchanged. The Court was noting that all of this information of which the lawyer is aware ultimately is part of the background that informs the advice given.

Similarly, in *Graham v. Prudential Ins. Co. of Am.*,[52] plaintiff was denied rights to convert an insurance policy following her treatment for cancer; the Court denied defendant's motion for summary judgment. The Court cited, inter alia, Rule 2.1 and noted: "It is rare to

---

[48] *See, e.g.*, United States v. Davita, Inc., 301 F.R.D. 676, 682 (N.D. Ga. 2014), on reconsideration in part, No. 1:07-CV-2509-CAP-JSA, 2014 WL 11531065 (N.D. Ga. May 21, 2014).

[49] Burton v. R.J. Reynolds Tobacco Co., 200 F.R.D. 661, 669 (D. Kan. 2001).

[50] Wise v. Washington Cty., No. CIV.A. 10-1677, 2015 WL 1757730, at *18 (W.D. Pa. Apr. 17, 2015).

[51] Henry v. Henry, No. 531717, 1994 WL 597378, at *3 (Conn. Super. Ct. Oct. 25, 1994).

[52] Graham v. Prudential Ins. Co. of Am., No. CV-05-S-102-NW, 2006 WL 8436807, at *2 (N.D. Ala. Jul. 12, 2006).

see a case still in litigation with such distasteful facts. The court cannot help but wonder how the amount spent in legal fees can justify the actual amount in controversy or cause at stake. At some point, members of what one hopes will continue to be a noble profession, must step back and carefully consider that one of the most important duties of attorneys is that of counselor and advisor." The Court noted that while "viewed in a vacuum" defendant's legal argument had "persuasive force," there were other facts that the Court found raised serious questions so as to deny the party's summary judgment motion; the above comment about Rule 2.1 apparently was meant to emphasize the responsibility of the lawyer to advise the client of the impact of such other factors on a legal result.[53]

These cited cases, however, focus on the evaluation of the legal merits and while they touch on the role of the lawyer as advisor, they do not go toward issues of morality or conscience or even public relations. To an extent, the issue is tied up with whether the lawyer was restrained by other factors from giving candid advice.[54]

Consequently, the application of Rule 2.1 may not always be apparent. It is well and good to note the factors that should be conveyed to the client to evaluate legal advice. Even so, offering non-legal advice may not be privileged in all circumstances as discussed above. This goes hand in glove with the requirements of Rule 1.4 to keep a client reasonably informed. Rule 1.4 further dictates that the lawyer also must "explain a matter to the extent reasonably necessary to permit the client to make informed decisions regarding the representation." Comment [5] to Rule 1.4 makes clear that what is reasonable is not one size fits all, and that the "[a]dequacy of communication depends in part on the kind of advice or assistance that is involved." Comment [6] indicates that "the information to be provided is that appropriate for a client who is a comprehending and responsible adult." It would not be possible to explain the legal meaning of a provision and its impact without providing a factual context for the client, and in such cases, the privilege is not lost.[55]

This is buttressed by Comment c to Section 20 of the Restatement (Third) of the Law Governing Lawyers (Restatement), which section requires the lawyer to keep the client "reasonably informed about the matter," which means that:

> The lawyer's duty to consult goes beyond dispatching information to the client. The lawyer must, when appropriate, *inquire about the client's knowledge, goals, and concerns* about the matter, and must be open to discussion of the appropriate course of action.[56]

---

[53] *Id.*

[54] *See, e.g.*, Lee v. State Farm Mut. Auto. Ins. Co., 249 F.R.D. 662, 689 (D. Colo. 2008) ("The Special Master believes there is a substantial question as to whether Rodman violated this Rule by failing to exercise independent professional judgment and render candid advice to Thorne. The Special Master further believes there is a substantial question as to whether Rodman's conduct in his representation of Thorne was materially affected by his prior and ongoing relationship with State Farm [emphasis supplied])."

[55] "Legal counsel does not always render, and is not always expected to render, exclusively legal assistance. Often business advice needs to be mixed with legal advice so that the legal advice is fully understood and followed by the client. Similarly, when legal documents are reviewed by a lawyer, it is common for the lawyer to correct grammatical mistakes and propose alternative language that will best serve the client's interests. When these non-legal services are mixed with legal services it does not render the legal services any less protected by the privilege. In fact, they both are protected when they are inextricably intertwined." *In re* Vioxx Prod. Liab. Litig., 501 F. Supp. 2d 789, 798 (E.D. La. 2007).

[56] Restatement (Third) of the Law Governing Lawyers § 20 (2000) Comment c (emphasis added).

If legal advice for purposes of privilege includes extra-legal considerations to put the advice in context, and the legal advice rendered as an advisor pursuant to Rule 2.1 must also include such context, then the obligation of communication must also include consideration of such factors. To the extent that soft law, or, more particularly, the UNGPs, affect the ability to implement legal advice, such commentary should be included. Telling a client they may lawfully do or not do something in a jurisdiction when 95 percent of the population in that jurisdiction holds a particular view as to the appropriateness, morally or otherwise, of the contemplated action or inaction certainly should be part of the context of the legal advice. For example, legal advice on corporate governance and obligations to shareholders would be part of the legal advice a lawyer gives to a company contemplating speaking out on a particular political issue, but other factors would inform that advice, of necessity.[57]

The concept of a broader approach to legal advice that takes into account other than purely literal applications of the law is also amplified in the comment to § 94 of the Restatement, which explains that a lawyer generally is precluded from counseling a client to violate the law. However, § 94 of the Restatement also has a provision that accommodates Rule 2.1: "(3) In counseling a client, a lawyer may address nonlegal aspects of a proposed course of conduct, including moral, reputational, economic, social, political, and business aspects."

Comment h to § 94 of the Restatement addresses this concept and elaborates that "a lawyer's advice to a client may properly include the lawyer's views concerning aspects of a proposed course of conduct that are not narrowly legal in nature. Such advice, when given as part of legal services provided to the client, is within the scope of § 72 [Attorney–Client Privilege—Legal Assistance as the Object of a Privileged Communication] for purposes of the attorney-client privilege, and it is within § 59 [Definition of "Confidential Client Information"] for purposes of the general duty of confidentiality (see § 60) [A Lawyer's Duty to Safeguard Confidential Client Information]. (Restatement (Third) of the Law Governing Lawyers § 94 (2000) Comment h)."

Of relevance in the context of business and human rights counsel is the additional admonition in Comment h that "[a] lawyer's advice on significant nonlegal aspects of a matter may be particularly appropriate when the client reasonably appears to be unaware of such considerations or their importance or when it should be apparent that the client expects more than narrow legal counsel."[58]

The Restatement also refers to the ethical obligations of competence and diligence, and requires lawyers to "proceed in a manner reasonably calculated to advance a client's lawful objectives, as defined by the client after consultation."[59] The word "reasonably" comes into play again. Reasonable legal advice cannot be separated from assessment of the facts, reputation, and other aspects of the client's business standing.

---

[57] *See, e.g.*, Cole, Thomas A., *Business and Politics: When Should Companies Take a Public Position?* Harvard Law School Forum on Corporate Governance, https://corpgov.law.harvard.edu/2021/05/06/business-and-politics-when-should-companies-take-a-public-position/.

[58] Restatement (Third) of the Law Governing Lawyers § 94 (2000).

[59] Restatement (Third) of the Law Governing Lawyers § 16 (2000); *see also* § 5, incorporating the disciplinary rules of the jurisdiction.

E. Mission Statements and Representations

Another area of hard law that becomes part of the advice given by a lawyer relates to what goes into a contract or mission statements. While parties are required to adhere to applicable law, certain statutory protections can be waived expressly. To the extent a jurisdiction does not have reporting requirements for compliance with the UNGPs, desired reporting requirements can be made part of a contract and become enforceable as a matter of contract law. Similarly, requiring that a party provide certifications of compliance can also be made part of the contract. If made as a representation, the breach will subject the party to damages; if made as a condition, a breach may invalidate the contract.[60]

A corporate entity may find itself liable based upon representations made in corporate mission statements. For example, in *Sibley v. St. Albans School*,[61] plaintiff claimed he relied on a statement on the defendant's website regarding an alleged assurance of admission; the Court analyzed it in terms of whether it actually constituted a representation and if so, whether it was false as a reasonable person would read it. Although certain cases have held that mission statements are generally not statements of fact on which a reasonable person could rely,[62] other cases actually have analyzed those statements to see if they were true or false; simply because a statement is a mission statement, it does not necessarily mean that it cannot be actionable.[63]

This is a particular area where the lawyer's role as advisor under Model Rule 2.1 is important. Careful drafting of a mission statement to ensure that the company is not overreaching in its promises on the one hand, or understating its prophylactic purposes on the other, requires consideration of more than simply legal principles. This is an area in particular where choice of law considerations may matter, particularly in terms of how a jurisdiction treats such representations in mission statements.

The lawyer should always be attentive to what the client puts out in publicly available documents. An example of this issue is found in *Barber v. Nestlé USA, Inc.*,[64] in which consumers purchasing cat food products sued manufacturers for violations of the California Unfair Competition Law based on alleged misrepresentations. The allegation was that defendant did not disclose that certain of its products were likely produced using forced labor, thereby creating a claim under California's unfair trade practices and false advertising statutes. By way of defense to the claim under the Unfair Competition law, defendant claimed a safe harbor based on another statute, California's Transparency in Supply Chains Act of 2010,

---

[60] Lincoln Nat. Corp. v. TakeCare, Inc., No. C 97-02193 CW, 1998 WL 281290, at *3 (N.D. Cal. May 11, 1998); *see also* M. K. Metals, Inc. v. Container Recovery Corp., 645 F.2d 583, 588 (8th Cir. 1981); *In re* LCS Homes, Inc., 103 B.R. 736, 743 (Bankr. E.D. Va. 1989) ("The failure of a condition is not a breach of contract, but it discharges the liability of the promisor whose obligations on the contract never mature.")

[61] Sibley v. St. Albans Sch., 134 A.3d 789, 813 (D.C. 2016).

[62] *See, e.g.*, Posluns v. Educ. Mgmt. Corp., LLC, No. 4:10-CV-01294 SWW, 2010 WL 5346886, at *7 (E.D. Ark. Dec. 21, 2010), aff'd, 436 F. App'x 724 (8th Cir. 2011) ("[M]ission Statement are not statements of fact sufficient to constitute misrepresentations . . . .").

[63] *See, e.g*, Dreyer v. Idaho Dep't of Health & Welfare, 455 F. Supp. 3d 938, 951 (D. Idaho 2020).

[64] Barber v. Nestle USA, Inc., 154 F. Supp. 3d 954 (C.D. Cal. 2015), aff'd, 730 F. App'x 464 (9th Cir. 2018).

which only requires that a company *disclose* whether it does the following, but not that it must do the following: "(1) engages in verification of product supply chains to evaluate and address risks of human trafficking and slavery; (2) conducts audits of suppliers to evaluate supplier compliance with company standards for trafficking and slavery in supply chains; (3) requires direct suppliers to certify that materials incorporated into its products comply with laws regarding slavery and human trafficking; (4) maintains internal accountability standards and procedures for employees or contractors who fail to meet company standards regarding slavery and trafficking; and (5) provides company employees and management with training on human trafficking and slavery."[65] The Court rejected plaintiff's claims under the safe harbor, finding that "the California legislature considered the situation of regulating disclosure by companies with possible forced labor in their supply lines and determined that only the limited disclosure mandated by § 1714.43 is required."[66]

Having addressed the statutory disclosure obligations, the Court then analyzed the claims of misrepresentation contained in eight separate statements that appeared in defendant's online documents such as its corporate business principles, supplier code, responsible sourcing guidelines, and a public report on its own business policies. It found that the online statements did set forth rigid guidelines for suppliers, but held no cause of action was stated because:

> no reasonable consumer who reads the four documents Plaintiffs identify in context could conclude that Nestlé's suppliers comply with Nestlé's requirements in all circumstances. On the contrary, Nestlé seems to anticipate a certain level of non-compliance. It is not shy about identifying for consumers the rules and expectations for its suppliers, but it does not mislead them into thinking that its suppliers abide by those rules and meet those expectations in every instance.[67]

Barber has been cited for its holding that there is no liability where the legislature permitted certain conduct or otherwise considered the situation and did not provide for a private right of action.[68] *Barber* was affirmed by the federal Ninth Circuit Court of Appeals. The First Circuit Court of Appeals, in a matter of first impression, has followed *Barber*, and did not allow a cause of action under the Massachusetts unfair trade practices statute or for common law unjust enrichment, based on an alleged failure to disclose that defendant's manufacture of chocolate product likely included child labor in its supply chain.[69]

Statements made in a company's securities law filings may also be the basis for claims of misrepresentation; however, even statements as to a company's ethics and standards of conduct may not be actionable if, whether as statements of fact or opinion they are considered

[65] *Id.* at 959.

[66] *Id.* at 961.

[67] *Id.* at 964. The Court noted that "[s]imilarly, Nestlé's Supplier Code is replete with evidence that its requirements represent an ideal, and not necessarily a reality." *Id.* at 963.

[68] Forsher v. J.M. Smucker Co., No. 5:19CV00194, 2020 WL 1531160, at *10 (N.D. Ohio Mar. 31, 2020).

[69] Tomasella v. Nestlé USA, Inc., 962 F.3d 60 (1st Cir. 2020).

"immaterial puffery," but if they are not too vague or general, and are deemed to be material, such "sufficiently specific" statements may be actionable as a fraud claim.[70]

Consequently, HRDD requires familiarity with the jurisdiction's unfair business practices and false advertising statutes, the particular statements appearing in the company's public documentation, and the governing statutes relating to regulation and disclosure obligations, to ascertain whether or not safe harbors exist for the public statements made by companies.

IV. Identification of Good Practices

UNGPs Principle 14 applies the responsibility to respect human rights to "all enterprises regardless of their size, sector, operational context, ownership and structure." That responsibility is a function of the "severity of the enterprise's adverse human rights impacts." The commentary to Principle 14 does recognize that corporate policies will take different forms, but that even small and medium-sized enterprises (SMEs) "can have severe human rights impacts." SMEs may be more likely to be involved in supply chain issues, either as suppliers to larger multinationals or in using components from them in their business. Since most lawyers in private practice are more likely to represent SMEs, it is important to recognize that the same ethical considerations noted above are raised for both SMEs and multinational companies. Notably, given that human rights violations are not always international but may be purely domestic, all lawyers should be attentive to the UNGPs and to Principle 14 in particular.

There have been several attempts to set forth best practice guidelines for lawyers relating to HRDD as concerns the UNGPs. Among the earlier sources are the IBA Practical Guide on Business and Human Rights for Business Lawyers (as well as a reference annex) (IBA Guide).[71] The US Department of State has also issued guidelines for implementation of UNGPs in certain transactions.[72] Another interesting document in this regard was issued by Shift, Oxfam, and Global Compact Network Netherlands, titled "Doing Business with Respect for Human Rights: A Guidance Tool for Companies."[73]

The IBA Guide states its purpose is to:

> set out in detail the core content of the UNGPs, how they can be relevant to the advice provided to clients by individual lawyers subject to their unique professional standards and rules (whether they are in-house or external counsel acting in their individual capacity or as members of a law firm) and their potential implications for law firms as business enterprises with a responsibility to respect human rights themselves.[74]

---

[70] *See, e.g., In re* Braskem S.A. Sec. Litig., 246 F. Supp. 3d 731, 754 (S.D.N.Y. 2017).

[71] IBA Practical Guide on Bus. & Human Rights for Bus. Lawyers, at 39, Int'l Bar Ass'n, (May 28, 2016) [hereinafter IBA Guide]. https://media.business-humanrights.org/media/documents/files/documents/IBA_Practical_Guide.pdf

[72] *See* US Department of State Guidance on Implementing the UN Guiding Principles for Transactions Linked to Foreign Government End-Users for Products or Services with Surveillance Capabilities, https://www.state.gov/wp-content/uploads/2020/10/DRL-Industry-Guidance-Project-FINAL-1-pager-508-1.pdf.

[73] https://www.businessrespecthumanrights.org/image/2016/10/24/business_respect_human_rights_full.pdf.

[74] IBA Guide at 7, found at https://www.ibanet.org/MediaHandler?id=d6306c84-e2f8-4c82-a86f-93940d6736c4.

The IBA Guide makes clear that regardless of whether they are in-house, in outside law firms, or otherwise,

> lawyers have specific and legally binding professional responsibilities and obligations, including the duty of independence. The UNGPs do not abridge this duty, which includes the duty to decide, within the limits of the law, how to act in their client's best interests, independently of expectations and pressures that are external to the lawyer–client relationship, subject of course to adherence by the lawyers with their professional and legal responsibilities.[75]

This concept, that the UNGPs do not abridge other ethical obligations, was also recognized by the New York City Bar Association's Policy Statement regarding the UNGPs.[76]

The IBA Guide also stresses that "the UNGPs may nevertheless be highly relevant to the advice or services to be rendered the client: i.e., where they are within the agreed scope of services (or mandate) to be provided (which may include a range of services, from very specific to highly general); where they are reflected or incorporated in relevant laws, or where they are permitted or encouraged to be considered by lawyers in their independent judgment under applicable professional standards of conduct." Importantly, nothing in the IBA Guide overrides the lawyer's other ethical obligations, and:

> should not be read (1) to restrict the right of effective access by clients to legal services provided by independent lawyers; (2) to restrict the obligation of lawyers to provide independent services to their clients (without being identified with their client or client's causes, or deemed complicit in their clients' activities, as contemplated by UN Basic Principle 18); (3) to restrict the representation of clients who may be highly unpopular (including those who have been accused of engaging in human rights harm), (4) to restrict the rights of clients to secure a robust defence to such claims or to seek judicial determination of human rights related issues; (5) to restrict the rights of clients to seek, and lawyers to provide, independent legal advice with respect to human rights issues or matters that have potential impacts on human rights; or (6) to define the factors that lawyers must, should, or are expected to, consider in their independent judgement, when providing advice or services to a client.[77]

The IBA Guide identifies five discrete practice areas and notes the type of legal advice and services that are relevant. Those practice areas are (1) corporate governance and enterprise risk management; (2) reporting and disclosure; (3) disputes; (4) contracts and agreements; and (5) development of and participation in human rights standards. In each of these areas, knowledge by the lawyer of the UNGPs has direct impact on the advice given, particularly

[75] *Id.* at 27.

[76] http://documents.nycbar.org/files/Working_Group_on_Business_and_Human_Rights_Policy_Statement.pdf.

[77] IBA Guide at 29, found at https://www.ibanet.org/MediaHandler?id=d6306c84-e2f8-4c82-a86f-93940d6736c4.

Another useful guidebook for lawyers is the publication by the Council of Bars and Law Societies of Europe (CCBE) titled *Corporate Social Responsibility and the Legal Profession: Guidance II*.[81] Among other things, this publication provides advice on how lawyers should address corporate social responsibility. It provides an example showing that, in counseling on project finance transactions, the UNGPs may be implicated as well as certain other human rights standards.

A report by the New York City Bar Association's Business and Human Rights Working Group that surveyed law firm experiences regarding the UNGPs highlights the "developments, successes and challenges" for lawyers in developing good practices.[82] It reinforces the ethical obligations discussed above in terms of the need for lawyers to understand the framework of both soft law and hard law in this area. A common theme of survey respondents in the report is that the more familiar clients are with the UNGPs, the more receptive they are to advice on them. As a best practice, lawyers and their firms should develop client information, in-house seminars, and other client education functions.

Lawyers should also encourage their firms to join organizations such as the Law Firm Sustainability Network, a group of law firms and legal departments that works collaboratively in the education and promotion of sustainability and corporate social responsibility goals. Like bar associations, this Network provides resources on these topics to its members.

With all of this in mind, the following are some concrete examples of how lawyers can offer legal advice that advances the UNGPs.

Example 1: Remain conversant with environmental, social, and governance factors, and integrate that understanding in the context of legal advice.

Business schools are adding training on environmental, social, and corporate governance factors (ESG) to their curricula.[83] While ESG shares the goals of corporate social responsibility (CSR), ESG is generally understood to relate to compliance with standards, while CSR is a voluntary, self-regulating business model.[84] To the extent that up-and-coming business leaders who will be running global companies are evaluating the importance of ESG considerations in investment and other economic decisions, lawyers advising such companies, in their role of advisor under ABA Model Rule 2.1, must understand the vocabulary and the context. Lawyers are trained to draft documentation, whether pleadings or contracts, that capture the goals of the client in feasible, achievable, and understandable ways. One of the problems

---

[81] https://www.ccbe.eu/fileadmin/speciality_distribution/public/documents/CSR/CSR_Guides___recommendations/EN_CSR_20140206_CSR-and-the-Legal-Profession-Guidance-II.pdf.

[82] https://www.nycbar.org/member-and-career-services/committees/reports-listing/reports/detail/response-to-request-for-input-on-business-and-human-rights.

[83] Sarah Murray, *Business Schools Urged to Integrate ESG Topics in Core Courses*, Financial Times, April 11, 2021, found at https://www.ft.com/content/64211d86-ef52-4cf5-ba38-0fe64e18b58f.

[84] https://www.businessleader.co.uk/what-is-the-difference-between-esg-and-csr/ Some further distinguish "Business and Human Rights" as its own area, reliant upon the framework of UNGPs, for example. *See, e.g.*, D. Allison-Hope and P. Munoz Quick, Human Rights Are Not Just an "ESG Factor," https://www.bsr.org/en/our-insights/blog-view/human-rights-are-not-just-an-esg-factor .

facing companies is misguided ESG policies, which can do more harm than good and alienate otherwise sympathetic boards and shareholders.[85] In short, so-called "moral money" or ethical investing as part of the business and human rights–ESG framework, requires the commercial or business lawyer to know more than just "the law" in helping companies craft their overall approach to ESG.

Example 2: Draft appropriate policies

In September 2020, Apple Inc. published a policy titled "Our Commitment to Human Rights" that expressly stated in the section on its commitment to international human rights that "[o]ur approach is based on the UN Guiding Principles on Business and Human Rights. *We conduct human rights due diligence to identify risks and work to mitigate them. We seek to remedy adverse impacts, track and measure our progress, and report our findings.*"[86] (emphasis added). This was approved by the company's Board of Directors and reportedly was in response to shareholder pressure. Lawyers advising Apple presumably will now be advising on compliance and implementation. As discussed above, under certain circumstances, such representations and commitments may be binding on a company, and some plaintiffs may have standing to assert they were injured in reliance on such statements.

Corporate policies have been argued in the context of Alien Tort Statute claims, and while violations of them may not be actionable as against the law of nations,[87] there is nonetheless reputational damage to consider. An example of this relates to Nestlé, which has been called "one of the most hated companies in the world"[88] because of claims of child labor in the Ivory Coast, even though the Alien Tort Statute claims against it were dismissed for failure to state a claim by the US Supreme Court.[89] The point is not to single out Nestlé or evaluate the claims, but essentially to raise the point that regardless of the legal "win," a company may be subject to non-legal pressures. There is also the possibility of shareholder activism. So the lawyer's involvement in drafting corporate documents and otherwise rendering advice requires full awareness of the risks and exposure for the client and should be geared towards achievement of the doable, and not purely the aspirational.

Example 3: Be aware of developments on the business judgment rule.

In *In re UnitedHealth Grp. Inc. Shareholder Derivative Litig.*,[90] the Supreme Court of Minnesota was asked to resolve the issue of to what extent a court, in approving a proposed

[85] Dambisa Moyo, *Hasty, Imperfect ESG Is not the Path for Business*, Financial Times, April 11, 2021, found at https://www.ft.com/content/7ed30ebd-0b05-41b8-a366-0acafc63c549.

[86] https://s2.q4cdn.com/470004039/files/doc_downloads/gov_docs/Apple-Human-Rights-Policy.pdf.

[87] Beanal v. Freeport-McMoRan, Inc., 969 F. Supp. 362, 384 (E.D. La. 1997), aff'd, 197 F.3d 161 (5th Cir. 1999); cf Alomang v. Freeport-McMoran Inc., No. CIV. A. 96-2139, 1996 WL 601431, at *1 (E.D. La. Oct. 17, 1996).

[88] *See, e.g.*, https://www.zmescience.com/science/nestle-company-pollution-children/. Nestlé addresses this directly on its own website: https://www.nestle.com/ask-nestle/human-rights/answers/nestle-child-labour-supply-chains.

[89] Nestlé USA, Inc. v. Doe, 141 S. Ct. 1931, 210 L. Ed. 2d 207 (2021).

[90] *In re* UnitedHealth Grp. Inc. S'holder Derivative Litig.,754 N.W.2d 544 (Minn. 2008).

settlement of a shareholder derivative action, must defer to the decision of a corporate special litigation committee ("SLC") to settle on certain terms. In answering this question, the Court explored the boundaries of the business judgment rule. It cited a New York Court of Appeals decision that held that "the embrace of the business judgment doctrine, involve[es] the weighing and balancing of legal, ethical, commercial, promotional, public relations, fiscal and other factors familiar to the resolution of many if not most corporate problems"[91] and noted other courts adopted that approach.[92] While recognizing disagreement, it nonetheless adopted the New York approach, noting among other factors that "[b]y its very nature, an individual's business judgment is a unique amalgamation of many factors, including but not limited to personal experience, education, and general business philosophy."[93]

Consequently, as detailed above, the lawyer's role as advisor encompasses more than just legal considerations. A company may be within its rights to fight a litigation claiming human rights abuses, and may well win, but a business decision to settle that considers such factors as public relations and the corporation's own general philosophy will be protected in jurisdictions adopting the New York approach.

V. Identification of Outstanding/Evolving Issues and Challenges

One developing area of hard law application relates to the "beneficiary" or B Corporation. Under traditional statutory and common laws, corporate fiduciary responsibilities focus on shareholder profit. The B Corporation now has more expansive obligations that include, as a matter of law and duty, the consideration of how its actions have a broader impact on employees, customers, suppliers, communities, and the environment. Currently, over 4,000 companies in some 70 countries across 150 industries certify their compliance with B Corporation requirements.[94] Several US states permit B Corporations. As companies take advantage of such B Corporations, there may be shareholder suits to compel certain actions in the area of business and human rights.

The UN Human Rights Council established an open-ended intergovernmental working group (OEIGWG) in 2014 to develop a treaty to address business and human rights. Most recently, on August 17, 2021, a third revised draft of Legally Binding Instrument to Regulate, in International Human Rights Law, the Activities of Transnational Corporations and Other Business Enterprises was released.[95] This draft of a proposed treaty emphasizes the role of the UNGPs and seeks to incorporate key aspects of the UNGPs into the proposed treaty. For example, within Section 1, Article 2, subpart 1(b) indicates its purpose is "[t]o clarify and ensure respect and fulfillment of the human rights obligations of business enterprises." Article

[91] Auerbach v. Bennett, 47 N.Y.2d 619, 633, 393 N.E.2d 994, 1002 (1979).

[92] *See supra* note 90. It also cited contrary approaches. *Id.* at 556.

[93] *Id.* at 556.

[94] https://www.bcorporation.net/en-us/faqs/how-many-certified-b-corps-are-there-around-world.

[95] https://www.ohchr.org/Documents/HRBodies/HRCouncil/WGTransCorp/Session6/LBI3rdDRAFT.pdf.

3.1 (scope) renders the instrument binding on all business enterprises. Under Section II, Article 8 provides that:

> 8.6. States Parties shall ensure that their domestic law provides for the liability of legal and/or natural persons conducting business activities, including those of transnational character, for their failure to prevent another legal or natural person with whom they have had a business relationship, from causing or contributing to human rights abuses, when the former controls, manages or supervises such person or the relevant activity that caused or contributed to the human rights abuse, or should have foreseen risks of human rights abuses in the conduct of their business activities, including those of transnational character, or in their business relationships, but failed to take adequate measures to prevent the abuse.
>
> 8.7. Human rights due diligence shall not automatically absolve a legal or natural person conducting business activities from liability for causing or contributing to human rights abuses or failing to prevent such abuses by a natural or legal person as laid down in Article 8.6. The court or other competent authority will decide the liability of such legal or natural persons after an examination of compliance with applicable human rights due diligence standards.

Where this ultimately leads is perhaps less important than its outline of principles that may resonate within national legislation. As of this writing, the third draft served as the basis for the negotiations at the seventh session of the OEIGWG, which occurred from October 25–29, 2021.

Separately, the UN Working Group on the Issue of Human Rights and Transnational Corporations and Other Business Enterprises has been meeting. Established in 2011, this group of five geographically diverse experts has a mandate to promote the effective implementation and dissemination of the UNGPs while identifying and promoting good practices and lessons learned, as well as engaging in other activities to give traction to the principles. Its website notes its promotional activities.[96]

Similarly, the Uniform Law Commission is presently studying supply chain transparency to determine if uniform state legislation is an appropriate and feasible mechanism for addressing business reporting requirements regarding human trafficking, child labor, or substandard production and facility standards.[97] Other countries have their own initiatives on addressing not only supply chain transparency and reporting but other aspects of business and human rights.[98]

---

[96] https://www.ohchr.org/en/issues/business/pages/wghrandtransnationalcorporationsandotherbusiness.aspx.

[97] https://www.uniformlaws.org/committees/community-home?CommunityKey=8b5ff376-8537-41c9-8dfb-928fd271d406.

[98] *See generally* Steven M. Richman, Esq., *Ethical Issues for Business Lawyers Under the United Nations Guiding Principles*, 51 Int'l Law. 423 (2018).

The ABA also has developed model contract clauses as part of its Contractual Clauses Project that relate to human rights due diligence.[99]

VI. Conclusion

Every lawyer is a human rights lawyer. Whether involving CSR, ESG, or business and human rights, corporate entities—particularly on the global scale—cannot view the law in isolation. As Oliver Wendell Holmes wrote in his 1881 *The Common Law*, "[t]he life of the law has not been logic: it has been experience. The felt necessities of the time, the prevalent moral and political theories, intuitions of public policy, avowed or unconscious, even the prejudices which judges share with their fellow-men, have had a good deal more to do than the syllogism in determining the rules by which men should be governed." The notion of "the prevalent moral and political theories" has particular resonance in the area of HRDD. At its most basic, a profit-driven corporation may well find that adherence to the UNGPs enhances its reputation and brand, and conversely, failure to do so can be damaging. Rigid adherence to the law is of little comfort in the face of a national consumer boycott led by activists. To be sure, not all demands must be met, but this is where the lawyer as advisor plays a core role. It is the function of the lawyer to advise, and legal advice as noted cannot be delivered in a vacuum. The lawyer who cannot give advice that takes into account the broader implications of otherwise lawful action is not delivering competent legal advice and is not in compliance with the role of advisor.

VII. Resources

Advocates for International Development. *Guide for the Legal Profession*. http://www.a4id.org/wp-content/uploads/2016/04/A4ID-Business-and-Human-Rights-Guide-2013-web.pdf.

American Bar Association. *A Lawyer's Guide to Key Business and Human Rights Documents*. https://www.americanbar.org/groups/human_rights/business-human-rights-initiative/key-business-and-human-rights-documents/.

American Bar Association. *ABA Model Rules of Professional Conduct*. https://www.americanbar.org/groups/professional_responsibility/publications/model_rules_of_professional_conduct/model_rules_of_professional_conduct_table_of_contents/.

Business and Human Rights Resource Centre. *Tools and Guidance*. https://www.business-humanrights.org/en/latest-news/tools-guidance/.

Council of Bars and Law Societies of Europe. *Code of Conduct for European Lawyers*. https://www.ccbe.eu/NTCdocument/EN_CCBE_CoCpdf1_1382973057.pdf

Council of Bars and Law Societies of Europe. *Corporate Social Responsibility and the Legal Profession*. https://www.ccbe.eu/fileadmin/speciality_distribution/public/documents/CSR/CSR_Guides___recommendations/EN_CSR_20140206_CSR-and-the-Legal-Profession-Guidance-II.pdf.

The Ethics of Commercial Contracting. 2013 NO. 3 RMMLF-INST PAPER NO. 14.

[99] https://www.americanbar.org/groups/human_rights/business-human-rights-initiative/contractual-clauses-project/.

International Bar Association. *IBA Practical Guide on Business and Human Rights for Business Lawyers* (as well as a reference annex). https://www.ibanet.org/MediaHandler?id=d6306c84-e2f8-4c82-a86f-93940d6736c4.

Tom Lininger. *Green Ethics for Lawyers*. 57 B.C. L. Rev. 61, 61 (2016).

Milton C. Regan, Jr. & Kath Hall. *Lawyers in the Shadow of the Regulatory State: Transnational Governance on Business and Human Rights*, 84 Fordham L. Rev. 2001 (2016).

Restatement (Third) of the Law Governing Lawyers (2000).

Steven M. Richman, Esq.. *Ethical Issues for Business Lawyers Under the United Nations Guiding Principles*, 51 Int'l Law. 423 (2018).

United Nations. *UN Basic Principles on the Role of Lawyers*. https://www.ohchr.org/en/professionalinterest/pages/roleoflawyers.aspx.

World Business Council for Sustainable Development. *Inclusive Business and Human Rights Toolkit*. https://humanrights.wbcsd.org/project/inclusive-business-human-rights-toolkit/.

4

French Due Diligence Law

François de Cambiaire and Alice Murgier

I. Introduction

Referring to French law as a pioneer in the field of human rights due diligence (HRDD) might seem odd given that France's two-century-old Civil Code is not usually regarded as one of the most innovative legal systems. However, the adoption of the French Duty of Vigilance Law of March 27, 2017 (Duty of Vigilance Law or the Law),[1] represented a breakthrough in HRDD for France, and set a precedent for the enactment of mandatory HRDD (mHRDD) regimes throughout the world. The Duty of Vigilance Law is the first cross-sectoral and enforceable mandatory human rights and environmental due diligence law worldwide, which imposes a duty of vigilance and a civil liability regime on companies for damages resulting from serious human rights abuses throughout their supply chain.[2]

Yet, employers' organizations and business representatives (notably the French Association of Private Enterprises (AFEP) and the Movement of French Enterprises (MEDEF), the two main business representative organizations) have criticized the Law for impeding the competitiveness of French businesses, claiming that the mHRDD requirements create an uneven playing field in international business and unclear or ineffective obligations.[3] At the

---

[1] Law No. 2017-399 of March 27, 2017 on the duty of care of parent companies and ordering companies, codified in Articles L.225-102-4 and 5 of the French Commercial Code (*see* https://www.legifrance.gouv.fr/dossierlegislatif/JORFDOLE000030421923/). *See also* https://www.novethic.fr/actualite/entreprise-responsable/isr-rse/devoir-de-vigilance-la-loi-definitivement-adoptee-144294.html; https://www.medef.com/fr/communique-de-presse/article/devoir-de-vigilance-une-loi-inefficace-qui-menace-notre-economie.

[2] *See* the recent study carried out for the European Commission: LISE SMIT ET AL, Study on Due Diligence Requirements through the Supply Chain: Final Report, BIICCL, CIVIC, LSE, January 2020.

[3] *See also* Duty of vigilance law Parliamentary debates, Senate Report n° 74 by Senator Mr. Frassa, October 14, 2015, page 8, mentioning the "economic risks" created by the law, accessible here: http://www.senat.fr/rap/l15-074/l15-0741.pdf.

by an intergovernmental task force mandated by the United Nations (UN) Human Rights Council in June 2014.[7] The Law also directly inspired the call for a similar system by the European Union (EU) and the European Commission. On February 23, 2022, the European Commission issued its long-awaited Proposal for a Directive on Corporate Sustainability Due Diligence (CSDD) to tackle human rights and environmental impacts across global value chains.[8] The Commission estimates that 13,000 EU companies and 4,000 third-country companies would be within the scope of the Proposed Directive.

The Commission's proposal (Corporate Sustainability Due Diligence and amending Directive (EU) 2019/1937) has aroused great interest, paving the way for uniform regulation at the European level and a civil liability mechanism applicable in the event of a failure to exercise due diligence, which is based on the French law. However, it has also generated disappointment, since the text would not enter into force until 2025 or 2026 at the earliest. In particular, the proposal relies on the adoption of codes of conduct by companies, the inclusion of clauses in contracts with their suppliers, and the use of private audits and sectoral initiatives. However, it is precisely the ineffectiveness of these measures that has been the basis of NGO advocacy for many years for the adoption of a binding duty of vigilance, as distinct from "tick-the-box" reporting obligations.[9]

Moreover, the possibility provided for by French law to refer a case to the Court, before any damage is done, so that a judge can order a company to respect its prevention obligations, is not explicitly envisaged in the Commission's proposal. The Commission also proposes a restrictive approach to environmental matters, which could exclude from the scope of the directive certain environmental damage currently covered by French law.

This chapter aims to share the authors' four years of experience with application of the Duty of Vigilance Law, based on the initial cases brought under the Law and on the lessons that can be drawn from these cases and the debates in progress before the authorities of the EU. Thus, Section II initially traces the inspiration and developments that led to the Law as well as the procedural background for the Law. Section III then provides an overview of the scope of the Law and the requirements of the vigilance plan (Vigilance Plan). Section IV examines the contributions and lessons learned from the first lawsuits filed on the basis of

---

[7] *See* Chairmanship of the OEIGWG [Open-ended inter-governmental working group], Elements for the Draft Legally Binding Instrument on Transnational Corporations and Other Business Enterprises with Respect to Human Rights, https://www.ohchr.org/sites/default/files/Documents/HRBodies/HRCouncil/WGTransCorp/Session3/LegallyBindingInstrumentTNCs_OBEs.pdf. *See also* S. Brabant, E. Savourey, "Law on the Corporate Duty of Vigilance – A Contextualised Approach," REVUE INTERNATIONALE DE LA COMPLIANCE ET DE L'ÉTHIQUE DES AFFAIRES – SUPPLÉMENT À LA SEMAINE JURIDIQUE ENTREPRISE ET AFFAIRES N° 50 du jeudi 14 décembre 2017, 91, available here: http://www.bhrinlaw.org/frenchcorporatedutylaw_articles.pdf.

[8] European Commission, Proposal for a Directive of the European Parliament of the Council on Corporate Sustainability Due Diligence and amending Directive (EU) 2019/1937, COM(2022) 71 final, available here: https://ec.europa.eu/info/sites/default/files/1_1_183885_prop_dir_susta_en.pdf.

[9] Business and Human Rights Resource Centre, « Directive sur le devoir de vigilance des entreprises : la proposition enfin dévoilée par la Commission doit impérativement être améliorée », 23 février 2022, https://www.business-humanrights.org/fr/derni%C3%A8res-actualit%C3%A9s/directive-sur-le-devoir-de-vigilance-des-entreprises-la-proposition-enfin-d%C3%A9voil%C3%A9e-par-la-commission-doit-imp%C3%A9rativement-%C3%AAtre-am%C3%A9lior%C3%A9e/; Le Monde, « Les ambitions contrariées de la directive européenne sur le devoir de vigilance », 23 February 2022, https://www.lemonde.fr/economie/article/2022/02/23/les-ambitions-contrariees-de-la-directive-europeenne-sur-le-devoir-de-vigilance_6114927_3234.html.

the law. Finally, Section V addresses the questions that remain outstanding in practice and the possibilities for the evolution of the mandatory human rights due diligence (mHRDD) regime in France and abroad.

II. Context for the Duty of Vigilance Law

A. Inspiration for the Law

This Law is the result of several legislative initiatives in 2013 and 2015, supported by many NGOs and promoted by the Member of Parliament Dominique Potier, particularly in response to the dramatic collapse of the Rana Plaza in Bangladesh on April 24, 2013, which led to the death of 1,138 Bangladeshi workers and more than 2,000 injured workers in the textile factories located there, which were subcontractors to many Western corporate groups. According to the parliamentary discussion, the Law is based on international soft-law references, such as the Organisation for Economic Co-operation and Development (OECD) *Guidelines for Multinational Enterprises*,[10] and the *UN Guiding Principles on Business and Human Rights* (UNGPs) adopted in 2011,[11] while going beyond them by enshrining a cross-cutting and binding legal obligation. The concept is also closely related to the duty of care concept known in common law countries, which is discussed in Subsection 3 below.

1. International Soft-law Principles

International law has seen a proliferation of due diligence soft-law instruments. The most well-known are the 2011 UNGPs, whose application and implementation were re-evaluated by the UN Working Group on Business and Human Rights in a 2021 report, on the 10th anniversary of the UNGPs,[12] and the OECD *Due Diligence Guidance for Responsible Business Conduct*, which was implemented in 2018 to serve as a practical supplement to the 2011 *OECD Guidelines for Multinational Enterprises*.[13] These due diligence instruments have been supplemented with the increasing implementation by businesses of corporate governance regulations, such as the AFEP-MEDEF Code, as well as ethical guidance and codes of conduct establishing voluntary standards.[14]

The failure of businesses to fully implement these international due diligence standards was tragically emphasized to Western jurists by an event that underlined the failure of multinational companies from Western countries to ensure the respect of human rights by their foreign partners in the least developed countries: the collapse of the Rana Plaza building. This tragic incident sparked great controversy because of the gross violations of labor law

[10] Organisation for Economic Co-operation and Development (OECD), *OECD Guidelines for Multinational Enterprises*, June 27, 2000, available at: https://www.refworld.org/docid/425bd34c4.html.

[11] United Nations, *Guiding Principles on Business and Human Rights: Implementing the United Nations "Protect, Respect and Remedy" Framework*, 2011.

[12] UN Office of the High Commissioner for Human Rights, *Business and Human Rights: Towards a Decade of Global Implementation*, https://www.ohchr.org/sites/default/files/Documents/Issues/Business/UNGPsBHRnext10/UNPGs10plus_Launch_report.pdf.

[13] OECD (2011), *OECD Guidelines for Multinational Enterprises*, OECD Publishing. http://dx.doi.org/10.1787/9789264115415-en.

[14] Code A–ep - MEDEF révisé de gouverneme't d'entreprise des sociétés cotées », January 2020, accessible here: https://www.medef.com/fr/content/code-afep-medef-revise-de-gouvernement-dentreprise-des-societes-cotees-janvier-2020.

standards that occurred there; safety standards were overlooked by the manufacturers, who, despite concerns over the structural stability of the building, threatened to retain the wages of workers who refused to come to work. This incident resulted in a global push to improve corporate social responsibility (CSR), specifically in France.[15]

Before the incident, few CSR instruments had been introduced in France. The 2010 "Grenelle II" law for environmental protection introduced a mandatory CSR annual report for companies who employ over 500 workers or have revenue greater than EUR€100 million.[16] Its scope was therefore limited and did not include enforcement mechanisms. Further, the "Loi Canfin," adopted on July 7, 2014, encourages companies to comply with international soft-law standards on business and human rights. It states: "France encourages companies headquartered in France and established abroad to implement the guiding principles set out by the OECD for multinational enterprises and the Guiding Principles on Business and Human Rights adopted by the United Nations Human Rights Council."[17] But these were only non-binding measures, that were being marginally applied by French companies.

2. *European Regulations in Specific Areas*

The Law was also influenced by the progress of certain specific EU regulations. These include sectoral obligations imposing a duty of care on companies with operations in the sensitive areas of raw materials: wood in 2010 and certain metals from conflict zones in 2017.[18,19] The EU also adopted a directive on non-financial reporting in 2014, which includes the obligation for companies and groups exceeding certain thresholds, to account for obligations relating to environmental, social, and employee-related matters, respect for human rights, anti-corruption and bribery.[20] This directive is currently under revision as a result of the Commission's recent proposal for a Corporate Sustainability Reporting Directive (CSRD)[21]

[15] Duty of vigilance law Parliamentary debates, Opinion n° 2625 of member of Parliament Ms. Le Loch, March 10, 2015: « Catastrophes like the Rana Plaza cannot re-occur without parent companies facing the consequences » (« Des drames comme le Rana Plaza ne peuvent se reproduire sans conséquences pour les sociétés mères »), accessible here: https://www.assemblee-nationale.fr/14/rapports/r2625.asp.

See also Duty of vigilance law Parliamentary debates, Senate Report n° 74 by Senator Mr. Frassa, October 14, 2015, page 9, accessible here: http://www.senat.fr/rap/l15-074/l15-0741.pdf.

[16] The 2010 Law on the national commitent to the environment (Loi n° 2010-788 du 12 juillet 2010 portant engagement national pour l'environnement, accessible here: https://www.legifrance.gouv.fr/loda/id/JORFTEXT000022470434/.

[17] Loi n° 2014-773 du 7 juillet 2014 d'orientation et de programmation relative à la politique de développement et de solidarité internationale, accessible here: https://www.legifrance.gouv.fr/loda/id/JORFTEXT000029210384/.

[18] Regulation (EU) No. 995/2010 of 20 October 2010 laying down the obligations of operators who place timber and timber products on the market (https://eur-lex.europa.eu/legal-content/EN/TXT/HTML/?uri=CELEX:32010R0995&from=FR).

[19] Regulation 2017/821 of 17 May 2017 laying down supply chain due diligence obligations for European Union importers of tin, tantalum, and tungsten, their ores, and gold originating from conflict-affected and high-risk areas ((https://eur-lex.europa.eu/legal-content/EN/TXT/HTML/?uri=CELEX:32017R0821&from=FR).

[20] Directive 2014/95/EU of 22 October 2014 amending Directive 2013/34/EU as regards disclosure of non-financial and diversity information by certain large undertakings and groups (https://eur-lex.europa.eu/legal-content/EN/TXT/?uri=CELEX%3A32014L0095).

[21] Proposal for a DIRECTIVE OF THE EUROPEAN PARLIAMENT AND OF THE COUNCIL amending Directive 2013/34/EU, Directive 2004/109/EC, Directive 2006/43/EC and Regulation (EU) No. 537/2014, as regards corporate sustainability reporting (https://ec.europa.eu/info/business-economy-euro/company-reporting-and-auditing/company-reporting/corporate-sustainability-reporting_en).

that would extend the scope of the companies covered to all large and all listed companies, require the audit (assurance) of reported information and strengthen the standardization of reported information by empowering the Commission to adopt sustainability reporting standards.

3. *Common Law Jurisprudence on the Duty of Care*

Although somewhat more indirectly, the Law was also inspired by the concept of a duty of care from case law in common law countries, pursuant to which a parent company can be held liable for the actions of its subsidiaries. Essentially, the duty of care principle rejects the strict limitation of responsibility by the parent company for any actions of its subsidiaries.

B. Progress Toward the Law

1. *Emergence of Liability for Lack of Vigilance in French Tort Law*

In France, as a result of the above-mentioned sources of inspiration, there has been a growing movement to improve compliance and corporate accountability for human rights abuses throughout the supply chain and of all French companies wherever they operate.

In the EU, a number of NGOs have been key drivers behind the Law through their calls for action and the launch of citizen mobilization campaigns to raise awareness regarding corporate accountability in the fields of human rights and environmental protection. These civil society movements have driven political will and resulted in the adoption of corporate reporting obligations, notably on environmental and human rights standards, both from French lawmakers directly and through the transposition of EU directives into French law.[22]

The concept of vigilance is not new in French law, but it has traditionally applied to individual responsibility of the company under the civil law principle of individual responsibility, which limits responsibility of a company for the acts of other companies. The fault of a subsidiary was thus treated as entailing the liability only of that company and not of the parent company, unless it could be shown that the parent interfered in the management of the subsidiary.

[22] These reporting obligations are contained in the following:

The 2001 law for New Economic Regulations (NRE) (Loi n° 2001-420 relative aux Nouvelles Régulations Économiques, 15 mai 2001, accessible here: https://www.legifrance.gouv.fr/loda/id/JORFTEXT000000223114/.

The 2010 Law on the national commitment to the environment (Loi n° 2010-788 du 12 juillet 2010 portant engagement national pour l'environnement, accessible here: https://www.legifrance.gouv.fr/loda/id/JORFTEXT000022470434/.

The 2016 decree issued in application of article 173-IV of the law on energy transition for green growth (which promotes circular economy, anti-waste policies and reporting on direct and indirect emissions) (Décret n° 2016-1138 du 19 août 2016 pris pour l'application de l'article L. 225-102-1 du code de commerce et relatif aux informations environnementales figurant dans le rapport de gestion des entreprises accessible here: https://www.legifrance.gouv.fr/loda/id/JORFTEXT000033053035/.

The 2017 executive order relating to the publication of non-financial information by certain large companies and certain corporations transposing the *non-financial reporting* European directive ("NFRD") dated October 22, 2014 (Décret n° 2017-1265 du 9 août 2017 pris pour l'application de l'ordonnance n° 2017-1180 du 19 juillet 2017 relative à la publication d'informations non financières par certaines grandes entreprises et certains groupes d'entreprises, accessible here: https://www.legifrance.gouv.fr/jorf/id/JORFTEXT000035401863/.

Referring to the existence of a vigilance obligation, which was merely based on case law and only concerned a corporate's own activities, French courts had held corporations accountable for damage caused by their activities, for example in cases of nuisance.[23] Also, in a number of high-profile decisions in the medical field, the Court of Cassation (Cour de Cassation) has established the lack of vigilance as a breach of a due diligence standard in determining that the company took inadequate measures to limit the risks arising from its activities.[24] This jurisprudence could be compared to the duty of care in the case of activities over which the company had control, although it always concerned a case of corporate liability for negligence and did not apply to the entire supply chain; nor did it allow for preventive action.

Specifically in its 2006 Distilbene decision, the Court of Cassation ruled that a pharmaceutical laboratory breached its duty of vigilance when it allowed the market launch of a drug without sufficient prior safety testing, based on the general civil liability provisions of the French Civil Code (articles 1231-1 and 1240).[25] In its decision, the Court of Cassation stated:

> However, considering the Court of Appeals noted that before 1971 and since 1953-1954, doubts existed concerning the safety of Distilbene and the experimental and scientific data reported the occurrence of very different types of cancer; and in addition, from 1971, numerous experimental studies and clinical observations recommended against the use of Distilbene. The Court was therefore able to conclude, without misinterpreting the expert reports that the company XXX, aware of these scientifically proven and identified risks, had taken no action when it should have, even as they were aware of conflicting results as to the advantages and disadvantages of the medicine. The Court concluded the company had failed its obligation of vigilance.[26]

[23] In neighborhood nuisance cases, courts have established the "abnormal neighborhood nuisance" (trouble anormal de voisinage) as a legal standard to establish a duty of care relating to one's activities on their property, including industrial companies. The notion of nuisance is strongly related to environmental damage and liability, as it includes air, water, and soil pollution, emissions, noise, etc.

See Cour de Cassation, Chambre civile 2, 19 novembre 1986, 84-16.379, accessible here: https://www.legifrance.gouv.fr/juri/id/JURITEXT000007017687/; Cour de Cassation, Chambre civile 2e, 28 mai 2009, n° 06-19.027.

[24] Cass. 1re civ. 7 March 2006 [2 judgments], appeals Nos. 04-16.179 and 04-16.180, Bull. civ. I, Nos. 142 and 143; RTD civ.2006, p. 565, obs. P. Jourdain; 1re esp., D. 2006, IR p. 812, and NDLR, accessible here: https://www.legifrance.gouv.fr/juri/id/JURITEXT000007050790/. See in particular the whereas of principle concerning doubts about the safety of a drug: "*UCB Pharma, which, in the face of these known risks and scientifically identified, had not taken any action, which it should have done even in the presence of conflicting results regarding the advantages and disadvantages, had failed in its duty of care*".

[25] French Civil Code, articles 1231-1 and 1240.

[26] Cass, *supra* note 24.

« la Cour d'Appel a constaté qu'existaient avant 1971 et dès les années 1953-1954 des doutes portant sur l'innocuité du distilbène que la littérature expérimentale faisait état de la survenance de cancers très divers et qu'en outre, à partir de 1971, de nombreuses études expérimentales et des observations cliniques contre-indiquaient l'utilisation du distilbène; qu'elle a pu en déduire sans dénaturer les rapports d'expertise, que la société UCB Pharma qui, devant ces risques connus et identifiés sur le plan scientifique, n'avait pris aucune mesure, ce qu'elle aurait dû faire même en présence de résultats discordants quant aux avantages et inconvénients, avait manqué à son obligation de vigilance ».

Other decisions using a general due diligence standard were decided by French courts on the basis of other civil liability provisions, including cases of neighborhood nuisance, as noted above, and cases in which a bank failed to exercise its duty of vigilance in supervising its clients' activities—the professional standard relating to a reasonably diligent banker.[27] Thus, the duty of diligence derived from civil case law, coupled with the UNGPs' soft-law principles derived from international law, served as seeds for development of the Duty of Vigilance Law.

2. *Affirmation of an Environmental Duty of Care*

In the environmental field, French law already included a general obligation of environmental vigilance based on Articles 1 and 2 of the Charter for the Environment (France amended its Constitution in 2005 to include the Charter for the Environment that lays out France's commitment to supporting the right to a 'balanced environment').[28] These articles, which provide that "[e]veryone has the right to live in a healthy environment" and that "[e]veryone has the duty to take part in the preservation and improvement of the environment," were included in the French constitutional texts in 2005. The existence of a general duty of vigilance for environmental damage was further affirmed in a 2011 Constitutional Court (Conseil constitutionnel) decision that provides: The rights and duties set out in general terms by the articles [of the Charter] are applicable not only to public powers and administrative authorities in their respective fields of competence, but also on all persons; that it follows from these provisions that *all persons are bound by duty of vigilance with regard to environmental damage which could result from their activity* (emphasis added).[29]

According to Mr. Franck Terrier, former President of the Third Civil Chamber of the Court of Cassation:

> As interpreted by the April 8, 2011 Constitutional Court decision, the Charter creates a duty of vigilance that is applicable not only to public powers and administrative authorities but to every person, each being required to respond to environmental damage that could result from their activity; and the right to a legal action cannot be restricted under conditions which distort its scope. These principles establish that it is up to the judges to bring them to life.[30]

---

[27] For neighborhood nuisance, *see Cour de Cassation, Chambre civile 2, 19 novembre 1986, 84-16.379*, accessible here: https://www.legifrance.gouv.fr/juri/id/JURITEXT000007017687/; Civ. 2e, 3 mars 2016, n° 14.14-534.
For the professional duty of vigilance bankers, *see* article L.333-2-1 of the French Consommation Code.
See also Cass. Com. 7 juillet 1996, n° 94-17.119, available here: https://blog.osezvosdroits.com/wp-content/uploads/2016/08/Cass.-Com.-7-juillet-1996-n%C2%B094-17.119.pdf; *Cass. Civ. 12 juillet 2005, n° 03-10.921*, accessible here: https://blog.osezvosdroits.com/wp-content/uploads/2016/08/Cass.-Civ.-12-juillet-2005-n%C2%B003-10.921.pdf.

[28] *Loi constitutionnelle n° 2005-205 du 1er mars 2005* relative à la Charte de l'environnement, accessible in English here: https://www.conseil-constitutionnel.fr/sites/default/files/as/root/bank_mm/anglais/charter_environnement.pdf.

[29] Decision n° 2011-116, QPC "*Michel z*", 8 April 2011.

[30] Nomenclature des préjudices environnementaux, Préface Franck TERRIER Président de la troisième Chambre civile de la Cour de cassation, p. 7.

The duty of environmental vigilance therefore applies to a wide range of companies. It not only implies a duty to prevent known risks, but also a duty of care against unforeseeable risks. Above all, preventive measures must be adapted to the severity and importance of the risk of damage incurred on the basis of the best available scientific evidence.[31]

C. Procedural Background for the Duty of Vigilance Law

In November 2013, a first legislative bill was introduced on the floor of the French Parliament in order to improve French companies' due diligence legal obligations.[32] After the first bill was rejected and another bill was introduced in February 2015, Members of Parliament discussed the proposed law during the following months. Notably, the role of civil society in the corporate due diligence process was heavily debated: some Members of Parliament criticized the fact that NGOs would have an ambivalent role as both judge and party, since they would be involved in the development of the plan within the company and subsequently would be likely to take legal action in the event of noncompliance.[33] They also argued that relevant civil society organizations should be involved in drafting the Vigilance Plan, which idea was ultimately included in the law as such:

> The vigilance plan is meant to be designed in cooperation with stakeholders within the society, through multi-party initiatives in specific sectors or in a given space, when appropriate.[34]

The Parliamentary debates stretched over several months, from March 2015 to February 2017.[35] Had it not been for the admirable determination of Member of Parliament Dominique Potier, who filed not less than three parliamentary reports supporting the adoption of the Law, the bill would not have passed. Indeed, Mr. Potier argued that the Law was a great

[31] United Nations, *Draft articles on Prevention of Transboundary Harm from Hazardous Activities, with commentaries*, Report of the International Law Commission on the work of its fifty-third session, UN Doc. A/RES/56/82 (2001), UN Doc. A/56/10, 2001: "*[w]hat can be considered a reasonable degree of vigilance or diligence may change over time; what may be considered an appropriate procedure, standard or rule and reasonable at one time may not be reasonable at [such other] time. Accordingly, the duty of care necessary to ensure that the obligation of States to stay updated regarding technological and scientific progress in the field of operational safety*", point 11, page 154, accessible here: https://legal.un.org/ilc/texts/instruments/english/commentaries/9_7_2001.pdf.

This indication on the notion of vigilance is entirely relevant to the duty of vigilance under French law (see "the definition of the duty of vigilance of the pharmaceutical laboratory" by A. GOSSEMENT, Liability of pharmaceutics laboratory with regard to marketed drugs, Recueil Dalloz 2004, p.2071).

[32] Bill regarding the duty of vigilance of parent companies and ordering companies, November 6, 2013, accessible here: https://www.assemblee-nationale.fr/14/propositions/pion1519.asp.

[33] Duty of vigilance law Parliamentary debates, Report n° 2627 by member of Parliament Mr. Serge Bardy, March 11, 2015, accessible here: https://www.assemblee-nationale.fr/14/rapports/r2627.asp. *See also* Duty of vigilance law Parliamentary debates, Senate Report n° 74 by Senator Mr. Frassa, October 14, 2015, accessible here: http://www.senat.fr/rap/l15-074/l15-0741.pdf.

[34] Article L.225-102-4-I of the French Commercial Code.

[35] Duty of vigilance law Parliamentary debates, https://www.senat.fr/dossier-legislatif/ppl14-376.html.

A. Scope of the Duty of Vigilance Law

1. *Definition of Covered Companies*

In order to fall within the law's scope, according to Article L.225-102-4 of France's Commercial Code, companies must satisfy three criteria: (i) be incorporated in France; (ii) the incorporation is in one of the commercial corporate forms (mainly limited liability companies and similar forms: *SA, SAS, SCA*); and (iii) the corporation employs over 5,000 employees in France, or 10,000 worldwide including within their direct and indirect subsidiaries in France and abroad, for a minimum of two consecutive financial years.[40] Companies are obligated to publish a Vigilance Plan, unless they can prove that they are owned by a parent company that is itself subject to the publication of a Vigilance Plan and is already complying with this obligation.[41] According to the list formulated by NGOs CCFD-Terre Solidaire and Sherpa, 265 French companies met these criteria in 2020.[42]

2. *Applicability in Multi-Tiered Supply Chains*

Beyond the determination of the companies subject to the publication of the Vigilance Plan, the question arises of defining the extent of the vigilance measures. In particular, should the Vigilance Plan exhaustively cover all of the company's suppliers and subcontractors, or is the vigilance limited to a direct relationship between the company and its suppliers and subcontractors?

The Duty of Vigilance Law provides that it applies to three levels of the parent company's entire value-chain: the first level is the parent company; the second level is the company's subsidiaries in which it directly or indirectly holds majority voting rights (or over which it exercises de facto control); and the third level is its subcontractors and suppliers, with whom the company shares an "established commercial relationship." The term "established commercial relationship" is not defined in the Law, but French case law has clearly expressed that the commercial relationship must be one that is "consistent, stable and habitual" in order to be considered established.[43] A "subcontracting relationship" was defined by a 1975 law, which states that "subcontracting is the operation by which a contractor entrusts through a subcontract, and under his responsibility, to another person called a subcontractor the execution of all or part of the business contract or part of the public contract concluded with the contracting authority."[44]

The authors advocate that the liability be applicable throughout the whole value chain: subsidiaries, suppliers, and subcontractors, direct and indirect. Limitation of this Law's scope to only first-tier suppliers and subcontractors would mean that the Duty of Vigilance Law is

[40] Article L.225-102-4 of the Loi de Vigilance.

[41] Alinea 2 of same article is providing that: "*Subsidiaries or controlled companies that exceed the thresholds mentioned in the first paragraph are deemed to comply with the obligations set out in this article if the company that controls them, within the meaning of article L. 233-3, draws up and implements a due diligence plan relating to the activity of the company and all the subsidiaries or companies it controls*".

[42] Terre Solidaire, Sherpa, « Le radar du devoir de vigilance: Identifier les entreprises soumises à la loi », 2020 edition, https://plan-vigilance.org/wp-content/uploads/2020/06/2020-06-25-Radar-DDV-Edition-2020.pdf.

[43] Cass. Com., 15 septembre 2009, n° 08-19200, Bull. IV, n° 110.

[44] Loi n° 75-1334 du 31 décembre 1975 relative à la sous-traitance, article 1.

largely ineffective. In the case of the Rana Plaza disaster, which was one of the sources that led to the adoption of the Law, the workers were employed by indirect suppliers of major multinational companies, who would not be liable if the scope was limited to a first-tier level.[45] Moreover, the Law's rapporteur cited "the example of a cascade of seventeen subcontractors (which) was thus delivered to your rapporteur during the hearings he organized."[46]

The question remains as to whether the Law applies beyond France's borders, and if so, how. The Duty of Vigilance Law applies to companies (commercial companies, as defined by case law) that are headquartered in France with subsidiaries abroad, as long as they employ over 10,000 workers on a global basis, and therefore, regardless of whether they are incorporated in France or another country. As long as there is an established commercial relationship with a French company covered under the Law, then human rights impacts and environmental risks occurring in the whole group's supply chain, including beyond France's borders, are covered under the Law. Since the Law applies to breaches of the duty of vigilance by a parent company headquartered in France through its commercial partners abroad, the Duty of Vigilance Law's scope can be regarded as indirectly extra-territorial.

However, the Law's application to indirect suppliers and subcontractors, other than those in the first tier, or stated otherwise, holding the parent company liable for its entire supply chain even in the case of complex and multi-tiered supply chains is debated by several authors.[47] Companies generally advocate that if they are held responsible for the activities of their entire supply chain, this would imply potential liability by the parent company for the acts of a third party over which the parent company exercises little to no influence to change the third party's harmful practices. The purpose of the due diligence process is to make the parent company liable—it is the most efficient remedy to any risks resulting from activities within the whole supply chain. This is a key outstanding issue regarding the Law's application, and decisions on the matter are eagerly expected.

B. The Vigilance Plan

The Duty of Vigilance Law imposes a duty to draft, publish, effectively implement, and report annually on the implementation of a Vigilance Plan.[48] The law thus mentions that the plan must be composed of the following five measures, which will be described and analyzed below:

> "1. A risk mapping intended for the identification, analysis and prioritization of the [risks and serious breaches resulting from the companies' activities];

---

[45] Sherpa, Vigilance Plans Reference Guidance, 2019, page 33, available here: https://www.asso-sherpa.org/wp-content/uploads/2019/02/Sherpa_VPRG_EN_WEB-VF-compressed.pdf.

[46] Duty of vigilance law Parliamentary debates, Report n° 2628 (November 2, 2016).

[47] Emmanuel Daoud, Solene Sfoggia, « Les entreprises face aux premiers contentieux de la Loi sur le devoir de vigilance », Revue des juristes de Sciences Po n° 16, January 2019, page 97, accessible here: http://www.avocatparis.org/system/files/worksandcommissions/e.-daoud-s.-sfoggia-premiers-contentieux-devoir-de-vigilance.pdf.

Sophie Schiller, « Exégèse de la Loi relative au devoir de vigilance des sociétés mères et entreprises donneuses d'ordre », *La Semaine juridique - Entreprise et affaires*, LexisNexis, 2017, page 4.

[48] Article L.225-102-4-I of the French Commercial Code.

2. Procedures for regular assessment of the situation of subsidiaries, subcontractors or suppliers with whom an established commercial relationship is maintained, with regard to risk mapping;

3. Appropriate actions to mitigate risks or prevent serious damage (. . .);

4. A mechanism for alerting and collecting alerts relating to the existence or identification of risks, established in consultation with representative trade union organisations in the said company; and

5. A system for monitoring measures implemented and evaluating their effectiveness."[49]

The law does not specify exactly what each of these measures should contain and how they should be applied in practice. Since no precise guidance has been provided under the Law, the French NGO Sherpa (specialist in investigating international financial and environmental crimes that played a principal role during parliamentary debates over this law) published comprehensive guidelines in order to specify the extent of the requirements.[50] Below, we will detail each requirement according to available guidance, provided by NGOs, and based on the first applications made by the companies themselves.

1. A Risk-Mapping Process

The Law prescribes that the risk-mapping process identify any risks and serious breaches resulting from companies' activities that have negative impacts on individuals' health, physical security, other human rights and fundamental freedoms, and the environment.

The level of mapping detail is not precisely defined by law. However, several references can be used to determine the level expected from companies. Guidance published by the NGO Sherpa has described, in a very precise manner and with reference to international standards, the methodology applicable to risk mapping. Sherpa's guidelines state that the risk mapping should include a sufficient amount of detail to enable any person to identify accurately the risks within the substantial and organisational perimeters of the group. Inaccurate risk mapping would not comply with the obligation of making public the Vigilance Plan as it should help identify risks and violations of human rights and environmental standards, which are necessarily specific.[51]

In determining the nature of this mapping requirement, a comparison can be made with the Sapin 2 Act, modeled on the UK Bribery Act,[52] and the US Foreign Corrupt Practices Act,[53] which provide for a similar obligation to establish risk mapping, even though it is spe-

[49] Sherpa, *supra* note 45, at 17, available here: https://www.asso-sherpa.org/wp-content/uploads/2019/02/Sherpa_VPRG_EN_WEB-VF-compressed.pdf.

[50] *Ibid*, note 46.

[51] L. 225-102-4, point 5 of the French Commercial Code: "*The vigilance plan and the report on its effective implementation are made public and included in the report mentioned in Article L. 225-102*". (original in French: "*Le plan de vigilance et le compte rendu de sa mise en œuvre effective sont rendus publics et inclus dans le rapport mentionné à l'article L. 225-102.*")

[52] United Kingdom Parliament, UK Bribery Act 2010, 2010 CHAPTER 23.

[53] The Foreign Corrupt Practices Act of 1977 (FCPA), Pub. L. 95-213, 91 Stat. 1494 (1977), 15 U.S.C. §§78dd-1, et seq.

cific to the fight against corruption.[54] France's Anti-Corruption Agency has recently published its guidelines detailing the objectives and modalities of mapping, as well as involvement of all management positions in the company.[55] However, in order to fulfil the overarching aim of the Duty of Vigilance Law, the risk-mapping process requires companies to shift their approach from one of risk management, which generally consists of internal audit operations aimed at identifying risks to the company itself, to a focus on risks to stakeholders' rights.

2. *Evaluation Procedures to Assess Subsidiaries, Subcontractors, and Suppliers*

Second, the parent company is required to develop and publish procedures for regular evaluations of its subsidiaries, in which it directly or indirectly holds majority voting rights, and subcontractors and suppliers with whom the company shares an established commercial relationship. These evaluations must cover all risks and serious violations that may occur in the entire supply chain. The obligation to assess the situation of these subsidiaries, subcontractors, and suppliers falls on the parent company because of the due diligence it must exercise on the activities it controls and on activities of entities that form part of its supply chain, including entities outside France.

Specifically, companies are legally required to determine and publish information about tools, methodology, objectives, and timetables used to identify and evaluate risks, which then facilitates an objective appraisal of the company's approach. The company should also publish information about its selection of indicators and methods used to develop its indicators, as well as the results of its evaluation of adverse human rights, labor rights and environmental impacts of the subsidiaries,' subcontractors,' and suppliers' activities. Publication of this data over several years will make it possible to identify gaps, shortcomings, and/or progress made.

3. *Appropriate Actions to Mitigate Risks or Prevent Serious Damage*

The importance of the previously mentioned risk mapping and supply chain assessment is indicated by the obligation, under the Law, for companies to demonstrate preventive, mitigation, and remedial measures for these risks and serious breaches throughout its supply chains.[56] A specific timeline for the formulation and implementation of appropriate measures should be identified for each risk, and serious harms identified.[57]

[54] Law on Transparency, the Fight Against Corruption and the Modernization of Economic Life, 2016. (Loi n° 2016-1691 du 9 décembre 2016 relative à la transparence, à la lutte contre la corruption et à la modernisation de la vie économique), available here: https://www.legifrance.gouv.fr/jorf/id/JORFTEXT000033558528/.

[55] French Anti-corruption Agency, Recommendations to help public and private legal entities to prevent and detect instances of corruption, influence peddling, misappropriation, illegal taking of interest, embezzlement of public funds and favoritism, 2021 https://www.agence-francaise-anticorruption.gouv.fr/files/2021-03/French%20AC%20Agency%20Guidelines%20.pdf.

[56] Article L.225-102-4-I 3° of the French Commercial Code.

[57] Article L.225-102-4-I of the French Commercial Code: « *The Vigilance Plan and the report on its effective implementation are made public and included in the report mentioned in Article L. 225-102* » (« *Le plan de vigilance et le compte rendu de sa mise en œuvre effective sont rendus publics et inclus dans le rapport mentionné à l'article L. 225-102* »).

According to the Law, such measures (actions) implemented by the company must be "reasonable."[58] This legal term can be understood as setting a minimum standard pursuant to which vigilance measures can be assessed as "adequate, proportionate, and feasible" from both business and practical perspectives.[59] Currently, lawyers and other legal professionals in France are debating the strength of the parent company's obligation as to whether these obligations should be considered as "obligations of means" rather than "obligations of results" (*obligation de moyens* or *obligation de résultat*). "Obligation of means" would mean that companies owing a duty of vigilance must mobilize all the resources at their disposal to perform their obligations under the Law, and the latter would mean companies must do everything they can to limit damage.

The authors advocate for a compromise between the two, to establish a "reasonable" standard according to the level of risk involved: companies would have to do all they can, considering the seriousness of risks and breaches. A simple obligation of means would not be sufficient to limit serious risks or ensure a remedy for a serious injury in situations where there is a risk or a violation of a fundamental right, for example in the case of severe environmental damage due to global warming. Indeed, a purely informative or documentary-like mechanism would not be sufficient to limit such particularly serious risk or to remedy the consequences of a serious injury. This approach is similar to the appraisal made by the UK Supreme Court in the *Vedanta* decision, described in detail below in Section V.D., for determining whether the parent company exercised a degree of control over the subsidiary that allows, under the law, for a duty of care to be ascribed to the parent company for persons harmed by the actions of the subsidiary. However, the nature of the parent company's obligation under the Duty of Vigilance Law is primarily preventive rather than remedial.

4. *Mechanism for Alerting and Collecting Alerts*

Companies must also establish a mechanism that alerts them to the existence of any impacts or risks, and it must do so in cooperation with stakeholders ("*parties prenantes*"), including trade union organizations considered to represent company employees. This measure reflects the requirement, under Principle 29 of the UNGPs, that companies establish or participate in operational-level grievance mechanisms. Businesses can either create their own grievance mechanism or participate in mechanisms established by other entities. Some civil society organizations and independent organizations have established these mechanisms, particularly in the field of labor rights. For example, the Fair Labor Association (FLA),[60] the Workers Rights Consortium (WRC),[61] the Ethical Trading Initiative (ETI),[62] and Social Accountability International (SAI)[63] are entities that have created such mechanisms.

[58] Article L.225-102-4-I 3° of the French Commercial Code.

[59] E. Daoud, S. Sfoggia, « Les entreprises face aux premiers contentieux de la Loi sur le devoir de vigilance », *Revue des juristes de Sciences Po*, n° 16, janvier 2019.

[60] www.fairlabor.org.

[61] www.workersrights.org.

[62] www.ethicaltrade.org.

[63] www.sa-intl.org.

It is recommended that implemented alert mechanisms be confidential and, if possible, be conducted by an independent entity, allowing individuals and entities to formulate a complaint relating to risks and/or impacts of the company's activities.[64] The accessibility, adaptability, security, and confidentiality of these mechanisms are essential to ensure effectiveness of the remedy. Indeed, companies must verify that complaints are not only properly sent and received, but also that they constitute an adequate legal basis for reparative measures, that is, remedies for the harms.

5. *System for Monitoring Measures Implemented and Evaluating Their Effectiveness*

Lastly, companies subject to the Duty of Vigilance Law must implement a monitoring scheme to follow up on measures taken to address the risks and violations the company has identified within its supply chain.

According to Sherpa guidance and case law relative to the civil obligation of a company to act as normally diligent, it is recommended that the company publish information about its monitoring in an accessible, clear, understandable, and exhaustive way, and in a manner that identifies and prevents risks and infringements. Regular updates must therefore be implemented as soon as a new risk is identified or a measure proves to be insufficient in addressing human rights harms and environmental risks.

The Vigilance Plan is primarily envisioned as a prevention tool to identity and report "severe violations of human rights and fundamental freedoms, serious bodily injury or environmental damage or health risks" resulting from operations of covered companies. Companies are responsible for identifying their risks and defining their priority actions in order to fully comply with obligations to prevent and report such violations, damage, or risks. Some have criticized this approach because it does not provide enough definitional clarity and guidance.[65] Others, mainly company representatives, praise the flexibility given to companies, which allows them to adapt the content of their Vigilance Plan to their particular situation instead of merely engaging in a "tick-the-box" exercise.[66]

---

[64] French Anti-corruption Agency, Recommendations to help public and private legal entities to prevent and detect instances of corruption, influence peddling, misappropriation, illegal taking of interest, embezzlement of public funds and favoritism, 2018, available here: https://www.agence-francaise-anticorruption.gouv.fr/files/2018-10/2017_-_Recommandations_AFA.pdf.

[65] P-L Périn, Devoir de vigilance et responsabilité illimitée des entreprises: qui trop embrasse mal étreint, RTD com. 2015, 215.

[66] Sandra Cossart, Tiphaine Beau de Loménie, Antoine Lubrani, « *Extension du domaine de la vigilance, la Loi sur le devoir de vigilance, au-delà de la compliance* », Revue des juristes de Science Po n° 16, January 2019, page 90, accessible here: https://www.asso-sherpa.org/wp-content/uploads/2019/02/Sherpa-Extension-du-domaine-de-la-vigilance.pdf. « *However, by restricting the duty of vigilance to internal vigilance procedures, it is to be feared that the desired corporate behavior change will be replaced by a "tick-the-box" approach regarding the required procedures, without these inducing a real change of paradigm in the Human Rights sphere.* » (translation from French: « *Néanmoins, en restreignant le devoir de vigilance à des procédures internes de vigilance, il est à craindre que le changement de comportement visé soit remplacé par une approche symbolique de "tickboxing" des procédures exigées sans que celles-ci induisent un véritable changement de paradigme dans l'approche des droits humains.* »)

6. *Stakeholder Involvement in the Development of the Plan*

According to article L.225-102-4, paragraph 4 of the Duty of Vigilance Law, "the plan is to be drawn up in association with the stakeholders." It appears that the Law only refers to stakeholders' consultation as a possibility for companies covered under the Law. But, during the parliamentary process, the role of the stakeholders, specifically the role of trade unions and NGOs, in elaborating the Vigilance Plan was considered crucial to ensuring that the Law would be fully effective.

The involvement of stakeholders, namely NGOs and trade unions, represents a cornerstone of the Duty of Vigilance Law. Indeed, it ensures the effectiveness of due diligence with respect to some risks and damage that companies may not wish to disclose (and may prefer to hide or attempt to conceal), particularly those operating in foreign countries or with complex supply chains. Recent human rights and climate jurisprudence emphasizes the prevailing role of NGOs in bringing such cases before French courts.[67] In practice, compliance with the obligations of the Vigilance Plan creates a quasi-obligation for companies, in our opinion, as the stakeholders are best able to alert the parent company and suggest appropriate measures to limit the risks and harms. In this connection, it should be noted that the draft EU directive on mHRDD developed by the European Parliament includes an obligation to consult stakeholders.[68]

C. Accountability Regime and Enforcement Mechanisms

The Law relies on self-regulation but also contains a judicial sanctions mechanism based on tort law civil liability provisions. This "form of marriage between soft and hard law"[69] has led certain authors to describe the Law as a form of "coregulation," a concept developed by the Perelman Center for Legal Philosophy.[70] The notion of "coregulation" is based on the recognition of the role played by private actors in regulation standards and a critical perspective on the State's monopoly in the production of regulatory standards.[71]

[67] The Conversation, *Climate change: when civil society multiplies legal actions* (Changement climatique, quand la société civile multiplie les actions en justice), March 23, 2017, accessible here: https://theconversation.com/changement-climatique-quand-la-societe-civile-multiplie-les-actions-en-justice-74191.

The Case of the Century (L'Affaire du Siècle), brought by the NGOs Notre Affaire à tous, Fondation Nicolas Hulot pour la Nature et l'Homme, Greenpeace France and Oxfam France; on February 3rd, 2021, the Court ruled that the French state was responsible for failing to fully meet its goals in reducing greenhouse emissions; English press release here: http://paris.tribunal-administratif.fr/content/download/179704/1761585/version/2/file/CP%20affaire%20du%20si%C3%A8cle_EN.pdf.

The People of Uganda v. Total case, in which it is alleged that Total breached its duty of vigilance obligations, was brought by the NGOs les Amis de la Terre France, Survie, AFIEGO, CRED, NAPE/Amis de la Terre Ouganda, and NAVODA; English press release here; https://www.foei.org/oil-company-total-faces-historic-legal-action-in-france-for-human-rights-and-environmental-violations-in-uganda-%E2%80%A8/.

The Perenco case, in which it is alleged that the company's activities in the Democratic Republic of Congo have led to unprecedented amounts of pollution, was brought by the NGOs Amis de la Terre France and Sherpa; English press release here: https://www.asso-sherpa.org/continuing-opacity-the-court-denies-access-to-information-on-perencos-oil-activities-2.

[68] Art. 5 of the Parliament draft directive (https://www.europarl.europa.eu/doceo/document/A-9-2021-0018_FR.html).

[69] P. Bas, Rapport de la commission mixte paritaire, n° 99 (2016-2017).

[70] Benoit Frydman, "Coregulation: a possible legal model for global governance", January 1, 2004

[71] T. Sachs, La Loi sur le devoir de vigilance des sociétés-mères et sociétés donneuses d'ordre: les ingrédients d'une corégulation, Rev. Trav. 2017. 380.

2. *Proving a Breach of the Law*

However, there is no presumption of causality under the Duty of Vigilance Law, although NGOs have called for one.[77] The fault of the parent company must also be established. This requires evidence of a failure to establish and/or effectively implement the Vigilance Plan according to the five criteria laid out above.[78] Any omission or inaccuracy in the company's Vigilance Plan will also be considered as a failure by the company to comply with its obligations under the Law.

As a result, the assessment is likely to focus on the meaning and applicability of "reasonable" in connection with the "measures" that the company takes to identify risks and prevent serious violations of human rights and fundamental freedoms, human health and safety, and the environment.[79] The transcript of the parliamentary debates on the Duty of Vigilance Law provides some guidance on this point. Certifications, labels, and partnerships with stakeholders were identified during the debates as measures companies can take to establish proof of an effective implementation of the Vigilance Plan.[80] In contrast, the mere imposition of general environmental, health and safety, and human rights objectives by the company on its commercial partners would not be considered an effective implementation of a Vigilance Plan.[81]

Claimants will likely refer to the standards and norms set by national regulations (including domestic civil liability laws), international agreements and international standards in force within the relevant fields of human rights, health, and environment as prima facie evidence in order to determine the existence of any risk or serious harm caused by the company's activities.[82] During the parliamentary debates, the following sources were identified as norms of reference: the OECD Guidelines for Multinational Enterprises (drawn up as

meeting, but requires judicial review. And this can only be achieved through a strong social control made possible by the publication of the due diligence plan and by a loose definition of the interest to act, the action being very broadly open ('any person justifying an interest to act')." (Order of Pre-Trial Determination, Tribunal judiciaire de Nanterre, 11 February 2021 RG No. 20/00915).

[77] ActionAid, Amnesty International, CCFD-Terre Solidaire and all, « Towards European Legislation on the Responsibility of Multinationals - Recommendations from organizations that have defended the French law on the duty of vigilance » (French title: Vers une législation européenne sur la responsabilité des multinationales - Recommandations d'organisations ayant défendu la Loi française relative au devoir de vigilance), December 2020, accessible here: https://ethique-sur-etiquette.org/IMG/pdf/recommandations-dv-ue-francais-web.pdf.

[78] Article L. 225-102-4-I of the French Commercial Code.

[79] P-L Périn, Devoir de vigilance et responsabilité illimitée des entreprises: qui trop embrasse mal étreint, RTD com. 2015, 215.

See also art. L. 225-102-4-I of the French Commercial Code.

[80] AN, report n° 2628, p. 79; S. Brabant, E. Savourey, A Closer Look at the Penalties Faced by Companies, Revue internationale de la compliance et de l'éthique des affaires 2017, n° 50.

[81] Sachs, *supra* note 71.

[82] "*Due diligence is an obligation of means and not of result. It consists of a series of appropriate measures with the aim of achieving an objective defined in a national or international standard, to respect a minimum level of prudence in the consideration of an external standard.*" (Dominique Potier, report n° 2628 registered on 11 March 2015, II.B.).

early as 1976 and revised in 2011);[83] the International Labour Organization (ILO) Tripartite Declaration of Principles concerning Multinational Enterprises and Social Policy (drafted in 1977 and revised in 2017);[84] the UN Global Compact (introduced in 2000); and at the EU level, the Green Paper on Corporate Social Responsibility.[85] Proof that the company or any entity within its supply chain which is covered under the Law has not complied with the applicable norm shall then be sufficient, pursuant to article 1382 of the French Civil Code, to establish liability on the basis of precise, serious, and consistent presumptions.

Moreover, it is necessary to prove that the company's lack of vigilance has caused the damage: either that the company has been the direct cause of the wrongdoing or, even when it is not directly responsible, that compliance with the obligations of the Law would have allowed it to avoid or limit the damage.[86] When choosing this last approach, the claimants should rely on the notion of "loss of opportunity" ("*perte de chance*," a French legal concept for remedies referring to the deprivation of the reasonably probable occurrence of a positive event or of the non-occurrence of a negative event) caused by the lack of vigilance from the parent company.[87]

IV. Good Practices: Lessons Learned from the Courtroom

This Section will deal with the lessons that can be drawn from the notification letters and lawsuits filed since the Law was passed.

A. Assessment of the First Years of Implementation

Since the Duty of Vigilance Law became effective on March 27, 2017, six companies have been cited (*mis en demeure*) for their failure to have Vigilance Plans that are in compliance with the Duty of Vigilance Law.[88] The breaches that have been identified relate to deforestation (Groupe Casino), climate change (TotalEnergies), labor rights (XPO Logistics, Teleperformance),[89] and the rights of Indigenous peoples (Electricité de France or EDF, Total Energies Uganda). Even though seven formal notices have been sent to point out breaches of

[83] Organisation for Economic Co-operation and Development (OECD), OECD *Guidelines for Multinational Enterprises*, June 27, 2000.

[84] International Labour Organization (ILO), *Tripartite Declaration of Principles concerning Multinational Enterprises and Social Policy*, March 2017.

[85] European Union Commission, *Green Paper Promoting a European Framework for Corporate Social Responsibility, 2001*, accessible here: https://ec.europa.eu/transparency/regdoc/rep/1/2001/EN/1-2001-366-EN-1-0.Pdf.

[86] Article L. 225-102-5 of the French Commercial Code.

[87] "It would be wrong not to act sufficiently to avoid what we knew . . . We can see the probative value of the unilateral juridical act!" (Mathilde Hautereau-Boutonnet. Première assignation d'une entreprise pour non-respect de son devoir de vigilance en matière climatique: quel rôle préventif pour le juge?. Recueil Dalloz, Dalloz, 2020, pp.609).

[88] For the sake of transparency, please note that the author is involved as claimants' counsel in the cases which have been brought against Total, XPO Logistics, and Casino.

[89] https://www.itfglobal.org/sites/default/files/node/news/files/XPO%20letter%202%20page%20summary%20in%20English.pdf.

of the Duty of Vigilance Law (with Total being the recipient of two), only three cases have moved forward to the stage of subpoenas to the companies for questioning on the noncompliance of their Vigilance Plans with the Law.

The first case against Total's subsidiary in Uganda highlights the need for lawyers to continue arguing evolving issues and unanswered questions before courts. In 2019, six NGOs, including Friends of the Earth, filed a lawsuit in France against French oil company Total, for allegedly failing to comply with the Duty of Vigilance Law in their mining project. They demanded Total revise its Vigilance Plan so that it included the contentious project in Uganda. After Total failed to comply within the three-month legal deadline, the plaintiffs filed a lawsuit before the Court of Nanterre, which is in a business district near Paris La Défense, on October 23, 2019. They made the same request before the Court as they had made to Total. On January 30, 2020, the Court of Nanterre declared itself incompetent to rule on the case involving Total's activities in Uganda, arguing that the matter was a commercial matter, and instead referred the matter to a commercial court.[90] The plaintiffs appealed the decision, but the Versailles Court of Appeals ruled in favor of Total and remanded the case to the commercial court.[91] The Court of Appeals did not rule on the merits of the case. This was disappointing for the claimants, and it seemed to settle the jurisdictional question, that is, until a second case was brought against Total for its climate inaction and noncompliance with the Paris Agreement.[92] This second case will be discussed in Section IV.B. below.

The third case was brought on September 21, 2020 by an international coalition of Brazilian, Colombian, American and French NGOs (OPIAC, COIAB, Canopée, Envol Vert, Mighty Earth, Notre Affaire à Tous, and Sherpa) against the French mass-market retail group Casino. This case demonstrates that the Law makes it possible to address major transnational issues such as deforestation and the illegal land-grabbing of Indigenous territories of the Amazon, which resulted from the beef stock supply chains, mainly located in Brazil and Colombia.[93] This action also highlights the importance of thorough investigation, which in this case was carried out by Brazilian reporters and journalists, who collected precise data on farms, suppliers, and wholesalers.

---

[90] Nanterre judicial court, interim order of January 30, 2020, N° 19/02833.

[91] Versailles Court of Appeals, December 10th, 2020, English here: https://www.business-humanrights.org/en/latest-news/total-uganda-case-the-court-of-appeal-of-versailles-remands-the-case-to-the-commercial-court/.

[92] Paris Agreement to the UN Framework Convention on Climate Change, Dec. 12, 2015, T.I.A.S. No. 16-1104: pursuant to Article 2, it is provided that: "*Holding the increase in the global average temperature to well below 2 °C above pre-industrial levels and pursuing efforts to limit the temperature increase to 1.5 °C above pre-industrial levels, recognizing that this would significantly reduce the risks and impacts of climate change.*"

[93] Envol Vert, « Groupe Casino : Eco-responsable de la déforestation », 8 October 2020, http://envol-vert.org/wp-content/uploads/2020/06/Rapport-Casino%C3%A9coresponsable-de-la-d%C3%A9forestation.pdf.

B. Lessons from the Total Climate Case: First Climate Litigation against a Carbon Major in France

The first climate litigation case against a carbon major, a major corporate emitter of CO_2, in France was initiated against Total SA with a formal notice in June 2019, followed by the filing of a claim against the company on January 28, 2020.[94] The claim was brought by a coalition comprised primarily of 14 French cities and regions and five NGOs, Notre Affaire À Tous (NAAT), Sherpa, ZEA, Ecomaires, and France Nature Environnement (FNE).

1. *Mandatory Nature of the Plan and Scope of the Requirements*

In this case, the claimants allege Total's Vigilance Plan does not provide sufficient measures in the face of climate change. This is an innovative legal basis for litigation under the Duty of Vigilance Law that requires courts to determine if international instruments regarding climate change can be a basis for mandatory requirements for the scope of the Vigilance Plan. The case is based on reports from the UN Intergovernmental Panel on Climate Change (IPCC)[95] and scientifically established evidence that the rising temperatures to date have already resulted in profound alterations to human and natural systems, extreme weather, droughts, floods, sea level rise, and biodiversity loss that are causing unprecedented risks to vulnerable persons and populations. The claim is based, on the one hand, on the Duty of Vigilance Law, and, on the other hand, on the Charter for the Environment and civil liability provisions.[96] The claimants are requesting that Total identify and adequately prevent risks and harms pertaining to human rights, health and safety, and the environment that are induced by climate change. As it stands, the action does not seek compensation for past damages; the plaintiffs are only seeking an injunction requiring Total to publish a compliant Vigilance Plan and to take immediate action to stop and prevent climate risks related to its activities. In particular, Total is being asked to significantly cut its emissions by reducing its oil and gas production, in order to limit the increase in global warming to within the 1.5° Celsius objective set out in Article 2 of the 2015 Paris Agreement.

The Court will have to rule on claimants' allegation that Total's Vigilance Plan is non-compliant since it fails to take into account the indirect CO_2 emissions (Scope 3) of Total's global group.[97] The Court will also have to determine whether Total has failed to take into account the climate standards, which provide a reasonable chance for States to limit global warming to 1.5° Celsius, pursuant to the 2018 IPCC report and in accordance with the provisions of Paris Climate Agreement. Indeed, the Duty of Vigilance Law is based on a risk-based

---

94 Hereinafter "the TOTAL Climate Case."

95 The Intergovernmental Panel on Climate Change (IPCC) is the UN body for assessing the science related to climate change. https://www.ipcc.ch/sr15/chapter/spm/.

96 Article 1252 of the French Civil Code.

97 According to the Greenhouse Gas (GHG) Protocol, greenhouse gas emissions are categorized into three groups or 'Scopes' by the most widely used international accounting tool, the Greenhouse Gas (GHG) Protocol. Scope 3 includes all other indirect emissions that occur in a company's value chain: https://ghgprotocol.org/scope-3-technical-calculation-guidance.

approach to persons, making the objectives set by the Paris Agreement potentially legally enforceable against companies. However, Total did not commit to becoming carbon neutral on its worldwide emissions outside the EU,[98] and announced that it maintains its growth objectives for oil and gas production, even though it has been demonstrated by reports from scientific climate organizations such as Carbon Tracker and Oil Change International that these areas of its business are far from compliant with the Paris Agreement.[99]

2. *Practical Procedural Clarification*

In addition, the Total climate case clarified the issue of jurisdiction between civil and commercial courts that was not specified in the Law itself. As noted above, in the very first decision rendered under the Duty of Vigilance Law against Total (Total Uganda) on January 30, 2020, the Nanterre Court declared that it did not have jurisdiction to hear the case, and that the case should be heard by the commercial court.[100] The decision was confirmed on appeal by the Versailles Court of Appeals on December 10, 2020,[101] but on December 15, 2021, the French Supreme Court (*Cour de cassation*) overturned the case, which will therefore return to the first instance to finally be examined on its merits.[102]

In contrast, in an order dated February 11, 2021 relating to the Total climate case, the Court of Nanterre issued a ruling diametrically opposed to the Total Uganda precedent made by the same court and the Versailles Court of Appeals; it held that the civil court should retain jurisdiction over the climate case against Total.[103] This judgment was confirmed on appeal by the Versailles Court of Appeals, which therefore reversed the position taken in its previous decision.[104] The Court confirmed the first instance judgment and based the civil judge's competence on the civil nature of the claims relating to ecological damage.

On November 30, 2021, in the electricité de France (EDF) case brought before the Paris Tribunal (*Tribunal judiciaire de Paris*), the pre-trial judge issued an order confirming the jurisdiction of the civil judge, while raising questions about the requirements of the formal

[98] Committing to climate neutrality by 2050: Commission proposes European Climate Law and consults on the European Climate Pact (https://ec.europa.eu/commission/presscorner/detail/en/IP_20_335.

[99] Climate change has been recognized as environmental harm by the Paris Administrative Court in the "Case of the Century" judgment of 2021: Tribunal administratif de Paris, N° 1904967, 1904968, 1904972, 1904976/4-1, February 3 2021, English press release here: http://paris.tribunal-administratif.fr/content/download/179704/1761585/version/2/file/CP%20affaire%20du%20si%C3%A8cle_EN.pdf. *See also* reports from Carbon Tracker (https://carbontracker.org/resources/) and Oil Change International (http://priceofoil.org/2020/09/23/big-oil-companies-still-failing-on-climate/.)

[100] Nanterre judicial court, interim order of January 30, 2020, N° 19/02833.

[101] Versailles Court of Appeals, December 10, 2020, English here: https://www.business-humanrights.org/en/latest-news/total-uganda-case-the-court-of-appeal-of-versailles-remands-the-case-to-the-commercial-court/.

[102] Cour de cassation, arrêt n° 893 FS-B, pourvoi n° 21-11.882, December 15, 2021, available here: https://www.courdecassation.fr/decision/61b99380ef20f6a61afc3611

[103] Nanterre Judicial Court, 1st Chamber, n° 20/00915, February 11, 2021, available here: https://www.actu-environnement.com/media/pdf/news-37043-ordonnance-tribunal-nanterre-total-devoir-vigilance.pdf.

[104] Versailles Court of Appeals, November 18, 2021, available here: https://www.actu-environnement.com/media/pdf/news-38574-DECISION-CA-Versailles-incident-competence.pdf

notices.[105] Lastly and most likely putting an end to the jurisdiction debate, a law was passed by the French Parliament on December 22, 2021, giving full jurisdiction to civil courts to rule over cases brought under the Duty of Vigilance Law.[106]

Since the remedies for noncompliance with the Law are civil remedies, civil courts should normally be considered to have jurisdiction to rule on serious harms causing physical and health damage, environmental damage, and all violations of human rights or fundamental freedoms. Also, in the authors' view, the fact that the duty of vigilance implies a decision from a corporate entity should not change the civil nature of the vigilance obligations toward the claimants, who are not commercial entities. According to the French legal concept of "actes mixtes," the noncommercial party should be able to bring its action before a civil court.[107]

Any country contemplating the adoption of a mHRDD regime will want to clearly specify the competent jurisdiction with the purpose of ensuring a fair and unbiased assessment by the court and, above all, the determination of sanctions that are sufficiently dissuasive to ensure that companies comply with their duty of vigilance. Although the French Constitutional Court censured the proposed provision of the Law providing for a civil fine of EUR€10 million, which provision is therefore not applicable, it should be noted that the German government has just adopted a law relating to the duty of vigilance that provides for fines of EUR€100,000–800,000, and up to 2 percent of turnover for companies with a turnover of more than EUR€400 million.[108]

V. Outstanding and Evolving Issues: The Future of the Law

Four years after passage of the Duty of Vigilance Law, cases brought before courts have started to draw the contours of the law. These new details have also allowed lawyers and legal professionals to see the potential future evolution of the law at the domestic level and how

---

[105] Ordonnance du juge de la mise en état, Tribunal de Paris, RG n° 10246, 30 novembre 2021, page 10, (original in French: « *L'objet des actions fondées sur les articles L.225-102-4 et L.225-102-5 du code de commerce par les droits qu'elles visent à préserver excède le strict cadre de la gestion de l'entreprise et concerne plus largement l'impact de son activité sur la société (. . .) Il sera en outre relevé que l'article L.225-102-5 du code de commerce fait référence au droit commun de la responsabilité civile, que le tribunal judiciaire est le « juge naturel » du contentieux de la responsabilité civile (. . .). Ces éléments conduisent à retenir pour ces deux actions la compétence du tribunal judiciaire de sorte que l'exception d'incompétence soulevée par la société EDF sera rejetée.* »)

[106] Article 56 of the law: « *Sub-section 2 of section 1 of chapter I of title I of book II of the code of judicial organization is supplemented by an article L. 211-21 worded as follows: "Art. L. 211-21.-The Paris judicial court hears actions relating to the duty of vigilance based on Articles L. 225-102-4 and L. 225-102-5 of the Commercial Code."* (original in French: Loi n° 2021-1729 du 22 décembre 2021 pour la confiance dans l'institution judiciaire, article 56: « *Art. L. 211-21.-Le tribunal judiciaire de Paris connaît des actions relatives au devoir de vigilance fondées sur les articles L. 225-102-4 et L. 225-102-5 du code de commerce* »), available here: https://www.legifrance.gouv.fr/jorf/id/JORFTEXT000044545992.

[107] Cass. Com., 18 novembre 2020, n° 19-19.463, « Uber ».

[108] Supply Chain Act (Lieferkettengesetz), June 11, 2021, available in German here: https://dserver.bundestag.de/btd/19/305/1930505.pdf.

See also Human Rights Watch, *Germany: New Supply Chain Law a Step in the Right Direction - Law's Gaps Should be Fixed by Next Government*, June 11, 2021, available here: https://www.hrw.org/news/2021/06/11/germany-new-supply-chain-law-step-right-direction.

it influences other European legal instruments. On February 23, 2022, the evaluation report on the Law was submitted by MEPs Dubost and Potier, the first rapporteur of the Law.[109]

This report points out several imperfections of the French law, already exposed in this chapter. The report also suggests that the threshold for companies to be subject to the duty of vigilance should be based on turnover and not on the number of employees, should include foreign companies, and should apply to all forms of corporate entities.

A. Compliance

The first question raised about the effectiveness of the Law is whether it ensures the compliance of companies with their legal obligations. The law is quite ambitious and corporate counsel should advise their clients on the scope of its obligations for companies.

An extremely comprehensive study published by the compliance and CSR consulting firm I-Point demonstrates that the risk-mapping and supply chain assessment information provided by companies under the Law is very general and there is no enforcement mechanism if the assessment is not done.[110] The report finds that businesses provide descriptions rather than using their obligations to identify, analyze, and prioritize risks, and to regularly assess the situation with subsidiaries, suppliers, and subcontractors, based on key performance indicators. This analysis shows that most of the Vigilance Plans published by the covered companies are insufficient and that the performance indicators used by the companies do not allow reasonable vigilance to be established. All too often, these are still purely internal and non-analytical audit tools without concrete application, neither adapted to the risks nor sufficiently monitored as required by the provisions of the Law. In addition, in January 2020, the French General Economic Council issued a report to the Treasury Department, in which it noted not only the absence of an official list of French companies that are covered by the Law, but also that the Law was scarcely applied by the covered companies.[111]

Among the 265 companies listed as covered companies by the NGOs Sherpa and CCFD-Terre Solidaire, it has been reported that 27 percent have still not published a Vigilance Plan. A company's Vigilance Plan should set out specific information about the company's identification, analysis, and prioritization of risks and impacts, how it regularly assesses the situation of its subsidiaries, suppliers and subcontractors, and the steps it takes to implement and monitor measures taken in response to the risks and impacts it identifies.

Therefore, these reports and the very first citations of companies mentioned above in Section IV on good practices emphasize that this type of legislation must come with strong

[109] Information report n° 5124 on the evaluation of the law of 27 March 2017 on the duty of vigilance of parent companies and contractors (https://www.assemblee-nationale.fr/dyn/15/rapports/cion_lois/l15b5124_rapport-information#).

[110] Development International e.V., *Devoir de Vigilance: Reforming Corporate Risk Engagement*, 2020, available here: https://www.ipoint-systems.com/fileadmin/media/downloads/Devoir-de-Vigilance_Loi-2017-399_Study_2020.pdf.

[111] The General Council of the Economy is a public policy inspection and control body attached to the Ministry of the Economy: Conseil général de l'économie, de l'industrie, de l'énergie et des technologies, « *Evaluation de la mise en œuvre de la Loi n° 2017-399 du 27 mars 2017 relative au devoir de vigilance des sociétés mères et des entreprises donneuses d'ordre* », janvier 2020.

regulator that is equivalent to the US Securities and Exchange Commission, has extended its monitoring over the compliance of listed companies with the NFRD requirements.[113]

During the public consultation on the revision of the NFRD, the AMF called for balanced participation of all stakeholders interested in non-financial reporting in order to ensure the relevance of this future regulation.[114] Involvement of stakeholders, who were previously absent from the non-financial reporting mechanism, would also align the two regimes more closely, leading to greater regulatory efficiency. In addition, since a Commission on Climate and Sustainable Development was appointed in July 2019,[115] it is likely that the AMF will further monitor the consistency between the non-financial information disclosed by a listed company under the NFRD and the information published within its Vigilance Plan. The AMF will likely address any breach by a company of its duty of vigilance obligation that could have a significant impact on the market.

The concurrent proposals to revise the CSRD and the draft CSDD aim to make reporting procedures more restrictive by introducing a duty of vigilance and sanctions through liability claims. However, the use of codes of conduct to define the obligations of vigilance of companies is worrying since they fail to allow the flexibility necessary for companies to adopt appropriate vigilance measures.

C. Applicability of Law to Groups Incorporated in France with Headquarters outside of France

The application of the Duty of Vigilance Law is based, as stated in Section III.A.1. above, on the dual criteria of the location of the headquarters in France as well as the threshold of employees in France (over 5,000) and abroad (over 10,000). However, a question remains as to the application of the Law to companies with headquarters outside of France.[116]

In the duty of vigilance formal notice sent in September 2019 to the logistics company XPO, headquartered in the United States and incorporated in France, the International Transport Workers' Federation (ITF) based its claim of noncompliance with the Law on investigations revealing serious breaches of labor regulations in France and in other countries in Europe. Thus, this case raises the question of the applicability of the Duty of Vigilance Law to violations by the US parent company of the group incorporated in France. The issue has

[113] Autorité des Marchés financiers, *Rapport 2019 sur la responsabilité sociale, sociétale et environnementale des sociétés cotées*, November 14, 2019, accessible here: https://www.amf-france.org/fr/actualites-publications/publications/rapports-etudes-et-analyses/rapport-2019-sur-la-responsabilite-sociale-societale-et-environnementale-des-societes-cotees.

[114] AMF response to the European public consultation on the review of the extra-financial directive, June 12, 2020, accessible here: https://www.amf-france.org/fr/actualites-publications/consultations-publiques/lamf-repond-la-consultation-publique-europeenne-sur-la-revue-de-la-directive-extra-financiere.

[115] The AMF's Climate and Sustainable Finance Committee brings together stakeholders on the subject of sustainable finance. Its role is to help the Authority to carry out its missions of both regulation and supervision on issues related to sustainable finance, more information here: https://www.amf-france.org/fr/lamf/notre-organisation/la-commission-climat-et-finance-durable.

[116] Schiller, *supra* note 47.

not been settled to date in French case law but may be the subject of future decisions by the French courts.

Discussions at the level of the EU have suggested that the proposed directive on mHRDD should apply to all companies operating within the EU, regardless of their nationality or location of their registered office and headquarters, which could result in the European duty of vigilance applying to US, UK, and Chinese companies.[117] Firstly, the Commission's recent proposal for a CSRD, revising the NFRD, would extend the scope of the companies covered to all large and all listed companies.[118] This measure aims to reduce the risk of "due diligence dumping" (i.e., choosing the registered office according to where the diligence regulations are less burdensome), especially in respect of Google, Apple, Facebook, and Amazon, whose dominant and tax-advantaged positions have been widely criticized, particularly since the COVID-19 pandemic, by penalizing European companies through the application of stricter regulations.

In addition, Article 2 of the Proposal for a Directive on Corporate Sustainability Due Diligence, issued by the European Commission on February 23, 2022, defines the scope of the Directive as: companies that, for a given year, had over 500 employees on average and had a net worldwide turnover of more than EUR€150 million in the last financial year for which annual financial statements have been prepared; companies that had more than 250 employees on average and had a net worldwide turnover of more than EUR€40 million in the last financial year for which annual financial statements have been prepared, provided that at least 50 percent of this net turnover was generated in certain sectors (textile, agriculture, and mineral extraction); finally, companies which are formed in accordance with the legislation of a third country, and either (i) generated a net turnover of more than EUR€150 million in the European Union for the given financial year or (ii) generated a net turnover between EUR€40 million and EUR€150 million in the European Union for the given financial year preceding the last financial year, provided that at least 50 percent of its net worldwide turnover was generated in one or more of the sectors listed above.[119]

---

[117] *See* article 2 of the proposed European Parliament resolution of March 10, 2021 with recommendations to the Commission on corporate due diligence and corporate accountability (2020/2129 (INL)):

> "*1. This Directive shall apply to large undertakings governed by the law of a Member State or established in the territory of the Union.*
>
> *(. . .)*
>
> *3. This Directive shall also apply to large undertakings, to publicly listed small and medium-sized undertakings and to small and medium-sized undertakings operating in high risk sectors, which are governed by the law of a third country and are not established in the territory of the Union when they operate in the internal market selling goods or providing services. Those undertakings shall fulfil the due diligence requirements established in this Directive as transposed into the legislation of the Member State in which they operate and be subject to the sanctions and liability regimes established by this Directive as transposed into the legislation of the Member State in which they operate.* », available here: https://www.europarl.europa.eu/doceo/document/TA-9-2021-0073_EN.html#title1.

[118] Proposal for a Directive of the European Parliament and of the Council amending Directive 2013/34/EU, Directive 2004/109/EC, Directive 2006/43/EC and Regulation (EU) No 537/2014, as regards corporate sustainability reporting (COM/2021/189 final): the sustainability reporting obligation would apply to all large companies as defined by the Accounting Directive (which the CSRD would amend) and, as of 2026, to companies.

[119] European Commission, Proposal for a Directive of the European Parliament of the Council on Corporate Sustainability Due Diligence and amending Directive (EU) 2019/1937, COM(2022) 71 final, available here: https://

D. Alignment of Common Law Duty of Care and the Duty of Vigilance Law

Recently, there has been an expansion in the duty of care jurisprudence that holds parent companies responsible for preventing and remedying violations of human rights by their subsidiaries and suppliers. According to Professor Béatrice Parance: "the assertion of a duty of vigilance from parent companies to prevent and remedy violations of human rights and damage to the environment and health is echoed in the progressive expansion of the duty of care in UK and Canadian case law."[120] Common law jurisprudence relating to the duty of care, as well as the Dutch case of *The People of Nigeria v. Shell*,[121] have particularly emphasized the need for an extra-territorial principle of liability of multinationals based on their negligence or wrongful conduct in connection with their global operations, as well as those of their subsidiaries and suppliers. Establishing the duty of care of the parent company for its subsidiaries has been a legal challenge in such cases, but in the current context of a globalized economy, it is a reality that multinational companies effectively control world operations from their headquarters.

The Supreme Court of the United Kingdom recognized a duty of care by the parent company in the well-known case of *Dominic Liswaniso Lungowa & Others v. Vedanta Resources Plc and KCM.*[122] Vedanta argued that it could not be shown that any of its actions relating to the mine's operation handled by its subsidiary KCM met the criteria of a common law duty of care. Vedanta was, it was said, merely an indirect owner of KCM, and as such, could not be held liable on the basis of its duty of care.[123] The Court disagreed and stated that the parent company Vedanta had a duty of care towards the Zambian claimants, which arose as a result of their assumption of responsibility for ensuring that its subsidiary KCM's mining operations did not cause harm to the environment or local communities, as evidenced by the very high level of control and direction that Vedanta exercised at all material times over the mining operations of KCM and its compliance with applicable health, safety, and environmental standards.[124]

The Okpabi decision, in early 2021, also rendered by the UK Supreme Court demonstrates the proximity existing between the duty of care and the duty of vigilance. It also underlines the broader coverage of the common law approach, namely, that its duty of care

---

ec.europa.eu/info/sites/default/files/1_1_183885_prop_dir_susta_en.pdf.

[120] Béatrice Parance, Elise Groulx, Victoire Chatelin « *Regards croisés sur le devoir de vigilance et le duty of care* ». Journal du droit international, (Clunet), janvier 2018, n° 1. With respect to Canadian case law, see also Choc c/ Hudbay Minerals, Inc, 2013 ONSC 1414; Garcia v. Tahoe Resources 2017 BCCA 39; and Araya v. Nevsun Resources Ltd, 2017 BCCA 401 Newbury JA.

[121] Eric DOOH and others v. Royal Dutch Shell PLC and others, 200.126.843 + 200.126.848, December 18, 2015 available here: http://deeplink.rechtspraak.nl/uitspraak?id=ECLI:NL:GHDHA:2015:3586; *See also* the final judgments in 2021, available here: https://www.rechtspraak.nl/Organisatie-en-contact/Organisatie/Gerechtshoven /Gerechtshof-Den-Haag/Nieuws/Paginas/Shell-Nigeria-liable-for-oil-spills-in-Nigeria.aspx

[122] Vedanta Resources Plc and another v. Lungowe and others [2019] UKSC 20, April 10, 2019, on appeal from EWCA Civ 1528, available here: https://www.supremecourt.uk/cases/docs/uksc-2017-0185-judgment.pdf.

[123] *Id.* at point 46 and seq.

[124] *Id.*, at point 50 and seq.

is based on the control exercised by the parent company rather than imposing conditions of nationality or employee thresholds, as is the case with the Duty of Vigilance Law.[125]

The need for an extra-territorial component to CSR is especially important when harm occurs in a country with less protective laws or enforcement of laws to redress human rights or environmental abuses through the courts of the parent company's home jurisdiction. Legal liability of the parent company therefore reflects the reality of the ultimate beneficial owner controlling the entity's activities. Corporate accountability, whether termed due diligence, duty of care, or duty of vigilance, will nevertheless require some level of harmonization. Case law developments will likely influence mHRDD, and vice versa, but these will also need to be harmonized in order to ensure that the legal obligations are clear to companies.

E. Extra-territorial Application of the Law

A question also arises about the application of French law to companies that do not have subsidiaries in France but have a relationship with a French partner subject to the publication of a Vigilance Plan. Whether French courts will accept jurisdiction in a case alleging liability of a subsidiary or supplier operating outside France that is sued alongside the French parent company under the Duty of Vigilance Law is a complex issue, and it will depend on the type of damages claimed and on the jurisdictional conflict rule. When damage or breach happens abroad (for instance, the collapse of Rana Plaza or the deforestation caused by Brazilian farms supplying the company JBS), and the Duty of Vigilance Law applicability criteria are not met (for example, if the company is not headquartered in France), the Court will have to determine what law is applicable to the case according to conflict of law rules. For instance, in the case of environmental damage, article 7 of the Rome II EU regulation stipulates that the applicable law is the law of the country where the event giving rise to damage occurred (*fait générateur*).[126] The issue is whether the location in question is the physical location of the damage (e.g., where the trees are being cut in a deforestation case, or where the oil has spilled in a pollution case) or the location of the headquarters of the company that is exercising its control over the activity that caused the damage. This last approach is the one that has been utilized in the recent UK duty of care cases cited above (*Vedanta*, *Okpabi*).

In addition, the question of extra-territoriality may arise with regard to evidence of risks or serious harms on which the claim is based against the parent company in France, when

[125] A UK-based parent company argued it had no duty of care relating to actions committed by its foreign subsidiary. The UK Court of Appeals agreed it did not have jurisdiction until 2021, when the Supreme Court allowed claimants to go forward with their claim that the UK-domiciled parent of the multinational group owed a duty of care to those allegedly harmed by acts of the foreign subsidiary (Okpabi and Others v. Royal Dutch Shell Plc and another [2018] EWCA Civ 191; and Okpabi and others (Appellants) v. Royal Dutch Shell Plc and another, 2021, UKSC 3, available here: https://www.supremecourt.uk/cases/docs/uksc-2018-0068-judgment.pdf.

[126] REGULATION (EC) No 864/2007 OF THE EUROPEAN PARLIAMENT AND OF THE COUNCIL of July 11, 2007 on the law applicable to non-contractual obligations (Rome II). Article 7 aims to harmonise the conflict of laws rules applied by Member States when dealing with disputes involving non-contractual obligations and means that one rule for choice of law in such disputes applies across all Member States.

such risks or harms are considered unlawful in France but remain lawful in another country or are not subject to any regulation in the State where the damage occurs.

Faced with these complex conflict of laws issues, the Duty of Vigilance Law has a great advantage in making it possible to judge whether a breach was committed in France as a result of damage occurring abroad. The Law is applicable when a serious breach of a voluntary commitment by the parent company is established or if there is an occurrence of a serious breach within the parent company's supply chain that is incompatible with national and international human rights and environmental standards. This will likely engender some interesting developments by French and foreign courts.

VI. Conclusion

Due diligence is emerging as a primary tool for corporate accountability to ensure multinational businesses take responsibility for their impacts on human rights and the environment. The French Duty of Vigilance Law is serving as an inspiration and a catalyst for States' due diligence laws, a proposed EU directive on mHRDD, and a draft UN treaty on business and human rights. These illustrate that the need for a due diligence regime is shared by governments, businesses, and stakeholders from civil law and common law systems. From the point of view of the civil law jurist, common law countries have an advantage thanks to their jurists' familiarity with the notions of duty of care and due diligence which were among the main sources of inspiration for the French legislation, and which constitute a general basis for corporate accountability.

However, many obstacles still remain to ensure that companies do not see due diligence legislation as an impediment to their entrepreneurial freedom. A general duty of vigilance should, in the authors' opinion, apply to all companies, whatever their field of activity and size, throughout their business activities. A due diligence regulation shows its full effectiveness when it pierces the corporate veil that would otherwise preclude courts from holding the parent company of a complex corporate group structure and multi-tiered supply chain liable. Companies can use human rights compliance and the integration of due diligence into their business models and commercial contracts as a strategic opportunity to distinguish themselves on the market and meet consumers' demands for increased transparency, while aligning with the needed ecological and social transition.

In summary, in the face of the global perils for the planet and its population, including climate change with its effect of global warming, and soil, air, and water pollution, mHRDD systems are indispensable legal tools that urgently need to be developed and harmonized.

VII. Resources

A. Caselaw

Cour de cassation, arrêt n° 893 FS-B, pourvoi n° 21-11.882, December 15, 2021, available here: https://www.courdecassation.fr/decision/61b99380ef20f6a61afc3611.

Eric DOOH and others v. Royal Dutch Shell PLC and others, 200.126.843 + 200.126.848, December 18, 2015, available here: http://deeplink.rechtspraak.nl/uitspraak?id=ECLI:NL:GHDHA:2015:3586.

Nanterre Judicial Court, 1st Chamber, n° 20/00915, February 11, 2021, available here: https://www.actu-environnement.com/media/pdf/news-37043-ordonnance-tribunal-nanterre-total-devoir-vigilance.pdf.

Nanterre Judicial Court, interim order of January 30, 2020, n° 19/02833, available here: https://www.doctrine.fr/d/TJ/Nanterre/2020/U6DF0C118D7D6A5C7216F.

Okpabi and Others v. Royal Dutch Shell Plc and another [2018] EWCA Civ 191, available here: https://www.bailii.org/ew/cases/EWCA/Civ/2018/191.html.

Okpabi and others (Appellants) v. Royal Dutch Shell Plc and another, 2021, UKSC 3, available here: https://www.supremecourt.uk/cases/docs/uksc-2018-0068-judgment.pdf.

Vedanta Resources Plc and another v Lungowe and others [2019] UKSC 20, April 10, 2019, on appeal from EWCA Civ 1528, available here: https://www.supremecourt.uk/cases/docs/uksc-2017-0185-judgment.pdf.

Versailles Court of Appeals, December 10, 2020, English here: https://www.business-humanrights.org/en/latest-news/total-uganda-case-the-court-of-appeal-of-versailles-remands-the-case-to-the-commercial-court/.

Versailles Court of Appeals, November 18, 2021, available here: https://www.actu-environnement.com/media/pdf/news-38574-DECISION-CA-Versailles-incident-competence.pdf.

B. Other Resources

Conseil constitutionnel, Décision n° 2017-750 DC du 23 mars 2017 (Loi relative au devoir de vigilance des sociétés mères et des entreprises donneuses d'ordre), accessible in English here: https://www.conseil-constitutionnel.fr/en/decision/2017/2017750DC.htm.

Duty of Vigilance Law of March 27, 2017, accessible in English here: https://www.business-humanrights.org/en/latest-news/french-duty-of-vigilance-law-english-translation/.

European Commission, Proposal for a Directive of the European Parliament of the Council on Corporate Sustainability Due Diligence and amending Directive (EU) 2019/1937, COM(2022) 71 final, February 23, 2022, available here: https://ec.europa.eu/info/sites/default/files/1_1_183885_prop_dir_susta_en.pdf.

Executive order relating to the publication of non-financial information by certain large companies and certain corporations transposing the non-financial reporting European directive ("NFRD") dated October 22, 2014 (Décret n° 2017-1265 du 9 août 2017 pris pour l'application de l'ordonnance n° 2017-1180 du 19 juillet 2017 relative à la publication d'informations non financières par certaines grandes entreprises et certains groupes d'entreprises, accessible here: https://www.legifrance.gouv.fr/jorf/id/JORFTEXT000035401863/.

French Anti-corruption Agency, *Recommendations to Help Public and Private Legal Entities to Prevent and Detect Instances of Corruption, Influence Peddling, Misappropriation, Illegal Taking of Interest, Embezzlement of Public Funds and Favoritism* (2021), https://www.agence-francaise-anticorruption.gouv.fr/files/2021-03/French%20AC%20Agency%20Guidelines%20.pdf.

French Commercial Code, articles L.225-102-4 and L.225-102-5 Law on transparency, the fight against corruption and the modernization of economic life, 2016 (Loi n° 2016-1691 du 9 décembre 2016 relative à la transparence, à la lutte contre la corruption et à la modernisation de la vie économique), available here: https://www.legifrance.gouv.fr/jorf/id/JORFTEXT000033558528/.

New Economic Regulations (NRE) Law (Loi n° 2001-420 relative aux Nouvelles Régulations Économiques, 15 mai 2001, accessible here: https://www.legifrance.gouv.fr/loda/id/JORFTEXT000000223114/.

Parliamentary debates of the Duty of Vigilance Law, Reports n° 4184 (March 11, 2015), n° 2628 (November 2, 2016), n° 4242 (November 23, 2016) by member of Parliament Mr. Potier

Report n° 2628: https://www.assemblee-nationale.fr/14/rapports/r2628.asp.

Report n° 4184: https://www.assemblee-nationale.fr/14/rapports/r4184.asp.

Report n° 4242: https://www.assemblee-nationale.fr/14/rapports/r4242.asp.

Sherpa, *Vigilance Plans Reference Guidance* (1st ed. 2019) available here: https://www.asso-sherpa.org/wp-content/uploads/2019/02/Sherpa_VPRG_EN_WEB-VF-compressed.pdf.

5

Human Rights Due Diligence Requirements Outside the United States

Esmira Hackenberg, Olivia Dean, and Shelley Marshall

I. Introduction

The aim of this chapter is to inform legal practitioners, civil society organizations, and consumers of the legal mechanisms currently debated and already enacted throughout the world in relation to human rights due diligence (HRDD) obligations for businesses. The proliferation of legal approaches may lead to a lack of clarity for businesses and advisors regarding to whom duties are owed, upon whom they are imposed, what sanctions may be applied, and what "effective remedy" may look like.

The chapter will describe current legal requirements for HRDD and disclosure-based mechanisms for the United Kingdom (UK), Australia, Canada, a range of countries in Europe, as well as guidelines in China; and explain how the law is being applied in practice with reference to case examples and good practices, where legislation has been in place for long enough for good practices to be established. This chapter's findings will provide useful guidance for legal practitioners and officers of transnational companies, which must adhere to domestic corporate reporting and conduct obligations.

II. Context: Overview of Background and Evolution in This Area

Laws that aim to give effect to the 2011 *United Nations' (UN) Guiding Principles on Business and Human Rights* (UNGPs)[1] have taken different forms around the world. The principles are characterized in three categories: (1) reporting and disclosure-based mechanisms, (2) duty of care and diligence mechanisms and duty of vigilance mechanisms, and (3) and trade-based mechanisms, with only (1) and (2) covered in this chapter.

Disclosure-based mechanisms have been favored by Anglo-American countries, including the United States, Australia, and the UK.[2] These do not mandate HRDD, but rather require reporting on efforts. Canada appears to be developing a hybrid approach. Duty of care and diligence mechanisms and duty of vigilance mechanisms are favored by European countries apart from the UK. Such mechanisms include mandatory (positive duties to conduct) HRDD, penalties when HRDD is not conducted to the standard expected, and, in some countries, liability for negligence where companies are found to contribute to human rights breaches in business relations. Duty of care and diligence requirements are found in the French Corporate Duty of Vigilance Law (the French Duty of Vigilance Law);[3] laws requiring due diligence for high-risk sectors like conflict minerals;[4] and laws requiring due diligence to uncover risks of child labor for consumers.[5] European approaches, excepting the French Duty of Vigilance Law and the proposed Swiss approach, are compared in this chapter. A further distinction in legal approaches is based on the types of harms the laws aim to mitigate. Some address broad human rights abuses, while others focus on eliminating modern slavery or are limited to child labor.

Effective HRDD processes include assessing actual and potential human rights impacts that the business enterprise may cause or contribute to through its own activities, or which may be directly linked to its operations, products, or services by its business relationships, and this should be done on an ongoing basis (UNGPs Principle 18). To prevent further human rights risks, business should integrate and act upon their due diligence findings and impact assessments by ensuring responsibility is delegated at appropriate levels within the business and incorporate sufficient budget allocation and oversight mechanisms (UNGPs Principle 19). Appropriate action depends on whether the business has caused or contributed to harms, whether the harms are directly linked to business operations, products, services, or

[1] United Nations Office of the High Commissioner for Human Rights, *Guiding Principles on Business and Human Rights*, UN Doc. HR/PUB/11/04 (Jun. 16, 2011).

[2] *See* Cal. Leg. SB 657 Transparency in Supply Chains Act (Cal. 2010); Modern Slavery Act 2015, c.30 (U.K); or *Modern Slavery Act 2018* (Austl.).

[3] The 2017 French model of due vigilance is the Loi n° 2017-399 du 27 mars 2017 relative au devoir de vigilance des sociétés mères et des entreprises donneuses d'ordre [LAW No. 2017-399 of March 27, 2017 relating to the duty of vigilance of parent companies and ordering companies (1), or Corporate Duty of Vigilance Law] (Fr.), described elsewhere in this volume.

[4] *See* Dodd-Frank Wall Street Reform and Consumer Protection Act, 12 U.S.C. § Rule 1502 (2015); and EU Parliament and Council of EU Regulation 2017/821 O.J. (L.130) 1.

[5] The 2017 Dutch model of due vigilance is titled Wet zorgplicht kinderarbeid [Child Labour Due Diligence Act] and came into force in 2020.

relationships; and whether the business has leverage over third-party suppliers.[6] Businesses should then track the implementation of responses (UNGPs Principle 20). Finally, to account and remedy any adverse human rights impacts, businesses should communicate findings to external stakeholders–in particular, to affected groups. Importantly, where businesses have identified that they have caused or contributed to human rights impacts, then they should either provide, or contribute to, an effective remedy through a legitimate process (UNGPs Principle 21).[7]

III. Legal/Regulatory/Voluntary Standards

This section analyzes legislative and voluntary approaches to HRDD that have been adopted outside the United States.

A. Disclosure-based Standards

Disclosure-based mechanisms require reporting on HRDD efforts, rather than positive duties to undertake HRDD or penalties for failing to undertake HRDD. Such approaches do not require entities to adopt substantive policies or procedures to address modern slavery. The aim of these laws is to drive enhancements to modern slavery compliance programs through transparency. This section summarizes the disclosure-based mechanisms in order both of their date of enactment and their strength: the UK Modern Slavery Act, the Australian Modern Slavery Act, the New South Wales Modern Slavery Act, and the proposed Canadian Modern Slavery Act.[8]

1. *The UK Modern Slavery Act 2015*

In response to the 2014 UN Palermo Convention[9] and associated protocols (which focused on transnational organized crime and the eradication of forced labor, human trafficking, and arms trafficking), the UK passed the Modern Slavery Act 2015 (the UKMSA). The UKMSA established the Office of the Anti-Slavery Commissioner to oversee the Act and introduced new criminal provisions and disclosure reporting obligations for large companies.

The UKMSA does not cover all human rights breaches, but a smaller subset of abuses. Part 1 of the UKMSA strengthens criminal and civil provisions for human trafficking and other criminal activity concerning slavery, servitude, forced or compulsory labor, and human trafficking. Part 5 deals with victims, including defenses for victim-offenders, protections for witnesses, and legal aid. Penalties include asset confiscation, reparation orders, and forfeiture of vehicles, boats, or aircraft. Additionally, prevention orders may be applied to high-risk

---

[6] *Id.* Principle 19(b).

[7] United Nations Office of the High Commissioner for Human Rights, *Guiding Principles on Business and Human Rights*, UN Doc. HR/PUB/11/04 (Jun. 16, 2011).

[8] Cal. Leg. SB 657 Transparency in Supply Chains Act (Cal. 2010); Modern Slavery Act 2015, c.30 (UK); or *Modern Slavery Act 2018* (Austl.).

[9] United Nations Convention Against Transnational Organised Crime, November 15, 2000, 2237 U.N.T.S. 319.

persons (for instance, to prevent foreign travel), and maritime orders may apply for situations such as the "hot pursuit" of vessels believed to contain trafficked persons.

The main obligations for companies covered by the UKMSA are reporting obligations set out in Part 6 titled "Transparency in supply chains." Section 54 specifically obligates businesses which supply goods or services, carry on business in the UK, and have an annual total turnover (total sales revenue) exceeding GBP£36 million (which includes turnover from domestic and foreign subsidiaries) to report on measures to address modern slavery in their business and supply chains via a "slavery and human trafficking (SHT) statement." Section 54 sets out six criteria that companies "may" include information about: (1) the organization's structure, business, and supply chains; (2) policies relating to slavery and human trafficking; (3) due diligence processes relating to SHT in its business and supply chains; (4) parts of its business and supply chains with risks of SHT and steps to assess and manage risks; (5) effectiveness in ensuring SHT is not taking place in its business, measured against self-identified performance indicators; and (6) any related training for staff. SHT statements must be signed by a member of the board of directors, approved by shareholders, and published on the homepage of the company's website. The UK Guidance to the UKMSA states that a company reporting that no action has been taken to address and mitigate modern slavery risks may be noncompliant.[10]

UK government reporting has highlighted high levels of noncompliance to the UKMSA. Initially, only 60 percent of companies produced any reporting at all, and many who did report did not fully comply. In October 2018, the UK Home Office communicated with more than 17,000 reporting entities, which included US-based multinationals, regarding failures to report or deficient reporting.

Complying with the UKMSA does not mean a business is conducting HRDD in line with the UNGPs. The most significant criticism is that the UKMSA does not mandate HRDD but focuses on a limited range of egregious human rights breaches. Problematically, the UK government did not commit to the imposition of fines or penalties for companies that fail to report; however, civil proceedings may be brought in the High Court for an injunction leading to a contempt of court order, or in Scotland for an action of specific performance of a statutory duty.[11] To date, such actions have not been taken.

Instead, the UK government relies on the scrutiny of civil society, ethical consumers, or responsible investors who possess no power to enforce legislation. In practice, the worst outcome for nonreporting entities, or poor reporters, is loss of reputation.[12] The UKMSA's effectiveness as a transparency measure remains limited by the absence of a public registry of statements and full list of all reporting entities.

More rigorous, mandatory HRDD legislation may be developed in the future in the UK. A coalition of UK-based nongovernmental organizations has prepared a draft UK HRDD bill

---

[10] UK Home Office, Transparency in Supply Chains etc. A Practical Guide, April 2020, at 6.

[11] Modern Slavery Act 2015, c.30, § 54(11) (UK).

[12] Patricia Carrier, *On Anti-Slavery Day: Is the UK Modern Slavery Act the Best Way to Tackle Modern Slavery?* Business and Human Rights Resource Centre (Oct. 16, 2020), https://www.business-humanrights.org/en/blog/marking-anti-slavery-day-is-the-uk-modern-slavery-act-the-best-way-to-tackle-modern-slavery/.

to facilitate their lobbying efforts,[13] which would mean far more extensive obligations than the UKMSA, in line with the European Union (EU) Directive on HRDD described later in this chapter.[14] The UK government's 2017 Joint Committee on Human Rights report proposed framing the UK HRDD model using a "failure to prevent" mechanism along the same lines as Section 7 of the 2010 UK Bribery Act.[15] Some UK businesses have come out in support of mandatory HRDD, including ASOS, plc, a British retailer,[16] and it seems likely that stronger HRDD legislation will be adopted in the UK in due course.

2. *The Australia Modern Slavery Act 2018*

The Australia Modern Slavery Act 2018 (AMSA) is a federal law designed to largely mirror the UKMSA. The AMSA requires companies based or operating in Australia with annual revenue of more than AUD$100 million to report annually on the risks of modern slavery in their operations and supply chains, and such companies' actions to address those risks[17] in an annual compliance statement which they can submit to the Modern Slavery Statements Register maintained on the Australian Border Force website at https://modernslaveryregister.gov.au/. As with the UKMSA, the AMSA gives much latitude in how a company "addresses" such risks, as set out below.

The term "modern slavery" is intended to "include all forms of trafficking in persons, slavery and slavery-like practices, and the worst forms of child labour."[18] The AMSA states that "modern slavery" includes all offences (as set out in division 270 and 271 of the federal Criminal Code). This includes human trafficking, which is defined as the movement of a person into, out of, or within Australia through the use of coercion, threats, or deception for certain exploitive end purposes. These exploitive end purposes are slavery, servitude, forced labor forced marriage, and debt bondage.[19]

Section 16 of the AMSA contains a reporting requirement that covers similar matters to those required under Section 54 of the UKMSA, but Australian annual compliance statements "must" include the following criteria: (1-2) the entities' structure, operations, and supply chains; (3) the risks of modern slavery practices within its operations and supply chains and controlled entities; (4) the actions taken by the entity and controlled entities to address those risks, including due diligence and remediation measures; (5) how the entity has assessed the effectiveness of such actions; (6) the process of consultation undertaken with owned or controlled entities; and (7) any other relevant information.

[13] https://corporatejusticecoalition.org/wp-content/uploads/2019/04/190417_UK-mHRDD-campaign-statement_FINAL-with-logos.pdf.

[14] Patrick Bourke and Stuart Neely, *First Steps Taken Towards a Mandatory Human Rights Due Diligence Law in the EU*, Norton Rose Fulbright (November 2020), https://www.nortonrosefulbright.com/en/knowledge/publications/00dce527/first-steps-taken-towards-a-mandatory-human-rights-due-diligence-law-in-the-eu#1.

[15] https://publications.parliament.uk/pa/jt201719/jtselect/jtrights/686/686.pdf.

[16] https://www.business-humanrights.org/en/latest-news/uk-asos-calls-for-mandatory-human-rights-due-diligence-legislation/.

[17] *Modern Slavery Act 2018* (Cth) s 3 (Austl.).

[18] Explanatory Memorandum, *Modern Slavery Act 2018* (Cth) para 46 (Austl.).

[19] Australian Government, *Responses to Questions on Notice*, 11 August 2017, p. 10.

The Section 16 reporting requirements differ from the UKMSA by requiring companies to describe the due diligence and remediation measures for suppliers and any owned or controlled entities, and the process of consultation with such entities. A company that publishes a SHT statement in compliance with the UKMSA may use the same statement for the AMSA.

Like the UKMSA, the AMSA has no penalties, such as fines, for noncompliance. The AMSA did not establish an Office of the Anti-Slavery Commissioner to oversee compliance, nor did it implement enforcement mechanisms for noncompliance such as submitting a defective report, or failing to report. Such noncompliance may result in the entity being requested by the relevant Minister to explain the failure to comply and/or undertake remedial action.[20] Failing this, the entity's identity and details of its noncompliance will be included in a Parliamentary report summarising overall compliance to the Act, where it is expected that "[p]ublicly identifying a noncompliant entity is likely to cause reputational damage . . . [which] will incentivise compliance."[21] Due to the economic effects of the COVID-19 pandemic, final timelines for first reports under the AMSA were extended to March 2021, so the effectiveness of this public "name and shame" approach will not be seen until 2022. One mechanism which may be a tool for enforcement consists of Australia's robust federal consumer protection laws. Substantial penalties apply if a company makes false or misleading representations about its goods or services,[22] or if they mislead the public about characteristics of goods or services,[23] such as a statement that goods, services, or supply chains are slavery free.

A voluminous 96-page Australian federal government guidance document was produced to explain what is required of reporting entities regarding HRDD, which makes express reference to the HRDD standards of the UNGPs and the Organisation for Economic Co-operation and Development (OECD) Guidelines for Multinational Enterprises (OECD Guidelines)[24] in explaining the Section 16 criteria, in particular with reference to "remediation and due diligence."[25] First reports were submitted in late 2020. A mandated three-year statutory review will provide opportunity for policy makers to review and address AMSA deficits, such as the absence of penalties and an Anti-Slavery Commissioner.

It is expected that few US companies will report under the AMSA, as only entities based in Australia with annual revenue exceeding AUD$100 million need to comply. For instance, if a company is a foreign-owned subsidiary of a parent company which has annual revenue of over AUD$100 million, neither that company nor the parent company need to report. Businesses can choose to voluntarily comply if they fall under the AUD$100 million threshold, and in doing so can submit an annual compliance statement to the Modern Slavery Statements Register.

---

[20] *Modern Slavery Act 2018* (Cth) s 16A (Austl.).

[21] Supplementary Explanatory Memorandum, *Modern Slavery Act 2018* (Cth), para 10 (Austl.).

[22] *Competition and Consumer Act 2010* (Cth) Sched 2, s 29(1) (Austl.).

[23] *Id.* at 33–34.

[24] OECD, *Guidelines for Multinational Enterprises*, (2011).

[25] Commonwealth Government, Commonwealth Modern Slavery Act 2018: *Guidance for Reporting Entities*, (2019) 29–30, 47–50.

Like the UKMSA, the AMSA has been criticized for falling short of the UNGPs framework by failing to address all human rights breaches, such as corporate land grabbing. Although the aim of the AMSA is to eliminate modern slavery in business and supply chains, Australian companies are not required to certify that their operations or supply chains are "slavery free."[26] However, the AMSA goes further than the UKMSA by encouraging the adoption of HRDD by reporting entities, and by mandating that Australian companies "must" report on all Section 16 criteria. However, Australian lawmakers have delegated the duty of enforcement of AMSA, by expecting civil society and consumers to read, understand, and act upon the disclosures and omissions of corporate statements; and the information contained within parliamentary reports on compliance with AMSA.

3. *The New South Wales Modern Slavery Act*

New South Wales (NSW) is Australia's most populous state, with Sydney as its capital. In response to concerns about the AMSA's weakness, NSW enacted its own Modern Slavery Act (NSWMSA) in June 2018. The effective date of the NSWMSA was delayed to allow for harmonization of federal and state legislation and is not yet effective.[27]

The NSWMSA applies to "commercial organisations" with (1) employees in NSW, (2) that supply goods and services for profit or gain, and (3) that have a total turnover (total sales revenue) of at least AUD$50 million, which is half the threshold of the AMSA. The NSWMSA was designed to capture only large state-based entities that did not meet the federal AUD$100 million threshold set by the AMSA. Therefore, the NSWMSA does not apply to commercial organizations that report under the AMSA. As such, multinationals doing business in Australia can avail themselves of this pre-emption provision. However, the lower turnover threshold of the NSWMSA is expected to capture a significant number of US companies not required to prepare an annual compliance statement under the AMSA.

The NSWMSA adopts the AMSA definition of modern slavery, covering exploitative practices including human trafficking, slavery, servitude, forced labor, debt bondage, and forced marriage, but extends this by including any conduct involving the use of any form of slavery, servitude, or forced labor to exploit children or adults within the supply chains of government agencies. No information is yet available about how to submit a compliance statement. This will presumably occur when an announcement is made about the commencement of the legislation.

Unlike the UKMSA and AMSA, the NSWMSA expressly stipulates that a person reporting information that they know or ought reasonably to know is materially false or misleading may be fined up to 10,000 penalty units. NSW penalty units are indexed each year; they are AUD$110 per unit in 2021, which equates to a fine of AUD$1.1 million. These penalties may be imposed if a commercial organization fails to prepare a modern slavery statement. Further, action may be taken under Section 307C of the NSW Crimes Act 1900 (Cth) for providing

---

[26] *Id.* at 39.

[27] NSW Government, *Modern Slavery*, https://www.nsw.gov.au/modern-slavery, (last visited May 25, 2021).

(Section 19(1)). In addition, under Section 19(2), every person or entity that knowingly makes a false or misleading statement or knowingly provides false or misleading information to the Minister or a person designated by the Minister to administer and enforce the CMSA, could be fined up to C$250,000. An officer, director, or agent of the person or entity who directed, authorized, assented to, acquiesced in, or participated in the commission of an offense also could be held liable for the offense.

The proposed CMSA also provides for the creation of an enforcement body with investigative powers (Section 14). It allows an enforcement person or body, defined under Section 15, to enter any place where they have reasonable grounds to believe there is anything to which this Act applies or any document relating to the administration of this Act. Powers on entry are defined and limited in Section 15(2).

The proposed CMSA also would amend the Customs Tariff to prohibit the importation into Canada of goods that are mined, manufactured, or produced wholly or in part by child labor (as defined in the proposed CMSA, described earlier in this section), or to prescribe the conditions under which those goods may be prohibited. The Customs Tariff already contains a similar prohibition on goods involving forced labor as part of the US-Mexico-Canada Agreement. The amendments to the Customs Tariff will be familiar to US companies as they are similar to provisions in federal US trade law (Section 307 of the Tariff Act of 1930 (19 U.S.C. § 1307)).

B. Duty of Care and Diligence Approaches

Duty of care and diligence approaches that place positive and mandatory duties on entities to adopt HRDD have been favored by the European Union (EU) and its Member States over disclosure-based mechanisms. The French Duty of Vigilance Law is covered elsewhere in this volume.

1. European Union Conflict Minerals Regulation

Regulation (EU) 2017/821 of the European Parliament and of the Council of May 17, 2017 laying down supply chain due diligence obligations for EU importers of tin, tantalum, and tungsten, their ores, and gold (3TG) originating from conflict-affected and high-risk areas (EU Regulation) came into effect on January 1, 2021.[29] The EU Regulation requires EU-based importers of 3TG minerals from all countries exporting 3TG minerals into the EU, to meet responsible sourcing standards established by the OECD in the OECD Due Diligence Guidance for Responsible Supply Chains of Minerals from Conflict-Affected and High-Risk Areas (OECD Minerals Guidance).[30]

---

[29] *See* https://eur-lex.europa.eu/legal-content/EN/TXT/?uri=uriserv%3AOJ.L_.2017.130.01.0001.01.ENG&toc=OJ%3AL%3A2017%3A130%3ATOC. *See also* European Commission, *The Regulation Explained*, https://ec.europa.eu/trade/policy/in-focus/conflict-minerals-regulation/regulation-explained/, (last updated Dec. 21, 2020).

[30] OECD, *Due Diligence Guidance for Responsible Supply Chains of Minerals from Conflict-Affected and High-Risk Areas*, (3rd ed. 2016).

HRDD obligations are created by Article 4, which requires EU metal and mineral importers to create management systems. This includes, but is not limited to, establishing standards for companies to conduct due diligence in their supply chains, engaging with their suppliers to incorporate their supply chain policies in contracts and agreements, establishing a grievance mechanism as an early-warning risk-awareness system or providing such mechanism through collaborative arrangements with other economic operators or organizations, or by facilitating recourse to an external expert or body, such as an ombudsman, and developing a traceability system for imported minerals.[31]

Article 5 establishes risk management obligations, which include: identifying and assessing the risks of adverse impacts in their mineral supply chains, and developing a strategy to respond to the identified risks designed so as to prevent or mitigate adverse impacts. In addition, Article 6 sets third-party audit obligations requiring the EU importers to carry out audits via an independent third party.

Article 7 requires that businesses must make compliance reports publicly available, including online.[32] There are two ways businesses can meet the reporting and disclosure requirements for EU importers created by Article 7. They can either provide reports from a third-party audit, or they can provide evidence of conformity with a government or industry association due diligence scheme. Under Article 8, such industry associations and groups of interested organizations having due diligence schemes in place, referred to as "scheme owners," may apply to the European Commission for the recognition of the supply schemes. If there is a failure to comply with the EU Regulation or deficiencies in a recognized supply chain due diligence scheme, the European Commission may grant the scheme owner an appropriate period of time to take remedial action. If the scheme owner fails or refuses to take the necessary remedial action, then the European Commission will withdraw the recognition of the scheme.

Each Member State will have to designate one or more competent authorities responsible for the application of the EU Regulation.[33] The enforcement of the EU Regulation will be up to the EU Member States, which are expected to implement appropriate checks of how EU importers comply with the EU Regulation. This includes auditing of records and on-the-spot inspections.[34] In case of violations of the EU Regulation, the EU Member State's competent authorities must issue a notice of remedial action to be taken by the EU importer.[35]

By June 30 of each year, the Member States are required to submit to the European Commission a report on the implementation of the EU Regulation, on remedial actions issued by their competent authorities, and on the independent third-party audits. This information

---

[31] *See* Dodd-Frank Wall Street Reform and Consumer Protection Act, 12 U.S.C. § Rule 1502 (2015); and EU Parliament and Council of EU Regulation 2017/821 O.J. (L.130) 1.

[32] EU Parliament and Council of EU Regulation 2017/821 O.J. (L.130), Article 7.

[33] *Id.* Article 10.

[34] Sascha Arnold, *The EU Conflict Minerals Regulation–New Due Diligence Requirements for Importers*, Freshfields Bruckhaus Deringer (Jun. 5, 2020), https://riskandcompliance.freshfields.com/post/102g8xx/the-eu-conflict-minerals-regulation-new-due-diligence-requirements-for-importer.

[35] EU Parliament and Council of EU Regulation 2017/821, O.J. (L.130), Article 16.

will be assessed by the European Commission to establish if the Member States' competent authorities are competent to impose penalties on the EU importers in the event of persistent failures to comply with their obligations. The European Commission may submit a legislative proposal to the European Parliament and to the European Council in this regard.[36]

US companies accustomed to reporting under the Securities and Exchange Commission rule promulgated pursuant to Section 1502 of the Dodd-Frank Wall Street Reform and Consumer Protection Act (US Conflict Minerals Rule),[37] targeting the same problem, will be largely familiar with the requirements under the EU Regulation. There are a few significant differences. The EU Regulation covers minerals sourced from any country, while the US Conflict Minerals Rule covers the same four minerals but limits such Rule's application to named countries (Democratic Republic of Congo, Zambia, Angola, Republic of the Congo (Brazzaville), Central African Republic, South Sudan, Uganda, Rwanda, Burundi, and Tanzania).

One of the criticisms of the EU Regulation is that its enforcement is at the Member State level, and there is no requirement for Member States to implement penalties for noncompliance.

2. *The Netherlands Child Labor Due Diligence Law*

The Netherlands Senate voted to adopt the Child Labor Due Diligence Act (Wet Zorgplicht Kinderarbeid) (Dutch Act) on May 14, 2019. According to the MVO Platform, a network of Dutch civil society organizations and trade unions which are active in the area of responsible business conduct, it is now up to the Dutch government to elaborate a number of important elements of the Dutch Act, in the form of general administrative orders, on which the Dutch Act's effectiveness will rest.[38] There is no effective date yet established for the Dutch Act, as the government must first elaborate a General Administrative Order (GAO) (Algemene Maatregel van Bestuur, AMvB).[39]

The Dutch Act applies to all companies, including foreign companies, regardless of their size or legal form, that sell or supply goods or services to Dutch consumers, including online sales, regardless of whether the company is based or registered in the Netherlands.[40] Foreign companies are entities from anywhere in the world that deliver their products or services to the Dutch consumers twice or more a year.[41] However, the government can exempt companies from certain sectors or categories if the risk of child labor is low. This exemption is yet

---

[36] *Id.* Article 17.

[37] *See* Dodd-Frank Wall Street Reform and Consumer Protection Act, 12 U.S.C. § Rule 1502 (2015).

[38] The MVO Platform, *Update: Frequently Asked Questions about the new Dutch Child Labour Due Diligence Law* (Jun. 3, 2019), https://www.mvoplatform.nl/en/frequently-asked-questions-about-the-new-dutch-child-labour-due-diligence-law/.

[39] *Id.*

[40] Ropes & Gray, *Dutch Child Labor Due Diligence Act Approved by Senate–Implications for Global Companies* (Jun. 5, 2019), https://www.ropesgray.com/en/newsroom/alerts/2019/06/Dutch-Child-Labor-Due-Diligence-Act-Approved-by-Senate-Implications-for-Global-Companies. For purposes of the Act, an end-user is the natural person or legal entity using or consuming the goods or purchasing the service. Companies that solely transport goods fall outside the scope of the law.

[41] The MVO Platform, *supra* note 38.

to be decided in the GAO.[42] The Act does not apply to businesses that simply transport goods to the Netherlands.

The obligations include: (1) a duty of due diligence to investigate if there is a "reasonable suspicion" (*redelijk vermoeden*) that goods or services have been created by use of child labor,[43] (2) a duty to develop and execute a plan of action (*plan van aanpak*) if there is a reasonable suspicion of child labor, and (3) a duty to issue a statement to the supervising authority, which is yet to be appointed. As per an explanatory memorandum that accompanied the legislative proposal, a "reasonable suspicion" constitutes a clear indication that goods or services materialized with the use of child labor. The law leaves it up to GAO to define the terms such as "a reasonable suspicion" and to specify what exactly adequate due diligence is.[44]

The statement will show that the companies have carried out the duty of due diligence in their entire supply chains (including beyond their tier-one suppliers).[45] Companies must only submit a statement once to a supervising authority, which is a regulator commissioned to monitor and enforce the Dutch Act. A supervising authority is to be appointed imminently by way of secondary legislation.[46] The regulator will publicize the statement in an online registry. There is currently no provision about the length of time it is valid. This is different from the UKMSA and the French Duty of Vigilance Law, which both require an annual statement. All statements will be published on the website of the regulator.

The Dutch Act provides that specific due diligence measures and the plan of action will be in line with the International Labour Organization (ILO) and International Organisation of Employers' (IOE) Child Guidance Tool for Business,[47] which is the set of guidelines to improve global supply chain governance, due diligence, and remediation processes in order to advance the elimination of child labor.

Noncompliance with the obligation to submit the statement will incur an administrative penalty of maximum 4,350 euros or, in the event this is not considered adequate, a fine of

---

[42] *Id.*

[43] The Act defines child labor as any form of work by children under the age of 18. The law considers Article 3 of the Worst Forms of Child Labor Convention of 1999, and references to slavery, trafficking, and prostitution. The Act also takes into account the Minimum Age Convention of 1973 with reference to specific details about "kinds of light work," for as long the work does not restrict the child's school or vocational attendance, health, safety, or morals. Kevin Braine and John Arvanitis, *Breaking Down the Dutch Child Labor Due Diligence Act*, Kroll (Jul. 2, 2019), https://www.kroll.com/en/insights/publications/compliance-risk/dutch-child-labor-due-diligence-act.

[44] Suzanne Spears & Olga Owczarek, *Mandatory Human Rights Due Diligence Laws: The Netherlands Led the Way in Addressing Child Labour and Contemplates Broader Action*, Allen & Overy (Sept. 2, 2020), https://www.allenovery.com/en-gb/global/news-and-insights/publications/mandatory-human-rights-due-diligence-laws-the-netherlands-led-the-way-in-addressing-child-labour-and-contemplates-broader-action#:~:text=The%20new%20Dutch%20legislation%20(available,chains%20if%20they%20find%20it.

[45] Elizabeth Forster, *Dutch Child Labour Due Diligence Law Adds to Growing Global Body of Corporate Human Rights Legislation*, Freshfields Bruckhaus Deringer (Jul. 22, 2019), https://sustainability.freshfields.com/post/102fo7y/dutch-child-labour-due-diligence-law-adds-to-growing-global-body-of-corporate-hum.

[46] *Id.*

[47] Kornel Olsthoorn & Rick Van't Hullenaar, *The Netherlands Adopts Business and Human Rights Legislation to Combat Child Labor*, Jones Day (Feb. 2020), https://www.jonesday.com/en/insights/2020/02/the-netherlands-tackling-child-labor-with-new-act

up to 8,700 euros will be imposed.[48] Noncompliance in exercising child labor due diligence and executing a plan of action may result in financial and legal enforcement actions, including imprisonment of the responsible director. Businesses will be subject to criminal liability, and/or an administrative fine of up to EUR€870,000 or 10 percent of its annual turnover (total sales revenue) in the preceding financial year. Repeated noncompliance with the law in the period of five years as of the imposition of an administrative fine is regarded an offense under the Dutch Economic Offences Act. The Dutch Act does not provide for a private right of action.

Stakeholders, including victims and consumers, can file a complaint with the regulator for noncompliance with any provision if they have been affected by a company's failure to comply. They can file a complaint only after the company has dealt with the complaint or the company has not responded to the complaint six months after the complaint was filed.[49]

The law encourages companies to participate in International Responsible Business Conduct (IRBC) agreements, which involve partnerships between business, government, unions, and NGOs that are set up by the Dutch government, and in other initiatives to identify, prevent, and mitigate use of child labor in global supply chains.[50] IRBC agreements are sectoral agreements with the partners to develop long-term strategies to tackle problems together and are based on the recommendations by the Social and Economic Council of the Netherlands in 2014.[51] IRBC agreements are voluntary, but they involve a firm commitment from the partners.[52]

The Dutch Act has been criticized because it exempts foreign entities defined as "unregistered" that do not have a permanent establishment in the country from conducting child labor due diligence if they sold goods and services less than twice in one calendar year. The Act will target foreign companies that are doing business with Dutch consumers consistently and not infrequently or in a single business transaction.[53]

It is expected that the Netherlands will develop broader HRDD legislation soon. In February 2021, four Dutch political parties (Christian Union, Greens, Socialists, Labour) circulated a draft law for consultation with key stakeholders. It covered human rights, labor rights, and environment, and the due diligence requirements are similar to the OECD Due Diligence Guidance for Responsible Business Conduct.[54]

---

[48] *Id.*

[49] Olsthoorn & Hullenaar, *supra* note 47.

[50] International RBC, *IRBC Agreements*, https://www.imvoconvenanten.nl/en (last visited May 25, 2021).

[51] *Id.*

[52] Council of Europe, *International Responsible Business Conduct (IRBC) Agreements*, (2014) https://www.coe.int/en/web/human-rights-intergovernmental-cooperation/-/international-responsible-business-conduct-agreements-irbc-.

[53] Braine & Arvanitis, *supra* note 43.

[54] OECD (2018), *OECD Due Diligence Guidance for Responsible Business Conduct*, online at: https://mneguidelines.oecd.org/OECD-Due-Diligence-Guidance-for-Responsible-Business-Conduct.pdf; *see also* Anneloes Hoff, *A Bill for Better Business: Dissecting the new Dutch Mandatory Human Rights Due Diligence Initiative*, Völkerrechtsblog, 5 May 2021, https://voelkerrechtsblog.org/a-bill-for-better-business/.

3. *German Due Diligence Act*

Germany passed HRDD legislation on June 11, 2021. By doing so, it implemented its 2016 National Action Plan (NAP) for the Implementation of the UNGPs,[55] which is a statement of government policy to protect against adverse human rights impacts by business in conformity with the UNGPs. The NAP stated that, if fewer than 50 percent of all companies based in Germany with more than 500 employees were undertaking HRDD processes with respect to their supply chains by 2020, legislation should be adopted requiring such companies to do so. The legislation, titled Strengthening of Corporate Due Diligence to Avoid Human Rights Impacts in Global Value Chains (Entwurf für Eckpunkte eines Bundesgesetzes über die Stärkung der unternehmerischen Sorgfaltspflichten zur Vermeidung von Menschenrechtsverletzungen in globalen Wertschöpfungsketten (Sorgfaltspflichtengesetz)) (the German Act) will enter into force in January 2023.[56]

The purpose of the proposed German Act is to ensure the protection of internationally recognized human rights and the environment in global supply chains.[57] The human rights covered are broad, encapsulating internationally recognized human rights contained in 16 international conventions, including, the ILO Convention Concerning Forced or Compulsory Labor and the International Convention on the Elimination of All Forms of Racial Discrimination, among others.

The German Act applies to companies that, regardless of their legal form, have their statutory seat, headquarters, or main office in Germany,[58] and have at least 3,000 employees. The employee threshold will be reduced to 1,000 employees in January 2024. The employee numbers include the employees of all companies, including temporary staff,[59] in the German company group, even if the group companies are domiciled overseas.[60] This also covers companies that are incorporated abroad under European or foreign law and whose head office, principal place of business or administrative headquarters is located in Germany.[61]

Most US companies operating in Germany will not be covered by the law. A company will be covered by the German Act if its key business decisions are made in Germany. According to the German Act, if the company's head office, principal place of business, administrative

---

[55] German Federal Foreign Office, National Action Plan Implementation of the UN Guiding Principles on Business and Human Rights, 2016–2020, (2017).

[56] Paul A. Davies, Michael D. Green, Joachim Grittmann, Stefan Bartz, & Alexander Wilhelm, *Additional ESG Obligations to Enter Into Force for German Companies*, Global Environment, Land & Resources (Mar. 10, 2021), https://www.globalelr.com/2021/03/additional-esg-obligations-enter-into-force-in-germany/.

[57] Act on Corporate Due Diligence Obligations in Supply Chains, https://www.bmas.de/SharedDocs/Downloads/DE/Internationales/act-corporate-due-diligence-obligations-supply-chains.pdf;jsessionid=71731FA3BE835852C39F24D5BEFF8C60.delivery1-replication?__blob=publicationFile&v=2

[58] Davies, Green, Grittmann, Bartz & Wilhelm, *supra* note 56.

[59] Roland Steinmeyer, Patrick Späth & Felix R. Werner, *Germany: German Federal Government Agrees on Act on Human Rights Due Diligence Obligations of Companies*, Mondaq, (Mar. 30, 2021), https://www.mondaq.com/germany/human-rights/1052448/german-federal-government-agrees-on-act-on-human-rights-due-diligence-obligations-of-companies.

[60] Davies, Green, Grittmann, Bartz & Wilhelm, *supra* note 56.

[61] Authors' translation of the German Act.

headquarters, or registered office is in Germany, it can be assumed that relevant decisions for supply chain risk management are made there.[62]

The German Act requires covered companies to exercise human rights and environmental due diligence requirements. The due diligence obligations include: (1) establishment of a risk-management system; (2) defining an in-house responsibility; (3) performing regular risk analyses; (4) adopting a policy statement on their human rights strategy; (5) establishing preventive measures within the company's own business unit and direct suppliers; (6) undertaking corrective action; (7) establishing a complaints procedure; (8) implementing due diligence for risks of indirect suppliers; and (9) documenting and reporting outcomes.[63]

Companies must implement risk assessments of corporate actions contributing to human rights abuses or environmental degradation, and they must take all appropriate preventative measures about procuring global business partners.[64] The obligations extend to companies' entire supply chain, meaning that they must be implemented by companies in their business activities and in relations with their direct suppliers. Indirect suppliers are also included if the company manages to receive confirmed information about the supplier's human rights violations.[65]

Due to the lack of specified criteria, it is yet to be seen how the authorities and the courts will determine the appropriateness of the measures. Some speculate that what constitutes appropriate measures is a matter for companies to assess.[66] Companies must demonstrate that they have implemented the statutory due diligence obligations that are appropriate and practicable to the individual situation of the respective company.

According to paragraph 4 of Article 1, the company must identify who is responsible for overseeing risk management and monitoring risk management; for example, by appointing a human rights officer. The management shall regularly, at least once a year, inform itself about the work of the responsible person or persons. The establishment of the position of a human rights officer reporting directly to the management board (*Vorstand*) is recommended. The company must provide the necessary tools to ensure appropriate monitoring.

According to paragraph 8 of Article 2, the company shall ensure that an internal company complaints procedure is in place in accordance with paragraphs 2 to 4, which enables persons to point out human rights and environmental risks or violations, and obliges companies to have publicly available, written procedures that are impartial, independent, and bound to secrecy, and ensure effective protection against disadvantage or punishment as a result of a complaint.

---

[62] *Id.*

[63] *Id.*

[64] Jan-Ove Becker, Lavanga Wijekoon, Courtney Osborn, Michael Congiu, and Stefan Marculewicz, *Germany Seeks to Mandate Human Rights Due Diligence for Companies and Their Global Partners*, LITTLER, (Apr. 25, 2019), https://www.littler.com/publication-press/publication/germany-seeks-mandate-human-rights-due-diligence-companies-and-their.

[65] Business and Human Rights Center, *German Parliament Passes Mandatory Human Rights Due Diligence Law* (Jun. 19, 2021), https://www.business-humanrights.org/en/latest-news/german-due-diligence-law/.

[66] Steinmeyer, Späth & Werner, *supra* note 59.

2014 Guidelines as to avoiding dealing with conflict minerals. CCCMC's 2014 Guidelines explicitly refer to the UNGPs.[71]

Chapter 2 of the 2014 Guidelines sets out eight minimum standards that cover organizational governance, fair operating practices, value chain management, human rights, labor issues, occupational health and safety, environment, and community involvement and engagement. The 2014 Guidelines note that companies should develop a HRDD process to identify, prevent, mitigate, and remedy adverse impacts on human rights, and that they should cooperate with the local community to effectively remedy those affected by adverse human rights impacts by way of a legitimate process. The human rights chapter (Clause 3.4) provides that companies should conduct risk-based supply chain due diligence in order to prevent engagement with minerals that may have funded or fuelled conflict (especially Clause 3.4.6).

The objective of the 2015 Guidelines is to operationalize and provide detail to Clause 2.4.6 of the 2014 CCCMC Guidelines for companies which are extracting and/or using mineral resources and their related products and are engaged at any point in the supply chain of minerals to identify, prevent, and mitigate their risks of directly or indirectly contributing to conflict, serious human rights abuses, and risks of serious misconduct.

The 2015 Guidelines use the UNGPs and the OECD *Due Diligence Guidance on Responsible Supply Chains of Minerals from Conflict-Affected and High-Risk Areas* (OECD Minerals Guidance) as their basis, and they promote integration and coordination with other related standards, regulations, and initiatives.

Section III specifies that the 2015 Guidelines apply to all Chinese companies which are extracting, trading, processing, transporting, and/or otherwise using mineral resources and their related products and are engaged at any point in the supply chain of mineral resources and their related products. This definition targets all Chinese companies which are engaged in both the upstream, i.e., resource exploration, extraction, trading, transporting, and storing up to processing, including refining, and/or smelting, and the downstream parts that are engaged in using mineral resources and their related products of the supply chain (for example, electronics, electrical appliances, instruments, jewellery, communications equipment, etc.). "Chinese company" in this regard means legal (for-profit) entities which are registered in China or overseas companies (including subsidiaries) which are wholly- or majority-owned or controlled by a Chinese entity or individual.

The 2015 Guidelines note that the extent of due diligence that is appropriate will depend on individual circumstances and will be affected by factors such as the size of the enterprise, the sector and nature of the products or services involved, as well as on the position of the company in the mineral supply chain, and the prevalence of risks in the supply chain.

A basic five-step model for carrying out risk-based supply chain due diligence is set out in Section IV of the 2015 Guidelines, in keeping with the UNGPs:

1. Establish strong company risk management systems.
2. Identify and assess risk in the supply chain.

[71] Karin Buhmann, *Chinese Human Rights Guidance on Minerals Sourcing: Building Soft Power*, 46(2) Journal of Current Chinese Affairs, 135–154 (2017).

3. Design and implement a strategy to respond to identified risks.
4. Carry out independent third-party audit at identified choke points in the supply chain (as indicated in the Audit Protocols).
5. Report on the process and results of supply chain risk management.

These five steps are elaborated in considerable detail in Section VII of the 2015 Guidelines. The 2014 and 2015 Guidelines are not compulsory and do not impose sanctions for noncompliance.

IV. Identification of Good Practices

The legislative advances in HRDD considered in this chapter suggest that US corporations operating across the OECD and China are advised to begin developing HRDD processes that go beyond those currently required under existing laws. The discussion of outstanding and evolving issues in the next section of this chapter shows that obligations to conduct HRDD obligations are likely to soon become broader and stricter, and will bring together human rights, social, and environmental due diligence. In this section we identify some good practices, noting that most of the legislation discussed in this chapter is new, not yet enforced, or only proposed. This means that for most of the legislation we considered, there are not yet examples of good practice to consider.

It is often those companies that were the subject of civil society campaigns around labor conditions in their supply chains in the 1990s that are advanced in conducting HRDD, transparency, and reporting on their efforts. Major apparel brand Nike has gone from attracting criticism and controversy over labor conditions in its supply chains to receiving praise for its reporting under the UKMSA. Criticized for its labor practices beginning in the 1990s, Nike took significant steps to improve its supply chains, releasing a global database of over 700 of its domestic and offshore factories in 2005. Although Nike transformed into an industry leader for supply chain transparency, it experienced a significant drop in sales and stock price from 2016, explained in part by competitive pressure and loss of market share from new apparel brands untainted by child and forced labor scandals. However, Nike continued its focus on transparency and in 2018 was chronicled as one of the leading reporters under the UKMSA.[72] Nike now publishes a code of conduct that its suppliers must follow. In addition to disclosing its global supplier list, Nike now publishes a "manufacturing map" on its website, enabling users to click on a region of the world which then displays detailed information such as the number of factories and workers, percentage of migrant and women workers, their average age, type of products made, and materials used.[73] One way Nike sets out to "assess and manage risks" is by carrying out audits by internal and external third parties (such as the Fair Labour Association)[74] against the "Supplier Code of Conduct and

[72] Mark Stevenson and Rosanna Cole, *Modern Slavery in Supply Chains: A Secondary Data Analysis of Detection, Remediation and Disclosure*, 12(3) Supply Chain Management, 81, 81–99 (2018).

[73] Nike Manufacturing Map, http://manufacturingmap.nikeinc.com/ (last visited May 25, 2021).

[74] Nike Inc. Statement on Forced Labor, Human Trafficking and Modern Slavery for Fiscal Year 2021, Nike, https://purpose.nike.com/nike-statement-on-forced-labor, (last visited Nov. 15, 2022).

Code Leadership Standards," which detail requirements for sustainability, safety, respect, and fairness, such as: minimising air emissions, having fire plans in place, invoking a minimum working age of 16, and ensuring on-time pay and hours which are not excessive.[75] The Code was updated in 2021 to augment foreign migrant worker requirements and construction safety requirements.

While this type of transparency and auditing is important to identify "symptoms" of poor workplace practices, scholars report that such practices are not effective in eliminating the "root causes" of modern slavery as they tend to be checklist processes used as a policing tool for tier-one suppliers, conducted every one to two years.[76] For instance, audits are useful in identifying and remedying blocked fire exits or poor chemical safety, which are easy for companies to identify and for suppliers to fix, but they are less helpful for criminal activity such as bonded labor. This is because the risks of criminal prosecution for the supplier may offer greater temptation for the supplier (or their supplier) to hide violations and falsify documents.[77] Further, workers are unlikely to disclose details such as working conditions and pay to an external auditor, for fear of repercussions such as termination.[78]

To address these problems, Nike supports multistakeholder initiatives such as the Freedom of Association Protocol. This initiative allows independent unions organizing sporting footwear workers in Indonesia to bring complaints and call on the assistance of brands such as Nike.[79] This means Nike goes beyond mere in-principle support for freedom of association, and instead provides effective support for independent unions in producer countries.

Intel provides an example of thorough adoption of HRDD and shows how this has resulted in new practices and new products. Its practices provide a model for how US companies can comply with the EU Regulation in particular, and how HRDD processes can add value to business. Intel is a large US-based computing organisation which uses 3TG to manufacture microchips, and acquires products from suppliers containing 3TG minerals, such as circuits and servers. As such, it is required to disclose information relating to ethical sourcing of 3TG minerals from the Democratic Republic of Congo via Section 1502 of the US Dodd-Frank Act. Intel has a large electronics supply chain including 11,000 suppliers across 90 countries. In 2014, Intel made the world's first conflict-free microprocessor by adopting a three-step approach to due diligence, including (1) mapping its supply chain, which included requiring suppliers to complete a "Conflict Minerals Reporting Template Survey" to understand risks relating to products, componentry, and sourcing; (2) implementing a responsible

---

[75] Nike Code of Conduct, Nike, (November 2020) < https://purpose-cms-preprod01.s3.amazonaws.com/wp-content/uploads/2021/02/23072112/Nike_2021_Code_of_Conduct.FINAL_.pdf, (last visited May 25, 2021).

[76] Jolyon Ford and Justine Nolan, *Regulating Transparency on Human Rights and Modern Slavery in Corporate Supply Chains: The Discrepancy Between Human Rights Due Diligence and the Social Audit*, 26(1) Australian Journal of Human Rights, 27, 34 (2020).

[77] Stevenson & Cole, *supra* note 73.

[78] Fair Work Ombudsman, An Inquiry into the Procurement of Cleaners in Tasmanian Supermarkets, 12, (Commonwealth of Australia, 2018).

[79] Tim Connor, Annie Delaney, and Sarah Rennie, *Non-judicial Mechanisms in Global Footwear and Apparel Supply Chains: Lessons from Workers in Indonesia*, Corporate Accountability Research (2016), https://corporateaccountabilityresearch.net/njm-report-xiv-indo-footwear.

minerals supply chain policy modelled on the OECD Minerals Guidance and overseen by the CEO and senior managers in technology and manufacturing; and (3) publicizing their due diligence expectations to direct suppliers, clients, and investors. This included standard-setting provisions in tenders and supplier contracts requiring adherence to the Intel Code of Conduct and the Responsible Business Alliance Code of Conduct, annual letters to suppliers, information posted on the Intel website, and company-wide training.[80]

A common weakness in HRDD practices in this early stage of adoption is in remediation. Good practices are best developed in communities of learning, such as sectoral approaches, multistakeholder organizations, and through involvement in worker-led compliance bodies such as the Fair Labor Association.

V. Identification of Outstanding/Evolving Issues

This section identifies outstanding and evolving challenges in relation to the implementation and operation of HRDD laws around the world. Likely future directions are also considered, such as the probable impact of the draft Business and Human Rights Treaty (UN Treaty) discussed below. The types of legislative developments that civil society is pushing for across the world are examined, providing an indication of likely future lobbying for reform and innovation in this area. The chapter has shown that that mandated HRDD has not yet been adopted outside the OECD. China has taken action in relation to conflict minerals, but this is only nonbinding soft law. If the UN Treaty is adopted, this will likely result in more countries outside the OECD adopting legislation of this type, but only if ratification is widespread.

A. Little Evidence of Development of Mandated HRDD Outside the OECD

There is slow progress to adopt business and human rights initiatives outside the OECD. China is the exception, here, as discussed earlier in this chapter. African countries are beginning to publish NAPs on business and human rights, focusing on different aspects of business impacts on human rights depending on their national contexts. Kenya's NAP is focused on five themes: land, environment, labor, revenue transparency, and access to justice. Zambia, Uganda, Liberia, and Morocco are also working on their own NAPs.[81] But while this shows some uptake of the principles of business and human rights, there is no evidence of moves to mandate HRDD in these countries.

---

[80] *See* Intel's policies at: https://www.intel.com/content/www/us/en/policy/policy-responsible-minerals.html; and review case study reporting by the European Partnership for Responsible Minerals, https://europeanpartnership-responsibleminerals.eu/blog/view/53242598/case-study-intel.

[81] Joseph Kibugu, *Is It Time for African Countries to Introduce Mandatory Due Diligence on Human Rights?* Business and Human Rights Resource Centre, (Jul. 29, 2019), https://www.business-humanrights.org/en/blog/is-it-time-for-african-countries-to-introduce-mandatory-due-diligence-on-human-rights/.

B. EU Due Diligence Directive

The EU is fast moving in the direction of far more expansive human rights and environmental due diligence requirements than those so far legislated or drafted in Member States.[82] On April 28, 2020, EU Commissioner for Justice Didier Reynders announced that the European Commission would introduce a legislative initiative in 2021 on mandatory due diligence for companies. In September 2020, the European Parliament Committee on Legal Affairs released a draft report with recommendations for the new EU HRDD Directive on corporate due diligence and corporate accountability,[83] and on March 10, 2021, the European Parliament, by a large majority, adopted a resolution with an annex that recommended a draft text for the content of a directive. In addition, on October 26, 2020, the European Commission launched a public consultation to gather further data and the views of stakeholders with regard to a possible initiative on sustainable corporate governance.[84] The European Green Deal also outlined the European Commission's commitment to the transformation of global value chains, by promoting new standards for sustainable growth.[85] Finally, on February 23, 2022, the European Commission published its long-awaited draft directive on "Corporate Sustainability Due Diligence amending Directive (EU) 2019/1937" (CSDD) which sets out mandatory human rights and environmental due diligence obligations for corporations, together with a civil liability regime to enforce compliance with the obligations to prevent, mitigate, and bring adverse impacts to an end.[86] The draft Directive will now undergo further review and debate, with its likely adoption by the European Parliament and subsequent implementation into domestic legal systems anticipated by 2027.

Under Article 2, Member State laws will cover companies with more than 500 employees on average and a net worldwide turnover of more than EUR 150 million in the last financial year for which annual financial statements have been prepared. A further category of companies covered will be high-risk sector companies that:

> had more than 250 employees on average and a net worldwide turnover of more than EUR 40 million in the last financial year for which annual financial statements have been prepared, provided that at least 50% of this net turnover was generated from one or more of the following sectors: the manufacture of textiles, leather and related products (including footwear), and the wholesale trade of textiles, clothing and footwear;

[82] External Policies, *Implementation of the UN Guiding Principles on Business and Human Rights*, External Study, Feb. 2017, PE 578.031 (E.P.); EP Research Service, *Towards a Mandatory EU System of Due Diligence for Supply Chains European Parliament*, PE 659.299 (Oct. 2020) (EU).

[83] EP Working Group on Responsible Business Conduct, *European Commission Promises Mandatory Due Diligence Legislation in 2021*, (Apr. 30, 2020), https://responsiblebusinessconduct.eu/wp/2020/04/30/european-commission-promises-mandatory-due-diligence-legislation-in-2021.

[84] European Commission, *Sustainable Corporate Governance*, https://ec.europa.eu/info/law/better-regulation/have-your-say/initiatives/12548-Sustainable-corporate-governance/public-consultation, (last visited May 25, 2021).

[85] European Commission, *A European Green Deal*, https://ec.europa.eu/info/strategy/priorities-2019-2024/european-green-deal_en, (last visited Aug. 26, 2021).

[86] European Council, *Proposal for a Directive on Corporate Sustainability Due Diligence and Annex*, (Feb. 23, 2022), https://ec.europa.eu/info/publications/proposal-directive-corporate-sustainable-due-diligence-and-annex_en.

> agriculture, forestry, fisheries (including aquaculture), the manufacture of food products, and the wholesale trade of agricultural raw materials, live animals, wood, food, and beverages; or the extraction of mineral resources regardless from where they are extracted, . . . the manufacture of basic metal products, other non-metallic mineral products and fabricated metal products (except machinery and equipment), and the wholesale trade of mineral resources, basic and intermediate mineral products.

If the draft is passed, revisions to the due diligence legislation in France, the Netherlands, Germany, and Switzerland would be required since the CSDD draft text is wider in scope in terms of the range of obligations and companies covered. Pursuant to Article 1, the CSDD covers "actual and potential human rights adverse impacts and environmental adverse impacts, with respect to their own operations, the operations of their subsidiaries, and the value chain operations carried out by entities with whom the company has an established business relationship." Under Article 3, "adverse environmental impact" means an adverse impact on the environment resulting from the violation of one of the prohibitions and obligations pursuant to broad range of international environmental conventions and "adverse human rights impact" means an adverse impact on protected persons resulting from the violation of one of the rights or prohibitions. Environmental and human rights international conventions are listed in the Annex.

The definition of "value chain" is broader than that in current EU Member States' HRDD legislation. Article 3(g) of the CSDD draft text defines a "value chain" to mean "activities related to the production of goods or the provision of services by a company, including the development of the product or the service and the use and disposal of the product as well as the related activities of upstream and downstream established business relationships of the company."

Under Article 4, companies must conduct comprehensive human rights and environmental due diligence as elaborated upon in Articles 5 to 11. Companies must integrate due diligence into all their corporate policies and have in place a due diligence policy (Article 5), and they must "take appropriate measures to identify actual and potential adverse human rights impacts and adverse environmental impacts arising from their own operations or those of their subsidiaries and, where related to their value chains, from their established business relationships" (Article 6). Companies must also "take appropriate measures to prevent, or where prevention is not possible or not immediately possible, adequately mitigate potential adverse human rights impacts and adverse environmental impacts that have been, or should have been, identified" (Article 7). The prevention action plan shall be developed in consultation with affected stakeholders. Article 9 sets out the requirement for a complaints procedure. Reporting is required under Article 11 through the publication on the company website of an annual statement in a language customary in the sphere of international business by April 30 each year.

Significantly, the CSDD draft text requires the adoption by covered companies of a plan to ensure that the business model and strategy of the company are compatible with the transition to a sustainable economy and with the limiting of global warming to 1.5 °C in line with the Paris Agreement. This is not a feature of HRDD legislation in any EU Member State, and will require significant amendment of existing Member State HRDD legislation, including that of France.

The CSDD draft text conceives of a significant role for supervising authorities. "Each Member State shall designate one or more supervisory authorities to supervise compliance with the obligations laid down in national provisions adopted" pursuant to Article 17, with adequate powers and resources to initiate an investigation on its own motion or as a result of substantiated concerns communicated to it, carried out with prior warning to the company, except where prior notification hinders the effectiveness of the inspection, pursuant to Article 18. This same article provides that where a failure to comply with national provisions is found, the company concerned will be given an appropriate period of time to take remedial action, if such action is possible. This may include the imposition of administrative sanctions or the triggering of civil liability in case of damages, in accordance with Articles 20 and 22. Article 21 provides for the creation of a European Network of Supervisory Authorities, composed of representatives of the supervisory authorities.

The CSDD draft text envisages Member States establishing effective, proportionate, and dissuasive penalties for infringements under Article 19. It also provides for the extension of the jurisdiction of EU courts to business-related civil claims brought against EU undertakings on account of violations of human rights caused by their subsidiaries or suppliers in third countries. US companies should take note of the proposal that the EU law would apply extraterritorially to non-EU entities selling goods and services in the single market.[87]

Like the French HRDD law, undertaking HRDD and reporting should act as a defense of sorts for offending companies. If a company has taken the actions referred to in Articles 7 and 8, it should not be liable for damages caused by an adverse impact arising as a result of the activities of an indirect partner with whom it has an established business relationship. The extent of liability will also be reduced by the company's efforts, insofar as they relate directly to the damage in question, to comply with any remedial action required of them by a supervisory authority, any investments made, and any targeted support provided pursuant to Articles 7 and 8, as well as any collaboration with other entities to address adverse impacts in its value chains.[88]

Taken as a whole, the CSDD draft text will no doubt usher in new legislation in Member States that do not yet have HRDD laws, and significant amendments for those that do.

C. UN Business and Human Rights Treaty

At its 26th session, on June 26, 2014, the UN Human Rights Council adopted resolution 26/9 in which it decided "to establish an open-ended intergovernmental working group on

---

[87] Bourke & Neely, *supra* note 14.

[88] Explanatory Memorandum to the Proposal for a Directive of the European Parliament and of the Council on Corporate Sustainability Due Diligence and amending Directive (EU) 2019/1937, Brussels, 23.2.2022, p. 17.

it risks overlooking and undermining the positive effects of many voluntary and soft-law standards.[91]

Regardless of how long it takes for the treaty be adopted, the third draft gives a sense of the likely direction of HRDD and company obligations.

VI. Conclusion

This chapter has shown that approaches to HRDD differ across the OECD. Disclosure-based mechanisms, which do not mandate HRDD, have been favored by Anglo-American countries while more stringent, mandatory duty of care and due diligence mechanisms and duty of vigilance mechanisms are favored by European countries. There is no evidence of mandatory HRDD requirements outside the OECD, although voluntary standards have been adopted by China.

The chapter has identified likely future trends. First, it seems likely that HRDD obligations will increase across the OECD. More stringent HRDD, which incorporates a broad range of human rights as well as environmental and social standards, will be adopted across the EU. There is a push in Anglo-American countries, particularly in the UK, to adopt mandatory HRDD, rather than a reporting approach. For the UK government, being seen simply to follow the lead of the EU could be criticised by those who see Brexit as an opportunity to diverge from common rules. While it may be some time before HRDD becomes mandatory in Anglo-American countries, it seems likely that the scope of the human rights covered by existing laws will expand beyond "modern slavery" in the UK, at least, to a wider range of human rights. Second, a process of convergence in practices seems likely amongst larger companies, as companies that operate across both the Anglo-American countries and Europe will be subject to mandatory HRDD or HRDD disclosure obligations, and will develop the capacity to conduct more rigorous HRDD throughout their operations and supply chains. This may result in a reduction of resistance from transnational business to the adoption of mandatory HRDD in Anglo-American countries in the longer term. Third, a UN Treaty on Business and Human Rights will place stronger obligations on States to place obligations on business to respect and protect human rights. This may not take the form of HRDD, but it will likely strengthen the penalties for violations by business when human rights are breached. Whatever the pathway taken in relation to future law reform, companies operating on a global basis, including US multinational corporations, would be well advised to add HRDD to their suite of business practices.

VII. Resources

An Act to Enact the Modern Slavery Act, 2020, Sen. Bill [S-216] (Can.).

Andreas Rötheli, Jacques Iffland, Valérie Menoud, Roman Graf, Beat Kühni, Matthias Wolf, Dominique Müller & Tobias Weber, *Switzerland: Counter-Proposal to Responsible*

[91] International Organisation of Employers, IOE Paper on State Policy Responses on Human Rights Due Diligence, (May 2018).

Business Initiative: Overview of New Duties for Companies, MONDAQ (Dec. 1, 2020), https://www.mondaq.com/corporate-and-company-law/1011262/counter-proposal-to-responsible-business-initiative-overview-of-new-duties-for-companies.

Business and Human Rights Center, *German Parliament Passes Mandatory Human Rights Due Diligence Law* (Jun. 19, 2021), https://www.business-humanrights.org/en/latest-news/german-due-diligence-law/.

China Chamber of Commerce of Metals, Minerals & Chemicals (CCCMC), *Guidelines for Social Responsibility in Outbound Mining Investment*, (2014). Beijing: The China Chamber of Commerce of Metals, Minerals & Chemicals, online http://www.cccmc.org.cn/docs/2017-08/20170804141709355235.pdf.

China Chamber of Commerce of Metals, Minerals & Chemicals Importers & Exporters, Chinese Due Diligence Guidelines for Responsible Mineral Supply Chains, *Beijing: The China Chamber of Commerce of Metals, Minerals and Chemicals*, (2015) https://mneguidelines.oecd.org/chinese-due-diligence-guidelines-for-responsible-mineral-supply-chains.htm.

Commonwealth Government, Commonwealth Modern Slavery Act 2018: Guidance for Reporting Entities, (2019) 29–30, 47–50.

Council of Europe, *International Responsible Business Conduct (IRBC) Agreements*, (2014) https://www.coe.int/en/web/human-rights-intergovernmental-cooperation/-/international-responsible-business-conduct-agreements-irbc-.

Dodd-Frank Wall Street Reform and Consumer Protection Act, 12 U.S.C. § Rule 1502 (2015)

EU Parliament and Council of EU Regulation 2017/821, O.J. (L.130).

European Commission, *Corporate Sustainability Reporting*, https://ec.europa.eu/info/business-economy-euro/company-reporting-and-auditing/company-reporting/non-financial-reporting_en#:~:text=Directive%202014%2F95%2FEU%20%E2%80%93,diversity%20information%20by%20large%20companies.&text=Companies%20are%20required%20to%20include,annual%20reports%20from%202018%20onwards.e, (last visited May 25, 2021).

European Commission, *Sustainable Corporate Governance*, https://ec.europa.eu/info/law/better-regulation/have-your-say/initiatives/12548-Sustainable-corporate-governance/public-consultation, (last visited May 25, 2021).

European Commission. *The Regulation Explained*. https://ec.europa.eu/trade/policy/in-focus/conflict-minerals-regulation/regulation-explained/, (last updated Dec. 21, 2020).

Explanatory Memorandum. *Modern Slavery Act 2018* (Cth) para 46 (Austl.).

Herbert Smith Freehills, *Switzerland Set to Adopt Human Rights Reporting and Limited Due Diligence Law After Referendum on Stricter Proposal Fails* (Dec. 4, 2021), https://www.herbertsmithfreehills.com/latest-thinking/switzerland-set-to-adopt-human-rights-reporting-and-limited-due-diligence-law-after.

International RBC. *IRBC Agreements*. https://www.imvoconvenanten.nl/en (last visited May 25, 2021).

Kevin Braine and John Arvanitis, *Breaking Down the Dutch Child Labor Due Diligence Act*, KROLL (Jul. 2, 2019), https://www.kroll.com/en/insights/publications/compliance-risk/dutch-child-labor-due-diligence-act.

Modern Slavery Act 2015, c.30, § 54(11) (U.K).

Modern Slavery Act 2018, (Cth) s 3 (Austl.).

NSW Government, *Modern Slavery*, https://www.nsw.gov.au/modern-slavery, (last visited May 25, 2021).

OEIGWG Chairmanship, Second Revised Draft of a Legally Binding Instrument to Regulate, in International Human Rights Law, The Activities of Transnational Corporations and Other Business Enterprises (Aug. 6, 2020), https://www.ohchr.org/Documents/HRBodies/HRCouncil/WGTransCorp/Session6/OEIGWG_Chair-Rapporteur_second_revised_draft_LBI_on_TNCs_and_OBEs_with_respect_to_Human_Rights.pdf.

Organisation for Economic Co-operation and Development, *OECD Due Diligence Guidance for Responsible Supply Chains of Minerals from Conflict-Affected and High-Risk Areas*, (3rd ed. 2016).

Roland Steinmeyer, Patrick Späth & Felix R. Werner, *Germany: German Federal Government Agrees on Act on Human Rights Due Diligence Obligations of Companies*, MONDAQ, (Mar. 30, 2021), https://www.mondaq.com/germany/human-rights/1052448/german-federal-government-agrees-on-act-on-human-rights-due-diligence-obligations-of-companies.

Ropes & Gray, *Dutch Child Labor Due Diligence Act Approved by Senate–Implications for Global Companies* (Jun. 5, 2019), https://www.ropesgray.com/en/newsroom/alerts/2019/06/Dutch-Child-Labor-Due-Diligence-Act-Approved-by-Senate-Implications-for-Global-Companies.

Ropes & Gray, *Mandatory Human Rights Due Diligence Initiative Brought to a Public Vote in Switzerland–Initiative Fails, Parliament Indirect Counterproposal Moves Forward* (Dec. 1, 2020), https://www.ropesgray.com/en/newsroom/alerts/2020/12/Mandatory-Human-Rights-Due-Diligence-Initiative-Brought-to-a-Public-Vote-in-Switzerland.

Sascha Arnold, *The EU Conflict Minerals Regulation–New Due Diligence Requirements for Importers*, FRESHFIELDS BRUCKHAUS DERINGER (Jun. 5, 2020), https://riskandcompliance.freshfields.com/post/102g8xx/the-eu-conflict-minerals-regulation-new-due-diligence-requirements-for-importer

Supplementary Explanatory Memorandum, *Modern Slavery Act 2018* (Cth), para 10 (Austl.).

The MVO Platform, *Update: Frequently Asked Questions about the New Dutch Child Labour Due Diligence Law* (June 3, 2019), https://www.mvoplatform.nl/en/frequently-asked-questions-about-the-new-dutch-child-labour-due-diligence-law/.

UK Home Office, *Transparency in Supply Chains etc. A Practical Guide*, April, 2020, at 6.

Wet zorgplicht kinderarbeid 2017, Principle17(a) (Neth.).

PART II

Approaching Human Rights Due Diligence Requirements

Section A: A Practical Approach

6

Human Rights Due Diligence and Corporate Governance

John F. Sherman III[1]

I. Putting Human Rights Due Diligence and Corporate Governance in Context

This chapter discusses the close relationship between corporate governance and human rights due diligence (HRDD). HRDD is a term that originated in the 2011 United Nations (UN) *Guiding Principles on Business and Human Rights* (UNGPs or Guiding Principles)[2] and is increasingly codified into mandatory law. HRDD is a unique, stakeholder-centric human rights risk management system that enables a business to identify and address the increasing strategic risks of its potential and actual involvement in human rights abuses.

The UNGPs were drafted by the late Harvard Kennedy School Professor John G. Ruggie, whom Kofi Anan, then the UN Secretary-General, had appointed in 2005 as his Special Representative on Business and Human Rights (SRSG). One of Professor Ruggie's key talents

[1] The author was privileged to work for many years with the late Harvard Kennedy School Professor John Ruggie. The author helped him shape, draft, and implement the 2011 United Nations *Guiding Principles on Business and Human Rights*. Prof. Ruggie passed away in September 2021. This chapter is dedicated to his memory. This chapter reflects the author's personal views only, and not those of any person or entity with whom he is or has been affiliated.

[2] UN Office of the High Commissioner for Human Rights, *Guiding Principles on Business and Human Rights: Implementing the United Nations "Protect, Respect and Remedy" Framework*, UN Doc. HR/PUB/11/4 (2011), https://www.ohchr.org/documents/publications/guidingprinciplesbusinesshr_en.pdf [hereinafter *Guiding Principles*].

that businesses will not infringe upon human rights in their operations and business relationships. Pillar Three is the need for greater access to remedy by persons whose human rights have been harmed by business, which is a responsibility of both States and businesses.

Pillar Two, the business responsibility to respect human rights, expects that corporate governance will provide a strong foundation to enable the corporation to avoid, mitigate, and remedy its involvement in human rights abuse. Pillar Two therefore expects that the board will approve and promulgate a public policy commitment to respect human rights. and ensure that the policy is embedded throughout the corporation, from top to bottom.[7] This means embedding the policy in the corporation's culture, that is, the way things are actually done.[8]

HRDD is an essential component of Pillar Two. It should be integrated into formal corporate governance processes, driven by active and effective leadership, and embedded in the authentic norms and values of corporate culture. HRDD expects that through engagement with stakeholders, a corporation will identify the risks of its involvement in human rights abuse from the perspective of the stakeholder; will make integrated and appropriate responses to those involved in those risks; will monitor its human rights performance; and will be prepared to disclose its human rights performance publicly, particularly to stakeholders where the risks of harm are severe.[9]

To be effective, HRDD must be more than formulaic :

> [H]uman rights due diligence is more about a consistent practice of reviewing how business decisions and actions may impact different people in different contexts, than it is about a single technical exercise; it is about the whole business, not just the actions of one function or set of experts; its success is a product in good part of the company's governance, leadership and culture, and cannot be achieved on the basis of mere checklists and compliance.[10]

In corporate governance terms, HRDD can be thought of as an internal control framework and enterprise risk management system that is necessary for the business to implement its high-level commitment to respect human rights, like the financial management systems that enable a company to ensure that a company's financial statements reflect reality. In human rights terms, HRDD enables a company to know and show that it is respecting human rights.

---

[7] *Guiding Principles, supra* note 2, at 16 (Principle 16).

[8] *See* John F. Sherman III, *Rights-Respecting Corporate Culture: Identifying The Cultural Norms and Values That Underpin Business Respect for Human Rights* (2019), Shift Valuing Respect Project, https://shiftproject.org/resource/rights-respecting-corporate-culture-cultural-norms-values-that-underpin-business-respect-for-human-rights/ (*Valuing Respect*) and Shift, *Leadership and Governance Indicators of a Rights Respecting Culture: 22 Practices and Behaviors That Help Foster Business Respect for Human Rights* (2021), (*Leadership and Governance Indicators*), https://shiftproject.org/resource/lg-indicators/about-lgis/.

[9] *Guiding Principles, supra* note 2, at 17–21 (Principles 17–21).

[10] Ruggie et al., *supra* note 5.

HRDD is distinguished from traditional business or legal due diligence in several ways:

First, HRDD is an ongoing process. In this sense, HRDD has more in common with ongoing due diligence systems, such as the legal and ethics compliance due diligence process of the US Sentencing Guidelines for Organizational Defendants, which the Delaware Chancery Court identified in its iconic *Caremark* case discussed later as a relevant soft-law standard for determining whether boards have met their fiduciary duty to oversee the company's legal compliance program.

Second, HRDD expects that companies will prioritize their attention to risks of severe impacts to the stakeholders, e.g., the scope, scale, and irremediability of the impacts. Likely severe risks of impact are called "salient risks."[11] This perspective should be incorporated into corporate enterprise risk management as discussed later on.

Third, HRDD is based on engagement with stakeholders. It therefore focuses first on identifying and addressing risk to persons whose basic dignity and equality are at risk from how business is done, rather than on harm to the business (although in the medium to long term, severe harm to people and harm to business will likely converge). Therefore, corporate boards and officers should ensure that the corporation has processes that provide for meaningful engagement with persons whose human rights will be affected by the business.

B. Corporate Governance and Culture

Corporate governance consists of the strategy and systems through which a corporation manages the relationships among its senior management, its board of directors, its shareholders, customers, employees, and other stakeholders, to meet the corporation's goals.[12] The board of directors is ultimately responsible for corporate governance, including the establishment of the corporation's goals. The corporation's senior officers are responsible for designing and implementing corporate governance systems, in order to provide assurance that the corporation will be able to meet those goals. As corporate fiduciaries, the general counsel and other top corporate legal officers also play an essential role in corporate governance by advising the board and senior management on what is legal and what is right in the corporation's best interests.[13]

It is a truism that corporate "culture eats strategy for breakfast." Corporate governance, combined with effective leadership, is designed to embed the corporation's norms and values deeply into the organization's culture. As a result, the board and senior management are responsible for getting the culture right. Corporate culture is actual, not aspirational, because it is "the way things are done." Achieving the right culture through corporate governance and leadership is the ultimate responsibility of the board and senior management.[14]

---

[11] The relationship between Enterprise Risk Management and HRDD is discussed in Section III.B below.

[12] European Commission (*EC*), *Green Paper on Corporate Governance in Financial Institutions and Remuneration Policies*, COM(2010) 284 https://op.europa.eu/en/publication-detail/-/publication/1788e830-b050-447c-8214-77ed51b13241.

[13] Ben J. Heineman, Jr., The Inside Counsel Revolution: Resolving the Partner-Guardian Tension, American Bar Association (2016).

[14] *See Valuing Respect* and *Leadership and Governance indicators*, *supra* note 8.

1. *Purpose of the Corporation*

A threshold corporate governance issue for business and human rights is the purpose of the corporation. This issue has been the subject of decades-old debate. The late economist Milton Friedman wrote in 1970 that the social responsibility of the corporation is to increase its profits.[15] The so-called Friedman doctrine is regarded as the foundation of the "shareholder primacy" view of corporate governance. It has been strongly criticized for encouraging companies to ignore the adverse impacts of their actions on non-shareholders:

> The Friedman doctrine was a precursor to and became a doctrinal foundation for an era of short-termism, hostile takeovers, extortion by corporate raiders, junk bond financing and the erosion of protections for employees, the environment and society generally, all in support of increasing corporate profits and maximizing value for shareholders.[16]

Some of the world's leading business associations strongly disagree with the doctrine of shareholder primacy. In the 2019 statement of the US Business Roundtable on the purpose of the corporation, more than 180 CEOs of major corporations signed a commitment "to lead their companies for the benefit of all stakeholders—customers, employers, suppliers, communities, and shareholders."[17] Moreover, major investors are showing increasing interest in a company's ability and willingness to consider and address stakeholder impacts, as seen by the increasing attention paid by investors to environmental, social, and governance (ESG) factors, including by the largest passive investors globally, such as BlackRock (US$6.3 trillion in assets under management), State Street Global Advisors (US$2.8 trillion), and the Government Pension Fund of Japan (US$1.4 trillion).[18]

In 2021, Exxon's shareholders voted to install two new board directors who are more focused on the need for the company to effectively address its climate change risk. Exxon's management strongly opposed the proposal, but major institutional investors, such as BlackRock, strongly supported it. As stated in the *New York Times*, "To corporate America, the upset was a clear sign that company boards and leaders need to pay attention to environmental, social and governance issues (known as E.S.G.)—or suffer rebukes."[19]

---

[15] Milton Friedman, *The Social Responsibility of Business is to Increase Its Profits*, N.Y. Times (Sept. 13, 1970), at 3, http://www.umich.edu/~thecore/doc/Friedman.pdf.

[16] Martin Lipton, *The Friedman Essay and the True Purpose of the Business Corporation* (Sept. 17, 2020), Wachtel, Lipton, Rosen, & Katz (2020) https://corpgov.law.harvard.edu/2020/09/17/the-friedman-essay-and-the-true-purpose-of-the-business-corporation/. *See also*, Malcolm Rogge, *Bringing Corporate Governance Down to Earth: From Culmination Outcomes to Comprehensive Outcomes in Shareholder and Stakeholder Capitalism*, Corporate Responsibility Initiative, Harvard Kennedy School April 2020 Working Paper No. 72, https://www.hks.harvard.edu/sites/default/files/centers/mrcbg/files/CRI_WP_72_Rogge.pdf.

[17] Business Roundtable, Statement on the Purpose of a Corporation, (2019), https://s3.amazonaws.com/brt.org/BRT-StatementonthePurposeofaCorporationJuly2021.pdf.

[18] COSO and WBCSD, *Enterprise Risk Management—Applying Enterprise Risk Management to Environmental, Social, and Governance-related Risks*, (2018), https://www.wbcsd.org/Programs/Redefining-Value/Making-stakeholder-capitalism-actionable/Enterprise-Risk-Management/Resources/Applying-Enterprise-Risk-Management-to-Environmental-Social-and-Governance-related-Risks *(ESG ERM Framework)*, (discussed further at note 26 *infra*), p. 4.

[19] Andrew Ross Sorkin, et al., *Wall Street Rebels against Exxon: A Small Activist Investment Fund Scored a Huge Win*, N.Y. Times (May 27, 2021), https://www.nytimes.com/2021/05/27/business/dealbook/exxon-mobil-engine-no-1.html?searchResultPosition=1.

The rise in ESG investing has shifted the purpose of the corporation debate from *whether* corporations should consider and address stakeholder interests to *how* they should do so.[20] As Professor Ruggie stated:

> The rise in ESG investing and the debate on repurposing the public corporation are not unrelated. Both express a view that the large public corporation should be more than a piece of private property that has been excavated and is insulated from its social and natural ecosystems. Both express a concern that the public corporation is not managing its adverse impacts on people and planet well enough. And both reflect a growing belief among investors and business leaders that there is unlocked value in creating shared value.[21]

A more extended discussion of the corporate purpose debate is beyond the scope of this chapter. Instead, the chapter focuses on whether, how, and the extent to which proper corporate governance standards in the most shareholder-protective state (Delaware) in the most shareholder-protective country (the United States) encourage corporations to address the risks of their involvement in human rights abuse.

2. *Corporate Governance Management Systems: Internal Control and Enterprise Risk Management*

Two complementary management systems are critical to effective corporate governance—internal control framework and enterprise risk management (ERM) systems. The board has responsibility for overseeing the effectiveness of both, and senior management is responsible for their effective design and implementation. Both systems were developed by the Committee of Sponsoring Organizations of the Treadway Commission (COSO) and are widely followed in and outside of the United States. COSO started as an initiative of five major private accounting and auditing associations formed in 1985 to combat corporate fraud, in response to major corporate financial scandals at the time. COSO has continued to develop authoritative frameworks and guidance on internal control, enterprise risk management, and fraud prevention.

In 1992, COSO published *Internal Control: Integrated Framework* (Internal Control Framework) and updated it in 2013.[22] The Internal Control Framework is not legally binding by itself, but it has been widely followed; a key example is the US Sarbanes-Oxley Act of 2002, which requires publicly-traded US companies to maintain systems of internal control.[23]

---

[20] John G. Ruggie, Caroline Rees, & Rachel Davis, *Ten Years After: From UN Guiding Principles to Multi- Fiduciary Obligations*, Business Human Rights Journal, First View, pp. 1–19 (May 3, 2021), https://doi.org/10.1017/bhj.2021.8.

[21] *Id.*

[22] COSO, *Guidance on Integrated Control* (2013), https://www.coso.org/sitepages/internal-control.aspx?web=1.

[23] Section 404(b) of the Sarbanes-Oxley Act of 2002, Public Law 107-204 (Jul. 30, 3003), 116 Stat. 745, 16 U.S.C. s. 7262(b), https://www.govinfo.gov/content/pkg/PLAW-107publ204/pdf/PLAW-107publ204.pdf.

In 2004, COSO published its *Enterprise Risk Management—Integrated Framework* (ERM Framework) which complements its Internal Control Framework by focusing more extensively on the management of risks to the enterprise.[24] COSO updated its ERM Framework in 2017.[25] In 2018, COSO and the World Business Council for Sustainable Development (WBCSD), published a guidance for applying ERM to ESG risks, which explicitly recommends applying HRDD to the management of human rights risks (ESG ERM Framework).[26]

a. Internal Control Framework Systems

The Internal Control Framework outlines a management system framework that enables a corporation to provide reasonable assurance to the external world regarding the achievement of its objectives, based on its control environment, risk assessment, control activities, information and communication, and monitoring.[27]

"Control environment" as used above is the first component of internal control and forms the foundation for the others; it sets the tone at the top and comprises the integrity and ethical values of the organization.[28] Since the control environment includes a corporation's commitment to ethics and integrity, it would naturally also include the corporation's top-level commitment to respect human rights.

The US Sentencing Guidelines for Organizational Defendants as an example of internal control One of the best-known examples of an internal control system is the US Sentencing Guidelines for Organizational Defendants (Sentencing Guidelines).[29] Although they are not legally binding by themselves, the Sentencing Guidelines establish a normative standard for an internal control system to prevent corporate involvement in crime.

The Sentencing Guidelines provide guidance to US federal judges in sentencing corporations that are convicted of crimes.[30] Under the Sentencing Guidelines, a corporation receives a lower sentence if can show that it had an effective compliance and ethics program to prevent criminal conduct by its employees.[31] In such a program, an organization must "exercise *due*

[24] COSO, *Enterprise Risk Management—Integrated Framework* (2004), https://egrove.olemiss.edu/cgi/viewcontent.cgi?article=1037&context=aicpa_assoc.

[25] COSO, *Enterprise Risk Management—Integrating with Strategy and Performance* (2017), https://www.coso.org/SitePages/Enterprise-Risk-Management-Integrating-with-Strategy-and-Performance-2017.aspx?web=1.

[26] *ESG ERM Framework*, *supra* note 18. As discussed later, the 'S' of ESG is heavily populated with human rights risks.

[27] Melvin Eisenberg, *Corporate Governance: The Board of Directors and Internal Control*, 19 Cardozo L Rev. 237 (1997) (*Eisenberg*), p. 242, https://papers.ssrn.com/sol3/papers.cfm?abstract_id=11400.

[28] Institute of Internal Auditors, Sarbanes-Oxley Section 404: A Guide for Management by Internal Controls Practitioners (2d ed., 2008), p. 15. Professor Michael Power states that internal control systems are "at the heart of a process by which organizations are being turned inside out and made into newly responsible actors" to meet the external expectations of society. Thomas Power, Organized Uncertainty, Designing a World of Risk Management (Oxford U. Press, 2007), p. 42.

[29] *See United States Sentencing Commission Guidelines Manual*, Chapter 8B.2.1, https://guidelines.ussc.gov/gl/§8B2.1 (*Sentencing Guidelines*) and *Eisenberg*, *supra* note 27, at 255–256.

[30] Eisenberg, *supra* note 27, at 256.

[31] The reference to "ethics" was added to the *Sentencing Guidelines* in 1994.

diligence to prevent and detect criminal conduct" and "otherwise promote an organizational culture that encourages ethical conduct and a commitment to compliance with the law"[32] (emphasis added).

The ongoing Sentencing Guidelines due diligence program consists of seven steps: (1) the organization should establish appropriate standards and procedures to reduce the likelihood of its involvement in crime; (2) the organization should administer the program by high-level persons; (3) the organization should ensure that the board is knowledgeable about the program and exercises reasonable oversight regarding its implementation and effectiveness; (4) the organization should communicate its standards widely; (5) the organization should monitor and audit compliance with these standards; (6) the organization should respond appropriately when violations occur, in order to prevent future ones; and (7) the organization should periodically assess the risk of criminal conduct and make changes as appropriate.[33] Echoes of this due diligence program can be heard in HRDD.

The use of the Sentencing Guidelines to inform Delaware fiduciary duty law In its landmark *Caremark* case,[34] the Delaware Court of Chancery addressed the importance of the Sentencing Guidelines to the board's fiduciary duty of loyalty to act in good faith to further the company's best interests. The case is important because the majority of US corporations are registered in the US state of Delaware, and because Delaware has the most highly developed law in the United States for the protection of shareholder interests.[35]

Caremark arose from a lawsuit by shareholders of Caremark, a health care company, against the company's board of directors, to recover losses arising from the company's indictment for violations by the company of US criminal laws, which had resulted in huge fines of over US$250 million.[36] The shareholders alleged that the board breached its fiduciary duty by failing to inform itself and senior management promptly about the likelihood of the company's involvement in criminal activities. The Court agreed that the board had such a duty but held that the board could be legally liable for the loss only if it "utterly failed" to ensure that a reasonable information and reporting system was in place.[37]

In its decision, the Court pointed to the Sentencing Guidelines, and the "powerful incentives" they provide for corporations to have compliance programs to detect legal violations, to report them to public authorities, and to take prompt action to remedy them.[38] It concluded that "any rational person attempting in good faith to meet an organizational governance authority would be bound to" take the Sentencing Guidelines into account.[39]

---

[32] *Sentencing Guidelines, supra* note 29, at Section 8B2.1(a).

[33] *Sentencing Guidelines, supra* note 29, at Section 8B2.1(b).

[34] *In re* Caremark International Inc. Derivative Litigation, 698 A.2d 959 (Del. Ch. 1996) (*Caremark*).

[35] *Caremark*, 692 A.2d at 970.

[36] *Caremark*, 698 A.2d at 961.

[37] In Stone v. Ritter, 911 A.2d 362, 369 (2006), the Delaware Supreme Court confirmed that the Court of Chancery had applied the correct standard in Caremark. It characterized the board's fiduciary duty of good faith as part of its duty of loyalty.

[38] *Caremark*, 698 A.2d at 969.

[39] *Id.* at 970.

The Court's use of the Sentencing Guidelines shows how a soft-law standard for an internal control system can shape a corporate fiduciary's responsibility. The Sentencing Guidelines are not legally binding on corporations, and are a feature of US federal law, not state corporation law. They come into play only where a corporation has been convicted of a federal crime. As a result, the Sentencing Guidelines are, in effect, soft law. But as is often the case, ignoring soft law can have a sharp bite.[40]

The fiduciary duty to affirmatively advance the best interests of the corporation Since the 1996 *Caremark* decision required proof that the board "utterly failed" in its oversight responsibilities, it is typically cited for the extreme difficulty of proving to facts sufficient to hold a board legally liable for its failure of oversight. However, plaintiff shareholders of Delaware companies have recently had better success in alleging less than an utter failure of oversight, where the oversight related to a critical part of the company's business. Beginning with *Marchand v. Barnhill* (2019), the Delaware Court concluded that shareholders of an ice cream company had stated a claim under *Caremark* by allegedly failing to provide for an *adequate* system of oversight and monitoring for food safety, because food safety was a critical part of the company's business.[41] In *In re Boeing* (2021), the Court ruled that an airline company's alleged failure to have an aircraft safety monitoring system in place to alert the board to yellow and red flags, despite two fatal plane crashes, stated a claim under *Caremark*.[42]

Liability questions aside, *Caremark* also stands for the proposition that in order to fulfill their duty of loyalty, fiduciaries have an affirmative duty of good faith to look to relevant soft-law standards, if doing so will further the corporation's best interests.[43] Georgetown Law Center Professor Chris Brummer and former Delaware Supreme Court Judge Leo Strine Jr. argue (in the context of furthering the human rights–infused goals of diversity, equity, and inclusion),[44] that this affirmative duty imposes a "normative obligation" on directors "to try to avoid the regulatory penalties, managerial turnover, stakeholder backlash, and overall reputational and financial harm that occurs when companies violate laws essential to

---

[40] Chris Brummer & Leo E. Strine, Jr., *Duty and Diversity*, U of Penn, Inst for Law & Econ Research Paper No. 21-08; Columbia Law and Economics Working Paper No. 642, VANDERBILT L. REV., March 2021 (Brummer & Strine), Forthcoming, https://papers.ssrn.com/sol3/papers.cfm?abstract_id=3788159.

[41] Marchand v. Barnhill, 212 A.3d 805 (Del. 2019).

[42] *In re* Boeing Co. Derivative Litig., C.A. No. 2019-0907-MTZ, 2021 Del. Ch. LEXIS 197 (Del. Ch. Sept. 7, 2021) (accessed April 2022). For an extensive discussion of the case, see Roy Shapira, *Max Oversight Duties: How Boeing Signifies a Shift in Corporate Law* (2022), 48 J. OF CORP. L., forthcoming, available at https://papers.ssrn.com/sol3/papers.cfm?abstract_id=4035952.

[43] Claire A. Hill, *Caremark as Soft Law*, 90 TEMPLE L. REV. 681 (2018), https://papers.ssrn.com/sol3/papers.cfm?abstract_id=3240667.

[44] The corporate goal of Diversity, Equity, and Inclusion (*DEI*) supports respect for internationally recognized human rights laws and the achievement of several sustainable development goals (SDGs). United Nations Office of the High Commissioner on Human Rights, *Empowerment, Inclusion, Equality: Accelerating sustainable development with human rights*, https://www.ohchr.org/Documents/Issues/MDGs/Post2015/EIEPamphlet.pdf

its core goals.[48] In other words, ERM "helps an entity to go where it wants to go and avoid pitfalls and surprises along the way."[49]

Like internal control systems, ERM also has a social and ethical dimension. It is one thing for a corporation to assess and tolerate risks to itself or other parties with whom it can share, shift, or hedge the risk. It is quite another for a corporation to manage risk in ways that stakeholders are forced to assume involuntarily and sometimes unknowingly.[50]

The 2018 ESG ERM Framework explicitly addresses how companies should manage their ESG risks, which include human rights risks. The "S" or social impact factor in ESG measures "how well a company manages its risks to people connected with its core business" and is therefore "heavily populated with labour and human rights elements."[51] Since the UNGPs are the authoritative global standard on business and human rights, company alignment with the UNGPs gives investors a better tool to use to predict a company's future human rights performance.[52]

In addition, HRDD is also relevant to the "G," or governance factor of ESG. Since HRDD must be integrated into corporate governance in order to be effective, the failure of a company to do so will likely reduce a company's governance, or "G" factor, as well.

Finally, HRDD is relevant to a company's "E", or environmental factor. The UN General Assembly voted overwhelmingly on July 26, 2022, to resolve that the right to a clean, healthy, and sustainable environment is a human right. In its Resolution, the UN noted that the UNGPs "underscore the responsibility of all business enterprises to respect human rights."[53]

Indeed, severe human rights harm can result from environmental impacts, such as climate change and reduction in biodiversity. As to climate change, on May 26, 2021, the Hague District Court in The Netherlands ordered Royal Dutch Shell (RDS) to reduce its CO_2 emissions, after concluding that RDS breached its duty of care imposed by a rule of unwritten law relating to social conduct under Dutch Civil Code Article 6:162. In so doing, the Court used the UNGPs and other soft-law instruments to define RDS's duty of care.[54]

---

[48] COSO, *ERM—Integrating Strategy with Strategy and Performance* (2017) https://www.coso.org/Documents/2017-COSO-ERM-Integrating-with-Strategy-and-Performance-Executive-Summary.pdf.

[49] COSO ERM 2004, *supra* note 24.

[50] John R. Boatright, *The Ethics of Risk Management in the Information Age*, Bentley University Center for Business Ethics, (Feb. 8, 2010), p. 25, http://d2f5upgbvkx8pz.cloudfront.net/sites/default/files/inline-files/boatright-monograph.pdf.

[51] John G. Ruggie & Emily K. Middleton, *Money, Millennials and Human Rights: Sustaining 'Sustainable Investing'* (2019) 10(1) Global Policy 144, https://www.hks.harvard.edu/sites/default/files/centers/mrcbg/working.papers/CRI69_FINAL.pdf

[52] *Id. See also, UN Guiding Principles Reporting Framework*, www.ungpreporting.org.

[53] United Nations General Assembly, *The human right to a clean, healthy and sustainable environment*, A/76/L.75 (Jul. 26, 2022), available at https://digitallibrary.un.org/record/3982508?ln=en.

[54] VERENIGING MILIEUDEFENSIE, etc. v. Royal Dutch Shell PLC, Court of The Hague, Case No. C/09/571932 / HA ZA 19-379 (English version) (May 26, 2021), https://uitspraken-rechtspraak-nl.translate.goog/inziendocument?id=ECLI:NL:RBDHA:2021:5339&_x_tr_sl=auto&_x_tr_tl=en&_x_tr_hl=en&_x_tr_pto=nui. In so doing, the Court used the UNGPs and other soft law instruments to define Royal Dutch Shell's duty of care. *See* Clifford Chance, *Climate Change, Human Rights and Corporate Duties – Dutch Court Issues Landmark Decision*, (May 27, 2021), https://www.cliffordchance.com/insights/resources/blogs/business-and-human-rights-insights/2021/05/climate-change-human-rights-and-corporate-duties-dutch-court-issues-landmark-decision.html.

As to the loss of biodiversity (seen as a contributor to pandemic disease such as COVID-19), the UN Special Rapporteur on human rights and the environment observed that businesses are involved in reducing biodiversity through "deforestation, land-grabbing, extracting, transporting and burning fossil fuels, industrial agriculture, intensive livestock operations, industrial fisheries, large-scale mining and the commodification of water and nature."[55]

The ESG ERM Framework notes that ESG risks, which were once considered "black swans," are now common and manifest quickly and significantly.[56] The ESG ERM Framework points out the increasing attention paid by investors to ESG factors, as discussed earlier in this chapter.

With respect to human rights specifically, in March 2021, BlackRock (a major passive investor that pays attention to ESG factors) issued its new policy regarding engagement with companies on human rights impacts. The policy states that as a matter of sound corporate governance and long-term value creation, companies should "implement processes to identify, manage, and prevent adverse human rights impacts that are material to their business, and provide robust disclosures on these practices" that align with the UNGPs, even though they are not legally binding.[57]

The ESG ERM Framework includes: (1) governance and culture; (2) strategy and objective setting; (3) performance; (4) review and revision; and (5) information, communication, and reporting.[58] The ESG ERM Framework focuses first on the need for systems and processes for effective corporate governance, "which provides the oversight, structure and culture needed to establish the goals of the organization, the means to pursue them and the ability to understand any associated risks."[59]

Unsurprisingly, the ESG ERM Framework points to the unique features of risk assessment under HRDD to evaluate and manage the company's involvement in human rights risks.[60] The UNGPs allow human rights risks to be included within broader ERM systems, "provided that the ERM identifies risks to rights-holders."[61] Therefore, the ESG ERM Framework recommends that in accordance with HRDD, corporations should prioritize attention to the risks of involvement in human rights abuse by the severity of the risk to the stakeholder. The

---

[55] *See* THE REPORT OF THE SPECIAL RAPPORTEUR, DAVID R. BOYD, ON THE ISSUE OF HUMAN RIGHTS OBLIGATIONS RELATING TO THE ENJOYMENT OF A SAFE, CLEAN, HEALTHY, AND SUSTAINABLE ENVIRONMENT, *HUMAN RIGHTS DEPEND ON A HEALTHY BIOSPHERE* (Jul. 15, 2020), A/75/161, https://undocs.org/A/75/161, paragraphs 76–77; *See also*, OFFICE OF THE HIGH COMMISSIONER ON HUMAN RIGHTS, HUMAN RIGHTS AT THE HEART OF THE RESPONSE: HUMAN RIGHTS, THE ENVIRONMENT, AND COVID-19: KEY MESSAGES, (2021), https://www.ohchr.org/Documents/Issues/ClimateChange/HR-environment-COVID19.pdf.

[56] *ESG ERM Framework, supra* note 18 and *supra* note 26, at 2.

[57] BlackRock, *Our approach to engagement with companies on their human rights impacts: Investment Stewardship* (Mar. 2021), https://www.blackrock.com/corporate/literature/publication/blk-commentary-engagement-on-human-rights.pdf.

[58] *ESG ERM Framework, supra* note 18 and *supra* note 26, at 2.

[59] *Id.* at 13.

[60] *ESG ERM Framework, supra* note 18 and *supra* note 26, at 54.

[61] *Guiding Principles, supra* note 2, 17 (Principle 17), Commentary.

ESG ERM Framework notes that risk management under HRDD is characterized by assessing risk from the perspective of the stakeholder, that stakeholder engagement is critical, and that findings of a risk assessment should be shared. As a result, the most severe risks require prioritized attention, even if they are relatively unlikely. For example, a highly unlikely risk of catastrophic harm to people (such as the failure of a tailings dam, the collapse of an oil drilling platform, or the meltdown of a nuclear power plant) would deserve priority attention from an HRDD perspective.[62]

3. *The Evolution of Human Rights Due Diligence from Soft to Hard Law*

The UNGPs originated as a soft-law norm. However, since their unanimous endorsement by the UN Human Rights Council in 2011, the UNGPs have enjoyed broad and swift uptake. The former UN High Commissioner for Human Rights, Zeid Ra'ad Al Hussein, described the UNGPs as "the global authoritative standard, providing a blueprint for the steps all States and businesses should take to uphold human rights."[63] The UNGPs are increasingly incorporated or reflected in law, regulation, judicial and administrative decision-making, public policy, multistakeholder norms, commercial and financial transactions, the practices and policies of leading companies, and the advocacy of civil society.[64]

In its comprehensive 2021 report, *UN Guiding Principles on Business and Human Rights at 10: The Impact of the UNGPs on Courts and Judicial Mechanisms*, prepared for the UN Business and Human Rights Working Group, the law firm Debevoise & Plimpton researched references to the UNGPs in judicial and quasi-judicial bodies around the world. It found few direct references. However, it predicted that the lack of direct references would change over time, based on such factors as legislation that makes HRDD mandatory or otherwise refers to the UNGPs; the advocacy of the UNGPs by plaintiffs and civil society; and the utilization by international courts and tribunals of the UNGPs as a standard to hold States accountable for failing to prevent adverse human rights abuse by businesses.[65]

a. The European Union Mandatory Human Rights Due Diligence Initiative and Other Legislation

Legislation is a key driver of the incorporation of the UNGPs into law. For the first five years after 2011, States encouraged voluntary business action by promulgating National Action Plans that outline their plans to implement the UNGPs.[66] In addition, States, particularly in

[62] *ESG ERM Framework*, *supra* note 26, at 55.

[63] Zeid Ra'ad Al Hussein, *Ethical Pursuit of Prosperity*, The L. Soc. Gazette, May 23, 2015, available at https://www.lawgazette.co.uk/commentary-and-opinion/ethical-pursuit-of-prosperity/5047796.article.

[64] John F. Sherman III, *Beyond CSR: The Story of the UN Guiding Principles on Business and Human Rights*, in Ray Lindsay and Roger Martella, Corporate Social Responsibility – Sustainable Business-Environmental, Social and Governance Frameworks for the 21st Century (Wolters Kluwer, 2020), Section 20.04, (*Beyond CSR*).

[65] Debevoise & Plimpton, *UN Guiding Principles on Business and Human Rights at 10: The Impact of the UNGPs on Courts and Judicial Mechanisms*, 15–16 (2021), https://www.debevoise.com/insights/publications/2021/07/un-guiding-principles.

[66] *See* UN Working Group on Business and Human Rights, *Guidance on National Action Plans on Business and Human Rights*, OHCHR (2016), https://www.ohchr.org/en/special-procedures/wg-business/national-action-plans-business-and-human-rights.

the EU, require companies to report on their human rights performance.[67] The United States, in its own procurement processes, requires sellers of products to the federal government to eliminate human trafficking from their supply chains.[68]

Beyond reporting, the United Kingdom (UK) authorized the seizure of imported goods manufactured in a manner involving human rights abuse.[69] In 2021, the US Customs Office has increased its seizure of goods manufactured by companies engaged in forced labor or other human rights abuses.[70] The threat of seizure can have huge adverse impacts; e.g., a Malayan company's US$1 billion listing in Hong Kong was delayed in order to resolve a US import ban based on multiple indicators of forced labor in its production processes.[71]

States have moved beyond National Action Plans, reporting requirements, and asset seizures to require corporations to engage in mandatory due diligence, starting with France in 2016[72] and The Netherlands in 2019.[73] Germany and Norway followed with their own legislation in 2021.[74] Similar mandatory due diligence legislative initiatives are underway

---

[67] *Id.*

[68] In 2012, the United States adopted the US Federal Acquisition Regulation, "Combatting Trafficking in Persons," FAR Subpart 22.17 and Part 52 (2012), https://www.federalregister.gov/documents/2015/01/29/2015-01524/federal-acquisition-regulation-ending-trafficking-in-persons, which requires all US government contractors to take detailed actions to eliminate human trafficking at all levels of their supply chains, including the development and implementation of compliance plans, with significant sanctions for noncompliance.

[69] In 2017, the UK adopted the Criminal Finances Act of 2017, https://www.legislation.gov.uk/ukpga/2017/22/contents/enacted, which authorizes UK prosecutors to seize property that was obtained by or "in connection with" gross human rights abuse, regardless of when the property was obtained.

[70] US Customs and Border Protection, *CBP issues Region-Wide Withhold Release Order on Products Made by Slave Labor in Xinjiang* (Jan. 13, 2021), https://www.cbp.gov/newsroom/national-media-release/cbp-issues-region-wide-withhold-release-order-products-made-slave.

[71] Scott Murdoch, et al., *Top Glove's $1 billion Hong Kong listing delayed amid U.S. ban imbroglio—sources*, (Jun. 1, 2021), https://www.nasdaq.com/articles/top-gloves-%241-bln-hong-kong-listing-delayed-amid-u.s.-ban-imbroglio-sources-2021-06-01-0.

[72] French Law on the Corporate Duty of Vigilance (2017), Loi no. 2017-399 d 27 Mars 2017 relative au devoir de vigilance des societies meres et des enterprises donneuses d'ordre, https://www.legifrance.gouv.fr/loda/id/JORFTEXT000034290626/. The French Law imposes human rights and environmental due diligence obligations on large French companies (including foreign firms with a significant French presence), with legal consequences for their violation. See Business and Human Rights Resource Center, *France's Duty of Vigilance Law* (Mar. 16, 2021), https://www.business-humanrights.org/en/big-issues/corporate-legal-accountability/frances-duty-of-vigilance-law/.

[73] The Netherlands Child Labor Duty of Care Act, https://zoek-officielebekendmakingen-nl.translate.goog/stb-2019-401.html?_x_tr_sl=auto&_x_tr_tl=en&_x_tr_hl=en&_x_tr_pto=nui ((accessed October 2021) (English translation) requires companies that sell goods to Dutch consumers (including foreign companies) to determine whether child labor occurs in their supply chains, and if so, to set out a plan of action on how to combat it and issue a statement showing its due diligence investigation and plan, violation of which would incur criminal penalties. See Business and Human Rights Resource Center, *Dutch Senate Votes to Adopt Child Labour Due Diligence Law* (March 16, 2021), https://www.business-humanrights.org/en/latest-news/dutch-senate-votes-to-adopt-child-labour-due-diligence-law/.

[74] *See* German Act on Corporate Due Diligence Obligations in Supply Chains of July 16, 2021, (Lieferkettensorgfaltspflichtengesetz-LkSG), https://www.bmas.de/SharedDocs/Downloads/DE/Internationales/act-corporate-due-diligence-obligations-supply-chains.pdf;jsessionid=4A3584DB6A2336FB861F7175C08F4C0E.delivery1-replication?__blob=publicationFile&v=2 (Unofficial English translation; and Norwegian Act relating to enterprises' transparency and work on fundamental human rights and decent working conditions, LOV-2021-06-18-99. Unofficial English translation at: https://lovdata.no/dokument/NLE/lov/2021-06-18-99#:~:text=The%20Act%20shall%20promote%20enterprises,fundamental%20human%20rights%20and%20decent. For a comparison of the German and Norwegian laws, see Markus Krajewski, Kristel Tonstad and Franziska Wohltmann, *Mandatory Human Rights Due Diligence in Germany and Norway: Stepping, or Striding, in the Same Direction?* Business and Human Rights Journal (2021), First View, 1–9, https://doi.org/10.1017/bhj.2021.43.

in Austria, Denmark, Finland, Switzerland, the UK, and elsewhere, and, most significantly, in the EU.[75] The French and Dutch laws, as well as the proposed EU legislation, have extra-territorial impact.

The French Duty of Vigilance Law and the Dutch Child Labor Law The French Duty of Vigilance law applies to direct or indirect subsidiaries of certain French companies that are organized and operate outside France, as well as to the activities of certain of their subcontractors and subsidiaries outside France.[76] It has been invoked as the basis for a claim by Mexican villagers against a Mexican subsidiary of a French company for failing to address the human rights risk of a wind farm electric project or the measures taken to prevent the violation of the rights of Indigenous peoples to free, prior, and informed consent, or adequate public participation in the decision-making process.[77]

The Dutch Child Labor law has broad extra-territorial impact. It requires companies to investigate whether there is a reasonable suspicion that goods or services to be supplied to Dutch consumers have been produced with child labor (whether or not the company is registered in The Netherlands), to determine whether child labor occurs in their supply chains, and if so, to set out a plan of action on how to combat it, and issue a statement showing its due diligence investigation and plan, violation of which would incur significant penalties, including a fine of up to 10 percent of the worldwide annual turnover of the company. Therefore, a non-Dutch company selling goods to Dutch consumers that were produced with child labor at remote tiers of the company supply chain could be subject to the Dutch Child Labor Law.[78]

The European Union Corporate Sustainability Due Diligence Draft Directive On February 23, 2022, the European Commission issued its *Draft Directive of the European Parliament and of the Council on Corporate Sustainability Due Diligence* (*CSDD*).[79] The CSDD sets forth a legislative proposal for adoption by the European Parliament and the Member States (the Council). The Parliament and the Council must agree upon a final text, which then must be transposed into national law of the Member States. The process could take several years.

The EU is the world's largest trading bloc. Its regulations have a global impact, known as the "Brussels Effect" in which EU regulation has become externalized in the practices

---

[75] Business and Human Rights Resource Center, *National & Regional Movements for Mandatory Human Rights & Environmental Due Diligence in Europe* (2019), https://www.business-humanrights.org/en/latest-news/national-regional-movements-for-mandatory-human-rights-environmental-due-diligence-in-europe/.

[76] ReedSmith Client Alert, *The New Duty of Vigilance Adopted in France Covers Much Broader Issues Than Anti-Bribery Compliance and Will Have Significant Extraterritorial Application* (2017), https://www.mondaq.com/france/human-rights/576816/the-new-duty-of-vigilance-adopted-in-france-covers-much-broader-issues-than-anti-bribery-compliance-and-will-have-significant-extraterritorial-application.

[77] Clifford Chance, *Legal Action Based on the French Vigilance Law Triggered By a Wind Farm Project in Mexico* (Jan. 11, 2021), https://www.cliffordchance.com/insights/resources/blogs/business-and-human-rights-insights/2021/01/legal-action-based-on-the-french-vigilance-law-triggered-by-a-wind-farm-project-in-mexico.html.

[78] Ropes & Gray Alert, *Dutch Child Labor Due Diligence Act Approved by Senate–Implications for Global Companies* (2019), https://www.ropesgray.com/en/newsroom/alerts/2019/06/Dutch-Child-Labor-Due-Diligence-Act-Approved-by-Senate-Implications-for-Global-Companies.

[79] Available at https://ec.europa.eu/info/publications/proposal-directive-corporate-sustainable-due-diligence-and-annex_en.

of companies from other countries, as has already happened with respect to privacy and consumer goods.[80] This is particularly true with respect to the CSDD since the CSDD's due diligence provisions would apply explicitly to large non-EU businesses doing business in the EU market.

The CSDD's stated purposes are to improve corporate governance practices; to avoid fragmentation of due diligence requirements; to increase corporate accountability for adverse impacts; to improve access to remedy; and to complement other EU measures that directly address sustainability challenges.[81]

The CSDD would therefore impose wide-ranging human rights and environmental due diligence duties that are derived from the UNGPs and the OECD Guidelines. It would apply to about 13,000 large EU companies and about 4,000 large third-country companies doing business in the EU, and smaller companies in high-risk sectors.[82] It would not include small to medium-sized enterprises (SMEs).[83]

To that end, the CSDD would require Member States to impose due diligence responsibilities on companies covered by the law. It would also impose duties on the directors of covered EU companies (but not on non-EU companies covered by the law).

In broad terms, the CSDD would require Member States: to ensure that companies integrate due diligence into all their corporate policies (Article 5); to identify actual and potential adverse human rights and environmental impacts (Article 6); to prevent potential adverse impacts (Article 7); to end actual adverse impacts (Article 8); to provide for complaint mechanisms (Article 9); to monitor their own operations and value chains (Article 10); to identify, mitigate, prevent, and remedy actual and potential adverse impacts on human rights in the environment and in the companies' own operations, their subsidiaries, and their supply chains; and to communicate their performance (Article 11).

To enforce its provisions, the CSDD relies on administrative supervision by appropriate authorities in Member States (Article 17), with significant investigative and sanctioning responsibilities (Articles 18 to 19). It also relies on civil liability for damages to injured persons arising from failure to adequately conduct due diligence as required by the law (Article 22). Companies can defend against civil liability claims by showing that they entered into contractual assurances with direct partners with whom they have an established relationship of compliance with the company's code of conduct or action plan, as confirmed by audits, where such assurances are cascaded down the supply chain (Articles 7, 8, and 22.) The CSDD charges the Commission with the task of developing guidance about voluntary model contract clauses (Article 13).

With respect to the directors of covered EU companies, the CSDD would require Member States to ensure that company directors "take into account the consequences of their decisions for sustainability matters, including, where applicable, human rights, climate change

---

[80] Anu Bradford, *The Brussels Effect*, 107 Northwestern Uni. L. Rev. 1(2012), https://scholarship.law.columbia.edu/cgi/viewcontent.cgi?article=1275&context=faculty_scholarship,

[81] *CSDD*, *supra* note 79, at 3.

[82] *Id.* at 16.

[83] *Id.* at 40.

and environmental consequences, including in the short, medium and long term" (Article 25). It requires them to set up and oversee due diligence policies and actions, with input from stakeholders and civil society, and to adapt the corporate strategy to take into its account adverse impacts and its measures to address them (Article 26).

There will be a vibrant debate before the EU Parliament and the European Council over the specific terms of the CSDD. Some of these issues are discussed in Section III below.

b. Human Rights Due Diligence as a Legal Duty of Care

In addition to State efforts to codify HRDD into statutes, HRDD has the potential to become the basis for a legal duty of care owed by corporations to avoid harming persons and society. Common law courts have often used normative standards as the basis for establishing tort-based legal duties of care to injured persons under domestic law. As Justice Learned Hand wrote in the famous *T. J. Hooper* case in 1932, "Courts must in the end say what is required; there are precautions so imperative even their universal disregard will not excuse their omission."[84] To date, violations of internationally recognized human rights laws have been rarely invoked to date to establish a common law duty of care, but that will likely change as HRDD becomes more deeply embedded in law, policy, and corporate practice. The change would be highly significant, since most multinational corporations are headquartered in common law jurisdictions, such as those in the United States, the UK, and Canada.

Although no courts have yet held that a common law duty of care to exercise HRDD exists, the Canadian Supreme Court set the stage for it in *Nevsun Resources, Inc. v. Araya.*[85] There, the Court recognized that customary international laws, including crimes against humanity, forced labor, and torture, are part of Canadian law, and that Canadian companies may be liable for the breach of these standards as a result of their overseas operations (in that case, arising from a Canadian company's mining operations in Eritrea). Professor Emeritus Douglas Cassel of Notre Dame Law School argues that all the elements are in place to establish a common law duty of care claim against a parent company for injuries to people and communities that result from its failure to conduct HRDD with respect to the operations of its foreign subsidiary.[86]

---

[84] T. J. Hooper, 60 F.2d 737, 738 (2d Cir. 1932) (Hand, J.), https://law.justia.com/cases/federal/appellate-courts/F2/60/737/1542549/. "[I]n most cases reasonable prudence is in fact common prudence; but strictly it is never its measure; a whole calling may have unduly lagged in the adoption of new and available devices. It may never set its own tests, however persuasive be its usages. *Courts must in the end say what is required; there are precautions so imperative even their universal disregard will not excuse their omission*" (emphasis added). The case is discussed *in Waitzer and Sarro*, (*infra*, n. 99), p. 825.

[85] Nevsun Resources Ltd. v. Araya, 2020 SCC 5 (CanLII), https://www.canlii.org/en/ca/scc/doc/2020/2020scc5/2020scc5.html.

[86] That is, there would be a proximate connection between the parent's conduct and the injury, the injury would be foreseeable, and liability would serve the public interest. Doug Cassel, *Outlining the Case for a Common Law Duty of Care to Exercise Human Rights Due Diligence*, 1 BUSINESS AND HUMAN RIGHTS LAW JOURNAL 2, 179–202 (2016), http://journals.cambridge.org/abstract_S2057019816000158. In addition, duty of care claims based on the UNGPs and HRDD can arise under statutes, too, as discussed at n. 54 above, regarding the 2021 Hague District Court decision involving Royal Dutch Shell, where the Court explicitly relied on the UNGPs to conclude that Royal Dutch Shell has breached its duty of care under a rule of unwritten law relating to social conduct under the Dutch Civil Code by not taking sufficient steps to reduce its CO_2 emissions.

in the wake of the 2013 Rana Plaza factory collapse, which is enforceable by arbitration; and (2) foreign investor–host State bilateral treaty arbitration, which may involve allegations that a State's increased efforts to protect human rights violate the rights of investors under bilateral treaties.[90]

4. *Business Benefits of Human Rights Due Diligence Other than Legal Compliance*

Complying with legal standards that reflect or incorporate HRDD is foundational for corporate governance. However, legal compliance is not the only reason for corporate fiduciaries to act affirmatively to ensure that HRDD is implemented into corporate governance. Doing so also furthers the best interests of the corporation.

The importance to ESG investors of company involvement in human rights abuse to investors has been discussed earlier, since such involvement implicates at least the 'S' factor, and perhaps the "E" and "G" factors as well. A company's involvement in human rights abuse is a leading indicator to ESG investors of the likelihood of risks to the business, and ultimately of lower ratings in potentially all three factors. Involvement in human rights abuse can harm the corporation's operations, finances, legal costs and liabilities, reputation, or staff recruitment and retention, among other things.

For example, conflicts between extractive companies and communities, and labor strikes and disruptions in the supply chain, can be very expensive. These conflicts disrupt production, prevent products from coming to market, jeopardize reputations, and divert senior management attention. The disruption of the global supply chain as a result of the COVID-19 pandemic has highlighted the fragility of supply chains to disruption.[91] In one famous case, an extractive company calculated that the disruption from disputes with communities, spread out over all its facilities over a two-year period, cost US$6.5 billion. Similar in terms of magnitude is the value of reputation.

Finally, it is estimated that over one-third of the market capitalization of FTSE350 companies is attributed to reputation, which is at risk when companies are involved in deaths to workers from the collapse of factories where workers are assembling their garments, or in sourcing from suppliers that use child or slave labor.[92]

---

[90] *Beyond CSR, supra* note 64, Section 20.04[K][2].

[91] John F. Sherman III, *Irresponsible Exit: Exercising Force Majeure Provisions in Procurement Contracts*, 6 Bus. & Hum. Rts. J., Cambridge University Press 1, 127–134 (2021), https://www.cambridge.org/core/journals/business-and-human-rights-journal/article/abs/irresponsible-exit-exercising-force-majeure-provisions-in-procurement-contracts/A1206F08637B7353E652857B9CDC9720.

[92] For a fuller description of these costs and the research that supports it, *see* Shift, Business, Human Rights and the Sustainable Development Goals: Forging a Coherent Vision and Strategy (2016), commissioned by the Business and Sustainable Development Commission, Section 4, http://s3.amazonaws.com/aws-bsdc/BSDC-Biz-HumanRights-SDGs.pdf. *See also* OECD and Columbia/SIPA Quantifying the Costs, Benefits and Risks of Due Diligence for Responsible Business Conduct, Framework and Assessment Tool (Jun. 13, 2016) https://www.oecd.org/industry/inv/mne/Quantifying-the-Cost-Benefits-Risks-of-Due-Diligence-for-RBC.pdf; Rachel Davis & Daniel Franks, Costs of Company-Community Conflict in the Extractive Sector, (2014), https://shiftproject.org/resource/costs-of-company-community-conflict-in-the-extractive-sector/.

II. The Corporate Legal Officer's Role

Under Delaware law, corporate officers are also fiduciaries, who owe duties of care and loyalty to the corporation.[93] Officers include corporate general counsel and other legal officers, if they are acting in their capacity as officers.[94] Although corporate legal officers partner with the CEO and other senior officers to manage the corporation's strategic risks, their affirmative fiduciary duty of loyalty and care is to the corporation itself. This creates an inevitable tension, where the general counsel and other in-house lawyers must "reconcile the dual—and at times contradictory—roles of being both a partner to the business leaders and a guardian of the corporation's integrity and reputation."[95]

As corporate fiduciaries, corporate legal officers have an affirmative duty to exercise their leadership of the legal function to further the best interests of the corporation when it comes to avoiding involvement in human rights abuse. There are many steps that a corporate legal officer can take to do so,[96] but here are three: (1) not undermining effective HRDD; (2) treating the potential for involvement in gross human rights abuse as a matter of legal compliance; and (3) not using legal privilege to chill the open discussion of human rights problems in the corporation in order to find and fix them.

A. Not Undermining Effective HRDD

According to the UN Office of the High Commissioner on Human Rights (OHCHR), corporate lawyers can impede the effective implementation of HRDD for their companies through an overly narrow focus on avoiding legal liability.[97] The tendency of corporate legal officers to focus mainly on liability avoidance or delay in the short term has resulted in their paying too little attention to their affirmative duty to promote the best interests of the corporation.[98] They tend not to focus on what a corporation can do, unless to confirm that the client's

---

[93] Gantler v. Stephens, 965 A.2d 695 (Del. 2009), https://caselaw.findlaw.com/de-supreme-court/1129452.html.

[94] Under Delaware law, a corporation cannot exculpate officers from liability for money damages for breach of the duty of care, as they can for board members. Edward B. Micheletti, Bonnie W. David, Andre D. Kinsey, *Recent Trends in Officer Liability*, Skadden, Arps, Slate, Meagher & Flom (Dec. 18, 2020), https://www.skadden.com/insights/publications/2020/12/insights-the-delaware-edition/recent-trends-in-officer-liability.

[95] Ben W. Heineman, Jr., *The Inside Counsel Revolution: Resolving the Partner-Guardian Tension* (ABA, 2016) p. 55. *See also*, Malcolm Rogge, *Vesting Transnational Corporate Responsibility in Natural Persons v. Legal Persons – What Matters Today?* Forthcoming in Corporate Citizen: New Perspectives on the Globalized Rule of Law, (Oonagh Fitzgerald, ed.) CIGI-McGill-Queen's University Press, 2020, https://papers.ssrn.com/sol3/papers.cfm?abstract_id=3570105.

[96] The leadership role of corporate counsel with respect to human rights is discussed in detail in John F. Sherman III *The Corporate General Counsel Who Respects Human Rights*, Legal Ethics J., Vol 24, 2021—Issue 1 (Oct. 7, 2021), Taylor & Francis Online, available at: https://doi.org/10.1080/1460728x.2021.1979731 .

[97] United Nations General Assembly (UNGA), The Report of the Working Group on the Issue of Human Rights and Transnational Corporations and Other Business Enterprises (Jun. 16, 2018) UN Doc. A/73/163 para 41, https://digitallibrary.un.org/record/1639520?ln=en.

[98] Brummer & Strine, *supra* note 40, at 64.

decided course of action is rational. Rather, they focus more on what a client should do to avoid legal liability, which is "typically, the most conservative path available."[99]

Such a narrow focus on liability avoidance has been used to justify a company's failure to mitigate and prevent toxic pollution and deny remedy to harmed persons and communities, where the "immediate costs of polluting would be borne by others, and any damages, penalties, or reputational harm for which the company or its managers ultimately might be accountable are discounted by both the probability of detection and the time lags between the decision to pollute and the detection of pollution, and between detection and enforcement."[100]

Professor Anita Ramasastry of the University of Washington Law School, and the former chair of the UN Business and Human Rights Working Group, has written that professional services providers, including lawyers, management consultants, architects, and others, typically do not identify human rights impacts and tailor their advice to prevent and mitigate those impacts, where such identification would likely have made a difference.[101] With respect to the legal profession, she calls out the need to go beyond counseling on avoiding liability to creative lawyering when it comes to human rights, citing as an example the 2003 negotiation of "a human rights undertaking between BP and Amnesty International regarding the BTC pipeline in the Caucasus region of Central Asia that would allow for evolving national human rights protection and stopping BP from raising certain claims against the government."[102]

B. Treating the Potential for Involvement in Gross Human Rights Abuse as a Matter of Legal Compliance, When Local Law Is Absent or Ineffective

The UNGPs specifically address the need for the legal function to take a leadership role in preventing the corporation's involvement in the most egregious forms of human rights abuse. Operating in areas of conflict often triggers a grave risk of gross human rights abuses, such as murder, rape, or torture, and corresponding impunity on the part of the relevant actors (which often include public security forces or armed groups). UNGPs Principle 23(c) therefore provides that businesses should treat "the risk of causing or contributing to gross human rights abuses as a legal compliance issue wherever they operate."

---

[99] Edward J. Waitzer & Douglas Sarro, *In Search Of Things Past And Future: Judicial Activism And Corporate Purpose*, 55(5) Osgood Hall L. J., 804 (Summer 2018), (*Waitzer and Sarro)*, https://digitalcommons.osgoode.yorku.ca/ohlj/vol55/iss3/5/.

[100] *Id.* at 797, citing Roy Shapira & Luigi Zingales, *Is Pollution Value-Maximizing? The DuPont Case*, NEBR Working Paper 23866 (2017), https://www.nber.org/papers/w23866.

[101] Anita Ramasastry, *Advisors or Enablers? Bringing Professional Service Providers into the Guiding Principles' Fold*, 6(2) Bus. & Hum. Rts. J., 293, 293–311 (Jun. 2021), https://doi.org/10.1017/bhj.2021.28. As one example, Prof. Ramasastry cites the advice given by the consulting firm McKinsey & Co to the US Dept. of Immigration and Customs Enforcement to cut food and medical care for immigrants placed in detention while awaiting adjudication on their asylum cases.

[102] *Id.* citing John F Sherman III, *Professional Responsibility of Lawyers under the UN Guiding Principles* (Apr. 2012), https://shiftproject.org/professional-responsibility-of-lawyers-under-the-guiding-principles/ and BTC Human Rights Undertaking (Sept. 22, 2003), https://subsites.bp.com/caspian/Human%20Rights%20Undertaking.pdf.

The Commentary to UNGPs Principle 23(c) provides that treating the risk of involvement in gross human rights abuses as a matter of legal compliance is required, "given the expanding web of potential corporate legal liability arising from extra-territorial civil claims, and from the incorporation of the provisions of the Rome Statute establishing specific corporate criminal responsibility and the jurisdiction of the International Criminal Court for those offences. In addition, corporate directors, officers, and employees may be subject to individual liability for acts that amount to gross human rights abuses."

UNGPs Principle 23(c) therefore directly asks the general counsel's office to take the lead in ensuring that the potential of involvement in gross human rights abuses is treated as a matter of legal compliance, rather than allowing other functions to decide whether the risk of such involvement to the company outweighs the costs of the risks to people.

C. Not Using Legal Privilege to Chill the Open Discussion of Human Rights Problems in the Corporation

As fiduciaries, corporate legal officers should help to foster a culture that respects human rights. One of the core norms and values of a rights-respecting culture is openness and learning.[103] This means searching out problems, trying to understand them, and fixing them. An open and learning culture entails: (a) actively searching for human rights problems of which the corporation is not already aware (for example, abuse in the remote tiers of its supply chain); (b) accepting responsibility when things go wrong (for example, by providing remedy when the corporation causes or contributes to abuse); and (c) being transparent about problems, even when they are not yet resolved.[104]

An example of a closed culture fostered by the corporate lawyers is the General Motors ignition key scandal, where the product safety and legal teams used legal privilege to slow-walk the investigation, discovery, and public disclosure of a design defect for 10 years. The defect had caused airbags not to deploy in accidents when the ignition key became loose and moved. This resulted in the deaths of 124 people, the recall of 300 million cars worldwide, and the payment of US$900 million in a Deferred Prosecution Agreement to the US government. An independent report to GM's Board strongly criticised the role of the legal department in fostering a closed culture, which chilled candid internal discussion and investigation of safety issues out of fear that discovery of problems could result in increased product liability awards in court.[105]

Similarly, in the UK's infamous British Post Office scandal, executives of the British Post Office, acting on the confidential advice of its lawyers, caused the criminal prosecution of hundreds of managers for stealing postal receipts, despite knowledge that the evidence of

---

[103] The other three authentic norms and values of a rights-respecting culture are respect for the dignity of all individuals and empathy with them, individual empowerment and responsibility, and coherence. *Valuing Respect*, *supra* note 8.

[104] *Id.*

[105] Anton R. Valukas (Jenner & Block), *Report to Board of Directors of General Motors Company Regarding Ignition Switch Recalls* (Attorney's Information Exchange Group, May 29, 2014), https://www.aieg.com/wp-content/uploads/2014/08/Valukas-report-on-gm-redacted2.pdf, (redacted copy).

stealing was not valid because it was based on fundamentally flawed accounting software. As the Evidence-Based Justice Lab of the University of Exeter observed, "Blame shifting of this kind can be a feature of corporate scandals. A key decision-maker says they were only following the advice of their lawyers; the lawyers say they were mere advisers, advising on or following instructions. The usual secrecy of legal advice encourages mutually assured irresponsibility."[106]

Of course, there is an inevitable tension between promoting the value of openness and learning, and the need for clients to be able to communicate in confidence with their legal counsel to assess their compliance with new mandatory HRDD laws.[107] This is particularly true as HRDD becomes mandatory and as the threat of legal violations becomes more widespread. Companies have an interest in protecting the "legitimate requirements of commercial confidentiality" under UNGPs Principle 17. This includes confidential attorney-client communications. Such communications need not be disclosed to affected stakeholders.

However, in the exercise of its fiduciary duty, the general counsel should ensure that even where the exercise of legal privilege may be technically justified, the organization does not use legal privilege reflexively to chill internal discussions that would identify and resolve human rights problems and build trust with external stakeholders.[108]

III. Going Forward

Due to the globalized impact of EU regulation, lawyers may wish to pay particular attention to the debate over the CSDD's provisions regarding directors' duties and over its proposed use of cascaded contractual assurances as a defence to civil liability claims.

A. Directors' Duties

As discussed above, the CSDD would require Member States to impose duties on directors to consider the consequences of their decisions on sustainability matters, including human rights, climate change, and the environment, and to oversee due diligence policies and actions, with input from stakeholders and society, and to adapt their corporate strategy accordingly. Not surprisingly, the directors' duty would not apply to non-EU companies and, therefore, would not have the same extra-territorial impact as the HRDD provisions.

The reform of directors' duties has been more controversial than mandatory HRDD, because the proposed reformation is not based on the same global consensus that produced the UNGPs. As a result, Professor Ruggie had voiced concern that linkage of the

---

106 Richard Moorehead, Karen Nokes, & Rebecca Helm, *Working Paper 4, Submission on Four Themes*, The Evidence-Based Justice Lab, Post Office Scandal Project (Oct. 29, 2021), 5, available at: https://www.postofficehorizoninquiry.org.uk/sites/default/files/2021-11/Moorhead.pdf.

107 Yousuf Aftab & Jonathan Drimmer, *Expert ESG Attorneys: How Corporate Sustainability Creates Legal Risk*, Corp. Gov. (Feb. 11, 2020), https://corpgov.com/lessons-from-cobalt-in-the-congo-how-corporate-sustainability-creates-legal-risk/.

108 John F. Sherman III & Amy Lehr, *Human Rights Due Diligence: Is it Too Risky?* (2010) Harvard Kennedy School Corporate Social Responsibility Initiative Working Paper No. 55, p. 15 https://www.hks.harvard.edu/sites/default/files/centers/mrcbg/programs/cri/files/workingpaper_55_shermanlehr.pdf.

EU directors' duty initiative with mandatory HRDD legislation might derail the passage of effective mandatory HRDD legislation.[109] Indeed, the proposed reform of directors' duties generated opposition by some business groups.[110]

In very broad terms, the thrust of the CSDD's language on directors' duties appears to make mandatory what is currently permitted but not yet mandated under Delaware law; namely, to act affirmatively in the company's sustainable best interests by considering impacts on human rights, climate, and the environment, and to put into place appropriate corporate governance measures to do so.

The directors' duty provisions have been welcomed by civil society commentators for making it clear that the board's duty to consider these impacts is no longer optional; but they have also been criticized for the vagueness and weakness of their language.[111]

B. HRDD as a Defense to Legal Liability and the EU Corporate Sustainability Due Diligence's Reliance on Contractual Assurances as a Defense

A key corporate governance issue is whether and the extent to which a corporation's implementation of HRDD should protect it from liability for not adequately managing the corporation's human rights risks. During the SRSG's UN mandate, an intervener suggested that the HRDD ought to provide immunity from legal claims arising from the involvement in human rights abuse, like the business judgment rule under Delaware law, which immunizes a board's actions from legal liability in a *Caremark*-type claim if the board's action is rational.[112] However, the Commentary to UNGPs Principle 17 flatly rejects automatic immunity. Rather, it states that evidence that a corporation took "every reasonable step to avoid involvement with an alleged human rights abuse" should help it to defend itself from a legal claim.

As a result, the UNGPs provide that to defend against a claim that a corporation's failure to conduct HRDD led to its involvement in human rights abuse, a corporation should be prepared to submit evidence to show that it took "every reasonable step" to avoid involvement in human rights harm through the exercise of HRDD. This requires more than pointing to the

---

[109] John G. Ruggie, *Letter to the European Commission regarding reform of directors duties* (Feb. 2021), https://www.business-humanrights.org/en/latest-news/john-ruggie-raises-concerns-about-adding-company-directors-duties-in-eu-mandatory-human-rights-due-diligence-legislation/.

[110] Sarah Anne Aarup, Barbara Moens, Giorgio Leali, & Hans von der Burchard, *Europe, Inc. Wins as EU Delays New Business Rules*, Politico (Mar. 21, 2021), https://www.politico.eu/article/europe-inc-puts-brussels-new-business-rules-on-ice/.

[111] John Morrison, Phil Bloomer, & Johannes Blankbach, *Human Rights Due Diligence and Corporate Boards: Reflections on European Commission Proposals Relating to Director Duties and Board Oversight*, IHRB and Dhaka Principles for Migration with Dignity (Mar. 9, 2022), available at: https://www.business-humanrights.org/en/blog/human-rights-due-diligence-and-corporate-boards-reflections-on-european-commission-proposals-relating-to-director-duties-and-board-oversight/.

[112] Report of the Special Representative of the Secretary-General on the issue of Human Rights and Transnational Corporations and Other Business Enterprises; John Ruggie, *Business and Human Rights: Further Steps toward the Operationalization of the "Protect, Respect and Remedy" Framework* A/HRC/14/27 (Apr. 9, 2010), par. 86, https://media.business-humanrights.org/media/documents/files/reports-and-materials/Ruggie-report-2010.pdf.

existence of its human rights policy on paper or listing the number of training sessions and the number of contracts with human rights provisions. These steps are important, but they do not explain why and how a company has taken these steps, how they fit into the company's overall HRDD efforts, and whether they are effective.

More fundamentally, the company should be prepared to defend itself by pointing to the specific HRDD policies, processes, and systems that it has integrated into its corporate governance, and to the leadership that it has exercised, in order to drive respect for human rights into the organization's culture.[113] In other words, the effective integration of HRDD into corporate governance will become critical to the defence of a claim under mandatory HRDD laws, even though it should not provide absolute immunity.

The EU CSDD's approach to defending against civil liability claims by alleged victims is much more limited, however. As noted earlier, the CSDD provides that a company can defend against a civil liability claim by relying upon appropriately verified contractual assurances from their established direct suppliers, of compliance with the company's code of conduct and preventative action plan, where the direct supplier cascades the contractual assurance requirement down the supply chain.

The contractual assurance defense must be reasonable. That is, the defense applies "unless it was unreasonable, in the circumstances of the case, to expect that the action actually taken, including as regards verifying compliance, would be adequate to prevent, mitigate, bring to and end or minimize the extent of the adverse impact." (Article 22(1)). Presumably, the purpose of this reasonableness standard is to prevent the contractual assurance and verification from becoming a formalistic, tick-the-box exercise that lacks substance.

Nevertheless, the CSDD's reliance on cascading contractual assurances from direct established suppliers is far less than demonstrating that a company used "every reasonable step" to avoid involvement in human rights impacts, as contemplated by the UNGPs. The reliance has triggered widespread concerns. The Dutch government has stated that the heavy reliance on such assurances risks the shifting of responsibility from companies covered by the CSDD to non-covered companies, such as SMEs or companies established in countries with weak protection of human rights or the environment. It further notes that contract clauses have not in the past been used to effectively counteract human rights violations and environmental damage and can lead large companies to offload their obligations to other companies in their supply chain.[114]

In addition, three leading international standard-setting authorities—the International Labour Organization (ILO), the Organisation for Economic Co-operation and Development (OECD), and the UN Office of the High Commissioner for Human Rights (OHCHR), have warned jointly against the risk of "box-ticking compliance approaches and overreliance on

---

[113] Shift, *Discussion Draft: Signals of Seriousness for Human Rights Due Diligence: How Can National Regulators Best Assess the Quality of a Company's HRDD Efforts under Potential EU Legislation?* (Feb. 2021), https://shiftproject.org/resource/signals-draft1/.

[114] W. B. Hoekstra, Dutch Minister of Foreign Affairs, *Richtlijn gepaste zorgvuldigheidsverplichting voor ondernemingen (Directive on Due Diligence for Companies)*, prepared by the Working Group on Assessment of New Commission Proposals, p. 6, April 7, 2022, available at: https://www.tweedekamer.nl/kamerstukken/brieven_regering/detail?id=2022Z06841&did=2022D13855.

c. The Private Law of Human Rights Due Diligence

Private commercial law is also incorporating UNGPs and HRDD concepts into contracts and agreements, thereby creating a new *lex mercatoria*, or private commercial law, of human rights. For example, when huge global business organizations such as FIFA (the world's largest and richest sports organization), require partners and suppliers to comply with these standards, including in FIFA World Cup tournaments, the results cascade throughout the supply chain.[87]

When huge multinational enterprises require their contractual counterparties to comply with the UNGPs, procurement staff and their lawyers are incentivized to address the deficiencies of current supply chain contracts from an HRDD perspective. These contracts are typically based on buyer-enforced supplier representations and warranties to meet human rights standards in the contract. However, the representations and warranties approach of existing supply chain contracts has been largely ineffective to improve human rights performance by suppliers; this is because so many suppliers lack the managerial and financial capacity to comply with both human rights and commercial performance standards (such as price, quantity, and timing of delivery of goods). Moreover, buyers often undercut the ability of low-margin suppliers with prices that make it impossible for workers to enjoy a living wage, and by last-minute changes in design and quantity. Doing so makes cheating and unauthorized subcontracting inevitable if the supplier wants to keep the business. Under such circumstances, the buyer's expectations of suppliers with respect to human rights performance is like "paying for a bus ticket and expecting to fly."[88] Buyers get what they pay for.

As a result, a Working Group of the Business Law Section of the American Bar Association (ABA) has drafted model supply chain contracts (ABA Model Contract Clauses) that would shift contracts from a representations and warranties regime to a HRDD regime, in which buyers and suppliers would share the responsibility of addressing supply chain human rights abuse.[89] The model contract clauses are suggestions only, but they indicate recognition of the need for corporate lawyers to help their clients address more effectively the problem of supply chain human rights abuse by incorporating HRDD principles into supply chain contracts.

Finally, private arbitration is increasingly being used to resolve business-related human rights disputes. Two examples are (1) the Bangladesh Accord, an agreement between about 200 Western garment companies and two trade unions to raise factory safety improvements

---

[87] John G. Ruggie & John F. Sherman III, *Adding Human Rights Punch to the New Lex Mercatoria: The Impact of the UN Guiding Principles on Business and Human Rights on Commercial Legal Practice*, 6 Journal of International Dispute Settlement 3, 455–461 (2015), https://scholar.harvard.edu/files/john-ruggie/files/adding_human_rights_punch_to_the_new_lex_mercatoria.pdf.

[88] Human Rights Watch, "*Paying for a Bus Ticket and Expecting to Fly": How Apparel Brand Purchasing Practices Drive Labor Abuses* (Apr. 2019) available at https://www.hrw.org/report/2019/04/23/paying-bus-ticket-and-expecting-fly/how-apparel-brand-purchasing-practices-drive.

[89] *Balancing Buyer And Supplier Responsibilities Model Contract Clauses To Protect Workers In International Supply Chains, Version 2.0*, https://www.americanbar.org/content/dam/aba/administrative/human_rights/contractual-clauses-project/mccs-full-report.pdf; John F. Sherman III, *No Need to Reinvent Wheels: Drafting Meaningful Human Rights Due Diligence through Model Suggested Supply Chain Contract Clauses*, Shift Viewpoint (Mar. 2001), https://shiftproject.org/aba-contract-clauses/.

contractual assurances" and urged coherence with international standards.[115] The UN *Principles for Responsible Investments* (UNPRI) echoed this concern.[116] Amnesty International expressed unease that the CSDD would restrict "access to remedy for victims of corporate human rights abuses by allowing companies to shift their responsibilities on to business partners using contractual assurances."[117] The French NGO Sherpa noted the historic ineffectiveness of reliance on company codes of conduct referenced in contracts and the audits of contract compliance as a means of improving human rights performance.[118]

Finally, Shift, the nonprofit center of expertise on the UNGPs that Prof. Ruggie chaired until his death last year, has echoed these and other concerns. However, it noted that the ABA Model Contract Clauses, drafted by a Working Group of the Business Law Section, referenced earlier, may address the concern that traditional supply contracts, which are based on top-down compliance with suppliers' representations and warranties, ignore buyer contributions to human rights impacts in the supply chain.[119]

The ABA Model Contract Clauses would move from a representations and warranties regime to a collaborative regime based on shared responsibility to exercise human rights due diligence, would require both parties to engage in responsible sourcing and purchasing practices, and would prioritize remedy to injured stakeholders over contract remedies between the parties for breach of the contract's human rights provisions. Using such contracts as a model might help to address some of the concerns raised with the current CSDD draft's reliance on cascaded contractual assurances.

In short, the role of HRDD as a defense to civil liability claims will be the subject of vibrant debate as the CSDD goes forward.

IV. Conclusion

HRDD is a familiar but unique form of business risk management developed by Professor Ruggie as SRSG to enable companies to know and show that they are respecting human rights under Pillar Two of the UNGPs. HRDD is familiar because it resonates with and is complementary to existing tools of corporate governance, such as internal controls and enterprise risk management, which enable a corporation to manage the relations among its

---

[115] *Joint letter by ILO, OECD, OHCHR Regarding The European Commission's Proposal for a Corporate Sustainability Due Diligence Directive* (Mar. 7, 2022), downloadable at: https://www.ilo.org/global/docs/WCMS_839276/lang–en/index.htm.

[116] *PRI Statement: European Commission Proposal on Corporate Sustainability Due Diligence* (Mar. 2, 2022), available at: https://www.business-humanrights.org/en/latest-news/pri-statement-european-commission-proposal-on-corporate-sustainability-due-diligence/.

[117] Amnesty International, *EU: Due Diligence Proposal 'A Missed Opportunity'* (Feb. 23, 2022), available at: https://www.amnesty.org/en/latest/news/2022/02/eu-due-diligence-proposal-a-missed-opportunity/.

[118] Sherpa, *Directive on Corporate Sustainability Due Diligence: The Proposal Finally Unveiled by the Commission Must Be Improved* (Feb. 23, 2022), available at: https://www.asso-sherpa.org/directive-on-corporate-sustainability-due-diligence-the-proposal-finally-unveiled-by-the-commission-must-be-improved.

[119] Shift, *The EU Commission's Proposal for a Corporate Sustainability Due Diligence Directive* (Mar. 2022), *see* authorities referenced at note 16, available at: https://shiftproject.org/resource/eu-csdd-proposal-analysis/.

shareholders, its staff and workers, its customers, its communities, and all other stakeholders affected by its operations and business relationships.

At the same time, HRDD is unique because its purpose is to enable the business to identify and address the risks of its involvement in human rights harm to vulnerable people, from their perspective, rather than solely the risks of harm to the business's commercial interests. By asking businesses to take the interests and views of stakeholders into account, HRDD adds to the long-standing debate over the shareholder-primacy purpose of the corporation. HRDD is premised on the belief that is not in the best interests of businesses, including shareholders, to ignore the adverse impacts of their decisions on stakeholders in the name of producing short-term returns for shareholders.

To fulfill its purpose, HRDD cannot be a superficial tick-the-box mechanism to be invoked whenever necessary to provide the equivalent of an insurance policy to officers and shareholders from legal claims based on involvement in human rights abuse. Rather, HRDD must be embedded into corporate governance as part of a whole-company system of identifying, preventing, mitigating, and addressing human rights risks. It is only when the company is truly serious about HRDD and does everything reasonably possible to prevent human rights harm, should the company's use of HRDD count in the company's favor in court.

At the end of day, the right relationship of HRDD to corporate governance is more than about meeting the minimum standards needed for legal compliance. In this regard, Professor Ruggie wrote that he "aligned himself with Amartya Sen, who insists that human rights are much more than laws' antecedents or progeny."[120] Rather, HRDD is a practical corporate governance tool that enables the business to meet the goal of respecting the dignity of all human beings in its operations and business relationships.

V. References

Judicial Cases

Canada

Nevsun Resources Ltd. v. Araya, 2020 SCC 5 (CanLII), https://www.canlii.org/en/ca/scc/doc/2020/2020scc5/2020scc5.html.

United States

Gantler v. Stephens, 965 A.2d 695 (Del. 2009), https://caselaw.findlaw.com/de-supreme-court/1129452.html/.

In re Caremark International Inc. Derivative Litigation, 698 A.2d 959 (Del. Ch. 1996).

Jane Doe 1, etc. v. Apple Inc 1, etc., US District Court for the District of Columbia, 16 December 2019, https://www.classaction.org/media/doe-et-al-v-apple-inc-et-al_1.pdf.

Stone v. Ritter, 911 A.2d 362, 369 (2006).

Teamsters Local 443 Health Svcs & Ins. Plan v. Chou, Delaware Court of Chancery, C.A. No. 2019-0816-SG (Memorandum Opinion, August 24, 2020), https://courts.delaware.gov/Opinions/Download.aspx?id=309790.

---

[120] Amartya Sen, *Elements of a Theory of Human Rights*, Philosophy and Public Affairs, 32, 319 (Autumn 2004), http://www.mit.edu/~shaslang/mprg/asenETHR.pdf.

The T. J. Hooper, 60 F.2d 737, 738 (2d Cir. 1932) (Hand, J.), https://law.justia.com/cases/federal/appellate-courts/F2/60/737/1542549/.

The Netherlands

VERENIGING MILIEUDEFENSIE, etc. v. Royal Dutch Shell PLC, Court of The Hague, Case No. C/09/571932 / HA ZA 19-379 (English version) (May 26, 2021), https://uitspraken-rechtspraak-nl.translate.goog/inziendocument?id=ECLI:NL:RBDHA:2021:5339&_x_tr_sl=auto&_x_tr_tl=en&_x_tr_hl=en&_x_tr_pto=nui.

Statutes and Regulations

US Federal Acquisition Regulation, *Combatting Trafficking in Persons*, FAR Subpart 22.17 and Part 52 (2012), https://www.federalregister.gov/documents/2015/01/29/2015-01524/federal-acquisition-regulation-ending-trafficking-in-persons.

US Sentencing Commission, Chapter Eight, *Sentencing of Organizations*, §8B2.1. Effective Compliance and Ethics Program (2015).

US Trafficking Victims Protection Reauthorization Act, 18 U.S.C. § 1595 et. seq.

United Kingdom Criminal Finances Act 2017, https://www.legislation.gov.uk/ukpga/2017/22/contents/enacted.

United Nations Materials

Report of the UN Working Group on the issue of human rights and transnational corporations and other business enterprises, *Guiding Principles on Business and Human Rights at 10: Taking Stock of the First Decade*, A/HRC/47/39 (April 22, 2021), https://www.ohchr.org/en/issues/business/pages/wghrandtransnationalcorporationsandotherbusiness.aspx.

UN General Assembly, *The Human Right to a Clean, Healthy, and Sustainable Environment*, A/76/L.75 (July 26, 2022), https://digitallibrary.un.org/record/3982508?ln=en.

UN Office of the High Commissioner for Human Rights, *Guiding Principles on Business and Human Rights: Implementing the United Nations "Protect, Respect and Remedy" Framework*, UN Doc. HR/PUB/11/4 (2011), https://www.ohchr.org/documents/publications/guidingprinciplesbusinesshr_en.pdf [hereinafter *Guiding Principles*].

UN Office of the High Commissioner for Human Rights, *The Corporate Responsibility to Respect Human Rights: An Interpretive Guide* (2012), https://www.ohchr.org/sites/default/files/Documents/Issues/Business/RtRInterpretativeGuide.pdf.

UN Office of the High Commissioner for Human Rights, *Human Rights at the Heart of the Response: Human Rights, the Environment, and Covid-19: Key Messages* (2021), https://www.ohchr.org/Documents/Issues/ClimateChange/HR-environment-COVID19.pdf.

UN Special Rapporteur David R. Boyd, on the issue of human rights obligations relating to the enjoyment of a safe, clean, healthy and sustainable environment, *Human Rights Depend on A Healthy Biosphere* (July 15, 2020), A/75/161, https://undocs.org/A/75/161.

United Nations Working Group on Business and Human Rights, *Guidance on National Action Plans on Business and Human Rights*, OHCHR (2016), https://www.ohchr.org/en/special-procedures/wg-business/national-action-plans-business-and-human-rights.

Mandatory HRDD Legislation and Initiatives

European Commission, *Green Paper on Corporate Governance in Financial Institutions and Remuneration Policies*, COM(2010) 284 https://op.europa.eu/en/publication-detail/-/publication/1788e830-b050-447c-8214-77ed51b13241.

European Commission, *Sustainable Corporate Justice, DG Justice, A3 Company Law Unit, Legislative and Possible Guidance*, Q1 2021, Ref. Ares (2020) 4034032–30/07/2020, https://media.business-humanrights.org/media/documents/files/documents/090166e5d21fb60c.pdf.

European Commission, DG Justice, *EC Sustainable Corporate Governance Initiative.—Summary Report—Public Consultation*, (May 18, 2021), https://media.business-humanrights.org/media/documents/EU_Commission_responses.pdf.

European Parliament, *Corporate Due Diligence and Corporate Accountability, European Parliament Resolution Of 10 March 2021 With Recommendations to the Commission On Corporate Due Diligence and Corporate Accountability* (2020/2129(INL)), https://www.europarl.europa.eu/doceo/document/TA-9-2021-0073_EN.html.

French Law on the Corporate Duty of Vigilance (2017), Loi no. 2017-399 d 27 Mars 2017 relative au devoir de vigilance des societies meres et des enterprises donneuses d'ordre, https://www.legifrance.gouv.fr/loda/id/JORFTEXT000034290626/.

German Act on Corporate Due Diligence Obligations in Supply Chains of July 16, 2021, (Lieferkettensorgfaltspflichtengesetz-LkSG), https://www.bmas.de/SharedDocs/Downloads/DE/Internationales/act-corporate-due-diligence-obligations-supply-chains.pdf;jsessionid=4A3584DB6A2336FB861F7175C08F4C0E.delivery1-replication?__blob=publicationFile&v=2 (Unofficial English translation).

The Netherlands Child Labor Duty of Care Act (2019), https://zoek-officielebekendmakingen-nl.translate.goog/stb-2019-401.html?_x_tr_sl=auto&_x_tr_tl=en&_x_tr_hl=en&_x_tr_pto=nui (English translation).

Norwegian Act relating to enterprises' transparency and work on fundamental human rights and decent working conditions, LOV-2021-06-18-99. Unofficial English translation at: https://lovdata.no/dokument/NLE/lov/2021-06-18-99#:~:text=The%20Act%20shall%20promote%20enterprises,fundamental%20human%20rights%20and%20decent.

Secondary Sources

Aarup, Sarah Anne, Moens, Barbara, Leali, Giorgio & Von Der Burchard, Hans, *Europe, Inc. Wins as EU Delays New Business Rules*, POLITICO (March 21, 2021), https://www.politico.eu/article/europe-inc-puts-brussels-new-business-rules-on-ice/.

Aftab, Yousuf, and Drimmer, Jonathan, *Expert ESG Attorneys: How Corporate Sustainability Creates Legal Risk* (Corp Gov, February 11, 2020) https://corpgov.com/lessons-from-cobalt-in-the-congo-how-corporate-sustainability-creates-legal-risk/.

Al Hussein, Zeid Ra'ad, *Ethical Pursuit of Prosperity*, THE LAW SOCIETY GAZETTE (March 21, 2015) available at: https://www.lawgazette.co.uk/commentary-and-opinion/ethical-pursuit-of-prosperity/5047796.article.

BlackRock, *Our Approach to Engagement With Companies on Their Human Rights Impacts*, Investment Stewardship (March 2021), https://www.blackrock.com/corporate/literature/publication/blk-commentary-engagement-on-human-rights.pdf. (accessed October 2021).

Boatright, John R., *The Ethics of Risk Management in the Information Age*, Bentley University Center for Business Ethics, (2010), http://d2f5upgbvkx8pz.cloudfront.net/sites/default/files/inline-files/boatright-monograph.pdf.

Brummer, Chris and Strine, Leo E., Jr., *Duty and Diversity*, U of Penn, Inst for Law & Econ Research Paper No. 21-08; Columbia Law and Economics Working Paper No. 642, Vanderbilt Law Review (March 2021), https://papers.ssrn.com/sol3/papers.cfm?abstract_id=3788159.

BTC Human Rights Undertaking (September 22, 2003), https://subsites.bp.com/caspian/Human%20Rights%20Undertaking.pdf.

Business & Human Rights Resource Center, *German Parliament Passes Mandatory Human Rights Due Diligence Law* (2021), https://www.business-humanrights.org/en/latest-news/german-due-diligence-law/.

Business and Human Rights Resource Center, *Dutch Senate Votes to Adopt Child Labour Due Diligence Law* (March 16, 2021), https://www.business-humanrights.org/en/latest-news/dutch-senate-votes-to-adopt-child-labour-due-diligence-law/.

Business and Human Rights Resource Center, *France's Duty of Vigilance Law* (March 16, 2021), https://www.business-humanrights.org/en/big-issues/corporate-legal-accountability/frances-duty-of-vigilance-law/.

Business and Human Rights Resource Center, *National & Regional Movements for Mandatory Human Rights & Environmental Due Diligence In Europe* (2019), https://www.business-humanrights.org/en/latest-news/national-regional-movements-for-mandatory-human-rights-environmental-due-diligence-in-europe/.

Business Roundtable, *Corporate Governance: Statement on the Purpose of a Corporation* (2019), https://www.businessroundtable.org/business-roundtable-redefines-the-purpose-of-a-corporation-to-promote-an-economy-that-serves-all-americans.

Cassel, Doug, *Outlining the Case for a Common Law Duty of Care to Exercise Human Rights Due Diligence* (2016) 1(2) Business and Human Rights Law Journal 179–202, http://journals.cambridge.org/abstract_S2057019816000158.

Clifford Chance, *Climate Change, Human Rights and Corporate Duties–Dutch Court Issues Landmark Decision*, (May 27, 2021), https://www.cliffordchance.com/insights/resources/blogs/business-and-human-rights-insights/2021/05/climate-change-human-rights-and-corporate-duties-dutch-court-issues-landmark-decision.html.

Clifford Chance, *Legal Action Based on the French Vigilance Law Triggered By a Wind Farm Project In Mexico* (January 11, 2021), https://www.cliffordchance.com/insights/resources/blogs/business-and-human-rights-insights/2021/01/legal-action-based-on-the-french-vigilance-law-triggered-by-a-wind-farm-project-in-mexico.html.

Committee of Sponsoring Organizations of the Treadway Commission (COSO), *Guidance on Integrated Control, Integrated Control—Integrated Framework* (2013), https://www.coso.org/sitepages/internal-control.aspx?web=1.

Committee of Sponsoring Organizations of the Treadway Commission (COSO) and the World Business Council for Sustainable Development (WBCSD), *Enterprise Risk Management–Applying Enterprise Risk Management to Environmental, Social and Governance-Related Risks*, (2018), https://www.wbcsd.org/Programs/Redefining-Value/Making-stakeholder-capitalism-actionable/Enterprise-Risk-Management/Resources/Applying-Enterprise-Risk-Management-to-Environmental-Social-and-Governance-related-Risks.

Davis, Rachel, and Franks, Daniel, *Costs of Company-Community Conflict in the Extractive Sec*tor, (2014), https://shiftproject.org/resource/costs-of-company-community-conflict-in-the-extractive-sector/ (accessed October 2021).

Debevoise & Plimpton, *UN Guiding Principles on Business and Human Rights at 10: The Impact of the UNGPs on Courts and Judicial Mechanisms* (2021), https://www.debevoise.com/insights/publications/2021/07/un-guiding-principles.

Eisenberg, Melvin, *Corporate Governance: The Board of Directors and Internal Control*, 19 Cardozo L Rev. 237 (1997) ("Eisenberg"), p. 242, https://papers.ssrn.com/sol3/papers.cfm?abstract_id=11400.

Fink, Larry, *A Sense of Purpose: Larry Fink's Annual Letter to CEOs*, Blackrock (2018), http://www.blackrock.com/corporate/investor-relations/larry-fink-ceo-letter.

Friedman, Milton, *The Social Responsibility of Business is to Increase Its Profits*, N.Y. Times (September 13, 1970), p. 3, http://www.umich.edu/~thecore/doc/Friedman.pdf.

Heineman, Ben W., Jr., *The Inside Counsel Revolution: Resolving the Partner-Guardian Tension* (ABA, 2016).

Hill, Clair A., *Caremark as Soft Law*, 90 Temple L Rev. 681 (2018), https://papers.ssrn.com/sol3/papers.cfm?abstract_id=3240667.

Human Rights Watch, '*Paying for a Bus Ticket and Expecting to Fly*': *How Apparel Brand Purchasing Practices Drive Labor Abuse*s (April 2019), https://www.hrw.org/report/2019/04/23/paying-bus-ticket-and-expecting-fly/how-apparel-brand-purchasing-practices-drive.

Institute of Internal Auditors, Sarbanes-Oxley Section 404: *A Guide for Management by Internal Controls Practitioners* (2nd ed. 2008).

Krajewski, Markus, Tonstad, Kristel, & Wohltmann, Franziska, M*andatory Human Rights Due Diligence in Germany and Norway: Stepping, or Striding, in the Same Direction?*, Business and Human Rights Journal (2021), First View, pp. 1–9, https://doi.org/10.1017/bhj.2021.43.

Lipton, Martin, *The Friedman Essay and the True Purpose of the Business Corporation* (September 17, 2020), Wachtel, Lipton, Rosen & Katz (2020) https://corpgov.law.harvard.edu/2020/09/17/the-friedman-essay-and-the-true-purpose-of-the-business-corporation/.

Micheletti, Edward B., David, Bonnie W., & Kinsey, Andrew D., *Recent Trends in Officer Liability*, Skadden, Arps, Slate, Meagher & Flom (December 18, 2020), https://www.skadden.com/insights/publications/2020/12/insights-the-delaware-edition/recent-trends-in-officer-liability (accessed October 2021).

Murdoch, Scott, Lee, Liz, & Daga, Anshuman, *Top Glove's $1 Billion Hong Kong Listing Delayed Amid U.S. Ban Imbroglio–Sources*, (June 1, 2021), https://www.nasdaq.com/articles/top-gloves-%241-bln-hong-kong-listing-delayed-amid-u.s.-ban-imbroglio-sources-2021-06-01-0.

Office of the US Trade Representative, *European Union*, https://ustr.gov/countries-regions/europe-middle-east/europe/european-union.

Organisation for Economic Co-operation and Development (OECD) and Columbia/SIPA Quantifying the Costs, Benefits and Risks of Due Diligence for Responsible Business Conduct, Framework and Assessment Tool (June 13, 2016) https://www.oecd.org/industry/inv/mne/Quantifying-the-Cost-Benefits-Risks-of-Due-Diligence-for-RBC.pdf.

Power, Thomas, *Organized Uncertainty, Designing a World of Risk Management* (Oxford U. Press, 2007).

Ramasastry, Anita, *Advisors or Enablers? Bringing Professional Service Providers into the Guiding Principles' Fold*, Bus. & Hum. Rts. J., 293, 293–311 (2021) https://doi.org/10.1017/bhj.2021.28.

ReedSmith Client Alert, *The New Duty of Vigilance Adopted in France Covers Much Broader Issues Than Anti-Bribery Compliance and Will Have Significant Extraterritorial Application* (2017), https://www.mondaq.com/france/human-rights/576816/the-new-duty-of-vigilance-adopted-in-france-covers-much-broader-issues-than-anti-bribery-compliance-and-will-have-significant-extraterritorial-application.

Rogge, Malcolm, *Bringing Corporate Governance Down to Earth: From Culmination Outcomes to Comprehensive Outcomes in Shareholder and Stakeholder Capitalism*, Corporate Responsibility Initiative, Harvard Kennedy School April 2020 Working Paper No. 72, https://www.hks.harvard.edu/sites/default/files/centers/mrcbg/files/CRI_WP_72_Rogge.pdf.

Ropes & Gray Alert, *Dutch Child Labor Due Diligence Act Approved by Senate– Implications for Global Companies* (2019), https://www.ropesgray.com/en/newsroom/alerts/2019/06/Dutch-Child-Labor-Due-Diligence-Act-Approved-by-Senate-Implications-for-Global-Companies.

Ruggie, John G., *The Social Construction of the UN Guiding Principles on Business and Human Rights*, 12 Jun. 2017, Harvard Kennedy School Faculty Research Working Paper Series, HKS Working Paper No. RWP17-030, https://www.hks.harvard.edu/publications/social-construction-un-guiding-principles-business-human-rights.

Ruggie, John G., *Letter to the European Commission Regarding Reform of Directors Duties* (February 2021), https://www.business-humanrights.org/en/latest-news/john-ruggie-raises-concerns-about-adding-company-directors-duties-in-eu-mandatory-human-rights-due-diligence-legislation/.

Ruggie, John G. and Middleton, Emily K., *Money, Millennials and Human Rights: Sustaining 'Sustainable Investing'* (2019) 10(1) Global Policy, https://www.hks.harvard.edu/sites/default/files/centers/mrcbg/working.papers/CRI69_FINAL.pdf.

Ruggie, John G., Rees, Caroline, and Davis, Rachel, *Making 'Stakeholder Capitalism Work: Contribution from Business & Human Rights*, Harvard Kennedy School Working Paper No. 76 (2020), p. 11, https://www.hks.harvard.edu/sites/default/files/centers/mrcbg/files/CRI_WP76.pdf.

Ruggie, John G., Rees, Caroline, and Davis, Rachel, *Ten Years After: From UN Guiding Principles to Multi-Fiduciary Obligations*, Bus. & Hum. Rts. J., First View, pp. 1–19 (May 3, 2021), https://doi.org/10.1017/bhj.2021.8.

Ruggie, John G. & Sherman, John F., III, *Adding Human Rights Punch to the New Lex Mercatoria: The Impact of the UN Guiding Principles on Business and Human Rights on Commercial Legal Practice* (2015) 6(3) J. of Int'l Disp. Settlement, 455, 455–461, https://www.hks.harvard.edu/publications/adding-human-rights-punch-new-lex-mercatoria-impact-un-guiding-principles-business-0.

Ruggie, John G., and Sherman, John F., III, *The Concept of 'Due Diligence' in the UN Guiding Principles on Business and Human Rights: A Reply to Jonathan Bonnitcha and Robert McCorquodale*, 6(3) The Eur. J. of Int'l L., (2017), https://academic.oup.com/ejil/article-abstract/28/3/921/4616676.

Sen, Amartya, "Elements of a Theory of Human Rights," Philosophy and Public Affairs, 32, 4, http://www.mit.edu/~shaslang/mprg/asenETHR.pdf (Autumn 2004).

Shapira, Roy & Zingales, Luigi, *Is Pollution Value-Maximizing? The DuPont Case*, NEBR Working Paper 23866 (2017), https://www.nber.org/papers/w23866.

Sherman, John F., III, *No Need to Reinvent Wheels: Drafting Meaningful Human Rights Due Diligence through Model Suggested Supply Chain Contract Clauses*, Shift Viewpoint (March 2001), https://shiftproject.org/aba-contract-clauses/.

Sherman, John F., III, *Exploring Human Rights Due Diligence*, Discussion Paper, Expert Meeting of North American Corporate and External Counsel (April 30, 2010), https://media.business-humanrights.org/media/documents/29c0373597a09aa834f2bdf87e93070fb6db345e.pdf.

Sherman, John F., III, *Professional Responsibility of Layers under the UN Guiding Principles* (April 2012), https://shiftproject.org/professional-responsibility-of-lawyers-under-the-guiding-principles/.

Sherman, John F., III, *Rights-Respecting Corporate Culture: Identifying the Cultural Norms and Values That Underpin Business Respect For Human Rights* (2019), Shift Valuing Respect Project, https://shiftproject.org/resource/rights-respecting-corporate-culture-cultural-norms-values-that-underpin-business-respect-for-human-rights/.

Sherman, John F., III, *Beyond CSR: The Story of the UN Guiding Principles on Business and Human Rights*, in Ray Lindsay, and Roger Martella, Corporate Social Responsibility – Sustainable Business-Environmental, Social and Governance Frameworks for the 21st Century (Wolters Kluwer, 2020), Section 20.04.

Sherman, John F., III, *Irresponsible Exit: Exercising Force Majeure Provisions in Procurement Contracts*, 6(1) Bus. & Hum. Rts. J., 127, 127–134 (2021), https://www.cambridge.org/core/journals/business-and-human-rights-journal/article/abs/irresponsible-exit-exercising-force-majeure-provisions-in-procurement-contracts/A1206F08637B7353E652857B9CDC9720.

Sherman, John F., III & Lehr, Amy, *Human Rights Due Diligence: Is it Too Risky?* (2010) HKS Corporate Social Responsibility Initiative Working Paper No 55, p. 15, https://www.hks.harvard.edu/sites/default/files/centers/mrcbg/programs/cri/files/workingpaper_55_shermanlehr.pdf.

Shift, Business, *Human Rights and the Sustainable Development Goals: Forging a Coherent Vision and Strategy* (2016), commissioned by the Business and Sustainable Development Commission, http://s3.amazonaws.com/aws-bsdc/BSDC-Biz-HumanRights-SDGs.pdf.

Shift, *Discussion Draft: Signals of Seriousness for Human Rights Due Diligence: How can national regulators best assess the quality of a company's HRDD efforts under potential EU legislation?* (February 2021), https://shiftproject.org/resource/signals-draft1/.

Shift, *Leadership and Governance Indicators of a Rights Respecting Culture: 22 Practices and Behaviors That Help Foster Business Respect for Human Rights* (2021), https://shiftproject.org/resource/lg-indicators/about-lgis/.

Sorkin, Andrew Ross, Karaian, Jason, Kessler, Sarah, de la Merced, Michael J., Hirsch, Lauren, & Livni, Ephrat, *Wall Street Rebels Against Exxon: A Small Activist Investment Fund Scored A Huge Win* (May 27, 2021), https://www.nytimes.com/2021/05/27/business/dealbook/exxon-mobil-engine-no-1.html?searchResultPosition=1.

US Customs and Border Protection, *CBP Issues Region-Wide Withhold Release Order on Products Made by Slave Labor in Xinjiang* (January 13, 2021), https://www.cbp.gov/newsroom/national-media-release/cbp-issues-region-wide-withhold-release-order-products-made-slave.

Valukas, Anton R. (Jenner & Block), *Report to Board of Directors of General Motors Company Regarding Ignition Switch Recalls* (Attorney's Information Exchange Group, 29 May 2014), https://www.aieg.com/wp-content/uploads/2014/08/Valukas-report-on-gm-redacted2.pdf. (accessed October 2021) (redacted copy).

Waitzer, Edward J. and Sarro, Douglas, *In Search Of Things Past And Future: Judicial Activism and Corporate Purpose*, 55(5) Osgood Hall L. J., 804, 804 (Summer 2018), https://digitalcommons.osgoode.yorku.ca/ohlj/vol55/iss3/5/.

7

Integrating Human Rights Due Diligence into Compliance Approaches

Anahita Thoms[1]

I. Introduction

This chapter addresses the interconnections between adverse human rights impacts and corruption and how human rights due diligence (HRDD) can be integrated into compliance approaches. The strong correlation between corruption in a State and significant human rights infringements by businesses has been increasingly recognized,[2] leading businesses to consider this interrelationship and appropriate measures to effectively prevent corruption and its negative impacts on human rights.

Although there is no definition of corruption in international law, corruption is most commonly described as the abuse of entrusted power for private gain.[3] Corruption can be divided into petty corruption, which is corruption of low-ranking public officials, and grand corruption/political corruption, which is corruption of persons holding high-level political office.[4] Regarding businesses, corruption can occur not only through a company's actions but

---

[1] I would like to thank Jan Dorwig and Kahraman Altun for their research and excellent support.

[2] UN Human Rights Council, Report of the Working Group on the Issue of Human Rights and Transnational Corporations and Oher Business Enterprises (Jun. 17, 2020), A/HRC/44/43, para. 8.

[3] Transparency International, *What Is Corruption*? <https://www.transparency.org/en/what-is-corruption#> (last visited Jan. 11, 2022).

[4] Distinction made by Nihal Jayawickrama in the report on the UN conference on anti-corruption, good governance, and human rights, A/HRC/4/71 (Feb. 12, 2007), para. 15.

also by the company's agent or business partners, particularly in regions where corruption is prevalent.[5]

Bribery is one of the most common types of corruption of relevance to businesses, and includes corrupt solicitation, acceptance, or transfer of value in exchange for official action.[6] A typical example of bribery is a payment to government officials in order to secure State contracts.[7] Another typical example of corruption related to businesses occurs when pharmaceutical companies grant benefits to doctors who prescribe their drugs.[8]

Generally, companies address corruption and human rights issues in completely separate processes. While they often have extensive anti-corruption compliance systems, most frequently, human rights risks are handled, if at all, by the supply chain team. However, companies could build HRDD processes based on their already existing compliance mechanisms. Over the past two decades, many corporations have developed anti-corruption compliance programs in response to the promulgation of national and international standards requiring companies to prevent, detect and respond to corruption throughout their global operations. Instead of creating a completely new work stream for human rights compliance, companies could, in various instances, extend their programs for the prevention of corruption to the protection of human rights and thereby benefit from synergy effects.

There are numerous advantages that businesses can reap from the "integration" of HRDD into their anti-corruption approaches. These include: making anti-corruption compliance more robust; saving financial and personnel resources by reducing the length of training processes; improving compliance efforts through sharing information and experiences; and preventing compliance fatigue engendered by multiple due diligence requirements.[9] Moreover, since corruption is an indicator for higher risks of human rights violations, integrating HRDD into anti-corruption approaches can help to identify geographical regions where heightened HRDD is advisable.[10]

This chapter begins with a presentation of the development of anti-corruption standards and an examination of the link between corruption and human rights violations in Section II. Section III then considers the existing legal and voluntary standards for addressing corruption and human rights violations before turning, in Section IV to good practices for how anti-corruption compliance measures and HRDD can be linked. Finally, outstanding issues will be identified in Section V, which is followed by a short conclusion in Section VI.

---

[5] Cf. UN Human Rights Council, *supra* note 2, at para. 47.

[6] Cornell Law School—Legal Information Institute, Bribery, <https://www.law.cornell.edu/wex/bribery> (last visited Jan. 11, 2022).

[7] Cf. CRI Group, Top 10 Bribery & Corruption Stories of 2020 (so far), Lexology, <https://www.lexology.com/library/detail.aspx?g=4996cda1-673e-4231-ba62-0f541a4d7c07> (last visited Jan. 10, 2022).

[8] *Id.*

[9] UN Global Compact Human Rights and Labour Working Group, Linking Human Rights and Anti-Corruption Compliance (2016), <https://www.unglobalcompact.org/library/5011> (last visited Jan. 10, 2022), p. 9.

[10] Cf. *Id.* p. 15; *See* Section IV.

II. Context

A. Development of Regulatory Requirements on Anti-Corruption

Economic globalization caused international organizations and global companies to place the topic of anti-corruption measures at the top of their agendas. As enterprises expanded into foreign markets, particularly those of developing countries, they encountered corruption, such as in the form of corrupt customs administrations, that proved to be ethical and financial obstacles to their conduct of business in these countries. Corruption, particularly bribery and embezzlement, essentially constituted non-tariff barriers that prevented companies from gaining a foothold in foreign markets. Corruption can still lead to theft and increased costs.[11]

Companies in the United States recognized this problem as they rapidly expanded overseas in in the 1950s and then had to take steps to ensure their compliance with the US Foreign Corrupt Practices Act,[12] following its adoption in 1977. However, it was not until the 1990's that the first anti-corruption treaty was adopted on a multilateral level, because many countries had previously viewed the topic of anti-corruption as an issue to be dealt with by national legislation.

At the United Nations (UN) level, the topic of corruption received little official attention for many years.[13] Then in 1989, the UN Crime Prevention and Criminal Justice Programme organized an interregional seminar that called for international technical cooperation and mutual legal assistance for measures against corruption.[14] Following several other conferences, the Programme developed the International Code of Conduct for Public Officials, which the General Assembly adopted in 1996 and recommended to UN Member States as a tool to guide their efforts against corruption.[15] Several days later, the General Assembly also adopted the Declaration against Corruption and Bribery in International Commercial Transactions.[16] This Declaration was a precursor to the adoption in 1997 by all Member States of the Organisation for Economic Co-operation and Development (OECD) of the Convention on Combating Bribery of Foreign Public Officials in International Business Transactions

---

[11] Calder, Corruption Is a Costly "Hidden" Tariff, GLOBAL TRADE, January 27, 2020, <https://www.globaltrademag.com/corruption-is-a-costly-hidden-tariff/#:~:text=The%20Organisation%20for%20Economic%20Co,and%20low%2Dmiddle%20income%20countries.&text=Combined%2C%20these%20effects%20will%20damage,welfare%20over%20the%20long%20run> (last visited Jan. 11, 2022).

[12] United States Foreign Corrupt Practices Act (1977) as amended, 15 U.S.C. §§ 78dd-1 et seq.

[13] Cf. Annan, Foreword to the Convention Against Corruption, <https://www.unodc.org/res/ji/import/international_standards/united_nations_convention_against_corruption/united_nations_convention_against_corruption.pdf> (last visited Jan. 10, 2022), p. iv.

[14] For an overview of the development that led to the UN Convention Against Corruption, please *see* Vlassis, The United Nations Convention Against Corruption - Origins and Negotiation Process <https://www.unafei.or.jp/publications/pdf/RS_No66/No66_16VE_Vlassis2.pdf> (last visited Jan. 11, 2022).

[15] UN General Assembly, International Code of Conduct for Public Officials Approved by Third Committee, Press Release (Oct. 31, 1996), GA/SHC/3372.

[16] UN General Assembly, United Nations Declaration against Corruption and Bribery in International Commercial Transactions (Feb. 21, 1997), A/RES/51/191.

(OECD Anti-Bribery Convention), which requires States parties to conform to a US model of preventing bribery and money laundering.[17]

During the negotiations of the UN Convention against Transnational Organized Crime, the topic of corruption was also discussed. However, the Ad Hoc Committee responsible for the negotiations of that convention concluded that the topic of corruption was so complex that it should be addressed in a separate convention. This led to the inclusion of only limited provisions on corruption in the UN Convention against Transnational Organized Crime that was adopted in 2000.[18] Therefore, the UN General Assembly established the Ad Hoc Committee for the Negotiation of a Convention Against Corruption in January 2001.[19] This committee negotiated the provisions of the treaty from 2002 to 2003. The UN Convention against Corruption (UNCAC) was then adopted by the UN General Assembly on October 31, 2003,[20] and 189 States are now parties.[21] The UNCAC is dedicated to the prevention and criminalization of corruption and provides for law enforcement measures and asset recovery to address its occurrence. Moreover, States parties to the UNCAC agree to cooperate with one another in the provision of mutual legal assistance that includes gathering and transferring evidence for use by another State in its own courts. States also commit to undertake measures to support the tracing, seizure, and confiscation of the proceeds of corruption. The near universal ratification of the UNCAC has led to an increase in the adoption of national anti-corruption legislation by States around the world. A study of the UN Office on Drugs and Crime shows that in 2017 the majority of States parties to the UNCAC had modified their anti-corruption legal framework so as to meet the Convention's criteria at least with regard to the criminalization of corruption, law enforcement measures, and international cooperation.[22]

Given these international and national developments, many companies have extended the scope of their due diligence process over the course of time and added work streams that focus on the implementation of anti-corruption measures. Legislation, such as the US Foreign Corrupt Practices Act and the United Kingdom Bribery Act,[23] requires pre-acquisition due diligence for a company to avoid being held financially liable under the principle of successor

[17] OECD, OECD Convention on Combating Bribery of Foreign Public Officials in International Business Transactions (1997), <http://www.oecd.org/daf/anti-bribery/ConvCombatBribery_ENG.pdf> (last visited Jan. 11, 2022).

[18] UN General Assembly, United Nations Convention against Transnational Organized Crime (Jan. 8, 2001), A/RES/55/25.

[19] UN General Assembly, An Effective International Legal Instrument against Corruption (Jan. 22, 2001), A/RES/55/61.

[20] UN General Assembly, United Nations Convention against Corruption (Oct. 31, 2003), A/RES/58/4.

[21] UN Office on Drugs and Crime, Signature and Ratification Status, <http://www.unodc.org/unodc/en/corruption/ratification-status.html> (last visited Jan. 11, 2022).

[22] UN Office on Drugs and Crime, State of Implementation of the United Nations Convention against Corruption <https://www.unodc.org/documents/treaties/UNCAC/COSP/session7/V.17-04679_E-book.pdf> (last visited Jan. 11, 2022).

[23] United Kingdom Bribery Act 2010 (c.23).

liability in merger and acquisition transactions if anti-corruption violations occurred prior to the transaction.[24]

B. Human Rights Due Diligence Standards

In contrast to anti-corruption due diligence, HRDD has only recently become a relevant topic for companies following the unanimous endorsement of the *UN Guiding Principles on Business and Human Rights*, by the UN Human Rights Council in 2011 (UNGPs).[25] Since then, corporate HRDD has been integrated into other policy frameworks, such as the *OECD Due Diligence Guidance for Responsible Business Conduct*.[26] The significance of such examinations for companies has risen as businesses' human rights violations have received increased public attention. These changes are reflected in the growing number of investors that are interested in the risk management capabilities of companies with respect to human rights.[27] Yet, just over one-third of companies in the European Union (EU) undertake due diligence taking all human rights into account and the majority of businesses limit their due diligence to first tier suppliers only.[28]

C. Linkages between Corruption and Human Rights Violations

International bodies, including the UN Office on Drugs and Crime and the UN Human Rights Council, as well as human rights think tanks and scholars, have over the past few years increasingly focused on the linkages between corruption and adverse human rights impacts. Corruption can be viewed as a structural obstacle to the enjoyment of human rights. It undermines the realization of almost all human rights, as almost every human right can be violated by corruption.[29] Corruption in the education sector can violate the right to education; in the health sector it can affect the right to medical services; and in the social welfare sector, the right to food may be infringed.[30]

---

[24] Oded/Ceulen, *Anti-Bribery Due Diligence in M&A Transactions: Have you Got it Covered?*, 6 IJMSR, 7 (2018), 14, 15.

[25] Human Rights Council, *Guiding Principles on Business and Human Rights: Implementing the United Nations "Protect, Respect and Remedy" Framework* (Mar. 21, 2011), A/HRC/17/31.

[26] OECD, *OECD Due Diligence Guidance for Responsible Business Conduct* (2018), <https://www.oecd.org/investment/due-diligence-guidance-for-responsible-business-conduct.htm> (last visited Jan. 11, 2022).

[27] UN Office of High Commissioner for Human Rights, *Corporate Human Rights Due Diligence: Emerging Practices, Challenges and Ways Forward* (2018), <https://www.ohchr.org/Documents/Issues/Business/ExecutiveSummaryA73163.pdf> (last visited Jan. 11, 2022).

[28] European Commission, Study on Due Diligence Requirements through the Supply Chain—Final Report (2020) <https://op.europa.eu/en/publication-detail/-/publication/8ba0a8fd-4c83-11ea-b8b7-01aa75ed71a1> (last visited Jan. 11, 2022), p. 16.

[29] UN Human Rights Council, Final Report of the Human Rights Council Advisory Committee on the Issue of the Negative Impact of Corruption on the Enjoyment of Human Rights (Jan. 5, 2015), A/HRC/28/73, para. 17.

[30] *Id.*

More specifically, corruption in the education sector may result in diminished resources for schools and students having to pay for books that should be free of charge or their being asked for sexual favors in exchange for better grades.[31] In the health and social welfare sectors, corruption can occur through the embezzlement of funds for medical supplies or food aid.[32] The right to food can also be violated if food of inadequate quality comes to the market because government officials fail to properly carry out their inspection duties in exchange for bribes.[33] To give another concrete example, if public authorities illegally allow companies to deforest a certain area in return for bribes, the right of the people living in this area to food, housing, and health may be violated.[34]

Similarly, the rights to equality before the law, access to justice, and a fair trial can be compromised when corruption pervades governments and legal systems.[35] For instance, if judges demand bribes for access to court services, the right of access to justice is violated. Furthermore, the corruption of court officials can lead to the impunity of corrupt individuals or entities.[36]

Additionally, corruption in business can result in adverse ramifications on the human rights of workers and local communities. For example, investors that pay bribes in exchange for obtaining land or favorable contract terms in a lease may violate land rights, including the right of local communities to the use of land, especially Indigenous peoples, which may severely impact the livelihood of these communities.[37] The effectiveness of supply chain due diligence can also suffer from corruption. For instance, companies and agents in the supply chain may pay bribes in order to avoid government health and safety inspections.[38]

As these examples illustrate, corruption can violate different human rights ranging from the right to education to the right to food.

Violations of human rights caused by corruption can be classified into three categories based on the impact upon the lives of individuals, groups, and communities.[39] First, corruption can negatively impact individuals, such as when individuals are unable or unwilling to bribe someone and are therefore denied access to public services. Second, corruption can have a collective negative impact on specific, identifiable groups of individuals, such as women, children, and persons with disabilities. For example, children from impoverished areas can be particularly affected by corruption in the education sector, which results in decreased spending on schools in those areas. Third, corruption can have a general negative impact on the

[31] UN Office on Drugs and Crime, Impact of Corruption on Specific Human Rights (2020), <https://www.unodc.org/e4j/en/anti-corruption/module-7/key-issues/impact-of-corruption-on-specific-human-rights.html> (last visited Jan. 11, 2022).

[32] *Id.*

[33] *Id.*

[34] UN Human Rights Council, *supra* note 29, para. 20.

[35] UN Office of the High Commissioner for Human Rights, The Human Rights Case against Corruption (Nov. 2013), HR/NONE/2013/120, p. 4; UN Human Rights Council, *supra* note 29, para. 17.

[36] UN Office on Drugs and Crime, *supra* note 31.

[37] Global Witness, Prof. De Schutter, International Corporate Accountability Roundtable (ICAR), *Tainted Lands - Corruption in Large Scale Land Deals* (Nov. 15, 2016), p. 1.

[38] UN Human Rights Council, *supra* note 2, para. 16.

[39] UN Human Rights Council, *supra* note 29, para. 20.

society at large. This occurs when corruption in the financial resources of a country diverts funds from the development of the country's social systems. This type of corruption can also negatively impact the realization of democracy and the implementation of the rule of law as people's confidence in their government and the functioning of its institutions is jeopardized.

Efforts to tackle corruption are undertaken through a criminal law approach with criminal investigations and prosecutions as the primary methods for identifying and holding perpetrators of corruption accountable. However, as demonstrated above, corruption is not only a criminal problem, but also has significant negative human rights impacts. Not only do corruption and adverse human rights impacts generally coincide geographically; they both also pose risks to the financial exposure and reputations of companies.[40]

Likewise, the challenges in managing corruption risks and avoiding adverse human rights impacts are similar. The company needs to identify inappropriate conduct that causes corruption and/or human rights infringements within its organization, in its business relationships, and in its supply chains.[41] It also needs to detect areas within its own operations, business partners, and suppliers that require screening to reveal potential behavior patterns that do not align with current anti-corruption measures and human rights.[42] This requires firms to implement due diligence that allows a quick and efficient analysis without giving cause for the delay of trade or services. Good practice examples for this are provided in Section IV.

III. Legal/Regulatory/Voluntary Standards

This section provides a brief overview of the most important standards concerning anti-corruption and HRDD. However, there are no business standards jointly covering human rights compliance and anti-corruption measures in one approach. A reason for this might be that international human rights conventions rarely mention corruption and international conventions dealing with corruption rarely mention human rights.[43]

A. Standards for Anti-Corruption Due Diligence

Among the sources for standards concerning anti-corruption due diligence are the UNCAC, adopted in 2003, and the OECD Anti-Bribery Convention, signed in 1997. Both conventions suggest a list of concrete measures that should be adopted by companies and that are quite similar. However, compared to the UN Convention, the OECD Anti-Bribery Convention is more detailed and specific.

The UNCAC is the first and only international treaty on anti-corruption that is multilateral, is legally binding, and covers multiple forms of corruption.[44] As mentioned above,

---

[40] Cf. UN Global Compact Human Rights and Labour Working Group, *supra* note 9, p. 6.

[41] Cf. *Id.* p. 4.

[42] Cf. *Id.* p. 15.

[43] International Council on Human Rights Policy, Corruption and Human Rights: Making the Connection (2009), p. 3; one exception noted is Council of Europe, Criminal Law Convention on Corruption (1999), <https://www.coe.int/en/web/conventions/full-list/-/conventions/treaty/173> (last visited Jan. 11, 2022), preamble.

[44] UN Office on Drugs and Crime, United Nations Convention against Corruption <http://www.unodc.org/unodc/en/corruption/uncac.html> (last visited Jan. 11, 2022).

almost all UN Member States have ratified this convention. In doing so, States parties have committed themselves in Article 12 para. 1 of the UNCAC to prevent corruption involving the private sector. The UNCAC suggests several concrete measures to achieve the prevention of corruption. The measures for the private sector include, among others, the development of a code of conduct (Article 12 para. 2(b)), measures regarding the identity of legal and natural persons involved in the establishment and management of corporate entities (Article 12 para. 2 (c)), restrictions on the professional activities of former public officials and on the employment of public officials by the private sector (Article 12 para. 2 (e)), and internal auditing controls (Article 12 para. 2 (e)).

The OECD Anti-Bribery Convention is a legally binding treaty focusing on the criminalization of bribery of foreign public officials. All 37 OECD countries and seven non-OECD countries have ratified the Convention.[45] In 2010 the Council of the OECD adopted a Good Practice Guidance on Internal Controls, Ethics and Compliance (OECD Good Practice Guidance) addressed to companies.[46] The OECD Good Practice Guidance is not legally binding and offers good practice examples for programs and measures to prevent and detect bribery of foreign officials. The examples include, among others, the installment of independent monitoring bodies such as internal audit committees with an adequate level of autonomy from management (Section A.4), the development of comprehensive ethics and compliance programs or measures (Section A.5), the development of financial and accounting procedures (Section A.7), periodic communication and documented training for all levels of the company (Section A.8) as well as disciplinary procedures (Section A.10) and internal confidential reporting systems and protection (Section A.11(ii)). The Guidance also suggests that business organizations and professional associations should provide support and assistance to businesses, especially small and medium-sized enterprises, in the development of their measures and programs *inter alia* by providing information, training, and advice (B). Since the Guidance provides that it should be viewed as flexible and adaptable and emphasizes that anti-corruption measures should be interconnected within a company's overall compliance framework, this argues for businesses connecting anti-corruption measures to HRDD and finding creative and effective solutions for integrating both.

B. Standards for Human Rights Due Diligence

The HRDD process to "identify, prevent, mitigate and account for how [businesses] address their adverse human rights impacts"[47] can be found in the UNGPs, which were unanimously endorsed by the UN Human Rights Council in 2011[48] and though not legally binding, are nev-

[45] OECD, OECD Convention on Combating Bribery of Foreign Public Officials in International Business Transactions (1997), <https://www.oecd.org/corruption/oecdantibriberyconvention.htm> (last visited Jan. 11, 2022).

[46] OECD, *Good Practice Guidance on Internal Controls, Ethics, and Compliance* (Feb. 18, 2010), <http://www.oecd.org/daf/anti-bribery/44884389.pdf> (last visited Jan. 11, 2022).

[47] *Guiding Principles, supra* note 25, at 22 (Principle 17).

[48] UN Human Rights Council, *supra* note 25.

ertheless widely accepted.[49] The human rights impacts to be identified by businesses include, at a minimum, those rights found in the International Bill of Human Rights (Universal Declaration of Human Rights,[50] International Covenant on Civil and Political Rights[51] and the International Covenant on Economic, Social and Cultural Rights[52]) and in the International Labour Organization (ILO) Declaration on Fundamental Principles and Rights at Work.[53]

Principles 17 to 21 in the UNGPs explain how companies should carry out HRDD. As a first step, they should assess actual and potential human rights impacts that the company might be involved in, even as a result of their business relationships (Principle 18). Then, the findings need to be integrated across the business's relevant internal functions and processes, and action must be taken (Principle 19). If a company has leverage to prevent or mitigate the adverse human rights impact of another entity, it should exercise it.[54] Finally, companies are supposed to track the effectiveness of their response to their findings (Principle 20) and communicate how they are addressing their human rights impacts (Principle 21).

The UNGPs and the OECD Good Practice Guidance on anti-corruption measures, described above, have several similarities and may thus be instituted together. Both demand action from all levels of a company and from all business functions.[55] Also, both demand frequent communication. While the OECD Good Practice Guidance requires communication on the company's measures regarding foreign bribery,[56] the UNGPs address a company's responsibility to provide information about its response to particular human rights impacts.[57] These communication obligations could easily be aligned. Furthermore, both standards oblige businesses to install a reporting process. While the OECD Good Practice Guidance suggests an internal and, where possible, confidential report process for complaints,[58] the UNGPs recommend an operational-level grievance mechanism, which would assist in generating feedback on the effectiveness of HRDD.[59] Therefore, consideration should be given to creating one reporting system to cover both anti-corruption and human rights complaints and concerns.[60]

---

[49] Cf. Deva, *Guiding Principles on Business and Human Rights: Implications for Companies*, European Company Law, Vol. 9, No. 2 (2012): 101, 101.

[50] A/RES/3/217 A (Dec. 10, 1948).

[51] A/RES/21/2200 (Dec. 16, 1966).

[52] *Id.*

[53] ILO, Declaration on Fundamental Principles and Rights at Work (Jun. 15, 1988), https://www.ilo.org/declaration/lang--en/index.htm (last visited Jan. 11, 2022).

[54] Human Rights Council, *supra* note 25, p. 18.

[55] *Id.*, OECD, *supra* note 46, at A.3.

[56] *Id.* at A.8.

[57] Human Rights Council, *supra* note 25, p. 20.

[58] OECD, *supra* note 46.

[59] Human Rights Council, *supra* note 25, p. 19.

[60] Cf. UN Global Compact Human Rights and Labour Working Group, *supra* note 9, p. 13 et seq; BIAC/IOE, *Connecting the Anti-corruption and Human Rights Agendas: A Guide for Business and Employers' Organisations* (Sep. 2020), <https://baselgovernance.org/sites/default/files/2020-09/2020-08-31-business-at-oecd-ioe-ac-hr-guide.pdf> (last visited Jan. 11, 2022).

C. Standards Covering Anti-corruption and Human Rights Due Diligence

Standards relating to both anti-corruption measures and HRDD can be found in the *OECD Guidelines for Multinational Enterprises* of 2011 (OECD Guidelines).[61] The OECD Guidelines are nonbinding recommendations to multinational enterprises on how to conduct responsible business in a global context.[62] In Part I, the OECD Guidelines recommend establishing compliance programs covering both human rights (Chap. IV.5) and anti-bribery (Chap. VII.2). With respect to human rights, the OECD Guidelines stress that the programs must be appropriate to the company's size, the nature of its business, and the risks (Chap. IV.5). The process of HRDD described by the OECD Guidelines (Chap. IV.45) is virtually the same as that described by the UNGPs. In addition, the OECD Guidelines mention that all programs should be reviewed on a regular basis (Chaps. VII.2 and IV.45). However, the OECD Guidelines address anti-corruption and human rights in separate chapters and do not link their suggestions for compliance with the law and relevant standards or assessment of potential or actual violations.[63]

Another document covering both areas without linking them is the UN Sustainable Development Goals (SDGs).[64] The SDGs were adopted by the UN General Assembly and are thus not legally binding but, rather, political goals. They refer to both anti-corruption and human rights. SDG 16.5 sets forth the target of substantially reducing corruption and bribery in all their forms. Human rights underpin the SDGs and constitute 90 percent of the goals and targets of the SDGs.[65] In contrast to the OECD Guidelines, however, the SDGs are not addressed to businesses but primarily provide general goals and targets for governments that are to be achieved by 2030.

IV. Good Practices

As indicated in the previous section, there are numerous advantages that can be garnered by businesses that integrate HRDD into anti-corruption compliance approaches. Prior to exploring good practices for businesses to do so, this section examines differences that affect this integration.

---

[61] OECD, OECD *Guidelines for Multinational Enterprises* (2011), <http://www.oecd.org/daf/inv/mne/48004323.pdf> (last visited Jan. 11, 2022).

[62] *Id.*

[63] Cf. *Id.*

[64] UN General Assembly, *Transforming Our World: the 2030 Agenda for Sustainable Development* (Sept. 25, 2015), A/RES/70/1.

[65] Rattray, *Human Rights and the SDGs—Two Sides of the Same Coin* (Jul. 5, 2019), <https://www.undp.org/blogs/human-rights-and-sdgs-two-sides-same-coin> (last visited Jan. 11, 2022).

A. Differences between Corruption and Adverse Human Rights Impacts

Although, as discussed above in Section II.B., corruption and adverse human rights impacts are interconnected, there are significant differences in their nature and the relevant analytical framework for their identification. Corruption risks for businesses, such as bribery, normally concern the actions of employees and other members of a company, while human rights risks are risks that the company's actions pose to employees or third parties, such as members of the local community. These can range from forced labor, unsafe working conditions, wage discrimination for equal pay, and sexual harassment to involvement in reprisals against members of civil society organizations that publicly criticize the company and its operations, and may even extend to restrictions on access to clean water by communities.[66] Thus, while anti-corruption measures are generally limited to a company's operations and employees, it is becoming increasingly important for companies to be sensitized to risks of human rights violations along their entire value chain and to pay particular attention to employment situations, community impacts, and health responsibilities.

Consequently, some tools commonly used to recognize corruption risks are not sufficient for identifying risks of adverse human rights impacts, in particular, financial auditing, which is the primary means relied upon by companies with respect to corruption.[67] Financial auditing refers to the review of the accounting processes and expenditures of a company. This can be either or both an internal or external process.[68] As a result, companies have come to realize that sustainable improvement goes further than simple compliance audits.[69] Instead, more comprehensive measures are required that actually improve conditions. While anti-corruption measures and HRDD can and should be linked, since the risk-framing analysis is fundamentally different for each of them, the approaches will not completely overlap. For instance, effective anti-corruption measures need the explicit and visible commitment from senior management to anti-corruption,[70] while effective HRDD should focus on assessing and adapting a company's activities that have adverse human rights impacts.[71] Consequently, although anti-corruption measures need a risk-based approach[72] and a strong external and internal communication of the management´s commitment, human rights due diligence is

[66] OECD, *supra* note 26, at Annex Q1.

[67] Suggesting non-financial auditing: UN Global Compact Human Rights and Labour Working Group, *supra* note 9, p. 14.

[68] Global Infrastructure Anti-Corruption Centre, Financial Controls (Apr. 10, 2020), <https://giaccentre.org/financial-controls/> (last visited Jan. 11, 2022), (11) Implement periodic financial audit.

[69] Shift, Respecting Human Rights Through Global Supply Chains—Workshop Report (Oct. 2012), <https://shiftproject.org/wp-content/uploads/2012/08/Shift_UNGPssupplychain2012.pdf> (last visited Jan. 11, 2022), p. 13.

[70] OECD, *supra* note 46, at A.1.

[71] *Guiding Principles, supra* note 25, at 24 (Principle 18).

[72] Cf. *Id.* at A.6.

more about mitigating existing impacts and changing the business operations of a company. Nevertheless, since both measures require the assessment of the entire company, they can be aligned.

B. Good Practices Regarding Anti-corruption and Human Rights Due Diligence

As a first step, business enterprises should review their current due diligence processes and examine if they can integrate a human rights focus into the anti-corruption aspects. While this evaluation should not be confused with conflating the two areas, it allows a quick and resource-saving way of establishing a HRDD regime, if this does not exist yet.

The following suggestions cover ways in which due diligence and anti-corruption approaches can be used together.

1. Set the Tone from the Top: Leveraging Senior Management Support

Strong, explicit, and visible senior management support is essential to embedding respect for human rights and anti-corruption measures into the corporate culture and for demonstrating the corporate commitment to these externally, especially vis-à-vis business partners.[73] Therefore, it is necessary to assign general oversight and responsibility for due diligence processes to senior management.[74] It might be practical to assign the specific responsibility for HRDD to a member of the senior management who already has corporate compliance responsibilities, like a chief compliance officer. However, to allow all senior managers to address the human rights impacts of the business and its business partners, they need to receive adequate training and direction from the chief executive officer. This also requires senior management to understand the importance of implementing comprehensive due diligence schemes that incorporate both anti-corruption and human rights.

This requirement is in line with the recommendation of the World Economic Forum (WEF) for boards of directors to develop a more holistic and integrated approach to ethics. The WEF suggests that they focus not only on detecting illegal conduct but also on ethical conduct in a broader sense.[75]

---

[73] BIAC/IOE, *Connecting the Anti-corruption and Human Rights Agendas: A Guide for Business and Employers' Organisations* (Sep. 2020), <https://baselgovernance.org/sites/default/files/2020-09/2020-08-31-business-at-oecd-ioe-ac-hr-guide.pdf> (last visited Jan. 11, 2022), p. 13; Explicitly for anti-bribery: OECD, *OECD Good Practice Guidance on Internal Controls, Ethics, and Compliance* (Feb. 18, 2010), <https://www.oecd.org/daf/anti-bribery/44884389.pdf> (last visited Jan. 11, 2022), A.1 and A.6.ii.

[74] OECD, *supra* note 26, p. 23.

[75] World Economic Forum, *Good Intentions, Bad Outcomes? How Organizations Can Make the Leap from Box-Ticking Compliance to Building a Culture of Integrity* (October 2020), <https://www3.weforum.org/docs/WEF_GFC_on_Transparency_and_AC_pillar2_good_intentions_bad_outcomes.pdf> (last visited Jan. 11, 2022), p. 6.

2. *Align Human Rights and Anti-corruption Policy Commitments*

The OECD Guidelines recommend that companies make public statements about their commitment to respect human rights and against bribery.[76] To save resources and ensure the effectiveness of these commitments, they could be aligned and expressed in the form of a single statement. In doing so, companies highlight that they are taking responsibility for compliance with all legal and regulatory requirements in the fight against corruption and that they are willing to adapt their business activities so as to avoid adverse human rights impacts.

3. *Add Human Rights Contractual Clauses*

The use of contractual clauses on anti-corruption measures by businesses is very common. In particular, US companies use anti-corruption compliance provisions in their agreements with intermediaries of their overseas businesses, including business development consultants, sales representatives, subcontractors, distributors, lawyers, and accountants.[77] Businesses are also increasingly including clauses, in contracts with suppliers, that obligate their contractual partners to identify and address adverse human rights impacts.[78] Enterprises need to ensure that contractual clauses are also enforced; this requires monitoring of the actual implementation of contractual clauses.

4. *Integrate Human Rights and Anti-corruption Procedures*

Companies will also want to build capacity in areas where anti-corruption and human rights efforts overlap. These areas include: key performance indicators and tracking metrics for internal control;[79] establishing joint reporting mechanisms to prevent compliance fatigue;[80] conducting joint trainings where feasible;[81] and integrating human rights impact assessment into non-financial anti-corruption auditing.[82] For example, key performance indicators and tracking metrics, and statistics that show the status and the success of a specific business process can include very different types of data depending on the type of the company, such as: the average cycle time of a workflow; the production rate of a certain unit; the percentage of products that pass a quality control; and employee turnover. While specialized training will be necessary for the personnel responsible for the company's human rights and anti-corruption strategies and procedures, joint training on these topics is an option in connection with general compliance training.

---

[76] OECD, *supra* note 61, at IV.44 (human rights) and VII.5 (anti-corruption).

[77] Boles, *The Contract as Anti-corruption Platform for the Global Corporate Sector*, 21 Univ. of Penn. J. of Bus. L., 4, (2008), 807, 819.

[78] European Commission, *supra* note 28, p. 16.

[79] Cf. UN Global Compact Human Rights and Labour Working Group, *supra* note 9, p. 12 et seq.

[80] Cf. *Id.* p. 13 et seq.

[81] Cf. BIAC/IOE, *Connecting the Anti-corruption and Human Rights Agendas: A Guide for Business and Employers' Organisations* (Sep. 2020), <https://baselgovernance.org/sites/default/files/2020-09/2020-08-31-business-at-oecd-ioe-ac-hr-guide.pdf> (last visited Jan. 11, 2022), p. 15.

[82] Cf. UN Global Compact Human Rights and Labour Working Group, *supra* note 9, p. 14.

The integration of a human rights impact assessment into non-financial anti-corruption auditing can increase the effectiveness of identifying adverse human rights impacts. For example, if an anti-corruption audit shows that officials in a country expect facilitation payments for factories to pass compliance inspections, the human rights impact assessment, which is part of the audit, will likely demonstrate that the same factories have human rights issues relating to working conditions of employees.[83]

5. *Combine Corruption and Human Rights Risk Assessments*

Companies should ensure that their screening of business partners (including suppliers) and client intakes cover both potential and actual human rights abuses and corruption. These aspects should be merged or augmented. Human rights–related questions should be added to forms for assessing potential corruption,[84] such as "know your customer" forms for business partners and screening forms for supply-chain entities; similarly, anti-corruption measures, such as anti-corruption agreements, should be added to HRDD and procurement questionnaires. Adding human rights questions to anti-corruption measures and vice versa not only avoids redundancies in work streams but also facilitates dialogue within the company and with business partners, suppliers, and stakeholders on prevention of adverse human rights impacts and corruption.[85]

There is a strong link between high levels of corruption in a State and widespread human rights abuses.[86] Corruption can signal a weak State structure, which should trigger heightened HRDD by a business.[87] The UN Working Group on the Issue of Human Rights and Transnational Corporations and Other Business Enterprises recommends that companies engage in heightened HRDD in conflict-affected regions.[88] Such regions show higher risks of human rights violations and are affected by war, violence, or persecution.[89] Among these regions are countries like Colombia, the Democratic Republic of Congo, Liberia, Myanmar, and Sierra Leone.[90] However, heightened HRDD seems to be necessary wherever State structures are generally weak. Since corruption and human rights abuses tend to occur in the same settings, collecting and analyzing regional data and sociopolitical information for both, where a company, its business partners, and suppliers operate, is advisable.

---

[83] *Id.* p. 14.

[84] Cf. *Id.* p. 15.

[85] Cf. *Id.* p. 15 et seq.; BIAC/IOE, Connecting the anti-corruption and human rights agendas: A guide for business and employers' organisations (Sep. 2020), <https://baselgovernance.org/sites/default/files/2020-09/2020-08-31-business-at-oecd-ioe-ac-hr-guide.pdf> (last visited Jan. 11, 2022), p. 17.

[86] *See* Section II.B.

[87] Working Group on the Issue of Human Rights and Transnational Corporations and Other Business Enterprises, Business, Human Rights and Conflict-affected Regions: Towards Heightened Action (Jul. 21, 2020), A/75/212, para. 17.

[88] *Id.* para. 106.

[89] Cf. *Id.* para. 1.

[90] *Id.*, para. 5.

6. *Establishing Cross-Functional Working Groups*

Cross-functional working groups within a company, that is, groups that include persons from different functions, such as the legal, human resources, compliance, finance, sales, and information technology sections, provide an opportunity to detect shared risks.[91] They also offer the possibility for collaboration, including in the development of systems to respond to detected corruption risks or adverse human rights impacts.[92] These working groups can be established on either a permanent or ad hoc basis, depending on the structure of the company and the type of business.[93]

7. *Partnering with Other Companies on Compliance Issues*

Companies should consider partnering with other companies within their industry to share knowledge and identify shared problems and strategies, such as industry-wide reputational risks and country-specific vulnerabilities.[94] Specifically, companies may share information about human rights or corruption-related incidents concerning a supplier of several companies. Small and mid-sized companies, who may not have the financial and personnel resources of larger companies to address corruption risks and human rights impacts, can particularly benefit from the support of business organizations and professional associations to obtain information, training, and general advice.[95]

V. Outstanding Issues

Even as the implementation of HRDD gains increasing importance for companies, they face several challenging issues. These include the rapidly evolving nature of compliance and HRDD requirements, the wide-ranging nature of potential adverse human rights impacts, and the current separation between corruption risks and human rights impacts, which issues are addressed in this section.

A. Changing Compliance Expectations

Compliance expectations are constantly changing, thus requiring continuous review and update of due diligence processes. A good example is the EU anti-money laundering legislation. Since 1991 the EU has adopted six directives in this field,[96] forcing the EU Member States to constantly adapt their national legislation and, thus, companies' actions to ensure

---

[91] United Nations Global Compact Human Rights and Labour Working Group, *supra* note 9, p. 17.

[92] *Id.* p. 17.

[93] Cf. *Id.* p. 18.

[94] Cf. *Id.*

[95] Explicitly for anti-bribery: OECD, *OECD Good Practice Guidance on Internal Controls, Ethics, and Compliance* (Feb. 18, 2010), <https://www.oecd.org/daf/anti-bribery/44884389.pdf> (last visited Jan. 11, 2022), B.

[96] The last directive being Directive (EU) 2018/1673 on combating money laundering by criminal law (also called "6AMLD").

compliance.[97] Similarly, the requirements for HRDD are rapidly evolving as soft-law standards from the UNGPs and the OECD Guidelines are codified into legislative requirements at the EU level and by EU Member States, following the initial legislation in this area by France, the French Corporate Duty of Vigilance Law, which forces companies to monitor their suppliers and subcontractors with regard to adverse human rights and environmental impacts.[98] Therefore, it is crucial that companies keep up to date with the pace of the developments. In addition, they should understand the necessity of widening their perspective. Compliance should not only focus on detecting and preventing illegal conduct but on sustainable and ethical business strategies.[99]

In addition to monitoring legal, regulatory, and case law developments related to businesses' responsibility to respect human rights, businesses need to constantly maintain awareness of the evolution in their own potential and actual human rights impacts, because the scope of adverse human rights that companies need to respect may change over time and thus should be subject to periodic review.[100]

B. Complexity of Adverse Human Rights Impacts

Another challenge for businesses is that the potential adverse human rights impacts of a company can cover an extensive array of human rights and they may have difficulty understanding the possible consequences of their actions on human rights. This challenge for businesses particularly arises in connection with the activities of entities in their corporate supply chains, which are often very complex; human rights violations increasingly occur at the end of the supply chain. Businesses' difficulty in understanding their human rights impacts contrasts with businesses' understanding of corrupt behavior, whose several forms are clearer to most companies due to extensive legislative developments in the past few decades.[101] Therefore, companies need to understand the variety of human rights risks they should be identifying and assessing.

Moreover, the extensive due diligence proceedings taken by companies to identify corruption are also a result of the clear laws that have been enforced to prevent bribery, embezzlement, and extortion. In contrast, the current legal framework for HRDD is not viewed as efficient, coherent, and effective by many companies.[102] As long as companies are not provided with legal certainty regarding their HRDD obligations, this will serve as an

[97] For the development of the legislation *see* ComplyAdvantage, *A Brief History of the AMLDS* (Aug. 18, 2020), <https://complyadvantage.com/blog/brief-history-amlds-part-one/> (last visited Jan. 11, 2022).

[98] Lavite, *The French Loi de Vigilance: Prospects and Limitations of a Pioneer Mandatory Corporate Due Diligence* (Jun. 16, 2020), <https://verfassungsblog.de/the-french-loi-de-vigilance-prospects-and-limitations-of-a-pioneer-mandatory-corporate-due-diligence> (last visited Jan. 11, 2022).

[99] Cf. World Economic Forum, *Good Intentions, Bad Outcomes? How Organizations Can Make the Leap from Box-Ticking Compliance to Building a Culture of Integrity* (Oct. 2020), <https://www3.weforum.org/docs/WEF_GFC_on_Transparency_and_AC_pillar2_good_intentions_bad_outcomes.pdf> (last visited Jan. 11, 2022), p. 6.

[100] OECD, *supra* note 61, commentary No. 40.

[101] *See* Section II.A.

[102] European Commission, *supra* note 28, p. 16.

impediment to their conducting adequate HRDD and integrating compliance and HRDD processes.

C. Separation of Corruption Risks and Human Rights Risks

Given the linkages between corruption risks and adverse human rights impacts, their separation in companies' processes and policies only aggravates the difficulty for companies to address them and prevents synergy effects that would benefit the entire due diligence process. For instance, screening suppliers for both anti-corruption and adverse human rights impacts in one process would save resources and improve results. Consequently, a joint focus would allow easier and more efficient tracking, execution, monitoring, and evaluation in carrying out due diligence. In addition, viewing anti-corruption, not as a separate area, but rather, in combination with human rights, would increase the role and use of HRDD by companies. However, the narrower focus by many companies on a "risk to business" approach when conducting due diligence is still prevalent. A paradigm shift needs to occur to place people at the center of businesses' attention.[103] A "risk to people" approach is better suited to address human rights infringements while at the same time maintaining measures to address corruption violations.

VI. Conclusion

To sum up, international anti-corruption standards have developed significantly since the 1990s, and many companies have adapted to this change by implementing extensive compliance systems. The accelerating shift in businesses' responsibilities with respect to human rights is occurring as soft-law standards for HRDD are turning into hard law through the adoption of legislative standards. Therefore, as companies proactively implement HRDD, they should consider how to link anti-corruption and HRDD, given the similarities in the processes and overlap in the occurrences of these two types of harms. However, due to the fundamentally different risk-framing analysis, they should not completely merge. While anti-corruption measures need to focus on the external and internal communication of a strong commitment and a risk-based approach, HRDD is more about identifying and mitigating potential and existing adverse impacts on persons and groups. Good practice examples for a sensible linkage include combining corruption and human rights risk assessments to identify high-risk zones, and cooperation among companies in both areas.

At the same time, tackling adverse human rights impacts requires a more detailed examination of the issue due to the extensive variety of possible human rights infringements that can be committed by enterprises—ranging, for example, from forced labor along the supply chain to the deprivation of land belonging to local communities. Therefore, and to help companies implementing human rights compliance systems, the current international legal framework needs to be augmented. This would facilitate States' coordination of their approaches to create hard law and would enable a level playing field for companies in different jurisdictions.

[103] SHIFT, *supra* note 69, p. 9.

Furthermore, international guidance is needed to assist companies to set up joint compliance programs that integrate corruption and human rights risks. These programs would allow companies to benefit from synergy effects of a joint system and facilitate their addressing adverse human rights impacts more effectively.

VII. Resources

A. Primary Sources

Annan, Foreword to the Convention Against Corruption, <https://www.unodc.org/res/ji/import/international_standards/united_nations_convention_against_corruption/united_nations_convention_against_corruption.pdf> (last visited Jan. 10, 2022), pp. iii–iv.

Business at OECD (BIAC)/International Organisation of Employers (IOE), *Connecting the Anti-corruption and Human Rights Agendas: A Guide for Business and Employers' Organisations* (Sep. 2020), https://baselgovernance.org/sites/default/files/2020-09/2020-08-31-business-at-oecd-ioe-ac-hr-guide.pdf (last visited Jan. 11, 2022).

Cornell Law School–Legal Information Institute, Bribery, https://www.law.cornell.edu/wex/bribery (last visited Jan. 11, 2022).

European Commission, Study on Due Diligence Requirements through the Supply Chain - Final Report (2020), https://op.europa.eu/en/publication-detail/-/publication/8ba0a8fd-4c83-11ea-b8b7-01aa75ed71a1 (last visited Jan. 11, 2022).

Global Witness, Prof. De Schutter, International Corporate Accountability Roundtable (ICAR), *Tainted Lands: Corruption in Large-scale Land Deals* (Nov. 15, 2016).

International Council on Human Rights Policy, Corruption and Human Rights: Making the Connection (2009).

International Labour Organization (ILO), *Conventions and Recommendations*, https://www.ilo.org/global/standards/introduction-to-international-labour-standards/conventions-and-recommendations/lang--en/index.htm (last visited Jan. 11, 2022).

International Labour Organization (ILO), *Declaration on Fundamental Principles and Rights at Work* (Jun. 15, 1988), https://www.ilo.org/declaration/lang--en/index.htm#:~:text=The%20ILO%20Declaration%20on%20Fundamental,our%20social%20and%20economic%20lives (last visited Jan. 11, 2022).

Organisation for Economic Co-operation and Development (OECD), OECD Convention on Combating Bribery of Foreign Public Officials in International Business Transactions (1997), https://www.oecd.org/corruption/oecdantibriberyconvention.htm (last visited Jan. 11, 2022).

Organisation for Economic Co-operation and Development (OECD), *Good Practice Guidance on Internal Controls, Ethics, and Compliance* (Feb. 18, 2010), http://www.oecd.org/daf/anti-bribery/44884389.pdf (last visited Jan. 11, 2022).

Organisation for Economic Co-operation and Development (OECD), *OECD Due Diligence Guidance for Responsible Business Conduct* (2018) https://www.oecd.org/investment/due-diligence-guidance-for-responsible-business-conduct.htm (last visited Jan. 11, 2022).

Organisation for Economic Co-operation and Development (OECD), *OECD Guidelines for Multinational Enterprises* (2011), http://www.oecd.org/daf/inv/mne/48004323.pdf (last visited Jan. 11, 2022).

Shift, Respecting Human Rights Through Global Supply Chains—Workshop Report (Oct. 2012), <https://shiftproject.org/wp-content/uploads/2012/08/Shift_UNGPssupplychain2012.pdf> (last visited Jan. 11, 2022).

Transparency International, *What Is Corruption?*, https://www.transparency.org/en/what-is-corruption# (last visited Jan. 11, 2022).

UN General Assembly, *An Effective International Legal Instrument against Corruption* (Jan. 22, 2001), A/RES/55/61.

UN General Assembly, *International Code of Conduct for Public Officials Approved by Third Committee*, Press Release (Oct. 31, 1996), GA/SHC/3372.

UN General Assembly, *United Nations Convention against Corruption* (Oct. 31, 2003), A/RES/58/4.

UN General Assembly, *United Nations Convention against Transnational Organized Crime* (Jan. 8, 2001), A/RES/55/25.

UN General Assembly, *United Nations Declaration against Corruption and Bribery in International Commercial Transactions* (Feb. 21, 1997), A/RES/51/191.

UN General Assembly, *Transforming our World: The 2030 Agenda for Sustainable Development* (Sept. 25, 2015), A/RES/70/1.

UN Global Compact Human Rights and Labour Working Group, *Linking Human Rights and Anti-Corruption Compliance* (2016), https://www.unglobalcompact.org/library/5011 (last visited Jan. 10, 2022).

UN Human Rights Council, Final Report of the Human Rights Council Advisory Committee on the Issue of the Negative Impact of Corruption on the Enjoyment of Human Rights (Jan. 5, 2015), A/HRC/28/73.

UN Human Rights Council, Report on the United Nations Conference on Anti-corruption, Good Governance and Human Rights (Feb. 12, 2007), A/HRC/4/71.

UN Human Rights Council, Report of the Working Group on the Issue of Human Rights and Transnational Corporations and Other Business Enterprises (Jun. 17, 2020), A/HRC/44/43.

UN Human Rights Council, *Guiding Principles on Business and Human Rights: Implementing the United Nations "Protect, Respect and Remedy" Framework* (Mar. 21, 2011), A/HRC/17/31.

UN Office of the High Commissioner for Human Rights, *Corporate Human Rights Due Diligence: Emerging Practices, Challenges and Ways Forward* (2018), https://www.ohchr.org/Documents/Issues/Business/ExecutiveSummaryA73163.pdf (last visited Jan. 11, 2021).

UN Office of the High Commissioner for Human Rights, *The Human Rights Case Against Corruption* (Nov. 2013), HR/NONE/2013/120.

UN Office on Drugs and Crime, *Impact of Corruption on Specific Human Rights* (2020), https://www.unodc.org/e4j/en/anti-corruption/module-7/key-issues/impact-of-corruption-on-specific-human-rights.html (last visited Jan. 11, 2022).

UN Office on Drugs and Crime, *Signature and Ratification Status*, http://www.unodc.org/unodc/en/corruption/ratification-status.html (last visited Jan. 11, 2022).

UN Office on Drugs and Crime, *United Nations Convention against Corruption* http://www.unodc.org/unodc/en/corruption/uncac.html (last visited Jan. 11, 2021).

Working Group on the Issue of Human Rights and Transnational Corporations and Other Business Enterprises, Business, Human Rights and Conflict-affected Regions: Towards Heightened Action (Jul. 21, 2020), A/75/212.

B. Secondary Sources

Alice Calder, *Corruption Is a Costly "Hidden" Tariff*, https://www.globaltrademag.com/corruption-is-a-costly-hidden-tariff/#:~:text=The%20Organisation%20for%20Economic%20Co,and%20low%2Dmiddle%20income%20countries.&text=Combined%2C%20these%20effects%20will%20damage,welfare%20over%20the%20long%20run (last visited Jan. 11, 2022).

ComplyAdvantage, *A Brief History of the AMLDS* (Aug. 18, 2020), https://complyadvantage.com/blog/brief-history-amlds-part-one/ (last visited Jan. 11, 2022).

CRI Group, *Top 10 Bribery & Corruption Stories of 2020 (so far)*, Lexology, https://www.lexology.com/library/detail.aspx?g=4996cda1-673e-4231-ba62-0f541a4d7c07 (last visited Jan. 10, 2022).

Jeffrey R. Boles, *The Contract as Anti-corruption Platform for the Global Corporate Sector*, 21 Univ. of Penn. J. of Bus. L., 4, 807–842 (2008).

Cannelle Lavite, *The French Loi de Vigilance: Prospects and Limitations of a Pioneer Mandatory Corporate Due Diligence* (June 16, 2020), https://verfassungsblog.de/the-french-loi-de-vigilance-prospects-and-limitations-of-a-pioneer-mandatory-corporate-due-diligence (last visited Jan. 11, 2022).

Surya Deva, *Guiding Principles on Business and Human Rights: Implications for Companies*, 9 Euro. Comp. L., 2, 101–109, (2012).

Sharon Oded/Daniel Ceulen, *Anti-Bribery Due Diligence in M&A Transactions: Have you Got it Covered?* 6 International Journal of Managerial Studies and Research (IJMSR), 7, 14–19, (2018).

Dimitri Vlassis, The United Nations Convention Against Corruption - Origins and Negotiation Process, https://www.unafei.or.jp/publications/pdf/RS_No66/No66_16VE_Vlassis2.pdf (last visited Jan. 11, 2022).

8

Making the Connection: Operational-Level Grievance Mechanisms and Human Rights Due Diligence

Lisa J. Laplante[1]

I. Introduction

Since the approval of the *United Nations Guiding Principles on Business and Human Rights* (UNGPs), there is a notable increase of discussion focused on company-based grievance mechanisms as important paths for redress sought by individuals and communities negatively impacted by company operations. Indeed, they are a featured part of the third pillar of the UNGPs, on access to remedy, which refers to them as operational-level grievance mechanisms (OGMs). Perhaps for that reason, one finds much less discussion on how these non-state, non-judicial mechanisms can also support an effective human rights due diligence (HRDD) process under the second pillar of the UNGPs, "The Corporate Responsibility to Respect Human Rights."

This chapter will explore this connection by highlighting how company-based grievance mechanisms are in fact intended by the UNGPs to be supportive of HRDD. At the same time, the author recognizes that the relationship between business grievance mechanisms and the HRDD process still remains relatively underexplored, leaving unanswered what this

[1] I would like to thank Cambrea Beller, Project Manager of the OGM Research Project at the Center for International Law and Policy, New England Law in Boston, for her invaluable assistance with research for this chapter.

relationship should consist of in terms of best practices. The author shares some recent developments in state regulation and policy as well as voluntary standards that suggest ways that the connection between company grievance mechanisms and due diligence can be more explicitly and consciously developed, arguing that more attention can be brought to this connection to enhance the success of not only due diligence processes, but also general compliance with business and human rights norms.

II. Context: The Evolution of Operational-Level Grievance Mechanisms within the Business and Human Rights Field

Although companies commonly maintain some type of complaint mechanism for handling issues raised by employees and consumers, they have historically rarely self-identified these venues as appropriate for resolving human rights issues.[2] This reality began to change upon the approval of the UNGPs in 2011, leading to a notable trend in which more companies identify internal complaint mechanisms as means for filing human rights grievances, which may be done not only by employees but also by external individuals and communities impacted by the company's operations.

Within the business and human rights field, these mechanisms are commonly referred to as OGMs. This is how they are referred to by the UNGPs, where they have a prominent place within pillar III, which emphasizes access to remedy for those negatively impacted by business operations.[3] Specifically, UNGP 29 sets forth: "To make it possible for grievances to be addressed early and remediated directly, business enterprises should establish or participate in effective operational-level grievance mechanisms for individuals and communities who may be adversely impacted."[4] Accordingly, most commentary on these redress mechanisms

---

[2] Ronald Berenbeim, Non-union Complaint Systems: A Corporate Appraisal (NY: The Conference Board, Report No. 770, 1980); Douglas McCabe, Corporate Nonunion Complaint Procedures and Systems: A Strategic Human Resources Analysis (1988); Avid B. Lipsky, Ronald L. Seeber & Richard D. Fincher, Emerging Systems for Managing Workplace Conflict: Lessons from American Corporations for Managers and Dispute Resolution Professionals (2003).

[3] *Good Practice Note: Addressing Grievances from Project-Affected Communities: Guidance for Projects and Companies on Designing Grievance Mechanisms*, Int'l Fin. Corp. 4 (2009), https://www.ifc.org/wps/wcm/connect/f9019c05-0651-4ff5-9496-c46b66dbeedb/IFC%2BGrievance%2BMechanisms.pdf?MOD=AJPERES&CACHEID=ROOTWORKSPACE-f9019c05-0651-4ff5-9496-c46b66dbeedb-jkD0-.g (describing operational-level grievance mechanism as, "a process for receiving, evaluating, and addressing project-related grievances from affected communities at the level of the company, or project"); *Community-Company Grievance Resolution: A Guide for the Australian Mining Industry*, Oxfam Austl., 7 (2010), https://www.oxfam.org.au/wp-content/uploads/2011/11/OAus-GrievanceMechanisms-0410.pdf (describing a company-level grievance mechanism as, "[a] company-supported, locally based and formalised method, pathway or process to prevent and resolve community concerns with, or grievances about, the performance or behavior of a company, its contractors or employees"); *Human Rights in the Mining & Metals Industry: Handling and Resolving Local Level Concerns and Grievances*, Int'l Council on Mining and Metals (2009), https://www.icmm.com/website/publications/pdfs/social-performance/2009/guidance_local-level-concerns-grievances.pdf (defining "complaints mechanism" as a "set of processes that a company may have in place to deal with local level concerns and grievances").

[4] *Guiding Principles on Business and Human Rights: Implementing the United Nations "Protect, Respect and Remedy" Framework*, UN Hum. Rts. Office of the High Commissioner 31 (2011), https://www.ohchr.org/documents/publications/guidingprinciplesbusinesshr_en.pdf [hereinafter UNGPs].

focuses primarily on their remedial functions as opposed to their relationship to due diligence.[5] United Nations (UN) bodies, such as the Office of the High Commissioner of Human Rights (OHCHR), have also tended to emphasize this function in their work on OGMs, although some connections have been drawn between OGMs and HRDD.[6] For example, through its Accountability and Remedy Project, the OHCHR produced guidance in 2020 on enhancing the effectiveness of non-State–based grievance mechanisms, in which it highlights connections between the effectiveness of OGMs and HRDD. Specifically, the guidance notes in *Policy Objective 13* that OGMs can help prevent future harms by "[c]ontributing to and influencing the human rights due diligence activities of relevant business enterprises by acting as an authoritative and credible source of expertise" as to the enterprises' human rights risks and harms, and to the appropriate actions to take in response to them.[7]

Indeed, a closer look at the UNGPs reveals that these grievance mechanisms were, in fact, envisioned as instruments that support HRDD. Specifically, the commentary to UNGP Principle 20 makes this linkage, stating, "operational-level grievance mechanisms can also provide important feedback on the effectiveness of the business enterprise's HRDD from those directly affected."[8] The commentary to UNGP Principle 29 further elaborates how OGMs support due diligence processes, through two key functions:

> First, they support the identification of adverse human rights impacts *as a part of an enterprise's ongoing human rights due diligence*. They do so by providing a channel for those directly impacted by the enterprise's operations to raise concerns when they believe they are being or will be adversely impacted. By analysing trends and patterns in complaints, business enterprises can also identify systemic problems and adapt their practices accordingly;
>
> Second, these mechanisms make it possible for grievances, once identified, to be addressed and for adverse impacts to be remediated early and directly by the business enterprise, thereby preventing harms from compounding and grievances from escalating. [emphasis supplied][9]

[5] Karin Lukas, Barbara Linder, Astrid Kutrzeba & Claudia Sprenger, Corporate Accountability: The Role and Impact of Non-Judicial Grievance Mechanisms (2016); Benjamin Thompson, *Determining Criteria to Evaluate Outcomes of Businesses' Provision of Remedy: Applying a Human Rights-Based Approach*, 2 Bus. and Hum. Rts. J. 55 (2017); Jonathan Kaufman & Katherine McDonnell, *Community-Driven Operational Grievance Mechanisms* 1 Bus. and Hum. Rts. J. 127 (2016); *Effective Operational-Level Grievance Mechanisms*, Int'l Commission of Jurists (2019), https://www.icj.org/wp-content/uploads/2019/11/Universal-Grievance-Mechanisms-Publications-Reports-Thematic-reports-2019-ENG.pdf.

[6] For example, the Office of the High Commissioner for Human Rights recently completed a study of non-State-based grievance mechanisms as part of its ongoing Accountability and Remedy Project that included a strong focus on company-based grievance mechanisms. *See* Improving Accountability and Access to Remedy for Victims of Business-Related Human Rights Abuse Through Non-State-Based Grievance Mechanisms, Rep. of the UN Office of the High Commissioner for Human Rights UN Doc. A/HRC/44/32 (2020); A/HRC/44/32/Add.1: ARP III Addendum: Explanatory Notes to Final Report, 3 June 2020. *See also*, Report of the Working Group on the issue of human rights and transnational corporations and other business enterprises: *Access to effective remedies under the Guiding Principles on Business and Human Rights: Implementing the United Nations Protect, Respect and Remedy Framework* A/72/162 (2017).

[7] *Id.* at 13.2.

[8] *Guiding Principles*, *supra* note 4, at 23 (referencing the commentary to Principle 20).

[9] *Id.* at 32 (referencing the commentary to Principle 29).

Ultimately, the primary way in which OGMs support HRDD processes is to reveal where a business must address not only potential risks but also actual harms that its operations, goods, or services contributed to or caused. As spelled out in the commentary to UNGP Principle 31, which outlines criteria for ensuring effective OGMs, these complaint mechanisms allow "regular analysis of the frequency, patterns and causes of grievances" which can in turn be used to "identify and influence policies, procedures or practices that should be altered to prevent future harm."[10] All of these commentaries support a company finding deliberate ways to strengthen the connection between a company's OGM and its human rights process.

While a fairly robust and large amount of literature exists regarding HRDD, much of it fails to examine the relationship between a company's OGM and HRDD process.[11] Only a handful of sources, including some industry and state guidelines as well as practitioner and academic commentary, do build off of the UNGP commentaries and recognize the link between the two mechanisms, assuming that the OGM operates effectively in accordance with the criteria laid out in UNGP Principle 31.[12]

Drawing on some of this guidance, the author offers a closer look at how an OGM can support a HRDD process. A useful starting point comes from the key steps laid out by the Organisation for Economic Co-operation and Development (OECD) *Due Diligence Guidance for Responsible Business Conduct* (OECD Guidance) for setting up an effective HRDD process.[13] These recommendations offered by the OECD were largely inspired by and

---

[10] *Id.* at 35.

[11] *See e.g.*, Björn Fasterling, *Human Rights Due Diligence as Risk Management: Social Versus Human Rights Risk*, 2 Bus. and Hum. Rts. J. 225 (2017) (discussing the effective integration of corporate HRDD processes without mentioning OGMs); Ralph Hamann et al., *Business and Human Rights in South Africa: An Analysis of Antecedents of Human Rights Due Diligence*, 87 J. Bus. Ethics 453 (2009); Björn Fasterling & Geert Demuijnck, *Human Rights in the Void? Due Diligence in the UN Guiding Principles on Business and Human Rights*, 116 J. Bus. Ethics 799 (2013); James Harrison, *Establishing a Meaningful Human Rights Due Diligence Process for Corporations: Learning from Experience of Human Rights Impact Assessment*, 31 Impact Assessment and Project Appraisal 107 (2013) (linking due diligence to a business's human rights impact assessment but failing to mention OGMs); Robert C. Bird et al., *Corporate Voluntarism and Liability for Human Rights in a Post-Kiobel World*, 102 Ky. L.J. 601 (2014); John F. Sherman, III & Amy K. Lehr, *Human Rights Due Diligence: Is It Too Risky?* (Corp. Soc. Resp. Initiative, Working Paper No. 55, 2010), https://www.hks.harvard.edu/sites/default/files/centers/mrcbg/programs/cri/files/workingpaper_55_shermanlehr.pdf; Doug Cassel, *Outlining the Case for a Common Law Duty of Care of Business to Exercise Human Rights Due Diligence*, 1 Bus. and Hum. Rts. J. 179 (2016) (failing to include an OGM as a part of a business's responsibility to exercise HRDD).

[12] *No Rights Without Remedies—An Assessment of Corporate Remedy Channels*, NYU Stern Ctr. for Bus. and Hum. Rts 4 (Oct. 24, 2017), https://issuu.com/nyusterncenterforbusinessandhumanri/docs/3-nyu-research-brief-oct17_60a5a7e903962d.

[13] *OECD Due Diligence Guidance for Responsible Business Conduct*, Org. for Econ. Co-Operation and Dev. 21 (2018), https://mneguidelines.oecd.org/OECD-Due-Diligence-Guidance-for-Responsible-Business-Conduct.pdf [hereinafter OECD Guidance]. The OECD Guidance provides a six-step process: (1) embed responsible business conduct (RBC); (2) identify and assess adverse impacts; (3) cease, prevent or mitigate; (4) track implementation and results; (5) communicate how impacts are addressed; (6) provide for or cooperate in remediation. The author's analysis does not include the first step of embedding RBC. Most of the literature reviewed on making a connection between OGMs and HRDD only focuses on these four steps (1) through (4), while a few publications simply assert that the establishment of an OGM falls into step (1). However, as argued here, a company cannot assume that an OGM, once established, is automatically linked to HRDD without more deliberate linkage, and the author's analysis provides suggestions on how that may be accomplished.

in line with those promoted by the UNGPs.[14] The following sections outline the symbiosis between an OGM and the key aspects of the OECD Guidance on developing an effective HRDD process.

A. Identify and Assess Adverse Impacts in Operations, Supply Chains, and Business Relationships

HRDD requires companies to identify the most significant risks and determine the appropriate response.[15] The complaints received through OGMs, whether from workers or members of communities, also help a company identify these risks by showing both actual and potential negative impacts.[16] In addition, an OGM can alert a company to emerging adverse impacts not identified through other risk assessment tools, especially those that are not ongoing but instead have a defined period of time in which they operate and a fixed conclusion, or that are not designed to detect all possible human rights impacts.[17] In particular, OGMs can bring special attention to how negative impacts "affect different groups in society," particularly when they adopt a gender perspective and pay special attention to people who may be at heightened risk of vulnerability or marginalization.[18]

B. Cease, Prevent, or Mitigate Adverse Impacts

In theory, an effective HRDD process leads a company to cease activities that cause or contribute to an identified human rights risk.[19] Similarly, OGMs are expected to lead companies to mitigate, or, when possible, prevent negative human rights impacts.[20] The literature identifies two main ways a business can use its OGM to serve this purpose.

First, an OGM functions as a warning system that allows for the early identification of human rights issues and better enables companies to effectively mitigate and prevent

[14] The OECD Guidance makes direct reference to the UNGPs as a resource for due diligence processes. *Id.* at 3. ("The UN Guiding Principles on Business and Human Rights as well as the ILO Tripartite Declaration of Principles Concerning Multinational Enterprises and Social Policy also contain due diligence recommendations, and this Guidance can help enterprises implement them.")

[15] *See Id.* at 25–27.

[16] *See* Mariana Aparecida Vilmondes Turke, *Business and Human Rights in Brazil: Exploring Human Rights Due Diligence and Operational-Level Grievance Mechanism in the Case of Kinross Paracatu Gold Mine*, 15 BRAZ. J. INT'L L. 222, 231 (2018); *Five Takeaways from the 2017 UN Forum on Business and Human Rights*, COVINGTON & BURLING LLP 3 (Dec. 8, 2017), https://www.cov.com/-/media/files/corporate/publications/2017/12/five_takeaways_from_the_2017_un_forum_on_business_and_human_rights.pdf; Caroline Rees, *Piloting Principles for Effective Company-Stakeholder Grievance Mechanisms: A Report of Lessons Learned*, HARV. KENNEDY SCH. CORP. SOC. RESP. INITIATIVE 9 (May 23, 2011), https://www.business-humanrights.org/sites/default/files/media/documents/ruggie/grievance-mechanism-pilots-report-harvard-csri-jun-2011.pdf; *Community Grievance Mechanisms in the Oil and Gas Industry*, IPIECA (2015), https://www.ipieca.org/resources/good-practice/community-grievance-mechanisms-in-the-oil-and-gas-industry/.

[17] Turke, *Id.* at 230.

[18] Improving Accountability and Access to Remedy, *supra* note 6, at 13.2(a).

[19] OECD Guidance, *supra* note 13, at 29.

[20] OECD Guidance, *supra* note 13, at 67; Turke, *supra* note 16; COVINGTON & BURLING LLP, *supra* note 16.

the adverse impact of its operations before the problems "escalate into unmanageable disputes."[21] It is argued that an effective OGM can even provide an incentive for a company to have an effective HRDD process in order to avoid the practical matter of handling numerous complaints and any negative consequences of these complaints filed against it.[22] In comparison, some due diligence processes, such as site-level assessments that occur both prior to and during a project, may not create a similar incentive because they are limited in scope and duration.

Second, complaints generated through an OGM may produce learning that leads a company to act proactively to revise its policies and practices based on a more comprehensive understanding of any recurrent issues.[23] The records of complaints received and resolved can be used by a company to analyze trends and patterns in complaints that reveal systemic issues, failure of company responses, and ways to correct company practices where needed.[24] Most importantly, this information can help to better identify "underlying reasons for concerns raised," thus assuring more sustainable prevention.[25] Here, Michele Law recommends that companies use this information to create "people-centered" maps of where a company fails to protect human rights to better inform how it makes changes to its policies and practices.[26]

[21] Anaïs Desjardins-Charbonneau, *Operational-Level Grievance Mechanisms: A New Approach to Human Rights for Mining Corporations*, Graduate Sch. of Pub. and Int'l Affairs Univ. of Ottawa 15, 36 (July 23, 2014), https://ruor.uottawa.ca/bitstream/10393/31560/1/DESJARDINS-CHARBONNEAU,%20Anaïs%2020145.pdf; Nadja Lidbeck, *The Lundin Case in Sudan According to the UN Guiding Principles*, Stockholm Univ. 37 (2016), http://www.diva-portal.org/smash/get/diva2:1081532/FULLTEXT01.pdf; Cindy Berman, Ben Rutledge & Samir Goswani, *Access to Remedy: Practical Guidance for Companies*, Ethical Trading Initiative 3 (2019), https://www.ethicaltrade.org/sites/default/files/shared_resources/Access%20to%20remedy_0.pdf; IPIECA, *supra* note 16, at 65; *see* Dr. Aidan McQuade, *Grievance Mechanisms, Remedies and Trade Unions: A Discussion Document*, Ethical Trade 6 (Dec. 2017), https://www.ethicaltrade.org/sites/default/files/shared_resources/grievance_mechanisms_remedies_and_trades_unions._eti._aidan_mcquade._dec_2017_final.pdf.; Rees, *supra* note 16, at 9; OECD Guidance, *supra* note 13, at 47; Turke, *supra* note 16, at 232; Laura Curtze & Steve Gibbons, *Access to Remedy—Operational Grievance Mechanisms*, Ergon (Oct. 25, 2017), https://www.ethicaltrade.org/sites/default/files/shared_resources/ergon_-_issues_paper_on_access_to_remedy_and_operational_grievance_mechanims_-_revised_draft.pdf.

[22] *Human Rights Due Diligence: Policy Measures for Effective Implementation*, CIDSE 12 (Sept. 16, 2013), https://www.cidse.org/2013/09/16/human-rights-due-diligence-policy-measures-for-effective-implementation/ ("[e]ffective mechanisms for access to remedy serve as an incentive for businesses to undertake proper human rights due diligence, and to repair harm done where they fail"); *Assessing the Effectiveness of Company Grievance Mechanisms*, CSR Europe 6 (Dec. 2013), https://static1.squarespace.com/static/5df776f6866c14507f2df68a/t/5e666810b7c6ef5fcd9bf296/1583769622168/MOC-A+Report.pdf.

[23] Turke, *supra* note 16; OECD Guidance, *supra* note 13, at 29; Ergon, *supra* note 21; Stuart Wallace, *Case Study on Holding Private Military and Security Companies Accountable for Human Rights Violations*, Frame (Apr. 28, 2016), http://www.fp7-frame.eu/wp-content/uploads/2016/08/25-Deliverable-7.5.pdf; CSR Europe, *supra* note 22, at 21.

[24] Rees, *supra* note 16, at 9.

[25] CSR Europe *supra* note 22, at 21.

[26] *See* Michele Law, *Can Operational Grievance Mechanisms Address Slavery? Innovation Issues – Summary of a Talk to the Nexus Working Group on Human Trafficking*, LinkedIn (June 15, 2017), https://www.linkedin.com/pulse/can-operational-grievance-mechanisms-address-slavery-innovation-law/; Wallace, *supra* note 19.

C. Track Implementation and Results of the Actions Taken to Address Impacts

An OGM helps a company track not only its human rights impacts through the type of grievance raised, but also the effectiveness of any of its responses to complaints and whether they were resolved, thus serving as a type of feedback loop.[27] During this internal assessment process, OGMs also help draw better attention to the experience of vulnerable or marginalized groups, who are often disproportionately impacted by company operations.[28] Moreover, the recommended monitoring of grievance mechanisms ensures a company will bring sustained attention to the types of complaints filed with a grievance mechanism, thus enabling the company to "identify new, emerging or endemic issues early on," thus feeding into the "Identify and Assess" step above, as well as "to assess the effectiveness of existing mitigation actions and take additional steps if necessary, thus directly feeding into broader human rights due diligence processes."[29] Additionally, this type of information generated by the operation of an OGM provides more qualitative data about company operations than merely tracking or ticking off the existence of processes and procedures put in place. It allows for more in-depth assessment of the effectiveness of changes and whether they are mitigating and preventing adverse impacts, as well as identifying possible new adverse impacts that may arrive from those changes.[30] Tracking the effectiveness of an OGM, as required by Principle 31 of the UNGPs, is also a better way to link it to a company's ongoing HRDD process to ensure the company maximizes its ability to capture information on potential and actual adverse impacts.[31]

Shift, an independent nonprofit organization that was created by advisors to Professor John Ruggie, who was special representative to the UN Secretary-General on human rights and transnational corporations and other business enterprises from 2005 to 2011, recommends that OGMs should be designed using an "eco-system approach" that allows for multiple ways to file a grievance or concern that could also flow into a due diligence process. A "single coordination point" would conduct an initial assessment of each complaint to then steer it to the appropriate remedial channel. This "tracking link" back to this coordination point "enable[s] the company to learn from the impacts that are occurring, feed into the company's HRDD processes, and to assess the effectiveness of the remediation eco-system as a whole."[32]

---

[27] *Human Rights Translated 2.0: A Business Reference Guide*, Castan Ctr. for Hum. Rts. L. 8 (2017); IPIECA, *supra* note 16, at 6.

[28] OECD Guidance, *supra* note 13, at 82; *Human Rights Translated 2.0*, *supra* note 27, at 8.

[29] Ergon, *supra* note 21.

[30] OECD Guidance, *supra* note 13, at 32, 82, 84; *See e.g., Codes of Practices Guidance*, Responsible Jewellery Council 45 (Apr. 23, 2019), https://www.responsiblejewellery.com/wp-content/uploads/RJC-COP-Guidance-April-2019.pdf. CSR Europe, *supra* note 22, at 21.

[31] Lidbeck, *supra* note 19, at 31; Turke, *supra* note 15, at 229.

[32] *Remediation, Grievance Mechanisms and the Corporate Responsibility to Respect Human Rights*, Shift 9 (May 2014), https://shiftproject.org/wp-content/uploads/2014/05/Shift_remediationUNGPs_2014.pdf.

D. Communicate Publicly How These Impacts Have Been Addressed

An effective HRDD process requires a company to communicate externally its findings and outcomes.[33] Similarly, effective OGMs are transparent and share information about the number and types of cases, the resulting outcomes of the grievance process, and how adverse impacts are being addressed.[34]

E. Provide for or Cooperate in Remediation When Appropriate

An effective HRDD process requires a company to enable remediation when such company has caused or contributed to an adverse impact.[35] Providing a remedy is a distinctive feature of an OGM, which is largely viewed as relevant to a remediation stage of addressing adverse impacts.[36]

A recent report issued by the UN Working Group on the Issue of Human Rights and Transnational Corporations and Other Business Enterprises (UN Working Group on Business and Human Rights) stresses the following:

> Where a business enterprise identifies that it has caused or contributed to an adverse impact, a key part of its responsibility is to provide for or cooperate in the remediation of such impacts through legitimate processes, which may involve State-based judicial and non-judicial mechanisms, as well as non-State–based grievance mechanisms. Business enterprises should establish or participate in effective operational-level grievance mechanisms, which should meet certain core criteria set out in Guiding Principle 31. Such mechanisms are critical to effective due diligence, reinforcing prevention by helping an enterprise to identify concerns and systemic problems and address grievances at an early stage, thereby preventing grievances from escalating.[37]

Thus, OGMs provide processes that enable a company to fulfill this responsibility to remediate issues that arise, while also ensuring affected populations have access to remedies

[33] OECD Guidance, *supra* note 13, at 33.

[34] *See* IPIECA, *supra* note 16, at 14; Ergon, *supra* note 21, at 27, 29.

[35] *Human Rights Translated 2.0*, *supra* note 27, at 9; OECD Guidance, *supra* note 13, at 34; Lidbeck, *supra* note 19, at 36.

[36] Lidbeck, *supra* note 19, at 16, 37; Dr. Aidan McQuade, *supra* note 21, at 5; *See Human Rights Translated 2.0*, *supra* note 27, at 9; *Injustice Incorporated: Corporate Abuses and the Human Right to Remedy*, Amnesty Int'l 17 (2014), https://www.amnesty.org/download/Documents/8000/pol300012014en.pdf. *See generally* Robert McCorquodale, *Survey of the Provision in the United Kingdom of Access to Remedies for Victims of Human Rights Harms Involving Business Enterprises*, Brit. Inst. of Int'l and Comp. L. 49–51 (July 17, 2015), https://corporate-responsibility.org/wp-content/uploads/2015/12/BIICL-McQuordale_-uk_access_to_remedies.pdf (discussing how OGMs provide a remedy, which complements the HRDD process).

[37] *The Report of the Working Group on the Issue of Human Rights and Transnational Corporations and Other Business Enterprises* A/73/163 (2018), para 12.

directly from the company, as opposed to a central office or judicial system, when negative impacts occur.[38]

Moreover, the remedy may be more appropriate because OGM outcomes are based on stakeholder engagement and dialogue.[39] Indeed, one of the other important ways that OGMs support due diligence processes is through their focus on stakeholder engagement, as urged by UNGPs Principle 31(h).[40] Indeed, commentators suggest that the most effective OGMs focus on dialogue with stakeholders in order to find agreed solutions that address and resolve complaints.[41] Ideally, the same stakeholder engagement policies used in grievance processes could be used during the due diligence process.

III. Trends in Voluntary Initiatives

While commentators flesh out the ways in which OGMs can support HRDD processes, there are some nascent, evolving trends in voluntary standards and initiatives that promote a connection between the two.

A. Direct Connections between Operational-level Grievance Mechanisms and Human Rights Due Diligence

As OGMs continue to draw more attention, one sees more voluntary standards explicitly requiring companies to include these OGMs as means for preventing and, if necessary, remedying negative human rights impacts.[42] Yet most of the time, the inclusion of an OGM maintains the conventional focus on remediation without making a clear connection to an HRDD process.[43] Of 38 voluntary initiatives focused on business and human rights which the author surveyed at the time of writing, only two standards explicitly require a company to implement an OGM in connection with HRDD: the Initiative for Responsible Mining Assurance (IRMA) and the Fair Wear Foundation Brand Performance Check Guide (FWF).

---

[38] Dr. Aidan McQuade, *supra* note 21; OECD Guidance, *supra* note 13, at 91; *Corporate Mechanisms and Access to Justice*, Bus., Hum. Rts. and Ne. Asia 115, https://www.hurights.or.jp/archives/other_publications/business_human_rights_and_northeast_asia/10_p105-118.pdf; Berman, Rutledge & Goswani, *supra* note 21, at 3; Responsible Jewellery Council, *supra* note 30, at 45. However, OGMs may not necessarily be suitable for all such grievances depending on the severity of the harm. *See* Lisa J. Laplante, *The Wild West of Company-Level Grievance Mechanisms: Drawing Normative Borders to Patrol the Privatization of Human Rights Remedies* (manuscript on file with author).

[39] *See* Turke, *supra* note 15, at 231; Maximilian J. L. Schormair & Lara M. Gerlach, *Corporate Remediation of Human Rights Violations: A Restorative Justice Framework*, 167 J. Bus Ethics. 475, 489–90 (Mar. 2019).

[40] *See Guiding Principles*, *supra* note 4, at 33–34.

[41] *Guiding Principles*, *supra* note 4, at 34; Turke, *supra* note 15, at 231.

[42] Lisa J. Laplante, *Corporate Accountability and Privatizing Remedies: Company Level Grievance Mechanisms Repairing Human Rights Harms* (manuscript on file with the author).

[43] *See, e.g.*, *FLA Workplace Code of Conduct and Compliance Benchmarks*, Fair Labor Assoc. (Oct. 5, 2011), https://sa-intl.org/programs/sa8000/. *Social Accountability 8000 International Standard*, Soc. Accountability Int'l (June 2014), https://2imd8u2t64kh14lne52j2jh2-wpengine.netdna-ssl.com/wp-content/uploads/2020/02/SA8000Standard2014.pdf.

1. *The Initiative for Responsible Mining Assurance (IRMA)*

The IRMA is an independent verification and certification program for mining companies. It specifically includes a section requiring HRDD that also requires companies to create an OGM to handle human rights complaints.[44] While the IRMA recognizes the primary remedial function of OGMs, it also cross-references them to HRDD.[45] Moreover, the periodic reporting requirements ask companies to report on identified issues, the methods used to identify human rights issues, as well as actions taken by the company to prevent, mitigate, and/or remediate the human rights grievances. The monitoring of the OGM includes actions that go toward supporting the purpose of the HRDD process, namely, to determine whether "changes need to be made to improve its effectiveness," or "if changes in company activities can be implemented to prevent or mitigate similar grievances in the future."[46]

2. *The Fair Wear Foundation Brand Performance Check Guide*

The Fair Wear Foundation (FWF) requires a complaints procedure, which is featured before a section on due diligence.[47] The FWF provides a "Check Guide" that directly links an OGM to HRDD, specifying:

> FWF advises member companies to conduct proper due diligence and assess possible risks for the subcontractors. Where additional risks are foreseen, FWF recommends to conduct an audit (for instance in the case of washing of denim). Whenever a complaint is received, the member company will be required to include this location in their monitoring system, regardless of whether it is a direct supplier or subcontractor.[48]

Thus, if a company participating in the FWF initiative receives a complaint about its operations, it must not only conduct additional due diligence on the matter, but also monitor the situation. Put simply, FWF recognizes that an OGM helps feed information into the initial due diligence step by serving as a type of alert that identifies potential risks.

B. Indirect Connections between Operational-level Grievance Mechanisms and Human Rights Due Diligence

Even though most voluntary standards do not explicitly make a connection between a company-led grievance mechanism and an HRDD process, the manner in which OGMs are expected to operate does provide inherent support of due diligence processes. Namely, this support arises because the primary purposes of an OGM is to identify actual or potential

---

[44] *IRMA Standard for Responsible Mining IRMA-STD-001*, Initiative for Responsible Mining Assurance 26 (June 2018), https://responsiblemining.net/wp-content/uploads/2018/07/IRMA_STANDARD_v.1.0_FINAL_2018.pdf.

[45] *Id.* at 30, 85.

[46] *Id.* at 33.

[47] *Brand Performance Check Guide*, Fair Wear Foundation 98, https://api.fairwear.org/wp-content/uploads/2011/12/online-brand-performance-check-guide-2016.pdf.

[48] *Id.* at 11.

adverse human rights impacts and to track the implementation and results of measures to address these issues, including remediation. Four voluntary standards, in particular, offer good examples of this less explicit, although equally important, connection between OGMs and due diligence.

1. *Aluminum Stewardship Initiative Performance Standard*

The Aluminum Stewardship Initiative (ASI) Performance Standard defines 59 environmental, social, and governance principles and criteria to address sustainability issues in the aluminum value chain.[49] The ASI Performance Standard states that due diligence requires access to remedy through formal processes without necessarily identifying the composition of those processes.[50] However, the ASI Performance Standard later states that a "Complaints Resolution Mechanism" is a formal process that provides access to remedy, although without any specific reference to its due diligence requirements.[51] The Complaints Resolution Mechanism functions as an OGM because it is a channel for all types of stakeholders (individuals and communities, workers, civil society groups) to file grievances, including human rights concerns, directly with the company.[52]

2. *Amfori Code of Conduct*

Amfori is a global business association dedicated to promoting open and sustainable trade; its membership includes 2,400 retailers, importers, brands, and associations from more than 40 countries.[53] The Amfori Code of Conduct encourages its members to "act with due diligence and develop the necessary management systems, policies and processes to a reasonable extent as well as effectively prevent and address any adverse human rights impacts that may be detected in the supply chain."[54] The Amfori Code of Conduct requires businesses to create OGMs as special protection for young workers in order to "prevent, identify and mitigate harm to young workers."[55] The Amfori Code of Conduct also recognizes that the OGM enables remediation, which effectively addresses human rights risk posed by the company.

3. *Global Reporting Initiative*

The Global Reporting Initiative (GRI) offers sustainability standards for organizations of any size, type, sector, or geographic location. In particular, the GRI promotes the "GRI 103" management approach that requires companies to adopt ways to help them avoid, mitigate,

---

[49] *ASI Performance Standard*, ALUMINUM STEWARDSHIP INITIATIVE (Dec. 2017), https://aluminium-stewardship.org/asi-standards/asi-performance-standard/.

[50] *See Id.* at 15.

[51] *Id.* at 23.

[52] *Id.* at 11, 23.

[53] *About Amfori*, AMFORI, https://www.amfori.org/content/about-amfori.

[54] *Amfori BSCI Code of Conduct*, AMFORI 3 (2017), https://www.amfori.org/sites/default/files/amfori%20BSCI%20COC%20UK_0.pdf.

[55] *Id.* at 7.

or remediate negative impacts, or to enhance positive impacts on the economy, environment, and society, which are considered "material topics."[56]

The GRI 103 describes how a reporting company can include due diligence in its management approach to support a focus on material topics, namely by instituting "a process to identify, prevent, mitigate and account for how an organization addresses its actual and potential negative impacts."[57] Similarly, if a company includes an OGM in its management approach, the report must include a description of the OGM, which is described as a "system consisting of procedures, roles and rules for receiving complaints and providing remedy."[58]

While the GRI 103 does not make an explicit connection between an OGM and HRDD, its explanation of the purpose of an OGM does reveal this interconnection. For example, the GRI standards expect OGMs to not only provide a remedy for the company's actual negative impacts, but also to identify prospective and actual negative impacts caused by the company and to reveal whether or not the adopted management approach to each material topic is effective.[59] Thus, the OGM feeds into the due diligence process by strengthening the latter's ability to identify, avoid, mitigate, or remediate adverse impacts while tracking the implementation of any company responses.

4. *International Council on Mining and Metals*

The International Council on Mining and Metals (ICMM) is an international organization dedicated to a "safe, fair and sustainable mining and metals industry."[60] It requires members to adopt 10 voluntary mining principles that set ethical standards regarding environmental, social, and governance issues that companies then disclose in an annual corporate sustainability report.[61] The ICMM has largely incorporated the UNGPs in a chapter on human rights, and pursuant to Principle 3 of these standards, companies are expected to respect human rights by undertaking HRDD as well as establishing an OGM. Companies are ultimately called upon to remediate "adverse human rights impacts that members have caused or contributed to," and to provide effective mechanisms that "seek[] resolution of grievances related to the company and its activities."[62] Although the ICMM does not make an explicit connection between an OGM as a means of providing remedy and the remediation aspect of due diligence, the language employed to describe the processes does facilitate such an interpretation.

---

[56] *GRI 103: Management Approach*, Global Sustainability Standards Board 2, 3, 8, 12 (2016), https://www.globalreporting.org/standards/media/1038/gri-103-management-approach-2016.pdf.

[57] *Id.* at 12.

[58] *Id.* at 8, 12.

[59] *Id.* at 6, 8, 10, 11.

[60] *About Us*, Int'l Council on Mining and Metals, https://www.icmm.com/en-gb/about-us.

[61] *Mining Principles: Performance Expectations*, Int'l Council on Mining and Metals 1 (2020), https://www.icmm.com/website/publications/pdfs/mining-principles/mining-principles.pdf.

[62] *Id.* at 2, 6.

IV. Legal and Regulatory Standards

As governments are beginning to recognize the importance of encouraging or even requiring companies to engage in some level of HRDD and putting in place regulations, a small number make a direct linkage between an OGM and a due diligence process. Specifically, out of 15 such pieces of regulation, only two made an explicit connection between OGMs and HRDD.

A. French Corporate Duty of Vigilance Law

In 2017, the French Parliament adopted the Corporate Duty of Vigilance Law that applies to the country's largest companies, requiring them to address adverse impacts linked to their activities as well as their suppliers and subcontractors in a vigilance plan required by Article 1 of the French law.[63] Article 2 states that if a company fails to comply with the requirements of establishing and implementing a vigilance plan, then it will be "liable and obliged to compensate for the harm that *due diligence* would have permitted to avoid. [emphasis supplied]"[64] They must also publish annual reports related to their compliance with the law.[65]

The Corporate Duty of Vigilance Law requires these companies to establish, implement, and publish an effective vigilance plan that amounts to a HRDD process (risk mapping, value chain assessment processes, mitigation and preventive actions, alert mechanisms, and a monitoring scheme to verify the plan's efficiency)[66] that includes "the reasonable vigilance measures to allow for risk identification and for the prevention of severe violations of human rights and fundamental freedoms, serious bodily injury or environmental damage or health risks resulting directly or indirectly from the operations of the company and of the companies it controls. . . ."[67]

In particular, the Corporate Duty of Vigilance Law requires an alert mechanism channel for the company to receive complaints of risks posed by the company and is based on stakeholder engagement.[68] This mechanism is also designed to collect and report on existing or actual risks and should be developed in working partnership with the trade union organizations' representatives of the company concerned.[69] The law provides only broad

[63] *See* LAW No. 2017-399 on the Duty of Vigilance of Parent Companies and Instructing Companies art. 1, 3 (March 27, 2017) [hereinafter Corporate Duty of Vigilance Law]; *See also Vigilance Plans Reference Guidance*, SHERPA 51–52 (2019), https://www.asso-sherpa.org/wp-content/uploads/2019/02/Sherpa_VPRG_EN_WEB-VF-compressed.pdf. The Vigilance Plan requires: "Any company that at the end of two consecutive financial years, employs at least five thousand employees within the company and its direct and indirect subsidiaries, whose head office is located on French territory, or that has at least ten thousand employees in its service and in its direct or indirect subsidiaries, whose head office is located on French territory or abroad, must establish and implement an effective vigilance plan."

[64] *Id.* Article 2.

[65] *Id.* Article 1.

[66] *Id.* Article 1; *see Compliance in France and the United States: A Combination of Corporate and Social Responsibility*, KRAMER LEVIN (Nov. 5, 2018), https://www.kramerlevin.com/en/perspectives-search/compliance-in-france-and-the-united-states-a-combination-of-corporate-and-social-responsibility.html.

[67] *Id.*

[68] *See* SHERPA, *supra* note 63, at 44.

[69] *See* Corporate Duty of Vigilance Law, *supra* note 63, Article 1.

guidance on this mechanism, which has prompted civil society to begin elaborating more guidelines. For example, the organization Sherpa recently published a guide on the Corporate Duty of Vigilance Law calling upon companies to develop these alert mechanisms in line with the UNGPs effectiveness principles related to OGMs.[70] The guide observes how these mechanisms improve upon the identification and prevention of risks as well as protect whistleblowers from retaliation.[71]

B. European Union Conflict Minerals Regulation

In May 2017, the European Union (EU) passed Regulation (EU) 2017/821 (Conflict Minerals Regulation), which includes a due diligence requirement for supply chains of companies importing minerals or metals consisting of tin, tantalum, tungsten, or gold originating from conflict-affected and high-risk areas.[72] As part of its due diligence plan, such EU importers must also "establish a grievance mechanism as an early-warning risk-awareness system; or provide such mechanisms through collaborative arrangements with other economic operators or organizations; or facilitate recourse to an external expert or body, such as an ombudsman."[73] Information from the grievance mechanism should then be used to "identify and assess the risks of adverse impacts in their mineral supply chain . . . against the standards of their supply chain policy."[74] After identifying and assessing the risks, EU importers of tin, tantalum, tungsten, and gold must implement a strategy to prevent or mitigate adverse impacts from the identified risks. Additionally, the Conflict Minerals Regulation calls on these companies to monitor and track the performance of their OGMs, including carrying out third-party audits of the OGM process and system, which in turn will support the due diligence process.

C. European Commission's Human Rights Due Diligence Directive

On March 10, 2021, the European Parliament considered and adopted an outline proposal for the "EU Directive on Mandatory Human Rights, Environmental and Good Governance Due Diligence" (Directive) to set on course the European Commission drafting of a formal legislative proposal to ensure more uniformity with regard to HRDD requirements imposed on

[70] *See* SHERPA, *supra* note 63, at 68.

[71] *Id.* at 44, 66.

[72] Regulation (EU) 2017/821 of the European Parliament and of the Council laying down supply chain due diligence obligations for Union importers of tin, tantalum and tungsten, their ores, and gold originating from conflict-affected and high-risk areas, https://eur-lex.europa.eu/legal-content/EN/TXT/PDF/?uri=OJ:L:2017:130:FULL&from=EN. The Regulation itself took effect in July 2017. However, the articles referenced in this chapter did not take effect until January 1, 2021.

[73] Regulation (EU) 2017/821, Article 4(e).

[74] Regulation (EU) 2017/821, Article 5(1)(a).

companies operating in the EU. The European Commission then published a draft Directive on February 23, 2022 setting out mandatory human rights and environmental due diligence obligations for corporations.[75] The draft Directive will undergo further review and debate, with the expectation of finally being adopted by the European Parliament closer to 2027.

As part of the basic obligation of Member States to ensure companies conduct human rights and environmental due diligence, the general framework contemplates the establishment of complaints procedures.[76] Indeed, Article 9 calls on Member States to "ensure that companies provide the possibility for persons and organisations . . . to submit complaints to them where they have legitimate concerns regarding actual or potential adverse human rights impacts and adverse environmental impacts with respect to their own operations, the operations of their subsidiaries and their value chains . . ."

Although Article 9 provides baseline guidance on setting up the grievance mechanisms and is silent on making a connection to the overall due diligence process, it can be read together with Article 6 to highlight that the Directive does make an explicit connection between the two. Specifically, Article 6 sets up the requirement that companies identify actual and potential adverse impacts arising from their operations and from their subsidiaries and suggests different quantitative and qualitative information that may inform this process, including information gathered "through the complaints procedure provided for in Article 9."[77]

Notably, the original proposal went even further to recognize the importance of making an explicit linkage between an OGM and a HRDD, indicating that

> [i]n order to be effective, a due diligence framework should include grievance mechanisms at the level of the undertaking or at sectoral level, and, in order to ensure that such mechanisms are effective, undertakings should take decisions informed by the position of stakeholders, when developing grievance mechanisms. Those mechanisms should allow stakeholders to raise reasonable concerns and should function as an early warning risk-awareness and mediation system.[78]

While the final draft does not offer as much detail on the importance of the relationship, it did maintain the connection to guide both Member States and companies in their conceptualization of how the two mechanisms work together.

---

[75] European Commission, *Proposal for a Directive of the European Parliament and of the Council Amending Directive 2019/1937/EU on Corporate Sustainability Due Diligence*, COM (2022) 71 final (Feb. 23, 2022), https://eur-lex.europa.eu/resource.html?uri=cellar:bc4dcea4-9584-11ec-b4e4-01aa75ed71a1.0001.02/DOC_1&format=PDF. [Hereinafter, "EU, The Directive"]

[76] Article 4, *Id.*

[77] Article 6(4), *Id.*

[78] European Parliament, Annex to Resolution of 10 Mar. 2021, Recommendation to the Commission on Corporate Due Diligence and Accountability ((2020/2129(INL)), 2021 O.J. (C 474) 11, 22., ¶ 47, https://www.europarl.europa.eu/doceo/document/TA-9-2021-0073_EN.html#title2

D. German Due Diligence Act

In June 2021 the German Federal Parliament adopted the "Act on Corporate Due Diligence in Supply Chains," which is scheduled to enter into force at the start of 2023.[79] The Act applies to both national and foreign companies with registered offices or branches in Germany and will begin to apply to companies with 3,000 or more employees; and then from 2024 onward, companies with 1,000 or more employees. Section 8 of the Act includes a requirement for a "complaints procedure" which calls on companies "to report human rights and environment-related risks as well as violations of human rights-related or environment-related obligations that have arisen as a result of the economic actions of an enterprise in its own business area or of a direct supplier." Similarly, Section 9 requires the enterprise to set up complaints procedures for reporting these same types of risks and problems as they relate to "the economic actions of indirect suppliers." While the law provides some guidance on how these complaints procedures should be implemented and maintained, it does not make an explicit link to the HRDD process, although it does require that "measures taken by the enterprise as a result of the complaints pursuant to Section 8 or Section 9(1)" be documented and included as part of the reporting obligations laid out in Section 10 of the law.

E. Government Regulations: Creating Opportunities for Operations-level Grievance Mechanism and Human Rights Due Diligence Linkage

Like voluntary codes, even if not explicitly required, some government regulations institute due diligence requirements that lead companies, in practice, to make their own linkage to a grievance mechanism in order to demonstrate they are complying with a due diligence requirement.

1. European Union Non-Financial Reporting Directive

In 2014, the EU issued Directive 2014/95/EU (Non-Financial Reporting Directive), which requires public-interest companies with at least 500 employees to prepare a non-financial statement containing information relating to, among other matters, respect for human rights as well as the due diligence processes implemented to identify, prevent, and mitigate adverse impacts. In reporting on their compliance, they must include information about their policies related to meeting these requirements as well as the outcome of these policies.[80]

While the Non-Financial Reporting Directive makes no specific reference to grievance mechanisms, companies subject to its mandate have nevertheless included information about

---

[79] Gesetz über die unternehmerischen Sorgfaltspflichten in Lieferketten [Act on Corporate Due Diligence Obligations in Supply Chains], July 16, 2021, Bundesgesetzblatt, Teil I, [BGBl I] at 2959 (Ger.), *translated* Federal Ministry of Labour and Social Affairs, Recent Publications, Act on Corporate Due Diligence in Supply Chains (Aug. 18, 2021), https://www.bmas.de/SharedDocs/Downloads/DE/Internationales/act-corporate-due-diligence-obligations-supply-chains.pdf

[80] Jessica L. Weber, et al., *Mandatory Nonfinancial Reporting in the EU: Implications for U.S. CPAs*, CPA J. (July 2018), https://www.cpajournal.com/2018/07/25/mandatory-nonfinancial-reporting-in-the-eu/.

OGMs when issuing their non-financial reports. For example, the ABB Group, a technology company, publishes an annual sustainability report in compliance with the Directive that describes multiple complaint channels available for reporting suspected human rights violations.[81] Similarly, Maersk, a shipping company, published a sustainability report that disclosed non-financial information, including a "complaint and grievance procedure."[82]

2. *United Kingdom Modern Slavery Act 2015*

The United Kingdom (UK) Modern Slavery Act 2015 (Modern Slavery Act) requires companies to "prepare a slavery and human trafficking statement for each financial year of the organization."[83] This statement must disclose the steps a company took during the financial year to ensure there is no slavery and human trafficking in its supply chains or any other part of its operations. Pursuant to the Modern Slavery Act, some companies have published a slavery and human trafficking statement that details their OGM policy. For example, the Financial Ombudsman Service, located in the UK government, publishes an annual statement under the Modern Slavery Act stating that one of its policies is "to reduce the risk of modern slavery and facilitate reporting of any potential slavery instances" and describes its OGM as a "speak up" policy.[84] While the Financial Ombudsman Service is not a company, its annual statement demonstrates that the Modern Slavery Act treats an OGM as a due diligence process, thereby indirectly linking OGMs to due diligence.

V. Government Business and Human Rights Policy Implementation through National Action Plans

In 2014, the UN Human Rights Council urged State Members to implement National Action Plans (NAPs) that would act as a roadmap for the practical implementation of measures concerning the UNGPs.[85] This has led approximately 49 countries, as of November 2020, to launch a process for developing a business and human rights NAP, with 24 having published their plans.[86] Of those countries with established NAPs, at the time of writing, only four explicitly link OGMs to a due diligence process.

---

[81] *Sustainability Report 2019: Leading Solutions for a Sustainable Future*, ABB 38 (2019), https://sustainabilityreport2019.abb.com/servicepages/downloads/files/sustainability_performance_2019_abb_csr19.pdf.

[82] *2019 Sustainability Report*, MAERSK 37 (2019), https://www.maersk.com/about/sustainability/reports.

[83] UK Modern Slavery Act 2015, Part 6(1).

[84] *The Modern Slavery Act*, FIN. OMBUDSMAN SERVICE (Mar. 31, 2020), https://www.financial-ombudsman.org.uk/modern-slavery-act.

[85] *See National Action Plan on Business and Human Rights: Chile*, NAT'L ACTION PLANS ON BUS. AND HUM. RTS., https://globalnaps.org/wp-content/uploads/2017/11/national-action-plan-on-business-and-human-rights_.pdf [hereinafter *Chilean NAP*].

[86] *See State National Action Plans on Business and Human Rights*, UN HUM. RTS. OFFICE OF THE HIGH COMMISSIONER, https://www.ohchr.org/en/issues/business/pages/nationalactionplans.aspx.

A. Chile

Chile first launched its NAP on August 21, 2017, but beginning in October 2019 began to update it with the aim of finalizing the process in March 2021.[87] The Chilean NAP details the manner in which an OGM supports its framework, which includes a linkage to a due diligence process, by serving two essential roles regarding a business's responsibility to respect human rights. Specifically, the NAP recognizes that OGMs "contribute in the determination of negative consequences over human rights as part of an enterprise's obligation *to act with due diligence in human rights*, and to allow the enterprise to respond to detected damages and repair the negative consequences directly at an early stage to avoid further damage or an escalation of claims. [emphasis supplied]"[88]

B. Colombia

Colombia launched its original NAP in December 2015 and adopted an updated NAP on December 10, 2020.[89] In the "Corporate Human Rights Due Diligence" section, the Colombian NAP states that it implemented a Task Force on Business and Human Rights to provide more understanding of the due diligence process, including determining the best manner in which enterprises can "establish easy-to-access, transparent and effective complaint and claims offices or mechanisms for prevention and mitigation and remedy of adverse human rights effects as may be caused by their activities."[90] Additionally, the Task Force will assist companies "through their complaint offices, [in] receiving and diligently managing the citizen and community claims" arising from "the adverse effects caused by their operations."[91] By creating the Task Force to develop strategies for companies to establish an effective OGM as a means to implement corporate HRDD, the Colombian NAP directly links OGMs to HRDD.

C. Germany

In December 2016, Germany adopted its NAP that specifically notes "[a] common understanding by all players worldwide of due diligence as described in the UN Guiding Principles is an indispensable means to this end."[92] Indeed, Germany expects all enterprises to introduce the process of corporate due diligence while taking into account their size, sector, and

---

[87] *Chile*, Nat'l Action Plans on Bus. and Hum. Rts., https://globalnaps.org/country/chile/ (last visited Mar. 6, 2021).

[88] *Id.* at 8.

[89] *See Colombia*, Nat'l Action Plans on Bus. and Hum. Rts., https://globalnaps.org/country/colombia/ (last visited Mar. 6, 2021). Colombia launched a second NAP on December 10, 2020, but it is not available yet. *Colombia Avanza Derechos Humanos y Empresa*, Global NAPs 6, https://globalnaps.org/wp-content/uploads/2018/04/pna-colombia-english.pdf [hereinafter *Colombian NAP*].

[90] *Id.* at 19.

[91] *Id.* at 19.

[92] *National Action Plan: Implementation of the UN Guiding Principles on Business and Human Rights 2016–2020*, Global NAPs 5, https://globalnaps.org/wp-content/uploads/2018/04/germany-national-action-plan-business-and-human-rights.pdf [hereinafter *German NAP*].

position in supply chains.[93] The German NAP defines the "core elements" of HRDD as including: "a human rights policy statement; procedures for the identification of actual or potential adverse impact on human rights; measures to ward off potentially adverse impacts and review of the effectiveness of these measures; reporting; [and] *a grievance mechanism.* [emphasis supplied]."[94] The German NAP provides guidance on the implementation of an OGM, with particular emphasis on including stakeholders in the design and operation of the mechanism while ensuring the protection of claimants.[95]

D. Slovenia

Slovenia adopted a NAP in November 2018 that closely follows the structure of the UNGPs, offering concrete actions to be taken to ensure their implementation.[96] Specifically, it explains that in order to comply with UNGP Principles 28, 30, and 31 regarding implementation of effective OGMs, the government will encourage companies "to strive for continuous development and to apply the relevant appeal mechanisms to address the alleged or potential violations of human rights in business processes, *also through human rights due diligence.* [emphasis supplied]."[97] The Slovenian NAP explains that HRDD in practice includes the implementation of "mechanisms for detecting, and responding to, violations and monitoring of, and reporting on, due diligence and respect for human rights."[98]

VI. Company Practice

There is still relatively limited in-depth analysis of company OGMs, with only a handful of commentators and scholars delving into their specific operations.[99] Most of these examinations are focused on a selection of case studies, while not necessarily providing a meta-analysis. To respond to this gap in understanding, the Center for International Law and Policy (CILP) at New England Law | Boston, which the author directs, established the Operational-Level Grievance Mechanism Research Project (OGM Project) in 2016 to conduct desktop research of grievance mechanisms established by companies to address complaints related to negative human right impacts raised by workers and communities where those companies operate.[100] Researchers conduct desktop research to log the development of companies of all sizes across

---

[93] *Id.* at 7.

[94] *Id.* at 8; *see also Id.* at 10 (stating that the "grievance mechanism of each enterprise and its whole process of corporate due diligence should be subjected to regular practice-based reviews to assess their effectiveness").

[95] *Id.* at 9. (OGMs are defined as a procedure for the "early identification of (actual or potential) adverse impacts.").

[96] *National Action Plan of the Republic of Slovenia on Business and Human Rights*, Global NAPs 42 (Nov. 2018), https://globalnaps.org/wp-content/uploads/2017/11/slovenia-bhr-nap-english.pdf [hereinafter *Slovenia NAP*].

[97] *Id.*

[98] *Id.* at 45.

[99] Grama, Benjamin, *Company-Administered Grievance Processes for External Stakeholders: A Means for Effective Remedy, Community Relations, or Private Power?*, 39 Wisconsin Int'l L. J. 71 (2022).

[100] *See Operational-Level Grievance Mechanism Research Project*, New England Law | Boston, https://www.nesl.edu/practical-experiences/centers/center-for-international-law-and-policy/projects/operational-grievance-mechanisms-project.

industries. The research focuses on the design, scope, process, and outcome of company OGMs that include the possibility of raising human rights complaints. While the OGM Project currently does not offer an evaluation per se of these OGMs, such as through Principle 31 of the UNGPs, it does supply information that could be used for this purpose. Furthermore, the OGM Project aims to generate meta-analysis of relevant trends in the field. As of December 2020, the OGM Project studied 290 companies, representing 21 industries, with 18 percent (53 companies) operating on a national scale and 82 percent (237 companies) operating on a multinational scale.

The OGM Research Project undertook a sampling of 281 companies within its database to determine whether or not companies recognize the role of OGMs in a due diligence process, including explicit linkage between the two. The overall findings reveal that only 16 percent (46 companies) make some connection between the two mechanisms, to varying degrees. Below are two companies that offer a representative look at how this practice is presented from a business perspective.[101] The author chose these two companies because they clearly and explicitly integrate an OGM into their HRDD process and provide further detail on the connection. Other companies that may appear to make a more conscious and explicit connection do not provide enough information on the connection to write a comprehensive analysis of how and why OGMs and HRDD are connected.

A. All Nippon Airways

All Nippon Airways (ANA), a Japanese airline company, having adopted a human rights policy, publishes an annual Human Rights Report. In a most recent report, the company dedicated one section to the establishment of a HRDD mechanism to demonstrate its commitment to human rights.[102] The due diligence process includes an evaluation of the company's operations to assess and mitigate risks. The company has also created a grievance mechanism to ensure stakeholder engagement throughout the entire HRDD process.

The ANA 2020 Human Rights Report goes as far as to include a section entitled "Human Rights Due Diligence/Grievance Mechanism" which explores how it includes an OGM in the company's due diligence process in order "to quickly gather information about latent and manifest human rights risks and effectively deal with [an] adverse impact that has been identified."[103] Notably, this new mechanism is intended to serve external stakeholders since ANA developed a different OGM for handling complaints from employees, customers, and shareholders.

---

[101] To learn more about this project, see the home website for the Operational-level Grievance Mechanism Research Project – New England Law | Boston. At https://www.google.com/url?sa=t&rct=j&q=&esrc=s&source=web&cd=&cad=rja&uact=8&ved=2ahUKEwjyxpOg7eLvAhVhFlkFHVFgBpkQIDAAegQIAxAO&url=https%3A%2F%2Fwebcache.googleusercontent.com%2Fsearch%3Fq%3Dcache%3A2K_5BV5y02cJ%3Ahttps%3A%2F%2Fwww.nesl.edu%2Fpractical-experiences%2Fcenters%2Fcenter-for-international-law-and-policy%2Fprojects%2Foperational-grievance-mechanisms-project%2B%26cd%3D1%26hl%3Den%26ct%3Dclnk%26gl%3Dus&usg=AOvVaw0XAPI-X2BAPx09rmPqFKFI

[102] *Human Rights Report 2020*, ANA (2020), https://www.ana.co.jp/group/en/csr/effort/pdf/Human_Rights_Report_2020_e.pdf.

[103] *Id.* at 31.

ANA reports that it monitors its OGM to ensure its compliance with the Effectiveness Criteria laid out in UNGP Principle 31, while leaving out any discussion of the direct linkage in supporting a HRDD process.[104] Considering the lessons learned, ANA began an ongoing discussion with an independent, third-party organization to design and develop a new OGM that better complies with the UNGPs and renews the company's commitment to improving "effective engagement and dialogue with relevant stakeholders."[105]

B. AngloGold Ashanti

AngloGold Ashanti is a global gold mining company founded in South Africa. In March 2016, AngloGold Ashanti created a Management Standard on Human Rights Due Diligence (Due Diligence Standard) and thereby uphold and promote fundamental human rights wherever the company does business in order to "contribute to building productive, respectful and mutually beneficial partnerships in the communities in which [it] operate[s]."[106] Specifically, this Due Diligence Standard requires AngloGold Ashanti to "take steps to prevent, mitigate and remediate adverse impacts that are identified through its assessment to have been or could be caused or contributed to by [the company], in line with the requirements of the Management Standard on Community Complaints and Grievances."[107] Notably, Ashanti's grievance mechanism predates its due diligence standards. Specifically, AngloGold Ashanti developed the Management Standard on Community Complaints and Grievances (Grievance Standard) in October 2011, setting up a process to create and implement an OGM that would resolve complaints and grievances from local communities at every mining site operated by the company.[108]

The stated purpose of the Grievance Standard is to support a due diligence process that identifies and addresses human right risks. For example, the AngloGold Ashanti OGM must be capable of handling serious concerns made against the site regarding its activities or impacts to "reduce opportunities for complaints and grievances to escalate into incidents" at the operational site.[109] In due diligence terms, the purpose of the OGM is to mitigate risks and prevent future recurrences. Along these lines, there is synergy with regard to the emphasis on stakeholder engagement in due diligence processes, with the Grievance Standard involving

[104] *Id.* at 31–32. Recently, this inspection revealed that ANA's existing whistleblower contact point does fully satisfy the eight effectiveness criteria detailed in UNGP 31. Specifically, ANA states that it fell short in ensuring the OGM was accessible, "as not all stakeholder groups including suppliers are aware of the existence of our mechanism"; predictable, because it "does not provide an indicative time frame for the procedure of our grievance mechanism"; and transparent, as ANA is "not providing sufficient information about the mechanism's performance."

[105] *Id.* at 31.

[106] *Management Standard: Human Rights Due Diligence*, AngloGold Ashanti 3 (Mar. 2016), https://www.anglogoldashanticolombia.com/wp-content/uploads/2016/12/HR-Due-Diligence-Standard-Final-Version-1.pdf.

[107] *Id.* at 8.

[108] *Management Standard: Community Complaints and Grievances*, AngloGold Ashanti 3 (Oct. 19, 2011).

[109] *Id.*

input and engagement of "its social partners and stakeholders . . . to enhance awareness of and trust in the mechanism."[110]

The fact that so few companies include a purposeful linkage between OGMs and HRDD points to a missed opportunity in the field. Any company intending to ensure a robust and effective HRDD process should also endeavor to include a deliberate focus on how to create OGMs, or draw upon existing grievance mechanisms, to better ensure their HRDD processes serve the ultimate purpose of preventing and remediating actual and potential adverse human rights impacts.

For example, they may establish better communication between the two mechanisms. One approach may include ensuring more formalized communication channels between company employees who oversee the two mechanisms or building into the design of their programming consistent reporting between the OGM and HRDD offices. Additionally, there may be built-in periodic reviews shared with the HRDD oversight body regarding the types of complaints filed with OGMs and their outcomes, especially if they point to underlying systemic problems that the company should seek to address at the macro level. A comprehensive record of the types of grievances filed can highlight systemic issues and reveal which business practices or policies need to change more broadly. Most importantly, to maximize its contribution to an HRDD process, the design and implementation of an OGM should aim to meet best practices, which arguably is still an underdeveloped and not fully understood field of practice.

VII. Conclusion

The often-overlooked relationship between OGMs and HRDD amounts to a missed opportunity to improve a company's ability to ensure its operations, services, and products do not negatively impact human rights of workers and communities. While this relationship between OGMs and HRDDs may be inherent or even occur naturally, it would improve the field to more consciously make the connection. This approach would ensure that such coordination and support is not left to happenstance, but instead is developed carefully to maximize the ability of companies to identify and where possible prevent and address negative human rights impacts.

There will need to be more study of how this linkage is done both in the design phase and in the implementation phase of a company's integration of a human rights approach. Understanding the unique characteristics of a more deliberate linkage can better guide company practices across industries. To begin to collect best practices will ensure that the explicit approach of linking OGMs and HRDD will better serve not only the goals of companies to comply with their obligation to respect human rights but will also provide assurances to workers and communities that they can fully enjoy their human rights without risk of negative impacts from companies operating where they work and live.

---

[110] *Id.* at 6.

VIII. Resources

European Parliament, Report with Recommendations to the Commission on Corporate Due Diligence and Corporate Accountability (Feb. 11, 2021), https://www.europarl.europa.eu/doceo/document/A-9-2021-0018_EN.pdf.

Organisation for Economic Co-Operation and Development, *OECD Due Diligence Guidance for Responsible Business Conduct*, Org. for Econ. Co-Operation and Dev. 21 (2018), https://mneguidelines.oecd.org/OECD-Due-Diligence-Guidance-for-Responsible-Business-Conduct.pdf.

Food and Agriculture Organization of the United Nations, *OECD-FAO Guidance for Responsible Agricultural Supply Chains* (2016).

Caroline Rees, *Piloting Principles for Effective Company-Stakeholder Grievance Mechanisms: A Report of Lessons Learned*, Harv. Kennedy Sch. Corp. Soc. Responsibility Initiative (May 23, 2011), https://www.business-humanrights.org/sites/default/files/media/documents/ruggie/grievance-mechanism-pilots-report-harvard-csri-jun-2011.pdf.

Responsible Jewellery Council, *Codes of Practices Guidance* (Apr. 23, 2019), https://www.responsiblejewellery.com/wp-content/uploads/RJC-COP-Guidance-April-2019.pdf.

Mariana Aparecida Vilmondes Turke, *Business and Human Rights in Brazil: Exploring Human Rights Due Diligence and Operational-Level Grievance Mechanism in the Case of Kinross Paracatu Gold Mine*, 15 Braz. J. Int'l L. 222 (2018).

9

Stakeholder Engagement

Shauna Curphey and Jared Cole

I. Introduction

"The key to human rights due diligence is the need to understand the perspective of potentially affected individuals and groups."[1] "Stakeholder engagement" is how business enterprises obtain this understanding. The *United Nations Guiding Principles on Business and Human Rights* (UNGPs) set forth the steps in the human rights due diligence process—identifying and assessing human rights risks, preventing or mitigating human rights harms, and tracking and communicating progress on both of those fronts—and stakeholder engagement is integral to each step.[2] Engagement is also essential to the design of accessible and effective grievance mechanisms, which are crucial to ensure that rights holders report abuses and thus serve as frontline monitors of the human rights situation on the ground. In short, without engagement, potential and actual abuses may go unrecognized, undetected, unreported, and due diligence will not produce positive human rights outcomes.

Thus, although the UNGPs use the term "stakeholder engagement" in relation to human rights due diligence, the underlying focus of engagement is "rights holders," which the UNGPs refer to as "potentially affected stakeholders."[3] Thus, rights holders are the people whose human rights—their lives and livelihoods and the panoply of rights that ensures they are free and equal in dignity—are potentially at risk from a company's decisions and operations. As

---

[1] UN Office of the High Commissioner for Human Rights, *The Corporate Responsibility to Respect Human Rights: An Interpretive Guide* (2012).

[2] Special Report of the Secretary General, *Guiding Principles on Business and Human Rights: Implementing the United Nations "Protect, Respect and Remedy" Framework*, 22–25 (2011).

[3] *Id.* at 20.

"potentially affected" individuals, rights holders are the only people with an existential stake in the due diligence process. Their perspectives are therefore distinct from, and more important than, those of other corporate stakeholders, such as investors and suppliers, which may have only financial or reputational interests at stake. Indeed, there is growing recognition by corporations that conducting stakeholder engagement in a manner that prioritizes and incorporates "bottom-up participation," in which rights holders drive the process, is the key to understanding and addressing their human rights impacts.[4]

This chapter therefore encourages sincere, direct engagement with rights holders, with the aim of securing meaningful human rights protections that rights holders experience in their communities and workplaces. Section II outlines the basic principles that underpin stakeholder engagement, while Section III explains how these principles work in practice. Section IV demonstrates the role of engagement at each step in the human rights due diligence process and draws from knowledge and practice of stakeholder engagement in other contexts to suggest appropriate methods. Section V outlines challenges to effective stakeholder engagement as well as the opportunities presented by emerging, bottom-up approaches and alternative models that center on the experiences and leadership of rights holders.

This chapter, however, does not set out to define one right way to conduct stakeholder engagement; nor does it provide comprehensive coverage of all the issues. Approaches will vary based on an enterprise's sector, its size, its business relationships, its potential impacts, and who comprises the rights holders that the enterprise potentially places at risk. Other chapters in this book cover particular issues related to stakeholder engagement in greater depth, such as gender-sensitive due diligence, consultation with indigenous peoples, and due diligence in high-risk security situations.

II. Background: Stakeholder Engagement in Principle

The UNGPs provide the framework for the role that stakeholder engagement plays in the human rights due diligence process, but provide little detail on what companies should actually do when they engage with rights holders. As a concept, stakeholder engagement embraces a variety of approaches, from top-down information-gathering on the one hand, to joint learning, accountability, and ownership on the other.[5] This section removes that ambiguity by drawing on a range of interpretive guidance to define what stakeholder engagement means in the context of effective human rights due diligence.

A. Human Rights Standards and Voluntary Guidance

The role of stakeholder engagement in human rights due diligence "reflects the entitlement of every human being to be treated with dignity."[6] In addition to this fundamental principle, stakeholder engagement is further grounded in the right to participate in the conduct of

[4] Rajiv Maher & Karin Buhmann, *Meaningful Stakeholder Engagement: Bottom-up Initiatives Within Global Governance Frameworks*, 107 Geoforum 231–234, 231 (2019).

[5] Frances Bowen, Aloysius Newenham-Kahindi & Irene Herremans, *When Suits Meet Roots: The Antecedents and Consequences of Community Engagement Strategy*, 95 J Bus Ethics 297–318, 304 (2010).

[6] UN Office of the High Commissioner for Human Rights, *supra* note 1, at 33.

public affairs and in the cultural life of the community, which are recognized in several international human rights instruments.[7] These include Article 25 of the International Covenant on Civil and Political Rights,[8] Article 15.1 of the International Covenant on Economic, Social and Cultural Rights,[9] Articles 7 and 8 of the Convention on the Elimination of All Forms of Discrimination Against Women,[10] Articles 41 and 42 of the International Convention on the Protection of the Rights of All Migrant Workers and Members of Their Families[11] and Articles 29 and 30 of the Convention on the Rights of Persons with Disabilities,[12] among others. In addition, the Indigenous and Tribal Peoples Convention of the International Labour Organization[13] and the United Nations Declaration on the Rights of Indigenous Peoples[14] recognize the right of indigenous peoples to participate in decision-making on certain matters that affect them directly.

With regard to the corporate responsibility to participate in stakeholder engagement specifically, the UNGPs[15] and the Organisation for Economic Co-operation and Development (OECD) *Guidelines for Multinational Enterprises* (OECD Guidelines) define the role of stakeholders in human rights due diligence.[16] The UNGPs state that the process of identifying human rights risks should: "involve meaningful consultation with potentially affected groups and other relevant stakeholders" and that tracking the effectiveness of company responses to those risks should "draw on feedback" from "affected stakeholders."[17] They also state that companies should communicate how they address human rights impacts, particularly "when concerns are raised by or on behalf of affected stakeholders."[18] The OECD Guidelines provide

[7] BRIGITTE HAMM & ANNE SCHAX, *Human Rights Due Diligence Through Stakeholder Engagement? The Case of a Copper-Gold Mine in the Philippines* 18 (Duisburg: Inst. for Dev. and Peace, U. of Duisburg-Essen) (INEF Report, 109/2015), https://www.uni-due.de/imperia/md/content/inef/report109.pdf.

[8] International Covenant on Civil and Political Rights, 19 December 1966, 999 UNTS 171 (providing, "every citizen shall have the right and opportunity . . . to take part in the conduct of public affairs").

[9] International Covenant on Economic, Social and Cultural Rights, *opened for signa*ture Dec. 16, 1966, 993 U.N.T.S. 3 (entered into force Jan. 3, 1976) (recognizing "the right of everyone to take part in cultural life").

[10] Convention on the Elimination of All Forms of Discrimination against Women, Dec. 18, 1979, 1249 U.N.T.S. 13; 19 I.L.M. 33 (1980) (recognizing the right of women to participate without discrimination and on equal terms in non-governmental organizations concerned with the public and political life of the country and in the work of international organizations).

[11] International Convention on the Protection of the Rights of All Migrant Workers and Members of their Families, New York, Dec. 18, 1990, entered into force July 1, 2003 2220 U.N.T.S. 93; 30 I.L.M. 1517 (1991) (recognizing the right of migrant workers to participate in the public affairs of their States of origin, and to consultation or participation in decisions concerning the life and administration of local communities in their States of employment).

[12] Convention on the Rights of Persons with Disabilities, May 3, 2008 A/RES/61/106, Annex I (recognizing the right of people with disabilities to fully participate in the conduct of public affairs and in cultural life without discrimination and on an equal basis with others).

[13] Convention (No. 169) concerning indigenous and tribal people in independent countries, 27 June 1989, 1650 U.N.T.S. 383 (entered into force 5 September 1991).

[14] United Nations Declaration on the Rights of Indigenous Peoples, Sep. 13, 2007, G.A. Res. 61/295, UN Doc. A/RES/61/295 (Sept. 13, 2007); 46 I.L.M. 1013 (2007).

[15] Special Report of the Secretary General., *supra* note 2.

[16] Organisation for Economic Co-operation and Development (OCED), *OECD Guidelines for Multinational Enterprises* (2011), http://mneguidelines.oecd.org/guidelines/.

[17] Special Report of the Secretary General., *supra* note 2, at 19, 22.

[18] *Id.* at 23.

that companies should "engage with relevant stakeholders in order to provide meaningful opportunities for their views to be taken into account in relation to planning and decision making for projects or other activities that may significantly impact local communities."[19]

Thus, the UNGPs and the OECD Guidelines leave stakeholder engagement largely open to interpretation. Indeed, the U.S. National Action Plan on Responsible Business Conduct, which presents US government efforts to promote responsible business conduct overseas, acknowledges that these frameworks are merely a starting point. It encourages businesses to treat the UNGPs and the OECD Guidelines "as a floor rather than a ceiling for implementing responsible business practices."[20]

Many resources exist, however, that define good practice. The UN Office of the High Commissioner for Human Rights (OHCHR) has issued an interpretive guide to the UNGPs,[21] and the OECD has issued guidance on due diligence specifically.[22] In addition, the UN Working Group on Business and Human Rights, an expert panel created by the UN Human Rights Council to promote the effective implementation of the UNGPs, has also addressed human rights due diligence in a report to the UN General Assembly.[23] The Working Group has also issued a roadmap for the next decade of implementation of the UNGPs that includes "more and better" stakeholder engagement as a primary goal.[24] These resources, along with contributions from civil society and scholars, help to clarify who stakeholders are and what stakeholder engagement means. The remainder of this section therefore draws from these sources to explain these core principles.

B. Who Are the Stakeholders?

Human rights due diligence focuses on the individuals or groups whose human rights have been affected, or may potentially be affected, by a company's operations, products, or services.[25] Consequently, for the business to engage these stakeholders, it must first determine who they are. As noted in Section I, these affected or potentially affected stakeholders are rights holders, and may be company employees or contractors, workers in supply chains, local communities near company operations, or consumers or end-users of products. Thus, rights holders may be internal or external to the company, close or distant from the company's

---

[19] OECD, *supra* note 16, at 20.

[20] US Dept. of State, *First National Action Plan for the United States of America*, 17 (2016), https://2009-2017.state.gov/e/eb/eppd/csr/naprbc/265706.htm.

[21] UN Office of the High Commissioner for Human Rights, *supra* note 1.

[22] OECD, *OECD Due Diligence Guidance for Responsible Business Conduct* (2018), http://mneguidelines.oecd.org/due-diligence-guidance-for-responsible-business-conduct.htm.

[23] Working Group on the Issue of Human Rights & Transnational Corporations and other Business Enterprises, *Report on Human Rights Due Diligence to the 2018 General Assembly* UN Doc. A/73/163 (2018).

[24] Working Group on Business and Human Rights, *UNGPs 10+ A Roadmap for the Next Decade of Business and Human Rights* (2021), https://www.ohchr.org/sites/default/files/2021-12/ungps10plusroadmap.pdf.

[25] UN Office of the High Commissioner for Human Rights., *supra* note 1, at 8.

headquarters, and protected (for example, by a strong trade union or regulatory enforcement) or marginalized (such as migrant workers or child laborers).[26]

Both the UNGPs and the OECD Guidelines direct businesses to pay special attention to impacts on marginalized groups because they face different risks and impacts.[27] These rights holders may include children, indigenous people, people belonging to ethnic or religious minorities, or people with disabilities, among others. In addition, in many contexts, women may face different or greater risks and impacts than men.

Where direct consultation with rights holders is not feasible, the UNGPs and the OECD interpretive guidance indicate that business enterprises may consult with credible rights holder representatives, which may include trade unions, local human rights defenders, or community-based organizations that have direct links to rights holders.[28] Care should be taken before consulting representatives, however, to determine whether they understand and represent the interests of rights holders, and if they exclude important perspectives, particularly those of marginalized groups.[29]

Human rights due diligence also entails engaging with other types of stakeholders that are relevant to a company's operations. For example, businesses may need to hold discussions or enter agreements with suppliers, who may need training, facility upgrades, or other support to implement protections for rights holders. Companies may also need to communicate with their investors, which have their own human rights due diligence obligations, to inform them on material risks that could impact investment decisions. Regulatory agencies, human rights experts, international human rights nongovernmental organizations (NGOs), industry associations, or multistakeholder initiatives may provide background knowledge on potential human rights risks and actual impacts.

Although these interactions are important to human rights due diligence, they are not equivalent to, or a replacement for, engaging directly with rights holders.[30] Most business enterprises already communicate with suppliers, investors, regulators, or even staff at international NGOs, and may already have established policies or procedures in place to govern those relationships. In contrast, stakeholder engagement focuses on "what potentially affected stakeholders want to discuss with the company in relation to the company's impacts."[31] There may be obstacles that prevent these conversations from being open and productive, such as power imbalances or geographic, language, social, or cultural barriers. Companies must be aware of and derive ways to overcome these barriers, however, if human rights due diligence is to have any impact on the ground, where rights holders live and work.

---

[26] Gwendolyn Remmert, Global Compact Network Germany, Madeleine Koalick, twentyfifty Ltd. & Luke Wilde, twentyfifty Ltd., *Stakeholder Engagement in Human Rights Due Diligence: A Business Guide* 13 (2014).

[27] Special Report of the Secretary General, *supra* note 2, at 20; OECD, *supra* note 16, at 32.

[28] *Id.*; OECD, *supra* note 22, at 48–49.

[29] Gwendolyn Remmert, et al., *supra* note 26, at 13.

[30] Shift, Oxfam, & Global Compact Network Netherlands, *Doing Business with Respect for Human Rights: A Guidance Tool for Companies* 97 (2016), https://www.businessrespecthumanrights.org/image/2016/10/24/business_respect_human_rights_full.pdf.

[31] *Id.*

C. What Does Stakeholder Engagement Mean?

Outside of the business and human rights context, what business enterprises conceive of as stakeholder engagement can take a variety of forms. It can mean sincere cooperation on the one hand, or serve as a means of manipulation on the other, where a company focuses on its own interests, such that any advantage to rights holders is secondary, unintended, and coincidental to the company's own long-term benefit.[32] It can be merely "transactional," a top-down interaction where the business transfers information or provides charity to a community, such as hosting an information session or building a school. Or it may be "transitional," involving two-way communication and consultation, such as stakeholder roundtables or community advisory groups.[33] Stakeholder engagement may also be transformational, where rights holders take a leadership role in framing problems and managing solutions, and both sides learn and benefit from the collaboration.[34]

As the principles that follow demonstrate, human rights due diligence emerges from dialogue, learning, and collaboration, and thus requires stakeholder engagement that falls on the transformational end of this spectrum, particularly when the human rights risks are complex or intractable. The leading implementation guidance—the UNGPs Interpretive Guide,[35] the OECD Due Diligence Guidance[36] and resources provided by the UN Working Group on Business and Human Rights, academics, and NGOs—points to several themes that, taken together, form the following foundational principles for this approach.

1. *Engagement Should Build Collaborative, Mutually Beneficial Relationships.*

Stakeholder engagement in human rights due diligence constitutes "an ongoing process of interaction and dialogue between an enterprise and its potentially affected stakeholders that enables the enterprise to hear, understand and respond to their interests and concerns, including through collaborative approaches."[37] Businesses should view rights holders "as partners,"[38] and thus engagement should be "meaningful" and conducted in "good faith."[39] Businesses should engage with the "genuine intention" of understanding how their activities negatively affect rights holder interests, and be prepared to address the problems identified.[40] It envisions building effective relationships as a means "to find ways to address impact in

[32] Michelle Greenwood, *Stakeholder Engagement: Beyond the Myth of Corporate Responsibility*, 74 J Bus Ethics 315–327, 320 (2007).

[33] Bowen, et al., *supra* note 5, at 304–305.

[34] *Id.* at 305–306.

[35] UN Office of the High Commissioner for Human Rights, *supra* note 1.

[36] OECD, *supra* note 22.

[37] UN Office of the High Commissioner for Human Rights, *supra* note 1, at 8.

[38] Working Group, *supra* note 24 at 47.

[39] OECD, *supra* note 22, at 20, 25.

[40] *Id.* at 49–50.

an agreed and sustainable way."[41] For example, "engagement could include participating in and sharing results of on-site assessments, developing risk mitigation measures," and including rights holders in "ongoing monitoring and designing of grievance mechanisms."[42] Thus, at a minimum, human rights due diligence envisions building relationships rather than a top-down, one-off event.[43]

2. *Companies Should Gather and Share Information at the Outset.*[44]

Businesses need baseline knowledge of their potential negative human rights impacts before they can identify who may be affected, and thus where they need to carry out due diligence. They also need to assess whether consulting with rights holders could put those individuals at risk of reprisals.[45] Likewise, in some situations, such as corporate land use or natural resource extraction, rights holders will need timely access to relevant information on how company operations may affect their interests so that they can participate fully and make informed decisions. This requires that companies communicate this information in formats that rights holders can access and understand.

3. *Communication Should Be Two-way and Responsive.*[46]

Many organizations make the mistake of treating their external relationships as unidirectional, extracting the information they need and leaving rights holders in the dark. But, as with any healthy relationship, it is essential that every engagement provides a clear mutual benefit to all who take part. Stakeholder engagement should be an interactive process, where the parties exchange viewpoints and ideas and aim to reach mutual understanding. It must also be responsive both in form and function. This means rights holders should have an opportunity to participate in designing the form of engagement and in carrying out engagement activities (such as meetings, workshops, or other consultations). It also means business enterprises should respect the function of engagement, namely to use what they learn to shape their decisions and, ultimately, prevent human rights abuses or mitigate harm.

4. *Potential Barriers to Participation, Including Power Imbalances, Should Be Addressed.*[47]

Stakeholder engagement requires sensitivity to barriers that may prevent people from speaking openly or participating fully. Between rights holders and company representatives, power imbalances, a history of distrust or poor relations, or fear of reprisal might prevent rights holders from speaking freely. Within a community, communication can break down due to divisions among rights holders on what are the most pressing human rights impacts or

---

[41] UN Office of the High Commissioner for Human Rights, *supra* note 1, at 44.

[42] OECD, *supra* note 22, at 19.

[43] Shift, Oxfam, and Global Compact Network Netherlands, *supra* note 30, at 96–97.

[44] OECD, *supra* note 22, at 18, 25–26; UN Office of High Commissioner for Human Rights, *supra* note 1, at 48.

[45] Shift, Oxfam, and Global Compact Network Netherlands, *supra* note 30, at 99.

[46] OECD, *supra* note 22 at 25, 49; UN Office of the High Commissioner for Human Rights, *supra* note 1, at 55.

[47] OECD, *supra* note 22, at 27, 51; UN Office of the High Commissioner for Human Rights, *supra* note 1, at 49, 50.

appropriate forms of mitigation. Human rights defenders can serve as a valuable source of information and ideas, but they are increasingly under threat in many places and may fear retaliation for speaking out.[48] Depending on the context, engagement methods should also take into account gender, language, culture, socioeconomic status, access to information, and other potential factors that may foreclose full involvement.

5. *Engagement Should Be Ongoing.*[49]

Engagement must begin before companies make major decisions or operating changes and should continue to respond to new developments or challenges. This repeated engagement is necessary to assess the adequacy of the company's response to the risks identified in the initial stages of due diligence, to identify whether and how risks have changed over time, and to assess and mitigate risks posed by project completion or company withdrawal from a supplier, location, or sector.

6. *Communication Should Be Direct Where Possible.*

Direct engagement "provides the best way to identify concerns" and foster appropriate business responses to human rights impacts.[50] While international human rights NGOs can provide valuable background information in easily accessible formats, such as good practice guidance[51] or reports on human rights abuses in a sector or a particular jurisdiction,[52] these cannot replace engagement with rights holders. In some cases, direct engagement on the ground may not be possible due to security concerns, financial constraints, or other practical barriers, and this may be particularly true for small or medium-sized enterprises.[53] In these situations, an accessible and effective operational-level grievance mechanism may provide the means to hear directly from rights holders on an ongoing basis.[54]

III. Stakeholder Engagement in Practice

The principles outlined above are easier said than done. This section helps to bridge the gap between principles and practice. It moves from what "rights holder" means as a concept, to how to actually identify and communicate with rights holders in a way that is meaningful

---

[48] Michel Forst, *Rep. of the Special Rapporteur on the Situation of Human Rights Defenders* 4–5 UN Doc. A/74/159 (2019).

[49] OECD, *supra* note 22, at 25, 27; UN Office of the High Commissioner for Human Rights, *supra* note 1, at 33–34, 37–38.

[50] Working Group on Business and Human Rights, *Corporate Human Rights Due Diligence – Getting Started, Emerging Practices, Tools and Resources: Companion Note II to the Working Group's 2018 report to the General Assembly* 10–11 A/73/163 (2018).

[51] See, e.g., Shift, Oxfam, and Global Compact Network Netherlands, *supra* note 30.

[52] *See, e.g.*, Global Witness, *Beef, Banks and the Brazilian Amazon*, https://www.globalwitness.org/en/campaigns/forests/beef-banks-and-brazilian-amazon/. (last visited Mar 20, 2021); Human Rights Watch, *Sparkling Jewels, Opaque Supply Chains* (2020), https://www.hrw.org/report/2020/11/24/sparkling-jewels-opaque-supply-chains/jewelry-companies-changing-sourcing (last visited Mar. 20, 2021).

[53] Working Group on Business and Human Rights, *supra* note 50, at 7–8.

[54] UN Office of the High Commissioner for Human Rights, *supra* note 1, at 66.

and productive. As a starting point, companies should approach stakeholder engagement as a team activity best practiced with a mix of company representatives and representatives of the different groups of rights holders who make up the primary stakeholders. It may also require subject matter experts, skilled facilitators, and field researchers. Small to medium-sized enterprises might not have the same resources available to them as larger organizations, but this does not mean that they cannot identify rights holders, understand their concerns, and bring them into the process of designing policy or monitoring adherence. Regardless of an organization's size, every effort to successfully engage rights holders will be shaped by the experience of local partners and their ability to build and maintain trust with different rights holder groups.

A. Identifying Rightsholders

As noted in Section II.B, rights holders are the people who are affected or potentially affected by a company's practices or operations, and may be direct employees, workers in supply chains, local communities, or consumers, among others. Initial desk research can help companies understand or get up-to-date information on how their sector or business model may negatively affect human rights and thus begin the process of identifying rights holders. Sources might include reports from governments, multilateral institutions, civil society organizations, multistakeholder initiatives, workers' representatives and trade unions, national human rights institutions, academics, and news reports.[55] The US National Action Plan on Responsible Business Conduct, for example, includes a list of resources for companies to gain an overview of the state of human rights and commercial conditions across the world, as well as reports that aid in understanding specific issues, such as child labor and human trafficking.[56] Where available, community-led human rights impact assessments can be particularly useful, as they are conducted by rights holders, often in tandem with a civil society organization.[57]

In some instances, past company violations may point to a need to focus on particular areas (for example, previous health and safety violations or instances of sexual harassment). Sources for this information might include existing internal legal reviews, health and safety inspections, or other compliance reviews.[58]

Once the relevant rights holder groups are identified, partnering with an organization that is trusted locally can be a good way to begin outreach. Involving neutral, local third parties to facilitate dialogue in the initial stages may help to bridge gaps and foster trust. In either scenario, a company planning to partner with an organization to facilitate the initial stages of stakeholder engagement will want to understand the following:

1. How does the organization identify rights holders and recruit their participation?
2. Have they worked with this specific group before?

[55] OECD, *supra* note 22, at 26.

[56] US Dept. of State, *supra* note 20, at 17–21.

[57] Gabrielle Watson, Irit Tamir & Brianna Kemp, *Human Rights Impact Assessment in Practice: Oxfam's Aapplication of a Community-Based Approach*, 31 Impact Assessment and Project Appraisal 118–127 (2013).

[58] OECD, *supra* note 22, at 26.

3. Do they understand local customs, culture, and language?
4. Are they able to identify and reach rights holders who may be marginalized or particularly vulnerable?
5. Does a previous engagement bias them or make them a more suitable partner?
6. Do previous engagements, other partners, or their alliances potentially affect how rights holders perceive them?
7. How are they protecting the privacy, security, and anonymity of rights holders?
8. Can they advise on the most appropriate way to recognize and reward the time and effort of the rights holders who eventually participate?

This assessment is critical. Companies that choose an inappropriate or inexperienced partner may not hear from rights holder groups facing serious human rights impacts, which will undermine the credibility and effectiveness of the due diligence process.

B. Addressing Barriers and Fostering Dialogue

Community acceptance, trust, and goodwill must be earned. The principles of stakeholder engagement outlined in Section II.B above require thoughtful planning to put into practice. This section offers some practical considerations in building collaborative relationships with rights holders.

Open and honest communication requires trust, and companies need to understand that trust is a process; it is not automatic. Trust is also deeply rooted in culture. Companies should ensure that their representatives, if they are not local, understand basic etiquette, along with local history, food, music, and norms. This show of respect will help build rapport with rights holders, but can go awry if overplayed. For example, if you're in Pittsburgh and you start talking about the Steelers, you had better know something about them.

Company representatives, or their local partner organizations, need a deep and nuanced understanding of trust within the rights holder groups with which they are working. For example, biases exist in every community, and companies need to be aware of them. In an area where there are tensions between groups, company representatives need to know if all rights holders are providing fair and honest input. Participants may hold back or misreport, but it is more likely that they may not be aware of their implicit bias or its impact on what they are sharing. In either case, a failure to recognize or understand these dynamics will result in inaccurate information. Credible local partners can help with these assessments.

It is also important to understand that trust is established and maintained over time, but it can be broken and lost immediately. A company's actions have far more value than the promises it makes. Many communities or rights holder groups are used to outsiders making and breaking promises, and therefore have good reason to be skeptical of those people and organizations they do not know. Company representatives should take care that when they say they or their company will do something, it actually gets done.

Company representatives should also understand that it takes time and effort for rights holders to participate in dialogue with them, that the company benefits from those efforts, and that those efforts should be compensated in some form. Regardless of the form of compensation, the time and effort of all people should be recognized and properly rewarded. Incentives can be financial or material, in the form of cash or goods, or they can be based on recognition or opportunity. An understanding of rights holders' context will help to determine the most appropriate form of compensation for sharing their time and knowledge. Although there are no invariable rules that dictate compensation, it is important to avoid providing compensation that would lead participants to accept risks, engage in activities to which they would otherwise strongly object, or lie or conceal information that would disqualify them from participation.[59] Compensation can also threaten the perceived legitimacy of the engagement if it appears that participants are being paid to oppose or support a particular position rather than voice their true opinions. These complex dynamics make compensation difficult to navigate. Credible local partners and rights holder representatives should advise on these issues.

Finally, it should be noted that the methods or formats in which dialogue takes place will vary depending on the context. In some cases, companies may need to contract with a third party to engage in a series of informational interviews to gain a full picture of potential impacts. Systematic recruitment of a wide pool of participants may not be necessary or feasible, however, for small or medium-sized business enterprises. Such businesses should still seek to identify opportunities for executives and managers to engage directly with rights holders, ideally in the locations where they live and work. When executives and managers meet with rights holders and spend time in their context, it humanizes the impact of their decisions and can shift company attitudes and drive efforts to respect human rights in practice.[60] In addition, regardless of the size of the enterprise, corporate representatives with decision-making authority should participate in conversations with rights holders about proposals that require company action. When company decision-makers do not take part in key meetings, rights holders can feel their time has been wasted and may lose trust in the process.

IV. Engagement and the Human Rights Due Diligence Process

Outside of human rights due diligence, many organizations are already actively engaged with their stakeholders. Marketing teams are running focus groups to understand the preferences of important audiences. Design teams are conducting qualitative research and employing codesign methods with potential users to explore new products and services. Customer satisfaction teams are gathering feedback to improve existing products and services. Human resources personnel are analyzing employee reviews and surveying staff to improve internal operations. Almost every team within a well-functioning organization looks for input to improve themselves and their output, by asking questions such as what do people need, does our current solution meet their needs, are we hitting our goals, what must change, how

[59] *See, e.g.*, Committee for Protection of Human Subjects, Compensation of Research Subjects (2017), https://cphs.berkeley.edu/compensation.pdf (last visited Mar. 21, 2021).

[60] David Kovick, *Meaningful Engagement with Affected Stakeholders*, Shift (2018), https://shiftproject.org/meaningful-engagement-with-affected-stakeholders/ (last visited Mar. 21, 2021).

does it need to change, how do people feel about things, and how are we doing with our commitments?

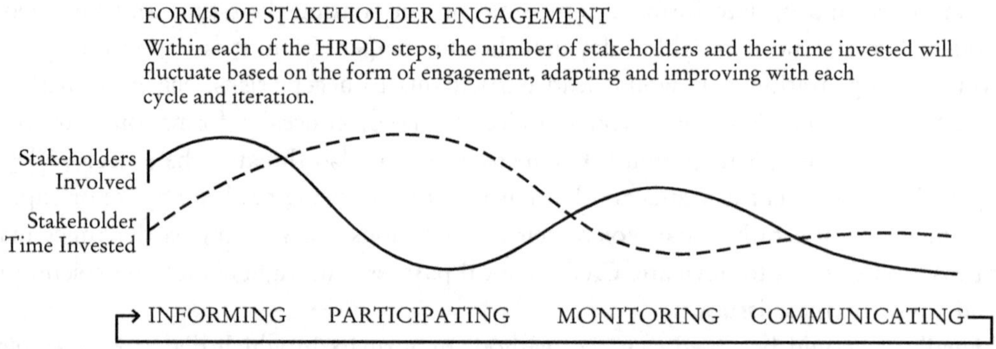

Figure 9.1 Spectrum of Stakeholder Engagement

All of the methods above can be used to improve human rights due diligence, from policy creation, to implementation and adherence, to reporting and remediation. The choice of method, number of stakeholders, and level of stakeholder participation will vary over the course of the due diligence process, as figure 9.1 illustrates. At the outset, where companies are gathering information to identify risks, larger numbers of stakeholders may provide discrete information through surveys or short interviews, whereas implementation of policies and compliance monitoring may require in-depth collaboration with a smaller group. The chart also shows that the process is ongoing. After communicating progress, companies should continue to check in with rights holders for their assessment on whether mitigation efforts are working, and then engage again more deeply to address any issues identified.

A. Identifying and Assessing Human Rights Risks and Impacts

The first step in human rights due diligence requires that companies identify and assess actual or potential adverse human rights impacts that they may cause or contribute to through their own activities, or that they are directly linked to through business relationships.[61] "The purpose is to understand the specific impacts on specific people, given a specific context of operations."[62] Stakeholder engagement at this step should also serve to prioritize which risks or impacts demand the most immediate action. It should also reveal whether rights holders have different perspectives than the company on what the human rights impacts are and how significant they may be and should identify the different perspectives within and between rights holder groups.[63]

For this step in the due diligence process, the shape that stakeholder engagement might take will vary depending on the context. Some companies may need a company-wide

[61] Special Report of the Secretary General, *supra* note 2, at 17.

[62] UN Office of the High Commissioner for Human Rights, *supra* note 1, at 19.

[63] *Id.* at 44.; OECD, *supra* note 22, at 27.

assessment, which may involve identifying known risks and impacts for the sectors in which the company operates and how those relate to the company, and then consulting with rights holders to verify findings and set priorities for action.[64] For new projects in a specific location, a full human rights impact assessment in that location may be appropriate. For a new product or service, stakeholder engagement might form part of the design process. Regardless of the form engagement takes, "the processes for assessing human rights impact should be systematic so that the various elements add up to a coherent overview of actual and potential human rights impact," that can accurately inform the subsequent steps in the due diligence process.[65]

In light of this variety, there is no one right way to engage with rights holders at this stage. Ideally, companies will employ a range of methods to gather information. These may include observational methods (what a researcher sees), conversational methods (what the rights holder says), and perhaps generative methods (what a rights holder makes and describes) that provide rights holders other ways of communicating what they are thinking or feeling.[66] In the latter, a rights holder may create a simple artifact or drawing that depicts an experience, aspiration, or fear, and talks through the logic and reasoning behind the artifact itself. This method is useful to uncover important insights that are difficult to describe, emotionally challenging, or may otherwise go overlooked. These qualitative methods may be combined with tools like surveys to gather more quantitative data in order to develop a baseline understanding of the rights holders' context. This approach of mixing methods allows answers to the most important questions to emerge in different ways, increasing confidence in cases where the answers are the most consistent.

In addition to these examples, further guidance is available on stakeholder engagement in specific contexts. The OECD has issued guidance for stakeholder engagement in the extractive sector.[67] The International Finance Corporation has guidance for stakeholder engagement at different stages of a project cycle: initial concept development, project planning, construction, operations, and finally downsizing, decommissioning, or divestment.[68] For companies seeking to fully understand the risks and impacts connected with a specific project, guidance exists for collaborative human rights impact assessments that are inclusive of and responsive to rights holders.[69]

---

[64] Gwendolyn Remmert, et al., *supra* note 26, at 24.

[65] UN Office of the High Commissioner for Human Rights, *supra* note 1, at 41.

[66] Elizabeth B. Sanders, *Generative Tools for Codesigning*, *in* Collaborative Design (2000).

[67] OECD, OECD Due Diligence Guidance for Meaningful Stakeholder Engagement in the Extractive Sector (2017), https://www.oecd-ilibrary.org/governance/oecd-due-diligence-guidance-for-meaningful-stakeholder-engagement-in-the-extractive-sector_9789264252462-en.

[68] Int'l Fin. Corp., Stakeholder Engagement: A Good Practice Handbook for Companies Doing Business in Emerging Markets (2007), https://www.ifc.org/wps/wcm/connect/affbc005-2569-4e58-9962-280c483baa12/IFC_StakeholderEngagement.pdf?MOD=AJPERES&CVID=jkD13-p.

[69] Columbia Center on Sustainable Investment, Danish Institute for Human Rights, and Sciences Po Law School Clinic, A Collaborative Approach to Human Rights Impact Assessments (2017), https://ccsi.columbia.edu/content/developing-collaborative-approach-human-rights-impact-assessments.

Fundamentally, this is the point where companies must determine the current state of rights holders' lives as the baseline. Does the introduction of your service, project, product, or policy improve or negatively impact the quality of people's lives as defined in the baseline over time? If things are trending downward, companies need to know that as clearly and as promptly as possible. Hopefully, this is measured and monitored, as discussed below.

B. Integrating Findings and Acting to Prevent and Mitigate Harm

"Integration" refers to a company's process for taking action on findings about potential or actual negative human rights impacts. It includes both operations and commitment sincerity. At this stage, rights holders can contribute ideas on appropriate actions to take, which in turn may foster trust and motivate their involvement in implementing and monitoring agreed-on solutions.[70] Representatives from rights holder groups will be essential to understanding how a particular policy has been introduced into the day-to-day lives of their community.

Through a mix of individual interviews and collaborative group work, it should be possible to verify if the company has handled the implementation process in a way that addresses the needs of rights holders. Beyond verifying that specific boxes have been checked, it is important to understand the flow of communication between the organization and the rights holders it impacts, as well as the flow of information between rights holder groups and among rights holders within them. It is also important to know how rights holders have been involved in the process of implementation, and if there is a clear process for reporting when something unexpected happens.

Starting with the baseline current state of rights holders' context, companies may see issues that need to be addressed immediately. Some situations may have clear solutions, in which case those solutions should be presented to rights holders to get their feedback. In many cases, rights holders will see potential problems that the company might have missed, and they can suggest alternatives. In the event that the solution to a specific problem is not clear, rights holders can generate a range of possible solutions drawn from their lived experience.

This process of codesign or co-creation can be done through rights holder–led narratives, describing preferred solutions or highlighting problems with the current solution; the more tangible the proposal, the better. For example, providing people with the opportunity to draw or even construct a model of their solution will allow for a more detailed conversation about their proposal.

All proposed solutions should be considered by a variety of internal and external stakeholders, prioritizing those most likely to be affected by the changes proposed. This process should be iterative and may take a few cycles before a proposed solution meets the needs of rights holders as well as organizational goals.

[70] OECD, *supra* note 22, at 29; Shift, et al., *supra* note 30, at 96.

C. Tracking and Communicating Progress

In keeping with the saying, "what gets measured gets managed," the UNGPs direct companies to track their progress on preventing and mitigating negative human rights impacts. Tracking progress facilitates learning and improvement over time, fosters internal company accountability, and contributes to external credibility.[71] Depending on the size and complexity of the business enterprise, it may involve a range of inputs, including performance reviews, assessment or audit data, trends in worker or other rights holder complaints, and direct rights holder feedback.

Rights holder participation at this stage is essential because it improves the accuracy and credibility of the company's tracking tools, enhances company understanding of the outcome and relevance of its efforts, builds knowledge and trust between rights holders and the company, and ultimately helps to ensure that human rights harms are prevented or addressed.[72] For example, in assessing a reduction in the number of reports of safety violations, qualitative feedback from rights holders may be necessary to determine if this reflects an actual reduction in incidents, or if intimidation or a loss of faith in the complaint system has affected rights holders' willingness to report violations.[73]

Participatory evaluation also reduces the risk or appearance of bias that can happen when companies measure and report on their own progress.[74] As the intended beneficiaries of prevention and mitigation efforts, rights holder input on appropriate metrics is vital, as it reflects their perspective on what success looks like. For example, rights holders, and the broader public, are more likely to accept quantitative information on environmental impacts if they are consulted first on the appropriate metrics and have input on selecting a neutral third party to perform the analysis.[75]

Rights holder participation at this stage involves far more than interviews during annual social audits. Although companies and the multistakeholder initiatives to which they belong have widely adopted social audits to track compliance with voluntary codes of conduct, a volume of research shows that they are largely ineffective at detecting or preventing human rights abuses or remediating harms.[76] The social auditing industry as a whole is facing mounting criticism for ignoring conflicts of interest, using inappropriate methodologies to detect worker rights violations, and not fostering real improvements.[77] In contrast to audits, which

---

[71] UN Office of the High Commissioner for Human Rights, *supra* note 1, at 52–53.

[72] Jana Mudronova, Stakeholder Voice: Learning from Affected Stakeholders to Better Evaluate Program Effectiveness and Outcomes 5 (2019), https://shiftproject.org/wp-content/uploads/2019/09/VRP_Stakeholder%20Voice.pdf.

[73] UN Office of the High Commissioner for Human Rights, *supra* note 1, at 60.

[74] *Id.* at 61.

[75] *Id.* at 53.

[76] Jolyon Ford & Justine Nolan, *Regulating Transparency on Human Rights and Modern Slavery in Corporate Supply Chains: The Discrepancy Between Human Rights Due Diligence and the Social Audit*, 26 Aust. J. Hum. Rts. 27–45 (2020), https://www.tandfonline.com/doi/full/10.1080/1323238X.2020.1761633 (last visited Sep 23, 2020).

[77] Opi Outhwaite & Olga Martin-Ortega, *Worker-driven Monitoring: Redefining Supply Chain Monitoring to Improve Labour Rights in Global Supply Chains*, 23 Competition and Change 378–396, 374 (2019).

treat rights holders as bystanders, rights holder participation can ensure "that responses are fit to context and provide individuals with the type of support they need, that will actually mitigate and prevent harm."[78]

Unfortunately, currently there is a large gap between the existing normative guidance on rights holder participation in monitoring and what companies are doing in practice. The recent UN Working Group on Business and Human Rights report on human rights due diligence has noted a "lack of common understanding about which metrics and indicators to use to track and evaluate performance," which may result in companies gathering and publishing information "that gives little insight into how their business actually affects the basic dignity and welfare of people."[79] The Working Group's roadmap for implementation of the UNGPs notes the need for businesses to "demonstrate use of credible methodologies" and input from rights holders "to show whether, and to what extent, human rights mitigations and remedy actions are leading to better outcomes for people."[80]

Companies are beginning to innovate in this area, however, in an effort to better understand and incorporate rights holder perspectives. Innovations include employing new methodologies, adapting existing evaluation approaches from other contexts, and deploying technology to hear from rights holders directly.[81] More work is needed, however, to evaluate the effectiveness of these new approaches and their appropriate use in different contexts. Toward that end, business and human rights practitioners are beginning to develop indicators to evaluate stakeholder engagement processes.[82]

Much depends on accessibility, trustworthiness, and uptake among users.[83] The Worker Engagement Supported by Technology (WEST) Principles, for example, recommend involving workers in the design of technology-oriented engagement tools, as well as building worker trust through engagement, and communicating results back to workers.[84] The Principles, developed by technology providers in consultation with employers, brands, and NGOs, thus acknowledge that effective monitoring systems require rights holder engagement up front in their design.

Part of the evaluation process should include communicating evaluation findings to relevant internal stakeholders, rights holders, or their respective representatives. This

---

78 Matthew Mullen, *Why Rightsholder Consultation Is the Gateway to Effective Human Rights Due Diligence*, Bus. and Hum. Rts, Res. Ctr. (2020), https://www.business-humanrights.org/en/blog/why-rightsholder-consultation-is-the-gateway-to-effective-human-rights-due-diligence/ (last visited Oct. 1, 2020).

79 Working Group on the Issue of Human Rights and Transnational Corporations and Other Business Enterprises, *supra* note 23, at 11.

80 Working Group, *supra* note 24, at 29.

81 Mudronova, supra note 72, at 10–16; Global Fund to End Modern Slavery, Using Employee Feedback to Assess Working Conditions: Identifying Risks Through Worker Engagement 8–10 (2020).

82 Lloyd Lipsett, Engaging Affected Stakeholders: Evaluating the Quality of Processes for Company-Community Engagement (2018), https://shiftproject.org/resource/engaging-affected-stakeholders-evaluating-the-quality-of-processes-for-company-community-engagement/.

83 Global Fund to End Modern Slavery, *supra* note 81, at 11–12.

84 Worker Engagement Supported by Technology, White Paper: Realizing the Benefits of Worker Reporting Digital Tools (2019), https://westprindsprod.wpengine.com/wp-content/uploads/2019/03/west_principles_white_paper-realizing_the_benefits_of_worker_reporting_digital_tools.pdf (last visited Oct. 1, 2020).

communication should inform rights holders regarding how their input was taken into account.[85] This transparency builds trust and demonstrates good faith. In addition, it allows rights holders to provide input on the analysis and, ultimately, to assess the adequacy of the company's efforts to prevent or mitigate human rights violations. To achieve these outcomes, companies should take care that the formats they use to communicate with rights holders are accessible, taking into account potential literacy, language, and cultural communication barriers.

D. The Role of Stakeholders in Grievance Mechanisms

Broadly speaking, a grievance mechanism is a formalized way to accept, assess, and resolve complaints. Grievance processes support due diligence by acting both as an early warning system to identify potential or recurring human rights violations, and as the means for rights holders to obtain a remedy when violations have occurred.[86] To serve these ends, a grievance mechanism "should not treat rights holders merely as recipients of remedy," but rather should be "at the service of rights holders, who should be consulted meaningfully in creating, designing, reforming and operating such mechanisms."[87] Indeed, the roadmap for the next 10 years of implementation of the UNGPs calls on businesses to ensure that rights holders are meaningfully involved in the design and performance of grievance mechanisms.[88]

Ultimately, a grievance mechanism must be known to, and trusted by, the rights holders for whom it is intended. In contrast, a poorly designed or implemented grievance mechanism, "can risk compounding a sense of grievance" among rights holders "by heightening their sense of disempowerment and disrespect by the process."[89] Rights holder input on the design and performance of a grievance mechanism is therefore essential. Indeed, the UNGPs indicate that operational-level grievance mechanisms, which are those administered by companies at a specific base of operation, must be based on engagement and dialogue.[90] At a minimum, this requires the following:

1. Developing an understanding of the operational context;
2. Consulting with rights holders on their needs and expectations of the grievance mechanism and following up regularly thereafter to ensure those are met;
3. Providing multiple opportunities and avenues for rights holders to contribute their views on the design and performance of the mechanism, including engaging proactively with those seeking to develop and implement worker-driven and community-driven grievance mechanisms; and

---

[85] SHIFT, ET AL., *supra* note 30, at 99.

[86] OECD, *supra* note 22, at 88–91.

[87] REPORT OF THE WORKING GROUP ON THE ISSUE OF HUMAN RIGHTS AND TRANSNATIONAL CORPORATIONS AND OTHER BUSINESS ENTERPRISES, at 8, UN Doc A/62/172 (2017).

[88] WORKING GROUP, *supra* note 24, at 33.

[89] Special Report of the Secretary General, *supra* note 2, at 39.

[90] *Id.* at 34.

4. Paying special attention to gender-based barriers and the needs of people who may be at heightened risk of vulnerability or marginalization.[91]

If rights holders have been engaged in the creation and implementation of policy, the processes of monitoring, grievance, and remediation should be clear to them, assuming organizational adherence has been honest and transparent. Assuming the process for filing a grievance is clear and individuals do not fear repercussions, rights holder engagement at this stage should be fairly straightforward.

That engagement should start by talking with the rights holders directly impacted by the grievance issue, as well as those peripherally related to the issue, to understand the nature of the grievance. Given the complexity of many grievances, it is often valuable to understand the complainant's concerns from as many angles as possible. For example, rights holder interviews should include direct questions, as well as ample time for narrative and visualization. Narrative allows the impacted individuals to express their experience in their own words, in a variety of ways. Visualization can happen through a wider range of inputs, such as diagramming or drawing, but fundamentally these methods encourage complainants to think about and communicate their experience in different ways.

Once the grievance has been fully articulated, rights holders should be included in the process of remediation. Questions to ask include: What do rights holders think needs to happen to address the immediate needs of the current situation? and; What do rights holders think needs to change to ensure that this situation does not occur again in the future? Those that have been impacted most directly often have suggestions for how to improve the situation and inform adjustments to policy.

V. Issues in Stakeholder Engagement

Recent research on human rights due diligence in practice indicates that most companies do not undertake stakeholder engagement that embraces the principles set forth in the existing normative guidance and outlined in this chapter. At the same time, there is growing recognition of worker-centered or rights holder-centered approaches as effective in preventing and remediating human rights harms. This section briefly describes these challenges and opportunities for stakeholder engagement in human rights due diligence.

A. The Status Quo: Far from Good Practice

The roadmap for the next decade of implementation of the UNGPs calls on States to "clarify that meaningful and ongoing consultation with potentially affected groups and other relevant stakeholders is integral to human rights due diligence."[92] Despite the crucial role that stakeholder engagement plays in human rights due diligence, generally accepted benchmarks

[91] REPORT OF THE WORKING GROUP ON THE ISSUE OF HUMAN RIGHTS AND TRANSNATIONAL CORPORATIONS AND OTHER BUSINESS ENTERPRISES, at 11–14, UN Doc. A/HRC/44/32 (2020).

[92] WORKING GROUP, *supra* note 24, at 36.

for how it should be done have not yet been formulated.[93] The potential for widely divergent practice threatens the legitimacy of human rights due diligence, as superficial, tick-the-box approaches will not only prove incapable of preventing abuses, they will also undermine good faith approaches that affect corporate decision-making and protect human rights.[94] This wide divergence in corporate practice is possible because under existing human rights due diligence legislation and the UNGPs, corporations are free to choose the form of stakeholder engagement they wish to undertake.

At present, engagement is company-driven, and this creates an inherent tension, as companies have little incentive to incur the cost of uncovering and addressing human rights risks and impacts, especially when full implementation of human rights due diligence "would essentially mean a change of business model for entire companies, and even for prevailing models in entire industries."[95] Research has shown that few companies have demonstrated meaningful engagement strategies. A survey of the human rights due diligence practices of companies in the mining and energy, financial services, pharmaceutical, and technology sectors found a reliance on desk-based research and external auditing to identify human rights impacts.[96] It also found that companies lacked grievance mechanisms that are available to rights holders who are not their employees.[97] Overall, it concluded that companies have not shifted their focus from risks posed to the business to risks faced by people, i.e., the potential human rights impacts faced by rights holders.[98]

Similarly, the 2020 Corporate Human Rights Benchmark, an assessment of the human rights disclosures of 229 companies in the agricultural, apparel, automotive manufacturing, ICT manufacturing, and extractive sectors, gave a human rights due diligence score of zero to nearly half the assessed companies.[99] The Benchmark, a project of the World Benchmarking Alliance to rank global companies on their human rights performance, also found that "[e]ven for those companies with robust commitments and management systems, these do not automatically translate at a practical level, with allegations of severe human rights violations regularly raised, even against some of the highest scoring companies."[100]

---

[93] Rajiv Maher & Karin Buhmann, *Meaningful Stakeholder Engagement: Bottom-Up Initiatives Within Global Governance Frameworks*, 107 Geoforum 231–234 (2019); Karin Buhmann, *Analysing OECD National Contact Point Statements for Guidance on Human Rights Due Diligence: Method, Findings and Outlook*, 36 Nordic J. of Hum. Rts. 390–410, 405–406 (2018).

[94] James Harrison, *Establishing a Meaningful Human Rights Due Diligence Process for Corporations: Learning From Experience of Human Rights Impact Assessment*, 31 Impact Assessment and Project Appraisal 107–117, 111, 114 (2013).

[95] V. Nelson, O. Martin-Ortega & M. Flint, Making Human Rights Due Diligence Work: An Analysis of Impact and Legal Options 39 (2020), https://fairtrade-advocacy.org/wp-content/uploads/2020/06/UoG-HRDD-Full-Report-60pp-FINAL-SECURED.pdf.

[96] Robert McCorquodale et al., *Human Rights Due Diligence in Law and Practice: Good Practices and Challenges for Business Enterprises*, 2 Bus. and Hum. Rts. J. 195–224 (2017).

[97] *Id.* at 208, 211.

[98] *Id.* at 222.

[99] World Benchmarking Alliance, *Corporate Human Rights Benchmark Rights Benchmark: 2020 Key Findings*, 3 (2020), https://assets.worldbenchmarkingalliance.org/app/uploads/2020/11/WBA-2020-CHRB-Key-Findings-Report.pdf.

[100] *Id.*

The UN Working Group on Business and Human Rights noted these issues in its report on human rights due diligence, pointing to an excessive reliance on tick-the-box approaches, "without meaningful engagement" with rights holders, "including engagement with vulnerable or at-risk groups and critical voices such as human rights defenders."[101] With regard to grievance mechanisms in particular, which are especially important as a backstop to identify risks or harms that other forms of engagement have missed, the Working Group has noted a need for "much greater emphasis to the needs, expectations and perspectives of the people for whose use these mechanisms are intended."[102] Overall, companies continue to rely on top-down approaches, with many weaknesses in implementation.[103]

Top-down approaches perpetuate power imbalances, which pose another obstacle to the type of stakeholder engagement envisioned by the UNGPs and described in this chapter. The large power differential between companies and rights holders can limit rights holders' perceived freedom of choice, particularly in situations of conflict with a company.[104] Power imbalances among rights holders can further sideline marginalized groups. Without clear guidelines and active measures to address these issues, companies can exploit these imbalances in an effort to "get the best deal," rather than act in good faith to uncover, assess, and address human rights risks.[105]

There is also the potential that human rights due diligence legislation will erode, rather than strengthen, the quality of stakeholder engagement. As more States contemplate mandatory human rights due diligence reporting, companies may treat engagement as a mere formality, necessary only to comply with legislation, rather than as an opportunity to improve how they do business.[106] A study of human rights due diligence reporting under the UK Modern Slavery Act, for example, found that fewer than 15 percent of companies report engaging directly with workers, and that many companies continue to rely on social audits, which are inadequate to detect abuses.[107] Similarly, studies of company reporting under the French Duty of Vigilance Law found that reporting on stakeholder engagement worsened, with few companies reporting "any detail on stakeholder engagement at all" or providing only vague information.[108] Other studies have highlighted that existing regulatory measures "have not

[101] Working Group on the Issue of Human Rights and Transnational Corporations and Other Business Enterprises, *supra* note 23, at 8.

[102] Report of the Working Group on the Issue of Human Rights and Transnational Corporations and Other Business Enterprises, *supra* note 91, at 4.

[103] Nelson, et al., *supra* note 95, at 16, 36.

[104] Rajiv Maher, *Squeezing Psychological Freedom in Corporate–Community Engagement*, 160 J. Bus. Ethics 1047–1066, 4–5 (2019).

[105] *Id.* at 14–17; *see also* Katherine McDonnell, Morvarid Bagheri & Shauna Curphey, *Addressing Corporate Activity That Negatively Impacts Natural Resources: Community-Led Engagement as a Path to Rights Compatible Remedies*, 49 Int'l L. News 5–10 (2021).

[106] Michelle Langlois, Human Rights Reporting in France 8 (2019), https://shiftproject.org/wp-content/uploads/2019/11/Shift_HumanRightsReportinginFrance_Nov27.pdf.

[107] Patricia Carrier, Modern Slavery Act: Five Years of Reporting (2020), https://media.business-humanrights.org/media/documents/Modern_Slavery_Act_2021.pdf.

[108] Nelson, et al., *supra* note 95, at 16.

delivered in terms of driving actual change in corporate behavior in practice."[109] These studies suggest that "there is a real risk that corporate practice focuses on reporting rather than exercising meaningful and effective due diligence."[110]

Even if human rights due diligence failures are linked to corporate liability for abuses, the extent of that liability "is likely to be much narrower" than the scope of issues that companies are expected to encompass in their human rights due diligence.[111] This "accountability gap" has led to calls for "regulators to look at additional measures that can incentivize companies to carry out the full scope" of human rights due diligence "to a suitably robust standard," as envisioned by the UNGPs.[112]

B. The Opportunities: Growing Recognition of Rightsholder-Driven Approaches

Although the UNGPs and the OECD Guidelines focus on how *companies* should carry out stakeholder engagement, diverse voices are calling for bottom-up, *rights holder*–driven approaches "whereby the stakeholder is at the center of the process, driving it, as opposed to being engaged from the top."[113] There is also an initiative under way to articulate a set of community principles to supplement the three-pillar "respect, protect, remedy" framework of the UNGPs, with a fourth pillar that underscores the importance of rights holder agency to the effective implementation of human rights protections.[114] In addition, several models have emerged that implicitly recognize that, apart from those perpetrating abuses, only rights holders "have the requisite knowledge and understanding of the various forms of abuse visited upon them every day to design effective systems to detect and prevent that abuse."[115] Through rights holder leadership, their lived experience can help uncover risks for abuse, identify alternatives, and guide future actions toward more equitable and rights-respecting outcomes.

Community-led human rights impact assessments (HRIAs) are gaining ground, and "offer a way for communities to assess the relevance and suitability of large investment in and around their territory and the extent to which it aligns with their own development priorities."[116] As with stakeholder engagement more broadly, benchmarks for "what effective

[109] European Commission. Directorate General for Justice and Consumers. et al., Study on Due Diligence Requirements Through the Supply Chain: Final Report 220 (2020), https://data.europa.eu/doi/10.2838/39830.

[110] Nelson, et al., *supra* note 95, at 43.

[111] Shift Project, Accountability as part of Mandatory Human Rights Due Diligence (2020), https://shiftproject.org/wp-content/uploads/2020/10/Shift_mHRDD_Accountability_October2020.pdf.

[112] *Id.* at 6.

[113] Maher & Buhmann, *supra* note 93, at 233.

[114] Harvard Law School International Human Rights Clinic, *Fourth Pillar: Community Principles for Business and Human Rights* (Mar. 21,2021) (first iteration draft on file with author).

[115] Greg Asbed & Steve Hitov, *Preventing Forced Labor in Corporate Supply Chains: The Fair Food Program and Worker-Driven Social Responsibility*, 52 Wake Forest L. Rev. 497–531, 514 (2017).

[116] Maher & Buhmann, *supra* note 93, at 233.

participation looks like" in HRIAs have not yet been fully developed, although research has contributed to defining good practice.[117] Recent research has proposed collaborative HRIAs, in which project-affected rights holders, a company, and potentially the host government or other stakeholders, work jointly to investigate and respond to the human rights impacts of a project.[118] It posits that, because collaborative HRIAs do not involve the perspectives of only one group, they "could help address the legitimacy challenge that standard HRIAs confront, providing a process that is more trusted by all stakeholders."[119]

Rights holder–led design of grievance mechanisms has also emerged as a new model. EarthRights International, an NGO focused on protecting human rights and the environment, has piloted Community-Driven Operational Grievance Mechanisms.[120] The model proceeds from the premise that dispute resolution processes should be designed and approved by rights holders if they are to "succeed in solving thorny problems between companies and the persons affected by their operations."[121]

In the field of product and service development, human-centered design (HCD) has become a common way of identifying opportunities for improving existing products or systems and engaging stakeholders, such as users, consumers, and customers, throughout the process, from initial identification of opportunity, to solution ideation and refinement, to solution testing and implementation. As the name suggests, HCD typically centers people's needs as a way of guiding the design process, rather than focusing on technology or business goals. Recently, concepts such as Design Justice have been bringing perspectives from community engagement, restorative justice, and social movements into the HCD process, creating space and providing the tools for designers and managers to engage with the "humans" within HCD as whole people, rather than simply thinking of them as users or consumers. Researcher, designer, and activist Sasha Costanza-Chock describes Design Justice as "an exploration of how design might be led by marginalized communities, dismantle structural inequality, and advance collective liberation and ecological survival."[122]

In the supply chain context, there is growing recognition that "workers should have a key role in designing and implementing monitoring processes that both identify workplace issues and provide redress for them."[123] The Coalition of Immokalee Workers, a Florida-based human rights organization focused on farmworkers in the supply chains of major food retailers, has pioneered the Worker-Driven Social Responsibility model with its creation of the Fair Food Program. The Program has proven uniquely effective in eliminating abuses

---

[117] Alejandro Gonzalez, Evaluating the Human Rights Impact of Investment Projects: Background, Best Practices and Opportunities 87 (2014), https://poderlatam.org/wp-content/uploads/2015/01/PODER-HRIA-Best-Practices-Dec-2014.pdf.

[118] Columbia Center on Sustainable Investment, et al., *supra* note 69.

[119] *Id.* at 16.

[120] Community-Driven Operational Grievance Mechanism (CD-OGM), EarthRights International, https://earthrights.org/what-we-do/corporate-accountability/cdogm/ (last visited Apr. 17, 2021).

[121] Jonathan Kaufman & Katherine McDonnell, *Community-Driven Operational Grievance Mechanisms*, 1 Bus. and Hum. Rts. J. 127–132 (2016).

[122] Sasha Costanza-Chock, Design justice: Community-led Practices to Build the Worlds We Need (2020).

[123] Ford & Nolan, *supra* note 76, at 111.

on participating farms, as evidenced by the dramatic improvement in compliance with its Code of Conduct over time, and workers' own accounts of their experience in the fields.[124] The UN Working Group on Business and Human Rights has praised the Program as "a ground-breaking accountability arrangement" that "through market incentives for growers and retailers, monitoring policies and, crucially, a robust and accessible mechanism to resolve complaints and provide remedy" delivers "respect for human rights and better living standards for workers."[125]

In the Worker-Driven Social Responsibility model, rights holders play the central role in identifying rights violations and managing solutions. Key features of the model include: (1) a code of conduct drafted by workers themselves; (2) worker-to-worker education on worker rights under the code of conduct; (3) a 24-hour, multilingual complaint hotline backed by investigators with the power to address allegations of violations of the code of conduct; (4) audits that include interviews with a minimum of 50 percent of workers; and, most importantly, (5) legally binding agreements with retail buyers creating market consequences for violations.[126] These agreements require that buyers suspend purchases from farming operations that are suspended from the program, which in turn gives participating farms a strong market incentive to avoid violations and remediate them when they occur.[127] As a result, workers trust and use the complaint system and become the central actors in protecting their own rights.

VI. Conclusion

Stakeholder engagement, when it constitutes sincere, direct, collaborative engagement with rights holders, has enormous potential to improve corporate human rights due diligence and, ultimately, to prevent human rights violations. Yet, the stakeholder engagement practices envisioned by the UNGPs and their existing interpretive guidance and described in this chapter require that companies cede some control over the human rights due diligence process but nonetheless act on its outcomes. Currently, this is a prospect that only the most committed companies have embraced. So far, there is little evidence that companies are willing to take the necessary steps to implement these engagement best practices. At the same time, new principles and models are emerging: community-led and collaborative impact assessments; Community-Driven Operational Grievance Mechanisms, Design Justice; and Worker-Driven Social Responsibility, in which workers and other rights holders are leading the way by creating and implementing models that realize engagement's potential to generate real change on the ground.

---

124 Fair Food Standards Council, Fair Food: 2018 Update (2019), https://www.fairfoodprogram.org/wp-content/uploads/2019/10/Fair-Food-Program-2018-SOTP-Update-Final.pdf; *see also* James Brudney, *Decent Labour Standards in Corporate Supply Chains: The Immokalee Workers Model*, *in* Temporary Labour Migration in the Global Era (2016).

125 *Coalition of Immokalee Workers Announces Walmart to Join Groundbreaking Fair Food Program*, BusinessWire (2014), https://www.businesswire.com/news/home/20140116006518/en/Coalition-of-Immokalee-Workers-Announces-Walmart-to-Join-Groundbreaking-Fair-Food-Program (last visited Mar. 21, 2021).

126 Asbed & Hitov, *supra* note 115, at 511–526.

127 *Id.* at 513.

VII. Resources

ARTURO ESCOBAR, DESIGNS FOR THE PLURIVERSE: RADICAL INTERDEPENDENCE, AUTONOMY, AND THE MAKING OF WORLDS. Durham and London: Duke University Press (2018).

Greg Asbed & Steve Hitov, *Preventing Forced Labor in Corporate Supply Chains: The Fair Food Program and Worker-Driven Social Responsibility*, 52 WAKE FOREST L. REV. 497–531 (2017).

Gwendolyn Remmert, Global Compact Network Germany, Madeleine Koalick, twentyfifty Ltd. & Luke Wilde, twentyfifty Ltd., *Stakeholder Engagement in Human Rights Due Diligence: A Business Guide* (2014).

Jana Mudronova, *Stakeholder Voice: Learning from Affected Stakeholders to Better Evaluate Program Effectiveness and Outcomes* (2019), https://shiftproject.org/wp-content/uploads/2019/09/VRP_Stakeholder%20Voice.pdf.

LINDA TUHIWAI SMITH, DECOLONIZING METHODOLOGIES: RESEARCH AND INDIGENOUS PEOPLES. London: Zed Books (2021).

Opi Outhwaite & Olga Martin-Ortega, *Worker-driven Monitoring: Redefining Supply Chain Monitoring to Improve Labour Rights in Global Supply Chains*, 23 COMPETITION AND CHANGE 378–396 (2019).

Organisation for Economic Co-operation and Development (OCED), *OECD Due Diligence Guidance for Responsible Business Conduct* (2018).

Rajiv Maher, *Squeezing Psychological Freedom in Corporate–Community Engagement*, 160 J BUS ETHICS 1047–1066 (2019).

SASHA COSTANZA-CHOCK, DESIGN JUSTICE: COMMUNITY-LED PRACTICES TO BUILD THE WORLDS WE NEED. MIT Press (2020).

SHIFT, OXFAM & GLOBAL COMPACT NETWORK NETHERLANDS, *Doing Business with Respect for Human Rights: A Guidance Tool for Companies* (2016).

UN Office of the High Commissioner for Human Rights, *The Corporate Responsibility to Respect Human Rights: An Interpretive Guide* (2012).

10

Gender-Responsive Human Rights Due Diligence

Constance Z. Wagner and Nancy Kaymar Stafford

I. Introduction

"The prevention of adverse impacts on people is the main purpose of human rights due diligence."[1] Human rights due diligence (HRDD) must include a focus on women,[2] including the social and institutional barriers of access to justice and the underlying discrimination they face, such as lack of knowledge of the procedure, societal stigmas, lack of capacity, and laws that do not meet women's needs.[3]

Since the adoption of the 2011 United Nations (UN) Guiding Principles on Business and Human Rights (UNGPs),[4] there has been an increasing recognition that businesses have a responsibility to respect human rights. At a minimum, these rights include those contained in (i) the International Bill of Human Rights, which consists of the Universal Declaration of Human Rights (UDHR),[5] the International Covenant on Economic, Social and Cultural

[1] Report of the Working Group on the Issue of Human Rights and Transitional Corporations and Other Business Enterprises, at 6, UN Doc. A/73/163 (July 16, 2018), https://undocs.org/A/73/163 [hereinafter, *Working Group Report*].

[2] For the purposes of this chapter, the term "women" includes women-identifying individuals.

[3] Laura Turquet, *Progress of the World's Women 2011-2012: In Pursuit of Justice*, UN Women 52–53 (2011).

[4] *Guiding Principles on Business and Human Rights: Implementing the United Nations 'Protect, Respect and Remedy' Framework*, UN Doc. HR/PUB/11/04 (2011), https://www.ohchr.org/documents/publications/guiding principlesbusinesshr_en.pdf [hereinafter, *Guiding Principles*] (Unanimously approved by the United Nations Human Rights Council in its resolution 17/4 of 16 June 2011).

[5] G.A. Res. 217 (III) A, Universal Declaration of Human Rights (Dec. 10, 1948) [hereinafter, *UDHR*].

Rights (ICESCR),[6] and the International Covenant on Civil and Political Rights (ICCPR),[7] and (ii) the principles concerning fundamental rights contained in the International Labour Organization (ILO) Declaration on Fundamental Principles and Rights at Work.[8] Depending on the circumstances, other international human rights instruments may have standards applicable to the individuals or groups requiring protection.[9] Steps towards greater normativity are under discussion, with the goal of a binding UN treaty on business and human rights.[10] Standards for gender-responsive HRDD (GR-HRDD) should be included in any such treaty.

Against this backdrop, HRDD has become an essential part of the way businesses meet their responsibility to respect human rights. According to UNGPs Principle 15(b), a business should implement a "human rights due diligence process to identify, prevent, mitigate and account for how they address their impacts on human rights."[11]

Although women have increasingly penetrated the global workforce, they still face greater hurdles when it comes to employment than men do. Women are overrepresented in informal and precarious employment. UN Women, officially known as the United Nations Entity for Gender Equality and the Empowerment of Women, notes that in developing countries, the share of women working in the informal sector is 4.6 percent higher than men, when agricultural workers are included, and an astounding 7.8 percent when agricultural workers are excluded.[12] Moreover, women are more detrimentally affected by climate change and environmental pollution, which may leave them with fallow land or require them to walk a longer way to fetch water, for example.[13] Women are often marginalized in formal employment settings, where they are paid less than their male counterparts and suffer sexual harassment and gender-based violence.[14] Women also face discrimination due to pregnancy or maternity-related issues, and are often overlooked for managerial positions.[15]

---

[6] G.A. Res. 2200A (XXI), International Covenant on Economic, Social and Cultural Rights, Dec. 16, 1966, 993 U.N.T.S. 3 (entered into force Jan. 3, 1976) [hereinafter, *ICESCR*].

[7] G.A. Res. 2200A (XXI), International Covenant on Civil and Political Rights, Dec. 16, 1966, 999 U.N.T.S 171 (entered into force Mar. 23, 1976) [hereinafter, *ICCPR*].

[8] International Labour Organization [ILO], ILO Declaration on Fundamental Principles and Rights at Work and its Follow-Up (Jun. 18, 1998), https://www.ilo.org/wcmsp5/groups/public/---ed_norm/---declaration/documents/normativeinstrument/wcms_716594.pdf.

[9] *Guiding Principles*, *supra* note 4, Commentary to UNGP 12, at 14.

[10] *At Last: A Draft UN Treaty on Business and Human Rights*, Business and Human Rights Resource Centre (Aug. 2, 2018), https://www.business-humanrights.org/en/latest-news/at-last-a-draft-un-treaty-on-business-and-human-rights/. The current draft calls for integrating a gender perspective into human rights due diligence. See https://www.ohchr.org/Documents/HRBodies/HRCouncil/WGTransCorp/Session6/LBI3rdDRAFT.pdf

[11] *Guiding Principles*, *supra* note 4, at 16.

[12] *Facts and Figures: Economic Empowerment*, unwomen.org, https://www.unwomen.org/en/what-we-do/economic-empowerment/facts-and-figures (last visited Dec. 30, 2020).

[13] Report of the Working Group on the Issue of Human Rights and Transnational Corporations and Other Business Enterprises, at 4–5, UN Doc. A/HRC/41/43 (May 23, 2019), https://media.business-humanrights.org/media/documents/files/documents/A_HRC_41_43.pdf [hereinafter, *Gender Dimensions Report*].

[14] *Id.*

[15] *Id.*

Because of deeply embedded gender roles within society, women are often confined to unpaid care work (caring for elderly parents or children) and domestic work. And even when women are paid, it is not on parity with men – on average 20 percent less across the globe.[16] The reality of the challenges faced by the vulnerable and marginalized is recognized in the UNGPs, which state that HRDD must address the "specific challenges that may be faced by indigenous peoples, *women*, national or ethnic minorities, religious and linguistic minorities, children, persons with disabilities, and migrant workers and their families" (emphasis added).[17] The challenge is even greater if a woman falls into more than one of these vulnerable and marginalized categories. For this reason, the UN Working Group on Business and Human Rights (UN Working Group), established by the Human Rights Council in 2011 and composed of five independent and geographically diverse experts, recommended that HRDD should be tailored to specific risks, should apply a gender lens, and should consider actual and potential adverse impacts and their specific effect on women.[18]

The economic benefits of performing GR-HRDD have been demonstrated. A study by the McKinsey Global Institute found that if women participated in the economy equally to men, it would add as much as US$28 trillion to the annual global GDP by 2025.[19] Yet, women still face systemic obstacles within corporate structures, which attests to the need for rigorous GR-HRDD.

This chapter is structured as follows. Section II will present context to the issue of GR-HRDD by providing an overview of women's human rights that are recognized in international treaties and other instruments. Section III will review voluntary standards on conducting GR-HRDD and guidance on incorporating a gender-responsive perspective into business operations more generally. Section IV will identify emerging good practices and evolving issues in GR-HRDD. Section V offers some concluding remarks. Section VI consists of a list of resources that the reader might find helpful for purposes of continuing work in this area.

II. Context

A. Overview of Gender-Responsive Human Rights Due Diligence

It is imperative that businesses conduct HRDD in order to fulfill their responsibility to respect human rights. HRDD should be integrated into all internal business operations and started early in supplier and other external commercial relationships. It is not something that should be perfunctory, taken lightly, or hurriedly addressed at the last minute. It should not just be

[16] *Id.*

[17] *Guiding Principles, supra* note 4, at 5.

[18] *Working Group Report, supra* note 1, at ¶ 13.

[19] *How Advancing Women's Equality Can Add $12 Trillion to Global Growth*, McKinsey Global Institute (Sept. 1, 2015), https://www.mckinsey.com/featured-insights/employment-and-growth/how-advancing-womens-equality-can-add-12-trillion-to-global-growth.

"checking the box" on a due diligence list, but an in-depth review of business operations. In order to address adverse impacts of business operations on women, HRDD must also be gender responsive. It should have a gender-sensitive lens and include a review of barriers to access and underlying discrimination that women face.

The history of women's human rights, as a part of international human rights law, has evolved. So too has GR-HRDD. Merely conducting gender-blind analysis during due diligence may not be sufficient, because risk assessments may come with an implicit gender bias. Therefore, HRDD must consider the specific risks associated with gender. Merely guaranteeing equal treatment is not enough. Not only do women need to be placed on an equal footing with men, but they also need the environment and tools to empower them to have an equal result as men (i.e., de jure and de facto equality).[20] As such, sometimes "non-identical treatment of women and men will be required in order to address" biological, social, and cultural constructs.[21] The result must be gender equality.

B. Women's Human Rights in International Law

The recognition of women's rights under international human rights law existed well before Hillary Clinton uttered her famous statement at the Fourth World Conference on Women that "human rights are women's rights. . . . And women's rights are human rights."[22] The Charter of the United Nations (UN Charter), adopted in 1945, was the first international text to specifically mention human rights and gender equality. Its preamble reaffirms faith in "fundamental human rights, in the dignity and worth of the human person, in the equal rights of men and women. . . .", while Articles 1, 55, and 76 of the UN Charter call for the promotion of "human rights and fundamental freedoms for all without distinction as to . . . sex. . . ."[23] To support the promotion of the rights of women, the UN established the Commission on the Status of Women (CSW) on June 21, 1946.[24] CSW "is the biggest global policy-making body dedicated exclusively to promoting gender equality and the empowerment of women."[25] Its establishment was a sign that the UN was taking the issue of women's rights seriously.

---

[20] *General Recommendation 25: Temporary Special Measures*, United Nations Committee on the Elimination of Discrimination Against Women 9 (2004), https://www.un.org/womenwatch/daw/cedaw/recommendations/General%20recommendation%2025%20%28English%29.pdf.

[21] *Id.*

[22] *First Lady Hillary Rodham Clinton: Remarks for the United Nations Fourth World Conference on Women*, un.org (Sept. 5, 1995), https://www.un.org/esa/gopher-data/conf/fwcw/conf/gov/950905175653.txt.

[23] UN Charter Preamble, ¶ 2, Article 1, 55, 76, https://www.un.org/en/about-us/un-charter/.

[24] *Commission on the Status of Women, Resolution adopted 21 June 1946*, Economic and Social Council Res. E/90 & E/84, ¶ 6 (Jun. 21, 1946), https://www.un.org/womenwatch/daw/csw/pdf/CSW_founding_resolution_1946.pdf.

[25] *Snapshot: What is CSW?* unwomen.org, https://www.unwomen.org/en/csw/csw-snapshot.

Keeping in mind that the UDHR, the first document detailing basic human rights obligations, was not adopted by the UN General Assembly until December 10, 1948,[26] it is remarkable that the CSW was established more than two years prior to this seminal document in human rights law. Article 2 of the UDHR, echoing the UN Charter, states that "[e]veryone is entitled to all the rights and freedoms set forth in the Declaration, without distinction of any kind, such as . . . sex. . . ."[27] The UDHR outlines important human rights that are critical for women, such as: equality before the law (Article 7); freedom of movement (Article 13); right to marry and have a family (Article 16); right to own property (Article 17); freedom of assembly and association (Article 20); right to social security (Article 22); right to work (Article 23); right to rest and leisure (Article 24); and right to adequate standard of living (Article 25).[28]

The rights in the UDHR were then expanded in two legally binding international agreements, adopted in 1966, the ICESCR[29] and the ICCPR.[30] The ICESCR requires States Parties to ensure women and men equal rights to the enjoyment of all rights enumerated in the covenant.[31] These rights include the rights to work,[32] equal pay,[33] healthy and safe working conditions,[34] promotion,[35] rest,[36] to form trade unions,[37] and maternity leave.[38] The ICCPR protects women's and men's equal rights to the enjoyment of all civil and political rights enumerated in the covenant.[39] Among other things, these include the rights to opinion,[40] peaceful assembly,[41] association,[42] and to vote and/or be elected.[43]

---

[26] *UDHR*, *supra* note 5.

[27] *Id.*

[28] There are many other critical rights outlined in the UDHR, as with other international instruments discussed, however, the authors are outlining those most useful in the area of GR-HRDD.

[29] *ICESCR*, *supra* note 6.

[30] *ICCPR*, *supra* note 7.

[31] *ICESCR*, *supra* note 6, at Article 3.

[32] *Id.* at Article 6(1). This right includes "the right of everyone to the opportunity to gain his living by work which he freely chooses or accepts."

[33] *Id.* at Article 7(a)(i). The article calls for women to be "guaranteed conditions of work not inferior to those enjoyed by men, with equal pay for equal work."

[34] *Id.* at Article 7(b).

[35] *Id.* at Article 7(c). The article states that this right is "subject to no considerations other than those of seniority and competence."

[36] *Id.* at Article 7(d). The article includes "reasonable limitation of working hours and periodic holidays with pay."

[37] *Id.* at Article 8.

[38] *Id.* at Article 10(2).

[39] *ICCPR*, *supra* note 7, at Article 3.

[40] *Id.* at Article 19(1).

[41] *Id.* at Article 21.

[42] *Id.* at Article 22(1), including the "right to form and join trade unions."

[43] *Id.* at Article 25(b).

Yet, despite these and various other instruments that addressed women's human rights,[44] "extensive discrimination against women" continued to exist.[45] This led to the CSW developing an additional treaty that would take its place among the other international human rights treaties and bring "the female half of humanity into the focus of human rights concerns."[46] This treaty is the Convention on the Elimination of All Forms of Discrimination against Women (CEDAW), which lays out the obligations of States to achieve substantive gender equality and entered into force in 1981. CEDAW requires States Parties "to take all appropriate measures to eliminate discrimination against women by any person, organization or enterprise"[47] and to remove prejudices, customs, stereotypes, and other practices that are based on the superiority/inferiority of either sex.[48] Moreover, CEDAW requires States Parties to eliminate discrimination against women in the field of employment,[49] requires equal remuneration and benefits,[50] and the protection of health and safety at work, including safeguarding reproduction.[51] Equally important are the prohibition against dismissal on the grounds of pregnancy[52] and the requirement for maternity leave.[53] To date, 189 States Parties have ratified CEDAW.[54]

International human rights law is the basis for businesses' formulation and implementation of GR-HRDD plans. For example, Article 2 of CEDAW, which states that States Parties must endeavor "to take all appropriate measures to eliminate discrimination against women by any person, organization or enterprise," raises an interpretive question about the role of business in eliminating such discrimination. The CEDAW Committee overseeing the

---

[44] Prior to a comprehensive women's rights treaty, there were several documents introduced to further women's rights, including: Convention on the Political Rights of Women, Mar. 31, 1953, 193 U.N.T.S. 135 (entered into force Jul. 7, 1954); Convention on the Nationality of Married Women, Feb. 20, 1957, 309 U.N.T.S. 65 (entered into force Aug. 11, 1958); Convention on Consent to Marriage, Minimum Age for Marriage and Registration of Marriages, Dec. 10, 1962, 521 U.N.T.S. 231 (entered into force Dec. 9, 1964); Convention against Discrimination in Education, Dec. 14, 1960, 429 U.N.T.S. 93 (entered into force May 22, 1962); Maternity Protection Convention, Jun. 28, 1952, 214 U.N.T.S. 321 (entered into force Sept. 7, 1955); Equal Remuneration Convention, Jun. 29, 1959, 165 U.N.T.S. 303 (entered into force May 23, 1953); Discrimination (Employment and Occupation) Convention, Jun. 25, 1958, 362 U.N.T.S. 31 (entered into force Jun. 15, 1960); and Convention Concerning Equal Opportunities and Equal Treatment for Men and Women Workers: Workers with Family Responsibilities, Jun. 23, 1981, 1331 U.N.T.S. 295 (entered into force Aug. 11, 1983).

[45] Convention on the Elimination of All Forms of Discrimination Against Women, *Preamble*, Dec. 18, 1979, 1249 U.N.T.S. 13 (entered into force Sept. 3, 1981) [hereinafter, *CEDAW*].

[46] *Introduction to Convention on the Elimination of All Forms of Discrimination against Women, New York 18 December 1979*, United Nations Office of the High Commissioner, https://www.ohchr.org/EN/ProfessionalInterest/Pages/CEDAW.aspx.

[47] *CEDAW*, *supra* note 45, at Article 2(e).

[48] *Id.* at Article 5(a).

[49] *Id.* at Article11(1).

[50] *Id.* at Article 11(1)(d).

[51] *Id.* at Article 11(1)(f).

[52] *Id.* at Article 11(2)(a).

[53] *Id.* at Article 11(2)(b).

[54] *See Parties to the International Convention on the Elimination of All Forms of Discrimination against Women*, United Nations Treaty Collection, https://web.archive.org/web/20120823144158/http://treaties.un.org/Pages/ViewDetails.aspx?src=TREATY&mtdsg_no=IV-8&chapter=4&lang=en (last viewed Nov. 17, 2020). It should be noted that the US has signed but not ratified CEDAW.

treaty's implementation provides General Recommendations that offer interpretive guidance. Although the General Recommendations are not binding, they are persuasive.

In its General Recommendation 28, the CEDAW Committee noted:

> Article 2 is not limited to the prohibition of discrimination against women caused directly or indirectly by States parties. Article 2 also imposes a due diligence obligation on States parties to prevent discrimination by private actors. In some cases, a private actor's acts or omission of acts may be attributed to the State under international law. States parties are thus obliged to ensure that private actors do not engage in discrimination against women as defined in the Convention.[55]

Moreover, the CEDAW Committee could not have been clearer on what it perceives to be gender-based discrimination when it noted:

> Although the Convention only refers to sex-based discrimination, interpreting article 1 together with articles 2(f) and 5(a) indicates that the Convention covers gender-based discrimination against women. . . . This definition points out that *any distinction, exclusion or restriction* which has the effect or purpose of impairing or nullifying the recognition, enjoyment or exercise by women of human rights and fundamental freedoms is discrimination, *even where discrimination was not intended*. This would mean that identical or neutral treatment of women and men might constitute discrimination against women if such treatment resulted in or had the effect of women being denied the exercise of a right because there was no recognition of the pre-existing gender-based disadvantage and inequality that women face.[56] (emphasis added).

Other sources on women's human rights relevant to HRDD by business are the Beijing Declaration and Platform for Action, the 2030 Agenda for Sustainable Development (2030 Agenda), and various ILO treaties and declarations. The Beijing Declaration and Platform for Action, adopted during the Fourth World Conference on Women in September 1995,[57] has been described as "the most comprehensive expression of States' commitments to the human rights of women."[58] The Beijing Declaration states that "[w]omen's rights are human rights" (para. 14) and "[w]omen's empowerment and their full participation on the basis of equality in all spheres of society . . .are fundamental for the achievement of equality,

[55] *Id.* at ¶ 13.

[56] Committee on the Elimination of Discrimination Against Women, *General Recommendation No. 28 on the core obligation of States parties under Article 2 of the Convention on the Elimination of all Forms of Discrimination against Women*, UN Doc. CEDAW/C/CG/28, at ¶ 5 (Dec. 16, 2010), https://undocs.org/CEDAW/C/GC/28.

[57] Fourth World Conference of Women, *Report of the Fourth World Conference on Women, Beijing, 4–15 September 1995*, UN Doc. A/CONF.177/20/Rev.1, chap. I, resolution 1, annexes I and II (Sept. 4–15, 1995) [hereinafter, *Beijing Declaration*].

[58] *Women's Rights are Human Rights*, United Nations Office of the High Commissioner of Human Rights 14, HR/PUB/14/2 (2014), https://www.ohchr.org/Documents/Events/WHRD/WomenRightsAreHR.pdf.

development and peace" (para. 13). In the Platform for Action, businesses are called upon, along with governments and civil society organizations, to take strategic action to eliminate discrimination against women and to achieve gender equality by addressing twelve areas of concern, including the increasing burden of poverty on women, unequal access to education and training, unequal access to health care, violence against women, inequalities in economic structures and policies relating to productive activity and access to resources, and inequalities in decision-making, among others (para. 44).

The 2030 Agenda, adopted by the UN General Assembly in 2015, sets forth an action plan for the international community consisting of 17 Sustainable Development Goals (SDGs) which "seek to realize the human rights of all and to achieve gender equality and the empowerment of all women and girls."[59] The 2030 Agenda "build[s] on the Millennium Development Goals [of 2000] and complete[s] what they did not achieve."[60] SDG 5, "[a]chieve gender equality and empower all women and girls," is operationalized by a series of aspirational targets that include eliminating all forms of discrimination and violence against women and girls, ensuring women's full participation in equal opportunities for leadership, and undertaking reforms to give women equal rights to economic resources including land.[61] The 2030 Agenda contemplates an active role for business in implementing the SDGs, including the goal of achieving gender equality.[62]

The ILO, which has played an important role in establishing fundamental rights in the workplace, developed several binding international conventions that support the principle of gender equality in employment. These include such gender equality principles as equal pay for equal work, nondiscrimination in employment on the basis of sex, equal employment opportunities and treatment for workers with family responsibilities, and support for women's reproductive rights.[63] Most recently, the ILO promulgated a convention focused on ending violence and harassment against women and men in the workplace.[64] Finally the ILO's Tripartite Declaration concerning Multinational Enterprises and Social Policy, which offers nonbinding guidelines to multinational enterprises, governments, and employers' and workers' organizations on workplace issues, not only calls on governments to promote equality and eliminate discrimination, promote equal pay for equal work, and eliminate workplace violence, but also calls on multinational enterprises to follow the principle of nondiscrimination in their business operations.[65]

---

[59] G.A. Res. A/RES/70/1, Preamble, *Transforming our world: the 2030 Agenda for Sustainable Development* (Oct. 21, 2015), https://www.un.org/en/development/desa/population/migration/generalassembly/docs/globalcompact/A_RES_70_1_E.pdf.

[60] *Id.*

[61] *Id.* targets 5.1, 5.2, 5.5, 5.a, at 18.

[62] *Id.* Goal 17 (promoting public private partnerships), at 26–27.

[63] Equal Remuneration Convention, *supra* note 44; Discrimination (Employment and Occupation) Convention, *supra* note 44; Workers with Family Responsibilities Convention, *supra* note 44; Maternity Protection Convention, *supra* note 44; and Maternity Protection Convention, Jun. 15, 2000, 2181 U.N.TS. 253 (entered into force Feb. 7, 2002).

[64] ILO, Violence and Harassment Convention, 2019 (No. 190).

[65] *Tripartite Declaration of Principles Concerning Multinational Enterprises and Social Policy*, The International Labour Organization (2001), https://www.ilo.org/wcmsp5/groups/public/@ed_emp/@emp_ent/documents/publication/wcms_101234.pdf, at ¶¶ 28, 29, 30, 43.

Women's human rights are a part of universal human rights, as outlined in treaties and other international instruments.[66] All businesses are required to respect such rights in line with the UNGPs. States and corporations must "take concrete steps to identify, prevent and remedy gender-based discrimination and inequalities in all areas of life."[67] A review of these rights and the gender impacts of business operations on such rights must be included in all due diligence plans. States and corporations are required to give special attention to women's unique experiences and the structural barriers to equality that they face, in line with international human rights law.[68]

C. The UN Guiding Principles and Gender-Responsive Human Rights Due Diligence

The UNGPs contain only a few references to women and gender-based issues. These references have been grouped by the UN Working Group, which is mandated to "promote the effective and comprehensive dissemination and implementation of the [UNGPs],"[69] into three categories or "gender windows." First, there is the general principle of nondiscrimination, meaning that businesses should implement the UNGPs without discrimination but with "due regard to the different risks that may be faced by women and men."[70] The second window acknowledges the need to integrate a gender perspective based on the situation, for example in conflict-affected areas or where there is a heightened risk of gender-based and sexual violence.[71] The third window highlights the need for business to consider additional standards, such as those outlined in human rights law for the protection of a particular group, including women.[72]

The UN Working Group also outlined comprehensive "gender guidance" for each of the 31 UNGPs,[73] which are all important for a gender-sensitive interpretation of the UNGPs. The following are some examples of the gender guidance, based on the UNGPs that expressly mention women or gender.

---

[66] In addition to the items noted above, there are several regional treaties that may be used to support GR-HRDD including: the African (Banjul) Charter on Human and People's Rights, Jun. 27, 1981, 21 I.L.M. 58 (entered into force Oct. 21, 1986); Protocol to the African Charter on Human and Peoples' Rights on the Rights of Women in Africa (Maputo Protocol), Jun. 27, 1981, 1520 U.N.T.S. 217 (entered into force Oct. 21, 1986); American Convention on Human Rights, Nov. 22, 1969, 1144 U.N.T.S. 123 (entered into force Jul. 18, 1978); European Convention on Human Rights, Nov. 4, 1950, 213 U.N.T.S. 221 (entered into force Sept. 3, 1953); and the SADC Protocol on Gender and Development, Aug. 17, 2008 (entered into force Feb. 22, 2013).

[67] *Gender Dimensions Report*, *supra* note 13, at 2.

[68] *Gender Lens to the UNGPs*, United Nations Office of the High Commissioner For Human Rights, https://www.ohchr.org/EN/Issues/Business/Pages/GenderLens.aspx [hereinafter, *Gender Lens*].

[69] Working Group on the Issue of Human Rights and Transnational Corporations and Other Business Enterprises, Overview, United Nations Office of the High Commissioner for Human Rights, https://www.ohchr.org/en/issues/business/pages/wghrandtransnationalcorporationsandotherbusiness.aspx.

[70] *Gender Dimensions Report*, *supra* note 13, at 9.

[71] *Id.*

[72] *Id.*

[73] *Id.* at Annex, p. 14.

UNGPs Principle 3 sets out what States should do to meet their duty to protect human rights. One of the primary difficulties is that States are failing to pass laws, or passing inconsistent or inadequate laws to protect women, and failing to enforce the laws they do have.[74] The Commentary to UNGPs Principle 3 notes that States' "[g]uidance to business enterprises on respecting human rights should indicate expected outcomes and help share best practices. It should advise on appropriate methods, including human rights due diligence, and how to consider effectively issues of gender, vulnerability and/or marginalization. . . ."[75] The gender guidance notes, in relation to UNGPs Principle 3, that both the "direct and indirect discriminatory effects" of laws and policies must be addressed by States, citing women's participation in the drafting or revision of laws that promote and ensure respect for human rights by businesses.[76]

UNGPs Principle 7 addresses the risk of gross human rights violations in conflict-affected areas. It calls on States to support businesses as they "assess and address the heightened risks of abuses, paying special attention to both gender-based and sexual violence."[77] The gender guidance suggests that women should also participate in peacebuilding efforts, including partnerships that work to change discriminatory social norms.[78]

UNGPs Principle 12 outlines the need for businesses to respect internationally recognized human rights, including those in the International Bill of Human Rights and the ILO's Declaration on Fundamental Principles and Rights at Work.[79] However, depending on circumstances, business enterprises may need to consider additional standards. The gender guidance notes that the rights outlined in CEDAW should be considered throughout a business's operations, and that gender policies should be integrated across all departments.[80]

UNGPs Principle 18 notes that businesses should assess actual or potential human rights impacts that may result from their operations. The Commentary to UNGPs Principle 18 requires that an assessment be done of proposed business activities to identify "who may be affected."[81] Women are often adversely affected by business operations, but those effects are not always considered when a new business endeavor is being proposed. Moreover, the effects of a business operation could be different on men and women. The gender guidance suggests using gender experts or consulting with affected women or women's organizations, including human rights defenders, to properly identify any harm to women.[82]

These are just a few examples of ways that the gender guidance can be used to help businesses comply with business and human rights due diligence responsibilities. However, "most States and business enterprises still pay little or inadequate attention to the diverse

[74] *Working Group Report*, *supra* note 1, at 9–10.

[75] *Guiding Principles*, *supra* note 4, Commentary to UNGP 3, at 5.

[76] *Gender Dimensions Report*, *supra* note 13, at 15.

[77] *Guiding Principles*, *supra* note 4, UNGP 7, at 9.

[78] *Gender Dimensions Report*, *supra* note 13, at 16.

[79] *Guiding Principles*, *supra* note 4, UNGP 12, at 13.

[80] *Gender Dimensions Report*, *supra* note 13, at 19.

[81] *Guiding Principles*, *supra* note 4, Commentary to UNGP 18, at 19.

[82] *Gender Dimensions Report*, *supra* note 13, at 21.

experiences of women in implementing their respective duties and responsibilities under the Guiding Principles."[83] Gender can no longer be ignored. The gender guidance provides information and real examples of how gender can be properly integrated into HRDD.

III. Voluntary Standards

Under the UNGPs, while States have the primary responsibility to protect human rights, businesses also have an independent responsibility to respect human rights, which includes adopting "a human rights due diligence process to identify, prevent, mitigate and account for how they address their impacts on human rights."[84] HRDD is an ongoing risk management process that businesses should follow in identifying, preventing, mitigating, and accounting for their efforts to address adverse human rights impacts caused by their operations. The four steps set forth in the UNGPs for HRDD consist of (1) identifying and assessing actual and potential human rights impacts of business activities, (2) integrating the findings of such impact assessment phase in business operations and initiating appropriate action to address the findings, (3) tracking the effectiveness of such responses, and (4) communicating externally about how adverse human rights impacts are addressed.[85]

Although the UNGPs include commentary for each principle, such guidance on the four steps in HRDD is general and does not outline or provide a framework for the particular steps that businesses should follow in undertaking HRDD.[86] The UNGPs also do not provide guidance on the process that should be used to integrate gender into HRDD, although the UNGPs do recognize that women are especially vulnerable to human rights abuses, may suffer different risks than those faced by men, and are susceptible to both gender-based and sexual violence, particularly in conflict-affected areas.[87] The UNGPs also recommend the use of additional human rights standards that address the adverse human rights impacts on women and other marginalized groups and the use of sex-disaggregated data in implementing the UNGPs, but do not elaborate on these points.[88]

Thus, the topic of GR-HRDD is still in its infancy. While there are no legally binding standards in this area, there is some voluntary guidance currently available on the processes that companies should follow in conducting GR-HRDD. The UN Working Group and the Organisation for Economic Co-operation and Development (OECD) have suggested some steps that should be followed to address gender issues in conducting HRDD. Other intergovernmental organizations and civil society organizations have developed guidelines and analytical tools for incorporating a gender perspective into business that can be used as a

---

[83] *Id.* at 12.

[84] *Id.*; *Guiding Principles, supra* note 4, UNGP Section 15(b), at 16.

[85] *Guiding Principles, supra* note 4, UNGP Sections 18–21, at 19–23.

[86] Additional guidance is provided in the Interpretive Guide to the UNGPs. However, such guidance is still somewhat general in nature. *See The Corporate Responsibility to Respect Human Rights: An Interpretive Guide*, UNITED NATIONS OFFICE OF THE HIGH COMMISSIONER FOR HUMAN RIGHTS, HR/PUB/12/02 (2012), https://www.ohchr.org/sites/default/files/Documents/Issues/Business/RtRInterpretativeGuide.pdf.

[87] *Guiding Principles, supra* note 4, UNGPs Sections 3, 7, 18, at 4–19.

[88] *Guiding Principles, supra* note 4, UNGPs Sections 13, 20, at 14, 22.

basis for GR-HRDD. These guidelines and tools, discussed below, provide examples of good practices, which are presented in Section IV.

A. Guidance on Conducting Gender-Responsive Human Rights Due Diligence under the UN Guiding Principles

1. UN Working Group–Report on Gender Dimensions of the Guiding Principles on Business and Human Rights

As noted above, the UN Working Group has issued guidance on the gender dimensions of the UNGPs as part of its mandate to integrate a gender perspective throughout its work on implementing the UNGPs.[89] The UN Working Group's 2019 report titled *Gender Dimensions of the Guiding Principles on Business and Human Rights* (Gender Dimensions Report) is part of its "gender lens to the UNGPs" project.[90] The Gender Dimensions Report identifies gender-differentiated impacts and discrimination involving women in the context of business, develops a three-step gender framework for the UNGPs, and provides specific guidance on application of the gender framework to the 31 principles of the UNGPs, including UNGPs 18 through 21, which outline the steps in the HRDD process.[91] It is the stated goal of the Gender Dimensions Report "to provide guidance to States and businesses on integrating a gender perspective in implementing the Guiding Principles" as well as "to raise awareness about the need for gender integration in the business and human rights field" and "to highlight good practices of gender integration implemented by States and businesses."[92]

The Gender Dimensions Report defines "gender" as "socially constructed roles of and power relations among men, women, and gender nonbinary persons, all of whom may be affected differently by business activities."[93] Although the Gender Dimensions Report focuses on women, the authors state that all references to "women" should be understood to include girls as well as transgender and intersex women.[94] They also note that attention should be paid to issues of intersectionality.[95] The guidance in the Gender Dimensions Report applies to all States and to all businesses, but it states that specific guidance for different types of businesses and for businesses operating in particular industries should be developed.[96]

The Gender Dimensions Report's gender framework is based on the UNGPs' references to gender and women as well as to international standards concerning women's rights.[97]

---

[89] This mandate is contained in UN Human Rights Council Res. 17/4, UN Doc. A/HR/RES/17/4, at 3 (Jul. 6, 2011); Working Group on the Issue of Human Rights and Transnational Corporations and Other Business Enterprises, *supra* note 69.

[90] *Gender Lens, supra* note 68.

[91] *Gender Dimensions Report, supra* note 13.

[92] *Id.* at 3.

[93] *Id.*

[94] *Id.* at 1, 3.

[95] *Id.* at 1.

[96] *Id.* at 4.

[97] *Id.* at 9–10.

The three-step framework consists of three pillars, namely (1) gender-responsive assessment, (2) gender-transformative measures, and (3) gender-transformative remedies. The Gender Dimensions Report states that a gender-responsive assessment will "respond to differentiated, intersectional and disproportionate adverse impacts on women's human rights as well as to discriminatory norms and patriarchal power structures."[98] Gender-transformative measures and gender-transformative remedies will be "capable of bringing change to patriarchal norms and unequal power relations that underpin discrimination, gender-based violence and gender stereotyping."[99]

For each of the three steps in the gender framework, the Gender Dimensions Report provides a series of specific actions that businesses can take in implementing the UNGPs.[100] As discussed in Section II, more specific guidance is provided in the form of an annex to the report in which the authors have applied the gender framework to propose gender guidance addressing each of the 31 UNGPs.[101] The application of the gender framework to UNGPs 18 through 21 covering the HRDD process is helpful to an understanding of how businesses should conduct their due diligence process because the authors provide several examples of best practices and illustrative actions that can be taken in conducting GR-HRDD.

2. *OECD – Due Diligence Guidance for Responsible Business Conduct; Sector-Specific Due Diligence Guidance for Garment and Footwear, Agricultural, and Mineral Sectors*

The OECD updated its *Guidelines for Multinational Enterprises* (OECD Guidelines) in 2011 to reflect changes in the business environment for international investment and multinational enterprises since the last update in 2000.[102] The OECD Guidelines are "non-binding principles and standards for responsible business conduct in a global context consistent with applicable laws and internationally recognized standards."[103] The update included the addition of a new chapter on the human rights responsibilities of multinational enterprises, which is consistent with the UNGPs. The OECD Guidelines contain only three brief references to the responsibility to respect women's human rights.[104] Although the OECD Guidelines recommend that enterprises carry out HRDD and describe a HRDD process that is aligned with the UNGPs, there is no reference to GR-HRDD.[105]

---

98 *Id.* at 10.

99 *Id.*

100 *Id.* at 11.

101 *Id.* Annex to *Gender Dimensions Report*, at 14–26.

102 *OECD Guidelines for Multinational Enterprises*, OECD Publishing 3 (2011), https://www.oecd.org/daf/inv/mne/48004323.pdf.

103 *Id.*

104 Such references are contained in the sections on human rights and employment and industrial relations. *Id.* at 32, 39, 41.

105 *Id.* at 34.

The OECD provided useful guidance on HRDD in the 2018 *OECD Due Diligence Guidance for Responsible Business Conduct* (OECD Guidance).[106] The purpose of the OECD Guidance is to help businesses "to understand and implement due diligence for RBC [responsible business conduct]" as well as "to promote a common understanding amongst governments and stakeholders on due diligence for RBC."[107] The OECD Guidance contains a six-step process for conducting HRDD, consisting of the following: (1) embed responsible business conduct into policies and management systems, (2) identify and assess adverse impacts in operations, supply chains, and business relationships, (3) cease, prevent or mitigate adverse impacts, (4) track implementation and results, (5) communicate how impacts are addressed, and (6) provide for or cooperate in remediation when appropriate.[108]

The OECD Guidance recognizes that, in assessing human rights impacts, businesses should pay special attention to vulnerable and marginalized groups such as women, and recommends taking into account how specific risks affect different groups, such as by applying a gender perspective to due diligence.[109] In a separate section entitled "How can an enterprise integrate gender issues into its due diligence?" the OECD Guidance provides examples of how real or potential adverse impacts may be specific to women or impact them differently. Such adverse impacts may arise in situations where women face severe discrimination, where the business activities significantly affect the local economy, environment, and access to land and livelihoods, in conflict and post-conflict areas, and in sectors and global supply chains that employ large numbers of women (such as apparel, electronics, tourism, health and social care, domestic work, agriculture, and cut flowers).[110]

The OECD Guidance suggests good practices for GR-HRDD, including the following: (1) collect and use sex-disaggregated data; (2) implement gender-sensitive and gender-responsive policies to address adverse impacts; (3) identify intersectionality issues affecting women; (4) support women's equal participation in consultations and negotiations; (5) examine whether women are compensated equitably; (6) create separate and safe spaces for women to express opinions on business decisions; (7) identify gender-specific trends and patterns and adverse impacts; and (8) assess whether grievance mechanisms are gender-sensitive.[111] More detailed guidance on such good practices linked to the OECD HRDD process has been developed by nongovernmental organizations focused on women's rights. An example is the publication titled *Gender-Responsive Human Rights Due Diligence Tool* (GR-HRDD Tool) developed by Plan International Netherlands and Girls Advocacy Alliance, which is organized around the six steps of HRDD spelled out in the OECD Guidance and

---

[106] *OECD Due Diligence Guidance for Responsible Business Conduct*, OECD (2018), http://mneguidelines.oecd.org/OECD-Due-Diligence-Guidance-for-Responsible-Business-Conduct.pdf [hereinafter, *OECD Guidance*].

[107] *Id.* at 9.

[108] *Id.* at 21.

[109] *Id.* at 41.

[110] *Id.*

[111] *Id.* at 41–42.

provides practical guidance for planning, implementing, and monitoring GR-HRDD.[112] The GR-HRDD Tool focuses on nine human rights principles that businesses can directly influence, namely nondiscrimination in recruitment, employment and training; fair wages and benefits at living wage level; reasonable work hours at decent conditions; no forced labor; lack of sexual harassment and abuse; safe and healthy work environments and access to basic needs and services; respect for freedom of association and the right to collective bargaining; legally binding employment relationships with clear contracts and conditions; and respect for property rights of women, including land ownership and access to natural resources.[113]

The OECD has also published sector-specific guidance on due diligence practice, some of which addresses how women's human rights may be disproportionately impacted by business operations. Such guidance includes sectors that employ large numbers of women including the garment and footwear, agricultural, and mineral sectors. The 2017 *OECD Due Diligence Guidance for Responsible Supply Chains in the Garment and Footwear Sector* and the 2016 *OECD-FAO Guidance for Responsible Agricultural Supply Chains* both address the need for businesses to identify and take action on particular risks faced by women, including sexual harassment and discrimination in labor practices.[114] The 2016 *OECD Due Diligence Guidance for Responsible Supply Chains of Minerals from Conflict-Affected and High-Risk Areas* provides a HRDD framework that businesses involved in mining and trade in minerals in conflict and high-risk areas can use to identify and address human rights abuses, including those impacting women, such as sexual violence.[115] Finally, the 2017 *OECD Due Diligence Guidance on Meaningful Stakeholder Engagement in the Extractive Sector* provides guidance on engaging with women as part of the due diligence process, including understanding the context of engagement, prioritizing engagement with impacted women, designing appropriate processes for engagement, and monitoring and evaluating such inclusive engagement.[116]

---

[112] *A Gender-Responsive Human Rights Due Diligence Tool*, Plan International Netherlands and Girls Advocacy Alliance 36 (2020), https://www.planinternational.nl/uploaded/2021/03/GAA-Report-GRDD-Part-1-ONLINE_DEF.pdf [hereinafter, *GR-HRDD Tool*]. *See also Women Win and Plan International Netherlands*, Gender-Responsive Due Diligence Platform, https://www.genderduediligence.org/.

[113] *GR-HRDD Tool*, *supra* note 112, at 10.

[114] *OECD Due Diligence Guidance for Responsible Supply Chains in the Garment and Footwear Sector: Module 2 on Sexual Harassment and Sex and Gender-Based Violence in the Workplace*, OECD 116–125 (2017), https://www.oecd.org/daf/inv/mne/Due-Diligence-Guidance-Responsible-Supply-Chains-Textiles-Footwear.pdf; *OECD-FAO Guidance for Responsible Agricultural Supply Chains*, OECD/FAO 26, 56 (2016), https://www.oecd-ilibrary.org/docserver/9789264251052-en.pdf?expires=1625008427&id=id&accname=guest&checksum=E852EE44062BE2730DD0668F221914D9.

[115] *OECD Due Diligence Guidance for Responsible Supply Chains of Minerals from Conflict-Affected and High-Risk Areas: Third Edition*, OECD 17–24 (Annex I, Annex II) (2016), https://www.oecd.org/daf/inv/mne/OECD-Due-Diligence-Guidance-Minerals-Edition3.pdf.

[116] *OECD Due Diligence Guidance for Meaningful Stakeholder Engagement in the Extractive Sector*, OECD 81–83 (Annex C) (2017), https://www.oecd.org/daf/inv/mne/OECD-Guidance-Extractives-Sector-Stakeholder-Engagement.pdf.

B. Guidance on Incorporating a Gender-Sensitive Perspective into Business Operations

1. *UN Women and the UN Global Compact – Women's Empowerment Principles*

UN Women, the UN entity dedicated to gender equality and the empowerment of women, launched a partnership with the UN Global Compact Office in March 2010 to "provide a holistic framework for companies to promote gender equality and women's empowerment in the workplace, marketplace and community and drive positive outcomes for society and business."[117] Such guidance, titled *Women's Empowerment Principles – Equality Means Business* (3rd ed., 2021) (WEPs), is "informed by international labour and human rights standards and grounded in the recognition that businesses have a stake in, and a responsibility for, gender equality and women's empowerment."[118]

The WEPs are "a primary vehicle for corporate delivery on gender equality dimensions of the 2030 Agenda on Sustainable Development and the [United Nations] Sustainable Development Goals."[119] The WEPs point out that "[g]ender equality and women's empowerment are at the center of this global agenda," building on internationally agreed principles embodied in the 1995 UN Beijing Declaration and Platform for Action and in gender equality conventions.[120]

Companies of any size and industry, including state-owned enterprises and cooperatives, along with industry associations and chambers of commerce, are invited to join the WEPs community.[121] They are encouraged to follow a multi-step process that includes considering a commitment, signing on as a member of the WEPs community, conducting a self-assessment, engaging with other companies to develop good practices, tracking progress towards gender equality and women's empowerment through use of key performance indicators, and voluntarily reporting on such progress.[122] As of March 1, 2021, over 5,000 companies in 141 countries have committed to implementing the WEPs.[123]

Companies who sign on to the WEPs voluntarily agree to adopt transparency and accountability measures, as well as to track progress towards gender equality and women's

---

[117] *Women's Empowerment Principles - Equality Means Business: Third Edition*, UN Women and UN Global Compact Office 7 (2021), https://www.weps.org/sites/default/files/2021-05/WEPS_BROCHURE.pdf [hereinafter, *WEPs*]. The UN Global Compact is "a strategic policy initiative for businesses that are committed to aligning their operations and strategies with ten universally accepted principles in the areas of human rights, labour, environment and anticorruption." *The UN Global Compact and the OECD Guidelines for Multinational Enterprises: Complementarity and Distinctions*, UN Global Compact Office and the OECD Secretariat (Dec. 2012), https://www.oecd.org/corporate/mne/34873731.pdf.

[118] *Id.*

[119] *Id. See also Transforming Our World: The 2030 Agenda for Sustainable Development*, United Nations Department of Economic and Social Development, https://sdgs.un.org/2030agenda.

[120] *WEPs, supra* note 117, at 17.

[121] *Id.* at 15.

[122] *Id.* at 9.

[123] *Id.*

empowerment.[124] Such companies are encouraged to implement policies of equal pay, equal opportunity for career advancement, paid parental leave, and zero tolerance for sexual harassment in the workplace, among others.[125]

More specifically, the WEPs consist of seven principles containing 34 action steps that businesses can take to promote gender equality, which can be summarized as follows: Principle (1), which states "establish high-level corporate leadership for gender equality," includes obtaining top-level commitments to gender equality and human rights, developing corporate policies and company-wide targets to achieve gender equality, consulting relevant stakeholders in formulating and implementing such goals, measuring progress and holding managers accountable for results, and eliminating discrimination against women in governance structures.[126] Principle (2), which states "treat all women and men fairly at work," includes providing equal pay and benefits, eliminating gender-based discrimination from workplace policies and practices including recruitment and retention of employees, appointing women to management positions and the board of directors, and putting in place family-friendly policies such as flexible work arrangements and access to child care.[127] Principle (3), which states "ensure the health, safety and well-being of all women and men workers," includes implementing policies to address the risk of workplace violence and sexual harassment (including a grievance mechanism), ensuring safe working conditions, and offering health insurance and allowing employees time off for medical appointments.[128] Principle (4), which states "promote education, training and professional development for women," includes establishing policies and programs to advance women and to encourage them to enter nontraditional job fields, ensuring equal access to company-provided education and training programs, providing networking and mentoring opportunities for women, and communicating the company's gender equality goals.[129] Principle (5), which states "implement enterprise development, supply chain and marketing practices that empower women," includes developing new business relationships with women-owned companies such as through a diversity supplier policy, requiring suppliers and other business partners to commit to gender equality practices, eliminating gender stereotyping from company marketing materials, and taking steps to avoid involvement in human trafficking or other exploitation through use of companies' products, services, or assets.[130] Principle (6), which states "promote equality through community initiatives and advocacy," includes conducting local outreach on gender equality and women's leadership through consultations, collaborations, and advocacy involving stakeholders, community leaders, and business partners, as well as

---

124 *Id.* at 15.

125 *Id.* at 13.

126 *Id.* at 28.

127 *Id.* at 30.

128 *Id.* at 33.

129 *Id.* at 36.

130 *Id.* at 39.

providing financial support for related community initiatives.[131] Principle (7), which states "measure and publicly report on progress to achieve gender equality," includes publicizing the company's policies and implementation plan for promoting gender equality, and measuring and reporting on progress using sex-disaggregated data and benchmarking.[132]

In addition to providing descriptions of the principles, the WEPs provide case studies entitled "WEPS Signatories in Action", which are examples of signatories' implementation of each of the seven principles.[133] These are drawn from a large collection of such examples submitted by companies and contained in a separate 2015 publication titled *Companies Leading the Way: Putting the Principles into Practice.*[134]

Finally, for each of the seven principles, the WEPs provide specific strategies that can be used to make and measure progress under the headings "How to Be Transparent."[135] These strategies are, in essence, assessment tools that are matched with a measurement framework. The WEPs note that such assessment tools must be derived from company-specific cultures and objectives, and the routes to achieving gender equality are diverse.[136]

2. *UN Women and the UN Global Compact – Women's Empowerment Principles Gender Gap Analysis Tool; Women's Empowerment Principles Transparency and Accountability Framework*

The WEPs provide a series of resources intended to assist signatories in assessing, implementing, tracking, and reporting on their progress on the seven principles. One such resource is the WEPs *Gender Gap Analysis Tool* (updated February 22, 2021) (WEPs Analysis Tool), which is an online self-assessment questionnaire for use in evaluating a company's policies and programs on gender equality across business functions, using such information to identify areas for needed improvement, and then setting future goals and targets.[137] The WEPs Analysis Tool asks questions in the areas of commitment, implementation, measurement, and transparency, which can be used as a framework for a company's development of an action plan.[138] The WEPs Analysis Tool has been described as translating "general principles on gender equality into indicators that could help frame gender-responsive HRDD."[139]

---

[131] *Id.* at 42.

[132] *Id.* at 45.

[133] *Id.* at 29, 31–32, 34–35, 37–38, 40–41, 43–44.

[134] *Companies Leading the Way: Putting the Principles into Practice*, UN Women & UN Global Compact Office (updated Sept. 2015), https://d306pr3pise04h.cloudfront.net/docs/issues_doc%2Fdevelopment%2FCompanies_Leading_the_Way_25_September_2015.pdf.

[135] *WEPs*, *supra* note 117, at 28, 30, 33, 36, 39, 42.

[136] *Women's Empowerment Principles – Equality Means Business: Second Edition*, UN Women & UN Global Compact Office 8–9 (2011), https://www.unwomen.org/sites/default/files/Headquarters/Attachments/Sections/Library/Publications/2011/10/Women-s-Empowerment-Principles_en%20pdf.pdf.

[137] *WEPs*, *supra* note 117, at 48. The WEPs Gender Gap Analysis Tool was last updated on Feb. 22, 2021, and is available at https://weps-gapanalysis.org/.

[138] *Id.*

[139] Joanna Bourke Martignoni & Elizabeth Umlas, *Gender-Responsive Due Diligence for Business Actors: Human Rights-Based Approaches*, University Of Geneva/Graduate Institute Geneva Academy of International

Another resource is the 2021 publication titled *WEPs Transparency and Accountability Framework: Creating Transparency on Gender Equality to Transform Business* (WEPs Framework), which can be used to measure progress on gender equality and women's empowerment and then report on such progress.[140] The WEPs Framework is organized around four categories of indicators covering such matters as the percentage of women and men employees, senior managers, and board members; ratio of women's to men's pay; percentage of women and men that are new hires, have received promotions, and are retained after taking parental leave; and the existence of mechanisms to respond to violence and harassment.[141] Signatories are encouraged to voluntarily report on their progress to the WEPs Secretariat for internal use only or to the public by placing the information on a WEPs Company Profile page.[142]

3. *UN Development Programme – Gender Equality Seal Certification Program for Public and Private Enterprises*

The UN Development Programme (UNDP) has sponsored the Gender Equality Seal Certification Program for Public and Private Enterprises (GES Program) in an effort to encourage the private sector to promote gender equality and women's empowerment in the business world and to contribute to the achievement of the SDGs Goal 5 (gender equality), Goal 8 (decent work and economic growth), Goal 10 (reduced inequalities), and Goal 17 (partnerships for the goals).[143] Originally piloted in Latin America starting in 2009, the GES Program has expanded to 14 countries in that region and in the Caribbean, with over 600 companies with more than 1,900 branches and business units having received the certification.[144] Since 2016, the GES Program has been expanded to include additional countries in Africa, the Asia-Pacific region, Eastern Europe and the Commonwealth of Independent States (CIS), and the Arab States, and the UNDP's Gender Equality Strategy for 2018-2021 calls for a further scaling up of the GES Program.[145]

The GES Program consists of both national certification programs developed with national governments and a certification program for multinational companies with regional operations or located in countries without a national certification program.[146] Both types

---

HUMANITARIAN LAW AND HUMAN RIGHTS 24 (2018), https://www.geneva-academy.ch/joomlatools-files/docman-files/Academy%20Briefing%2012-interactif-V3.pdf.

[140] *WEPs*, *supra* note 117, at 58; *WEPs Transparency and Accountability Framework: Creating Transparency on Gender Equality to Transform Business*, UN WOMEN & UN GLOBAL COMPACT OFFICE (2021), https://asiapacific.unwomen.org/en/digital-library/publications/2021/03/creating-transparency-on-gender-equality-to-transform-business.

[141] *Id.* at 62.

[142] *Id.*

[143] *The Gender Equality Seal Programme*, UNDP, https://www.genderequalityseal.org/programme; *UNDP Gender Equality Strategy for 2018-2021*, UNDP (2018), https://www.undp.org/publications/undp-gender-equality-strategy-2018-2021; *UN Sustainable Development Goals*, UNITED NATIONS DEPARTMENT OF ECONOMIC AND SOCIAL AFFAIRS, https://sdgs.un.org/goals.

[144] *The Gender Equality Seal Programme*, *supra* note 143.

[145] *Id.*

[146] *Id.*

of programs are voluntary and are based on a Gender Equality Management System implemented by companies through a multi-step process involving (1) adopting a written gender equality policy, (2) establishing a gender equality committee, (3) training employees at all levels on gender equality, (4) conducting an internal organizational self-assessment of policies and practices, (5) developing a company policy and action plan for gender equality, (6) implementing the policy and action plan, (7) conducting a third party audit to verify compliance with the plan, (8) receiving a Gender Equality Seal at the Bronze, Silver, or Gold level, (9) monitoring progress towards gender equality, and (10) taking action to improve and maintain the Gender Equality Seal.[147]

The stated aim of the GES Program is to encourage companies to develop and implement gender equality policies that include eliminating gender wage gaps, advancing women in leadership positions, improving work-life balance of employees, increasing women's presence in male-dominated jobs, eliminating sexual harassment in the workplace, adopting inclusive language in corporate communications, and promoting women in business and along value chains.[148] In order to develop such policies, companies should first follow step 4 above by completing a self-assessment to determine their level of gender equality. This can be done by using a digital tool called the Equality@Work Online Platform that "gathers quantitative and qualitative data and collects an opinion survey, producing a set of [key performance indicators] to measure gender gaps and calculate a Gender Equality Index (GEI) that measures the degree of equality of an organization."[149] The GEI is expressed as a percentage, with 100 percent indicating gender equality.[150] The key performance indicators in this digital tool appear designed to detect and track the gender gaps in companies' policies mentioned above that the GES Program aims to address. Although the key performance indicators used in the self-assessment are not specifically linked to detecting and preventing human rights abuses, several of the categories do touch on categories of women's human rights, such as discrimination in employment and sexual harassment in the workplace. To that extent, the GES Program and its multi-step process can be helpful to companies in determining where potential human rights violations may arise in their business operations and are therefore relevant to the identification and assessment phase of HRDD. In addition, steps 5 and 6 are relevant to the phase of HRDD that consists of addressing adverse human rights impacts, while steps 7 and 9 are relevant to the phase of HRDD that involves tracking the effectiveness of such company responses.

4. EDGE Certification

Another gender equality certification program for business was developed by the Economic Dividends for Gender Equality (EDGE) Certification Foundation, originally founded as the

---

147 *Id.* The Bronze Seal symbolizes a commitment to close gender gaps and to promote gender equality. The Silver Seal symbolizes that actions to close gender gaps have been implemented effectively. The Gold Seal symbolizes that gender gaps have been effectively closed.

148 *Id.*

149 *Id.*

150 *Equality@Work Online Platform*, UNDP, https://www.genderequalityseal.org/equalityatwork/.

Gender Equality Project.[151] The EDGE Certification, which was launched at the Davos World Economic Forum in 2011, consists of an online tool that businesses can use to assess and track gender equality within their organizations.[152] Upon completion of the online assessment and an audit by an independent third-party, businesses receive certification at one of three levels, namely assess, move, and lead, with each higher level representing a progressively increasing commitment to gender equality.[153]

C. Guidance on Gender-Sensitive Issues in Specific Areas of Concern

UN agencies, nongovernmental organizations, and other organizations focused on business and human rights have developed additional guidelines and frameworks addressing particular areas of concern for women, including workers' rights in supply chains, workplace health, and land tenure. Some prominent examples are discussed in this Section III.C. because such advice may be relevant for businesses seeking to address these issues in their HRDD processes.

1. BSR – Making Women Workers Count: A Framework for Conducting Gender-Responsive Due Diligence in Supply Chains; Gender Equality in Codes of Conduct Guidance; Gender Equality in Social Auditing Guidance

BSR, a global organization that consults with the world's leading companies on sustainable business practices, has developed detailed guidance for GR-HRDD in supply chains that is based on the gender framework in the Gender Dimensions Report and is titled *Making Women Workers Count: A Framework for Conducting Gender-Responsive Due Diligence in Supply Chains* (BSR Framework).[154] The BSR Framework states that the Gender Dimensions Report holds brands responsible for requiring their suppliers to respect women's human rights and to track their actions to do so.[155] The purpose of the BSR Framework is to provide recommendations to both brands and suppliers on how best to conduct GR-HRDD along all four phases, namely "phase 1, assess and analyze; phase 2, integrate and act; phase 3, track; and phase 4, communicate."[156]

The BSR Framework notes that the lack of reliable data on women and global supply chains and the barriers women face has led to companies adopting policies that fail to benefit

[151] *About Us*, EDGE, https://edge-cert.org/about-us/.

[152] *Id.*

[153] *What is EDGE Certification?* EDGE, https://edge-cert.org/certifications/. As of June 30, 2021, there are 200 businesses from 44 countries representing 29 different industry sectors that are EDGE certified. EDGE, Home, https://edge-cert.org.

[154] *Making Women Workers Count: A Framework for Conducting Gender-Responsive Due Diligence in Supply Chains*, BSR (2019), https://www.bsr.org/reports/BSR_Gender_Data_Impact_Framework_Report.pdf [hereinafter, *BSR Framework*].

[155] *Id.* at 5.

[156] *Id.* at 5.

women equally with men and may negatively harm women in some instances.[157] The reason is that many brands and suppliers are not familiar with the use of gender data and may lack the systems required for collection and analysis of such data.[158]

For this reason, the BSR Framework places heavy emphasis on use of gender-disaggregated data and introduces the Gender Data and Impact Tool (GDI Tool) as a component of phase 1 of GR-HRDD. The GDI Tool is designed to enable brands to determine the type of data that should be collected by suppliers to assess gendered impacts, the manner of collecting such data, the analysis of the data and identification of root causes of gendered impacts, and understanding the supplier practices and conditions that would lead to gender equality in the workplace.[159] The GDI Tool consists of three steps: (1) collection of gender-disaggregated data, (2) analysis of gender data, and (3) development of an action plan based on the results.[160] The GDI Tool uses two categories of key performance indicators, with the first category comprised of workforce indicators providing a profile of the gender composition of the workforce and its performance on such measures as absenteeism, turnover, and productivity, and the second category comprised of worker impact indicators providing information on women's agency, health and safety, economic opportunity, leadership opportunities, violence and harassment, and sexual and reproductive health and rights and unpaid care.[161]

The GDI Tool is only one component of the guidance on conducting GR-HRDD that the BSR Framework provides. Other components of phase 1 (assess and analyze) include reviewing brand sourcing practices that may negatively impact women by creating adverse working conditions and reviewing country-specific context and risks for female workers.[162] Phase 2 (integrate and act) recommends steps for brands and suppliers to prioritize the most pressing issues impacting women based on the data collected in phase 1, defining adequate measures to remedy negative impacts and setting measurable targets, and implementing internal processes and systems to track progress towards such goals.[163] Phase 3 (track) covers guidance on tracking progress against worker outcomes and achievement of targets set in phase 2.[164] Phase 4 (communicate) suggests ways that brands and suppliers can communicate their efforts to promote gender equality in the workplace both internally and externally and also recommends aligning communications about the GDI Tool indicators with the WEPs and the SDGs when communicating with stakeholders.[165]

BSR has published additional guidance on gender equality issues in the business context. Two such publications are directly relevant to the issue of GR-HRDD. In a 2017 publication titled *Gender Equality in Codes of Conduct Guidance*, the authors provide a "gender-sensitive

[157] *Id.* at 6.

[158] *Id.* at 5.

[159] *Id.* at 28.

[160] *Id.* at 30.

[161] *Id.* at 31 (Tables 1.3 and 1.4).

[162] *Id.* at 20–28.

[163] *Id.* at 62–68.

[164] *Id.* at 70, 72.

[165] *Id.* at 74–81.

analysis of codes of conduct principles - with the primary focus on women" and recommend changes to existing corporate codes of conduct to promote gender equality in the workplace.[166] The guidance notes that although corporate codes of conduct have been viewed as an important tool to eliminate poor employment practices in supply chains by providing a framework for implementation of good working conditions, gender and women's rights are not addressed comprehensively.[167] Recommendations to remedy this situation cover proposed changes and additions to clauses in corporate codes of conduct addressing workplace discrimination, equal pay and family-friendly benefits, forced labor, overtime pay, harassment and abuse, health and safety, and freedom of association and collective bargaining, among other issues.[168]

Another BSR publication from 2018 dealing with a related topic is titled *Gender Equality in Social Auditing Guidance* and provides recommendations on integrating gender considerations into such audits, which are integrally linked to corporate codes of conduct as a way to assess compliance.[169] Traditionally, however, social audits have focused on issues that can be verified through documentation checks and have been unsuccessful at uncovering less visible social issues pertaining to women's rights, including freedom of association, discrimination, and sexual harassment.[170] The guidance suggests methods for conducting gender-sensitive audits, such as by checking company policies and conducting worker interviews.[171]

2. *Ethical Trading Initiative – Gender and the Base Code; Gender and Human Rights Due Diligence*

The Ethical Trading Initiative (ETI), an alliance of businesses, trade unions, and nongovernmental organizations seeking to promote workers' rights, has developed guidance intended to assist companies in identifying and responding to gender issues in their supply chains.[172] Such guidance refers to the ETI Base Code, which is a code of good labor practices based on the ILO's conventions.

ETI's 2018 publication titled *Gender and the Base Code* explains the importance of gender equality for business, the gender aspects of the ETI Base Code, and the steps necessary to integrate gender equality considerations and women's human rights into global supply

[166] *Gender Equality in Codes of Conduct Guidance*, BSR 5 (2017), https://www.bsr.org/reports/BSR_Gender_Equality_in_Codes_of_Conduct_Guidance.pdf.

[167] *Id.* at 14.

[168] *Id.* at 6–11.

[169] *Gender Equality in Social Auditing Guidance*, BSR 11 (2017), https://www.bsr.org/reports/BSR_Gender_Equality_in_Social_Auditing_Guidance.pdf.

[170] *Id.*

[171] *Id.* at Section 2, Section 3.

[172] *Base Code Guidance: Gender Equality, Part A – Gender and the Base Code*, Ethical Trading Initiative (2018), https://www.ethicaltrade.org/sites/default/files/shared_resources/Base%20code%20guidance%2C%20gender%20equality%2C%20Part%20A.pdf; *Base Code Guidance: Gender Equality, Part B – Gender and Human Rights Due Diligence*, Ethical Trading Initiative (2018), https://www.ethicaltrade.org/sites/default/files/shared_resources/Base%20code%20guidance%2C%20gender%20equality%2C%20Part%20B.pdf.

chains.[173] The guidance emphasizes that gender equality is a central issue for workers' rights and advocates for achieving the SDGs and the UNGPs.[174] Gender-related issues and potential human rights risks for women workers in global supply chains are identified for each of the following ETI Base Code principles: "employment is freely chosen, freedom of association and the right to collective bargaining is respected, working conditions are safe and hygienic, child labor shall not be used, living wages are paid, working hours are not excessive, no discrimination is practiced, regular employment is provided, and no harsh or inhumane treatment is allowed" (including sexual harassment and gender-based violence).[175]

Another ETI publication from 2018 titled *Gender and Human Rights Due Diligence* provides advice on integrating gender equality and women's human rights into impact assessments in HRDD in the context of global supply chains and taking necessary steps to integrate gender equality into such operations, consisting of "(i) how to integrate a gender sensitive approach into their due diligence assessments[,] (ii) what to consider when integrating gender equality at corporate and decision-making levels[,] (iii) how to design and implement gender transformational activities that will enhance women's rights, and (iv) how to monitor and report progress."[176] Although such guidance is drafted to align with a HRDD framework developed by ETI, rather than the UNGPs HRDD framework, the steps outlined are nevertheless helpful for businesses conducting HRDD in their global supply chains.[177] The guidance recommends that companies adopt a strategy consisting of two pathways, with the first consisting of "looking in" by conducting an internal company organizational and systems gender assessment and strategy review, and the second consisting of "looking out" by reviewing gender equality and respect for women's rights in company supply chains.[178] The most salient recommendations for conducting GR-HRDD along both pathways are securing company leadership's commitment for gender equality, undertaking gender equality analysis to understand the context of women's workplace issues and their root causes, taking action to address workplace issues including violence against women through engagement and collaboration with women's rights organizations and trade unions, and collecting, tracking, and communicating progress about companies' gender strategy and gender-related activities, including analyzing and regularly reviewing gender-disaggregated quantitative and qualitative data.[179]

---

173 *Base Code Guidance: Gender Equality, Part A – Gender and the Base Code*, *supra* note 172, Section 1, at 2.

174 *Id.*

175 *Id.* Section 3, at 9–19.

176 *Base Code Guidance: Gender Equality, Part B – Gender and Human Rights Due Diligence*, *supra* note 172, Section 1, at 2.

177 *Id. See also Human Rights Due Diligence Framework*, ETI (2016), https://www.ethicaltrade.org/sites/default/files/shared_resources/eti_human_rights_due_diligence_framework.pdf.

178 *Base Code Guidance: Gender Equality, Part B – Gender and Human Rights Due Diligence*, *supra* note 172, Section 1, at 6.

179 *Id.* at 5.

3. *UN Foundation – Framework for Corporate Action on Workplace Women's Health and Empowerment*

The UN Foundation, in conjunction with the UN Global Compact and the UN Population Fund, developed the 2019 *Framework for Corporate Action on Workplace Women's Health and Empowerment* (Health Framework), which provides comprehensive guidelines that companies may follow to promote women's well-being in global supply chain workplaces.[180] The Health Framework emphasizes the need for companies to invest in women's health and empowerment due to the large number of women working in the global supply chain, estimated at more than 190 million in the 40 countries where estimates were available, and the high percentage of female supply chain workers in such industries as "garments, textiles, shoes, coffee, tea, cocoa, flowers, electronics, and hospitality," estimated at between 50 percent and 85 percent of the workforce.[181] Such investments have been neglected by companies in the past, but are called for in light of the SDGs, especially Goal 3 (good health and well-being) and Goal 5 (gender equality).[182] The Health Framework emphasizes that there is a business case for these investments because they can increase productivity by lowering employee absenteeism and turnover.[183] This issue is so important that an initiative, the Private Sector Action for Women's Health and Empowerment, was launched to work with companies that have large supply chains and employ millions of women as workers, in order to improve their health and well-being.[184]

Companies are encouraged to implement Workplace Women's Health and Empowerment programs addressing three elements, namely "health, protection from violence and harassment, and economic empowerment," with health, which includes reproductive health, as the most important aspect.[185] Both companies who use supply chains (buyers) and suppliers are encouraged to participate in a four-step process consisting of (1) assessing women's workplace issues related to the three pillars of empowerment, (2) setting priorities and measurable targets that are responsive to assessed needs of women workers, (3) taking action to implement education and services programs on women's health and empowerment, and (4) measuring the impact of health and empowerment initiatives on workers as well as improving and communicating results.[186] The Health Framework focuses on both programs and policies that will lead to systemic changes in the way business is conducted.[187]

---

[180] *Framework for Corporate Action on Workplace Women's Health and Empowerment*, UN Foundation, UN Global Compact & UN Population Fund (2019), https://docs.wixstatic.com/ugd/01ff14_f00e5ea53ad64b60b2f6f9bbe597d4e5.pdf.

[181] *Id.* at 2.

[182] *Id.*

[183] *Id.*

[184] Private Sector Action for Women's Health and Empowerment, https://www.universalaccessproject.org/workplace-wh-psa-initiative. (last visited Jul. 6, 2021).

[185] *Framework for Corporate Action on Workplace Women's Health and Empowerment, supra* note 180, at 2.

[186] *Id.* at 5–13. The three pillars of empowerment are: "worker health & well-being education and services; Protection from violence and harassment; and Economic empowerment and professional development."

[187] *Id.* at 3.

4. *The Population Council, et al. – Workplace Health Facility Guidelines and Management Benchmarks*

The Population Council, a nongovernmental organization that conducts research on science and public health issues and helps build research capacity in developing countries, in conjunction with the United States Agency for International Development, BSR, and other organizations, published the *Workplace Health Facility Guidelines and Management Benchmarks* (Health Facility Guidelines) in 2015.[188] These are voluntary health and management guidelines for corporations and their supply chains, intended to promote good practices for access to health services and more effective use of health resources at workplaces in the developing world.[189] The Health Facility Guidelines build on the WEPs and are based on internationally recognized primary health care standards.[190]

The Health Facility Guidelines state that they are designed in part to assist companies in implementation of the UNGPs' mandate that businesses respect human rights and perform HRDD.[191] The Health Facility Guidelines are relevant to HRDD because they provide advice and indicators for a three-part self-assessment by businesses of (1) their workplace health services ("what practices and standards should be met by the health facility and its staff at the workplace"), (2) their management systems ("how health services and staff should be managed by the enterprise"), and (3) corporate leadership and policies relating to workplace health services ("how leadership should support achievement of health standards and better management of health operations").[192]

The Health Facility Guidelines are not focused exclusively on women's health issues, but they place a strong emphasis on ensuring gender equity in workplace health services, a topic that is frequently overlooked.[193] Recommended steps include the following: understanding the health concerns of women workers, collecting and analyzing sex- and age-disaggregated health data, providing reproductive health services and products, seeking input from women and men workers in developing health plans, and addressing violence, harassment, and threats to women and men workers.[194]

5. *Food and Agriculture Organization of the United Nations –Voluntary Guidelines on the Responsible Governance of Tenure of Land, Fisheries and Forests in the Context of National Food Security*

The Food and Agriculture Organization of the United Nations (FAO) published *Voluntary Guidelines on the Responsible Governance of Tenure of Land, Fisheries and Forests in the*

---

[188] *Workplace Health Facility Guidelines and Management Benchmarks*, The Population Council, Et. Al. (2015), https://evidenceproject.popcouncil.org/wp-content/uploads/2015/10/Health-Facility-Guidelines-and-Management-Benchmarks_FINAL_October-2015.pdf.

[189] *Id.* at 1.

[190] *Id.* at 3.

[191] *Id.* at 3.

[192] *Id.* at 1.

[193] *Id.* at 9, 20.

[194] *Id.* at 9, 10, 22.

Context of National Food Security (FAO Guidelines) in 2012.[195] These are voluntary guidelines intended "to provide guidance to improve the governance of tenure of land, fisheries and forests with the overarching goal of achieving food security for all and to support the progressive realization of the right to adequate food in the context of national food security."[196]

Land tenure is a women's human rights issue because land is a critical economic resource for the rural poor who depend on agriculture for their livelihood. However, many women in the developing world have less access, control, and ownership of land than men, which limits women's economic opportunities and leaves them vulnerable to poverty, food insecurity, and other dangers. For this reason, improving women's land tenure has become an aspect of women's empowerment.[197]

Although the FAO Guidelines go beyond women's rights, there is a strong focus on gender equality, including the principle that "States should ensure that women and girls have equal tenure rights and access to land, fisheries and forests independent of their civil and marital status."[198] The FAO Guidelines contain numerous additional principles on gender equality and the steps companies need to take to ensure that they respect equal rights over land and natural resources as part of their responsibility to respect human rights and land tenure rights and to conduct due diligence to avoid infringing on such rights.[199]

IV. Good Practices and Emerging Issues

This Section IV will outline good practices and emerging issues in the area of GR-HRDD, which are drawn from the guidance discussed in Section III. The focus will be on an overview of the good practices highlighted in the gender frameworks contained in the Gender Dimensions Report and in the OECD Guidance.[200] Many of these good practices are reflected in GR-HRDD frameworks developed by nongovernmental organizations, including the BSR Framework and GDI Tool and the GR-HRDD Tool.[201]

A. Embed Gender Equality into a Company's Operations by Developing a Written Policy Complying with Relevant Legal Standards and Obtaining Top-Level Commitment to Such Policy

An important step in the GR-HRDD process is for top-level company management to recognize the importance of such due diligence and commit to implementing it, because of the

[195] *Voluntary Guidelines on the Responsible Governance of Tenure of Land, Fisheries and Forests in the Context of National Food Security*, Food and Agricultural Organization of the United Nations (2012), http://www.fao.org/3/i2801e/i2801e.pdf.

[196] *Id.* at iv.

[197] *See Gender and Access to Land*, Food and Agricultural Organization of the United Nations (2002), http://www.fao.org/3/y4308e/y4308e.pdf, at Section 3 (Why is Gender an Issue in Access to Land).

[198] *Voluntary Guidelines on the Responsible Governance of Tenure of Land, Fisheries and Forests in the Context of National Food Security*, *supra* note 195, at 5 (Principle 3B(4)).

[199] *Id.* at 4 (Principles 3A(3.2)).

[200] *Gender Dimensions Report*, *supra* note 13, at 11; *OECD Guidance*, *supra* note 106, at 41–42.

[201] *GR-HRDD Tool*, *supra* note 112, and accompanying text.

responsibility of businesses of all types and sizes to respect human rights, including women's human rights. Some companies may not wish to voluntarily conduct GR-HRDD, unless and until they are legally required to do so. Even in the absence of binding legal norms, however, some companies may become more motivated when presented with empirical evidence that businesses that actively support gender equality tend to make better business decisions and ultimately make more money.[202] High-level commitment to gender equality is essential because it signals the importance of GR-HRDD to lower-level managers, supervisors, and employees, as well as to external stakeholders.

As part of this process, companies may need to build support and capacity for gender equality by educating both management and staff about the international legal norms supporting gender equality discussed in Section II, as well as federal, state, and local laws that may protect women from discrimination and guarantee their rights. A company's policy should be tailored to conform to relevant legal norms. As an example of this, the GR-HRDD Tool recommends referring to the nine human rights principles that businesses can directly influence.[203]

Company policies on gender equality should be in writing and should clearly assign responsibilities for implementation internally to managers and staff in relevant business units and functional areas such as human resources and legal. These steps are necessary for the policy to be integrated into management systems and operationalized within the organization.

Gender-sensitive business policies should be communicated internally to employees, as well as externally to suppliers, other business partners, and other external stakeholders, so that there is a common understanding about the company's commitment. The importance of compliance should be emphasized in all business operations.

B. Evaluate Existing Company Policies and Management Systems for Adherence to International Gender Equality Norms and National Legal Requirements on Gender Equality

Existing company policies and management systems should also be assessed to ensure they are consistent with the company's gender equality policy. Some companies may have existing policies that refer to human rights in such areas as marketing, procurement, health and safety, finance, and communication or public relations. However, such policies may not refer specifically to gender issues, and in some cases they may interfere with the company's gender equality policy. One example of how companies might avoid such problems is by subscribing to and implementing the WEPs, which represent a company's commitment to its seven principles intended to promote gender equality.[204]

---

[202] *Diveristy Wins: How Inclusion Matters*, McKinsey & Company (May 19, 2020), https://www.mckinsey.com/featured-insights/diversity-and-inclusion/diversity-wins-how-inclusion-matters#.

[203] *GR-HRDD Tool*, *supra* note 112, at 36 and accompanying text.

[204] *WEPs*, *supra* note 117, at 27.

C. Require Business Partners in the Supply Chain to Conduct GR-HRDD and to Implement Gender-Sensitive Policies

Although companies should first take steps to embed gender-sensitive human rights policies in their own business operations, it is also considered a good practice for companies to require suppliers and other significant business partners to adopt such policies. This can be accomplished by including such a requirement in contracts or in codes of conduct backed up by social audits. Some suppliers and business partners may be unfamiliar with HRDD generally and with GR-HRDD in particular. If this is the case, companies may need to provide training and other resources to such counterparties in order to develop their capacity to conduct such due diligence.[205]

D. Conduct a Risk Assessment of Gender-Specific Human Rights Impacts

Companies should conduct an assessment of their business operations and relationships, including their supply chains, to determine whether they are causing or contributing to gender-specific human rights risks and adverse impacts. Companies need to understand that gender can be important in determining the likelihood that a risk will arise as well as the type of impact that may occur, which may be different for women than for men. For example, women may be more likely to experience sexual harassment and gender-based violence than men. Requiring women to work overtime due to an accelerated production timeline may be more burdensome for women due to their household and childcare responsibilities than for men. The purpose of such analysis is to enable companies to take steps to avoid and address adverse impacts that are identified. Examples of areas that should be examined include long-term investment decisions, day-to-day operations and processes, the life cycle of goods and services that are produced, and the economic, cultural, and geographical contexts in which the company operates.

The steps in the risk analysis process include determining what data is required, what processes should be used to collect such data, assessing risks and whether they give rise to actual and potential gender-specific impacts, and prioritizing the most significant risks that should be addressed most urgently. It may also be useful to determine the root causes for the most significant risks and identify those that stem from systemic issues such as cultural norms or from flaws in company processes that unduly burden women employees. The risk assessment process should cover both internal and external factors. Internal risks are those considered preventable because they stem from unauthorized, illegal, or incorrect decisions that can be avoided. External risks are beyond the control of companies and are attributable to political, cybersecurity, social, technological, legal, economic, or environmental factors. Some of the assessment tools described in Section III, such as the BSR Framework and GDI Tool and the GR-HRDD Tool, are useful for this purpose.[206]

---

[205] *Implement Step 1*, GENDER-RESPONSIVE DUE DILIGENCE PLATFORM, https://www.genderduediligence.org/implement-grdd/step-1/.

[206] *BSR Framework*, *supra* note 154; *GR-HRDD Tool*, *supra* note 112 and accompanying text.

E. Collect and Analyze Sex-Disaggregated Data and Use Outcome Indicators

Conducting effective GR-HRDD requires the collection and analysis of data and the use of outcome indicators to assess the true impact of business activities on women. It is important for such data to be disaggregated by sex, a point that is emphasized in the Gender Dimensions Report, both for the risk assessment phase as well as for the tracking phase.[207] This is necessary to provide an accurate account of women's working conditions and experiences and to develop effective responses if negative impacts are identified. The GDI Tool that is part of the BSR Framework emphasizes the need for sex-disaggregated data, including such measures as the gender composition of the workforce and the workforce performance broken down by gender on such measures as absenteeism, turnover, and productivity, as well as gender-specific information on health and safety issues, economic opportunity, leadership opportunities, violence and harassment, and sexual and reproductive health and rights.[208]

F. Recognize Differences Among Women and Identify Intersectionality Issues Affecting Women

Women do not constitute a homogeneous group, but rather are differentiated based on numerous factors, including age, race and ethnicity, religion, educational level, income level, health status, family status, presence of a disability, and sexual orientation and identity, among others. Because of these significant differences, women may be differentially impacted by business operations. GR-HRDD should take these differences into account in conducting risk assessments and tracking the effectiveness of remedial measures. In particular, businesses should recognize that some women may experience multiple forms of discrimination based on the presence of additional factors besides their sex, a concept referred to as intersectionality.

G. Engage with Stakeholders, Including Women Employees, Women's Organizations, and Gender-Equality Experts, in the Policy Formulation and Impact Assessment Processes

Good practice requires that businesses engage with key stakeholders in the formulation and implementation of a gender equality policy. Internal stakeholders, including employees, trade unions, and workers' councils, should be part of this process. It is of paramount importance that women employees be central participants. Women should be given the opportunity to voice their experiences and concerns in a safe environment, which may mean without their

[207] *Gender Dimensions Report*, *supra* note 13, Commentary to UNGPs 18 and 21, at 21–22.

[208] *BSR Framework*, *supra* note 154 and accompanying text.

supervisors and managers present. In addition, managers and staff who are charged with implementing the policy should be included to create a shared understanding of the company's responsibility to protect women's human rights and to provide an opportunity for buy-in.

External stakeholders might also be included. For example, companies that have strong business relationships with suppliers and others in the value chain should consult such parties, especially when the gender equality policy is to be included in supplier codes of conduct. Women's rights organizations, both international and local, and gender-equality experts might also provide helpful input. Such organizations and experts could provide gender context on particular industry sectors and insights on the political, legal, and customs frameworks that may impact the business climate in countries where companies operate.

H. Implement Gender-Sensitive Policies to Address Adverse Impacts of Company Operations on Women, Including Preventing and Remedying Harms Caused to Women

After conducting a gender-sensitive risk assessment that identifies actual or potential adverse impacts on women caused by business operations, companies should take steps to remedy actual impacts and also to prevent further negative impacts and to reduce such risks for the future. Such action might consist of stopping or finding alternatives to its own business activities that cause or contribute to adverse impacts. For example, the company that has identified a gender pay gap might take steps to remove such pay disparity in the future or to compensate women for lost income for past work. A company might prevent a potential negative impact on women who choose to return to work after childbirth but do not have a source of childcare by introducing a workplace day care center. In the case of external risks that are not preventable by a company, a business mitigation strategy should focus on identifying, designing, and testing responsive strategies. For example, cultural norms that prevent or discourage women from taking certain jobs might be counteracted through employment practices to actively recruit and train female employees.

Effective remediation of gender-related human rights abuses may call for companies to establish internal grievance mechanisms to provide safe and confidential redress, for example in the case of sexual harassment and gender-based violence. Such mechanisms should be viewed as a supplement to State-level judicial mechanisms and other remedies, about which women should be informed.

In the case of identified adverse impacts that are directly linked to the activities of suppliers or other business partners, companies should use their leverage to influence their business partners to prevent or mitigate such impacts. For example, a company that identifies a supplier operating a factory with unsafe working conditions for women might require such entity to take steps to improve such working conditions. This might be accomplished through use of contract terms or supplier codes of conduct.

I. Take Steps to Track Progress on Gender Equality, to Periodically Evaluate the Effectiveness of Gender-Sensitive Remedial Measures, and to Communicate Such Progress to Stakeholders

GR-HRDD should be conducted on an ongoing basis in order to achieve the goal of gender equality. A meaningful process will include further steps to track, evaluate, and communicate to stakeholders whether the company's policy goals have been achieved. This entails identifying key performance indicators and measurement tools to track the effectiveness of policies and processes, awareness and competencies on gender-related issues by managers and employees, and achievement of outcomes tied to respect for human rights principles. This analysis should be based upon the use of sex-disaggregated data drawn from sources such as employee interviews and satisfaction surveys, onsite visits, document reviews, social audits, grievance mechanisms, and human resources records. Actual monitoring of progress can be based upon evaluation instruments such as third-party audits, company self-assessments, and review of supplier self-assessment reports.

Communication on progress towards gender equality to both internal and external stakeholders is a recommended good practice consisting of reporting of adverse risks, actions taken to address such risks, and the results of such actions. Employees and their representatives such as trade unions and workers' councils, investors, customers, and suppliers and other business partners are among the constituents that should receive such communication as part of corporate communications and branding activity.

Reporting on progress towards gender equality might be included in the annual sustainability reports that many companies now routinely issue voluntarily or pursuant to legal requirements that governments are increasingly putting into place. Such reporting is often based upon global frameworks, such as the Global Reporting Initiative Sustainability Reporting Standards, which could be used to report on gender-related measurements in such areas as employment, diversity and equal opportunity at work, training and education, and nondiscrimination.[209] Another helpful framework is the *UNGP Reporting Framework* developed by Shift and Mazars, which can be used to assist companies in complying with the expectation in the UNGPs that companies report on their human rights performance.[210]

J. Conduct Advocacy for Gender Equality, Such as by Engaging with Governments and Other Stakeholders to Reform Discriminatory Laws

Although neither the UNGPs nor the OECD Guidance include advocacy as part of the HRDD process, some commentators have suggested that businesses should take steps to identify systemic risk factors related to gender-based human rights abuses in their risk assessments and should lobby governments and engage with other stakeholders to reform discriminatory laws.

---

[209] *Sustainability Reporting Standards*, Global Reporting Initiative, https://www.globalreporting.org. *See GR-HRDD Tool, supra* note 112, at 105.

[210] *UNGP Reporting Framework*, Shift & Mazars LLP, https://www.ungpreporting.org/. *See GR-HRDD Tool, supra* note 112, at 105.

V. Conclusion

Empowering women is considered a critical strategy in today's global business environment. But all too often women are marginalized and relegated to low-paid and hazardous jobs in the formal sector or work in informal sectors with unstable income and lack of legal protections, where they face systemic discrimination and, often, sexual harassment and gender-based violence.

Under the UNGPs, HRDD requirements apply to both States and businesses. On October 2, 2020, the 25th anniversary of the Beijing Declaration and Platform for Action, over 100 States recommitted themselves to the efforts that began 25 years earlier.[211] In 1995, they committed to "addressing . . . constraints and obstacles and thus enhancing further the advancement and empowerment of women all over the world, and agree that this requires urgent action in the spirit of determination, hope, cooperation and solidarity, now and to carry us forward into the next century."[212] Moreover, they agreed to implement the corresponding Platform for Action.[213] The Platform for Action is the most comprehensive global agenda for the empowerment of women and the achievement of gender equality. Little progress has been made over those 25 years.[214] The inclusion of gender-responsiveness in all areas of HRDD is an important step to securing fundamental rights for all.

Platitudes about the importance of women's rights can no longer stand as a substitute for action. While some States and some businesses have taken steps to implement the UNGPs, it has often been with dilution or pushback, and others have failed to take any action at all. The business world will remain apathetic about addressing gender issues until forced to do so. Meanwhile, women continue to bear the brunt of human rights abuses. GR-HRDD by business is the starting point and must be a part of any binding international treaty on business and human rights.

VI. Resources

A. Intergovernmental Organization Resources

Organisation for Economic Co-operation and Development, *Due Diligence Guidance for Responsible Business Conduct* (2018).

Organisation for Economic Co-operation and Development, *OECD Due Diligence Guidance for Responsible Supply Chains in the Garment and Footwear Sector* (2017).

Organisation for Economic Co-operation and Development, *OECD Due Diligence Guidance for Responsible Supply Chains of Minerals from Conflict-Affected and High-Risk Areas* (2016).

---

[211] *Press release: At UN high-level meeting, world leaders reignite the vision of the Beijing Platform for Action, the most transformative agenda for advancing gender equality*, UN Women (Oct. 2, 2020), https://www.unwomen.org/en/news/stories/2020/10/press-release-leaders-reignite-the-vision-of-the-beijing-platform-for-action.

[212] *Beijing Declaration*, *supra* note 57, at ¶ 7.

[213] *Id.* at ¶ 38.

[214] *Gender equality: Women's Rights in Review 25 Years after Beijing*, UN Women 2 (2020), https://www.unwomen.org/sites/default/files/Headquarters/Attachments/Sections/Library/Publications/2020/Gender-equality-Womens-rights-in-review-en.pdf.

Organisation for Economic Co-operation and Development, *OECD-FAO Guidance for Responsible Agricultural Supply Chains* (2016).

United Nations, Convention on the Elimination of All Forms of Discrimination Against Women (1981).

UN Development Programme, *Gender Equality Seal Certification Program for Public and Private Enterprises.*

UN Food and Agriculture Organization, *Voluntary Guidelines on the Responsible Governance of Tenure of Land, Fisheries and Forests in the Context of National Food Security* (2012).

United Nations Foundation, United Nations Global Compact, and United Nations Population Fund, *Framework for Corporate Action on Workplace Women's Health and Empowerment* (2019).

UN Office of the High Commissioner of Human Rights, *Women's Rights are Human Rights* (HR/PUB/14/2) (2014).

UN Women and UN Global Compact Office, *Women's Empowerment Principles – Equality Means Business* (3rd ed. 2021).

UN Women and UN Global Compact Office, *Women's Empowerment Principles Gender Gap Analysis Tool* (2021).

UN Women and UN Global Compact Office, *Women's Empowerment Principles Transparency and Accountability Framework* (2021).

UN Working Group on Business and Human Rights, *Gender Dimensions of the Guiding Principles on Business and Human Rights* (A/HRC/41/43) (2019).

B. Civil Society Resources

Bourke Martignoni, Joanna and Unlas, Elizabeth, *Gender-Responsive Due Diligence for Business Actors: Human Rights-Based Approaches* (University of Geneva/Graduate Institute Geneva Academy of International Humanitarian Law and Human Rights) (2018).

BSR, *Gender Equality in Codes of Conduct Guidance* (2017).

BSR, *Gender Equality in Social Auditing Guidance* (2018).

BSR, *Making Women Workers Count: A Framework for Conducting Gender-Responsive Due Diligence in Supply Chains and Gender Data and Impact Tool* (2019).

Edge Certification Foundation, *Edge Certification Tool.*

Ethical Trading Initiative, *Gender and the Base Code* (2018).

Ethical Trading Initiative, *Gender and Human Rights Due Diligence* (2018).

Plan International Netherlands and Girls Advocacy Alliance, *Gender-Responsive Human Rights Due Diligence Tool* (2020).

The Population Council, et al., *Workplace Health Facility Guidelines and Management Benchmarks* (2015).

11

Human Rights Due Diligence Practices for Adequate and Effective Consultation with Indigenous Peoples

Thomas Andrew O'Keefe

I. Introduction

The United Nations (UN) estimates that there are some 370 million Indigenous peoples living around the world in over 90 countries.[1] Due to widespread marginalization and discrimination, Indigenous peoples often find themselves mired in poverty and, therefore, especially vulnerable to the negative impacts of business activities. While Indigenous peoples may represent only about 5 percent of the world's population, "estimates indicate that over half of the world's remaining mineral resources may be located in their territories."[2] Consequently, there is considerable risk that government licenses or concessions for development and investment activities will detrimentally impact Indigenous peoples' relationship to their lands and cause environmental degradation and pollution.[3]

[1] A Business Reference Guide: United Nations Declaration on the Rights of Indigenous Peoples 4 (United Nations Global Compact Office 2013).

[2] Cathal M. Doyle, Indigenous Peoples, Title To Territory, Rights and Resources 3 (Routledge 2015).

[3] Christina Binder, *The UNDRIP and Interactions with International Investment Law* in Jessie Hohmann & Marc Weller, Eds., The UN Declaration on the Rights of Indigenous Peoples: A Commentary 87 (Oxford University Press 2018).

This chapter examines the legal obligation of prior consultation arising under the International Labour Organization Convention 169 on Indigenous and Tribal Peoples (ILO 169)[4] as well as the principle of free, prior, and informed consent contained in the UN Declaration on the Rights of Indigenous Peoples (UNDRIP).[5] The chapter then explores how both ILO 169 and the UNDRIP have influenced the development of a series of guidelines and standards for businesses whose activities may detrimentally impact Indigenous peoples. The chapter also discusses how these guidelines and standards can be used to fashion a business enterprise's internal human rights due diligence policies and practices to ensure it supports, respects, and promotes the human rights of Indigenous peoples, including adequate and effective consultation.

This chapter's geographical focal point is the Western Hemisphere since this is the area of the world with the largest concentration of Indigenous peoples, in some cases making up close to, if not the majority of, a country's population, and the greatest number of States that have ratified international legal instruments requiring prior consultation with Indigenous peoples. In addition, the inter-American human rights system has the most extensive substantive jurisprudence on consultation and consent. Hence, the Americas offer a plethora of examples that provide practical guidance for countries in other regions of the world on what constitutes adequate and effective consultation, not to mention decades of cumulative errors to avoid.

A. Who Are Indigenous Peoples?

Given the diversity of Indigenous peoples, no single definition has been adopted by the contemporary international legal community, and a combination of subjective and objective criteria is often used.[6] One criterion underpinning most definitions is that of self-identification. Given that the establishment of States has often come at the cost of sacrificing Indigenous rights and identity, perhaps it is better that there be no explicit definition of who constitutes Indigenous peoples, as "one way of ensuring that Indigenous rights thrive is to challenge the sole right of States to determine who the Indigenous peoples within their territory are."[7]

Self-identification is also the criterion preferred by ILO 169, although Article 1 also offers a set of suggested criteria:

> (a) tribal peoples in independent countries whose social, cultural and economic conditions distinguish them from other sections of the national community, and whose status

[4] International Labour Organization, *Indigenous and Tribal Peoples Convention No. 169*, 27 Jun. 1989, available at: https://www.ilo.org/dyn/normlex/en/f?p=NORMLEXPUB:12100:0::NO::P12100_ILO_CODE:C169 [accessed 12 Jun. 2021].

[5] UN General Assembly, *United Nations Declaration on the Rights of Indigenous Peoples*, resolution adopted by the General Assembly on 13 Sept. 2007, A/RES 61/295, available at: https://undocs.org/A/RES/61/295 [accessed 12 Jun. 2021].

[6] A Business Reference Guide, *supra* note 1, at 8.

[7] Joshua Castellino & Cathal Doyle, *Who Are 'Indigenous Peoples'?*, in The UN Declaration on the Rights of Indigenous Peoples: A Commentary, *supra* note 3, at 37.

is regulated wholly or partially by their own customs or traditions or by special laws or regulations;

(b) peoples in independent countries who are regarded as [I]ndigenous on account of their descent from the populations which inhabited the country, or a geographical region to which the country belongs, at the time of conquest or colonization or the establishment of present state boundaries and who, irrespective of their legal status, retain some or all of their own social, economic, cultural and political institutions.[8]

B. Why Indigenous Peoples Receive Special Treatment in International Law

Although the Indigenous rights regime is "rooted in centuries-long dynamics of colonial dispossession and normative debates in Western legal thought," the development of this regime is a "recent process catalyzed by the emergence of Indigenous peoples as political actors in the international area, and the successful re-articulation of their historical demands and strategies to fit, while creatively transforming, the logics and mechanisms of the late-twentieth-century human rights machinery."[9] In the 1970s, for example, the demands of Indigenous peoples "resonated within what had become a central component of the UN human rights agenda, the campaign against racial discrimination in all its forms."[10]

Indigenous peoples have obtained recognition, under international human rights law, due to their cultural distinctiveness.[11] The UN Committee on the Elimination of Racial Discrimination (CERD)—which has a well-established record on addressing discrimination against Indigenous peoples—has noted that Indigenous peoples are "vulnerable to patterns of discrimination that have deprived them, as groups, of the enjoyment of their property and distinct ways of life, and hence calls upon . . . [UN members States] to take special measures to protect Indigenous cultural patterns and traditional land tenure."[12] In particular, "[o]ne of the most aggravating forms of discrimination against Indigenous peoples occurs when they are deprived of the collective possession and traditional use of their land for the sake of economic interests."[13] The right of Indigenous peoples to "hold specific collective rights aimed at ensuring the preservation of their cultural identity" is recognized in international human rights law and "the requirement of consultation with Indigenous peoples serves as a guarantee for the realization of such collective rights."[14] This is a noteworthy development, because international human rights have traditionally been understood as applying only to

[8] ILO 169, *supra* note 4.

[9] S. James Anaya & Luis Rodríguez-Piñero, *The Making of the UNDRIP*, in The UN Declaration on the Rights of Indigenous Peoples: A Commentary, *supra* note 3, at 38.

[10] *Id.* at 42.

[11] Maria Victoria Cabrera Ormaza, The Requirement of Consultation with Indigenous Peoples in the ILO 61 (Brill/Nijhoff 2017).

[12] S. James Anaya & Luis Rodríguez-Piñero, *supra* note 9, at 47.

[13] Cabrera Ormaza, *supra* note 11, at 65.

[14] *Id.* at 147.

individuals rather than groups.[15] This special recognition of Indigenous peoples under international law is also reflected in the *United Nations Guiding Principles on Business and Human Rights* (UNGPs),[16] in connection with human rights due diligence, as discussed in detail in Section IV below.

II. Context

Although the Americas are not unique in experiencing violent clashes that result from an actual or perceived failure to adequately consult with Indigenous communities detrimentally impacted by natural resource extraction and economic development projects, the region provides several striking examples. Among the most emblematic was the use in 2009 of armed force in Peru's Amazonian province of Bagua to counter protests by Indigenous peoples who opposed legal changes that facilitated energy, mining, and agricultural concessions on Indigenous lands. The violence resulted in the deaths of 34 people (mostly policemen) and hundreds of injured.[17] Southern Chile has been convulsed by continuous clashes with the Mapuche Indigenous community over energy and forestry projects that have left scores dead and led to incalculable economic losses. These clashes began in the early 1990s with the construction of the massive Pangue-Ralco hydroelectric dams along the Bio-Bio River with funding from the International Finance Corporation (IFC).[18] Bolivia, despite having an Indigenous president, was the scene of bloodshed in 2011 over efforts to build a Brazilian-funded highway through the Isiboro Secure National Park and Indigenous Territory (TIPNIS) in the eastern part of the country.[19] The dispute pitted Aymara- and Quechua-speaking migrants involved in coca production, who formed the base of the Bolivian president's constituency, against Indigenous residents of the TIPNIS.

To minimize social conflicts with Indigenous communities, businesses would be wise to incorporate consultation and consent requirements within their corporate human rights due diligence policies and approaches. Aside from making good business sense, private sector companies are increasingly expected to conduct their affairs in a way that upholds human rights and does not interfere with a government's obligations under international human rights instruments such as ILO 169. In fact, companies are not absolved by "States' failed responsibilities and possible omissions regarding prior and adequate consultation," and "due diligence includes certain obligations with regard to Indigenous peoples' right to be consulted on projects affecting them irrespective of [. . .] State obligations in this regard."[20]

---

[15] Martin Scheinin & Mattias Àhrén, *Relationship to Human Rights, and Related International Instruments*, in The UN Declaration on the Rights of Indigenous Peoples: A Commentary, *supra* note 3, at 67.

[16] Guiding Principles on Business and Human Rights (United Nations 2011).

[17] Lila Barrera-Hernández, *Peruvian Indigenous Land Conflict Explained*, Americas Q. (Jun. 12, 2009), https://www.americasquarterly.org/article/peruvian-indigenous-land-conflict-explained/.

[18] Lila Barrera-Hernández, *Got Title; Will Sell: Indigenous Rights to Land in Argentina and Chile*, in Aileen McHarg et. al., eds., Property and the Law in Energy and Natural Resources, 193–196 (2009).

[19] AQ Editors, *TIPNIS Protestors Retake March After Negotiations Fail*, Americas Q. (Oct. 11, 2011), https://www.americasquarterly.org/blog/tipnis-protesters-retake-march-after-negotiations-fail/.

[20] Jessika Eichler, Reconciling Indigenous Peoples' Individual and Collective Rights 57 (Routledge 2019).

In addition, there is a growing trend in Europe and at the UN to make human rights due diligence principles mandatory for businesses. For example, France passed a law in 2017 that requires companies with a substantial presence in the country to adopt "reasonable vigilance measures to allow for risk identification and for the prevention of severe violations of human rights and fundamental freedoms, serious bodily injury or environmental damage or health risks resulting directly or indirectly from the operations of the company and of the companies it controls."[21] The CERD, for its part, has emphasized "the need for home State regulation to ensure that extractive corporations registered in their jurisdictions respect Indigenous peoples' rights."[22] Furthermore, multilateral lending agencies such as the Asian Development Bank, the European Bank for Reconstruction and Development, and the Inter-American Development Bank have also developed performance standards that include a consent requirement and are applicable not only to these lending agencies but must also be adhered to by any company seeking their financing for investment projects that may impact Indigenous peoples.[23] In addition, the International Council on Mining and Metals committed its members in 2013 to seek free, prior, and informed consent for new projects and changes to existing projects that are likely to significantly impact Indigenous communities.[24]

III. Legal and Regulatory Framework

A. International Labour Organization Convention 169

Enacted in 1989, ILO 169 recognizes a role for Indigenous and tribal peoples in any endeavor that may impact their lives and the lands they occupy or otherwise utilize and is binding on States that have ratified it. The fact that the first significant legal treaty to articulate the rights of Indigenous peoples under international law emanated from a body associated with the protection of workers is explained by the ILO's involvement in efforts between the 1920s and 1950s to ameliorate the harsh treatment of Indigenous workers, particularly in the Andean region of South America, where conditions bordered on slavery.[25] To date, ILO 169 has been ratified by 23 countries, the majority of which (15) are in the Western Hemisphere. Neither the United States nor Canada is a signatory to ILO 169.

Article 6 of ILO 169 affirms that Indigenous peoples should be consulted in good faith with respect to legislative or administrative measures that may affect them, with the objective of achieving agreement or consent to the proposed measures. In addition, a State party should, when appropriate, ensure that studies are carried out in cooperation with Indigenous peoples to assess the social, spiritual, cultural, and environmental impact on them of planned

[21] Elise Groulx Diggs, Mitt Regan, & Beatrice Parance, *Business and Human Rights as a Galaxy of Norms*, 50 Geo. J. of Int'l L. 309, 312 (2019). Companies that fail to meet their vigilance obligations are liable for damages, although a plaintiff has the burden of proving that failure to adhere to the law led to the harms that occurred. *Id.* at 313.

[22] Doyle, *supra* note 2, at 211.

[23] *Id.* at 202.

[24] Doyle, *supra* note 2, at 231.

[25] Cabrera Ormaza, *supra* note 11, at 24–32.

development activities, and that these studies be considered as fundamental criteria for the implementation of these activities (Article 7(3)).

Article 15(2) of ILO 169 requires governments to consult with Indigenous peoples where the State retains ownership of minerals or resources before permitting exploration or exploitation of such resources. In addition, where possible, Indigenous peoples shall participate in the benefits and receive compensation for any damages that may result from a natural resource extraction activity. Article 15(2) is tied to two collective rights recognized by ILO 169: the right of Indigenous peoples to own and possess traditionally occupied lands (Article 14(1)), and the right to participate in the use, management, and conservation of resources pertaining to those lands (Article 15(1)). Consultation also "contributes to the protection of the cultural integrity of Indigenous peoples by ensuring that these communities take part in assessing measures with the potential to impact their cultural relationship with their land and natural resources."[26]

Article 16 of ILO 169 requires that where the relocation of Indigenous peoples is deemed a necessity, the government must obtain their "free and informed consent" before removal. Indigenous peoples shall also have the right to return to their traditional lands as soon as relocation is feasible (Article 16(2)) and shall be fully compensated for their losses and injury (Article 16(5)). Compensation can include lands of quality and legal status at least equal to that of lands previously occupied, suitable to provide for present needs and future development (Article 16(4)).

B. United Nations Declaration on the Rights of Indigenous Peoples

In 2007, the UN General Assembly adopted the UNDRIP that introduced the concept of free, prior, and informed consent with respect to projects that have a significant impact on Indigenous peoples and/or their way of life. Only four countries, namely Australia, Canada, New Zealand, and the United States, voted against adoption of the UNDRIP, based, in part, on concerns that free, prior, and informed consent might be interpreted as an absolute "right to veto" applicable uniquely to Indigenous peoples.[27] However, all four countries expressed general acceptance of the core principles and values and eventually reversed their position and formally endorsed the UNDRIP, albeit with Canada and the United States emphasizing that it is not binding on signatory States.[28]

Article 32(2) of the UNDRIP specifically requires that States shall consult and cooperate in good faith with the Indigenous peoples concerned through their own representative institutions in order to obtain their free and informed consent prior to the approval of any project affecting their lands or territories and other resources, particularly in connection with the development, use, or exploitation of mineral, water, or other resources.

---

[26] *Id.* at 63.

[27] Doyle, *supra* note 2, at 161. These four countries, perhaps not surprisingly, are home to the world's major natural resource extractive companies, many of which have operations in Indigenous territories both at home and abroad.

[28] Anaya & Rodríguez-Piñero, *supra* note 9, at 60. *See, also*, Doyle, *supra* note 2, at 163.

The UNDRIP also requires the free, prior, and informed consent of impacted Indigenous peoples:

1. whenever they are forcibly removed from their lands or territories, with the added proviso that no relocation may occur until after an agreement on just and fair compensation and, where possible, with the option of return (Article 10);
2. before the adoption and implementation of legislative or administrative matters that may affect Indigenous peoples (Article 19);
3. before authorizing the storage or disposal of hazardous materials in the lands or territories of Indigenous peoples (Article 29(2)).

Free, prior, and informed consent, at a minimum, requires "that the relevant consultations should not be a mere formality, but, rather, should be conducted in good faith and with the objective of finding a common agreement."[29] The term free "implies that the process of consultation should be conducted in the absence of any type of coercion and pressure"; prior suggests "that consultations should take place before undertaking an action or implementing a project"; and, informed "means that Indigenous peoples should receive satisfactory information in relation to the relevant measure or project."[30] Free "also implies allowing sufficient time for the engagement process to occur, so that [I]ndigenous communities do not feel rushed, or believe that the process was mere window-dressing."[31]

Unlike ILO 169, which is a legally binding treaty for ratifying States, the UNDRIP is not legally binding on the State except to the extent that the State has incorporated specific UNDRIP provisions into its domestic legal framework. Although this is also the official US position, some legal scholars argue that its adoption at the UN "with overwhelming support, and coupled with the important subsequent endorsements by the four States that at the time of adoption voted against the Declaration, provides strong support for the contention that many of the substantive provisions of the UNDRIP reflect and express norms of customary international law."[32] In particular, key provisions in the UNDRIP, "including its land rights provisions and the necessary participation of Indigenous peoples in decisions which affect them, are generally considered as a codification of customary international law."[33]

C. Inter-American Human Rights System

The inter-American human rights system, which monitors, promotes, and protects human rights in all 35 member countries of the Organization of American States (OAS), has attempted to inject greater uniformity into the myriad interpretations by national governments of what

---

[29] Mauro Barelli, *Free, Prior, and Informed Consent in the UNDRIP*, in The UN Declaration on the Rights of Indigenous Peoples: A Commentary, *supra* note 3, at 248.

[30] *Id.* at 250.

[31] Amy K. Lehr, Indigenous Peoples Rights and the Role of Free, Prior, and Informed Consent 14 (United Nations Global Compact 2014).

[32] Scheinin & Àhrén, *supra* note 15, at 64.

[33] Binder, *supra* note 3, at 89.

constitutes adequate and effective consultations with Indigenous peoples. This has been accomplished both through case law developed by the Inter-American Court of Human Rights and recommendations issued by the Inter-American Commission on Human Rights. The Inter-American Court of Human Rights has "held that the duty of States to consult Indigenous peoples must now be regarded as a general principle of international law" and, in the case of large-scale development or investment projects, States "have a duty to not only consult with Indigenous peoples, but also to obtain their free, prior, and informed consent."[34] The inter-American human rights system also recognizes the special relationship between Indigenous peoples and their ancestral lands as "the fundamental basis for the maintenance of their physical and cultural integrity, their economic survival and for the protection of Indigenous peoples' rights to land and natural resources."[35] In this regard, the Inter-American Court of Human Rights has established three safeguards that apply to large-scale projects affecting Indigenous peoples: (1) their effective participation in the project plans; (2) a reasonable benefit from such plans; and (3) no issuing of concessions or licenses until an independent body carries out an environmental and social impact assessment.[36]

On June 15, 2016, the OAS General Assembly approved the American Declaration on the Rights of Indigenous Peoples (American Declaration)[37] over Canadian and US objections, with Colombia dissenting from two provisions related to consultations to obtain free, prior, and informed consent as well as another concerning military actions on Indigenous lands.[38] Pursuant to Article XXVIII(3) of the American Declaration, States "with the full and effective participation of [I]ndigenous peoples, shall adopt measures necessary to ensure that national and international agreements and regimes provide recognition and adequate protection for the cultural heritage of [I]ndigenous peoples and intellectual property associated with that heritage. In adopting such measures, consultations shall be held to obtain the free, prior, and informed consent of [I]ndigenous peoples." Similarly, States "shall consult and cooperate in good faith with the [I]ndigenous peoples concerned, through their own representative institutions, in order to obtain their free, prior and informed consent before adopting and implementing legislative or administrative measures that may affect them" (Article XXIII(2)). Furthermore, States "shall consult and cooperate in good faith with the [I]ndigenous peoples concerned through their own representative institutions in order to obtain their free and informed consent prior to the approval of any project affecting their lands or territories and other resources, particularly in connection with the development, utilization or exploitation of mineral, water, or other resources" (Article XXIX(4)). As the American Declaration's provisions are incorporated into the domestic legal framework of OAS member States and

[34] Barelli, *supra* note 29, at 257–258.

[35] Cabrera Ormaza, *supra* note 11, at 172.

[36] Claire Wright & Alexandra Tomaselli, Eds., The Prior Consultation of Indigenous Peoples in Latin America 2 (Routledge 2019).

[37] OAS General Assembly, *American Declaration on the Rights of Indigenous Peoples*, resolution adopted by the General Assembly, 15 Jun. 2016, AG/RES. 2888 (XLVI-O/16).

[38] The full text of the American Declaration, including objections and reservations by States, is found in OAS General Secretariat, Forty Sixth Regular Session of the OAS General Assembly Proceedings: Volume 1, 167–190 (2016), which can be accessed electronically at: http://www.oas.org/en/council/AG/ResDec/.

interpreted by bodies in the inter-American human rights system, this may generate clearer guidance on the separate but interrelated obligations of consultation and free, prior, and informed consent.

IV. Voluntary Guidelines and Standards

The UN and the Organisation for Economic Co-operation and Development (OECD) have developed a set of principles while the IFC has performance standards, all of which offer useful guidance for companies drafting their own human rights due diligence standards so as to ensure adequate and effective consultation with Indigenous communities impacted by their business activities. Equally as helpful in this regard is the UN Global Compact (UNGC) *Business Reference Guide* on the UNDRIP.

A. United Nations

On June 16, 2011, the UN Human Rights Council unanimously endorsed the UNGPs developed by the Special Representative of the UN Secretary-General on the issue of human rights and transnational corporations and other business enterprises. The UNGPs, which elaborated upon the UN's "Protect, Respect, and Remedy" framework, contains not only the obligations of States to protect against human rights abuses by business enterprises, but also the responsibility of business enterprises to respect human rights, in recognition of their role as social institutions performing specialized functions.

The Commentary to Guiding Principle 3 concerning the State's duty to protect acknowledges that governments when advising business enterprises on appropriate methods to respect human rights, including due diligence, need to consider "the specific challenges that may be faced by [I]ndigenous peoples."[39] Furthermore, the Commentary to Guiding Principle 12, on the responsibility of business enterprises to respect human rights, emphasizes that companies may need to consider additional standards related to the human rights of individuals belonging to specific groups or populations, such as Indigenous peoples, specifically recognized in UN instruments.[40] These standards include both the obligation of prior consultation found in ILO 169, as the ILO has been a specialized agency within the UN system since 1946, as well as the UNDRIP's principle of free, prior, and informed consent.

Guiding Principle 18, on the need to gauge human rights risks, notes that one important means of assessing such risks is for business enterprises to engage in meaningful consultation with potentially affected groups and other relevant stakeholders. The Commentary to Guiding Principle 18 emphasizes that this means paying "special attention to any particular human rights impacts on individuals from groups or populations that may be at heightened risk of vulnerability or marginalization" such as Indigenous peoples.[41] To ensure an accurate assessment of human rights impacts, the Commentary to Guiding Principle 18 also suggests

---

[39] Guiding Principles on Business and Human Rights, *supra* note 16, at 5.

[40] *Id.* at 14.

[41] *Id.* at 20.

that business enterprises "should seek to understand the concerns of potentially affected stakeholders by consulting them directly in a manner that takes into account language and other potential barriers to effective engagement."[42] Finally, the Commentary to Guiding Principle 20, on the need to verify whether adverse human rights impacts are being addressed, recommends that business enterprises "should make particular efforts to track the effectiveness of their responses to impacts on individuals from groups or populations that may be at heightened risk of vulnerability or marginalization," such as Indigenous peoples.[43]

More generally, with respect to businesses' responsibility to respect the human rights of Indigenous peoples, Guiding Principle 11 requires business enterprises to address adverse human rights impacts. The Commentary notes that this includes "taking adequate measures for their prevention, mitigation and, where appropriate, remediation."[44] Guiding Principle 15 provides further elaboration:

> In order to meet their responsibility to respect human rights, business enterprises should have in place policies and processes appropriate to their size and circumstances, including:
>
> (a) A policy commitment to meet their responsibility to respect human rights;
>
> (b) A human rights due diligence process to identify, prevent, mitigate and account for how they address their impacts on human rights;
>
> (c) Processes to enable the remediation of any adverse human rights impacts they cause or to which they contribute.[45]

B. United Nations Global Compact

A Business Reference Guide: United Nations Declaration on the Rights of Indigenous Peoples (Business Reference Guide) was launched in 2013 by the UNGC. The UNGC, created in 2000, is the largest corporate social responsibility initiative in the world in terms of the number of businesses that have signed on and that acknowledge their responsibility to respect human rights.[46] The *Business Reference Guide* is the culmination of nearly two years of discussions involving Indigenous peoples, civil society groups, and private sector enterprises. It recommends that companies interacting with Indigenous peoples adhere to a set of fundamental "best practices" that include:

1. Adopt and implement a formal policy (whether on a stand-alone basis or within a broader human rights policy) addressing [I]ndigenous peoples' rights and committing the business to respect [I]ndigenous peoples' rights;

---

42 *Id.* at 20.

43 *Id.* at 23.

44 *Id.* at 13.

45 *Id.* at 15–16.

46 Further information on the UNGC is available at: https://www.unglobalcompact.org/.

2. Conduct human rights due diligence to assess actual or potential adverse impacts on [I]ndigenous peoples' rights, integrate findings and take action, track and communicate externally on performance;
3. Consult in good faith with [I]ndigenous peoples in relation to all matters that may affect them or their rights;
4. Commit to obtain (and maintain) the free, prior and informed consent of [I]ndigenous peoples for projects that affect their rights, in line with the spirit of the UN Declaration;
5. Establish or cooperate through legitimate processes to remediate any adverse impacts on [I]ndigenous peoples' rights; and,
6. Establish or cooperate with an effective and culturally appropriate grievance mechanism.[47]

The *Business Reference Guide* emphasizes that "[i]t is crucial that [I]ndigenous peoples with whom the business interacts and works are engaged in the process of developing, implementing and reviewing the [business's] policy early in the development process" and that "[b]usinesses should conduct pre-engagement analysis to understand the specific needs and interests of [I]ndigenous peoples and develop an outreach and communication strategy for engaging with them."[48]

The *Business Reference Guide* highlights that consultation is not an end in and of itself but a process that must achieve the goal of obtaining consent.[49] In particular, it states that "[c]onsent can be understood as a formal, documented social license to operate" and that Indigenous peoples "have the right to give or withhold consent, and in some circumstances, may revoke consent previously given."[50] In fact, the *Business Reference Guide* recommends that if free, prior, and informed consent for a business activity that may impact Indigenous land, territory, or resources "is not granted, then the activity should not proceed."[51] The *Business Reference Guide* also emphasizes that businesses "should not take advantage of a power imbalance" nor should Indigenous peoples ever "be under the impression that the project will go ahead whether they participate or not."[52] Furthermore, it underscores that "prior" implies "that consent is to be sought sufficiently in advance of any authorization or commencement of activities" and that respect be shown for however long the Indigenous consultation and consensus processes may require.[53] Finally, the *Business Reference Guide* warns about "the potential legal risks, which include those arising from the possibility of complicity in rights abuses, if projects are pursued against the wishes of the affected Indigenous peoples."[54]

---

[47] A Business Reference Guide, *supra* note 1, at 11.

[48] *Id.* at 13.

[49] Doyle, *supra* note 2, at 229.

[50] A Business Reference Guide, *supra* note 1, at 28.

[51] *Id.* at 70.

[52] *Id.* at 27.

[53] *Id.*

[54] Doyle, *supra* note 2, at 229–230.

C. Organisation for Economic Co-operation and Development

The *OECD Guidelines for Multinational Enterprises* (OECD Guidelines) is a set of voluntary principles and standards for responsible business conduct, jointly developed by the 37 member governments of the OECD plus Argentina, Brazil, Egypt, Latvia, Lithuania, Morocco, Peru, and Romania that are applicable to multinational enterprises operating in or from their territories. The OECD Guidelines were last updated in 2011 and include a human rights chapter premised on the UNGPs to address adverse impacts to human rights and the environment, caused or contributed to by an enterprise, or directly linked to its operations, products, or services as a result of business relationships (including supply chains). Implementation of the OECD Guidelines is supported by so-called National Contact Points that assist businesses in taking appropriate measures as well as providing a mediation and conciliation platform for resolving practical issues that may arise. The *OECD Guidelines* do not specifically address situations involving Indigenous peoples, however, other than to point out in Commentary 40 to Article IV that business enterprises should respect the human rights of individuals belonging to specific groups or populations that require particular attention, such as Indigenous peoples.[55]

The *OECD Due Diligence Guidance for Responsible Business Conduct* (Due Diligence Guidance) offers more detailed suggestions for engaging or consulting with impacted or potentially impacted Indigenous peoples in the context of human rights due diligence, emphasizing that consultation with Indigenous peoples is a human right in and of itself.[56] Meaningful engagement with Indigenous peoples involves the timely sharing of the relevant information needed for them to make decisions; and the information must be provided in a way they can understand and access.[57] Moreover, engagement and consultation are to be undertaken in a manner that encourages businesses to identify and remove barriers to stakeholder engagement such as language, culture, gender and power imbalances, and divisions within the community so as to ensure engagement and consultation are effective.[58] Given the previously noted inadequacies in implementation and/or enforcement of consultation and consent obligations by governments, the OECD warns that if business enterprises choose to operate in countries where the government does not fulfil its human rights obligations, this does not absolve the enterprise of its responsibility to provide a remedy where a business has contributed to an adverse human rights impact.[59] In addition, in those contexts in which a host government is not fulfilling its human rights obligations, business enterprises may use their leverage with the local or national government to encourage change, for example, through better enforcement of laws and regulations.[60]

[55] OECD Guidelines For Multinational Enterprises 32 (OECD Publishing 2011).

[56] OECD Due Diligence Guidance for Responsible Business Conduct 50 (OECD 2018).

[57] *Id.* at 18.

[58] OECD, *supra* note 56, at 51.

[59] *Id.* at 89.

[60] *Id.* at 76.

D. International Finance Corporation

The IFC, a member of the World Bank Group based in Washington, D.C., that provides lending to the private sector for investment projects, issued a series of *Performance Standards on Environmental and Social Sustainability* and associated Guidance Notes in 2012 that apply not only to the IFC but also to companies that receive IFC financing, be it in the form of a loan or equity.

IFC Performance Standard 7 on Indigenous Peoples, one of eight *Performance Standards on Environmental and Social Sustainability*, is specifically focused on issues arising from projects impacting Indigenous communities.[61] Private sector companies are required to undertake an engagement process with potentially impacted Indigenous communities that includes stakeholder analysis and engagement planning, disclosure of information, consultation, and participation in a culturally appropriate manner. This process of informed consultation and participation should involve the Indigenous peoples' own representative bodies and organizations, as well as members of the larger Indigenous community, and should provide enough time for Indigenous peoples' decision-making processes (Paragraph 10 to Performance Standard 7).

Free, prior, and informed consent is required, according to Guidance Note 7 that accompanies Performance Standard 7, for certain IFC-funded initiatives whenever the design, implementation, and expected outcomes of a project result in:

1. Impacts on lands and natural resources subject to traditional ownership or under customary use;
2. Relocation of Indigenous Peoples from lands and natural resources subject to traditional ownership or under customary use;
3. Significant impacts on critical cultural heritage that is essential to the identity and/or cultural, ceremonial, or spiritual aspects of Indigenous Peoples' lives, including natural areas with cultural and/or spiritual value such as sacred groves, sacred bodies of water and waterways, sacred trees, and sacred rocks; or,
4. Use of cultural heritage, including knowledge, innovations or practices of Indigenous Peoples for commercial purposes.[62]

The IFC also emphasizes in the same Guidance Note that the process and outcome of free, prior, and informed consent "do not require unanimous support from all members of Affected Communities of Indigenous Peoples."[63] However, other than for projects necessitating relocation, the IFC's interpretation of what should happen in the absence of Indigenous peoples' consent is at, best, ambiguous.[64] Other ambiguities include an implication that

[61] The full text of *Performance Standards on Environmental and Social Sustainability*, including Performance Standard 7 on Indigenous Peoples, is available at: https://www.ifc.org/wps/wcm/connect/24e6bfc3-5de3-444d-be9b-226188c95454/PS_English_2012_Full-Document.pdf?MOD=AJPERES&CVID=jkV-X6h.

[62] Guidance Note 7: Indigenous Peoples 10 (IFC 2012).

[63] *Id.* at 11.

[64] Doyle, *supra* note 2, at 206.

consent may not be required until after implementation, and the role that Indigenous peoples themselves are entitled to play in defining and implementing the consent processes.[65]

Performance Standard 7 and its affiliated Guidance Note also suffer from certain structural limitations including: (1) reliance on the private sector borrower implementing the project for actual enforcement; (2) increasing use of financial intermediaries that further distances the IFC from project oversight; (3) no direct recourse by impacted communities to the IFC for noncompliance; and (4) no contractual link of the State to the IFC agreement with the private sector borrower, even though the State is legally obligated to oversee implementation of the consultation process.[66]

V. Identification of Outstanding and Evolving Issues

A. Varying Interpretations of Consultation

ILO 169's prior consultation obligations and, to a lesser extent, the UNDRIP principle of free, prior, and informed consent of Indigenous peoples, have been incorporated into the domestic legal frameworks of many Western Hemisphere countries through national legislation and/or national court decisions. Significant variations exist, however, as to what triggers the obligation to consult and when it must occur, what constitutes appropriate consultation, who is deemed to be Indigenous, who specifically within a community must be consulted, what entity does the consulting and in what manner, as well as what constitutes meaningful consent and the ramifications, if any, should consent not be obtained. The fact that the consultation requirement is addressed in different legal instruments and by multiple legal contexts in both the international and domestic legal systems, adds to the uncertainty about its scope and content.[67] This situation is aggravated by the fact that the "general position of the ILO supervisory bodies has been that the requirement of consultation is an obligation of process, which means that it does not impose the duty to obtain the consent of the Indigenous community affected."[68]

Even in cases where the letter of the national law may have been strictly followed, this will not always avoid social conflict and even violent confrontations with Indigenous communities who feel they were not adequately consulted or properly compensated for damages sustained as a result of a government-authorized investment or development project. This is exacerbated by the fact that in cases where the UNDRIP's free, prior, and informed consent obligation is subsumed within the consultation requirement arising out of ILO 169, this does not, in general, provide for Indigenous communities exercising any type of veto power. Such an expansive notion of consent would constitute an expression of full self-determination and territoriality, something anathema to governments sensitive to any infringement of national sovereignty. Accordingly, this situation often leads to misunderstandings on the part of Indigenous communities which, not unreasonably, interpret consent as a right to reject any type

[65] *Id.* at 206–207.

[66] Doyle, *supra* note 2, at 207–208.

[67] Cabrera Ormaza, *supra* note 11, at 5–6.

[68] *Id.* at 2.

of investment project that threatens their way of life or will permanently displace them from ancestral lands.

B. Limitations on Indigenous Peoples' Right to Genuine Self-Determination as Manifested in a Lack of Veto Power

Despite the proclamation in Article 3 of the UNDRIP that Indigenous peoples have the right to self-determination, the ramifications of what this entails remain highly contested. For example, even Article 46(1) emphasizes that nothing in the UNDRIP may be construed as authorizing or encouraging any action which would dismember or impair, totally or in part, the territorial integrity or political unity of sovereign and independent States. Accordingly, the UNDRIP is "not designed to end the relationship of domination between polities called 'States' and peoples termed 'Indigenous.'[69]

A limited conception of self-determination also impacts the UNDRIP's requirement of free, prior, and informed consent and whether this obligation grants Indigenous peoples a "veto power" over the State, "[a]s full consent is an expression of full self-determination."[70] The argument against such an expansive notion of consent "is usually justified as an expression of State sovereignty" and "the necessity of economic development and the fulfillment of the government's social responsibilities" even if the model of development of Indigenous peoples may not, for example, favor extractive exploitation.[71] Under this approach, "the promotion of extractive projects requires a legal framework that recognizes Indigenous rights as only being related to social and economic participation in the project" but "not rights of self-determination and territoriality expressed in their right to provide consent."[72]

C. Tensions between Indigenous Peoples' Individual and Collective Rights

As previously noted, recognition of the collective rights of Indigenous peoples is a novelty in international law, as human rights have been traditionally centered around the individual. This recognition of collective rights, however, can create tensions between respect for the human rights of individuals versus those of the whole community. For example, carrying out a consultation with a traditional council made up only of male elders risks overlooking the viewpoints of not only women, but also youth, and may lead to violations of their rights. In such a scenario, for example, short-term pecuniary interests that may motivate elderly persons can override the long-term interests of younger people in limiting sociocultural and environmental harm generated by an extractive investment project.

---

[69] Steven Newcomb, *Domination in Relation to Indigenous ("Dominated") Peoples in International Law* in Irene Watson, Ed., Indigenous Peoples As Subjects of International Law 28 (Routledge 2018).

[70] Roger Merino, *Law and Politics of Indigenous Self-Determination: The Meaning of the Right to Prior Consultation*, in Irene Watson, Ed., Indigenous Peoples As Subjects of International Law 28 (Routledge 2018), at 131.

[71] *Id.* at 139.

[72] Merino, *supra* note 70, at 132.

VI. Identification of Good Human Rights Due Diligence Practices

Human rights due diligence is understood as the process through which enterprises can identify, prevent, mitigate, and account for how they address the actual and potential adverse human rights impacts in their own operations, supply chains, and other business relationships, as an integral part of business decision-making and risk management systems.[73] Due diligence "reflects the assumption that preventing harms is preferable to imposing liability after harms are inflicted, and that corporations are in the best position to determine how to do so."[74] Human rights due diligence is not necessarily the same thing as corporate due diligence for legal compliance purposes, because the focus is not on the risk to the company *per se* but rather on stakeholders who are affected by its operations.[75] Accordingly, meaningful stakeholder engagement is important throughout the duration of a project, including when assessing actual or potential adverse impacts on human rights. In the case of Indigenous peoples, stakeholder engagement or consultation is a human right in and of itself.

Based on ILO 169 and the UNDRIP—as well as the guidance provided by international, regional, and multilateral institutions such as the Inter-American Court of Human Rights, the OECD, the IFC, and the UN—businesses should formulate human rights due diligence standards that include consultation policies and processes for all projects that will or may impact Indigenous communities, including their lands, natural resources, and water supplies subject to traditional ownership or under customary use. At a minimum, these internal processes require that the company:

1. Consult with actual or potentially impacted Indigenous communities in good faith, which includes:
   a. respecting traditional decision-making structures;
   b. providing all relevant information promptly and in a manner that accounts for language and other potential barriers to effective engagement;
   c. providing the community with adequate time to make determinations; and,
   d. not taking advantage of power imbalances.
2. Conduct culturally appropriate consultations before any type of government authorization is granted or any action occurs to initiate the activity or begin implementing the project;
3. Engage an independent and technically capable entity to carry out an environmental and social impact assessment prior to the commencement of any large-scale project;
4. Include the Indigenous community in the design of any impact assessment, including seeking input on what should be examined; and

[73] OECD GUIDELINES FOR MULTINATIONAL ENTERPRISES, *supra* note 55, at 23.

[74] Groulx Diggs et. al., *supra* note 21, at 316.

[75] *Id.* at 316–317.

5. Obtain, as a result of consultations, and maintain through subsequent stakeholder engagement, the "free, prior, and informed" consent of the relevant Indigenous community. This means that consent previously given can subsequently be revoked.

A 2010 report by the Inter-American Commission on Human Rights provides guidance for ensuring that the collective interest of an Indigenous community does not prevail to the detriment or exclusion of individual members.[76] The report recommends that all members of a community should be fully and accurately informed of the nature and consequences of the process and provided with an effective opportunity to participate individually or collectively.[77] The requirement of full participation is not met whenever: members of a community have not been afforded a full and effective role in the selection, authorization, or mandate of those who act on behalf of the community; the corresponding claims are promoted by a particular band, clan, or segment of the community; or appropriate consultations among the members of the entire community are not carried out at the moment of adopting substantial decisions affecting the rights or interests of the community.[78]

A Good Practice Note on *Indigenous Peoples Rights and the Role of Free, Prior and Informed Consent*, prepared by Amy Lehr, was endorsed by the UNGC Human Rights and Labor Working Group in 2014. It emphasizes that consent "means an agreement to a company activity, not merely consultation" and "[i]t can be understood as a formal, documented social license to operate."[79] This agreement should ideally be in writing and state:

1. The nature of the project;
2. Any benefits that will accrue to the community;
3. Mitigation steps the company will take to address risks;
4. The stage of the project that the agreement includes;
5. Project milestones at which the company would need to obtain consent for additional activities or other planned steps; and
6. Monitoring mechanisms or any other means through which the community and company will continue to engage.[80]

In addition to detailing benefits and mitigation steps to address risks in the written agreement itself, a company must also track the effectiveness of responses to negative impacts and be prepared to offer just and fair compensation to an Indigenous community for any damages that arise from its activity or project. To facilitate this, a company should also establish an effective and culturally appropriate grievance mechanism.

Because business enterprises are not constrained by sovereignty concerns, a good practice is for a company to obtain consent premised on an expansive conception of Indigenous

[76] Inter-American Commission on Human Rights, Indigenous and Tribal Peoples' Rights Over Their Ancestral Lands and Natural Resources 107 (OAS 2010).

[77] *Id.* at 107.

[78] Inter-American Commission on Human Rights, *supra* note 76, at 107.

[79] Lehr, *supra* note 31, at 16.

[80] *Id.* at 18.

self-determination. As recommended by the UNGC's *Business Reference Guide*, if—after a thorough consultation with all relevant members of an Indigenous community—the free, prior, and informed consent for a business activity that impacts Indigenous land, territory, or resources is not forthcoming, then the activity should not proceed. Companies fearful of losing business opportunities to less scrupulous—and ultimately more short-sighted—competitors should heed the advice contained in the *OECD Due Diligence Guidance for Responsible Business Conduct* and use their leverage with local or national governments to lobby for enforcement of an interpretation of consent by Indigenous Peoples that encompasses a veto power.

VII. Conclusion

Although governments have the primary responsibility to consult with and obtain the free, prior, and informed consent of Indigenous peoples before authorizing investment or development projects, the business sector's increasing acknowledgment of its human rights responsibilities represents a dynamic and potentially significant development in terms of achieving full compliance with both separate but intertwined requirements of consultation and consent. Undoubtedly this development has been furthered by years of work in connection with the UNGPs to ensure that respect for human rights is a global standard of expected conduct for all business enterprises, and that this obligation "exists independently of States' abilities and/or willingness to fulfil their own human rights obligations."[81] Furthermore, this development is also an outgrowth of practical considerations attributable to the experiences of companies who, in the recent past, have forfeited millions of dollars due to operational delays, were forced to abandon concessions, or even faced government revocation of previously granted concessions, in response to ongoing Indigenous protests.[82] In addition, equity investors with investment risk management concerns are emerging as important guarantors of corporate consultation and consent with Indigenous communities, particularly in the extractive industry.[83]

The ultimate test of whether a company's human rights due diligence policies related to consultation and consent have value is the extent to which they avoid the types of social conflict and violence that have characterized investment and development projects where there was an actual or perceived failure to adequately consult detrimentally impacted Indigenous communities. In this regard, it is important for companies to "recognize the distinction between legal requirements and socially responsible and sustainable practices that go above and beyond the bare minimum legal framework."[84] In fact, it is now incontestable that the right of Indigenous peoples to give or withhold free, prior, and informed consent falls within

---

[81] Guiding Principles on Business and Human Rights, *supra* note 16, at 13.

[82] Lehr, *supra* note 31, at 7.

[83] Doyle, *supra* note 2, at 240.

[84] Charlotte Teal, Sharon Singh, & Radha Curpen, *Corporate Social Responsibility and Indigenous Rights* in Alan S, Gutterman Et. Al., Eds, The Lawyer's Corporate Responsibility Deskbook 197 (American Bar Association 2019).

the universe of rights which corporations are expected to respect independently of whatever consultation and consent requirements may be incumbent on a government.[85]

VIII. Resources and References

AQ Editors, *TIPNIS Protestors Retake March after Negotiations Fail.* Americas Quarterly, October 11, 2011, https://www.americasquarterly.org/blog/tipnis-protesters-retake-march-after-negotiations-fail/

Barrera-Hernández, Lila. *Peruvian Indigenous Land Conflict Explained,* Americas Quarterly, June 12, 2009, https://www.americasquarterly.org/article/peruvian-indigenous-land-conflict-explained/.

Cabrera Ormaza, María Victoria. The Requirement of Consultation with Indigenous Peoples in the ILO. Leiden: Brill/Nijhoff, 2017.

Doyle, Cathal M. Indigenous Peoples, Title to Territory, Rights and Resources. Abingdon, UK: Routledge, 2015.

Eichler, Jessika. Reconciling Indigenous Peoples' Individual and Collective Rights. Abingdon, UK: Routledge, 2019.

Global Sustainability Standards Board. *GRI 411: Rights of Indigenous Peoples 2016.* Amsterdam: Global Reporting Initiative, 2018. Available at: https://www.globalreporting.org/standards/media/1026/gri-411-rights-of-indigenous-peoples-2016.pdf.

Groulx Diggs, Elise, Mitt Regan, & Beatrice Parance. *Business and Human Rights as a Galaxy of Norms.* Georgetown J. of Int'l L. 50, 309–362, (2019).

Gutterman, Alan S., Margaret M. Cassidy, Travis Miller & Ashley C. Walter, eds. The Lawyer's Corporate Social Responsibility Deskbook. Chicago: American Bar Association, 2019.Hohmann, Jessie & Marc Weller, eds. The UN Declaration on the Rights of Indigenous Peoples: A Commentary. Oxford: Oxford University Press, 2018.

International Finance Corporation (IFC). *Guidance Notes to Performance Standard 7 on Indigenous Peoples.* Washington, DC: IFC, 2012. Available at: https://www.ifc.org/wps/wcm/connect/9baef8f6-9bd9-4d95-a595-7373059081d4/GN7_English_2012.pdf?MOD=AJPERES&CVID=mRQk089

International Finance Corporation (IFC). *Performance Standards on Environmental and Social Sustainability.* Washington, DC: IFC, 2012. Available at: https://www.ifc.org/wps/wcm/connect/24e6bfc3-5de3-444d-be9b-226188c95454/PS_English_2012_FullDocument.pdf?MOD=AJPERES&CVID=jkV-X6h

Inter-American Commission on Human Rights. *Indigenous and Tribal Peoples' Rights Over Their Ancestral Lands and Natural Resources.* Washington, D.C.: Organization of American States, 2010. Available at: https://www.oas.org/en/iachr/indigenous/docs/pdf/AncestralLands.pdf.

[85] Doyle, *supra* note 2, at 278.

Lehr, Amy K. *Indigenous Peoples Rights and the Role of Free, Prior, and Informed Consent.* United Nations Global Compact, 2014. Available at: https://d306pr3pise04h.cloudfront.net/docs/issues_doc%2Fhuman_rights%2FHuman_Rights_Working_Group%2FFPIC_Indigenous_Peoples_GPN.pdf

McHarg, Aileen, Barry Barton, Adrian Bradbrook, & Lee Godden, eds. Property and the Law in Energy and Natural Resources. Oxford: Oxford University Press, 2010.

Organisation for Economic Co-operation and Development (OECD). *OECD Due Diligence Guidance for Responsible Business Conduct.* Paris: OECD Publishing, 2018. Available at: http://mneguidelines.oecd.org/OECD-Due-Diligence-Guidance-for-Responsible-Business-Conduct.pdf

Organisation for Economic Co-operation and Development (OECD), *OECD Guidelines for Multinational Enterprises.* Paris: OECD Publishing, 2011. Available at: http://www.oecd.org/daf/inv/mne/48004323.pdf

UN Guiding Principles on Business and Human Rights. New York: United Nations, 2011. Available at: https://www.ohchr.org/documents/publications/guidingprinciplesbusinesshr_en.pdf

UN Global Compact. A Business Reference Guide: United Nations Declaration on the Rights of Indigenous Peoples. New York: UN Global Compact Office, 2013. Available at: https://d306pr3pise04h.cloudfront.net/docs/issues_doc%2Fhuman_rights%2FIndigenousPeoples%2FBusinessGuide.pdf

Watson, Irene, ed. Indigenous Peoples as Subjects of International Law. Abingdon, UK: Routledge, 2018.

Wright, Claire & Alexandra Tomaselli, eds. The Prior Consultation of Indigenous Peoples in Latin America. Abingdon, UK: Routledge, 2019.

Section B: Specific Challenges

12

The United Nations Guiding Principles on Business and Human Rights and Global Supply Chains

Andrea Shemberg and Bettina Braun

I. Introduction[1]

The *UN Guiding Principles on Business and Human Rights* (UNGPs) have profoundly influenced current thinking about companies' responsibility for their involvement in human rights abuses. This chapter focuses on one key aspect: how the UNGPs elaborate the *scope* of a company's responsibility to respect human rights, and what this implies for a company's responsibilities for human rights within its supply chains.[2]

Human rights risks in the context of supply chains have gained much attention over the past three decades, initially due to the emblematic cases of severe labor rights abuses in the 1990s, when complex supply chains rapidly expanded. Nike's use of sweatshop labor in

[1] The views expressed do not necessarily reflect the positions of the German Institute for Human Rights or the Global Business Initiative on Human Rights. The authors wish to thank Ana María Uribe for providing valuable research assistance.

[2] This chapter points to several public reports of company practice to offer examples relevant to the text. However, the inclusion of company policies and links does not indicate that the author has verified the quality of their human rights due diligence, nor does it indicate that the companies are necessary leaders or demonstrating best practices.

Indonesia and child labor in Pakistan to sew footballs are two such well-known cases.[3] Even as the UNGPs were being developed between 2005 and 2011, the question of scope of a company's responsibility for respecting human rights was often framed in terms of "how many tiers down" a company's responsibility ought to flow in its supply chains.

Instead of focusing on a specific number of tiers for which the business is responsible, the UNGPs elaborate that the business's scope of responsibility for adverse impacts on human rights extends across all business relationships—and is not limited to suppliers. A company's scope of responsibility for human rights impacts therefore includes those that occur through franchisee relationships, joint ventures, investor/investee relationships, customer and client relationships, and mergers and acquisitions, among others. Additionally, the UNGPs require a company to assess its impacts on all internationally recognized human rights, not just labor rights. The idea elaborated in the UNGPs, that a company can not only cause and contribute to human rights harms, but also be directly linked to human rights abuses through *all* of its business relationships, reflects the evidentiary findings of the UN Special Representative of the Secretary-General on the Issue of Human Rights and Transnational Corporations and Other Business Enterprises (SRSG) regarding the de facto relationship of a company's involvement in human rights abuses.[4] The expanded scope of responsibility "put business relationships squarely on the business and human rights map."[5]

The Office of the UN High Commissioner for Human Rights (OHCHR) Interpretive Guide (OHCHR Interpretive Guide), which provides guidance on understanding and applying the UNGPs, defines "business relationships" as:

> those relationships a business enterprise has with business partners, entities in its value chain and any other non-State or State entity directly linked to its business operations, products or services. They include indirect business relationships in its value chain, beyond the first tier, and minority as well as majority shareholding positions in joint ventures.[6]

This definition better reflects stakeholder expectations and opened up greater possibilities for collective action to tackle systemic issues that perpetuate human rights abuses in the context of commercial activities.

---

[3] *See* New Idea, *Nike Sweatshops: Inside the Scandal*, https://www.newidea.com.au/nike-sweatshops-the-truth-about-the-nike-factory-scandal (last visited September 12, 2021); International Labour Organization, *Elimination of Child Labour in the Soccer Ball Industry in Sialkot, Pakistan: Evaluation Report*, Doc. PAK/97/MO1/USA (1997-1999), https://www.ilo.org/wcmsp5/groups/public/---asia/---ro-bangkok/---sro-new_delhi/documents/publication/wcms_440159.pdf.

[4] John Ruggie (UN Special Representative of the Secretary-General on the Issue of Human Rights and Transnational Corporations and Other Business Enterprises), *Report of the Special Representative of the Secretary-General on the issue of human rights and transnational corporations and other business enterprises, Addendum: Corporations and human rights: A survey of the scope and patterns of alleged corporate-related human rights abuse*, UN Doc. A/HRC/8/5/Add.2 (2008).

[5] The Institute for Human Rights and Business (IHRB) & The Global Business Initiative on Human Rights (GBI), *State of Play: The Corporate Responsibility to Respect Human Rights in Business Relationships*, at 10 (2012), https://www.ihrb.org/pdf/state-of-play/State-of-Play-Full-Report.pdf.

[6] UN Office of the High Commissioner for Human Rights (OHCHR), *The Corporate Responsibility to Protect Human Rights: An Interpretive Guide*, at 5, UN Doc. HR/PUB/12/02 (2012).

The UNGPs' elaboration of a company's responsibility for human rights abuses across all business relationships has practical implications within supply chains. Specifically, it has implications for: companies pursuing human rights due diligence and identifying risk; legislators forging rules concerning company responsibilities for human rights; lawyers advising commercial clients; and individuals bringing grievances under legal or other processes. This chapter will explore those implications by examining the UNGPs' elaboration of the scope of responsibility in Section II and exploring the UNGPs' influence as evidenced by current regulatory and soft law developments in Section III. The chapter will then conclude, in Section IV, by highlighting several open questions and challenges regarding respecting human rights in the context of supply chains. This chapter focuses on supply chains, but it should not be forgotten that human rights risks in other types of business relationships, including those mentioned above, are increasingly the focus of lawsuits and of legislative and soft law developments.[7]

II. Context

A. From Supply Chain to Value Chain Thinking

In 2008, the SRSG clearly defined the root cause of the business and human rights "problem" as not simply the result of companies as bad actors (as some advocates had done) or as the result of economic globalization itself (as others had done), but instead as the result of global "governance gaps." Specifically, he stated:

> The root cause of the business and human rights predicament today lies in the governance gaps created by globalization—between the scope and impact of economic forces and actors, and the capacity of societies to manage their adverse consequences. These governance gaps provide the permissive environment for wrongful acts by companies of all kinds without adequate sanctioning or reparation. How to narrow and ultimately bridge the gaps in relation to human rights is our fundamental challenge.[8]

Overcoming the challenges of narrowing and bridging the governance gaps related to human rights, according to the SRSG, would not be the work of a single human rights treaty or only of legislators. He observed that "[t]here is no single silver bullet solution to the institutional misalignments in the business and human rights domain. Instead, all social actors—States, businesses, and civil society—must learn to do many things differently."[9]

[7] *See e.g.*, Vedanta Resources Plc and Konkola Copper Mines Plc v Lungowe and Ors. (Respondents) [2019] UKSC 20. Rhiannon Hoyle and Andrew Peaple, *Financial Impact of Brazil Dam Catastrophe Weighs on BHP BILLIton*, Wall St. J. (Nov. 9, 2015), https://www.wsj.com/articles/dam-burst-costs-could-break-1-billion-analyst-says-1447043902. *See also* Anna Triponel, *Human Rights and M&A: It's No Longer about the "Why"; It's Now about the "How,"* Thomas Reuters Practical Law (May 14, 2019) https://uk.practicallaw.thomsonreuters.com/w-020-2360?transitionType=Default&contextData=(sc.Default)&firstPage=true.

[8] John Ruggie (UN Special Representative of the Secretary-General on the Issue of Human Rights and Transnational Corporations and Other Business Enterprises), *Protect, Respect and Remedy: A Framework for Business and Human Rights*, § 3, UN Doc. A/HRC/8/5 (Apr. 7, 2008).

[9] *Id.*, § 7.

The SRSG designed the UNGPs as an authoritative foundation that would serve as a single reference point for guiding this learning so that shifts in behavior of many actors would cohere and create cumulative impact. Consequently, the UNGPs serve as a tool to catalyze the creation of new governance systems, including state-based (rules), civil (stakeholder initiatives and pressure), and corporate rules and systems, to ultimately bridge the governance gaps in global business.

The scope of the "responsibility to respect human rights" in business relationships, defined in Principle 13 of the UNGPs, encompasses (i) those abuses the company causes or contributes to through its own activities or (ii) "human rights impacts that are directly linked to their operations, products or services by their business relationships, even if they have not contributed to those impacts."[10]

"Contribution," as elaborated further by the OHCHR Interpretive Guide,[11] encompasses the company's acts that contribute to the wrongs of another entity—including those with whom the company has a business relationship, such as joint venture partners, customers, or suppliers. A company changing product requirements for suppliers that forces them to violate labor standards is one example of "contribution."[12] Common law lawyers will be familiar with this reasoning from tort law liability concepts.

The "directly linked" concept was innovative because it attaches responsibility to companies irrespective of their own contribution to the potential or actual harm. This responsibility reflects stakeholder expectations that malfeasance, whether deep in supply chains or carried out by distributors, end-users, or business partners, taints the product, the service, and the corporate operations. Importantly, attaching responsibility to those companies directly linked to human rights harms through their business relationships incentivizes "parent companies and companies at the apex of producer or buyer-led value chains to use whatever **leverage** they have in relation to their subsidiaries, contractors and other actors in their network of business relationships to improve respect for human rights. They should establish clear policies and operational procedures that embed respecting rights throughout their entire value chain system."[13] Furthermore, placing responsibility on companies, which potentially flows through all business relationships via the concept of direct linkage, helps alter management's tendency to look only at the human rights risks over which a company can exercise some commercial control, such as those in the major first-tier suppliers. This expanded scope of responsibility more accurately reflects the reality that the severe risks to people that lie deep in global value chains or relate to end-use of products will require collective action of many actors to make positive change.[14]

---

[10] UN OHCHR *Guiding Principles on Business and Human Rights*, § 13, UN Doc. HR/PUB/11/04 (2011).

[11] UN OHCHR, *supra*, note 6, at 16–17.

[12] *Id.*

[13] John Ruggie, Keynote Address, *Conference on Business & Human Rights: Towards a Common Agenda for Action*, Shift & the Finnish Presidency of the Council of the EU (Dec. 2, 2019) (emphasis added), https://shiftproject.org/resource/john-ruggie-keynote-finland2019/.

[14] *See* Letter from John Ruggie, Board Chair of Shift and Berthold Beitz Professor at Harvard Kennedy School, to Peter Altmaier, Hubertus Heil, Gerd Müller, Federal Ministers of Germany for Economic Affairs and Energy, Labor

Both the UNGPs and the *OECD Guidelines on Multinational Enterprises* (OECD Guidelines), a set of responsible business conduct standards that date from 1976 and are aligned with the UNGPs, use the term "value chain" instead of "supply chain." "Value chain" is defined as follows in the OHCHR Interpretive Guide:

> A business enterprise's value chain encompasses the activities that convert input into output by adding value. It includes entities with which it has a direct or indirect business relationship and which either (a) supply products or services that contribute to the enterprise's own products or services, or (b) receive products or services from the enterprise.[15]

Therefore, value chain thinking looks at an entity's upstream and downstream and direct and indirect relationships. This approach brings into sharp relief many situations that have created headlines in recent years, such as Toyota trucks being used by Al-Qaeda and ISIS,[16] facial recognition technology sold to police departments and then deployed to violate rights, such as the right to peaceful assembly and association,[17] and the misuse of bicycles as weapons against peaceful protestors by police departments in the context of Black Lives Matter protests.[18] Although these situations would not normally be seen to be related to Toyota's supply chain, tech firms, or bicycle brands, respectively, they now fall squarely within the scope of a business's responsibility to respect human rights in connection with its value chain under international standards on business and human rights.

The UNGPs were designed, therefore, to move companies, policy makers, and others beyond supply chain thinking to that of business relationships, and in the context of their production of products and services, to think across value chains. This shift to value chain thinking is the reason why The Coca-Cola Company undertook a series of studies of human rights risks associated with sugar production. The public report on their efforts begins: "As part of a commitment to respect human rights across our value chain, the company initiated third-party studies to evaluate key human rights risks in top sugar sourcing countries."[19] Nestlé also has activated value chain analysis regarding human rights impacts,[20] and Heineken

---

and Social Affairs & Economic Cooperation and Development (Mar. 9, 2021), https://shiftproject.org/wp-content/uploads/2021/03/Shift_John-Ruggie_Letter_German-DD.pdf.

15 UN OHCHR, *supra*, note 6, at 8.

16 Nathan Pemberton, *U.S. Government Wants to Know: Why Does ISIS Only Drive Toyotas?* New York Magazine (Oct. 8, 2015), https://nymag.com/intelligencer/2015/10/us-govt-asks-why-does-isis-drive-toyotas.html.

17 Andrews K. Hunton, *UK Court of Appeal Finds Automated Facial Recognition Technology Unlawful in Bridges v South Wales Police*, Privacy & Information Security Law Blog (Aug. 12, 2020), https://www.huntonprivacyblog.com/2020/08/12/uk-court-of-appeal-finds-automated-facial-recognition-technology-unlawful-in-bridges-v-south-wales-police/.

18 Robert Annis, *The Police Are Weaponizing Bikes. Should Brands Stop Selling to Them?* Bicycling (Jun. 10, 2020), https://www.bicycling.com/news/a32816784/police-force-bicycles-black-lives-matter-protests/.

19 The Coca-Cola Company, *Human Rights in The Coca-Cola Company Sugar Supply Chain: Lessons and Opportunities*, at 1 (2019), https://www.coca-colacompany.com/content/dam/journey/us/en/policies/pdf/human-workplace-rights/addressing-global-issues/human-rights-in-the-coca-cola-sugar-supply-chain.pdf.

20 Nestlé, *Our Material Issues across the Value Chain*, https://www.nestle.com/sites/default/files/asset-library/documents/creating-shared-value/our-material-issues-across-the-value-chain.pdf.

and ABN Amro have been working on human rights risk mapping in their value chains, as have many other companies.[21]

B. How the UNGPs Influence Approaches with Buyers

As described above, the UNGPs have shifted the idea of what companies should do to manage human rights risks by expanding a company's responsibility to apply throughout its business relationships and value chains. The company's human rights responsibility in its value chain is broad and relates to indirect business relationships as well as customers, clients, and end-users. A focus on a company's relationships with entities in its supply chain demonstrates how the UNGPs require a shift in the way companies have traditionally and generally managed human rights risks.

For example, prior to the UNGPs' endorsement in 2011, buyer companies were increasingly requiring first-tier (and sometimes second- or third-tier) suppliers to apply certain labor and working conditions standards. Still today, companies often include representations and warranties of labor conditions in their supply contracts and conduct audits to verify compliance.[22] This approach may be useful for discrete issues that can be enforced in a compliance fashion based on audits, for example on the quality of worker housing or verification of the availability of information on harmful substances in the workplace. From a UNGPs perspective, however, this approach is potentially problematic for at least two reasons.

First, supplier codes of conduct or contractual clauses tend to focus on supplier behavior and fail to consider how the buyer company's terms, conditions, and pressures affect the supplier's behavior. The UNGPs expect that buyers, when addressing human rights abuses in supply chains, should assess the adverse effects of their own buying behavior. Purchasing practices such as "timing demands, pricing pressures, and last-minute order modifications, as well as a lack of due diligence—turning a blind eye—to human rights issues"[23] can contribute to human rights abuses in the supply chain. A sole focus on supplier behavior and supplier codes of conduct without changing buying behavior in such situations is unlikely to get at some of the root causes of human rights abuses.

Secondly, supplier codes of conduct can also distort the practices of suppliers by forcing them to prioritize selected human rights risks irrespective of the real risks to people in any given context. The UNGPs expect companies to take a proactive approach that identifies and prioritizes their actual salient human rights risks in the supply chain, no matter what kind of human rights might be impacted, without a predetermination as to which rights are most

---

[21] David Vermijs, *How Value Chain Mapping Is Helping Companies Respect Human Rights*, Shift Project (Mar. 2019), https://shiftproject.org/how-value-chain-mapping-is-helping-companies-respect-human-rights/.

[22] IHRB & GBI, *supra*, note 5, at 103.

[23] David V. Snyder, Susana Maslow & Sarah Dadush, *Balancing Buyer and Supplier Responsibilities: Model Contract Clauses to Protect Workers in International Supply Chains*, 77 Business Lawyer (ABA) (forthcoming in winter 2021-2022) (manuscript version 2.0 at 4), https://ssrn.com/abstract=3829782. For research, *see also* Richard Locke, Matthew Amengual & Akshay Mangla, *Virtue Out of Necessity? Compliance, Commitment and the Improvement of Labor Conditions in Global Supply Chains*, MIT Sloan Research Paper No. 4719-08 (Oct. 3, 2008), http://dx.doi.org/10.2139/ssrn.1286142.

important. This proactive approach is beginning to take hold in at least some companies,[24] even while countries have adopted regulatory norms related to specific labor rights in supply chains, such as modern slavery and child labor standards.[25]

The UNGPs make it clear that responsibility for ensuring respect for human rights in the supply chain is the responsibility of all entities in the supply chain. This means that even though large, consumer-facing companies may receive heightened pressure because they are more likely to be the subject of media headlines and advocacy campaigns, all companies have an identical responsibility, recognized by the UNGPs, to respect human rights. Consequently, the UNGPs harmonize expectations, thereby providing the basis for all companies to ask their respective suppliers about their human rights policies and human rights due diligence processes. If companies throughout the supply chain follow the UNGPs, this creates a cascade of harmonized expectations.

Harmonized expectations facilitate suppliers' ability to meet those expectations because doing so is an efficient way to satisfy all buyers. Harmonized expectations also facilitate collaboration among companies to strengthen the management and leadership of their mutual suppliers to strengthen their human rights due diligence processes. The Responsible Business Alliance is one such example of a collaboration born of harmonized expectations.[26] There are also several good examples of lead companies working with suppliers in a manner that recognizes their own responsibility under the UNGPs and strengthens their suppliers' capacity to implement international human rights standards.[27]

The Global Business Initiative on Human Rights (GBI), a business-led membership organization engaged in peer learning to help companies implement the UNGPs, has fostered collaboration between buyer companies and suppliers.[28] Several member companies have invited their major suppliers to join peer learning processes held worldwide and have even successfully encouraged major suppliers to become full-fledged members.

---

[24] *See, e.g.*, ERICSSON, Salient Human Rights Risk, https://www.ericsson.com/en/about-us/sustainability-and-corporate-responsibility/responsible-business/responsible-sourcing/human-rights-in-our-supply-chain/salient-human-rights-aspects (last visited Sept. 9, 2021); H&M, *Salient Human Rights Issues* (2020), https://hmgroup.com/wp-content/uploads/2021/03/Salient-Human-Rights-Issues-2020.pdf; and PEPSICO, *PepsiCO Global Human Rights Statement* (Jun. 2017), https://www.pepsico.com/docs/default-source/sustainability-and-esg-topics/human-rights-and-salient-issues-statement.pdf?sfvrsn=a65299a3_3.

[25] *See Modern Slavery Act 2015*, c. 30 (Eng.); *Modern Slavery Act 2018*, No. 153 (Austl.); and NEW ZEALAND GOVERNMENT, *Plan of Action against Forced Labour, People Trafficking and Slavery* (2020), https://www.mbie.govt.nz/dmsdocument/13568-combatting-modern-forms-of-slavery-plan-of-action-against-forced-labour-people-trafficking-slavery.

[26] *See* Responsible Business Alliance, https://www.responsiblebusiness.org/ (last visited Feb. 11, 2021).

[27] *See* MARKS & SPENCER, Supplier Management, https://corporate.marksandspencer.com/sustainability/food-and-household/supplier-management (last visited Sept. 9, 2021); UNILEVER, *Human Rights Report: Creating a Fairer and More Socially Inclusive World* (2020), https://www.unilever.com/Images/unilever-human-rights-report-2020_tcm244-558516_en.pdf; HEWLETT PACKARD ENTERPRISE, Supply Chain Responsibility, https://www.hpe.com/us/en/about/human-progress/supply-chain-responsibility.html (last visited Sept. 9, 2021); and Sundeep Singh, *Safeguarding Human Rights across BHP's Supply Chain*, BHP (Dec. 9, 2019), https://www.bhp.com/news/prospects/2019/12/safeguarding-human-rights-across-bhps-supply-chain.

[28] *See* GLOBAL BUSINESS INITIATIVE ON HUMAN RIGHTS, gbihr.org.

The extended scope of buyer entities' responsibility for their supply chains, irrespective of the distance between the company and the human rights abuse in the supply chain, increases the importance of the buyer's screening of suppliers on the basis of suppliers' capacity to manage their human rights risks in their own operations as well as their supply chains. Consequently, instead of merely relying on suppliers meeting performance-based contractual obligations primarily verified through audits, buyer companies focus on identifying suppliers with human rights risk management systems or with the potential and willingness to develop them.

Companies across the globe have largely welcomed the UNGPs' expanded scope of responsibility for their supply chains and other business relationships. Indeed, there is growing business support for mandatory rules on human rights due diligence to align with the UNGPs. For example, in September 2021, a cross-sectoral group of industry organizations and major companies issued a public letter in support of mandatory European rules on human rights and environmental due diligence in line with international standards.[29] In December 2021, a similar letter was issued by industry associations and responsible business initiatives.[30] Likewise, a group of investors worth US$5 trillion called on governments to institute mandatory human rights due diligence measures for companies.[31] While interest in legal certainty and a level playing field are also influencing the position of businesses on the issue of human rights due diligence legislation, the leverage that results from harmonized standards and a legal requirement applicable throughout the entire supply chain is surely also appealing to buyer firms.

In sum, the UNGPs broadened the companies' scope of responsibility to include all human rights impacts that occur through their business relationships. This has moved considerations of human rights risks from a supply chain perspective to a value chain perspective including clients, customers, and end-users as well as suppliers. In the specific context of supply chains, this responsibility includes indirect suppliers and in the context of multi-tiered and complex supply chains, the UNGPs harmonize expectations by recognizing the responsibility of buyers and an identical responsibility for every company in the supply chain. The UNGPs are designed to assist in driving momentum for collective action around preventing, mitigating, and remediating the worst human rights abuses first, no matter how many tiers down in the supply chain these abuses occur. The broadened idea of responsibility of companies for human rights abuses in their supply chains also has influenced the development of legislation, case law, soft law standards, and practitioner guidance. These influences are reviewed in the next Section.

---

[29] Statement from Adidas AG, Aldi Nord, and 24 other companies, *Support for EU Framework on Mandatory Human Rights and Environmental Due Diligence* (Sept. 2, 2020), https://media.business-humanrights.org/media/documents/EU_Business_Statement_Mandatory_Due_Diligence_02092020.pdf.

[30] *See* Industry Association and Responsible Business Initiatives Joint Statement, "*Ensuring Harmonisation and Consistency Across Due Diligence Frameworks,*" at https://www.amfori.org/sites/default/files/Statement%20harmonisation%20of%20due%20diligence%20frameworks.pdf.

[31] Investor Alliance for Human Rights, *Investors with US$5 Trillion Call on Governments to Institute Mandatory Human Rights Due Diligence Measures for Companies* (Apr. 21, 2020), https://investorsforhumanrights.org/news/investor-case-for-mhrdd.

III. Hard and Soft Law Norms Relevant to Supply Chains That Reflect the UNGPs

This Section highlights how the UNGPs are influencing hard and soft law developments regarding company responsibilities for human rights impacts in the context of complex and multi-tiered supply chains. Legal developments in this area are increasing at a rapid pace, particularly in the European Union (EU), but also the United States and worldwide. Indeed, in the United States, even specific state laws are being developed to address supply chain human rights issues.[32] This Section does not provide an exhaustive description of global supply chain regulation or company supply chain practices. Instead, it furnishes examples to assist legal practitioners with identifying the influence of the UNGPs on hard and soft law developments. The intention is therefore to contribute to lawyers' confidence in using the UNGPs and aligned international standards and guidance, such as that produced by the OECD, to advise clients, with or in multi-tiered and complex supply chains, on human rights.

A. Legal and Regulatory Developments

1. 2017 French Duty of Vigilance Law – Scope Still Unclear[33]

The French law is explored in detail in chapter 4 of this book. However, two points concerning the law and its approach to supply chain due diligence are of importance to the discussion in this chapter. First, it appears that the scope of responsibility under the law extends to subcontractors and suppliers when they have an "established commercial relationship" with the parent company or the companies that the parent company controls. The definition of "established commercial relationship" is still unclear, but it is interesting that instead of defining the scope of responsibility by number of tiers in a supply chain, the law looks to the potentially more inclusive ambit of "established commercial relationships," in line with the UNGPs focus on business relationships.[34] It is not entirely clear whether this term only covers direct suppliers or also extends to suppliers further embedded in the supply chain.[35] A case filed in March 2021 by Brazilian and Colombian civil society organizations against the supermarket chain Casino for deforestation linked to sales of beef may help clarify this point.[36] Additionally, there is a lack of clarity about the breadth of human rights

---

[32] *See e.g.*, Fashion Sustainability and Social Accountability Act, Assembly Bill A8352, (Oct. 20, 2021) https://www.nysenate.gov/legislation/bills/2021/A8352.

[33] Loi 2017-399 du 27 mars 2017 [Law 2017-399 of March 27, 2017 on the Duty of Care of Parent Companies and Ordering Companies], Journal Officiel de la République Française, Mar. 28, 2017.

[34] Stéphane Brabant, Charlotte Michon, Elsa Savourey, *The Vigilance Plan: Cornerstone of the Law on the Corporate Duty of Vigilance*, Revue Internationale de la Compliance et de L'Éthique des Affaires – Supplément à la Semaine Juridique Entreprise et Affairs N° 50 (Dec. 14, 2017).

[35] European Commission, Directorate-General for Justice and Consumers, Torres-Cortés, F., Salinier, C., Deringer, H., et al., *Study on Due Diligence Requirements through the Supply Chain: Final Report, Publications Office* (2020), https://data.europa.eu/doi/10.2838/39830.

[36] Business & Human Rights Resource Centre, *French Supermarket Giant Casino Sued Over Links to Amazon Deforestation* (2021), https://www.business-humanrights.org/en/latest-news/french-supermarket-giant-casino-sued-over-links-to-amazon-deforestation/.

covered. The law does not specify which human rights and environmental impacts should be the focus of businesses. However, in line with the UNGPs, it asks them to proactively identify risks before taking appropriate action.

2. *Dutch Efforts to Expand Supply Chain Law to All Human Rights*

The Dutch Child Labor Due Diligence Law, passed in May 2019, requires companies to investigate their supply chain to identify whether there is a reasonable presumption that their goods and/or services have been produced by child labor. Where this is the case, the company is required to draw up an action plan setting out measures to address these risks.

At the time of writing, the Dutch Parliament has proposed replacing this law with a new Responsible and Sustainable International Business Act.[37] The bill, submitted in March 2021, would expand the scope of protection to include all human rights, not just child labor. It would assign a duty of care to all companies, irrespective of size, and impose due diligence obligations on large companies to identify human rights risks in their business relationships. Whereas the due diligence obligation only falls on large companies, which are presumably more able to shoulder the administrative burden, the generalized duty of care may make it easier to sustain tort claims against small and medium-sized enterprises for human rights harms in their value chains. The duty of care and due diligence requirements integrated into the draft bill were influenced by the recent Dutch court case *Milieudefensie et al. v Royal Dutch Shell plc* explored below.[38]

In December 2021, after the EU announced another delay in publishing a draft Directive containing human rights due diligence obligations (further discussed below in Subsection viii), the Dutch Foreign Trade and Development minister announced that the Netherlands would go forward to introduce a national human rights and environmental due diligence law.[39]

3. *Milieudefensie et al. v Royal Dutch Shell plc (26 May 2021)*[40]

In May 2021, a Dutch court held that Royal Dutch Shell (RDS) is required to reduce its own greenhouse gas emissions as well as those emissions generated by end-users of its products, termed "Scope 3 emissions." This was a landmark decision for a host of reasons, including that the Court specifically referenced the UNGPs and the OHCHR Interpretive Guide in defining the scope of RDS's responsibility. It confirmed a company's responsibility for its value chain, from suppliers through to end-users. The Court also differentiated, consistent

[37] Tweede Kamer der Staten-Generaal [Second Chamber of the Parliament], Bill for Responsible and Sustainable International Business Act (submitted Mar. 11, 2021), https://www.tweedekamer.nl/kamerstukken/wetsvoorstellen/detail?cfg=wetsvoorsteldetails&qry=wetsvoorstel%3A35761.

[38] Anneloes Hoff, *A Bill for Better Business: Dissecting the New Dutch Mandatory Human Rights Due Diligence Initiative*, Völkerrechtsblog (May 5, 2021), https://voelkerrechtsblog.org/a-bill-for-better-business/ (last visited September 9, 2021). *Infra* Subsection iii.

[39] MVO Platform, *Dutch Minister Announces National Corporate Due Diligence Legislation*, European Coalition for Corporate Justice (Dec. 6, 2021), https://corporatejustice.org/news/dutch-minister-announces-national-corporate-due-diligence-legislation/.

[40] Rechtbank Den Haag, 26 mei 2021, C/09/571932 (Vereniging Milieudefensie et al./Royal Dutch Shell plc) (Neth.), https://uitspraken.rechtspraak.nl/inziendocument?id=ECLI:NL:RBDHA:2021:5339.

with the UNGPs, the expectations on RDS in addressing emissions, determined by whether the emissions emanate from RDS entities or relate to RDS's business relationships, including its end-users.[41]

4. *German Supply Chain Law – Timidly Beyond Tier One*

In June 2021, the German Parliament passed the Supply Chain Act now known as "Law on Corporate Due Diligence in Supply Chains."[42] The law entered into force on January 1, 2023 and applies to all Germany-based companies or subsidiaries with more than 3,000 employees as of 2023, and 1,000 employees as of 2024.

In several ways the law diverges from the UNGPs, but in others it reflects movement toward recognition of the UNGPs as a core standard related to multi-tiered supply chains.[43] For example, the law delineates a specific set of human rights it expects companies to address,[44] and while the list of rights is quite broad, it omits important rights, including those related to gender-based violence and Indigenous peoples.[45] The law focuses on responsibility for tier 1 suppliers, but it also stipulates that if a company obtains "substantiated knowledge" of a possible violation beyond the first tier, it should "carry out a risk analysis" and take appropriate measures to address the risk.[46]

Another interesting feature of the law, consistent with the UNGPs, is that it requires companies to implement purchasing practices that minimize human rights risks in recognition that purchase prices or lengths of contracts can have an important impact on the human rights risks in suppliers' facilities.[47]

5. *Norwegian Transparency Act*

In June 2021, Norway passed the "Åpenhetsloven," or Transparency Act.[48] It requires large companies domiciled in Norway or selling products or services in Norway to: conduct human rights due diligence in accordance with the OECD Guidelines, which are fully aligned with

---

[41] SHEARMAN & STERLING, *Milieudefensie v. Shell – A Landmark Court Decision for Energy and Energy-Intensive Companies* (2021), https://www.shearman.com/Perspectives/2021/06/Milieudefensie-v-Shell--Landmark-Court-Decision-For-Energy-Companies (last visited Oct. 25, 2022).

[42] Lieferkettensorgfaltspflichtengesetz (LkSG) [Act on Corporate Due Diligence in Supply Chains], BGBl. I at 2959 (2021) https://www.bgbl.de/xaver/bgbl/start.xav?start=//*%5B@attr_id=%27bgbl121s2959.pdf%27%5D#__bgbl__%2F%2F*%5B%40attr_id%3D%27bgbl121s2959.pdf%27%5D__1644514035237. BUSINESS & HUMAN RIGHTS RESOURCE CENTRE, German Parliament Passes Mandatory Human Rights Due Diligence Law (Jun. 16, 2021), https://www.business-humanrights.org/en/latest-news/german-due-diligence-law/ (last visited Sept. 9, 2021).

[43] John Ruggie, Board Chair of Shift, *supra* note 14.

[44] LkSG, *supra* note 42, Article 1 ("protected legal positions within the meaning of this Act are those arising from the conventions of the protection of human rights listed in nos. 1 to 11 of the Annex").

[45] LIEFERKETTENGESETZ, *What the New Supply Chain Act Delivers, and What It Does Not*, https://lieferkettengesetz.de/wp-content/uploads/2021/06/Initiative-Lieferkettengesetz_Analysis_What-the-new-supply-chain-act-delivers.pdf at page 5 (last visited Feb. 11, 2022).

[46] LkSG, *supra* note 42, Article 9 para 3.

[47] LkSG, *supra* note 42, Article 6 para 3(2).

[48] Act Relating to Enterprises' Transparency and Work on Fundamental Human Rights and Decent Working Conditions (Transparency Act), LOV-2021-06-18-99, unofficial translation https://lovdata.no/dokument/NLE/lov/2021-06-18-99.

the UNGPs; report on their due diligence practices; and answer information requests from any person on how they address adverse human rights impacts. The Transparency Act's scope of responsibility reflects the UNGPs' approach: due diligence obligations apply to a company's operations, its supply chain, and its business partners. The law defines the "supply chain" as any part of the supply chain providing goods, services, or other input, from the raw material stage to the finished product and "business partners" as those who are not part of the supply chain but directly provide goods or services to the company. The legal commentary clarifies that a company's "operations" include parent companies and subsidiaries, and that the definitions of "supply chain" and "business partners" read together should be interpreted in line with the OECD Guidelines' definition of "business relationship."[49]

6. *Modern Slavery Legislation Addressing Operations and Supply Chains*

Domestic legislation has rapidly expanded worldwide regarding labor-related human rights abuses, including forced labor and other forms of modern slavery, in the form of reporting guidelines and import bans. The UK,[50] Australia,[51] and the state of California have passed such reporting legislation.[52] These legislative approaches consistently address company operations and their supply chains. None of the legislative acts place tier limits on companies' responsibility to identify the risks and take action to address such human rights abuses.

The United States is the first country to repeatedly block imports of goods connected to forced labor,[53] although Canada seized imports under a similar law for the first time in November 2021.[54] Under Section 307 of the Tariff Act of 1930, US Customs and Border Protection (CBP) can issue Withold Release Orders (WROs) to stop the import of goods "produced, or manufactured wholly or in part in any foreign country by convict labor or/and forced labor or/and indentured labor. . . ." CBP has increasingly targeted forced labor; it issued 31 different WROs in the last three years, with 912 shipments detained in the fourth quarter of 2021 (Oct 1, 2021–Dec. 31, 2021) alone.[55]

---

[49] Markus Krajewski, Kristel Tonstad & Franyiska Wohltmann, *Mandatory Human Rights Due Diligence in Germany and Norway: Stepping, or Striding, in the Same Direction?* BUSINESS AND HUMAN RIGHTS JOURNAL 6(3) at 556 (2011), https://www.cambridge.org/core/journals/business-and-human-rights-journal/article/mandatory-human-rights-due-diligence-in-germany-and-norway-stepping-or-striding-in-the-same-direction/85815FE5F1D1F64208B0068B7FBBECF8.

[50] *See Modern Slavery Act 2015*, c. 30 (Eng.) and UK GOVERNMENT AND HOME OFFICE, *Transparency in Supply Chains: A Practical Guide* (Jul. 22, 2021), https://www.gov.uk/government/publications/transparency-in-supply-chains-a-practical-guide/transparency-in-supply-chains-a-practical-guide.

[51] *Modern Slavery Act 2018*, No. 153 (Austl.), https://www.legislation.gov.au/Details/C2018A00153.

[52] *See California Transparency in Supply Chains Act of 2010* (Civil Code Section 1714.43) and CALIFORNIA DEPARTMENT OF JUSTICE, The California Transparency in Supply Chains Act: A Resource Guide (2015), https://oag.ca.gov/sites/all/files/agweb/pdfs/sb657/resource-guide.pdf.

[53] *See Tariff Act of 1930* (19 U.S.C. § 1307) and U.S. CUSTOMS AND BORDER PROTECTION, Forced Labor (September 10, 2021), https://www.cbp.gov/trade/programs-administration/forced-labor.

[54] Steven Chase, *Canada Seizes Goods Made with Forced Labour from China; MPs Urge More Action for Uyghurs*, THE GLOBE AND MAIL (Nov. 15, 2021), https://www.theglobeandmail.com/politics/article-canada-seizes-goods-made-with-forced-labour-from-china-mps-urge-more/.

[55] US Customs and Border Protection, *Forced Labor*, CBP.GOV, https://www.cbp.gov/trade/forced-labor (last visited Feb. 2, 2022).

CBP does not have to meet a high burden of proof to issue a WRO, and it is sufficient if CBP has information which "reasonably but not conclusively indicates" that the goods are in violation of the Tariff Act.[56] Upon issuance of a WRO, companies have three months to contest the WRO and show that no forced labor was involved in the production of the goods by making "every reasonable effort to determine the source of the merchandise and of every component thereof and to ascertain the character of labor used in the production of the merchandise and each of its components. . . ."[57]

The Tariff Act does not distinguish between the tiers of a supply chain. Rather, if any entity in the production process used forced labor, the goods fall under the terms of the Act, and CBP has not shied away from forcing companies to look far into their supply chains. In preparation for a WRO banning products connected to Xinjian Production and Construction Corps, CBP sent some companies a questionnaire, asking them to disclose the identity of entities in their supply chain all the way to the extraction of raw materials, in an effort to understand connections to forced labor in Xinjiang.[58] A month later, CBP issued a regional ban on all cotton products from Xinjiang, with the acting Commissioner for US Customs and Border Protection clearly signaling to companies to "know your supply chains."[59]

7. *EU and US Conflict Minerals Regulation Due Diligence in the Whole Supply Chain*

An EU regulation, the Conflict Minerals Regulation, in force since January 1, 2021, imposes supply chain due diligence obligations on EU importers of tin, tantalum, and tungsten, their ores, and gold originating from conflict-affected and high-risk areas.[60] EU businesses importing these minerals must verify that they have not been produced in a manner that funds conflict, for example, by purchasing in a manner that provides funding to armed groups. The regulation's due diligence steps follow those of the *OECD Due Diligence Guidance for Responsible Supply Chains from Conflict-Affected and High-Risk Areas*.[61] Whereas the EU regulation narrows the range of human rights abuses that firms must proactively identify, it does require them to evaluate the entire supply chain and use due diligence designed in line with the UNGPs.

Similarly, Section 1502 of the US Dodd-Frank Act requires US listed companies to disclose whether they use tin, tungsten, tantalum, and gold, so-called "conflict minerals," and whether

[56] 19 C.F.R. § 12.42 (e).

[57] 19 CFR § 12.43 (b).

[58] Finbarr Bermingham, *Xinjiang: US Moves Swiftly to Enforce Ban on Cotton Products Linked to Forced Labour*, South China Morning Post (Dec. 4, 2020, 9:00pm), https://www.scmp.com/economy/china-economy/article/3112595/xinjiang-us-moves-swiftly-enforce-ban-cotton-products-linked.

[59] See Ana Swanson, *U.S. Bans All Cotton and Tomatoes from Xinjiang Region of China*, NY Times (Jan. 13, 2021), https://www.nytimes.com/2021/01/13/business/economy/xinjiang-cotton-tomato-ban.html.

[60] (EU) 2017/821 of the European Parliament and of the Council of 17 May 2017, 2017 OJ (L 130).

[61] OECD, *OECD Due Diligence Guidance for Responsible Supply Chains from Conflict-Affected and High-Risk Areas* (Apr. 2016), https://www.oecd.org/corporate/mne/mining.htm. *See also* European Commission, *The Regulation Explained*, www.ec.europa.eu (last accessed Feb. 10, 2022), https://ec.europa.eu/trade/policy/in-focus/conflict-minerals-regulation/regulation-explained/.

these minerals originate in the Democratic Republic of the Congo or an adjoining country. In such a case, reporting companies must submit a "Conflict Minerals Report," which should include a description of the due diligence measures undertaken. The OECD has stated that its *Due Diligence Guidance for Responsible Supply Chains from Conflict-Affected and High-Risk Areas* can be used to generate a compliant Dodd-Frank "Conflict Minerals Report."[62]

8. *EU Nonfinancial Reporting Directive – Human Rights Risks through Business Relationships*

The EU Non-financial Reporting Directive (Directive), adopted in 2014, requires large companies to disclose information about how they operate and manage social and environmental challenges.[63] It covers risks associated with *business relationships*, and thereby aligns with the UNGPs. The Directive covers approximately 6,000 large companies and groups across the EU. Covered companies must publish an annual report on their policies and implementation of environmental protection, social responsibility and treatment of employees, respect for human rights, anti-corruption and bribery, and diversity of the company's board. Covered companies also are required to report how they manage the risks they have identified.[64]

9. *European Union Proposed Directive on Corporate Sustainability Due Diligence*

On February 23, 2022, the European Commission published a proposal for a Corporate Sustainability Due Diligence Directive,[65] which aims to introduce human rights and environmental due diligence obligations on some large EU and foreign companies selling products and services within the EU. The proposal includes administrative supervision as well as civil liability for harms caused by a failure to conduct due diligence.

The scope of the due diligence elaborated in the draft Directive includes a company's own operations, subsidiaries, and "established business relationships" along the value chain. The definitions clarify that a direct or indirect relationship can be "established" if it is "expected to be lasting, in view of its intensity or duration and which does not represent a negligible or merely ancillary part of the value chain."[66] The recitals highlight that if a relationship is "established," "then all linked indirect business relationships should also be considered as established regarding that company."[67]

---

[62] OECD, *OECD Work on Responsible Mineral Supply Chains & the U.S. Dodd-Frank Act* (Oct. 2011), https://www.oecd.org/daf/inv/mne/OECD-Guidance-and-Dodd-Frank-Act.pdf.

[63] Directive 2014/95/EU of the European Parliament and of the Council of 22 October 2014, 2014 OJ (L 330).

[64] *See* Article 19a & Article 20a, literal (d) of Directive 2014/95/EU, of The European Parliament and of The Council of 22 October 2014 amending Directive 2013/34/EU on Disclosure of Non-financial and Diversity Information by Certain Large Undertakings and Groups, 2014 O.J. (L 330), 1.

[65] Proposal for a Directive of the European Parliament and the Council on Corporate Sustainability Due Diligence and amending Directive (EU) 2019/1937, COM (2022) 71 final, https://eur-lex.europa.eu/legal-content/EN/TXT/?uri=CELEX%3A52022PC0071.

[66] *Id.* Article 3(f).

[67] *Id.* recital 20.

The proposal therefore looks at the value chain, including, potentially, end-users and customers, but at the same time it seems to exclude short or informal business relationships. Members of the UN Working Group on Business and Human Rights and other stakeholders have criticized this approach for a number of reasons,[68] including (i) that the novel concept of "established business relationships" can create confusion, (ii) that this concept drives the Directive away from alignment with the UNGPs, (iii) that this limitation on due diligence could exclude important business relationships from the scope of due diligence, and (iv) that the reliance on "established business relationships" could create incentives for companies to enter into short and unstable business relationships.[69]

In the next steps, the EU Council and the European Parliament (EP) will review the proposal.[70] The EP has previously encouraged alignment of the legislative initiative with the UNGPs. The EP, on March 10, 2021, adopted a legislative initiative report (504 votes in favor, 79 against, and 112 abstentions) that set forth recommendations to the EU Council on corporate due diligence and accountability and included a draft directive. The report called on the EU Council to pass legislation that encompasses the entire value chain, without a distinction between business relationships, and addresses all human rights.[71]

Time will tell if through the course of the legislative process the limitation of the value chain to "established business relationships" will be dropped, and, if it stays, what business relationships will be considered to be "established."

B. Soft-Law Standards and Practitioner Guidance for Human Rights Risks

1. OECD Guidelines for Multinational Enterprises—*Application to Harms through Direct Linkage*

The OECD Guidelines, as noted above, are a set of responsible business conduct (RBC) standards that originally date from 1976. They are part of the OECD Declaration on International Investment and Multinational Enterprises that was intended to facilitate direct investment among OECD Members. One important and unique requirement of the OECD Guidelines is that adhering governments, now numbering 46, are tasked with establishing a mechanism to hear complaints that arise from conduct of the multinational either in the

---

[68] Ramasastry, A., Remarks via videoconference, *EU Human Rights and Environmental Due Diligence in Global Value Chains*, hosted by the RBC Working Group of the European Parliament (Mar. 2, 2022), https://www.ohchr.org/sites/default/files/2022-03/20220302-WG-remarks.pdf.

[69] *See e.g.*, Shift, *Shift's Analysis of the EU Commission's Proposal for a Corporate Sustainability Due Diligence Directive* (Mar. 2022), https://shiftproject.org/wp-content/uploads/2022/03/Shift_Analysis_EU_CSDDProposal_vMarch01.pdf; Danish Institute for Human Rights, *Legislating for impact: analysis of the proposed EU corporate sustainability due diligence directive* (Mar. 2022), https://www.humanrights.dk/publications/legislating-impact-analysis-proposed-eu-corporate-sustainability-due-diligence.

[70] Steps of the Procedure 2022/0051/COD, https://eur-lex.europa.eu/procedure/EN/2022_51 (last accessed Apr. 10, 2022).

[71] *See* European Parliament Resolution of 10 Mar. 2021 with Recommendations to the Commission on Corporate Due Diligence and Corporate Accountability, Article 7 (2020/2129(INL)).

home state of the multinational or in the country where allegations of failures to follow the OECD Guidelines arise. The mechanisms are termed National Contact Points (NCPs) and the complaints are referred to as Specific Instances.[72]

Although the 2000 revision to the OECD Guidelines included some high-level and vague language pointing to the responsibilities of companies in the context of business relationships,[73] it was the 2011 revision, modeled on the UNGPs, that clarified that human rights due diligence is expected across an enterprise's business relationships, even without the presence of an equity relationship, or an "investment nexus" as it is termed, under the OECD Guidelines, between firms. As stated by John Ruggie and his co-author Tamaryn Nelson:

> The updated Guidelines of 2011 expanded their scope, stating that MNEs should avoid causing or contributing to adverse impacts on the social, environmental and other interests related to the Guidelines, not only through their own activities but also through their business relationships. The text explicitly states that the 'Guidelines concern those adverse impacts that are either caused or contributed to by the enterprise, or are directly linked to their operations, products or services by a business relationship.' The latter is defined as 'relationships with business partners, entities in the supply chain and any other non-State or State entities directly linked to its business operations, products or services.' Therefore, MNEs should carry out risk based due diligence efforts to identify, prevent and mitigate adverse impacts throughout its extended enterprise and business relationships. That issue is now settled principle.[74]

Thus, the expanded scope of businesses' responsibility under the OECD Guidelines, based on the UNGPs, means that there is no need to find an "investment nexus" to hold businesses responsible for human rights violations in their supply chains, and that the lack of an "investment nexus" is no longer a legitimate basis for NCPs to reject a claim. This change to the OECD Guidelines effectively ended one of the most commonly used reasons for NCPs to reject Specific Instances.[75]

2. *OECD Supply Chain Guidance*

Following the important 2011 revision of the OECD Guidelines, the OECD issued several authoritative guides, including the *OECD Due Diligence Guidance on Responsible*

---

[72] OECD, *About the* OECD Guidelines for Multinational Enterprises, http://mneguidelines.oecd.org/about/ (last visited Sept. 9, 2021).

[73] John Ruggie & Tamaryn Nelson, *Human Rights and the OECD Guidelines for Multinational Enterprises: Normative Innovations and Implementation Challenges*, at 17 (Harvard Kennedy School of Government, 2015), https://www.hks.harvard.edu/sites/default/files/centers/mrcbg/programs/cri/files/workingpaper.66.oecd.pdf.

[74] *Id.* at 17 (citations omitted).

[75] Joris Oldenziel, Joseph Wilde-Ramsing & Patricia Feeney, *10 Years On: Assessing the Contribution of the OECD Guidelines for Multinational Enterprises to Responsible Business Conduct*, at 11 (OECD Watch, 2010), https://www.somo.nl/wp-content/uploads/2010/06/OECD-Watch-10-Years-On.pdf.

Business Conduct,[76] and several sectoral guides, including a guide on garment and footwear,[77] agriculture,[78] and conflict minerals[79] (OECD Guides), which explore how to perform human rights due diligence in supply chains in a manner consistent with the OECD Guidelines and the UNGPs. The OECD Guides reflect the shifts described in Section II, as they require companies to evaluate their supply chains proactively and prioritize salient risks by considering the whole spectrum of internationally recognized human rights.[80] In addition, the OECD Guides provide for the responsibility of buyer firms and explore ways to implement the responsibility for human rights risks throughout the companies in the entire supply chain, including through capacity building, support, and training.[81]

3. *Model Contract Clauses*

The American Bar Association (ABA) was the first national bar association to formally endorse the UNGPs. In March 2021, a Working Group of the ABA Business Law Section published a set of model contract clauses for international supply chains.[82] While the scope of the model clauses primarily covers labor rights, the model clauses are aligned with the UNGPs' approach to responsibility. The model clauses explicitly recognize the potential role of the buyer in positively or negatively influencing labor standards throughout the supply chain and recognize an identical scope of responsibility for respecting human rights by all businesses throughout the supply chain.[83]

IV. Good Practices – Due Diligence in Complex Supply Chains and Value Chains

This Section provides specific examples of the practices that companies and other actors are undertaking to address human rights harms upstream and downstream in complex supply chains consistent with the scope of responsibility laid out in the UNGPs and described in this

[76] OECD, *OECD Due Diligence Guidance for Responsible Business Conduct* (2018), https://www.oecd.org/investment/due-diligence-guidance-for-responsible-business-conduct.htm.

[77] OECD, *OECD Due Diligence Guidance for Responsible Supply Chains in the Garment and Footwear Sector* (2017), https://mneguidelines.oecd.org/responsible-supply-chains-textile-garmentsector.htm.

[78] OECD, *OECD-FAO Guidance for Responsible Agricultural Supply Chains* (2016), https://www.oecd.org/daf/inv/investment-policy/rbc-agriculture-supply-chains.htm.

[79] OECD, *OECD Due Diligence Guidance for Responsible Supply Chains of Minerals from Conflict-Affected and High-Risk Areas* (2016), https://mneguidelines.oecd.org/mining.htm.

[80] *See, e.g.*, OECD, *OECD Due Diligence Guidance for Responsible Supply Chains of Minerals from Conflict-Affected and High-Risk Areas*, at 40 – Section D (2016), https://mneguidelines.oecd.org/mining.htm.

[81] *Id.*

[82] American Bar Association, Contractual Clauses Project, https://www.americanbar.org/groups/ human_rights/business-human-rights-initiative/contractual-clauses-project/ (last visited Sept. 9, 2021). (However, the American Bar Association has not officially endorsed the Project's final report.)

[83] John F. Sherman, *No Need to Reinvent Wheels: Drafting Meaningful Human Rights Due Diligence through Model Suggested Supply Chain Contract Clauses*, Shift Project (Mar. 2021), https://shiftproject.org/aba-contract-clauses/.

chapter.[84] These examples demonstrate behavior that the UNGPs set out to catalyze: collaborative and collective action to cohere around the most severe risks to people, no matter where the risks occur in the value chain. This includes prioritizing issues that are embedded deep within a supply chain as well as risks associated with end-users, as opposed to merely working horizontally across all tier 1 suppliers on predetermined human rights issues, such as labor rights.

A. Dutch Banking Agreement: Value Chain Mapping and Work on Leverage

In October 2016, the Dutch Banking Sector Agreement on Human Rights (DBA) was signed by Dutch ministers, bankers, and civil society representatives. The DBA is one of a series of "covenants" on responsible business conduct developed for various industry sectors in the Netherlands. Under the DBA, 11 Dutch banks committed to work together with civil society, trade unions, and governmental offices to meet their responsibilities to respect human rights, as set out in the OECD Guidelines and the UNGPs. The DBA was effective during a three-year period and ended in December 2019.[85]

The DBA has been written about and criticized by academics and civil society organizations, and the final report evaluating the agreement also contains sharp criticisms of the effort.[86] However, what is notable about this three-year process under the DBA is the work carried out by the multistakeholder group, comprised of representatives of banks, civil society, and the Dutch government, to map the value chains in gold, palm oil, and cocoa, and its exploration of ways to build and exercise leverage. The group not only wholeheartedly accepted that banks have a responsibility for human rights impacts to which they are directly linked through their business relationships, but also oriented the thrust of their work toward understanding how best this responsibility should be implemented.

The report of the multistakeholder working group described the importance of value chain mapping in this way:

> Human rights impacts occur in a variety of ways across the globe on a daily basis. Banks have obligations under the UN Guiding Principles (among others) and the manner in

[84] Whereas the practices laid out below are useful for illustrative purposes, the author has not conducted any independent assurance work to confirm that the illustrated practices have been impactful. Additionally, a good practice on one issue or in one initiative should not be taken as single evidence that the company acts in line with the UNGPs.

[85] SOCIAAL-ECONOMISCHE RAAD [Government and Parliament on Social and Economic Policy], *Dutch Banking Sector Agreement* (Neth.), https://www.imvoconvenanten.nl/en/banking (last visited Sept. 10, 2021).

[86] *See* (i) Benjamin Thomson, *The Dutch Banking Sector Agreement on Human Rights: An Exercise in Regulation, Experimentation or Advocacy?*, UTRECHT LAW REVIEW 14(2), at 84–107, http://doi.org/10.18352/ulr.440; (ii) INVESTESG, *NGOs After Evaluation of Dutch Banking Sector Agreement: Legislation Needed to Ensure Respect for Human Rights* (Aug. 24, 2020), https://investesg.eu/2020/08/24/ngos-after-evaluation-of-dutch-banking-sector-agreement-legislation-needed-to-ensure-respect-for-human-rights/ (last visited Sept. 10, 2021); and (iii) BANKTRACK, *Dutch Banking Sector Agreement on Human Rights*, https://www.banktrack.org/campaign/dutch_banking_sector_agreement_on_human_rights (last visited Sept. 10, 2021); and (iv) MONITORING COMMITTEE FOR THE DUTCH BANKING SECTOR AGREEMENT ON INTERNATIONAL BUSINESS CONDUCT REGARDING HUMAN RIGHTS, Final Monitoring and Progress Report (Jul. 13, 2020), https://www.imvoconvenanten.nl/-/media/imvo/files/banking/banking-final-report-2020.pdf.

which this is fulfilled depends on their role in their financing relationships with clients. Evaluating their impact requires a nuanced approach in order to have the best information and perspective available. One of the tools that is considered beneficial to this end is value chain mapping. This allows banks to pinpoint where the impact of its involvement can be found and how they can apply leverage to mitigate or address human rights impacts. Specifically, value chain mapping helps to:

- Clarify responsibility: Which responsibilities should banks take into account, according to the UN Guiding Principles and the OECD Guidelines?
- Prioritize efforts: Where do the most severe human rights impacts occur and, subsequently, on what should banks, with the support of other parties, first focus their efforts?
- Understand Leverage: How exactly are banks connected to human rights impacts and where can they create most leverage in the value chain to effectively prevent, mitigate, and remediate these impacts?
- Analyze solutions: What are the root causes and challenges in a particular value chain and how best can they be addressed, including identifying who needs to be involved?[87]

Irrespective of the successes or failures of the DBA, it demonstrates how cooperation among multistakeholder actors can be catalyzed to collectively undertake value chain mapping. For example, a cosmetics company that sources relatively small amounts of thousands of commodities likely has minimal leverage to address human rights harms in its value chains. Yet, collective value chain mapping with other companies and stakeholders, which includes building consensus around the most severe impacts and identifying points where leverage can be exercised by actors collaboratively, offers greater opportunities for taking meaningful action.

B. Accord on Fire and Building Safety in Bangladesh: Collective Action on Severe Human Rights Harms

Dhaka, Bangladesh, was the site of history's worst industrial disaster in the garment industry. On April 24, 2013, an eight-story building collapsed, killing 1,129 garment workers.[88] The disaster highlighted the lethal labor and safety conditions for workers sewing clothes for major western brands including H&M, Primark, and Mango.

Two multistakeholder initiatives were formed as a result of the disaster. These initiatives "illustrate the promise of collective action to leverage change. Importantly, these initiatives

[87] Sociaal-Economische Raad [Government and Parliament Advisor on Social and Economic Policy], *Value Chain Working Group: Cocoa Value Chain Analysis*, at 13–14 (2018), https://www.imvoconvenanten.nl/-/media/imvo/files/banking/news/IMVO-Cocoa-value-chain-analysis-EN.pdf?la=en&hash=91B8FC85E9D19D85 3EBC27A9167F06C7 (last visited September 10, 2021).

[88] Steven Greenhouse & Elizabeth A. Harris, *Battling for a Safer Bangladesh*, N.Y. Times (Apr. 22, 2014), https://www.nytimes.com/2014/04/22/business/international/battling-for-a-safer-bangladesh.html (last visited Sept. 10, 2021).

are not just about voluntary philanthropic contributions to development, but also the product of a recognized responsibility of companies to address severe human rights risks in their supply chains."[89]

One initiative ceased in 2018, but the *Accord for Health and Safety in the Textile and Garment Industry* was renewed in 2021 and has an expanded number of signatories.[90] This agreement between workers, factory managers, and apparel companies contains a number of innovations that reflect the responsibility of buyer companies and supplier factories for the well-being of workers, including: the legal enforceability of brands' commitments; independent oversight of brand compliance; the obligation to pay prices to suppliers sufficient to support safe workplaces; and the obligation to cease doing business with any factory that refuses to operate safely.[91]

The Accord is a good example of the type of collective action the UNGPs aim to incentivize: companies in complex supply chains collaborating with international organizations, governments, and civil society and using their collective leverage to address human rights harms where they are most severe. Between 2013 and 2018 more than 38,000 inspections were carried out, and almost 200 factories lost their contracts due to failure to correct safety standards.[92]

While the Accord is a good example of collective action in response to a severe risk, it is designed for specific challenges and is not a tool that will address all human rights issues in global supply chains. For example, the Accord does not provide a remedy for garment workers killed or injured in the Rana Plaza disaster or for their families. The Accord focuses efforts on so-called tier 2 suppliers, leaving smaller suppliers who mainly work on the subcontracting level untouched.[93] A global value chain approach more aligned to the UNGPs would also look at smaller suppliers who are subcontracted. So far, these subcontractors continue to escape scrutiny even as major brands step up their due diligence efforts.

---

[89] Letter from John Ruggie, Board Chair of Shift and Berthold Beitz Professor at Harvard Kennedy School, to Guy Ryder, Director General of the International Labour Office, at 2 (May 30, 2016), https://media.business-humanrights.org/media/documents/files/documents/Ruggie-letter-Ryder-30-May-2016.pdf.

[90] International Accord for Health and Safety in the Textile and Garment Industry (Sept. 1, 2021), https://bangladesh.wpengine.com/wp-content/uploads/2021/08/1-September-International-Accord-on-Health-and-Safety-in-the-Textile-and-Garment-Industry-public-version.pdf; *See* Clean Clothes Campaign, *Which Brands Care about Workers' Safety?*, https://cleanclothes.org/campaigns/protect-progress/brand-tracker (last visited Sept. 10, 2021) for a current list of signatories.

[91] *See* Worker Rights Consortium, *Bangladesh Accord*, https://www.workersrights.org/our-work/bangladesh-accord/ (last visited Sept. 10, 2021).

[92] Lauren Cochrane, *Fashion Brands Sign New Deal on Bangladesh Garment Workers' Safety*, The Guardian (Aug. 26, 2021), https://www.theguardian.com/global-development/2021/aug/26/fashion-brands-sign-new-deal-on-bangladesh-garment-workers-safety (last visited Sept. 10, 2021).

[93] Chris Reinhardt & Elizabeth D. Herman, *Inside Bangladesh's Garment Industry, Second Largest in the World*, The World (Aug. 14, 2014), https://www.pri.org/stories/2014-08-14/inside-bangladeshs-garment-industry-second-largest-world (last visited Sept. 10, 2021).

C. Coca-Cola and Responsibility to Address Human Rights Risks in the Value Chain

As the scope of responsibility under the UNGPs is aimed at motivating all companies within a value chain to catalyze improvements in human rights conditions, it is useful to compare how The Coca-Cola Company expressed its responsibilities for human rights risks in its supply chain before and after the adoption of the UNGPs.

In 2004, and thus prior to the UNGPs, Human Rights Watch (HRW) published a report identifying the problem of hazardous child labor in sugarcane harvesting in El Salvador that revealed that some of the sugar in question was sold through a supply chain to The Coca-Cola Company. The report describes the company's response as only encompassing a responsibility for human rights issues in direct suppliers:

> Coca-Cola's written response to the information provided by Human Rights Watch did not deny the likelihood that children harvested the raw sugarcane used in producing the refined sugar that went into its beverages bottled in El Salvador. **Instead, Coca-Cola's extensive response addressed only its direct suppliers**: 'Our review has revealed that none of the four cooperatives identified in the letter supplied any products directly to The Coca-Cola Company, and neither TCCC [The Coca-Cola Company] nor the Salvadoran bottler have any commercial contracts with these farm cooperatives.' (emphasis added)[94]

In a response to HRW following the adoption of the UNGPs, The Coca-Cola Company stated that its evaluation of labor issues in its sugar supply chain included non-direct suppliers, such as mills and farms, and that it was working to improve human rights practices, including through efforts to influence the practices of suppliers deep in its supply chain. As the company noted in its 2019 report, *Human Rights in The Coca-Cola Company Sugar Supply Chain: Lessons and Opportunities*:

> Through our due diligence efforts, we have **identified risks in our agricultural supply chain.** The Sustainable Agriculture Guiding Principles (SAGP) **set expectations of our agricultural ingredient suppliers** to address sustainability challenges specific to agriculture. The SAGP expand on the SGP [Supplier Guiding Principles for direct and authorized suppliers] and provide targeted guidance encompassing environmental and social principles. These policies help ensure that, **as a system, we create a positive impact in the communities where we operate, mitigate social and environmental risks and remediate issues when they arise.** Collaboration across the company, system and suppliers is key to creating an **opportunity for mills and farms to improve their**

[94] Human Rights Watch, *El Salvador Turning a Blind Eye: Hazardous Child Labor in El Salvador's Sugarcane Cultivation*, at 60, Vol. 16, No. 2 (Jun. 2004), https://www2.ohchr.org/english/bodies/hrc/docs/ngos/HRW_ElSalvador_HRC97.pdf. The Coca-Cola Company did follow up on the HRW report, conducting a study in 2014 on the issues raised. *See* UL, *Review on Child and Forced Labor and Land Rights in El Salvador's Sugar Industry*, The Coca-Cola Company (2015), https://www.coca-colacompany.com/content/dam/journey/us/en/policies/pdf/human-workplace-rights/addressing-global-issues/ul-elsalvador-coca-cola-company-report.pdf.

human rights practices. As we work together, we are focused **on monitoring, capacity building (e.g. training managers of mill-owned and operated farms and independent farms) and best practice sharing** (emphasis added).[95]

D. Microsoft's Work to Explore Impacts of Artificial Intelligence – Focus on End Use

Microsoft, inspired by the UNGPs' scope of responsibility, worked with a consultancy firm to study the potential human rights impacts of artificial intelligence on end-users. This exercise, which was intended to assess human rights impacts, aimed to help Microsoft prepare for the integration of safeguards as new AI technologies are researched, developed, and deployed in the market.[96] This human rights risk assessment may even have led Microsoft to quite publicly refuse to sell certain technologies to police in the United States.[97] Thus, Microsoft identified end use—a value chain issue as opposed to a traditional supply chain issue—as one of their most important human rights risks under a UNGPs analysis.

V. Outstanding Issues Regarding Human Rights Due Diligence and Complex Supply Chains

This Section will very briefly flag some key open questions, evolving issues, and challenges for companies looking to implement the UNGPs with respect to supply chains.

A. Continuing Harms of Suppliers

In a similar manner to environmental law and employment law, human rights law, a branch of public international law, recognizes the concept of continuing violations or continuing harm.[98] In the context of business and human rights, the impacts of certain human rights abuses continue until a remedy is provided. For example, when victims of wrongful land expropriation and environmental damage, which can impact peoples' health, welfare, and livelihoods and their ability to carry out cultural practices, are denied access to a remedy, these constitute continuing harms.

This begs the question, from a UNGP perspective, of what the challenges are that arise for companies when they forge relationships with suppliers who are responsible for

---

[95] The Coca-Cola Company, *supra* note 19, at 2.

[96] Microsoft & Article One Advisors, *Human Rights Impact Assessment (HRIA) of the Human Rights Risks and Opportunities Related to Artificial Intelligence (AI)* (2018), https://www.articleoneadvisors.com/case-studies-microsoft (last visited Sept. 10, 2012).

[97] *See* Joseph Menn, *Microsoft Turned Down Facial-recognition Sales on Human Rights Concerns*, Reuters (Apr. 17, 2019), https://www.reuters.com/article/us-microsoft-ai-idUSKCN1RS2FV (last visited Sept. 10, 2021); *see also* Zak Doffman, *Is Microsoft AI Helping to Deliver China's "Shameful" Xinjiang Surveillance State?* Forbes (Mar. 15, 2019), https://www.forbes.com/sites/zakdoffman/2019/03/15/microsoft-denies-new-links-to-chinas-surveillance-state-but-its-complicated/?sh=4bf349c33061 (last visited Sept. 10, 2021).

[98] UN International Law Commission, *Responsibility of States for Internationally Wrongful Acts* (2005), Annex to General Assembly Resolution 56/83 of 12 Dec. 2001, and corrected by UN Doc. A/56/49(Vol. I)/Corr.4., https://legal.un.org/ilc/texts/instruments/english/draft_articles/9_6_2001.pdf.

continuing harms? The existence of continuing harms places the company on notice of not only actual harms but also potential malfeasance by the supplier and the need to mitigate potential future harms. A number of issues then arise. With respect to continuing harms, to what extent does responsibility lie with the buyer firm? Where the buyer exacerbates the continuing harm through its acts or omissions, or makes it less likely that those harms are remediated, can the buyer be held responsible for contributing to the harms? If so, what are the steps that companies can take to ensure they do not contribute and are not viewed as contributing to continuing harms? Irrespective of legal agreements between the supplier and the buyer that may apportion liability and protect companies from being legally liable for legacy issues, the expectations of stakeholders, including investors, based on the UNGPs, relating to buyer responsibility for continuing harms are unsettled now.

B. Customer Requirements Regarding Indirect Suppliers

Increasingly, customers are requiring their direct suppliers to perform human rights due diligence. This has been happening in the law firm space too, where clients ask firms for their human rights policy and want to understand firms' human rights practices before entering into a formal relationship with them.[99] In some contexts, customer requirements have gone further; customers are requiring their suppliers to take concrete actions with respect to their own suppliers to ensure management of human rights issues. The supplier may even be asked to set up a supervisory board to help oversee progress on human rights issues in their own potentially problematic supplier(s). Over the past decade, these requests have become more complex and sophisticated as companies better understand their own links to human rights harms through multi-tiered supply chains. This trend is likely to continue.

C. The Effects of the Global Pandemic—Building Human Resilience in Global Supply Chains

The devastating human impacts of the COVID-19 global pandemic have had long-lasting impacts on business. COVID-19 also has highlighted human rights issues in global supply chains. One of the most important issues is the vulnerability of workers deep in global supply chains to lead company responses to global shutdowns. Whereas some companies went into high gear to support their suppliers by prepaying orders, offering loans or other support, or ensuring seafarers deep in supply chains got to safe harbors, other companies did quite the opposite.[100] The dramatic impacts of cancelling orders or refusing to pay producers was

[99] Catie Shavin & Anna Triponel, *Law Firm Business and Human Rights Peer Learning Process: Emerging Practice, Insights and Reflections – Workshop Report* at 7 (Nov. 2016). https://www.globalgovernancewatch.org/library/doclib/20161130_LawFirmBHRPeerLearningProcessReport.pdf (last visited Feb. 23, 2022).

[100] *See, e.g.*, Global Business Initiative on Human Rights, *COVID-19 and Contract Non-Performance: Wise Companies Are Guided by Business and Human Rights Thinking* (Apr. 4, 2020), https://gbihr.org/updates/covid-19-and-contract-non-performance-wise-companies-are-guided-by-business (last visited Sept. 10, 2021); World Ports Sustainability Program, Over 300 companies and organizations join forces to help resolve a humanitarian crisis on the world's oceans (Jan. 26, 2021), https://sustainableworldports.org/over-300-companies-and-organizations-join-forces-to-help-resolve-a-humanitarian-crisis-on-the-worlds-oceans/ (last visited Sept. 10, 2021).

arguably one of the first visible business and human rights issues that arose in the spring of 2020. Newspapers worldwide showed photographs of large swaths of workers, who produce goods in global supply chains, summarily dismissed from their jobs. These workers, often living in company-offered accommodations far from home or even outside their own country, had no support to return home or reach a place of safety.[101]

The challenge for those working on the management of human rights risks in the headquarters of buyer companies, however, was how to get decision-makers to make a priority of the human rights of workers at the bottom of the supply chain while employees in headquarters were also experiencing impacts. Although sustainability departments within multinational companies may operate in a manner that reflects the understanding that the company's responsibility flows through its entire supply chain and that the severity of risks should guide prioritization, the pandemic's complex impacts that affected every part of large companies made that prioritization more challenging.

Companies also have faced great difficulty in performing human rights due diligence during the pandemic. The onsite, in-person monitoring of supply chain human rights performance and worker voice programs, which are based on in-person interviews and engagement with workers, have largely been halted or their frequency reduced.[102] Some companies have created innovative online tools to try to continue monitoring the most problematic suppliers. Additionally, the pandemic has heightened interest in and catalyzed the development of technological solutions for supply chain monitoring.[103] However, monitoring human rights performance at a distance is simply not an effective long-term solution, especially where it replaces stakeholder engagement on sensitive human rights issues in an in-person setting.

D. Supply Chain Synergies in Corruption and Business and Human Rights Practices

During the past year, the discussion of how to identify and take advantage of anti-corruption and business and human rights practices has begun in earnest. Although this discussion has been ongoing for some time,[104] there is now heightened attention to the issue, perhaps because of growing legislative efforts on human rights due diligence alongside longer-standing anti-corruption laws.[105] The connection between these two agendas is also important in the

[101] *See* Sushmita S. Preetha & Zyma Islam, *Is Foul Play the New Normal?: 1,931 Brands Bent on Shifting $3.7b Contagion Losses to Bangladesh Garment Exporters*, The Daily Star (Jun. 26, 2020), https://www.business-humanrights.org/en/latest-news/bangladesh-1931-brands-have-delayed-cancelled-37bn-worth-of-orders-from-garment-factories-during-covid-19/; *and* UN Virtual Forum on Responsible Business and Human Rights 2020, *Impact of Covid-19 on Migrant Workers in India* (Jun. 9, 2020), https://www.youtube.com/watch?v=gNwgB63KXPc.

[102] Neil Hodge, *Managing Supply Chain Risks in the Covid-19 Era*, International Bar Association, https://www.ibanet.org/article/AF613016-91EE-43DD-BF37-7B39EA7EF8E3 (last visited Sept. 13, 2021).

[103] *See, e.g.*, Uzair Amir, *Garment Workers in a Covid-19 World: Re-Inventing a Broken System*, Ulula (May 26, 2020) https://ulula.com/garment-workers-in-a-covid-19-world-re-inventing-a-broken-system/.

[104] Johana Drewert & Kaustuv Banerjee, *Linking Human Rights and Anti-Corruption Compliance*, UN Global Compact (2016), https://www.globalcompact.de/migrated_files/wAssets/docs/Korruptionspraevention/Publikationen/Human_Rights_and_Anti_Corruption_Compliance.pdf.

[105] *See* (i) The International Organisation of Employers (IOE) and Business at OECD, *Connecting the Anti-Corruption and Human Rights Agendas: A Guide for Business and Employers' Organisations* (Sept. 2020),

context of complex, global supply chains, because similar challenges are seen in both areas. Leveraging the learning from more advanced anti-corruption practices may be helpful.[106]

VI. Conclusion

The UNGPs broadened the scope of responsibility of companies for human rights harms and has led them to consider impacts that occur through business relationships, which encompass business partners and the entire value chain, including indirect suppliers, customers, and end-users. Within multi-tiered and complex supply chains, the UNGPs recognize the responsibility of not only buyer companies for human rights impacts, but also every company involved in the supply chain, thereby harmonizing expectations. Finally, the UNGPs have altered the focus from labor standards to all internationally recognized human rights. These developments, fostered by the UNGPs, have led to collective action that coheres around preventing, mitigating, and remediating the worst human rights abuses first, no matter how many tiers down the supply chain the abuses take place. These shifts, related to supply chains, have in turn influenced important hard law and soft law standards, including legislation, case law, and practitioner guidance. Where legislation worldwide may not yet fully reflect the UNGPs' concepts and approaches to the scope of responsibility described in this chapter, there is a definite trend toward a broader scope of responsibility for companies, and some laws already fully take on the UNGPs approach. For lawyers advising companies that must satisfy rules in multiple jurisdictions, respond to fast-developing legislation, and meet the expectations of a range of stakeholders regarding human rights, working to meet the UNGPs is an effective way to pursue all of these goals at once.

VII. Resources

There is a plethora of resources, tools, and guides on Human Rights Due Diligence. Those are not included here. The resources listed below tend to focus on supply chain issues in particular or modern slavery, given recent legislative developments on the theme.

American Bar Association (ABA), *Model Contract Clauses (MCCs 2.0) and a Responsible Purchasing Code of Conduct (the Buyer Code)* (2021), https://www.americanbar.org/groups/human_rights/business-human-rights-initiative/contractual-clauses-project/aba-business-law-section-working-group-releases-model-contract-c/.

---

https://www.ioe-emp.org/index.php?eID=dumpFile&t=f&f=147731&token=c0fecaf2120d7faf7e4214377a1754ab8170fd88; (ii) UN Working Group on Business and Human Rights, *Guidance on National Action Plans on Business and Human Rights* (Dec. 2014), https://www.ohchr.org/documents/issues/business/unwg_%20napguidance.pdf; (iii) Letter from the OECD to the UN OHCHR on Connecting the Business and Human Rights and Anti-Corruption Agendas (2020), https://www.ohchr.org/Documents/Issues/Business/2020Survey/IRO_NHRIS/OECD.docx; and (iv) Rocio Paniagua & Bonnie Groves, *Lessons from Past Approaches Towards Human Rights and Corruption Point to Pursuing Them Together in Future*, International Bar Association (IBA) (May 2021), https://www.ibanet.org/lessons-from-past-approaches-towards-human-rights-and-corruption?sap-outbound-id=A34CB9D4DD4DF5254624A2D8F7476BAF859D9E17&utm_source=SAPHybris&utm_medium=email&utm_campaign=151&utm_term=Copy%20of%20BHR%20eBulletin%20July%20%2721___Read%20more...&utm_content=EN#_edn16.

[106] *See, e.g.*, TRACE International, *Leveraging Anti-Bribery Compliance Programs to Address Human Rights in a Post-COVID-19 World*, https://www.traceinternational.org/resource-center (not publicly available) (last visited Sept. 13, 2021).

BICCL & Norton Rose Fullbright, *Making sense of managing human rights issues in supply chains report and analysis*, (2018) https://www.biicl.org/documents/1939_making_sense_of_managing_human_rights_issues_in_supply_chains_-_2018_report_and_analysis_-_full_text.pdf?showdocument=1.

Dutch Banking Sector Agreement (2018), https://www.imvoconvenanten.nl/en/banking/news.

Interactive Map for Anti-Human Trafficking Organizations (2018), www.modernslaverymap.org (a collaboration of the ILO, the International Organization on Migration, the UN Global Compact and others).

Lise Smit, Claire Bright, et. al., *Study on Due Diligence Requirements through the Supply Chain*, European Commission (2020), https://op.europa.eu/en/publication-detail/-/publication/8ba0a8fd-4c83-11ea-b8b7-01aa75ed71a1/language-en.

Organisation for Economic Co-operation and Development (OECD), *OECD Due Diligence Guidance for Responsible Business Conduct* (2018), https://www.oecd.org/investment/due-diligence-guidance-for-responsible-business-conduct.htm (includes links to other relevant documents).

Responsible Sourcing Tool, www.responsiblesourcingtool.org (a collaboration of the US State Department's Office to Monitor and Combat Trafficking in Persons, Verité, Made in a Free World & The Aspen Institute).

Shift, *Putting Principles into Practice* (2012), https://www.hks.harvard.edu/sites/default/files/centers/mrcbg/programs/cri/files/Shift-Workshop-Report-2_Respecting-Human-Rights-Through-Global-Supply-Chains.pdf

United Nations Office of the High Commissioner for Human Rights (UN OHCHR), *The Corporate Responsibility to Respect: An Interpretive Guide* (2012), www.ohchr.org/Documents/Issues/Business/RtRInterpretativeGuide.pdf.

United Nations Office of the High Commissioner for Human Rights (UN OHCHR), *Expert Group Meeting: Human Trafficking & Global Supply Chains* (2012), https://www.ohchr.org/en/issues/trafficking/pages/globalsupplychains.aspx.

13

Leveraging the Financial Sector for Human Rights

Margaret G. Wachenfeld

I. Introduction

The financial sector can be a powerful force to reinforce respect for human rights. The financial system is the lifeblood of the economy and as such can play a positive role in supporting poverty alleviation and contributing to the realization of human rights. But for many human rights advocates, the financial sector can also be a destructive force, as epitomized by the global financial crisis in 2007 to 2009. It was a financial and economic crisis, but it was also a human rights crisis. Millions of jobs were lost, homes were repossessed, public services cut, and social protection systems were overwhelmed. The crisis undermined the human rights to housing, food, water, health, education, and other human rights through its impacts on jobs, incomes, and livelihoods. Moreover, the negative impact of the crisis on peoples' human rights persisted long after the financial system stabilized, due to subsequent austerity measures. The intergenerational effects continue to reverberate on the lives of those affected and in the rise of populist politics in the postcrisis period.

The financial crisis highlighted how globalized financial markets can deeply affect human rights. The financial system is now so large, integrated, and pervasive that the lives of people around the planet are inextricably intertwined with its cycles. The financialization of the world economy over the past 30 years now means that the amount of money available and the size of financial markets have grown much faster than economic output.[1]

[1] David Kinley, Necessary Evil: How to Fix Finance by Saving Human Rights (2018), https://global.oup.com/academic/product/necessary-evil-9780190691127?cc=be&lang=en&.

This significant shift toward financialization pushes in exactly the opposite direction from the human rights principle of accountability: rather than being able to readily identify a company that is responsible for human rights impacts, financialization introduces layers of financial instruments, structures, and actors that obscure those responsible and dissipate responsibility. With so many layers, potentially hidden behind complex structures and aggregations of transactions, it becomes literally impossible to identify and hold accountable those responsible for human rights impacts. The significance of financialization for human rights realization has not been fully recognized by the human rights community, which has tended to focus on impacts and defined areas of the financial space that can be addressed through processes such as human rights due diligence.[2]

As set out in a paper on human rights and the financial system prepared for the United Nations (UN) Environment Programme's (UNEP) Inquiry into a Sustainable Financial System, there are at least three levels of interaction between human rights and the financial system.[3] First, there is the systemic level of regulation of the financial sector, which operates at both the international and national levels. While human rights are just starting to make their way into some areas of specific regulation by forward-looking national regulators, human rights have yet to be considered at the international level of financial standard setting, even though human rights set out a vision of the key values and fundamental social goods that are essential to stable societies and sustainable economies. Second, there is the company level, where financial institutions, including banking, investment, and insurance firms, like other business sectors, are expected to respect human rights. Third, there is the consumer level, where financial institutions in certain segments of the market interact directly with consumers. Human rights underpin many consumer protection legal frameworks to protect people from harm and defend against injustice.

This chapter focuses on the company level, addressing the application of the *UN Guiding Principles on Business and Human Rights* (UNGPs)[4] by financial institutions. This typically includes integrating human rights into risk management systems and carrying out human rights due diligence processes to address human rights risks in their relationships with their clients. However, as this introduction and selected sections of the chapter highlight, the broader relationship between the financial sector and human rights is far more complex than just human rights due diligence. Even at the company level, developments to date have really only begun to scratch the surface of areas of financing where potential human rights impacts are more identifiable. There are many areas of finance that are likely to escape the application of due diligence processes because they simply cannot be fitted into the due diligence template. Applying human rights principles to more complex financial products like derivatives

---

[2] Mary Dowell-Jones, *The Global Financial Crisis: A Human Rights Response* (2009) (unpublished with the author).

[3] Margaret Wachenfeld, Motoko Aizawa & Mary Dowell-Jones, *Human Rights and Sustainable Finance: Exploring the Relationship*, (2016), UNEP Inquiry on a Sustainable Financial System and The Institute for Human Rights and Business, Inquiry Working Paper 16/01, Section 3.5.1., http://apps.unep.org/publications/index.php?option=com_pub&task=download&file=011960_en [hereinafter UNEP Inquiry Human Rights Report].

[4] UN Human Rights Office of the High Commissioner, *Guiding Principles on Business and Human Rights—Implementing the United Nations "Protect, Respect and Remedy" Framework* (2011). New York and Geneva: United Nations, https://www.ohchr.org/documents/publications/guidingprinciplesbusinesshr_en.pdf.

will take far more thinking and interaction between financial specialists and human rights specialists; and yet, understanding how such types of transactions affect society and particularly the most vulnerable in society may well be critical to understanding and managing systemic risk in the financial system. While this chapter focuses on the evolving norms and practice around due diligence, it is important for practitioners not to lose sight of the bigger picture.

This chapter is organized as follows. Section II briefly sets out the context, looking at the role of financial institution involvement leading up to the adoption of the UNGPs. Section III then provides a lengthier overview of the legal, regulatory, and voluntary initiatives that have developed since the adoption of the UNGPs and the updated Organisation for Economic Co-operation and Development (OECD) *Guidelines on Multinational Enterprises* (OECD Guidelines) in 2011 to begin to address the application of these frameworks to the financial sector.[5] Section IV provides a brief overview of good practices, while pointing to existing guidance for more detail. As closing remarks, Section V highlights some significant challenges ahead and Section VI briefly draws conclusions.

II. Context

Prior to the endorsement of the *"Protect, Respect, Remedy" Framework for Business and Human Rights* by the UN Human Rights Council in 2008[6] and the subsequent implementing guidance in the form of the UNGPs in 2011, some financial institutions were already paying attention to human rights issues. A select group of socially responsible investors developed investment products conditioned on respecting human rights, often based on exclusions of particular types of projects or specific countries. Investors were important participants in divestment movements driven by human rights concerns in apartheid South Africa and Sudan, for example. Financial institutions that joined the UN Global Compact, created in the year 2000, were required to commit to the two human rights principles included in the Compact.[7] The Business Leaders Initiative on Human Rights (BLIHR), which was formed in 2003 by a group of seven leading companies, including a bank, explored the ways that human rights standards and principles can inform issues of corporate responsibility and corporate governance.[8] BLIHR developed early guidance for companies and financial institutions seeking clarity on what they could and should do to respect human rights.[9]

---

[5] Organisation for Economic Co-operation and Development (OCED) (2011), *OECD Guidelines for Multinational Enterprises*, OECD Publishing, http://dx.doi.org/10.1787/9789264115415-en [hereinafter OCED].

[6] UN Human Rights Council, *Protect, Respect and Remedy: A Framework for Business and Human Rights: Report of the Special Representative of the Secretary-General on the Issue of Human Rights and Transnational Corporations and Other Business Enterprises*, John Ruggie (Apr. 7, 2008), A/HRC/8/5, https://www2.ohchr.org/english/bodies/hrcouncil/docs/8session/A-HRC-8-5.doc.

[7] https://www.unglobalcompact.org/what-is-gc/mission/principles.

[8] *See*, John Ruggie, *Business and Human Rights: The Evolving International Agenda*, (2007), footnote 31, https://www.hks.harvard.edu/sites/default/files/centers/mrcbg/programs/cri/files/workingpaper_38_ruggie.pdf.

[9] *See, for example*, BLIHR, UN Global Compact, A Guide for Integrating Human Rights into Business Management (1st ed. 2006), available at: https://www.unglobalcompact.org/library/13.

A few forward-looking investors and banks were engaged in the development of the UNGPs, and in the 2011 update of the OECD Guidelines, which occurred in parallel with the adoption of the UNGPs and which added a new chapter on human rights that was aligned with the UNGPs. But, for the most part, the financial sector was absent from the development of these two foundational normative frameworks for business and human rights. Civil society organizations (CSOs)[10] were not absent, however, and realized early on that the UNGPs and the human rights chapter of the OECD Guidelines set expectations for the financial sector and could be used to challenge financial sector practice. They lost little time in doing so. Given the growing questions on the application of these two normative frameworks to the financial sector, new and existing initiatives began exploring the implications of these frameworks for this sector, which are examined briefly in Section III below.

III. Legal/Regulatory/Voluntary Standards

This Section provides a brief and selective overview of some of the most significant standard-setting, regulatory, and voluntary developments on the application of the UNGPs and the OECD Guidelines to the financial sector.

A. Standards and Standards Interpretation from Relevant International Organizations

The UN Office of the High Commissioner for Human Rights (OHCHR) and the OECD are the sources of the relevant normative standards in the business and human rights field. Their work in elaborating how these standards apply to the financial sector thus represents authoritative interpretive guidance. They address core issues on the applications of these frameworks to this sector and thus are a clear starting point for practitioners seeking guidance.

The additional UN agency, UNEP, through both the Inquiry on a Sustainable Financial System (see Subsection 3 below) and the UNEP Finance Initiative (UNEP FI), develops authoritative guidance on the application of the UN Sustainable Development Goals (SDGs),[11] the Paris Agreement under the UN Framework Convention on Climate Change,[12] and other global standards relevant to the finance sector, as well as addressing human rights. UNEP established the UNEP FI program following the Rio Earth Summit in 1992. This program works with banks, insurers, and investors on sustainable finance and is active in convening

[10] "CSOs" is typically used to refer to a wide array of organizations: community groups, nongovernmental organizations [NGOs], labor unions, indigenous groups, charitable organizations, faith-based organizations, professional associations, and foundations.

[11] The SDGs are a collection of 17 interlinked global goals designed to be a "blueprint to achieve a better and more sustainable future for all." They were adopted in 2015 by the United Nations General Assembly and are intended to be achieved by the year 2030. *See* https://sdgs.un.org/goals. UN General Assembly Resolution A/RES/70/1 (Oct. 21, 2015), *Transforming Our World: The 2030 Agenda for Sustainable Development*, https://www.un.org/en/development/desa/population/migration/generalassembly/docs/globalcompact/A_RES_70_1_E.pdf.

[12] UN Framework Convention on Climate Change, Conference of the Parties, Report of the Conference of the Parties on Its Twenty-first Session, held in Paris from 30 November to 13 December 2015, Adoption of the Paris Agreement, FCCC/CP/2015/10/Add.1, https://unfccc.int/sites/default/files/resource/docs/2015/cop21/eng/10a01.pdf.

discussions and issuing guidance on a wide range of sustainable finance topics.[13] The guidance can help practitioners understand how these related global standards can be applied to the financial sector in the context of financial transactions.

1. *The UN Office of the High Commissioner for Human Rights*

Soon after the adoption of the UNGPs and the updated OECD Guidelines, CSOs posed a set of questions to the OHCHR and the OECD, as well as to the former UN Special Representative to the Secretary-General on Business and Human Rights, Professor John Ruggie, about whether these frameworks apply to the financial sector, and if so, how. They all replied with separate but coordinated and definitive "yes," clarifying that the frameworks do apply to all actors in the financial sector, even minority investors, no matter how small the holdings.[14] The OHCHR issued additional interpretive guidance on the UNGPs in the form of letters responding to requests for clarifications, focused on explaining how core UNGP terms and concepts apply to the financial sector. Two letters in 2013 addressed how Pillar II of the UNGPs on "The Corporate Responsibility to Respect" applies to investors. One of those letters provided advice that addresses the UNGPs' "involvement" framework, (i.e. whether a business "causes, contributes to or is directly linked to a human rights impact") clarifying what being "directly linked" means in the context of investment and the extent to which minority shareholders and investment in sovereign bonds are covered by this provision (UNGP Principle 13 [also citing UNGP Principle 14]).[15] The second letter addressed whether the UNGPs apply to institutional investors holding minority shareholdings (UNGP Principle 14), whether such shareholdings constitute a "business relationship" within the meaning of UNGP Principle 13(b), and the role of "leverage" in such circumstances (UNGP Principle 19).[16] A third and later letter, issued in 2017, addressed the application of the UNGPs to banking, exploring issues such as factors that would influence how a bank is "involved" with an adverse human rights impact (UNGP Principle 13); the responsibilities of banks with respect to remedy in situations where a bank has contributed to an adverse human rights impact (UNGP Principle 22); and the role of operational-level grievance mechanisms (UNGP Principle 29).[17] OHCHR has also taken an active interest in assessing how development finance institutions address human rights.[18]

[13] *See* https://www.unepfi.org/.

[14] OECD, *Expert Letters and Statements on the Application of the OECD Guidelines for Multinational Enterprises and UN Guiding Principles on Business and Human Rights in the Context of the Financial Sector* (Jun. 2014), https://mneguidelines.oecd.org/global-forum/GFRBC-2014-financial-sector-document-3.pdf.

[15] UN Human Rights Office of the High Commissioner, *Advice to the OECD on the Application of the Guiding Principles to the Financial Sector* (Nov. 2013), https://www.ohchr.org/Documents/Issues/Business/LetterOECD.pdf.

[16] UN Human Rights Office of the High Commissioner, *Response to SOMO on the Application of the UNGPs to Minority Shareholdings of Institutional Investors* (2013), https://www.ohchr.org/Documents/Issues/Business/LetterSOMO.pdf.

[17] UN Human Rights Office of the High Commissioner, *Response to Request from BankTrack for Advice Regarding the Application of the UN Guiding Principles on Business and Human Rights in the Context of the Banking Sector* (2017), https://www.ohchr.org/Documents/Issues/Business/InterpretationGuidingPrinciples.pdf.

[18] *See* the UN Human Rights Office of the High Commissioner page on development finance institutions, with resources and submissions critiquing the environmental, social, and information policies of these banks and their independent accountability mechanisms, https://www.ohchr.org/EN/Issues/Development/Pages/DFI.aspx.

2. *The Organisation for Economic Co-operation and Development*

The OECD Working Party on Responsible Business Conduct issued a similar series of clarifications on applying the OECD Guidelines to the financial sector, including how the term "business relationship" applies to client relationships and the interpretation of "cause, contribute and directly linked" in the context of the financial sector.[19] These early questions were prompted, in particular, by one of the early cases following the 2011 update on the application of the OECD Guidelines' human rights chapter to the financial sector. The case was brought to the Norwegian National Contact Point (NCP) against the State's sovereign wealth fund, managed by Norges Bank Investment Management (NBIM).[20] NCPs are government-appointed bodies that handle cases as nonjudicial grievance mechanisms under the OECD Guidelines. NBIM maintained that as a minority investor, the OECD Guidelines did not apply to it; however, the Norwegian NCP determined that the OECD Guidelines apply to the financial sector, including minority investors. It clarified that the responsibility to respect human rights applies to both institutional investors and the enterprises in their portfolios. The NCP concluded that NBIM had failed to observe the OECD Guidelines in a number of ways, notably that its due diligence system was too limited. While NBIM addressed children's rights, it did not address the full scope of internationally recognized human rights as set out in the OECD Guidelines.[21]

The case prompted the Government of Norway to request that the OECD Working Party on Responsible Business Conduct launch a project to develop detailed due diligence guidance for the financial sector on the application of the OECD Guidelines. The first guidance addressed institutional investors (*Institutional Investor Guidance*),[22] and like other OECD due diligence guidance,[23] was developed with a multistakeholder advisory group of institutional investors, governments, CSOs, and other experts. Interestingly, clarifying terminology proved to be one of the early challenges in developing the guidance. For example, terms such as "risk," "due diligence," and "leverage" have different meanings under the OECD Guidelines than they do in the investment world. The Institutional Investor Guidance contains an entire annex that explains the differences in terminology and the implications for understanding the application of the OECD Guidelines to the financial sector.

---

[19] OECD, *Scope and Application of 'Business Relationships' in the Financial Sector under the OECD Guidelines for Multinational Enterprises* (Jun. 2014), https://mneguidelines.oecd.org/global-forum/GFRBC-2014-financial-sector-document-2.pdf and OECD, *Due Diligence in the Financial Sector: Adverse Impacts Directly Linked to Financial Sector Operations, Products, or Services by a Business Relationship* (Jun. 2014), https://mneguidelines.oecd.org/global-forum/GFRBC-2014-financial-sector-document-1.pdf.

[20] *See* the Norwegian NCP decision at https://www.responsiblebusiness.no/dialog-og-mekling/enkeltsaker/forum-vs-nbim-2/.

[21] Margaret Wachenfeld, *Recent Decisions Clarify Investor Responsibility to Address Human Rights Concerns: How the OECD Guidelines for Multinational Enterprises Relate to Investors* (Oct. 7, 2013), Responsible Investor, https://www.responsible-investor.com/articles/ncp-decision-analysis.

[22] OECD, *Responsible Business Conduct for Institutional Investors: Key Considerations for Due Diligence under the OECD Guidelines for Multinational Enterprises* (2017), https://mneguidelines.oecd.org/RBC-for-Institutional-Investors.pdf [Institutional Investor Guidance].

[23] *See* the list of due diligence guidance on the application of the OECD Guidelines here: http://mneguidelines.oecd.org/duediligence/.

The Institutional Investor Guidance identifies key actions for asset managers and asset owners under each of the three core steps set out in the UNGPs and the OECD Guidelines, namely: (1) adopting a human rights policy commitment and embedding it in the investor's policies and management systems; (2) due diligence (identifying and assessing adverse impacts, preventing and mitigating adverse impacts, and accounting for impacts through tracking and communicating); and (3) processes to support remedy of human rights harms.[24] The Guidance goes beyond just the due diligence steps and addresses the full set as all three steps play an integral role in supporting the corporate responsibility to respect human rights and are therefore treated as a package. For each step, the Institutional Investor Guidance addresses key considerations, challenges, and existing practices specific to the investment sector to make the guidance as practical as possible.

The second guidance developed by the OECD on responsible business conduct for the financial sector is the *Corporate Lending and Securities Underwriting Guidance* (Corporate Lending Guidance).[25] It uses the same structure as the Institutional Investor Guidance in addressing the full set of three steps but is specifically geared to the challenges posed by corporate lending and securities underwriting transactions for banks and other financial institutions. The Guidance specifically aims to fill a gap in the market. A group of commercial and state-owned banks and export credit agencies from around the world have adopted the Equator Principles,[26] a leading environmental and social management risk management framework for determining, assessing, and managing environmental and social risk in project finance. However, those Principles cover only a fraction of most of the Equator Banks' lending activities, leaving a vacuum with respect to the vast majority of transactions. The Corporate Lending Guidance focuses on a wider set of transactions, covering the full sweep of transactions that could be characterized as corporate lending or securities underwriting, thus filling the gap. For the CSOs that follow the financial sector, the Corporate Lending Guidance represents important clarifications related to the due diligence and responsible conduct expected of banks across seven key areas: (1) the relationship of banks to adverse impacts and remedy; (2) bank-level grievance mechanisms; (3) transparency and client confidentiality; (4) sustainability responsibilities; (5) public policy advocacy; (6) engagements with rights holders; and (7) disengagement and divestment.[27]

The third, and likely final, guidance from the OECD on responsible business conduct in the financial sector addresses project finance and asset-backed finance. It is expected to be finalized during the course of 2021 and is likely to follow the same model as the other two

---

[24] Institutional Investor Guidance, Section 2.

[25] OECD, *Due Diligence for Responsible Corporate Lending and Securities Underwriting: Key Considerations for Banks Implementing the OECD Guidelines for Multinational Enterprises* (2019), https://mneguidelines.oecd.org/final-master-due-diligence-for-responsible-corporate-lending-and-securities-underwriting.pdf [Corporate Lending Guidance].

[26] https://equator-principles.com/wp-content/uploads/2020/05/The-Equator-Principles-July-2020-v2.pdf.

[27] Bank Track and OECD Watch, *The OECD Due Diligence for Responsible Corporate Lending and Securities Underwriting: An Analysis and Briefing for Civil Society Organisations on the Strongest Elements for Use in Advocacy* (Nov. 2019), https://www.banktrack.org/download/the_oecd_due_diligence_for_responsible_corporate_lending_and_securities_underwriting/oecd_watchbanktrack_briefing.pdf.

guidance documents, covering the three key steps of the UNGPs and OECD Guidelines, but with issues and actions geared to addressing the specifics of project finance and asset-backed finance transactions.

3. *United Nations Environment Programme*

UNEP is another UN agency that has taken a strong interest in the financial sector, recognizing the significant role the sector can play in supporting sustainable and inclusive companies and projects—if the sector is prompted to do so by regulation and market measures. It launched the influential UNEP Inquiry into a Sustainable Financial System (Inquiry) in 2014 to advance strategies for aligning the financial system with the goals of sustainable development.[28] The Inquiry is a leading international platform focused on transforming the global financial system to deliver an inclusive, green economy. The Inquiry worked with national regulators in more than 20 countries on national processes, published approximately 90 reports and working papers, and serves as the Secretariat for the G20's Green Finance Study Group. Given UNEP's mandate as the UN agency responsible for coordinating responses to environmental issues within the UN system, the majority of papers commissioned by the Inquiry focused on the environmental dimensions of a sustainable financial system, including the impact of the growing climate crisis. However, it commissioned one paper on the human rights dimension of the financial system.[29] As noted in the Section I introduction, the paper sets out a broad, three-level framework for analyzing the complex relationship between human rights and the financial system, recognizing that the individual transactions of financial institutions are just one part of the financial system.

The UNEP FI works with financial institutions and has a Social Issues Advisory Group that has been exploring the relationship between human rights and the finance sector since 2006.[30] UNEP FI first developed the "Human Rights Tool" in 2007 and updated it in 2014 to provide guidance for finance practitioners on human rights impact management. It includes background information on human rights and finance, and a focus on specific issues relating to different industry sectors, geographies, and specific human rights issues.[31] The UNEP FI program has since adopted a number of frameworks that broadly support the UNGPs and the OECD Guidelines, although they do not reference those initiatives directly. These frameworks include the Principles for Responsible Banking,[32] the Principles for Sustainable Insurance,[33] and the Positive Impact Initiative[34] that focuses on financing the SDGs.

Significantly, UNEP FI has addressed the legal issues emanating from institutional investors' fiduciary duties to address environmental, social, and governance (ESG) issues over three "generations" of legal studies. Fiduciary duties have been interpreted as prohibiting

---

[28] https://unepinquiry.org/.

[29] UNEP *Inquiry Human Rights Report.*

[30] https://www.unepfi.org/social-issues/social-issues/.

[31] https://www.unepfi.org/humanrightstoolkit/.

[32] https://www.unepfi.org/banking/bankingprinciples/.

[33] https://www.unepfi.org/psi/.

[34] https://www.unepfi.org/wordpress/wp-content/uploads/2018/10/PI-Flyer-2019.pdf.

institutional investors from considering ESG issues unless they are material to financial return. The studies set out to clarify the legal frameworks and interpretation of this important concept, based on detailed legal analysis across a range of common law and civil law jurisdictions. The first-generation report, the 2005 "Freshfields Report," found that institutional investors could incorporate financially material ESG issues as part of their fiduciary duties.[35] The second-generation report, first published in 2015 and revised in 2019, "Fiduciary Duty in the 21st Century,"[36] clarified that integrating ESG issues into investment decision-making is not just permissible, but required in many jurisdictions. The purpose of this report was "to end the debate" about whether fiduciary duty is a legitimate barrier to institutional investors integrating ESG issues into their investment processes.[37] The third-generation report, running from 2019 to 2021 and titled "A Legal Framework for Impact,"[38] is seeking to go a step further. The Paris Agreement and the SDGs have raised institutional investor awareness about global sustainability challenges, and these investors are increasingly considering "sustainability impact duties" such as decarbonization targets, commitments to quality of life, gender equality, and other human rights issues. The third-generation report seeks to understand and analyze how institutional investors can manage both their fiduciary duties and sustainability impact duties, and what happens if they are in conflict, based on the analysis of laws and jurisprudence in 11 jurisdictions. The third-generation report will prepare and publish legal analysis, as well as practical recommendations, for institutional investors and regulators seeking to assess and account for sustainability impacts in investment decision-making as a core part of investment activity.

B. International Financial Standard-Setting Bodies

The 15 international financial standard-setting bodies (SSBs) that sit at the apex of the international financial regulatory system establish the standards that guide national financial regulatory and supervisory authorities around the world in developing their own national financial sector regulatory frameworks.[39] Their work is of less immediate relevance to practitioners in a practical sense, but it is nonetheless important for practitioners to know the source of overall regulatory guidance for the sector and to foresee regulatory trends that will eventually be cascaded down to national regulatory frameworks.

The SSBs include international organizations like the International Monetary Fund and the World Bank Group, international committees like the Basel Committee on Banking Supervision and the Financial Action Task Force, and privately funded bodies like the International Accounting Standards Board and the International Auditing and Assurances Board.

---

[35] Freshfields, Bruckhaus, Deringer, *A legal framework for the integration of environmental, social and governance issues into institutional investment: Produced for the Asset Management Working Group of the UNEP Finance Initiative* (2005), UNEP Finance Initiative.

[36] PRI, UNEP FI, et al. *Fiduciary Duty in the 21st Century* (2019), https://www.fiduciaryduty21.org/.

[37] *Id.* Executive Summary.

[38] https://www.unepfi.org/investment/legal-framework-for-impact/.

[39] *See* FSB, *Standard-Setting Bodies in the Compendium*, www.fsb.org/what-we-do/about-the-compendium-of-standards/wssb/.

Because these international standard setters and their standards are so influential in guiding national standard setting, incorporating human rights issues into their standards or requiring processes for consideration of the regulatory impact on human rights would have a ripple effect throughout the financial system. Until recently, there was no indication that the SSBs took account of the human rights impacts of financial system reforms, or of even wider ESG risks that would signal that the standard setters are cognizant of the two-way interaction between systemic sustainability risks and financial system risks.[40]

One of the 15 SSBs, the International Organization of Securities Commissions (IOSCO), has been the most active in moving into the ESG space, which is not too surprising given the rising attention to ESG in the investment community. IOSCO recognized that "sustainability issues in general, and climate-related issues in particular, pose important challenges in meeting its core objectives—investor protection, market efficiency and mitigation of systemic risks—making these issues relevant from a regulatory perspective."[41] It issued a statement in 2019 on the importance of ESG disclosure[42] and in 2020 set up a Task Force on Sustainable Finance.[43] It issued a 2020 report on sustainable finance titled "Sustainable Finance and the Role of Securities Regulators and IOSCO," which provides an overview of current initiatives, includes references to human rights at several points, and identifies the need for IOSCO to play a key role in this area, based on gaps that were identified.[44] Significantly, this report noted that it conducted a 2019 survey among securities regulators and found that "[a]ll regulators that responded to the survey indicate that they recognize the impact of sustainability matters in the financial markets, particularly in relation to securities regulators' mandates . . .,"[45] which signals the need for further future work on these issues. Another SSB that also regulates financial institutions that have corporate and consumer clients, the International Association for Insurance Supervisors, only just started to address climate change in 2020 but not ESG issues more broadly.[46]

C. Regional/National Regulators

Awareness of regional (in the case of the European Union [EU]) and national regulation are clearly important for practitioners to be able to advise clients on existing and forthcoming regulatory requirements. Keeping an eye on leading jurisdictions helps practitioners spot emerging regulatory trends that may eventually come to their own jurisdiction.

---

[40] Motoko Aizawa, Danny Bradlow, Margaret Wachenfeld, *International Financial Regulatory Standards and Human Rights: Connecting the Dots*, 15 MJIEL 2–44 (2018) https://digitalcommons.wcl.american.edu/cgi/viewcontent.cgi?article=1951&context=facsch_lawrev.

[41] UNEP *Inquiry Human Rights Report*, Section 3.2.1–3.2.2.

[42] International Organization of Securities Commissions (IOSCO), *Statement on Disclosure of ESG Matters by Issuers* (Jan. 18, 2019), https://www.iosco.org/library/pubdocs/pdf/IOSCOPD619.pdf, [hereinafter IOSCO].

[43] IOSCO, *IOSCO Steps Up Its Efforts to Address Issues Around Sustainability and Climate Change* (Apr. 14, 2020), https://www.iosco.org/news/pdf/IOSCONEWS564.pdf.

[44] IOSCO, *Sustainable Finance and the Role of Securities Regulators and IOSCO* (Apr. 2020), https://www.iosco.org/library/pubdocs/pdf/IOSCOPD652.pdf.

[45] *Id.* at 16.

[46] https://www.iaisweb.org/uploads/2022/01/201013-Application-Paper-on-the-Supervision-of-Climate-related-Risks-in-the-Insurance-Sector1.pdf.

1. *European Union*

The EU is by far the most advanced globally on sustainable finance regulation. It has adopted a whole range of laws on the financial sector that bind its 27 Member States.[47] The EU has set out its ambitions to develop a financial system that supports sustainable development in its Sustainable Finance Strategy, with an updated Strategy expected in 2021, and its Sustainable Finance Action Plan already underway.[48] Several of the regulatory actions already adopted under the Sustainable Finance Action Plan, discussed below, are significant for human rights.

The Sustainable Finance Disclosure Regulation (SFDR) is the first financial law in the EU to include specific requirements on human rights. The SFDR requires financial institutions to disclose how they are addressing sustainability.[49] It captures a wide range of financial institutions that have a presence in the EU or market products in the EU.[50] The SFDR sets important new requirements on what the EU terms the "double materiality" principle.[51] The first part of the double materiality requirement addresses the impacts of sustainability risks on financial returns.[52] "Sustainability risks" include "environmental, social and employee matters, respect for human rights, anti-corruption and anti-bribery matters."[53] This may alone have been significant—to see human rights included within the list of factors that could potentially have a material impact on financial returns and therefore be worthy of disclosure. But it is the second part of the double materiality approach that is particularly significant from a human rights point of view. The SFDR requires disclosure of the "principal adverse impacts of investment decisions on sustainability factors,"[54] namely the impact of investments on human rights, and other sustainability issues. The SFDR also requires: a statement on due diligence policies with respect to those impacts, information about policies on the identification and prioritization of principal adverse sustainability impacts, and disclosure against a set of indicators of "principal adverse impacts" that include indicators on human rights and a description of any actions taken or planned to address the adverse impacts.[55] The SFDR refers to the UNGPs and the OECD Guidelines in the recitals and is clearly influenced by the two international frameworks in requiring that investors disclose information not only about their due diligence policies, but also about the outcomes of those policies, namely whether financial transactions have adverse human rights impacts and the steps financial institutions have or will take to address them.

---

[47] *See* https://ec.europa.eu/info/departments/financial-stability-financial-services-and-capital-markets-union_en#responsibilities.

[48] https://ec.europa.eu/info/publications/sustainable-finance-renewed-strategy_en.

[49] Regulation (EU) 2019/2088 of the European Parliament and of the Council of 27 November 2019 on sustainability-related disclosures in the financial services sector, [hereinafter SFDR], https://eur-lex.europa.eu/legal-content/EN/TXT/?uri=CELEX:32019R2088.

[50] Insurers, pension funds, alternative investment fund managers, banks when providing portfolio management—*see* SDFR Article 2.

[51] Explained in the European Commission guidelines on reporting climate-related information (2019), https://ec.europa.eu/finance/docs/policy/190618-climate-related-information-reporting-guidelines_en.pdf.

[52] SFDR Article 3.

[53] SFDR Article 2.

[54] SFDR Article 4.

[55] SFDR Article 4.

The EU regulatory authorities charged with developing regulatory technical standards under the SFDR (European Supervisory Authorities [ESAs]) proposed a preliminary set of key indicators on "principal adverse impacts" covering climate and environmental matters and social, employee, respect for human rights, anti-corruption and anti-bribery matters in summer 2020. These indicators would always be considered as leading to principal adverse impacts. They include a range of human rights issues, from human rights policies and due diligence to child labor and board gender diversity.[56] There was, somewhat predictably, strong pushback from industry associations, and the EU regulators have now delayed the final adoption by at least a year until late 2021 or early 2022.[57] The ESAs issued a draft regulatory technical standard (RTS) in February 2021; the Commission is expected to adopt it by the end of May 2021 and to finalize the date of application.[58] The annex includes the proposed indicators of principal adverse impacts on human rights, albeit with changes that indicate that the regulator, unsurprisingly, is not very conversant with human rights normative standards as it made some unexpected changes in the indicators.[59]

The SFDR and the RTS impose additional disclosure requirements for investments with a specific focus on the promotion of environmental or social characteristics.[60] For these investments, the draft RTS added a significant requirement not specifically included in the consultation draft: in addition to requiring that the financial market participant disclose how it has taken into account the indicators for principal adverse impacts, they must also show whether the investments are aligned with the OECD Guidelines and the UNGPs, including the principles and rights set out in the eight fundamental conventions identified in the Declaration of the International Labour Organization on Fundamental Principles and Rights at Work and the International Bill of Human Rights. The objective is to bring the human rights disclosures under SFDR in line with the "minimum safeguards" in the EU Taxonomy Regulation (see below).

The SFDR is important for several reasons. To begin with, it is one of the first financial regulations in the world to refer to human rights, the UNGPs, and the OECD Guidelines. Given the scope of the SFDR, it is a very significant regulatory reinforcement of these two important frameworks that reaches a broad range of financial institutions—those that have a

---

[56] European Supervisory Authorities (ESAs), *ESAs Consult on Environmental, Social and Governance Disclosure Rules* (Apr. 23, 2020), https://www.esma.europa.eu/press-news/esma-news/esas-consult-environmental-social-and-governance-disclosure-rules, [hereinafter ESAs].

[57] Rachel Owens & Maria Van Der Heide, *EU Must Hold Firm on Delayed Sustainable Finance Disclosure Rules* (Dec. 4, 2020), Responsible Investor, https://www.responsible-investor.com/articles/eu-must-hold-firm-on-delayed-sustainable-finance-disclosure-rules.

[58] ESAs, *ESAs Issue Recommendations on the Application of the Regulation on Sustainability-related Disclosures* (Feb. 25, 2021), https://www.esma.europa.eu/press-news/esma-news/esas-issue-recommendations-application-regulation-sustainability-related.

[59] For example, the consultation paper for the draft referred to the UNGPs; those references were replaced with a reference to the UN Global Compact principles. ESAs, *Final Report on draft Regulatory Technical Standards with regard to the content, methodologies and presentation of disclosures pursuant to Article 2a(3), Article 4(6) and (7), Article 8(3), Article 9(5), Article 10(2) and Article 11(4) of Regulation (EU) 2019/2088* (Feb. 25, 2021), https://www.esma.europa.eu/sites/default/files/library/jc_2021_03_joint_esas_final_report_on_rts_under_sfdr.pdf.

[60] SFDR Article 8–11.

presence in the EU or market products in the EU inside the EU. Second, it requires financial institutions to consider the adverse impacts of their transactions on human rights, not just on their financial returns. This is a direct reflection of the approach of the UNGPs and the OECD Guidelines. In requiring financial institutions to look at both types of impacts, it reinforces the "double materiality" approach that will be incorporated into the 2021 revisions of the EU Non-Financial Reporting Directive (Non-Financial Disclosure Directive), the EU law that sets sustainability reporting requirements for companies.[61] This reinforcement is an important signal in the upcoming "battle" among international regulators and organizations setting standards for ESG disclosure over whether disclosure should be about financial materiality only or instead about double materiality.[62] Third, the SFDR is expected to drive more systematic attention to ESG issues, including human rights, among financial institutions. For some financial institutions, minimum compliance with the regulation will already be a stretch; but other, more forward-thinking financial institutions, seeing the regulatory "writing on the wall," may use these and other regulatory requirements to realign their investment objectives and approaches more fundamentally with the SDGs and the international human rights standards that underpin them.[63]

The EU Taxonomy Regulation (Taxonomy Regulation)[64] seeks to promote investment with sustainability objectives and reduce "greenwashing."[65] It is a classification tool to help investors, companies, issuers, and project promoters navigate the transition to a low-carbon, resilient, and resource-efficient economy. The Taxonomy Regulation sets performance thresholds for economic activities across a wide range of industries that must be met to be considered "sustainable" within the meaning of the Taxonomy Regulation. Importantly, any economic activity seeking a sustainability classification must also show that it meets the "minimum safeguards" defined in the Taxonomy Regulation—that means demonstrating alignment with the OECD Guidelines and the UNGPs.[66] The Taxonomy Regulation is important because it

[61] Directive 2014/95/EU of the European Parliament and of the Council of 22 October 2014 amending Directive 2013/34/EU as regards disclosure of non-financial and diversity information by certain large undertakings and groups Text with EEA relevance, OJ L 330, 15.11.2014, p. 1–9, https://eur-lex.europa.eu/legal-content/EN/TXT/?uri=CELEX%3A32014L0095; and *see* https://ec.europa.eu/info/business-economy-euro/company-reporting-and-auditing/company-reporting/non-financial-reporting_en.

[62] For a useful overview, see Carlos Tonero, *A New Dawn for Mandatory ESG Reporting: How It Came About . . . and What to Expect Next*, Responsible Investor (Dec. 22, 2020), https://www.responsible-investor.com/articles/a-new-dawn-for-mandatory-esg-reporting-how-it-came-about-and-what-to-expect-next.

[63] *See* Danish Institute for Human Rights, *The Human Rights Guide to the Sustainable Development Goals*, https://sdg.humanrights.dk/.

[64] Regulation (EU) 2020/852 on the establishment of a framework to facilitate sustainable investment, and amending Regulation (EU) 2019/2088 https://eur-lex.europa.eu/legal-content/EN/TXT/?uri=celex:32020R0852 [hereinafter Taxonomy Regulation].

[65] Greenwashing is the process of conveying a false impression or providing misleading information about how a company's products are more environmentally sound. In this case it refers to the marketing of investment products as greener or more sustainable than they really are. It is a term that also describes unsubstantiated claims to deceive consumers into believing that a company's products are environmentally friendly. See the US Federal Trade Commission (FTC) page on environmental claims. https://www.ftc.gov/tips-advice/business-center/guidance/environmental-claims-summary-green-guides.

[66] Taxonomy Regulation, Article 18.

makes clear that respect for human rights is a core requirement for a business activity to be considered sustainable and thus a core part of the transition to a net zero economy.[67] The Taxonomy Regulation thus provides a significant legal basis for the concept and the practice of "just transition" in responding to the climate crisis. "Just transition" puts the concerns and rights of workers and communities front and center in climate transition planning and is therefore relevant in connecting the climate change and business and human rights agendas.[68]

The EU is also in the process of amending two other relevant pieces of legislation that apply to all companies, including those in the financial sector, that will further regulate business and human rights. As noted above, the EU is revising the Non-Financial Disclosure Directive that already required disclosure of a company's policies and approaches to human rights.[69] The 2021 update is expected to deepen and broaden the scope of expected disclosure. The EU is also expected to issue a draft Directive in 2021 on mandatory environmental and human rights due diligence that will likely apply to all companies in the EU, with potential adjustments for small, medium-sized, and micro enterprises.[70]

2. *United States*

Regulatory actions in the United States under the Trump Administration (2017 to 2021) moved in the opposite direction of the EU. The United States does not have an overall strategic approach to sustainable finance.[71] Instead of opening the way for investors to more actively consider ESG issues, the US Department of Labor (DOL) in 2020 issued a new rule that would have required private retirement plans and asset managers to change how they approach ESG-focused investments. Under the new rule, ESG factors would have only been considered when they are pecuniary, meaning when such factors would have a material effect on the risk or return of an investment.[72] Despite the overwhelming opposition among the thousands of comments received supporting ESG in the US market, the DOL adopted the rule in 2020.[73]

---

[67] Kelly Levin and Chantal Davis, *What Does "Net-Zero Emissions" Mean? 6 Common Questions* (Answered updated Aug. 12, 2020), https://www.wri.org/blog/2019/09/what-does-net-zero-emissions-mean-6-common-questions-answered.

[68] Institute for Human Rights and Business, *Connecting the Just Transitions and Business & Human Rights Agendas* (Dec. 2020), https://www.ihrb.org/focus-areas/just-transitions/briefing-connecting-just-transitions-business-human-rights-agendas.

[69] Directive 2014/95/EU of the European Parliament and of the Council of 22 October 2014 amending Directive 2013/34/EU as regards disclosure of non-financial and diversity information by certain large undertakings and groups Directive 2014/95/EU of the European Parliament and of the Council of 22 October 2014 amending Directive 2013/34/EU as regards disclosure of non-financial and diversity information by certain large undertakings and groups Text with EEA relevance OJ L 330, 15.11.2014, p. 1–9 https://eur-lex.europa.eu/legal-content/EN/TXT/?uri=CELEX%3A32014L0095 and *see* https://ec.europa.eu/info/business-economy-euro/company-reporting-and-auditing/company-reporting/non-financial-reporting_en.

[70] *See* https://www.business-humanrights.org/en/big-issues/mandatory-due-diligence/.

[71] Nor is the United States a member of the International Platform on Sustainable Finance, https://ec.europa.eu/info/business-economy-euro/banking-and-finance/sustainable-finance/international-platform-sustainable-finance_en.

[72] Joseph Lifsics, *The Department of Labor's ESG-less Final ESG Rule* (Nov. 24, 2020), Harvard Law School Forum on Corporate Governance, https://corpgov.law.harvard.edu/?s=ESG&is_v=1.

[73] Julie Gorte, et. al, *Public Comments Overwhelmingly Oppose Proposed Rule Limiting the Use of ESG in ERISA Retirement Plans* (Aug. 20, 2020), https://www.ussif.org/Files/Public_Policy/DOL_Comments_Reporting_FINAL.pdf.

Similarly, President Trump–appointed Chairman of the US Securities and Exchange Commission (SEC), Jay Clayton, made clear his skepticism on ESG while he was in office.[74] The SEC did not adopt a general requirement on ESG disclosure, despite a recommendation from its Investor-as-Owner Subcommittee of the SEC Investor Advisory Committee to do so.[75] Similar to the DOL rule, letters in opposition to the changes vastly outnumbered those in support.[76] A General Accounting Office report released in 2020 evaluating the state of public company disclosures related to ESG issues, covered the SEC's role in oversight of ESG disclosures, and options to improve and regulate ESG disclosures.[77]

The Biden administration (2021 to 2025) has signaled a complete shift in position, demonstrating far stronger support of a sustainable finance agenda[78] early on in its tenure. This was expected, given President Biden's strong statements on addressing climate change and commitment to rejoin the Paris Agreement on Climate Change.[79] Within the first few months of the new administration, in March 2021, the DOL released an enforcement policy statement setting out its intention to revisit its recently published final rules on ESG investments issued in the waning days of the Trump administration.[80] The DOL stated that it will not enforce the rule or otherwise pursue enforcement actions against any plan fiduciary based on a failure to comply with those final rules, but it did not provide any clear indications of how it will modify the rules.[81] The DOL noted in particular that stakeholders conveyed the message that the DOL rules had "already had a chilling effect on appropriate integration of ESG factors in investment decisions."[82]

---

[74] SEC Chairman Jay Clayton, *Remarks at Meeting of the Asset Management Advisory Committee* (May 27, 2020), https://www.sec.gov/news/public-statement/clayton-amac-opening-2020-05-27#_edn8.

[75] *Recommendation from the Investor-as-Owner Subcommittee of the SEC Investor Advisory Committee Relating to ESG Disclosure* (May 14, 2020), https://www.sec.gov/spotlight/investor-advisory-committee-2012/recommendation-of-the-investor-as-owner-subcommittee-on-esg-disclosure.pdf.

[76] *Id.*

[77] Government Accountability Office (GAO), *Disclosure of Environmental, Social, and Governance Factors and Options to Enhance Them* (Jul. 2020), https://www.gao.gov/assets/710/707949.pdf.

[78] Leslie Norton, *The Biden Era Could Be a Boon to Sustainable Investing* (Nov. 23, 2020), Barrons, https://www.barrons.com/articles/the-biden-era-could-be-a-boon-to-sustainable-investing-51606131000, Suzanne Smetana, State Street Global Advisors, *ESG and the Biden Presidency* (Feb. 19, 2021), https://corpgov.law.harvard.edu/2021/02/19/esg-and-the-biden-presidency/. *See also* Hunton Andrews Kurth, *A Preview of ESG Regulation under the Biden Administration*, XI National Law Review (Feb 16, 2021), https://www.natlawreview.com/article/preview-esg-regulation-under-biden-administration, Lewis Braham, *Biden Administration Will Reverse the Department of Labor's Ruling on ESG Funds, Analysts Say*, Barrons (Jan. 31, 2021), https://www.barrons.com/articles/biden-administration-will-reverse-the-department-of-labors-ruling-on-esg-funds-analysts-say-51612094408.

[79] *See 9 Key Elements of Joe Biden's Plan for a Clean Energy Revolution*, https://joebiden.com/9-key-elements-of-joe-bidens-plan-for-a-clean-energy-revolution/.

[80] Department of Labor (DOL), *U.S. Department of Labor Statement Regarding Enforcement of Its Final Rules on ESG Investments and Proxy Voting by Employee Benefit Plans* (Mar. 10, 2021), https://www.dol.gov/sites/dolgov/files/ebsa/laws-and-regulations/laws/erisa/statement-on-enforcement-of-final-rules-on-esg-investments-and-proxy-voting.pdf.

[81] Ropes & Gray, *Department of Labor Announces Non-Enforcement Policy for Trump-Era ESG and Proxy Voting Rules* (Mar. 11, 2021), https://www.ropesgray.com/en/newsroom/alerts/2021/March/Department-of-Labor-Announces-Non-Enforcement-Policy-for-Trump-Era-ESG-and-Proxy-Voting-Rules.

[82] DOL, *US Department of Labor Statement Regarding Enforcement of Its Final Rules on ESG Investments and Proxy Voting By Employee Benefit Plans* (Mar. 10, 2021), https://www.dol.gov/sites/dolgov/files/ebsa/laws-and-regulations/laws/erisa/statement-on-enforcement-of-final-rules-on-esg-investments-and-proxy-voting.pdf.

Similarly, the SEC rapidly signaled important shifts to reverse a number of Trump administration policies on climate change and ESG more broadly. The Acting Head of the SEC noted in March 2021 that there is "really no historical precedent for the magnitude of the shift in investor focus . . . over the last decade toward the analysis and use of climate and other ESG risks and impacts in investment," and that consequently, "no single issue has been more pressing for me than ensuring that the SEC is fully engaged in confronting the risks and opportunities that climate and ESG pose for investors, our financial system, and our economy."[83]

In February 2021, the SEC's Division of Corporation Finance noted it will enhance its focus on climate-related disclosure in public company filings and stated that the SEC staff would begin reviewing existing disclosures as part of a process of updating the SEC's 2010 climate change guidance.[84] In early March 2021, the SEC also announced the creation of a Climate and ESG Task Force in the SEC's Division of Enforcement.[85] In a statement also in March 2021, the Acting Head of the SEC noted that the Commission will take critical steps toward a comprehensive ESG disclosure framework aimed at producing the consistent, comparable, and reliable data that investors need.[86] In April, its Acting Director of Corporate Finance issued a wide-ranging discussion on ESG disclosures, noting the need to keep pace with developments affecting investors, public companies, and the capital markets; the virtues of achieving a single global ESG reporting framework; and indicating that SEC policy on ESG disclosures will need to be both "adaptive and innovative."[87]

Also in April 2021, the SEC issued an ESG risk alert that describes the areas on which the staff will focus in examinations of registered investment advisers' and funds' ESG offerings. The risk alert notes that the rapid growth in demand, increasing number of ESG products and services, and lack of standardized and precise ESG definitions present risks of confusion among investors if investment advisers and funds have not clearly and consistently articulated how they define ESG and how they use ESG-related terms, especially when offering products or services to retail investors. It noted that the staff will evaluate whether firms are "accurately disclosing their ESG investing approaches and have adopted and implemented policies, procedures, and practices that accord with their ESG-related disclosures."[88] The risk alert goes on to identify a whole series of problematic and misleading statements and practices based on recent examinations.

---

[83] Acting SEC Chair Alison Herren Lee, *A Climate for Change: Meeting Investor Demand for Climate and ESG Information at the SEC* (Mar. 15, 2021), https://www.sec.gov/news/speech/lee-climate-change.

[84] Acting Chair Allison Herren Lee, *Statement on the Review of Climate-Related Disclosure* (Feb. 24, 2021).

[85] SEC, Press Release, *SEC Announces Enforcement Task Force Focused on Climate and ESG Issues* (Mar. 4, 2021).

[86] Acting SEC Chair Alison Herren Lee, *A Climate for Change: Meeting Investor Demand for Climate and ESG Information at the SEC* (Mar. 15, 2021), https://www.sec.gov/news/speech/lee-climate-change.

[87] Acting Director, Division of Corporation Finance John Coates, *ESG Disclosure—Keeping Pace with Developments Affecting Investors, Public Companies and the Capital Markets* (Mar. 11, 2021), https://www.sec.gov/news/public-statement/coates-esg-disclosure-keeping-pace-031121?utm_medium=email&utm_source=govdelivery.

[88] SEC, Division of Examinations, *Risk Alert: The Division of Examinations' Review of ESG Investing* (Apr. 9, 2021), https://www.sec.gov/files/esg-risk-alert.pdf.

The SEC has also changed course on shareholder resolutions, reaffirming that proposals cannot be excluded if they concern socially significant issues.[89] In March 2021, the SEC made two rulings on shareholder resolutions at oil and gas companies on emissions reductions that signaled a clear shift to climate change and ESG becoming an issue "front and center" at the SEC. In another reversal, the SEC allowed proposals on systemic racism that were not permitted under the Trump SEC. These changes indicate that shareholders will find a far more receptive environment to presenting resolutions at annual meetings under the Biden administration SEC.[90]

The increased attention to ESG issues among US regulators is important to the human rights area because many "S" issues are in fact human rights issues (see also Subsection D.2. below). But human rights issues are not only related to the "S" in ESG. As the acting head of the SEC noted, climate change presents heightened risks for marginalized communities, linking it to racial justice. She clearly framed "human capital, human rights, climate change" as "fundamental to our markets, and investors."[91] This signals increasingly focused and sophisticated regulatory attention to these concerns.

D. Selected Voluntary Initiatives

1. *Government Initiatives—Dutch International Responsible Business Conduct Agreements*

The Dutch Government has initiated a series of "international responsible business conduct agreements" focused on the application of the UNGPs and the OECD Guidelines in several sectors, including the financial sector, with separate agreements covering banking, insurance, and pension funds.[92] The agreements are voluntary, bringing together participants from the private sector, civil society, and trade unions, and they set out the steps and standards companies in the sector will take to meet the UNGPs and the OECD Guidelines. The government plays an active role in overseeing the agreement negotiation and implementation process. The banking sector agreement, which closed at the end of 2019, produced studies on human rights in selected supply chains of projects financed by banks, discussion papers on leverage and remediation,[93] and an analysis on transparency in light of confidentiality obligations, among other topics.[94] Work on the responsible business conduct agreements for insurance and pension funds is ongoing in 2021.

[89] Acting Chair Alison Herren Lee, *A Climate for Change: Meeting Investor Demand for Climate and ESG Information at the SEC* (Mar. 15, 2021), https://www.sec.gov/news/speech/lee-climate-change.

[90] Paul Verney, *The Tide Has Turned: SEC Sides with Investors and Civil Society on Shareholder Resolutions*, RESPONSIBLE INVESTOR (Mar. 25, 2021), https://www.responsible-investor.com/articles/the-tide-has-turned-sec-sides-with-investors-and-civil-society-on-shareholder-resolutions.

[91] Acting Chair Alison Herren Lee, *A Climate for Change: Meeting Investor Demand for Climate and ESG Information at the SEC* (Mar. 15, 2021), https://www.sec.gov/news/speech/lee-climate-change.

[92] https://www.imvoconvenanten.nl/en/agreements.

[93] *See also*: https://shiftproject.org/dutch-banks-government-unions-and-civil-society-sign-groundbreaking-agreement-on-business-and-human-rights/.

[94] https://www.imvoconvenanten.nl/en/banking/about-this-agreement/publicaties.

2. *Investor Initiatives*

Institutional investors have been some of the most active in applying the UNGPs and the OECD Guidelines, prompted by the broader shift within the investment community on incorporating ESG considerations into their investment choices and decision-making. This has also been prompted in part by early cases involving investors before NCPs under the OECD Guidelines, and in particular the case involving NBIM, discussed in Section III.A.2. above. ESG considerations have "raced to the top" of the agenda for many investors in the closing of the decade up to 2020. Just in the period from 2018 to 2020, over $100 billion flowed into investment products focused on ESG issues.[95] While superior returns on investment in firms with ESG policies and practices have played a strong role in the building momentum, numerous studies and commentaries highlight a growing range of reasons to pay attention to such factors, including the growth in regulatory requirements.[96]

While the "E" and the "G" have dominated ESG discussions to date, the "S" is rapidly rising up the agenda. The COVID-19 pandemic[97] and the US "Black Lives Matter" protests drawing renewed attention to racial inequality[98] have catapulted "S" topics further up investors' agendas. And while human rights are also relevant to the "E" and the "G," they are most firmly rooted in the "S" dimension and provide a normative clarity and framework to the "S" agenda that is missing from current approaches to "S" issues, which are often presented as a hodge-podge list with no clear reference framework.[99] Viewing the issues through a human rights framework helps make sense of the many "S" issues that are human rights issues: this includes the issues around workers, human capital, workplace standards, nondiscrimination, and diversity, but also issues around broader relations with customer and communities, inequalities, privacy, and freedom of expression, to name just a few. Some investors are beginning to appreciate that understanding an investee company's approach to human rights also provides a bellwether on how forward-looking the company is in dealing with a whole range of other societal challenges as well.[100]

---

[95] Barclays Bank, *10 ESG Themes for 2020*, https://www.investmentbank.barclays.com/content/dam/barclaysmicrosites/ibpublic/documents/our-insights/10_Trends_ESG_2020/Barclays-ESG-2020-Trends-Slideshow.pdf.

[96] Gunnar Friede et al., *ESG and Financial Performance: Aggregated Evidence from More than 2000 Empirical Studies*, 5 J. of Sustainable Fin. & Inv., 210, 210–233 (Oct. 2015), and *see*, Aviva Investors, *Investment Research: Time for a Brave New World?* (2017), Appendix 3. *See for example*, Witold Henisz, Tim Koller & Robin Nuttall, *Five Ways That ESG Creates Value*, McKinsey Quarterly (Nov. 14, 2019), https://www.mckinsey.com/business-functions/strategy-and-corporate-finance/our-insights/five-ways-that-esg-creates-value.

[97] Kosmas Papadopoulos, Rodolfo Araujo & Simon Toms, *ESG Drivers and the COVID-19 Catalyst*, Harvard Law School Forum on Corporate Governance (Dec. 27, 2020), https://corpgov.law.harvard.edu/2020/12/27/esg-drivers-and-the-covid-19-catalyst/#more-135227.

[98] Seymour Burchman, Barry Sullivan & Julia Thorner, *Racial Equity on the Board Agenda*, Harvard Law School Forum on Corporate Governance, (Nov. 16, 2020), https://corpgov.law.harvard.edu/2020/11/16/racial-equity-on-the-board-agenda.

[99] Fiona Reynolds & John Ruggie, *What Institutional Investors Need to Know about the S in ESG* (Oct. 22, 2020), PRI, https://www.unpri.org/pri-blogs/what-institutional-investors-need-to-know-about-the-s-in-esg/6635.article and Margaret Wachenfeld, *Strengthening the 'S' in ESG: What New Developments in Human Rights and Business Bring to the Table for Investors*, in Karen Wendt (Ed.), Responsible Investment Banking: Risk Management Frameworks, Sustainable Financial Innovation and Softlaw Standards (2015).

[100] Institute for Human Rights and Business and ICCR, *Investing the Rights Way: A Guide for Investors on Business and Human Rights* (2013), https://www.ihrb.org/focus-areas/finance/report-investing-the-rights.

The UN-backed Principles for Responsible Investment (PRI), whose 3,000 member signatories have US$120 trillion of assets under management, is a membership organization for institutional investors that is supported by, but not part of, the UN, and that works to achieve a sustainable global financial system.[101] PRI signatories commit to six principles on responsible investment and report annually on their responsible investment activities.[102] PRI has organized a number of "collaborative engagements" on human rights among its members that involve joint discussions on human rights with targeted companies.[103] In 2020, the PRI set out clear expectations for PRI investors themselves, and not just the companies they invest in, based on human rights standards, and provided recommendations on the integration of respect for human rights into investment practices.[104] It also developed a five-year work program to prompt its members to apply the UNGPs and the OECD Guidelines consistently across their operations.[105]

The Interfaith Center on Corporate Responsibility (ICCR), a long-standing leader in the United States from the early days of socially responsible investment, has been active on a wide range of human rights issues, both through advocacy with governments and collaborative engagements with investee companies.[106] In 2018, it launched the Investor Alliance on Human Rights as a collective action platform for responsible investment that is grounded in respect for human rights.[107] It also developed a toolkit to support investors in applying the UNGPs and the OECD Guidelines.[108]

Other groupings of institutional investors have joined together to support specific initiatives to raise the human rights profile with investee companies and prompt further disclosure of human rights information that is relevant for investment decision-making. Several investors have collaborated with human rights organizations to develop the Corporate Human Rights Benchmark (CHRB) that benchmarks over 230 of the largest companies in the world on their human rights records.[109] Investors use the CHRB data to inform engagement with investee companies as part of investment decision-making, and in advocacy with governments.[110]

---

[101] https://www.unpri.org/pri/about-the-pri.

[102] https://www.unpri.org/reporting-and-assessment/the-reporting-process/3057.article.

[103] https://www.unpri.org/sustainability-issues/environmental-social-and-governance-issues/social-issues/human-rights-and-labour-standards.

[104] PRI, *Why and How Investors Should Act on Human Rights* (2020), https://www.unpri.org/human-rights-and-labour-standards/why-and-how-investors-should-act-on-human-rights/6636.article.

[105] https://www.unpri.org/human-rights-and-labour-standards/why-and-how-investors-should-act-on-human-rights/6636.article.

[106] https://www.iccr.org/about-iccr.

[107] https://investorsforhumanrights.org/about.

[108] https://investorsforhumanrights.org/investor-toolkit-human-rights.

[109] https://www.corporatebenchmark.org/.

[110] https://www.business-humanrights.org/en/latest-news/letter-investor-statement-calling-on-companies-to-improve-performance-on-the-corporate-human-rights-benchmark/.

3. *Banking Sector Initiatives*

In 2003, a small group of private sector banks formed the Equator Principle Association (EP Association) at the invitation of the International Finance Corporation (IFC) and adopted the Equator Principles (Equator Principles).[111] The first set of Equator Principles were revised in July 2006 to align with the newly adopted IFC Performance Standards that set out environmental and social requirements for certain project finance transactions.[112] In doing so, the Equator Principle banks in principle accepted the human rights requirements incorporated in the IFC Performance Standards.[113] The growing number of Equator Principle banks have nonetheless been under continued scrutiny by a range of CSOs for human rights impacts in the projects they finance.[114] In 2020, responding to growing pressure from human rights and climate change campaigns to update the Equator Principles to respond to both these sets of concerns, the EP Association updated the Equator Principles to include new, brief provisions on human rights, with a specific reference to the UNGPs and to carrying out human rights due diligence.[115] However, the update did not include commitments to establishing grievance mechanisms at the banks or the EP Association, a long-running campaign demand from several CSOs. The EP Association has noted that it is keeping the issue of remedy under the UNGPs under consideration.[116]

The informal "Thun Group," named for a town in Switzerland where one of the banks is headquartered, is a group composed largely of European banks formed to work together to understand how human rights can be respected and promoted across the breadth of different banking activities. The Thun Group produced two rounds of discussion papers setting out their positions, which were tested through a series of hypotheticals. Though the initiative was welcomed by stakeholders, some of the Thun Group's interpretations of the application of the UNGPs were not. The 2017 Thun Group Discussion Paper prompted responses from the former UN Special Representative to the Secretary-General on Business and Human Rights, the UN Working Group on Business and Human Rights, and others, as did the 2018 revision.[117]

4. *Insurance Sector Initiatives*

The insurance sector has been far less active, or at least less visible, in addressing human rights. The UNEP FI Principles for Sustainable Insurance do not explicitly address human rights, but instead, address ESG factors more broadly.[118] Apart from an early guidance

[111] https://www.mizuhogroup.com/sustainability/business-activities/investment/equator/about.

[112] https://equator-principles.com/.

[113] https://www.ifc.org/wps/wcm/connect/topics_ext_content/ifc_external_corporate_site/sustainability-at-ifc/publications/ibhr_ifc_sustainability_framework.

[114] Bank Track, *Tracking the Equator Principles*, https://www.banktrack.org/page/tracking_the_equator_principles.

[115] https://equator-principles.com/wp-content/uploads/2020/05/The-Equator-Principles-July-2020-v2.pdf.

[116] Equator Principles Association, *EPA Response to Feedback during Review of the EPs*, https://equator-principles.com/wp-content/uploads/2019/11/EPA-response-to-feedback-received-during-review-of-EPs-11-11-19.pdf.

[117] *See* https://www.business-humanrights.org/en/latest-news/thun-group-of-banks-releases-new-paper-on-implications-of-un-guiding-principles-for-corporate-investment-banking/.

[118] https://www.unepfi.org/psi/the-principles/ (2012).

document from a group of insurance companies on human rights,[119] there has been very little to indicate what, if any, work the sector is doing to address human rights. This is surprising, given that insurance can play a role in supporting their corporate clients to respect human rights by providing a service that ensures that human rights harm can be compensated.[120]

IV. Identification of Good Practices

As highlighted in Section III above, there is a growing range of authoritative interpretations and existing guidance for the financial sector that specifically address the application of the UNGPs and the OECD Guidelines in the sector. These provide useful starting points for understanding the state of play to date but only begin to scratch the surface of the complexities of the application of human rights principles by financial institutions across their full range of financial transactions.

As a preliminary matter, while the focus may continue to be on due diligence, practitioners should not lose sight of the importance of all three key steps that underpin the corporate responsibility to respect human rights, set out below. Much of the existing guidance for the financial sector covers the full sweep of the responsibility to respect, even though it may be labelled as "due diligence" guidance. A few selected highlights for each step of the UNGPs and the OECD Guidelines drawn from existing discussions to date are set out below.[121]

A. Policy Commitment to Respecting Human Rights and Embedding Human Rights in Management Systems

The first step is for financial institutions to recognize that they have a responsibility to respect human rights, just like other businesses. Banks and investors are increasingly developing human rights policies that may be stand-alone policies or incorporated into relevant policies on sectoral or high-risk issues.[122] The more mature policies identify the financial institution's own commitments, describe how it will be embedded in its corporate procedures and processes, and assign responsibility for implementation across relevant departments of the financial institution. These policies typically also set human rights expectations for the companies they finance. Without the specific recognition by the financial institution of its own responsibility to respect human rights and the accompanying institutional, procedural, and budgetary allocation of responsibility to implement those commitments, consideration of human rights impacts can too easily become just another risk screen for lending and

---

[119] CRO Forum, *Human Rights and Corporate Insurance* (2014).

[120] For further explanation on the role of insurance with respect to human rights, *see* UNEP Inquiry Human Rights Report, Section 3.5.1.

[121] For more details on these points, *see in particular* the guidance developed by the OECD in applying the OECD *Guidelines* to the financial sector: https://mneguidelines.oecd.org/rbc-financial-sector.htm.

[122] *See for example*, the NBIM Expectations on Human Rights and Children's Rights, https://www.nbim.no/en/publications/ and ABN Amro's Human Rights Statement, https://assets.ctfassets.net/1u811bvgvthc/31STNCr1gNbb4AhiHCcsQ7/6b28984c36003ea610a362eb9e213560/ABN_AMRO_Human_Rights_Statement_2020.pdf.

investment portfolios or a tickbox exercise that does not accord human rights the prioritization it deserves.

B. Human Rights Due Diligence

1. Identification and Assessment of Human Rights Risks and Impacts

Institutional investors and banks are developing a range of scoping and screening tools to identify potential human rights risks when entering into financial transactions. Professor Ruggie, the author of the UNGPs, coined the phrase "knowing and showing" as a shorthand to describe human rights due diligence. Identifying potential and actual human rights impacts is the "knowing" part of the process. Approaches used range from developing a set of red-flag criteria around transactions that might pose a higher human rights risk based on the country, sector, business model, or other high-risk categories, to incorporating human rights issues into data management systems that pull a wide range of information into ESG scoring systems in order to identify potential human rights issues. Managers of larger investment portfolios are developing more structured, systematic, and innovative systems to identify and use decision-relevant information on human rights.

As to assessment of the financial institution's role with respect to clients' adverse human rights impacts, much of the discussion to date has focused on the issue of how to apply the UNGPs concepts of "involvement" in an adverse human rights impact to financial institutions. In particular, whether a financial institution is "contributing" to an impact or whether it is only "directly linked" through its business relationship with its client has been a consistent point of discussion. The distinction is significant because it relates to which parties in a transaction have a responsibility for remedying the adverse impacts. A financial institution will always be "directly linked" to the human rights impacts of its clients. In these cases, the financial institution should use its leverage to prompt the client to take action to remedy the harm, but the financial institution is not expected to take a role in the remedy, though it can do so. If the financial institution contributes to the harm alongside a client, it is expected to contribute to the remedy as well. Distinguishing between contribution and direct linkage in turn relies on several factors that, in particular, point to the importance of the quality of the due diligence.[123] Banks and other financial institutions, including private equity firms, may be in a position to contribute to adverse human rights impacts and therefore need to consider whether their due diligence processes are sufficient to identify and manage human rights impacts in order to avoid situations contributing to adverse impacts.[124]

---

[123] As the discussion to date among the investment community has been among large-scale institutional investors with very small percentages of holdings in companies, they are considered only directly linked in the vast majority of cases. *See* Institutional Investor Guidance, p. 34. That assumption does not necessarily apply to private equity transactions where investors may hold much larger shares and exercise much more control. See the elaboration of the factors that are relevant in the Corporate Lending Guidance, pp. 43–47.

[124] *See* Bank Track's Human Rights Benchmark (2019), p. 15 https://www.banktrack.org/hrbenchmark.

2. *Prevention and Mitigation of Human Rights Risks and Impacts*

Banks and institutional investors can use a range of actions to prevent and mitigate human rights impacts through their own processes, such as maintaining exclusion lists that exclude high-risk projects from financing. They can do their own due diligence so they are informed of the key human rights issues in the sector and the transaction so as to be able to judge whether a client's proposed prevention and mitigation measures are sufficient. Financial institutions are expected to "exercise their leverage" with their clients in the UNGPs sense, rather than the usual financial sector use of the term.[125] Under the UNGPs, "exercising leverage" is about using the various tools a financial institution has to persuade and require clients to address human rights in the operations financed. In addition to using its commercial leverage to provide or withhold finance or provide financial incentives, financial institutions will typically have a wider range of tools to exercise leverage than they may have realized or used. They can raise issues early with clients, ensure that clients are doing human rights due diligence on a project or operation, provide expertise to clients on how to address issues, and incorporate human rights requirements and conditions into loan or other legal agreements to provide legal grounding for exercising leverage. Investors can use their collective voice and pressure in discussions with investee companies through engagement to persuade them to change practices, and they can use shareholder resolutions and voting to prompt investee companies to adopt policies and a systematic approach to identifying and managing human rights issues.

3. *Tracking*

Tracking is about taking a systematic approach to measuring human rights performance both within a transaction and across the financial institution's portfolio, understanding the trends, and adjusting internal systems and processes to improve performance. The rising focus on ESG means that financial institutions are developing more sophisticated approaches and systems to pull and analyze a wide range of ESG information and track it over time for individual clients and across their portfolios. Human rights information can and should be part of these systems, which can include information on client human rights performance drawn from company sustainability reports, tracking human rights controversies that involve clients, using new tools such as human rights benchmarking, and establishing relationships with CSOs that provide relevant information.

4. *Communication and Disclosure*

This is the "show" dimension of "knowing and showing" under the UNGPs. Financial institutions, like other businesses, are expected under the UNGPs and the OECD Guidelines to communicate publicly what they are doing to address human rights. Large financial institutions in the EU are already required to report on human rights under the EU Non-Financial

[125] *See* Section III.A.2 above and the discussion on terminology which is explained further in the Institutional Investor Guidance.

Reporting Directive, and some are going further in reporting on human rights.[126] With respect to reporting on specific client operations, financial institutions are typically bound by client confidentiality requirements when it comes to disclosing information about their clients and the impacts they may be having on human rights. However, pressure from CSOs has led to debates and further re-examination of the appropriate boundaries of client confidentiality provisions typically used in financial transactions in light of the public interest and normative expectations set by the UNGPs to disclose meaningful information about how human rights concerns are being addressed.[127]

C. Processes to Enable the Remediation of Adverse Human Rights Impacts

As in other sectors, the issue of which party is responsible for remedying adverse human rights impacts has been the source of much discussion and debate, because responsibility for remedy comes closer to issues of legal liability. Financial institutions, like other businesses, are expected under the UNGPs to individually and collectively establish or participate in operational-level grievance mechanisms that can address and resolve human rights concerns early.[128] This is challenging for financial institutions, because they are typically at least one-step removed from the actual impacts on the ground which their clients have caused or to which their clients have contributed. Nonetheless, such mechanisms are not unheard of—multilateral development banks already had grievance mechanisms in place to hear complaints about the projects they finance long before the UNGPs.[129] The Dutch Banking Sector Responsible Business Conduct Agreement, mentioned in Section III.D.1, developed a paper on the role of banks in remedy that lays out a wide range of steps banks can take themselves and with their clients in enabling and providing remedy.[130]

---

[126] *See for example* ING Bank's Human Rights Report (2018), https://www.ing.com/MediaEditPage/2018-Human-rights-report-ING-Groep-N.V.htm.

[127] *See* Nauta Dutilh, *Legal Report on the Possibilities for Increased Transparency in Light of the Adhering Banks' Client Confidentiality Obligations* (2017), https://www.imvoconvenanten.nl/-/media/imvo/files/banking/news/nautadutilh-legal-report.pdf?la=en&hash=1AAD2F201AD97A7B4F7C4B28493C87AD and see Bank Track, "*We Are Unable to Comment on Specific Customers . . .,*" *Challenging Banks on Client Confidentiality* (2019), https://www.banktrack.org/article/world_s_biggest_banks_routinely_hide_links_to_human_rights_and_environmental_abuses_behind_client_confidentiality_study.

[128] *See for example*, Oxfam and Bank Track, *Developing Effective Grievance Mechanisms in the Banking Sector* (2018), https://www.banktrack.org/article/banktrack_and_oxfam_australia_call_on_banks_to_ensure_access_to_remedy_for_victims_of_human_rights_abuses.

[129] *See* the Independent Accountability Mechanisms Network, http://independentaccountabilitymechanism.net/.

[130] Dutch Banking Sector Agreement, *Discussion paper: Working Group Enabling Remediation* (2019), https://www.imvoconvenanten.nl/-/media/imvo/files/banking/paper-enabling-remediation.pdf and David Kovick, *Rethinking Remedy and Responsibility in the Financial Sector* (May 2019), https://shiftproject.org/rethinking-remedy-and-responsibility-in-the-financial-sector/.

V. Identification of Outstanding/Evolving Issues and Challenges

There is no longer any question about whether the UNGPs and the OECD Guidelines apply to financial institutions and financial transactions. They clearly do. The issue now is how they do so. Significant progress in beginning to unpack that question has been made, as highlighted throughout this chapter. However, numerous challenges remain to better align the financial system and sector with human rights; several are highlighted below.

One, the interaction of UNGPs concepts with legal principles that shape financial practice—including materiality, fiduciary duty, and the interplay between disclosure and client confidentiality—will require business and human rights practitioners to collaborate with their colleagues advising on financial transactions to develop appropriate advice about how the two sets of concepts can be balanced and applied together. These interactions could also usefully explore how other areas of financial practice, such as anti-corruption and anti–money laundering systems, could provide valuable models and information to address human rights issues.[131]

Two, financial institutions will be increasingly required by law or via other mechanisms such as stock exchange listing requirements, or just through rising expectations, to demonstrate that they are applying the UNGPs and doing so effectively. Neither the regulators nor the public may be very clear about how that is to be done, but they will nonetheless expect financial institutions to be able to "know and show" that they are doing so effectively. This should prompt reflection on how much more transparent they can be about their systems and outcomes.

Three, practitioners will want to track the rapidly evolving discussions on ESG disclosure standards and understand how they relate to the due diligence processes that should be the source of the information that is disclosed.[132] Practitioners will also need to be able to "sort the wheat from the chaff." Unsurprisingly, given the growing interest in sustainable finance and human rights within the financial sector, there has been a veritable explosion of specialist ESG service providers that scrutinize companies' ESG performance and sell this information to institutional investors and others,[133] and of ESG practices in the financial,

---

[131] *See for example,* the Finance against Slavery and Trafficking Initiative, https://www.fastinitiative.org/.

[132] *See for example*, John Coates, US Securities and Exchange Commission, on Saturday, March 13, 2021 *ESG Disclosure—Keeping Pace with Developments Affecting Investors, Public Companies and the Capital Markets,* https://corpgov.law.harvard.edu/2021/03/13/esg-disclosure-keeping-pace-with-developments-affecting-investors-public-companies-and-the-capital-markets/ and Mark S. Bergman, Brad S. Karp, Richard A. Rosen, Paul, Weiss, Rifkind, Wharton & Garrison LLP, *ESG Disclosures: Frameworks and Standards Developed by Intergovernmental and Non-Governmental Organizations* (2020), https://corpgov.law.harvard.edu/2020/09/21/esg-disclosures-frameworks-and-standards-developed-by-intergovernmental-and-non-governmental-organizations/.

[133] *See for example*, some like Vigeo-Eiris and Sustainalytics have been in the ESG "space" for a long time and have well-established track records.

legal,[134] and accountancy fields to respond to these demands. Some of these may be supported by a clear understanding and expertise on human rights, but arguably others have jumped on the bandwagon. Practitioners will need to help clients sort through the complexity, explaining that data scraping based on searches for "human rights" should not be equated with a serious approach to due diligence processes that seek to identify and address human rights impacts.[135]

Four, business and human rights practitioners should already be looking ahead to anticipate future developments in the field. The push on sustainable finance to redirect financial flows, the anticipated introduction of mandatory human rights and environmental due diligence law in the EU, and the climate change and biodiversity crises provide a clear signal. This means practitioners should already be working with their environmental law colleagues and the sustainability departments in financial institutions to explore how human rights and environmental due diligence can be better aligned to achieve synergies through due diligence processes to reduce interlinked adverse impacts and achieve better sustainability outcomes.[136]

Five, current developments highlighted in this chapter involve only a fraction of the world's financial regulators and financial institutions and an even smaller fraction of the world's financial transactions, so much work remains to be done.

VI. Conclusion

It is clear that pressure from regulators, CSOs, and, increasingly, the general public concerned about sustainability and sustainable finance will continue to build on financial institutions. This will include pressure to address human rights directly and systematically. The UNGPs were not developed as a legal standard, even though the human rights due diligence concept was deliberately adapted from other due diligence processes (legal, financial, technical) that are familiar to business. But the push toward developing mandatory due diligence legislation means that the application of the UNGP concepts will continue to harden into hard law, and as a result the concepts within them are likely to be seriously contested and tested, including through legal challenges. Their application to the financial sector adds additional layers of complexity, especially around the UNGPs' "involvement framework" and the related issue of the appropriate role of financial institutions in enabling or providing remedy alongside clients.

Practitioners can prepare themselves in a number of ways. A few recommendations are provided.

---

[134] This has in turn led to integrated ESG legal practices; *see* Carla Parson, Paul Watchman & Vanessa Wood, *The Rise of ESG Law Firms Part I:* Responsible Investor (Oct. 26, 2020).

[135] ". . . a shift toward stakeholder capitalism is unlikely to be a presentation on the metrics, and far more likely to be the conversation an executive is having with his teenage children at the dinner table." Alison Taylor, *The Psychology of Shifting to Stakeholder Capitalism* (Mar. 10, 2021), https://www.ethicalsystems.org/the-psychology-of-shifting-to-stakeholder-capitalism/.

[136] *See for example*, IHRB, *Connecting the Climate Change and Business & Human Rights Agendas* (Dec. 2020), https://www.ihrb.org/focus-areas/just-transitions/briefing-connecting-climate-change-business-human-rights-agendas.

A. Understand the Broader Context

First, as noted in the Section I introduction, practitioners interested in the application of human rights to the financial sector should build an understanding of the many different ways and levels that human rights can apply to the financial sector and should consider "the bigger picture."

Second, with the rise of sustainable finance and stakeholder capitalism, financial institutions and their advisors need to be prepared to engage in this broader debate and their role in it. Practitioners will also need to be prepared to understand and articulate how human rights interact with sustainable finance frameworks, and to defend the inclusion of human rights but also to be flexible in being able to adapt important human rights principles and processes to new areas. At the same time, the human rights community and practitioners must remain alert to an increasingly visible tendency to cast the private sector as the actor that "saves" the SDGs and the Paris Agreement, focusing only on positive contributions. While it is important that the financial sector, like other business sectors, seriously engages on contributing to realizing the SDGs, addressing adverse human rights impacts should be an integral part of every transaction, even those intended to support important societal goals.

B. Build and Maintain Knowledge about Existing Developments

On a more practical basis, as a start, practitioners advising financial institutions should familiarize themselves with the existing guidance highlighted in the chapter and monitor emerging themes and guidance coming from authoritative sources: the UN-related initiatives, notably OHCHR, PRI, and UNEP FI, as well as OECD, that are very active in the space, and from the development finance institutions that have both commercial mandates as well as public development mandates and are incorporating human rights requirements into their financing.[137]

Developing a better understanding of what the human rights community considers good practice among financial institutions is another good place to start. The CSO BankTrack has developed a Human Rights Benchmark that evaluates 50 of the largest private sector commercial banks globally against a set of 14 criteria based on the requirements of the UNGPs.[138] It is one example from a growing list of CSOs that regularly track and report on human rights issues at financial institutions and continue to raise emerging issues.[139]

[137] UN Human Rights Office of the High Commissioner, *Draft OHCHR Benchmarking Study on DFI Safeguards and Due Diligence Frameworks against the UN Guiding Principles on Business and Human Rights (working document to be updated periodically)* (Sept. 2019), https://www.ohchr.org/Documents/Issues/Development/DFI/OHCHR_Benchmarking%20Study_HRDD.pdf.

[138] https://www.banktrack.org/hrbenchmark and *see* Financial Services Human Rights Benchmark, https://law-fshrb.sydney.edu.au/; and *see* White & Case, *Human rights benchmarks: Corporate performance rankings on the rise* (2020), https://www.whitecase.com/publications/insight/bhr-benchmarks-2020/human-rights-benchmarks-corporate-performance-rankings-rise.

[139] For example, other CSOs include SOMO, Oxfam, Global Witness, WWF, and ShareAction, among others.

Keeping an eye on regulatory developments outside the United States, particularly among leading jurisdictions like the EU, helps provide insight on emerging regulatory trends.[140]

C. Be Prepared to Challenge Existing Practices

Practitioners need to be prepared to work with financial institution clients that in turn must work with their clients to address human rights issues—even where that requires challenging existing practices in the sector. The responsibility to respect human rights applies even where there is no law requiring respect for human rights, the law is not enforced, or the law itself undermines respect for human rights. That position, clearly articulated in these frameworks, may be surprising or even an anathema to many in the sector where success is measured by financial prowess rather than finance's more traditional role of contributing to the real economy. There is much work to be done within the human rights and legal practitioner community to address the challenge of realizing human rights values within the context of 21st-century finance, so that "investors and financial leaders take values as seriously as valuation, culture as seriously as capital."[141] Legal practitioners have their own responsibility to respect human rights and to advise clients, even recalcitrant clients, accordingly; those who do not may find themselves with more scrutiny than expected as sustainable finance gathers pace.[142] The initiatives and practice to date have broken important ground and opened the gates for more detailed and robust discussions and development of innovative practices.

VII. Resources

Dutch Banking Sector Agreement, *Discussion Paper: Working Group Enabling Remediation* (2019), https://www.imvoconvenanten.nl/-/media/imvo/files/banking/paper-enabling-remediation.pdf.

Institute for Human Rights and Business and ICCR, *Investing the Rights Way: A Guide for Investors on Business and Human Rights* (2013), https://www.ihrb.org/focus-areas/finance/report-investing-the-rights.

Investor Alliance for Human Rights, *Investor Toolkit on Human Rights* (2020), https://investorsforhumanrights.org/sites/default/files/attachments/2020-05/Full%20Report-%20Investor%20Toolkit%20on%20Human%20Rights%20May%202020c.pdf.

Margaret Wachenfeld, Motoko Aizawa, & Mary Dowell-Jones, *Human Rights and Sustainable Finance: Exploring the Relationship* (2016), UNEP Inquiry on a Sustainable Financial System and the Institute for Human Rights and Business, Inquiry Working Paper 16/01 https://unepinquiry.org/publication/human-rights/.

---

[140] *See also* the UNEP Inquiry, which has limited attention to human rights, is nonetheless pushing regulatory developments in the sustainable finance area.

[141] Christine Lagarde, Managing Director, International Monetary Fund, *Economic Inclusion and Financial Integrity*, Conference on Inclusive Capitalism (2014).

[142] Law Students for Climate Accountability: The 2020 Law Firm Climate Change Accountability Scorecard, https://static1.squarespace.com/static/5f53fa556b708446acb4dcb5/t/5f755753f217027860728759/1601525603800/Law+Firm+Climate+Change+Scorecard.pdf.

Organisation for Economic Co-operation and Development, *Due Diligence in the Financial Sector: Adverse Impacts Directly Linked to Financial Sector Operations, Products, or Services by a Business Relationship* (Jun. 2014), https://mneguidelines.oecd.org/global-forum/GFRBC-2014-financial-sector-document-1.pdf.

Organisation for Economic Co-operation and Development, *Due Diligence for Responsible Corporate Lending and Securities Underwriting: Key Considerations for Banks Implementing the OECD Guidelines for Multinational Enterprises* (2019), https://mneguidelines.oecd.org/final-master-due-diligence-for-responsible-corporate-lending-and-securities-underwriting.pdf.

Organisation for Economic Co-operation and Development, *Expert Letters and Statements on the Application of the OECD Guidelines for Multinational Enterprises and UN Guiding Principles on Business and Human Rights in the Context of the Financial Sector* (Jun. 2014), https://mneguidelines.oecd.org/global-forum/GFRBC-2014-financial-sector-document-3.pdf.

Organisation for Economic Co-operation and Development, *Scope and Application of 'Business Relationships' in the Financial Sector under the OECD Guidelines for Multinational Enterprises* (Jun. 2014), https://mneguidelines.oecd.org/global-forum/GFRBC-2014-financial-sector-document-2.pdf.

Organisation for Economic Co-operation and Development, *Responsible Business Conduct for Institutional Investors: Key Considerations for Due Diligence under the OECD Guidelines for Multinational Enterprises* (2017), https://mneguidelines.oecd.org/RBC-for-Institutional-Investors.pdf.

PRI, *Why and How Investors Should Act on Human Rights* (2020), https://www.unpri.org/human-rights-and-labour-standards/why-and-how-investors-should-act-on-human-rights/6636.article.

PRI, UNEP FI, et al., *Legal Framework for Impact* (2021), https://www.unpri.org/policy/a-legal-framework-for-impact.

UN Office of the High Commissioner on Human Rights, *Advice to the OECD on the Application of the Guiding Principles to the Financial Sector* (Nov. 2013), https://www.ohchr.org/Documents/Issues/Business/LetterOECD.pdf.

UN Office of the High Commissioner on Human Rights, *Response to Request from BankTrack for Advice Regarding the Application of the UN Guiding Principles on Business and Human Rights in the Context of the Banking Sector* (2017), https://www.ohchr.org/Documents/Issues/Business/InterpretationGuidingPrinciples.pdf.

UN Office of the High Commissioner on Human Rights, *Response to SOMO on the Application of the UNGPs to Minority Shareholdings of Institutional Investors* (2013), https://www.ohchr.org/Documents/Issues/Business/LetterSOMO.pdf.

14

Environmental Law and Climate Change

Carlos de Miguel Perales and Austin Pierce

I. Introduction

While human rights law has traditionally developed separately from environmental law, there has been increasing recognition that the "human" cannot be separated from the "environment." Discussions around climate change have accelerated the propulsion of environmental and human rights concerns into more integrated, though still somewhat amorphous, dialogue. This interaction is multidirectional. For example, climate change can exacerbate both acute and chronic natural disasters—ranging from flooding and wildfire to water scarcity and instability in the food supply.[1] These impacts not only damage physical, environmental, and social infrastructure, but they are also expected to be worse for already vulnerable communities, such as marginalized and Indigenous peoples.[2]

Generally, the interaction between environmental and human rights concerns can be subdivided into three main categories:

1. **Traditional Environmental Issues with Human Rights Implications.** For example, air pollution can exist on a scale that impacts, among other things, the life and health of persons. Similarly, eradication of certain species or ecosystems can vitiate local or Indigenous communities' ability to have cultural continuation.

---

[1] Intergovernmental Panel on Climate Change, Climate Change and Land: An IPCC Special Report at 10, 17 (P.R. Shukla et al. eds., 2019), https://www.ipcc.ch/srccl/.

[2] US Global Change Research Program, *Summary Findings*, in Fourth National Climate Assessment Volume II: Impacts, Risks, and Adaptation in the United States (2018), https://nca2018.globalchange.gov/.

2. **Traditional Human Rights Issues with Environmental Implications.** This has been called the "greening" of human rights, i.e., a trend in which some have called for the protection of environmental quality as an extension of existing human rights obligations, such as the rights to life and health.[3]
3. **A Human Right to Environmental Quality.** Multiple countries, though not the United States, have enshrined a human right to a healthy environment in their constitutions.[4] The United Nations Human Rights Council also endorsed such a right in October 2021.[5] Climate change has increased pressure to substantiate this right, though with varying degrees of success.[6]

Separately, the concept of "rights of the environment" (i.e., investing nature with its own rights), although a relatively fringe concept, has been articulated and incorporated into the laws of certain countries.[7]

Each form of interaction can raise concerns for business operations, but they can be managed by effective due diligence. Just as the "human" and the "environment" cannot be wholly separated, human rights impacts cannot be fully considered without considering impacts to, and from, the environment. Therefore, this chapter focuses on the "identify" prong of human rights due diligence as it relates to environmental law, to assist human rights practitioners in identifying environmental issues with potential human rights impacts.

II. Context: Evolution of Environmental Law and Its Interaction with Human Rights

Environmental law is a broad field. It includes both areas that are core—virtually always included within its ambit—and areas that are more peripheral, related to environmental concerns but only sometimes included in its scope. Core areas include such topics as pollution (whether of air, water, or soil), waste management, and the protection and conservation of natural resources, including wildlife. Peripheral areas vary in their degree of connection but include such topics as cultural heritage, visual and aesthetic resources, and noise and smell impacts. As other environmental concerns receive attention, they can be incorporated into

[3] *See* John Knox, *Greening Human Rights*, Open Democracy (Jul. 14, 2015), https://www.opendemocracy.net/en/openglobalrights-openpage/greening-human-rights/; Alan Boyle, *Human Rights and the Environment: What Next?* 23 Eur. J. Int'l L. 613, 614 (2012).

[4] UN Env't. Programme, Environmental Rule of Law: Fist Global Report 158 (2019), https://www.unenvironment.org/resources/assessment/environmental-rule-law-first-global-report.

[5] UN Human Rights Council, *The Human Right to a Safe, Clean, Healthy and Sustainable Environment*, A/HRC/48/L.23 (Oct. 5, 2021), https://undocs.org/a/hrc/48/l.23/rev.1.

[6] *See, e.g.*, Juliana v. United States, 217 F.Supp. 3d 1224 (9th Cir. 2016); Aji P. v. State of Washington. 2021 Wash. App. LEXIS 237 (Wash. Ct. App. 2020).

[7] The idea has gained greatest traction in the Andean region. *See* Law No. 071, Ley de Derechos de la Madre Tierra ("Law of the Rights of Mother Earth"), Dec. 21, 2010 (Bolivia), http://www.planificacion.gob.bo/uploads/marco-legal/Ley%20N%C2%B0%20071%20DERECHOS%20DE%20LA%20MADRE%20TIERRA.pdf; *see also* Const. of Ecuador Article 71–74 (2008). However, it is not unique to that region. *See, e.g.*, Te Awa Tupua (Whanganui River Claims Settlement) Act 2017 (N.Z.), http://www.legislation.govt.nz/act/public/2017/0007/latest/whole.html#DLM6831461.

the scope of environmental law, oftentimes starting on the periphery and moving closer to the core as they receive greater attention and increase in importance. Because of this, the range of subjects covered by environmental law has grown beyond mere pollution prevention to incorporate topics such as site restoration; protection for natural and cultural resources; and, increasingly, sustainability.

Just as the scope of environmental law can grow, so too can the scope of areas within the field. For example, water protection primarily focused on surface waters before expanding to drinking water and certain sources of groundwater.[8] Sustainability, though a nascent area, has seen similar developments, as there is increasing recognition of its social dimension.[9]

Climate change, and the dialogue it has provoked, is responsible for much of this recognition. However, climate impacts too have been subject to expanded understandings over time. For example, although the United Nations Framework Convention on Climate Change was drafted in 1992,[10] human rights language in the context of discussions of climate change only entered international legal dialogue in the late 2000s.[11] This consideration of human rights in relation to climate change in turn presaged developments on the broader recognition of a link between the environment and human rights more generally,[12] as well as more affirmative statements on the bidirectional impact human rights and environmental issues can have on each other.[13]

Concrete legal action in response to the recognition of their impacts upon one another has been slow. However, as countries take action to regulate sustainability efforts (particularly those related to climate change),[14] this is likely to change. For example, the European Union (EU) has adopted regulations to establish criteria for various business activities to be

[8] *Compare* Clean Water Act, 33 U.S.C. § 1251(a)(1), *with* Safe Drinking Water Act ("SDWA"), 42 U.S.C. § 300f *et seq. and* County of Maui, Hawaii v. Hawaii Wildlife Fund, 140 S.Ct. 1462 (2020).

[9] *See, e.g.*, Proposed Directive on Corporate Sustainability Due Diligence (Feb. 23, 2022), https://eur-lex.europa.eu/legal-content/EN/TXT/?uri=CELEX%3A52022PC0071 ("CSDDD Proposal").

[10] *United Nations Framework Convention on Climate Change* (Mar. 21, 1994), https://unfccc.int/resource/docs/convkp/conveng.pdf.

[11] *See, e.g.*, Human Rights Committee Resolution 7/23, *Human Rights and Climate Change*, A/HRC/RES/7/23 (Mar. 28, 2008), https://ap.ohchr.org/documents/E/HRC/resolutions/A_HRC_RES_7_23.pdf; Malé Declaration on the Human Dimension of Global Climate Change (2007), http://www.ciel.org/Publications/Male_Declaration_Nov07.pdf.

[12] *See, e.g.*, Human Rights Committee Resolution 19/10, *Human Rights and the Environment*, A/HRC/RES/19/10 (Apr. 19, 2012), https://www.right-docs.org/doc/a-hrc-res-19-10/.

[13] United Nations, Human Rights Committee, *Framework Principles on Human Rights and the Environment*, A/HRC/37/59 (Jan. 24, 2018), https://www.ohchr.org/en/issues/environment/srenvironment/pages/frameworkprinciplesreport.aspx; Paris Agreement, Paris, Dec. 12, 2015, https://unfccc.int/sites/default/files/english_paris_agreement.pdf; Exec. Order 14008, Sections 203(b), 219, 3 C.F.R. 7619, 7623, 7629 (Jan. 27, 2021) https://www.whitehouse.gov/briefing-room/presidential-actions/2021/01/27/executive-order-on-tackling-the-climate-crisis-at-home-and-abroad/.

[14] *See, e.g.*, Council Directive, 2014/95 2014 O.J. (L. 330) (EU), https://eur-lex.europa.eu/legal-content/EN/TXT/?uri=CELEX%3A32014L0095 ("EU NFRD"); European Parliament, Human Rights Due Diligence Legislation – Options for the EU (2020), https://www.europarl.europa.eu/RegData/etudes/BRIE/2020/603495/EXPO_BRI(2020)603495_EN.pdf; James Shaw, *New Zealand First in the World to Require Climate Risk Reporting*, Beehive.govt.nz (Sep. 15, 2020), https://www.beehive.govt.nz/release/new-zealand-first-world-require-climate-risk-reporting (last visited Mar. 18, 2021); Fed NGFS, https://www.federalreserve.gov/newsevents/pressreleases/bcreg20201215a.htm.

considered "sustainable."[15] Although the primary focus of these regulations is environmental sustainability, they also incorporate "minimal safeguards" to address social sustainability concerns like human rights.[16]

Additionally, sustainability laws have been complemented, and in many cases preceded, by a push to integrate environmental, social, and governance (ESG) factors into business and investment decisions. This change has involved an increasing recognition of how environmental concerns interrelate with other fields, such as human rights. Many investors have noted that considering and managing the full array of risks associated with ESG concerns can have a direct benefit on a company's financial performance over time.[17] ESG and sustainability are heavily intertwined, in many cases differing more in audience and nomenclature than substance. Regardless of terminology, the concepts will likely continue to influence each other into the future.[18]

For example, civil society and various international bodies, as well as certain investors and industry groups, have created various ESG frameworks and standards that can inform and provide a benchmark for business behavior in the absence of hard legal requirements.[19] Oftentimes, these "soft law" standards provide the basis for eventual codification of expectations into hard law. For example, several efforts to regulate company disclosures on climate change have directly referenced the recommendations of the Taskforce for Climate-Related Financial Disclosures (TCFD), which established an influential framework for companies' voluntary climate disclosures.[20] Such influences are likely to increase in the future as governments consider further regulations on ESG and sustainability topics, including those involving the intersection of the environment and human rights.

III. Environmental Standards of Particular Importance for Human Rights

The development of environmental law has resulted in a panoply of applicable standards. While the specific formulation may vary by jurisdiction, the discussion in this Section outlines

[15] *See* Council Directive 2020/852 (2020) O.J. (L. 198) (EU), https://eur-lex.europa.eu/legal-content/EN/TXT/PDF/?uri=CELEX:32020R0852&from=EN ("EU Sustainable Taxonomy Regulation").

[16] *Id.* at Article 3(c), 18.

[17] *See, e.g.*, UN Principles for Responsible Investing, A Practical Guide to ESG Integration for Equity Investing 115 (2016), https://www.unpri.org/download?ac=10.

[18] *See, e.g.*, Moody's Analytics, NGFS Advocates Environmental Risk Analysis for Financial Sector (Sep. 10, 2020), https://www.moodysanalytics.com/regulatory-news/sep-10-20-ngfs-advocates-environmental-risk-analysis-for-financial-sector; Network for Greening the Financial System (NGFS), A Sustainable and Responsible Investment Guide for Central Banks' Portfolio Management (2019), https://www.ngfs.net/sites/default/files/medias/documents/ngfs-a-sustainable-and-responsible-investment-guide.pdf.

[19] Examples include international organizations, like the United Nations' Guiding Principles on Business and Human Rights, as well as private parties such as CDP, https://www.cdp.net/en, and Greenhouse Gas Protocol, https://ghgprotocol.org/.

[20] Climate Risk Disclosure Act, H.R. 3623, 116th Cong. § 8 (2019) (proposed); *Guidelines on Non-financial Reporting: Supplement on Reporting Climate-related Information*, 2019/C 209/01, 2 (Jun. 20, 2019), https://eur-lex.europa.eu/legal-content/EN/TXT/PDF/?uri=CELEX:52019XC0620(01)&from=EN.

common elements of those areas of environmental law which are most likely to have human rights implications. However, given the scope of environmental law, the pertinent topics may vary depending on the business activity in question. For example, distinct regulatory regimes, in addition to standard environmental laws, often regulate particular industries, such as mining,[21] pipelines,[22] and agriculture and bioengineering.[23]

A. Project Assessments

Many jurisdictions require a review of potential environmental impacts prior to project approval[24] or prior to the approval of certain plans or programs. In general, to trigger requirements for formal assessments, a project must be "likely to have significant effects on the environment by virtue, inter alia, of [its] nature, size or location."[25] In addition to traditional environmental elements—such as air emissions or impacts to wildlife—these assessments often require a review of the human environment, e.g., social, cultural, and aesthetic aspects.[26]

Other regimes can supplement the required scope of review. Several countries require consultations with Indigenous peoples prior to projects that may impact such groups.[27] Moreover, new laws can create additional requirements. For example, an Australian Court recently ruled that the Human Rights Act of 2019 meant that human rights impacts could serve as the basis for objection to a mining lease or environmental permit.[28] Certain voluntary frameworks, such as the Equator Principles, also have assessment requirements for their member companies.[29]

---

[21] *See, e.g.*, Surface Mining Control and Reclamation Act, 30 U.S.C. chapter 25 (1997). *See also* Global Industry Standard on Tailings Management, International Council on Mining & Metals (Aug. 2020), https://globaltailingsreview.org/wp-content/uploads/2020/08/global-industry-standard_EN.pdf.

[22] *See, e.g.*, 49 C.F.R. Part 192 (2020); Law on Trunk Pipelines, No. 20-V (Jun. 22, 2012) (Kazakhstan), http://adilet.zan.kz/eng/docs/Z1200000020.

[23] *See, e.g.*, Council Directive 2001/18, 2001 O.J. (L. 106) (EU), https://eur-lex.europa.eu/legal-content/EN/TXT/?uri=celex%3A32001L0018.

[24] *See, e.g.*, Decreto Presidencial 117/20, 2020 (Angola) ("Angola Decreto 117/20), http://extwprlegs1.fao.org/docs/pdf/ang194840.pdf; Council Directive 2011/92, (2011) O.J. (L. 026) (EU) ("EU Directive 2011/92"), https://eur-lex.europa.eu/legal-content/EN/TXT/?uri=celex%3A32011L0092; Decreto 20/2017, Sistema de Evaluación Ambiental de Permisos y Autorizaciones para el Uso Sostenible de los Recursos naturales [Environmental Assessment System for Permits and Authorizations for the Sustainable Use of Natural Resources], La Gaceta, Diario Oficial [L/G/] (Nov. 29, 2017) (Nicaragua) ("Nicaragua Decreto No. 20-2017"), http://extwprlegs1.fao.org/docs/pdf/nic177024.pdf, National Environmental Policy Act of 1969 [NEPA], 42 U.S.C. §§ 4321 et seq. (1969).

[25] *See, e.g.*, EU Directive 2011/92, *supra* note 24, Article 2.

[26] *See* NEPA, *supra* note 24, at § 101; Angola Decreto 117/20, *supra* note 24, Article 4.1.

[27] For more information, *see* chapter 11 by Tom O'Keefe on Indigenous peoples.

[28] Waratah Coal Pty Ltd v Youth Verdict Ltd & Ors [2020] QLC 33 (Astl.), https://archive.sclqld.org.au/qjudgment/2020/QLC20-033.pdf.

[29] *See, e.g.*, The Equator Principles (Jul. 2020), https://equator-principles.com/wp-content/uploads/2020/05/The-Equator-Principles-July-2020-v2.pdf.

B. Air and Climate

Although "climate" has become a veritable buzzword, air regulations already have a substantial history in the field of environmental law. Air regulation primarily focuses on emissions of pollutants—both those with localized and broader impacts.[30] Regulatory standards are primarily set to address concerns to human health; for example, the US Congress established the Clean Air Act "to promote the public health and welfare" by reducing the prevalence of various air pollutants.[31] Sources of these pollutants are often subject to permitting, with emissions thresholds that they cannot exceed if the source is to remain in compliance, as well as the imposition of procedural or technological requirements.[32] Certain pollutants also have regulated emissions markets (e.g., cap-and-trade); these establish a cap on total emissions of a pollutant by all regulated entities but allow for entities to trade those emissions allowances.[33] Over time, the general trend has been greater regulation, either by rules for new pollutants or tighter thresholds for already regulated pollutants.

Climate change has led air regulators to focus more intensely on greenhouse gases (GHGs, primarily methane and carbon dioxide), though regulators' approaches have varied. In addition to emissions thresholds or technological prescriptions,[34] jurisdictions are increasingly implementing other measures, such as establishing GHG taxes or emissions trading systems for GHGs.[35,36]

Because of the relative novelty of climate policy, the predominant regulatory mechanisms may change significantly. For example, in the United States, the Biden Administration has committed to a "government-wide approach" to climate action,[37] which has included regulatory action across agencies as well as the recent passage of the Inflation Reduction Act, which includes a variety of initiatives to propel the energy transition.[38] This is expected to include action to address climate change through financial, environmental, and other types of policy. Given the scope of climate issues, they may require globally coordinated regulation. Financial institutions, both corporations and regulatory bodies, have already taken significant steps to

---

[30] Council Directive 96/62, 1996 O.J. (L. 296) (EU), https://eur-lex.europa.eu/legal-content/EN/TXT/PDF/?uri=CELEX:31996L0062&from=EN; United States, Clean Air Act, 42 U.S.C Chapter 85.

[31] 42 U.S.C. § 7401.

[32] *See, e.g.*, NOM-025-SSA1-2014, Salud Ambiental. Valores límite permisibles para la concentración de partículas suspendidas PM10 y PM2.5 en el aire ambiente y criterios para su evaluación, Diario Oficial (Aug. 20, 2014); 40 C.F.R Part 60 (2020) (discussing performance standards for stationary sources of air pollutants in various industries).

[33] *See, e.g.*, 40 C.F.R. Part 73 (1993).

[34] *See, e.g.*, Regulations Respecting Reduction in the Release of Methane and Certain Volatile Organic Compounds (Upstream Oil and Gas Sector), SOR/2018-66 (Can.), https://laws-lois.justice.gc.ca/PDF/SOR-2018-66.pdf.

[35] *See, e.g.*, Canada, Greenhouse Gas Pollution Pricing Act, (S.C. 2018, c. 12, s. 186), https://laws-lois.justice.gc.ca/PDF/G-11.55.pdf. *But see* In the Matter of the Greenhouse Gas Pollution Pricing Act [2020], S.C. 74 (Can. Alta. C.A.) (on appeal to Supreme Court of Canada), https://www.canlii.org/en/ab/abca/doc/2020/2020abca74/2020abca74.html?resultIndex=1.

[36] *See, e.g.*, Regional Greenhouse Gas Initiative, https://www.rggi.org/; Council Directive 96/61, 2003 O.J. (L. 275) (EU), https://eur-lex.europa.eu/legal-content/EN/TXT/?uri=celex%3A32003L0087.

[37] Exec. Order 14008, Section 201, 3 C.F.R. 7619, 7622 (Jan. 27, 2021).

[38] Inflation Reduction Act, Pub. L. No. 117-169 (2022).

collaborate and develop the data frameworks necessary to reduce emissions attributable to financial portfolios, and continued collaboration is likely in this area and others.[39]

C. Water

Clean water is necessary for both life and many human needs and activities, which makes access to sufficient quantities of the substance of paramount importance. As with air, water-related regulations have primarily focused on pollutants entering the medium. But water comes in several varieties: surface, ground, drinking, precipitation. These several varieties can be subject to differing regulation. Generally, limits are set for the discharge of pollutants into surface bodies[40] as well as for certain underground bodies of water.[41] However, there is increasing recognition that water systems are interconnected,[42] encouraging coordination between these standards.

Water is also a natural resource, which entails another set of regulations. For example, many jurisdictions require suppliers of drinking water to ensure certain quality levels.[43] Some jurisdictions, particularly where water is scarce, also thoroughly regulate water use.[44] Water scarcity is predicted to grow to impact more than half the world's population by 2050;[45] therefore, regulations on water use may become more prevalent, which can have direct bearing on human rights. In the meantime, voluntary frameworks have developed to review companies' contributions to water scarcity problems and their management.[46]

D. Waste

In general, waste regulations govern the proper classification of waste and its associated generation, storage, management, transport, and disposal, as well as criteria for landfills and other waste disposal facilities.[47] Although regulations can establish many classifications of

---

[39] *See* TCFD Pilot Projects-Banking, UN ENV'TL. PROGRAMME FIN. INITIATIVE ("UNEP FI"), https://www.unepfi.org/banking/tcfd/; NGFS, A CALL FOR ACTION: CLIMATE CHANGE AS A SOURCE OF FINANCIAL RISK (Apr. 2019), https://www.ngfs.net/sites/default/files/medias/documents/ngfs_first_comprehensive_report_-_17042019_0.pdf.

[40] *See, e.g.*, 40 C.F.R. § 122.44; Brazil, CONAMA 357/05, http://pnqa.ana.gov.br/Publicacao/RESOLUCAO_CONAMA_n_357.pdf.

[41] *See, e.g.*, 40 C.F.R. Part 146; Council Directive 2000/60, 2000 O.J. (L. 327) (EU) ("EU Directive 2000/60"), https://eur-lex.europa.eu/legal-content/EN/TXT/?uri=CELEX:32000L0060.

[42] *See, e.g.*, *County of Maui*, *supra* note 8 (discussing connection of groundwater to surface water); EU Directive 2000/60, *supra* note 41 (discussing impact of inland waters on coastal ecosystems).

[43] *See, e.g.*, SDWA, *supra* note 8; Council Directive 98/83, 1998 O.J. (L. 330) (EU), https://eur-lex.europa.eu/legal-content/EN/TXT/?uri=CELEX:31998L0083.

[44] *See, e.g.*, Water Law, 5719–1959, SH No. 57 p. 173 (Isr.), https://www.knesset.gov.il/review/data/eng/law/kns3_water_eng.pdf.

[45] UN WORLD WATER DEVELOPMENT REPORT, WATER AND CLIMATE CHANGE at 26 (2020), https://www.unwater.org/publications/world-water-development-report-2020/.

[46] *See, e.g.*, CDP, Water, https://www.cdp.net/en/water.

[47] *See, e.g.*, Resource Conservation and Recovery Act ("RCRA"), 42 U.S.C. § 6901 *et seq.*; Lei 12305/10, Article 13, 2 de Agosto de 2010, Lex, Agosto 2010 (Braz.) ("Brazil Law 12305/10"), http://www.planalto.gov.br/ccivil_03/_ato2007-2010/2010/lei/l12305.htm.

waste, the primary difference is between hazardous and nonhazardous wastes, which is typically dependent upon analysis and comparison to prescribed standards.[48] Hazardous wastes are subject to more stringent requirements, discussed further in Section III.E below.

Regulations evolve alongside understandings of wastes. Plastics are a recurrent example due to their prevalence and deleterious impacts. Restrictions on microplastics,[49] as well as single-use plastic,[50] are becoming more prevalent. Similarly, with the proliferation of electronic products, laws related to e-waste are also being promulgated.[51] In addition to regulating novel wastes, several of these rules are related to the establishment of a "circular economy," i.e., one in which a majority of waste products are recycled as inputs of production.[52] Broader adoption of a circular economy will likely require further regulation on waste management and recycling.

E. Hazardous Substances and Remediation

Although many substances are subject to regulation under environmental law, they do not all pose the same magnitude of harm. Substances that pose a particular risk to the environment or human health and well-being are subject to regulation as "hazardous" substances, which are subject to more stringent regulation than other substances.[53] Typically, jurisdictions regulate all phases of a hazardous substance's life (i.e., "cradle-to-grave"): generation, storage, handling, transport, and disposal.[54] Certain regulations may apply to all hazardous substances covered under the rule,[55] but others depend on the nature of the substance in question or the manner in which it is used.[56] Regulations may also vary based on the quantity of the substance in question.[57]

---

[48] *See, e.g.*, RCRA, *supra* note 47, at 42 U.S.C. § 6903(5) (2014); Brazil Law 12305/10, *supra* note 47, Article 13(II) (expressing the difference between "hazardous" and "non-hazardous" wastes for purposes of the statute).

[49] *See, e.g.*, Microbead-Free Waters Act of 2015, Pub. L. No. 114-114, 129 Stat. 3129, https://www.congress.gov/114/plaws/publ114/PLAW-114publ114.pdf; The Environmental Protection (Microbeads) (England) Regulations 2017 (Eng.), https://www.legislation.gov.uk/uksi/2017/1312/contents/made.

[50] *See, e.g.*, Council Directive 2019/904, 2019 O.J. (L. 155) (EU), https://eur-lex.europa.eu/eli/dir/2019/904/oj; Law 17/2019 Law Relating to the Prohibition of Manufacturing, Importation, Use and Sale of Plastic Carry Bags and Single-Use Plastic Items (Aug. 10, 2019), (Rwanda), https://www.environment.gov.rw/fileadmin/user_upload/Moe/Publications/Laws/Law_relating_to_the_prohibition_of_manufacturing__importation__use_and_sale_of_plastic_carry_bags.pdf.

[51] *See, e.g.*, Council Directive 2012/19, 2012 O.J. (L. 197) (EU), https://eur-lex.europa.eu/legal-content/EN/TXT/?uri=CELEX:32012L0019.

[52] *See, e.g.*, *Communication from the Commission to the European Parliament, the Council, the European Economic and Social Committee and the Committee of the Regions*, COM (2020) 98 final (Mar. 11, 2020), https://eur-lex.europa.eu/legal-content/EN/TXT/?qid=1583933814386&uri=COM:2020:98:FIN; Basic Act for Establishing a Sound Material-Cycle Society, Law No. 110 of 2000 (Japan), https://www.env.go.jp/recycle/circul/kihonho/law.html.

[53] *See, e.g.*, 42 U.S.C. § 6903(5) (2014) (defining "hazardous" waste as a subcategory of solid waste).

[54] *See, e.g.*, 42 U.S.C. §§ 6922–6924 (1984); Council Directive 2008/98/EC, Article 17–19, 2008 O.J. (L. 312) (EU) ("EU Directive 2008/98"), https://eur-lex.europa.eu/legal-content/EN/TXT/?uri=CELEX:32008L0098.

[55] *See, e.g.*, 40 C.F.R. Part 262 (2019).

[56] *See, e.g.*, 49 C.F.R. Part 173 (2003); Council Directive 67/548, Article 8(b), 1976 O.J. (196) (EU) ("EU Directive 67/548"), https://eur-lex.europa.eu/legal-content/EN/TXT/PDF/?uri=CELEX:31967L0548&from=en.

[57] *See, e.g.*, 40 C.F.R. § 302.5; EU Directive 2008/98, *supra* note 54, Article 29(3); EU Directive 67/548, *supra* note 56.

Related to the regulation of hazardous substances, jurisdictions prescribe requirements for remediation should such substances be released into the environment at certain "action levels." Such remediation is typically of two types: (1) fault-based liability and (2) strict liability. Fault-based remediation is a causal-based theory triggered when a company is required to clean up a release from the company's operations or facilities in violation of the law.[58] Strict liability remediation does not depend on an actor's action or omission but rather on its "status" such as "owner," "operator," "transporter," or "arranger"; liability is triggered whenever environmental contamination, or a threat of such contamination, occurs, without regard to the actor's fault or compliance with law.[59]

As with nonhazardous pollutants, society's understanding of hazardous substances evolves over time; therefore, both the regulation of hazardous substances and remediation of such substances are subject to change. However, not all such changes increase burdens on companies; in efforts to rehabilitate contaminated properties, the United States amended the onerous requirements of the Comprehensive Environmental Response, Compensation, and Liability Act (CERCLA) to provide "safe harbors" for lenders to incentivize investment as well as to promote the reuse of brownfield properties.[60]

F. Natural and Cultural Resources

Environmental law also contains a substantial body of laws and regulations focused on the protection and conservation of natural and cultural resources. This body of law boasts a wide variety of foci, so the discussion here is an especially high-level overview of this area. In addition to water,[61] jurisdictions regulate rights to procure oil, gold, and other minerals.[62] But environments are more than their inorganic elements. Many jurisdictions also regulate impacts to flora and fauna,[63] including certain enhanced protections for threatened or

[58] *See, e.g.*, *Learn about Corrective Action*, EPA, https://www.epa.gov/hw/learn-about-corrective-action (last visited Nov. 3, 2020); Council Directive 2004/35, Article 3(1)(b), 2004 O.J. (L. 143) (EU), https://eur-lex.europa.eu/legal-content/EN/TXT/PDF/?uri=CELEX:02004L0035-20190626&qid=1568193390794&from=EN.

[59] *See, e.g.*, Comprehensive Environmental Response, Compensation, and Liability Act of 1980 § 107, 42 U.S.C. § 9607; Law No. 25,675 Article 28, (Nov. 28, 2002) (Arg.), https://www.argentina.gob.ar/normativa/nacional/ley-25675-79980/texto; National Environmental Management Act of 1998, Article 28 (S. Afr.), https://www.gov.za/sites/default/files/gcis_document/201409/a107-98.pdf. *See also* Chief Pule Shadrack VII Bareki NO and Another v. Gencor Limited and Others, 2006 (8) BCLR 920 (T) (S. Afr.), (South Gauteng High Court, 2010), https://cer.org.za/virtual-library/judgments/high-courts/chief-pule-shadrack-vii-bareki-no-and-another-v-gencor-limited-and-others-2006-8-bclr-920-t.

[60] *See* Small Business Liability Relief and Brownfields Revitalization Act, Pub. L. No. 107-118, 115 Stat. 2356 (2002), https://www.govinfo.gov/app/details/PLAW-107publ118#:~:text=An%20act%20to%20provide%20certain,revitalization%2C%20to%20enhance%20State%20response.

[61] *See supra*, Section III.C.

[62] *See, e.g.*, Law No. 18097, Ley Orgánica Constitucional sobre Concesiones Mineras (Jan. 7, 1992), Diario Oficial [D.O] (Chile), https://www.bcn.cl/leychile/navegar?idNorma=29522; Minerals and Mining Act, 2006, 703 (Ghana), http://extwprlegs1.fao.org/docs/pdf/gha85046.pdf.

[63] *See, e.g.*, Convention on the Conservation of European Wildlife and Natural Habitats ("Berne Convention"), (Sept. 19, 1979), E.T.S. 104, https://rm.coe.int/1680078aff; Ley General de Vida Silvestre, Diario Oficial de la Federación [DOF] 03-07-2000, últimas reformas DOF 19-01-2018 (Mex.), https://www.diputados.gob.mx/LeyesBiblio/pdf/146_200521.pdf.

endangered species.[64] In addition to natural resources, many jurisdictions also have protections for cultural resources.[65]

These protections may apply to entire areas instead of particular sites, whether for the protection of natural or cultural heritage.[66] Also, as discussed briefly above, there is a movement that has gained some traction to recognize rights for aspects of nature, including natural features such as rivers and mountains.[67]

IV. Good Practices for Identifying Risks in Environmental Due Diligence

The standards discussed in Section III necessitate substantial environmental due diligence. However, the scope varies by context. Due diligence for building a power plant will differ from that for providing financing to a company, which will both differ from a company's own enterprise risk management. Therefore, this Section IV discusses tools and practices that are used to identify potential environmental risks that may have human rights components; these start with practices applicable in due diligence for projects and transactions before discussing good practices generally associated with sustainability and ESG (including climate). Not every matter will involve all of the documentation and practices discussed herein.

As an initial note, specialists in this area of law should be incorporated into the process at an early stage. Environmental law is a broad and technical discipline. The early involvement of specialists can help to identify issues earlier and, oftentimes, address them more economically.

A. Traditional Environmental Assessments

Environmental assessments are prepared by technical consultants or government officials with subject-matter expertise in the area of assessment to evaluate the environmental characteristics of the assets or operations in question. Where prepared, these assessments often contain substantial information about the subject site/project/operation, including history, condition, and potential impacts. These assessments typically come in two forms: (1) impact assessments, and (2) site assessments. Both types of assessments are, aside from any explicit

---

[64] *See, e.g.*, Berne Convention, *supra* note 63, Article 1.2; United States, Endangered Species Act (1973), 16 U.S.C. Chapter 35.

[65] *See, e.g.*, National Historic Preservation Act (1966), 54 U.S.C. § 300101 et seq.; National Museums and Heritage Act (2012) Cap. 216 (Kenya), http://extwprlegs1.fao.org/docs/pdf/ken137136.pdf; Law No. 28296, Ley General del Patrimonio Cultural de la Nación, 2004 (Peru), http://www.congreso.gob.pe/Docs/comisiones2017/Comision_de_Cultura_y_Patrimonio/files/ley-28296-ley-general-patrimonio-cultural-nacion.pdf.

[66] *See, e.g.*, Convention Concerning the Protection of the World Cultural and Natural Heritage ("UNESCO Convention") (Nov. 16, 1972), http://portal.unesco.org/en/ev.php-URL_ID=13055&URL_DO=DO_TOPIC&URL_SECTION=201.html; Convention Africaine Sur la Conservation de la Nature et des Ressources Naturelles, 1968, https://en.unesco.org/sites/default/files/afr_convention_maputo_2003_freorof.pdf; Convention on Wetlands of International Importance especially as Waterfowl Habitat (Feb. 2, 1971) ("Ramsar Convention"), https://www.ramsar.org/sites/default/files/documents/library/current_convention_text_e.pdf.

[67] *See supra* note 7.

social sub-focus, often one step removed from human rights concerns. However, they can identify the environmental catalysts for human rights impacts.

1. *Impact Assessments*

Environmental impact assessments are typically associated with the review of projects proposed for development. They assess the ambit of environmental impacts associated with the project if it will require any form of significant government support.[68] This support can take the form of financing, the approval of discretionary permits, or otherwise.

Such assessments are substantial undertakings and generally are not prepared unless required, due to the time and cost associated; however, where prepared they can contain a host of information about environmental impacts. They often come in at least two levels of detail, with the level required typically being determined by the anticipated project impact after a base-level review.

Because impact assessments are supposed to review the entire sphere of environmental impacts associated with a project, they can be troves of information for assessing potential human rights concerns related to the environmental impacts of a project. In many cases, these assessments also contain sections on socioeconomic and land use impacts, as well as a consideration of "environmental justice," i.e., an examination of the distribution of burdens and benefits across the communities impacted by the project. Although they are not required to examine all environmental minutiae associated with a project, impact assessments should consider sufficient impacts in all pertinent categories so as to perform a fulsome review of a proposed project's effect on the environment (including the human environment). In addition to a review of direct impacts, a review of indirect and cumulative impacts can often reveal human rights impacts associated with a project.

2. *Site Assessments*

Environmental site assessments (ESAs) are often associated with transactions such as acquisitions or financings, or with projects that do not reach the scale as to require an impact assessment. They examine the subject site and, in some instances, a particular "zone of impact" around it. ESAs are typically narrower in scope than impact assessments. They come in different forms depending on the matter in question.

The most common type of ESA is known as a "Phase I" ESA. The Phase I assesses whether there is a risk of environmental contamination at or from the site.[69] This determination may be based on site history, such as if the land in question was ever used for extractive industries, chemical processing, landfills, or other forms of heavy industry. The reason for the popularity of this sort of assessment is the high costs and scope of liability to remediate contamination. If the venture in question is being financed or using certain insurance

---

[68] *See, e.g.*, Nicaragua Decreto No. 20-2017, *supra* note 24, Article 14–16; U.S. Dep't of Energy Off. of NEPA Oversight, Environmental Assessment Checklist (Aug. 1994), https://www.energy.gov/nepa/downloads/environmental-assessment-checklist-doe-1994.

[69] *ASTM E1527-13, Standard Practice for Environmental Site Assessments: Phase 1 Environmental Site Assessment Process*, ASTM Int'l, https://www.astm.org/Standards/E1527.htm (last visited Dec. 21, 2020).

protections, the lender/insurer may require a Phase I as a condition to its services. In some instances, liability can be curtailed by performing "all appropriate inquiries" prior to acquiring or doing business on a site,[70] and a Phase I is the most common way to demonstrate this. Subsequent assessments, such as a "Phase II" (i.e., an analysis of the chemical constituents in the soil and groundwater against various risk thresholds), may be required depending on the results of the Phase I.

Many Phase I's are also accompanied by limited compliance assessments. These generally focus on permitting and enforcement actions. Such assessments can help parties performing due diligence to quickly identify potential issues; however, they are often limited to document reviews and visual inspections concurrent with other site visits.

Depending on the project, certain other assessments may be required. Projects involving construction on any sizeable plot of land (typically greater than an acre) may need to engage expert consultants to assess impacts to wetlands, protected species, or cultural heritage, among others. Similarly, projects in densely populated areas may be subject to assessments of noise, odor, particulate matter, etc.[71] Even where such assessments are not required, it is often best to obtain them if there is a reasonable expectation of potential concerns.

B. Company Disclosures

For transactions involving pre-existing companies, due diligence should include a review of information published by the company. For public and certain other regulated companies, this should begin with a review of mandated disclosures. Often, these require a discussion of major environmental and human rights risks, as well as of any significant litigation or contentious government proceedings.[72] Additionally, a general review of the company's website can help to define the scope of review and highlight potential items of concern.

Increasingly, companies are also publishing voluntary disclosure reports. These come under many labels—ESG, sustainability, corporate social responsibility—and are often focused on highlighting the positive aspects of companies' environmental and social sustainability performance. However, under pressure from investors and others, these reports are also beginning to incorporate more thorough analysis of companies' ESG risk/opportunity profiles, as well as discussions of companies' strategies to manage them.

Although these voluntary reports are at present subject to few formal requirements, a host of third-party frameworks have proliferated to guide their structure and content.[73]

---

[70] 42 U.S.C. §§ 9601(35), (40) (2018); 40 C.F.R. § 312.20 (2005).

[71] *See, e.g.*, Port Metro Vancouver, Project & Environmental Review: Guidelines – Environmental Noise Assessment (July 2015), https://www.portvancouver.com/wp-content/uploads/2015/05/PER-Noise-Assessment-Guidelines-FINAL-2015-07-09.pdf.

[72] *See, e.g.*, 17 C.F.R. §§ 229.103, 229.105 (2020); EU NFRD, *supra* note 14.

[73] Aside from TCFD, some of the more commonly used standards are published by the Global Reporting Initiative, the Sustainability Accounting Standards Board, and the Science-Based Targets Initiative. Additionally, several industry-specific standards have developed to address the particular requirements of their target industries. Often, these are published through various industry bodies, such as the International Council on Mining & Metals or the International Petroleum Industry Environmental Conservation Association.

While some frameworks are more influential than others, the mere selection of one standard over another does not necessarily reflect the quality of the information. Companies cannot align with every third-party framework, and many factors may influence the selection of a particular standard. Ultimately, what matters is that disclosures address how companies are assessing and managing their ESG profile and that such management is successful.

C. Plans and Policies

As with company disclosures, a company's plans and policies can help to detail a company's environmental risk exposure. Even more so, these plans and policies provide insight into the protocols or systems a business has in place to manage those risks. Labels may vary between documents; however, as used here, plans tend to deal more with acute issues directly related to the company's operations (e.g., spills by companies storing large quantities of hazardous materials or discoveries of artifacts by earthmoving operations), whereas policies address more systemic or thematic topics (e.g., GHG emissions, water use, etc.).

Certain documents may be required, e.g., spill prevention plans for certain activities. These tend to be rather formulaic; however, they can be particularly helpful where they are not necessarily required. For example, many climate and sustainability policies are tied to a company's ESG goals instead of to legal requirements. And in certain instances, such plans/policies may be implemented as alternatives to legal restrictions.[74]

The detail in such documents will vary, but both procedural and substantive elements matter. In reviewing these documents, those performing due diligence should look not only at subject-matter content but also at information on how the document was developed; who is responsible for its implementation; references to third-party frameworks; and incorporation of mechanisms to obtain further information on implementation and report concerns or potential violations. Additionally, if policies contain any aspirational goals or targets, those should be reviewed against the company's disclosures for any updates on progress.

D. Government Databases

Government agencies in many countries maintain databases about permitting and enforcement actions. These can be invaluable resources for due diligence on companies or sites, because they can help to address whether companies are in compliance with existing legal requirements and any potential contamination or other concerns that may be outstanding. Databases with more extensive records can also be used to assess histories of (non-)compliance by potential acquisition/investment targets or histories of sites being considered for various projects.

[74] *See, e.g.*, Endangered and Threatened Wildlife and Plants; 12-Month Finding on a Petition to List Greater Sage-Grouse (Centrocercus urophasianus) as an Endangered or Threatened Species, 80 Fed. Reg. 59857, 59858 (Oct. 2, 2015) (to be codified at 50 C.F.R. pt. 17) (finding listing of the greater sage grouse to be unwarranted, citing in significant part conservation efforts and plans established to protect the species), https://www.federalregister.gov/documents/2015/10/02/2015-24292/endangered-and-threatened-wildlife-and-plants-12-month-finding-on-a-petition-to-list-greater.

E. Stakeholder Comments

Discussions with business stakeholders are often limited in the transactional context. Phase I ESAs typically incorporate an interview of those knowledgeable with site operations; similarly, environmental due diligence may involve an interview of company representatives to ascertain the overall function of its environmental management systems. But this is generally the extent of any stakeholder interviews in a transactional or project context.

In such situations, public documents can be important stand-ins. A search for local permit protests or filings by local community members or groups in administrative dockets can help to ascertain the overall degree of concern from local communities about business operations. Similarly, any litigation filed, whether by local communities or investors, can help to identify environmental issues and their impacts on those stakeholders.

F. Sustainability Due Diligence

Due diligence performed to assess sustainability or ESG topics is still in its nascency. However, sustainability is increasingly seen as a fundamental part of environmental due diligence. Therefore, companies should incorporate at least basic sustainability diligence into their standard environmental due diligence and risk management processes. Major environmental foci for sustainability include: (1) climate change; (2) water use; (3) electronic waste; (4) the "circular economy"; (5) biodiversity; and (6) ecosystem impacts.

In a transactional context, common practice is to limit due diligence to topics covered by legal requirements; however, companies are increasingly concerned with "reputational risks" and their "social license to operate." In many cases, ESG topics can typically be addressed obliquely by expanding the scope of existing reviews. For example, due diligence can incorporate ESG topics by reviewing voluntary disclosures or policies relating to them. Similarly, various environmental assessments already discuss GHG emissions and impacts to both water and wildlife. Expanding these can incorporate the sustainability aspects in a more fulsome review.

For companies assessing their own sustainability profile, the following good practices can be used to identify ESG-related environmental risks.

1. Stakeholder Engagement

Understanding stakeholder positions and engagement can be an effective way to identify environmental impacts, particularly those with human rights components. Ideally, stakeholder engagement will be a dialogue. From a practical perspective, people are more likely to approve of a project if they feel that they have had a say in the form it takes. From a due diligence perspective, ongoing outreach that gives stakeholders a voice can help the company to identify concerns before they become actual problems.

This dialogue can take several forms. Companies can set up periodic meetings with community leaders or townhalls. Or companies may perform periodic customer and employee engagement surveys, using the findings to identify potential weak spots in company practices and potential means of addressing them.

In certain instances, consultations with local communities may be required. For example, in many countries, projects with the potential to impact Indigenous communities require consultations with such communities.[75] And projects receiving funding from certain sources may require consultations if there are potential impacts on local communities.[76] Even when such consultations are not required, substantial projects should consider performing them, because they can help to identify potential environmental and human rights issues early on and, if performed with open ears, can even help to garner community support for ventures.

In addition to such periodic, formally solicited input, companies should also consider maintaining a hotline for anyone to report concerns at any time, depending on the actual circumstances of their business. It is good practice for this hotline to be anonymous, and the company should prohibit retaliation against parties reporting in good faith. This improves both the credibility and effectiveness of the hotline. However, as a final note, the company should require that all reports to the hotline be thoroughly investigated and any problems thus discovered addressed. It should by no means be an unattended drop box.

2. *Supply Chain Management*

The dependence of a company on certain products and services for their own operations, paired with the lack of direct oversight of supply chain operations, means that even well-operated companies may have environmental and human rights issues embedded in the production process for their products. Therefore, companies are increasingly required to assess their supply chains for compliance with environmental and human rights standards, though such requirements are not yet universal.[77]

Meeting these expectations while avoiding the liability concerns associated with oversight is a continual balancing act. Companies can, however, examine the products and services required for their operations and assess how they are being procured against an internal policy or policies (such as a vendor code of conduct) that the company has established. This policy should be tailored to the company but can be based on certain third-party protocols. Although this is an area ripe for continued evolution,[78] companies should in general require their suppliers to periodically both confirm compliance with their policy and provide supporting documentation, as appropriate.

---

[75] Indigenous and Tribal Peoples Convention (1989), https://www.ilo.org/dyn/normlex/en/f?p=NORMLEXPUB:12100:0::NO::P12100_ILO_CODE:C169 ("ILO Convention 169").

[76] *See, e.g.*, Int'l Fin. Corp., IFC Performance Standards on Environmental and Social Sustainability (Jan. 1, 2012), https://www.ifc.org/wps/wcm/connect/c02c2e86-e6cd-4b55-95a2-b3395d204279/IFC_Performance_Standards.pdf?MOD=AJPERES&CVID=kTjHBzk.

[77] *See, e.g.*, Loi 2017-399 du 27 mars 2017 relative au devoir de vigilance des sociétés mères et des enterprise donneuses d'ordre [Law 2017-399 of March 27, 2017 on the Duty of Vigilance of Companies and Ordering Companies], Journal Officiel de la République Française [J.O.] [Official Gazette of France], (Mar. 27, 2017), https://www.legifrance.gouv.fr/jorf/id/JORFTEXT000034290626/; Gesetz über die unternehmerische Sorgfaltspflichten in Lieferketten [LkSG] [Supply Chain Due Diligence Act], (Jun. 11, 2021) (Ger.), https://dserver.bundestag.de/btd/19/305/1930505.pdf; CSDDD Proposal, *supra* note 8. *See also* 15 U.S.C. § 78m(p) (2015) (requiring disclosure on certain conflict minerals sourcing).

[78] *See infra* Pierce & Perales, Section V.

3. *Environmental, Social, and Governance (ESG) Assessments*

As with environmental assessments, there are increasingly available tools and subject-matter experts to help companies assess their ESG impacts and risk profile. Such assessments are increasingly being expected by stakeholders, particularly for climate change. Therefore, climate is used as an example to discuss good practices for such assessments, though they can be applicable to other ESG assessments as well. The "Final Recommendations" of the TCFD are generally regarded as the exemplary framework with which companies should align their climate disclosures.[79] A major component of the TCFD recommendations is an assessment of the resilience of a company's strategy against various scenarios, i.e., "scenario analysis." This should include scenarios to assess impacts of climate change transition risks, such as new technology or regulation, as well as physical risks, such as changes in the distribution or frequency of extreme weather events or climatic conditions such as temperature and precipitation. However, TCFD provides limited guidance on how to actually perform such scenario analysis.

To fill this gap, several organizations have developed tools to model certain common possible scenarios. The International Energy Agency annually discusses various policy scenarios for the energy sector,[80] and the Intergovernmental Panel on Climate Change selected and defined a series of "representative concentration pathways" for temperature increase that can be of use in physical scenario analysis.[81] Additionally, different economic sectors may establish conventions or good practices for climate scenario analysis. For example, in the financial sector, several tools have been developed to help financial institutions assess their financed emissions and the associated transition risks.[82] Companies should look for any such frameworks applicable to their sector in order to inform their scenario analysis, and companies without the capacity to perform such quantitatively intensive analyses in-house should engage expert consultants to assist in the process.

Nevertheless, not all data will be quantitative. Companies should make sure to collect and assess qualitative data when performing these assessments. Important information cannot always be presented quantitatively, and qualitative information provides instructive context for any quantitative metrics. However, where available, quantitative information can reduce the potential ambiguity of wholly qualitative information, and it is often seen as more objective than qualitative data. Therefore, achieving a balance of both types of data will typically produce the best assessment.

---

[79] *See generally* Task Force on Climate-Related Fin. Disclosures, Final Report: Recommendations of the Task Force on Climate-related Financial Disclosures (Jun. 2017), https://assets.bbhub.io/company/sites/60/2020/10/FINAL-2017-TCFD-Report-11052018.pdf.

[80] *See, e.g.*, International Energy Association, World Energy Outlook 2020, IEA.org (Oct. 2020), https://www.iea.org/reports/world-energy-outlook-2020.

[81] *See Scenario Process for AR5: Representative Concentration Pathways*, Intergovernmental Panel on Climate Change (last modified Nov. 4, 2019), https://sedac.ciesin.columbia.edu/ddc/ar5_scenario_process/RCPs.html

[82] *Credit for Climate Action*, Harvard Law School Forum on Corporate Governance (Apr. 8, 2021), https://corpgov.law.harvard.edu/2021/04/08/credit-for-climate-action/.

4. *Risk Management Frameworks—A Note on Governance*

In identifying risk, sometimes the issue is a breakdown in communication across different aspects of the company. Risk management frameworks help companies to vet for risk in their operations at a macro-level. Environmental risks have a substantial history, but these have largely been focused on risks from contamination or other compliance concerns. Sustainability risks are yet to be fully integrated into companies' traditional risk management processes. Importantly, sustainability often touches on multiple existing risks, augmenting them. For example, companies already must be concerned about availability of materials required for their products, such as water. Climate change is not just a novel risk; it increases the probability and likely severity of other risks, such as drought conditions that could lead to water stress. Similarly, as countries take action to address climate change, it adds another element to already existing regulatory risk management. Therefore, integrating sustainability concerns requires more than simply adding a novel risk "stripe" to companies' risk management processes. It requires a reconceptualization of multiple existing risk areas to address relevant aspects of sustainability.

This process may require substantial time and resources on the part of a company. However, it can be streamlined by involving all pertinent parties early on. This will likely involve members of Environmental, Health, and Safety ("EHS"), legal, and operations teams, and may include others, particularly any that are industry-specific. Moreover, it must involve all levels of the company. Board identification of risks does not preclude the need for risk identification protocols for frontline operations, and vice versa.

The above describes a handful of good practices for companies to identify environmental risks that may have human rights impacts. However, good practices are by their very nature relative. As additional attention is paid to environmental issues, particularly those related to sustainability, what is considered "good practice" is likely to change. Companies should be prepared to routinely assess their practices to ensure they are effective.

V. Outstanding and Evolving Issues in the Environment–Human Rights Nexus

Environmental law is a dynamic field, and the increased focus on climate change and sustainability has highlighted many unsettled questions. These are likely to receive enhanced focus in the coming years, with multiple implications for human rights as well. This Section V discusses some of the main evolving issues in the environment–human rights nexus.

A. Climate

The magnitude of the threat of climate change demands an urgent response. While global climate action has hit various snags, it is likely that more formal climate regulations will develop in the coming years.

These will likely come from several sources. Direct regulation of emissions is becoming more prominent, but countries are also aware of a wider array of tools they can use to influence behavior. Governments are particularly attracted to financial levers, due to their immediate importance to companies. For example, multiple regulators have called for financial institutions to perform climate stress tests of their operations. Similarly, there is increased emphasis on climate-related disclosures. In addition to new proposed requirements from the US Securities and Exchange Commission,[83] the EU has expanded on its disclosure requirements. Building on the guidance to the Non-Financial Reporting Directive (NFRD), which requires certain large companies to disclose on a host of ESG-related topics, the EU has started revisions to the NFRD and issued rules discussing the criteria for business activities to claim substantial contribution to climate change mitigation and adaptation efforts.[84] Climate will also continue to be incorporated in environmental assessments, which could influence the issuance of required project authorizations.

In addition to government requirements, there will likely continue to be increased pressure from both investors and civil society for businesses to further address climate risk. For example, multiple large financial institutions have committed to achieving net zero financed emissions by 2050.[85] Most, if not all, of these financial institutions do not currently have a baseline to determine what their "financed emissions" consist of, and after determining this they will also need to develop strategies to reduce their emissions in line with their commitments. The contents of these policies will likely have a significant effect on companies' behavior, as they have the potential to directly impact companies' access to capital.

There is a separate question on the degree to which human rights will be incorporated into any of these climate regulations or policies. Though there have been efforts to develop climate change–related legal instruments from a human rights perspective, thus far the instruments that have typically most influenced companies' approach to climate change have been direct emissions regulations and financial-related requirements. However, any laws or policies developed to specifically address climate and human rights may also inform how the issue is addressed by businesses.

B. Sustainability

Climate is one quasi-independent issue under the broader umbrella of sustainability. The urgency of climate change has allowed it to serve the roles of harbinger and catalyst. However, it ultimately is only one, if the most immediately pressing, matter among a family of issues related to the relationship between humanity and environmental systems. This entails a substantial reanalysis of certain social, legal, and economic institutions.

---

[83] The Enhancement and Standardization of Climate-Related Disclosures for Investors, Release Nos. 33-11042; 34-94478 (proposed Mar. 21, 2022) (to be codified at 17 CFR 210, 229, 232, 239, and 249), https://www.sec.gov/rules/proposed/2022/33-11042.pdf.

[84] *What the CSRD Could Mean for Companies in the EU*, Latham & Watkins Client Alert (Apr. 26, 2022), https://www.lw.com/admin/upload/SiteAttachments/Alert%202953.v3.pdf. *See also* Implementing and Delegated Acts for Regulation (EU) 2020/852 (Taxonomy), available at: https://ec.europa.eu/info/law/sustainable-finance-taxonomy-regulation-eu-2020-852/amending-and-supplementary-acts/implementing-and-delegated-acts_en.

[85] These include Bank of America, Citigroup, Goldman Sachs, JPMorgan Chase, Morgan Stanley, and Wells Fargo. *See, e.g.*, Eamon Barrett, *Wells Fargo Is the Last of the Big Six Banks to Issue a Net-zero Climate Pledge. Now Comes the Hard Part*, FORTUNE (Mar. 9, 2021), https://fortune.com/2021/03/09/wells-fargo-climate-carbon-neutral-net-zero/.

The language of "sustainability" has found particular purchase in the EU, where it has informed several recent rules.[86] For example, the EU Sustainable Taxonomy Regulation establishes criteria for financial products, and related business activities, to be considered sustainable.[87] While this regulation does not obviate traditional financial markets, it does include requirements that financial products not meeting the sustainability criteria indicate that fact, thereby requiring even traditional financial products to interface with the lens of sustainability.[88]

Below are several of the other main themes that will continue to evolve under the general focus on sustainability.

1. *Life Cycle Considerations*

Managing waste is a problem that has long plagued humanity, and marginalized communities have often borne the brunt of the adverse impacts of waste management systems, which can directly affect these peoples' basic human rights to life and health. The sheer volume of waste associated with contemporary consumerism is antithetical to sustainability. To address this, there has been an increased emphasis on life cycle considerations for businesses' products and services. Part of this is the "circular economy," the idea of using wastes or disposed products as inputs for new products; this idea has already received mention in certain EU documents.[89] Whereas waste regulations, and related due diligence, have traditionally focused on proper handling and disposal, the "circular economy" concept will likely see increasing pressures for disposal to give way to recycling and beneficial reuse, whereby companies do not send wastes to disposal sites but instead send them to other businesses to make use of them in products or projects (e.g., the use of ash in concrete or of worn tires in asphalt). Many companies may already try to find uses for waste products, particularly where they are valuable or costly to dispose of, but more wide-scale implementation will likely entail more substantial waste stream organization and logistics at several steps in the value chain.

Another effect of an increased focus on life cycle considerations is that it can recontextualize products and their impacts. New pollutants are regularly identified.[90] However, life cycle considerations mean that certain pollutants that were previously identified but ignored suddenly have renewed importance. Consider microplastics; while plastic pollution initially focused on macroplastics, the response to which generally just required collection and disposal of use-size items, an increasing body of work has looked at how these macroplastics continue to impact the environment postmortem as they decompose into tiny (but persistent) particles, making them a different sort of pollutant. Microplastics are ubiquitous and can be found in both seafood and drinking water, which has led many to question potential impacts to human health. This change in scope, brought about at least in part by an

[86] Latham & Watkins Client Alert, *supra* note 84.

[87] Council Directive 2020/852, 2020 O.J. (L. 198) (EU), https://eur-lex.europa.eu/legal-content/EN/TXT/PDF/?uri=CELEX:32020R0852&from=EN ("EU Sustainable Taxonomy Regulation").

[88] *Id.* Article 7.

[89] *See, e.g., Id.* Article 9, 13.

[90] *See, e.g., Per- and Polyfluoroalkyl Substances (PFAS)*, EPA, https://www.epa.gov/pfas (last visited Dec. 18, 2020).

increased emphasis on sustainability, will require novel environmental solutions. Here again, a circular economy will likely play a substantial role.

2. *Natural Capital: Biodiversity and Ecosystems*

Recent attention has also focused on other natural systems, such as the important role of biodiversity and the complex ecology on which life depends.[91] Like climate response and the circular economy, the protection and restoration of biodiversity and ecosystems is a major environmental objective of recent EU rulemaking.[92] However, the technical implementation of protections for biodiversity and ecosystems is particularly challenging due not only to the wide variety of constituent elements involved (the number of species and their interactions with each other and other features of their surroundings) but also the dynamism inherent in the systems.

To address this variety, some legal guidance has adopted the language of "natural capital" as a catch-all term.[93] As a parallel to human capital or financial capital, natural capital is a measure of the various assets and services (such as erosion control, coastline protection, crop pollination, or viability as a nursery for a species) found in nature that provide economic value. As with other forms of capital, it can be depleted. Natural capital can also be particularly difficult to generate or replace. It depends upon a well-functioning environment, and damage to either the structure or diversity of habitats and ecosystems can fundamentally alter natural capital stocks.

Currently, references to natural capital in the law are rare. However, there is increasing recognition of the role such capital plays in human life. Among myriad other benefits, wetlands mitigate floods, forests reduce erosion, and shellfish reefs filter water. All these areas also provide a host of resources ranging from food to dyes to medicine; and for certain communities (such as Indigenous communities) a particular ecosystem may be integral to their survival and way of life. As recognition of the value of these services continues to grow, it is possible that governments will develop legal regimes to protect ecosystem quality, acknowledging that it is as important as air or water quality for public health and welfare. First steps have already been taken on this matter. Among other initiatives, a parallel to the TCFD has been established in the Taskforce for Nature-Related Financial Disclosures,[94] and the OECD

---

[91] *See* Anthony D. Barnosky *et al.*, *Has the Earth's Sixth Mass Extinction Already Arrived?* 471 NATURE 51 (2011); Gerardo Ceballos *et al.*, *Vertebrates on the Brink as Indicators of Biological Annihilation and the Sixth Mass Extinction*, 24 PNAS 13596 (Jun. 1, 2020); Belinda Reyers & Elizabeth R. Selig, *Global Targets That Reveal the Social-Ecological Interdependencies of Sustainable Development*, 4 NATURE ECOLOGY & EVOLUTION 1011 (2020);

[92] Latham & Watkins Client Alert, *supra* note 84.

[93] *See, e.g.*, EU Comm'n, Guidelines on non-financial reporting (methodology for reporting non-financial information), 2017 O.J. (L. II) C 215/1, C215/15, https://eur-lex.europa.eu/legal-content/EN/TXT/PDF/?uri=CELEX:52017XC0705(01)&from=EN. *See also Natural Capital Protocol*, Natural Capital Coalition (Jan. 14, 2021), https://capitalscoalition.org/capitals-approach/natural-capital-protocol/?fwp_filter_tabs=training_material.

[94] *See* Taskforce for Nature-related Financial Disclosures, *How It Works*, https://tnfd.info/how-it-works/.

has released a guide on biodiversity and natural capital considerations for economic and fiscal policy.[95]

3. *Other*

Although water is a topic that has long been within the realm of environmental law, it is a subject of renewed focus under the auspices of sustainability. Water also maintains a particularly intricate relationship with climate; although the focus on climate has been GHG emissions, the resulting changes in precipitation patterns have a direct impact on water availability in various regions across the globe. As discussed in Section III.C above, the legal requirements surrounding water use often relate to the prevalence of water in the jurisdiction. However, even beyond climate, water stress has continued to grow in various locations, and sustainable water use regimes may need to be developed.

Increasingly, discussions on sustainability contain a direct human rights and social component as well. For example, the EU Sustainable Taxonomy Regulation also incorporates "minimum safeguards" for social issues—alignment with the *OECD Guidelines for Multinational Enterprises* and the UN Guiding Principles on Business and Human Rights, including the principles and rights set out in the eight fundamental conventions identified in the Declaration of the International Labour Organisation on Fundamental Principles and Rights at Work and the International Bill of Human Rights—into the criteria for sustainability.[96] The Technical Expert Group consulting on this regulation suggested that, in future, social sustainability categories should be incorporated alongside the environmental sustainability categories in the regulation's criteria.[97]

The combination of nascency and urgency makes trends regarding sustainability particularly dynamic. What was considered standard, or even best practice, a few years ago may be seen as woefully outdated today. This is likely to continue for some time, particularly as these topics begin to be comprehensively incorporated into legal regimes.

C. Supply Chain Due Diligence

Supply chain due diligence could be seen as an aspect of sustainability; however, like climate, it is at least independent enough to merit a separate discussion. As noted above, jurisdictions are increasingly expecting businesses to inspect their supply chains for various ESG considerations, including environmental and human rights impacts.[98] However, there is substantial

---

[95] OECD, BIODIVERSITY, NATURAL CAPITAL AND THE ECONOMY: A POLICY GUIDE FOR FINANCE, ECONOMIC AND ENVIRONMENT MINISTERS (2021), https://www.oecd-ilibrary.org/environment/biodiversity-natural-capital-and-the-economy_1a1ae114-en;jsessionid=bkm5F359AUtN_VKd9A9sgqHb.ip-10-240-5-73.

[96] EU Sustainable Taxonomy Regulation, *supra* note 87, at Article 18.

[97] EU TECHNICAL EXPERT GROUP ON SUSTAINABLE FIN., TAXONOMY: FINAL REPORT OF THE TECHNICAL EXPERT GROUP ON SUSTAINABLE FINANCE 10, 51 (2020), https://ec.europa.eu/info/sites/info/files/business_economy_euro/banking_and_finance/documents/200309-sustainable-finance-teg-final-report-taxonomy_en.pdf (discussing incorporation of minimum social safeguards and potential inclusion of social criteria to potential eligibility in addition to environmental aspects of sustainability).

[98] *See* CSDDD Proposal, *supra* note 9; Loi, *supra* note 77; California Transparency Act, S.B. 657, 2009 Reg. Sess. (Ca. 2010).

variation in these laws. Some, such as the Dodd-Frank Act's conflict minerals provisions, are primarily disclosure oriented.[99] They rely on the perceived shame associated with disclosing undesired behavior as an incentive for companies to correct their behavior without any legally compulsory changes. However, the increasing trend is for governments to require companies to proactively ensure compliance in their supply chains, both for human rights as well as for any environmental impacts that may affect human rights.[100]

D. Future Interaction between Environmental and Human Rights Due Diligence

As has been discussed throughout this chapter, human rights and environmental law developed independently but have the potential for overlap in many areas. Both are also receiving increased attention throughout society as part of the push for a greater consideration of environmental and social impacts, particularly the impacts of businesses. Because of this, there are natural questions of how the relationship between environmental law and human rights law will develop going forward.

Although environmental and human rights law can inform each other and may even need to be used together to address certain intersectional matters, they are ultimately distinct areas of law. They developed independently and with different motivations; therefore, particularly in the short term, no one should expect these areas to converge or even to begin invariably including questions pertaining to the other in their due diligence processes. Certain topics within each are, at least currently, still typically seen through only an environmental or human rights lens. However, it is much more likely that specialists in these areas will need to engage in sustained dialogue, and it is possible that additional overlaps may be identified to draw them into even greater synergy.

VI. Conclusion

The "human" and the "environment" are inextricably linked. Therefore, it should be no surprise that environmental and human rights issues are converging in several areas. As both environmental law and its nexus with human rights continue to evolve, particularly in light of the increasing awareness of the importance of sustainability, companies' due diligence in these topics becomes ever more vital. Both areas of law are specialized and involve a wide array of sub-topics, and some of these sub-topics have more prominent overlap with the other area of law than others. This chapter provides an overview of the major current and developing topics within environmental law, as well as good practices for identifying environmental issues during the due diligence process. Because of the complexity of these matters, parties should strongly consider involving specialist environmental counsel when there is the potential for environmental concerns. However, the contents of this chapter should provide human rights practitioners with the facility to begin dialogue on environmental issues.

---

99 15 U.S.C. § 78m(p) (2015).

100 *See, e.g.*, Supply Chain Due Diligence Act, *supra* note 77.

VII. Resources

There are many resources cited throughout this chapter that readers should consider referencing; however, the following are a selection of initial sources—previously cited and otherwise—that can help interested readers further their understanding of this space.

A. Legal Standards

Although these vary by jurisdiction, the following laws and treaties have been particularly influential in the conceptualization of environmental law.

United States

Clean Air Act, 42 U.S.C Chapter 85

Clean Water Act, 33 U.S.C. Chapter 26

Comprehensive Environmental Response, Compensation, and Liability Act, 42 U.S.C. Chapter 103

Endangered Species Act, 16 U.S.C. Chapter 35

National Environmental Policy Act, 42 U.S.C. Chapter 55

National Historic Preservation Act, 54 U.S.C. § 300101 *et seq.*

Resource Conservation and Recovery Act, 42 U.S.C. Chapter 82

Safe Drinking Water Act, 42 U.S.C. Chapter 6A

European Union (EU)

Access to Environmental Information Directive: Council Directive 2003/4, 2003 O.J. (L. 41), https://eur-lex.europa.eu/eli/dir/2003/4/oj.

Ambient Air Quality Directive: Council Directive 2008/50, 2008 O.J. (L. 152), https://eur-lex.europa.eu/legal-content/EN/TXT/PDF/?uri=CELEX:02008L0050-20150918&from=EN.

Environmental Impact Assessment Directive: Council Directive 2011/92, 2011 O.J. (L. 26), https://eur-lex.europa.eu/legal-content/EN/TXT/?uri=CELEX: 32011L0092.

Habitats Directive: Council Directive 92/42, 1992 O.J. (L. 206), https://eur-lex.europa.eu/legal-content/EN/TXT/?uri=celex%3A31992L0043.

Industrial Emissions Directive: Council Directive 2010/75, 2010 O.J. (L. 334), https://eur-lex.europa.eu/legal-content/EN/TXT/?uri=CELEX:32010L0075.

Non-Financial Reporting Directive ("NFRD"): Council Directive 2014/95, 2014 O.J. (L. 330), https://eur-lex.europa.eu/legal-content/EN/TXT/?uri= CELEX%3A32014L0095.

Registration, Evaluation, Authorisation, and Restriction of Chemicals ("REACH") Regulation: Council Reg. No. 2006/1907, 2006 O.J. (L. 396), http://publications.europa.eu/resource/cellar/ab8123f5-83ef-4659-90f6-4e12f33b30da.0005.02/DOC_1.

Sustainable Taxonomy Delegated Acts: *Implementing and delegated acts for Regulation (EU) 2020/852* (Nov. 20, 2020), https://ec.europa.eu/info/law/sustainable-finance-taxonomy-regulation-eu-2020-852/amending-and-supplementary-acts/implementing-and-delegated-acts_en.

Sustainable Taxonomy Regulation: Council Directive 2020/852, 2020 O.J. (L. 198).

Waste Framework Directive: Council Directive 2008/98, 2008 O.J. (L. 312), https://eur-lex.europa.eu/legal-content/EN/TXT/?uri=CELEX:32008L0098.

Water Framework Directive: Council Directive 2000/60, 2000 O.J. (L. 327), https://eur-lex.europa.eu/legal-content/EN/TXT/?uri=CELEX:32000L0060.

International

Aarhus Convention: *Convention on Access to Information, Public Participation in Decision-Making and Access to Justice in Environmental Matters*, Aarhus (Jun. 25, 1998), https://unece.org/fileadmin/DAM/env/pp/documents/cep43e.pdf.

Aichi Biodiversity Targets: Strategic Plan for Biodiversity 2011-2020 (Aichi Biodiversity Targets): CBD Dec. X/2, UN Doc. UNEP/CBD/COP/DEC/X/2 (Oct. 29, 2010), https://www.cbd.int/doc/decisions/cop-10/cop-10-dec-02-en.pdf.

Convention on Biological Diversity, Rio de Janeiro (Jun. 5, 1992), United Nations Treaty Series, vol. 1760, No. 30619, p. 79, https://treaties.un.org/Pages/ViewDetails.aspx?src=TREATY&mtdsg_no=XXVII-8&chapter=27&clang=_en.

Convention on the International Trade in Endangered Species of Wild Flora and Fauna, Washington, DC (Mar. 3, 1973), *United Nations Treaty Collection*, vol. 993, No. 14537, p. 243, https://treaties.un.org/pages/showDetails.aspx?objid=0800000280105383.

Kyoto Protocol, Kyoto (Dec. 11, 1997), *United Nations Treaty Series*, vol. 2303, no. 30822, p. 162, https://treaties.un.org/Pages/ViewDetails.aspx?src=TREATY&mtdsg_no=XXVII-7-a&chapter=27&clang=_en.

Montreal Protocol on Substances That Deplete the Ozone Layer, Montreal (Sep. 16, 1987), *United Nations Treaty Series*, vol. 1522, no. 26369, p. 3, https://treaties.un.org/doc/Publication/UNTS/Volume%201522/v1522.pdf.

Paris Agreement, Paris (Dec. 12, 2015), https://unfccc.int/sites/default/files/english_paris_agreement.pdf

United Nations Convention on the Law of the Sea, Montego Bay (Nov. 16, 1994), *United Nations Treaty Series*, vol. 1833-35, no. 31363, p. 3, https://treaties.un.org/Pages/showDetails.aspx?objid=0800000280043ad5.

United Nations Framework Convention on Climate Change (UNFCCC) (Mar. 21, 1994), https://unfccc.int/resource/docs/convkp/conveng.pdf.

B. Organizations

The following organizations include legal organizations as well as entities that are thought leaders or otherwise significant in the realm of environmental matters.

California Environmental Protection Agency, https://calepa.ca.gov/.

Environmental Law Institute, https://www.eli.org/.

European Environment Agency, https://www.eea.europa.eu/.

Food and Agriculture Organization of the United Nations, http://www.fao.org/home/en/.

Intergovernmental Panel on Climate Change, https://www.ipcc.ch/.

International Union for Conservation of Nature, https://www.iucn.org/.

International Water Law Project, https://www.internationalwaterlaw.org/.

United Nations Division for Sustainable Development, https://sdgs.un.org/.
United Nations Environment Programme, https://www.unep.org/.
United States Environmental Protection Agency, https://www.epa.gov/.
World Heritage Center, https://whc.unesco.org/en/.
World Resources Institute, https://www.wri.org/.
World Water Council, https://www.worldwatercouncil.org/en.

C. Reports and Publications

The following provide insights and information on various of the topics discussed in this chapter.

American Bar Association (ABA), *Environment, Energy, and Resources: The Year in Review*, https://www.americanbar.org/groups/environment_energy_resources/publications/year_in_review_home/.

The Environmental Law Reporter (ELR), https://elr.info/.

David Reidmiller et al., *Fourth National Climate Assessment* (2018), https://nca2018.globalchange.gov/.

Latham & Watkins, *The Book of Jargon – Environmental, Social, & Governance*, https://www.lw.com/bookofjargon-apps/boj-environmental-social-governance.

D. Third-Party Frameworks/Standards

There are myriad such regimes; those below are a mere selection.

CDP (formerly the "Carbon Disclosure Project"), https://www.cdp.net/en.

Equator Principles, https://equator-principles.com/about/.

Global Reporting Initiative, *GRI Standards* (2020), https://www.globalreporting.org/how-to-use-the-gri-standards/gri-standards-english-language/.

International Finance Corporation, *Performance Standards on Environmental and Social Sustainability* (2021), https://www.ifc.org/wps/wcm/connect/Topics_Ext_Content/IFC_External_Corporate_Site/Sustainability-At-IFC/Policies-Standards/Performance-Standards.

Organisation of Economic Co-operation and Development (OECD), *OECD Guidelines for Multinational Enterprises* (2011), http://mneguidelines.oecd.org/guidelines/.

Sustainability Accounting Standards Board, *SASB Standards* (2021), https://www.sasb.org/standards/download/.

Task Force on Climate-Related Fin. Disclosures, *Final Report: Recommendations of the Task Force on Climate-related Financial Disclosures* (2017), https://assets.bbhub.io/company/sites/60/2020/10/FINAL-2017-TCFD-Report-11052018.pdf.

United Nations Principles

UNEP Finance Initiative, *Principles for Responsible Banking*, https://www.unepfi.org/banking/bankingprinciples/.

UN Principles for Responsible Investment, https://www.unpri.org/.

15

Due Diligence in Conflict-Affected and High-Risk Areas

Morvarid Bagheri

I. Introduction

Companies operating in conflict-affected or high-risk areas (CAHRA) face significant barriers to conducting business responsibly. CAHRA may be fragile, failing, or turbulent states or regions with weak governance zones.[1] Governments of CAHRA may be failing to carry out their core functions or be in the midst of armed conflict, post-conflict development, or political instability. Citizens in CAHRA may be experiencing repression or widespread human rights abuses, violence, insecurity, or ineffective, weakened, or collapsed institutions, governance, or infrastructures.[2]

The risk of complicity in human rights abuses is heightened for businesses operating in CAHRA.[3] Companies' actions often cause them to become caught in a "conflict spiral" whereby they "unwillingly or unknowingly cause or exacerbate conflict and consequentially face new and largely unforeseeable human rights risks."[4] To identify and address the

[1] Institute for Business and Human Rights, *From Red to Green Flags: The Corporate Responsibility to Respect Human Rights in High-Risk Countries*, 3 (2011) at 25 [hereinafter Green Flags].

[2] *OECD Due Diligence Guidance for Responsible Supply Chains of Minerals from CAHR Areas* (3rd ed., 2016) at 13 [hereinafter OECD].

[3] Special Rep. of the Sec'y Gen., *Guiding Principles on Business and Human Rights: Implementing the United Nations "Protect, Respect and Remedy" Framework*, Hum. Rts. Council, UN Doc. A/HRC/17/31 (Mar. 21, 2011), UNGP 23 [hereinafter *Guiding Principles*].

[4] Swisspeace, *Enhanced Human Rights Due Diligence in Conflict Affected and High-Risk Areas*, at 6 (2016) [hereinafter Swisspeace].

heightened risks of triggering new conflicts or exacerbating existing ones and thereby contributing to human rights violations,[5] companies must enhance each stage of the human rights due diligence (HRDD) framework set forth in the *United Nations Guiding Principles* (UNGPs)[6] and discussed in chapter 2 of this book, with additional procedures derived from conflict sensitivity methodology (CSM)[7] to conduct enhanced human rights due diligence (EHRDD) on all operations in or linked to CAHRA. EHRDD through CSM enables companies to understand the CAHRA context.[8] It also allows companies to systematically assess, address, track, and communicate about their adverse impacts on both conflict dynamics and salient human rights issues.[9]

The conflict spiral involves two categories of conflicts that emerge due to businesses' operational impacts in CAHRA, both of which can be addressed through EHRDD. First, existing conflicts among groups may be directly or indirectly exacerbated by business, such as through payments to armed groups, as has occurred in Sudan, Liberia, Angola, or Columbia, or through discriminatory hiring practices that result in "exacerbating perceptions of injustice, exclusion, inequality, and human rights abuses."[10] Second, the impact of business operations on the CAHRA may trigger new conflicts,[11] which may arise (i) between the community and company, such as in the case of protests around mining operations in Peru or South Africa,[12] and/or (ii) within communities, such as in Ghana,[13] where disputes have emerged as to who profits from the company's presence, creating "ideological discrepancies between those favoring economic development and . . . those trying to protect traditional ways of living."[14]

Section II of this chapter provides a contextual overview of CSM in relation to HRDD, to assist lawyers and others with understanding how HRDD should be approached in CAHRA. Section III identifies standards on complicity in international crimes and key industry-specific regulatory and voluntary frameworks relative to HRDD in CAHRA. Section IV then discusses good practices for community engagement and offers a seven-step framework within

---

[5] Andreas Graf & Andrea Iff, *Respecting Human Rights in Conflict Regions: How to Avoid the 'Conflict Spiral,'* 2 Bus. and Hum. Rts. J. 1 at 123 (2017) [hereinafter Graf].

[6] *Guiding Principles, supra* note 3.

[7] Working Group on the Issue of Human Rights and Transnational Corporations and other Business Enterprises (WGBHR), *Business, Human Rights and Conflict-Affected Regions: Towards Heightened Action,* Gen. Assembly, UN Doc. A/75/212 at 22 (Jul. 21, 2020) [hereinafter A/75/212]; Swisspeace, *supra* note 4, at 14.

[8] JustPeace Labs, *Conflict Sensitivity for the Tech Industry* at 11 (Aug. 2020) [hereinafter JustPeace].

[9] International Alert, *Conflict-Sensitive Business Practice: Guidance for Extractive Industries* at 12 (2005) [hereinafter CSBP]; *Graf, supra note 5*, at 113; Swisspeace, *supra* note 4, at 14, 22.

[10] JustPeace, *supra* note 8, at 11, 13.

[11] A/75/212, *supra* note 7, at 11; International Alert, *Human Rights Due Diligence in Conflict-affected Settings: Guidance for Extractives Industries*, prepared by Yadaira Orsini and Roper Cleland [hereinafter IA].

[12] Graf, *supra* note 5, at 114; Swisspeace, *supra* note 4, at 23.

[13] Charles Gyan & Abena Ampomah, *Effects of Stakeholder Conflicts on Community Development Projects in Kenyase*, 6 SAGE Open J. 1 (Mar. 4, 2016).

[14] Graf, *supra* note 5, at 126.

the four stages of HRDD, which results in EHRDD that incorporates CSM. Section V identifies key outstanding areas, Section VI concludes the chapter, and Section VII offers a list of resources for legal practitioners conducting EHRDD in CAHRA.

II. Contextual Overview

The UN Working Group on Business and Human Rights (UNWG) first linked CSM to HRDD in 2014 by calling on States to identify steps in their National Action Plans[15] for integrating CSM in HRDD processes to help companies conduct EHRDD in CAHRA.[16] CSM, which is rooted in the international development and humanitarian assistance fields,[17] shares several similarities with HRDD. Both methodologies use context analysis and impact assessment tools to understand human rights and conflict contexts, respectively, and to identify adverse impacts of operations on the respective contexts.[18] Both also apply risk mitigation and prevention techniques to address adverse impacts.

Key differences are that HRDD applies in all contexts and begins by analyzing risk areas where the scale, scope, and irremediability of consequences of human rights impacts are most severe on individuals, whereas CSM applies only in CAHRA and begins by analyzing societal undercurrents and identifying consequences of impacts on conflict dynamics.[19] CSM nonetheless parallels and supplements the four stages of HRDD methodology. For example, the conflict context and impacts analyses of CSM's first stage uncover information relevant to the human rights context and impact analyses of HRDD's first stage. Seven steps for enhancing HRDD with CSM to conduct EHRDD, which essentially requires applying a conflict sensitivity lens to the design and implementation of the entire HRDD process,[20] are outlined in Section IV of this chapter.

III. Standards

This section outlines existing legal, regulatory, and voluntary standards relating to HRDD and responsible business operations in CAHRA. Section III(A) discusses applicable international standards for complicity in mass atrocity crimes. Section III(B) examines existing regulatory frameworks on conflict minerals, and Section III(C) outlines industry-specific voluntary initiatives for the extractive, private security, and technology sectors.

---

[15] National Action Plans are "policy documents in which a government articulates priorities and actions that it will adopt to support the implementation of international, regional, or national obligations and commitments with regard to a given policy area or topic." *See* https://globalnaps.org/about/.

[16] *See,* CSBP, *supra* note 9; UN WGBHR, Gen. Assembly, UN Doc. A/69/263 at 14 (Aug. 5, 2014) [hereinafter A/69/263].

[17] *Id.* at 6; Graf, *supra* note 5, at 118.

[18] JustPeace, *supra* note 8, at 13; Graf, *supra* note 5, at 123, 132.

[19] Graf, *supra* note 5, at 120; *See infra* Section IV.

[20] A/75/212, *supra* note 7, at 14, 23.

A. Complicity in International Crimes

Corporations can become complicit in gross human rights violations that amount to mass atrocity crimes (MAC), such as war crimes, crimes against humanity, or genocide, committed by third parties against civilian populations. EHRDD through CSM, discussed in Section IV, enables companies to identify and address situations that may legitimize or assist the commission of MAC and minimize exposure to civil or criminal liability for the company, its officers, and its staff. War crimes constitute serious violations of international humanitarian law; they include forced labor,[21] natural resource plunder, and gender- or sexual-based violence when committed in situations of international or non-international armed conflict, such as regional wars and local insurgencies.[22] Crimes against humanity involve widespread or systematic attacks or inhumane acts directed at civilian populations, including gender and sexual-based violence, deportation, imprisonment, torture, persecution, apartheid, enforced disappearance, enslavement, extermination, or murder.[23] Genocide involves committing murder, preventing births, transferring children, or inflicting mental or bodily harm with the intention to physically destroy a national, ethnic, racial, or religious group in whole or in part.[24]

In situations of international or non-international armed conflict, company activities become closely linked with conflict if they substantially assist or encourage the commission of MAC, resulting in complicity.[25] Companies can also be complicit in crimes against humanity or genocide where there is no ongoing armed conflict. Directors and staff can face individual criminal liability[26] if they knowingly provide "practical assistance or encouragement that" substantially affects the commission of a MAC.[27] Civilian superiors can be held "responsible for crimes committed by their subordinates" if they knew or should have known the crime would be committed and failed to exercise control to prevent its commission or report it to authorities for investigation and prosecution.[28]

Recent developments signal an openness at the international level toward the recognition of corporate criminal liability for MAC, such as the adoption of the Malabo Protocol by the African Union,[29] the incorporation of corporate liability in the Draft Articles on the Prevention and Punishment of Crimes against Humanity,[30] and calls to amend the Rome Statute

[21] Geneva Conventions I, II, and III.

[22] Rome Statute.

[23] *Id.* at Article 7.

[24] UN Convention on the Prevention and Punishment of the Crime of Genocide, Article 2 (1948).

[25] *Guiding Principles* 12, Commentary and Guiding Principles 23, Commentary, *supra* note 3; *Q&A: International Humanitarian Law and Business: Ten questions to Philip Spoerri, ICRC Director for International Law and Cooperation*, Int'l Rev. of the Red Cross, vol. 94, number 887, Autumn 2012, pp. 1125–1134, at 1126–1127; OECD Guidelines, 32, http://www.oecd.org/daf/inv/mne/48004323.pdf; ICRC, Business and International Humanitarian Law (2006), https://www.icrc.org/en/doc/resources/documents/misc/business-ihl-150806.htm.

[26] Global Centre for the Responsibility to Protect (GCR2P), Preventing corporate involvement in mass atrocity crimes: Implementing the UN Guiding Principles on Business and Human Rights, by Rachel Davis, Managing Director, Shift, Policy Brief, March 2016 at https://s156658.gridserver.com/media/files/2016-business-and-r2p.pdf [hereinafter GCR2P].

[27] *Guiding Principles* 17, Commentary, *supra* note 3.

[28] The mens rea for civilian superior is "should have known," as provided in the Rome Statute Article 28(b)(i); Spoerri at 1131–1132, *supra* note 25.

[29] African Union, Malabo Protocol.

[30] Draft Articles on the Prevention and Punishment of Crimes against Humanity.

to recognize criminal liability for corporations.[31] The concept of corporate criminal liability is recognized in many countries, including the United States, United Kingdom, Netherlands, France, Italy, Spain, Switzerland, and Canada.[32] Many of them also allow for the exercise of extra-territorial jurisdiction in their domestic courts over MAC committed abroad when there is a sufficient territorial nexus to the crime, perpetrator, or victims.[33] International humanitarian law also obliges all States to investigate and prosecute war crimes committed on their territory or by their nationals, and extends the right to vest extra-territorial jurisdiction in national courts over such crimes.[34]

1. Modes of Involvement in Mass Atrocity Crimes

The UNGPs outline three modes of corporate involvement in MAC: direct linkage, contribution, and causation. These are discussed below, and, in practice, correspond with modes of legal liability for companies and personnel. The risks of involvement in MAC should always be treated as legal compliance issues.[35] Examples of involvement include aiding and abetting forced labor; expelling people from their communities; contaminating air, land, or water; hiring members of an armed party to a conflict or abusive security forces; selling chemical products to be used as weapons;[36] or financing international crimes.[37]

Companies most commonly become involved in MAC due to direct or indirect business relationships linked to their operations, products, or services with State or non-State entities involved in their commission.[38] This includes acquiring or inheriting land, natural resources, or other assets through an entity in a global supply chain or multi-tiered value chain that obtained them by committing MAC.[39] Companies in the electronics, automotive, and consumer goods sectors may use conflict minerals sourced through their global supply chains. Similarly, those engaged in the exploration for natural resources, infrastructure building, or agriculture projects may gain access to land obtained by pillaging and/or forced displacement,[40] such as through a joint venture with the State[41] or a "crony-led" company, thereby institutionalizing the impacts of war crimes.[42]

---

[31] Marie Davoise, *All Roads Lead to Rome: Strengthening Domestic Prosecutions of Businesses through the Inclusion of Corporate Liability in the Rome Statute*, OpinioJuris, (Jul. 25, 2019), http://opiniojuris.org/2019/07/25/all-roads-lead-to-rome-strengthening-domestic-prosecutions-of-businesses-through-the-inclusion-of-corporate-liability-in-the-rome-statute/.

[32] Clifford Chance, Corporate Criminal Liability Brochure (Apr. 2016) https://www.cliffordchance.com/content/dam/cliffordchance/briefings/2016/04/corporate-criminal-liability.pdf.

[33] Spoerri at 1132, *supra* note 25.

[34] *Id.* at 1127.

[35] *Guiding Principles* 17, Commentary, *supra* note 3.

[36] Spoerri at 1131, *supra* note 25.

[37] *Red Flags: Liability Risks for Businesses Operating in High-Risk Zones*, https://redflags.info/, [hereinafter Red Flags].

[38] GCR2P, *supra* note 26, at 2.

[39] *Id.* at 3.

[40] Spoerri at 1129, *supra* note 25.

[41] GCR2P, *supra* note 26.

[42] A/75/212, *supra* note 7, at 17.

Contribution may include facilitating or motivating another entity or person to commit MAC or acting in parallel with State or non-State actors, including State officials or other entities, "such that the cumulative effect of behavior causes" the MAC.[43] Private security companies and companies in the extractive or information and communication technologies (ICT) sectors are at higher risk of contributing to MAC. For example, private security companies may aid or train armed forces. Extractive companies may provide supplies or transportation to security forces involved in MAC, and ICT companies may fuel online hate campaigns.

Causation, the third mode, is a common form of involvement for corporate human rights abuses, such as of labor rights,[44] but less relevant to MAC. Companies nonetheless risk inadvertently fueling MAC by exacerbating underlying conflict drivers in a CAHRA.[45] These risks can be addressed through EHRDD, discussed in Section IV.[46]

B. Regulatory Standards

In 2014 and 2021, regulations entered into force in the United States and the European Union (EU), respectively, to increase transparency about the presence of the "conflict minerals" tin, tantalum, tungsten, or gold (3TG), sourced from CAHRA, in companies' global supply chains. In places like the eastern region of the Democratic Republic of Congo, Afghanistan, Central African Republic, and Colombia, armed militias control 3TG production processes, particularly in artisanal and small-scale mines, tax local miners to fund military campaigns, expose them to severe health and safety risks, and commit forced labor, murder, and rape against women and children.[47] These laws aim to limit the sourcing of conflict minerals and incorporate variations of the five-step due diligence framework for downstream and upstream companies elaborated in the *OECD Due Diligence Guidance for Responsible Supply Chains of Minerals from CAHRA* (OECD Guidance):[48] (1) establishing strong company management systems; (2) identifying and assessing supply chain risks; (3) designing and implementing a strategy to respond to identified risks; (4) carrying out third-party audits of supply chains; and (5) reporting on supply chain due diligence.[49]

The US Dodd-Frank Wall Street Reform and Consumer Protection Act (Dodd-Frank)[50] incorporated the OECD five-step framework by requiring all companies listed on US exchanges to disclose in annual conflict minerals reports to the US Securities and Exchange Commission, whether they manufacture or use products in their supply chains containing 3TG sourced from the Democratic Republic of Congo or an adjacent country and measures

---

[43] GCR2P, *supra* note 26, at 3.

[44] John Ruggie, *Corporations and Human Rights: A Survey of the Scope and Patterns of Alleged Corporate-Related Human Rights Abuse*, UN Doc. A/HRC/8/5/Add.2 (May 2008).

[45] GCR2P, *supra* note 26, at 4.

[46] JustPeace, *supra* note 8, at 15.

[47] GCR2P, *supra* note 26.

[48] *OECD, supra* note 2.

[49] *OECD Due Diligence Guidance for Minerals: 5-Step Framework for Upstream and Downstream Supply Chains*, available at http://mneguidelines.oecd.org/5%20Step%20Framework_A3.pdf.

[50] United States, Dodd-Frank Wall Street Reform and Consumer Protection Act, Pub. L. No. 111-203 (Jul. 21, 2010), Section 1502, entered into force in 2014.

taken to exercise due diligence. The EU Conflict Minerals Regulation is broader in scope and application, covering companies importing concentrated or processed metals or mineral ores from any CAHRA.[51] It also echoes the OECD Guidance and Dodd-Frank in requiring supply chain due diligence on 3TG mining and processing.[52] While these laws require mandatory disclosures by companies, they fail to impose penalties when 3TG is sourced from CAHRA, thus functionally relying on the reputational impacts of reporting.[53]

Several countries have also incorporated principles from the International Code of Conduct for Private Security Service Providers (ICOC)[54] in domestic regulations governing the conduct of their contractors with private security companies.[55] The ICOC is a voluntary code discussed below that assists private security companies, including providers of armed or unarmed security services,[56] to reduce their security-related human rights risks.[57] For example, in 2011, the US Congress directed the Department of Defense to require operational and business practice standards for contractors providing private security functions in military operations.[58] It resulted in the development of standards and a certification process,[59] which builds on ICOC and offers guidelines for management systems with auditable criteria.[60] These regulatory developments suggest that voluntary standards concerning the impact of corporate activities in CAHRA, such as the OECD Guidelines and others discussed in Section III(C) below, are transforming into normative frameworks.[61]

C. Voluntary Standards

The high risks of contributing to MAC for the private security company, extractive, and ICT sectors in CAHRA have resulted in the development of industry-specific voluntary standards for these sectors, which incorporate CSM and HRDD processes.[62] These include: the ICOC

[51] Regulation (EU) 2017/821 of the European Parliament and of the Council of 17 May 2017 (Effective Jan. 1, 2021); for list of countries see, https://www.cahraslist.net/.

[52] China has also issued guidelines based on the UNGPs and the OECD Guidance concerning conflict minerals in supply chains. *See* China Chamber of Commerce of Metals, Minerals and Chemicals Importers and Exporters, Chinese Due Diligence Guidelines for Responsible Mineral Supply Chains (2015).

[53] Dorothée Baumann-Pauly and Justine Nolan, Business and Human Rights: From Principles to Practice (2016, London) at 38 [hereinafter Baumann-Pauly].

[54] International Code of Conduct for Private Security Service Providers (2010) [hereinafter ICOC].

[55] Switzerland Federal Act on Private Security Services Provided Abroad (2013).

[56] ICOC, *supra* note 54, https://www.icoca.ch/en/the_icoc#b-definitions.

[57] https://biz.sdg.humanrights.dk/salient-issue/human-rights-and-security.

[58] US National Defense Authorization Act, 2011, Section 833, Standards and Certification for Private Security Contractors, operational and business practice standards.

[59] Office of the Assistant Secretary of Defense for Sustainment, Private Security Companies Standards, https://www.acq.osd.mil/log/LOG_CSD/psc_Standards.html.

[60] ANSI/ASIS PSC.1-2012 (R2017), Management System for Quality of Private Security Company Operations – Requirements with Guidance, https://webstore.ansi.org/Standards/ASIS/ansiasispsc2012.

[61] https://www.researchgate.net/publication/279331850_Human_Rights_Due_Diligence_for_Corporations_From_Voluntary_Standards_to_Hard_Law_at_Last.

[62] Swisspeace, *Conflict Sensitivity: Taking It to the Next Level,* Working Papers at 45–46 (Feb. 2016).

for the private security sector; the Extractive Industries Transparency Initiative (EITI)[63] and the Voluntary Principles on Security and Human Rights (VPSHR)[64] for the extractive sector;[65] and the Global Network Initiative (GNI) for the ICT sector, including telecommunications, internet, and hardware companies.[66]

1. *International Code of Conduct for Private Security Companies*

The International Code of Conduct for Private Security Companies (ICOC) is a sector-wide code for private security companies that articulates principles applicable to operations in CAHRA.[67] Signatories pledge to respect the human rights of, and fulfill international humanitarian law responsibilities toward, all persons affected by their activities, including personnel, communities, clients, suppliers, and shareholders. It was created in 2010 through a multi-stakeholder initiative convened by the Swiss government in response to a September 2007 incident when Blackwater Private Security guards hired by the United States to secure a military convoy opened fire on civilians in Baghdad's Nisour Square.[68] The International Code of Conduct Association,[69] composed of governments, private security companies, and civil society, was created in 2013 to serve as ICOC's oversight mechanism of companies' reporting and alleged violations.[70]

The ICOC requires signatory companies to take steps to deter, monitor, report, and address their adverse human rights impacts by establishing effective internal governance frameworks.[71] It restricts the use of force to circumstances of self-defense and defense of others, and requires all personnel be trained in international humanitarian law and international human rights law, and that any detentions comply with these standards.[72] It also acknowledges the prevalence of gender-based violence in CAHRA and requires personnel to "remain vigilant for all instances of [such] violence and, where discovered, report such instances to competent authorities."[73]

The ICOC prohibits personnel from participating in, encouraging, or seeking to benefit from national or international crimes, including torture, enforced disappearance, forced labor, hostage-taking, sexual or gender-based violence, human trafficking, the trafficking of

[63] *Extractive Industries Transparency Initiative* (2003), www.eitransparency.org.

[64] Voluntary Principles on Security and Human Rights (2000), https://www.voluntaryprinciples.org/the-principles/[hereinafter VSPHR].

[65] UN Interagency Framework Team for Preventive Action, Extractive Industries and Conflict: Toolkit and Guidance for Preventing and Managing Land and Natural Resources Conflict (2012).

[66] *Global Network Initiative*, MSIntegrity, https://www.msi-integrity.org/gni/.

[67] ICOC, *supra* note 54, D (13) at 6.

[68] Baumann-Pauly, *supra* note 53, at 161 (chapter by Anne-Marie Buzatu).

[69] *Articles of Association*, International Code of Conduct for Private Security Providers' Association, https://icoca.ch/wp-content/uploads/2020/10/ICoCA-Articles-of-Association.pdf

[70] *About Us*, International Code of Conduct Association (ICoCA), https://icoca.ch/about/.

[71] *ICOC, supra* note 54, para. 6(d).

[72] *Id.* para. 55, 30–33.

[73] *Id.* para. 38.

weapons or drugs, child labor, and extrajudicial, summary, or arbitrary executions.[74] It also requires the exercise of due diligence in the selection and vetting of personnel and subcontractors, including reviewing criminal and military records, and determining fitness to carry weapons.[75] Moreover, it requires ensuring all subcontractors are ICOC signatories who also act diligently in selecting, vetting, and training their personnel.[76]

2. *Extractive Industries Transparency Initiative*

The Extractive Industries Transparency Initiative (EITI), initiated by the UK Department for International Development in 2002, was developed to promote transparency about payments made by extractive companies to governments in resource-rich countries by making information about government revenues from business activities, contractual terms, and beneficial ownership more publicly available.[77] EITI-supporting companies are expected to "engage in rigorous procurement processes, including due diligence in respect to partners and vendors," and identify beneficial owners of joint ventures, contractors, and other business partners. Companies must also publicly disclose beneficial owners, taxes, and payments made to any of the 55 EITI-implementing member countries.

They must also declare their support for the 12 EITI Principles relating to increased transparency over payments and revenues in the extractive sector,[78] and "support the operationalization of countries' decisions to disclose future licenses and contracts entered into that govern the exploration and exploitation of oil, gas and minerals in accordance with the recommendations in the EITI standard."[79] It is a bottom-up effort to address the resource curse, where natural resource wealth in less diversified economies becomes linked to conflict, corruption, and political instability.[80] However, it has been criticized for focusing on a symptom rather than the cause, which may be linked to States' revenue mismanagement.[81]

3. *Voluntary Principles on Security and Human Rights*

The Voluntary Principles on Security and Human Rights (VPSHR) offer guidance to extractive companies on conducting their security arrangements in a manner that respects human rights in CAHRA.[82] Established in 2000, and formulated by governments, businesses, and non-governmental organizations, they offer a set of standards, operationalized in the VPSHR

[74] *Id.* para. 22, 35–42.

[75] *Id.* para. 45, 48, 50.

[76] *Id.* para. 16, 18, 50, 51.

[77] Baumann-Pauly, *supra* note 53, at 149–150 (chapter by Scott Jerbi).

[78] EITI Principles can be found at: https://eiti.org/collections/eiti-standard.

[79] EITI International Secretariat, Expectations for EITI Supporting Companies (Jun. 2018), https://eiti.org/documents/expectations-eiti-supporting-companies.

[80] David Goldwyn & Andrea Clabough, *Confronting the Resource Curse: Advice for Investors and Partners*, Working Paper on the Role of Foreign Direct Investment in Resource-Rich Regions (Feb. 2020), p. 2, available at: https://www.bakerinstitute.org/sites/default/files/2020-02/import/fdi-goldwynclabough-confronting-the-resource-curse.pdf [hereinafter Goldwyn].

[81] Red Flags, *supra* note 37, at 69.

[82] VSPHR, *supra* note 64.

Implementation Guidance Tools,[83] to help companies address human rights implications and severe security risks and ensure respect for international humanitarian law.[84] The VPSHR's four modules may be used together or as stand-alone toolkits for specific purposes; they cover stakeholder engagement, risk assessment, relations with public security forces, and relations with private security providers.[85] The initiative has been criticized for having inadequate monitoring and reporting requirements and accountability mechanisms.[86]

4. *Global Network Initiative*

ICT companies operating in CAHRA can become complicit in State censorship or be forced to disclose online user activity.[87] They can also fuel conflict through the spread of misinformation and hate campaigns, as in Myanmar, where online hate speech fueled genocide.[88] The Global Network Initiative (GNI) offers guidelines on responsible decision making, multi-stakeholder collaborations, governance, accountability, and transparency,[89] to help ICT companies limit adverse impacts on the rights to privacy and freedom of expression.[90]

IV. Good Practices

Following a note in subsection A below on community engagement in CAHRA, subsection B outlines seven steps derived from CSM along the four stages of HRDD: stage I, impact assessment; stage II, prevention and mitigation; and stages III and IV, tracking and reporting. These steps can be taken to supplement HRDD procedures to conduct EHRDD on business operations in or linked to CAHRA. They may be integrated into existing HRDD protocols or conducted as a stand-alone process after conducting HRDD,[91] but an integrated approach enables conflict sensitivity findings to better inform the HRDD process.[92]

A. Community Engagement

Companies should consult with communities and civil society regularly about the risks and impacts of their operations in CAHRA. Consultations should always be inclusive and in line with CSM. Processes should be structured to enable participation by different gender

83 IFC, International Council on Mining and Metals, and IPIECA, VPSHR Implementation Guidance Tools (2012) available at https://www.ipieca.org/resources/good-practice/voluntary-principles-on-security-and-human-rights-implementation-guidance-tools/ [hereinafter IGT].

84 IA, *supra* note 11, at 41–42.

85 IA, *supra* note 11.

86 Baumann-Pauly, *supra* note 53, at 150 (chapter by Scott Jerbi).

87 *Id.*, at p. 136 (chapter by Michael Samway).

88 A/HRC/39/64, Report of the independent international fact-finding mission on Myanmar (Sep. 2018), available at https://undocs.org/en/A/HRC/39/64.

89 GNI Implementation Guidelines.

90 Global Network Initiative, *Implementation Guidelines*, https://globalnetworkinitiative.org/implementation-guidelines/.

91 CSBP, *supra* note 9, at 33; Swisspeace, *supra* note 4, at 22.

92 Jonathan Goodhand, Tony Vaux, & Robert Walker. *Conducting Conflict Assessments: Guidance Notes*, Department for International Development, London, (January 2022), https://webarchive.nationalarchives.gov.uk/ukgwa/20100522033040/http:/www.dfid.gov.uk/Documents/publications/conflictassessmentguidance.pdf [hereinafter DFID].

identities and consider the intersections of gender with other identity factors which may hinder participation, when engaging with communities to map stakeholders in step one of EHRDD, described below. Local observers and third-party sources, such as aid agencies, can provide or help with gathering information about groups that may not be easily visible to outsiders,[93] including through safe environments via bilateral aid agencies.[94]

Companies must also ensure the protection of all persons with whom they engage in CAHRA during due diligence processes to allow them to feel safe criticizing the company or government.[95] Consultations should be conducive to marginalized groups communicating their concerns without fear of reprisals or harm.[96] Companies must also consider any risks posed to those who engage, including surveillance, arrest, threats, or retaliation from other community members.[97] Where political repression, discrimination, or violence against women or minorities is a norm, human rights defenders, political activists, journalists, or minority groups may also be at risk. Women are among the most affected by companies and are least visible and accessible to them in CAHRA. Without proper support from third-party experts, it is hard for companies to be both inclusive and conflict-sensitive.[98]

Moreover, where governments lack the capacity or will to safeguard human rights, communities may turn to companies for assistance. From the viewpoint of some CAHRA communities, rights are directly linked to values and traditions and are often articulated in social, economic, and cultural terms.[99] The community may believe foreign companies operating on their land or using their natural resources should demonstrate appreciation for the benefits received by ensuring reciprocal benefits to them. They may expect respect for their traditions and values, including concerning the environment, and common courtesy, hospitality, and generosity.[100] Notably, companies working with a State, through joint ventures or as suppliers, may be perceived locally as complicit in that State's human rights violations.[101]

State rule of law deficiencies increase public expectations and unmanaged community perceptions trigger conflicts in CAHRA. Sincere and meaningful engagement with local communities is a valuable tool for diffusing risks and enables both sides to understand the needs and expectations of the other.[102] This requires an understanding of and respect for local cultures and traditions, locals' perceptions of the company, and their understanding of human

---

[93] CSBP, *supra* note 9, at 24.

[94] *OECD Guidance for Responsible Business Conduct*, table 4, http://mneguidelines.oecd.org/OECD-Due-Diligence-Guidance-for-Responsible-Business-Conduct.pdf.

[95] JustPeace, *supra* note 8, at 14.

[96] *Id.* at 18; Green Flags, *supra* note 1, at 51.

[97] CSBP, *supra* note 9, at 24.

[98] *Id.*; Jana Naujoks, *Human Rights Due Diligence and Gender Sensitivity in Conflict-Affected Settings: Advancing Sustainability in Renewable Energy*, International Alert (Oct. 19, 2018) [hereinafter Naujoks].

[99] CDA Collaborative Learning Projects, Community Perspectives on the Business Responsibility to Respect Human Rights in High-Risk Countries at 11 (Oct. 2010) (based on interviews with local communities in Afghanistan, Colombia, the Philippines, and Sudan) [hereinafter CDA].

[100] *Id.* at 11; Green Flags, *supra* note 1, at 51.

[101] *Guiding Principles* 17, Commentary, *supra* note 3.

[102] Green Flags, *supra* note 1, at 44, 49, 51.

rights.[103] Developing a genuine relationship with affected communities can demonstrate respect and allows companies to learn about grievances and discuss what can and cannot be done to address them.[104] These and other CSM measures should guide all community interactions in CAHRA.[105]

B. Four Stages of Human Rights Due Diligence

1. Human Rights Due Diligence Stage I

Companies can enhance the first stage of their HRDD by taking the four steps outlined below.[106] These additional steps involve identifying links between business activities, human rights impacts, and conflict dynamics, and distinguishing between human rights abuses arising from existing conflicts and those linked to company operations. They include a conflict analysis at step one, analysis of the conflict/human rights nexus at step two, a conflict impact analysis (CIA) at step three, and prioritization of impacts at step four.[107] A human rights context assessment (HRCA) and a human rights impact assessment (HRIA) under the first stage of HRDD should be conducted in preparation for steps two and four, respectively. The HRCA, HRIA, and four steps outlined below constitute the first stage of EHRDD in CAHRA. Unmanaged adverse impacts of operations on issues identified at step one lead companies to become caught in conflict spirals. These can be managed through steps five and six in the second and third stages of EHRDD, respectively, and discussed later in this Section IV(B).

Step 1 Conflict Analysis: Step one involves the systematic analysis of the drivers, actors, and dynamics of conflicts and social cohesion. This analysis informs HRDD when human rights implications are assessed at step two.[108] Below are steps for conducting a conflict analysis:

(a) Conflict drivers: Conflict analyses begin by identifying the drivers, structures, and causes of conflicts, or issues subject to societal tensions. This is done by assessing contextual factors that have or could cause or exacerbate violent or non-violent conflicts. As the Institute for Business and Human Rights has noted about CAHRA:

> The law may be weak and poorly enforced or easily circumvented. The State may not fully control its territory or may exercise control by repression. Security may not be provided, or it may protect assets but not people. Water, health, transport, and education may be functionally absent or may benefit some but not others. Opportunities for employment may not exist or may be determined by ethnicity or patronage. Some groups in the society may believe that their aspirations can only be met through violence.[109]

---

[103] *Id.* at 49.

[104] *Id.* at 44, 49, 51.

[105] CSBP, *supra* note 9, at 13.

[106] A/75/212, *supra* note 7, at 10.

[107] Graf, *supra* note 5, at 125.

[108] Swisspeace, *supra* note 4, at 24.

[109] Green Flags, *supra* note 1, at 3.

These circumstances should be identified, because they often lead companies to contribute to gross human rights abuses. Conflict drivers are mapped through various categories, and a diverse range of categories are relevant and must be considered.[110] Conflicts are explained through such categories as socioeconomic conditions and historic narratives of past injustices, discussed below. Diminished or contested State authority or legitimacy also drives conflicts and is linked to heightened security risks for the company. The availability of natural resources, combined with the presence of corruption, competition over access and benefits, and flourishing shadow economies also drive conflicts. These circumstances often relate to local communities not benefiting from revenue flows from foreign investments, including in natural resources.[111] Below are categories of key factors that have or could cause or exacerbate violent or nonviolent conflicts that should be identified by businesses:

States, laws, and security: weaknesses in State capacity; quality of infrastructure, social services, and justice systems;[112] failures of political will; lack of popular participation in political processes; political exploitation of differences; gaps in legislation concerning minimum wage, workplace safety, sexual harassment, and other labor issues; poorly drafted legislation that limits the rights to access information, restricts the freedoms of assembly, association, or expression, hinders gender equality or community consultations;[113] presence of non-State armed groups, criminal gangs, or political insurgencies; unreliable State security forces; exacerbated gender-based violence;[114] poorly controlled or contested borders, legacies of past conflicts, and overlapping social, political, and economic tensions.[115]

Socioeconomics and legacies: size, regional distribution, and ethnic makeup of local populations; unemployment, poverty, inflation, and food insecurity levels; proximity to markets; tensions over language, religion, and ethnicity; socioeconomic inequalities and disparities based on regional or ethnic grounds, including access to jobs, markets, education, credit, and other opportunities;[116] adverse impacts of other companies; unresolved ethnic conflicts or land claims; perceptions shaped by histories of repression, discrimination, or State-formation processes.

(b) Conflict actors: After identifying conflict drivers, conflict actors should be analyzed by identifying (i) stakeholders who are most at risk of being negatively impacted by conflict, noting differentiated impacts on women and girls, children, indigenous peoples, migrants, and disabled persons;[117] (ii) grievances, or feelings of dissatisfaction among groups who have

---

[110] Taylor O'Connor, *How to Conduct Your Own Conflict Analysis: A User-friendly Guide*, Medium (Dec. 1, 2020), https://medium.com/skilluped/how-to-conduct-your-own-conflict-analysis-c37f4cfc1726.

[111] Goldwyn, *supra* note 80, at 2; *See*, Global Witness, *Building for the Long-Term: Avoiding the Resource Curse in Afghanistan*, (2014).

[112] CSBP, *supra* note 9, at 36.

[113] *Id.* at 44, 34–35.

[114] *Guiding Principles* 7, Commentary, *supra* note 3.

[115] Green Flags, *supra* note 1, at 77; DFID, *supra* note 92, at 12.

[116] CSBP, *supra* note 9, at 36, 37; DFID, *supra* note 92, at 12.

[117] Swisspeace, *supra* note 4, at 25.

been or perceive themselves to have been disadvantaged as a result of (a) identified conflict drivers, (b) the company's local operations or relationships or (c) from the interaction of both;[118] (iii) local actors who can influence conflict drivers, including unintentionally, and the company itself;[119] and (iv) mobilizers using resources and grievances to mobilize others for violence, such as criminal gangs, and for social cohesion, such as community leaders, religious groups, and trade unions, although human rights defenders should be "differentiated from parties to the conflict, even if they share the same claims."[120] Additionally, the relationships of various groups should be mapped, including their violent and nonviolent interactions and perceptions of interactions,[121] and their motives, incentives, and capacities to influence conflict.[122] This mapping should also consider how conflict structures incentivize decisions.[123] A political economy lens should be used to understand how groups may benefit from instability and identify economic and political interests in perpetuating conflict, political crises, or poverty.[124]

(c) Resilience factors: The resilience factors to be identified include conditions, institutions, and processes through which communities can prevent, mitigate, and resolve conflicts. An example is institutions linking separate societal sectors or interests. State capacity to contain conflicts and address grievances without perpetuating marginalization should also be assessed.[125] Indications of State capacity include the independence of judges and lawyers,[126] public confidence in judicial processes, and the role of informal rules or traditional legal systems.[127]

(d) Conflict dynamics: Lastly, "the system of interactions and relationships among grievances, resilience factors, and key mobilizers"[128] should be analyzed to determine conflict dynamics, such as long-term trends, triggers for violence, potential future conflict scenarios, and capacities for managing them.[129]

Step 2 Human Rights Context Nexus: Step 2 involves evaluating the HRCA against the conflict analysis conducted pursuant to Step 1, to determine how the human rights context

---

[118] Introduction Section; CSBP, *supra* note 9, at 37; DFID, *supra* note 92, at 15.

[119] JustPeace, *supra* note 8, at 11.

[120] A/75/212, *supra* note 7, at 11.

[121] Swisspeace, *supra* note 4, at 23.

[122] Naujoks, *supra* note 98, at 14.

[123] USAID, *Conflict Assessment Framework* 2.0 at 15 (2012) https://pdf.usaid.gov/pdf_docs/PNADY740.pdf [hereinafter USAID].

[124] DFID, *supra* note 92, at 8.

[125] *Id.* at 16.

[126] *Id.* at 12, 15.

[127] IA, *supra* note 11, at 37.

[128] USAID, *supra* note 123, at 16.

[129] DFID, *supra* note 92, at 10.

and conflict dynamics influence each other. This is done by assessing the interplay of company activities and conflict dynamics to determine whether human rights abuses are causes or consequences of conflict dynamics, and the human rights implications of conflict risks.[130] Human rights abuse that fuels conflicts among stakeholders or causes tensions to escalate into violence should be flagged,[131] as should conflict actors involved in both driving conflicts and perpetuating human rights violations.[132]

Step 3 Conflict Impact Analysis: Step three is the CIA, which involves the analysis of how company operations may adversely impact conflict dynamics, through interaction with conflict structures and actors identified in the conflict analysis. Salient conflict issues are those "through which the company has the most far-reaching actual or potential impact on conflict dynamics."[133] Two categories of salient conflict issues should be noted: impacts the company has on stakeholders through its operations, and those by others that are directly linked to the company's operations, products, or services by its business relationships.[134] Impacts on conflict dynamics in CAHRA can translate to company involvement in the commission of MAC. Examples of such involvement include contaminating air, land, or water; aiding and abetting forced labor; hiring members of parties to conflicts; engaging abusive security forces; or expelling people from their land.[135] Companies' impacts on conflict dynamics can be understood by examining: (a) the effects of the resources distributed by the company on groups in the community and its role in the market through various means, such as wages, prices, and profits; (b) the influence of the company on the legitimization of local actors, such as the police, and (c) the company's effects on land and water.[136]

(a) Distribution and markets: To generate fair and equal employment amid poverty, inequality, and corruption in CAHRA may be "the single most significant contribution" a company can make.[137] However, unrepresentative recruitment can deepen divides in situations of ethnic, religious, or tribal tensions, or when positions are offered to those favored by the State.[138] Hiring practices can thus either build bridges along conflict lines or be used to entrench divisions. Impacts on local wages, prices, and communities' ability to access raw materials to generate income should also be analyzed. Notably, women often operate in informal markets, which are less visible and at higher risk of being disturbed by company operations.[139]

---

130 Naujoks, *supra* note 98, at 15.

131 Swisspeace, *supra* note 4, at 24.

132 CSBP, *supra* note 9, at 46.

133 Swisspeace, *supra* note 4, at 24, 25, 27.

134 Green Flags, *supra* note 1, at 123.

135 Red Flags, *supra* note 37.

136 Graf, *supra* note 5, at 124.

137 *Id.*

138 Green Flags, *supra* note 1, at 74; Graf, *supra* note 5, at 124.

139 Green Flags, *supra* note 1, at 60.

(b) Legitimization: Business should not influence the legitimacy of MAC committed by others, such as by "solidifying the status of resettlements" where there was "forced displacements along sectarian lines," thereby institutionalizing the impacts of war crimes.[140] Moreover, relying on "police services in a situation of turmoil" may "further strengthen divisions,"[141] and use of judicial processes may provoke abuse of the complainant or offender.[142]

(c) Land and water: Companies' use of natural resources, where communities depend on them for livelihoods, increases scarcity, value, and competition for access. Company operations often diminish enjoyment of the right to water,[143] and degradation and expropriation of land and other resources can threaten people's survival. Land may also be "more than an economic asset," having sanctity or representing "history, place, culture, religion and identity."[144] Women are often disproportionately impacted, as their access to and management of natural resources may differ from men's, such as when they lack recognized rights to hold title to land.[145]

Step 4 Human Rights Impacts Nexus: To understand the full scope of human rights impacts in CAHRA, companies must assess their impacts on conflict dynamics, through a CIA, as well as on human rights contexts, through an HRIA. Companies should then identify the human rights implications of their conflict impacts at step four. This step involves determining how salient human rights issues identified in the HRIA and salient conflict issues identified in the CIA relate to each other, and prioritizing them. Salient issues identified in the HRIA and CIA should be categorized as either: (1) salient under both the CIA and HRIA; (2) salient under the CIA, but unlikely to implicate human rights; or (3) salient under the HRIA, but unlikely to impact conflict dynamics.[146]

Category 1 issues should be prioritized based on severity of impacts on human rights and the likelihood that they will materialize.[147] Category 2 issues should be prioritized based on their relevance to conflict and/or human rights.[148] Notably, conflict risks often affect how company operations impact rights identified in the HRIA and may implicate new rights that were not deemed relevant.[149] Category 2 issues and their human rights implications are often ignored or under-prioritized in HRIAs due to not being perceived as salient human rights issues. This step should also systematically assess escalating human rights risks and help prioritize human rights issues.

---

140 A/75/212, *supra* note 7, at 17.

141 Graf, *supra* note 5, at 125.

142 Green Flags, *supra* note 1, at 120.

143 *Id.* at 87.

144 *Id.* at 88.

145 A/75/212, *supra* note 7, at 14.

146 Swisspeace, *supra* note 4, at 25–27.

147 A/75/212, *supra* note 7, at 11; Green Flags, *supra* note 1, at 119.

148 Graf, *supra* note 5, at 125.

149 A/75/212, *supra* note 7, at 10.

2. *Human Rights Due Diligence Stage II*

Step 5 Prevention and Mitigation: In addition to ensuring compliance with laws and applicable standards identified in Section III, respecting human rights in CAHRA requires designing and implementing preventive and mitigating measures to address impacts on both conflict dynamics and human rights contexts.[150] If impacts identified at step four in Stage I of HRDD as category one (salient under the CIA and HRIA) and category two (salient under the CIA but not HRIA) issues are left unmanaged, they can spiral and intensify human rights risks. Measures addressing category three (salient under the HRIA but not CIA) issues should also take conflict risks into consideration. Examples are provided below of ways to address some of the adverse impacts on distribution in markets, legitimization, and land and water, which may have been identified at step three in Stage I of EHRDD, and of the vital roles of remedies and collaboration in CAHRA:

(a) Distribution and markets: Who is chosen to represent the company and in what capacity are consequential in CAHRA. The company's presence should neither sustain nor worsen discrimination on grounds of sex or gender.[151] Affirmative action plans for disadvantaged groups and hiring and workplace principles that cut across ethnic or racial divides, such as the Sullivan[152] and MacBride Principles,[153] can be used to avoid entrenching divisions.[154] Companies should address any adverse impacts on local prices or disturbance to informal markets and people's access to raw materials, and should maximize core benefits to communities, such as economic development. They may use quotas for local hires; provide long-term training to raise skills, use local suppliers and contractors; build capacity for local businesses; and help local suppliers, contractors, and businesses raise their human rights standards.

(b) Legitimization: Companies should not engage local suppliers or contractors involved in harmful practices, solidify the status of forced displacement, or fail to investigate and monitor harmful behaviors. Screening business relationships is particularly important in post-conflict settings, to identify links with parties to a conflict and avoid involvement in MAC. Contracts should address use of local police and private and public security services and reference the ICOC. All contracts should also reflect standards and contain "right of termination" clauses for acts such as paying bribes or abusing international labor, nondiscrimination,

---

[150] Green Flags, *supra* note 1, at 123.

[151] *Id.* at 7.

[152] *Sullivan Principles*, Boston University Trustees, https://www.bu.edu/trustees/boardoftrustees/committees/acsri/principles/; *See also The Global Sullivan Principles*, University of Minnesota Human Rights Library, http://hrlibrary.umn.edu/links/sullivanprinciples.html.

[153] *McBride Principles*, University of Minnesota Human Rights Library, http://hrlibrary.umn.edu/links/macbride.html.

[154] Both were developed in the 1980s to help US companies avoid subsidizing systematic discriminatory labor practices against religious and racial minorities in Northern Ireland and South Africa; *See*, Christopher McCrudden, *Human Rights Codes for Transnational Corporations: What Can the Sullivan and MacBride Principles Tell Us?* at 168, 170 (Oxford University Press, 1999).

environmental, or freedom of association standards.[155] Moreover, referral of non-criminal complaints by the company to judicial processes should be avoided where it would raise risks of abuse or retribution.[156]

(c) Land and water: Where operations diminish enjoyment of the right to water,[157] depredation of land or other resources affects people's livelihood, or land appropriation has caused resettlement or destruction of property, neither compensation nor replacement infrastructures alone may be sufficient remedies. Support for alternative livelihoods may also be necessary. The remediation of harms to the environment or sacred resources, which represent more than economic assets, may similarly require restoration to pre-investment conditions or measures to minimize harm, accompanied by tailored compensation determined through participatory community processes.[158] When neither company nor judicial solutions provide redress, alternative forms of remedy should be considered, but the company should not act as adjudicator.[159]

(d) Remedial measures: Unsettled grievances drive conflicts and multiply human rights risks in CAHRA. An integral part of EHRDD thus involves effectively resolving complaints against the company. This may be through apologies, negotiations that consider power imbalances, and the provision of remedy through non-judicial mechanisms, based on consultation with affected stakeholders.[160] Remedial measures and grievance mechanisms should be informed by insights gained from the conflict analysis and CIA, designed and implemented in collaboration with affected communities and in line with the requirements of legitimacy, accessibility, predictability, equitability, rights-compatibility, and transparency enumerated in the UNGPs.[161]

(e) Collaboration: Another critical element of CSM is fostering conditions under which the company can begin to meet its own responsibilities.[162] This involves supporting "institutions, processes and individuals which help prevent and address violent conflict,"[163] such as by exploring opportunities for constructive engagement with States to advocate for legal reform and socioeconomic development.[164] Companies should also harness "the potential of multi-

---

[155] Green Flags, *supra* note 1, at 71, 76, 123.

[156] UN Principles for Responsible Contracts (UNPRC) Principle 6, Commentary at 22.

[157] Green Flags, *supra* note 1, at 87.

[158] Graf, *supra* note 5, at 125; Green Flags, *supra* note 1, at 123.

[159] John Ruggie, Business and Human Rights: Further steps toward the operationalization, UN Doc. A/HRC/14/27 (Apr. 9, 2010).

[160] Green Flags, *supra* note 1, at 122, 126.

[161] A/69/263, *supra* note 16.

[162] Green Flags, *supra* note 1, at 125; Swisspeace, *supra* note 4, at 29; Graf, *supra* note 5, at 131.

[163] Graf, *supra* note 5, at 121.

[164] Green Flags, *supra* note 1, at 35, 52; UN Global Compact, https://www.unglobalcompact.org/.

stakeholder initiatives to lobby host governments on relevant human rights matters,"[165] and maintain transparency with policy level stakeholders who can become key counterparts,[166] such as by advocating for the fair allocation of resources in local operating regions, building local capacity for strengthening institutions, and supporting "media and civil society to hold local government accountable."[167]

3. *Human Rights Due Diligence Stage III*

Step 6 Tracking: This step involves designing and implementing conflict-sensitive processes for tracking measures and communicating about actions taken, to supplement the third and fourth stages of HRDD. Businesses should track the effectiveness of measures taken to address conflict impacts and assess the effects of measures taken to address human rights impacts while ensuring conflict sensitivity.[168] The differentiated impacts of measures on men and women should also be captured.[169] Conflict dynamics change, which should trigger updates of steps one and three of EHRDD, and reassessments of measures and their impacts.

4. *Human Rights Due Diligence Stage IV*

Step 7 Reporting: Finally, companies should communicate about their conflict-related impacts and measures to supplement their human rights reporting at the fourth stage of HRDD. Social and sustainability reporting can be combined and submitted to one constituency, with the primary function being to measure the company's non-business performance. Reporting should be understood as a bottom-up process, flowing up the system (in contrast to company policies that flow down); the principal audience should be those impacted by the business's activities, not the international audience that is normally the focus when designing communications strategies.[170] Companies should share information about potential impacts with affected stakeholders,[171] capturing "the attitudes and treatment of external parties."[172] Reporting should also include measures taken to address gaps and avoid adverse conflict and human rights impacts,[173] as well as applicable soft law guidelines.[174]

To increase transparency, well-structured reporting processes should be created before operations have had significant impacts, and baselines should be set before projects begin. These can be developed through self-assessments or external audits; they help companies show progress, track their human rights impacts, "and distinguish them from the impacts

---

165 Green Flags, *supra* note 1, at 42.

166 Shift, *Human Rights Due Diligence in High Risk Circumstances: Practical Strategies for Businesses* (Mar. 2015), at 19, https://shiftproject.org/wp-content/uploads/2015/03/Shift_HRDDinhighriskcircumstances_Mar2015.pdf.

167 Green Flags, *supra* note 1, at 73.

168 Swisspeace, *supra* note 4, at 32.

169 CSBP, *supra* note 9, at 46.

170 Green Flags, *supra* note 1, at 106.

171 A/69/263, *supra* note 16, at 19.

172 Green Flags, *supra* note 1, at 106.

173 Swisspeace, *supra* note 4, at 34.

174 Green Flags, *supra* note 1, at 42.

of others."[175] Companies should communicate with local communities about their tax and royalty payments and ensure the process for gathering and publishing data does not risk the safety of stakeholders or personnel or further fuel conflicts.[176]

V. Outstanding Issues

While the UNGPs clarify what is expected from business and States in CAHRA, according to the UNWG, "home States of businesses . . . can do more to ensure that their companies" respect international humanitarian law and international human rights law while operating in CAHRA.[177] The UNWG particularly called on States to help companies conduct EHRDD by identifying steps in their National Action Plans for integrating CSM in HRDD processes.[178] The UNWG also notes that the "expansion of mandatory due diligence means" concerns about business in CAHRA "should gain traction faster, including an expectation of" EHRDD, and that "lessons learned of implementing conflict minerals regulations across multiple jurisdictions offers insights transferable to a broader set of policy issues" in CAHRA.[179]

Additionally, more action is required to ensure that communities' rights to access and use of land, water, and other resources are protected, and that violations are remedied effectively. Michael Posner has observed a need for standards for the conduct of multinational food and beverage companies in CAHRA,[180] which confront "widespread use of child labor on family farms, dismal wages, excessive work hours and unsafe working conditions," and that businesses often face risks "that directly clash with their business models," resulting in "complicated operational hurdles."[181] Moreover, assistance managing "revenues wisely and improv[ing] standards of conduct for foreign investors"[182] may be required in new resource-producing countries, including "countries unfamiliar with significant, high-value resource wealth," where "discoveries and resource development" are under way, such as in Guyana, Senegal, Mauritania, Mozambique, and potentially Gambia, Suriname, and Tanzania.[183]

VI. Conclusion

A company's human rights responsibilities in CAHRA are both outcome and process oriented, "determined by the steps it takes, not only the results it achieves."[184] Companies face heightened risks of becoming engaged in conflict and multiplying human rights risks in CAHRA. To identify and address adverse impacts linked to these risks, they must conduct EHRDD on

---

175 *Id.* at 106.

176 Swisspeace, *supra* note 4, at 33, 35; Green Flags, *supra* note 1, at 52, 73.

177 A/75/212, *supra* note 7, para. 22; *See* A/HRC/17/32.

178 Green Flags, *supra* note 1; A/69/263, *supra* note 16, at 14.

179 A/75/212, *supra* note 7, p. 21.

180 Baumann-Pauly, *supra* note 53, p. 174–176 (chapter by Michael Posner).

181 *Id.*

182 Goldwyn, *supra* note 80, at 2.

183 *Id.*

184 Green Flags, *supra* note 1, at 123.

all operations linked to CAHRA. Section IV outlined the seven steps through which EHRDD can be conducted by integrating CSM into all four stages of HRDD. Companies operating in CAHRA should also adhere to applicable standards identified in Section III.

VII. Resources

Graf, Andreas and Iff, Andrea, *Enhanced Human Rights Due Diligence in Conflict Affected and High-Risk Areas*, SWISSPEACE (2016), https://www.connectingbusiness.org/system/files/2018-11/Enhanced-Human-Rights-Due-Diligence-in-Conflict-Affected-and-High-Risk-Areas.pdf.

Graf, Andreas and Iff, Andrea, *Respecting Human Rights in Conflict Regions: How to Avoid the 'Conflict Spiral'*, 2 BUS. AND HUM. RIGHTS J. 1 (2017).

Human Rights and Business Dilemmas Forum, https://hrbdf.org/.

Institute for Business and Human Rights, *From Red to Green Flags: The Corporate Responsibility to Respect Human Rights in High-Risk Countries* (2011), https://www.ihrb.org/pdf/from_red_to_green_flags/complete_report.pdf.

International Alert, *Conflict-Sensitive Business Practice: Guidance for Extractive Industries* (2005), https://www.international-alert.org/publications/conflict-sensitive-business-practice-guidance-extractive-industries/.

International Alert *Human Rights Due Diligence in Conflict-affected settings: Guidance for Extractives Industries,* prepared by Orsini, Yadaira and Cleland, Roper (2018), https://www.international-alert.org/wp-content/uploads/2021/08/Economy-Human-Rights-Due-Diligence-Guidance-EN-2018.pdf.

Organisation for Economic Co-operation and Development (OECD), *Risk Awareness Tool for Multinational Enterprises in Weak Governance Zones* (2006), https://www.oecd.org/daf/inv/corporateresponsibility/36885821.pdf.

Shift, *Human Rights Due Diligence in High Risk Circumstances: Practical Strategies for Businesses* (Mar. 2015), https://shiftproject.org/wp-content/uploads/2015/03/Shift_HRDDinhighriskcircumstances_Mar2015.pdf.

United Nations Global Compact, *Business Guide for Conflict Impact Assessment and Risk Management* (Jun. 2002), http://www.unglobalcompact.org/docs/issues_doc/Peace_and_Business/BusinessGuide.pdf.

United States Agency for International Development, *Conflict Assessment Framework* (version 2.0) (2012), https://www.dmeforpeace.org/peacexchange/wp-content/uploads/2015/10/Conflict-Assessment-Framework-Revised-CAF-2.0.pdf.

Index

T